D0340076

What Went Wrong

[What Went Wrong]

HOW THE 1% HIJACKED THE AMERICAN MIDDLE CLASS . . .
AND WHAT OTHER COUNTRIES GOT RIGHT

George R. Tyler

BENBELLA BOOKS, INC.
DALLAS, TEXAS

COVER CHART

The chart on the front cover shows the changes in total labor compensation between 1985 and 2008 for production employees in manufacturing, adjusted for inflation using the Consumer Price Index. Total compensation is comprehensive employer costs including: wages, bonuses, benefits, government taxes, and fees. This time series was chosen because it is the most uniform international data set on wages covering the past three decades. A chart depicting the time series for wage data alone would be similar.

Source: "International Hourly Compensation Costs for Production Workers in Manufacturing (wages, all benefits, social insurance expenditures, and labor-related taxes)," Department of Labor, Bureau of Labor Statistics, Washington, http://www.bls.gov/fls/pw/ichcc_pwmfg1_2.txt, March 2011, and "Consumer Price Index," OECD.StatExtracts Organisation for Economic Co-operation and Development (OECD), Paris, December 2012, http://stats.oecd.org/Index.aspx?DatasetCode=MEI_PRICES#.

BenBella Books, Inc.
10300 N. Central Expressway
Suite #530
Dallas, TX 75231

www.benbellabooks.com
Send feedback to feedback@benbellabooks.com

Printed in the United States of America
10 9 8 7 6 5 4 3 2 1

Library of Congress Cataloging-in-Publication Data is available for this title.
Tyler, George R.
What went wrong : how the 1% hijacked the American middle class . . . and what other countries got right / by George R. Tyler.
pages cm
Includes bibliographical references and index.
ISBN 978-1-937856-71-7 (trade cloth : alk. paper)—ISBN 978-1-937856-72-4 (ebook)
1. Wealth—United States. 2. Elite (Social sciences—United States. 3. Capitalism—United States. I. Title.
HC110.W4T95 2013
330.973--dc23

2013009618

Editing by Erin Kelley
Copyediting by Dori Perrucci
Proofreading by Rainbow Graphics and Cape Cod Compositors, Inc.
Cover design and interior art by Sarah Dombrowsky
Text design and composition by Elyse Strongin, Neuwirth & Associates, Inc.
Printed by Berryville Graphics

Distributed by Perseus Distribution
www.perseusdistribution.com

To place orders through Perseus Distribution:
Tel: 800-343-4499
Fax: 800-351-5073
E-mail: orderentry@perseusbooks.com

May Alexia and Ti's generation prosper from the spirit of Marcia McGill and Hubert H. Humphrey

CONTENTS

Section One

THE BEGINNING

CHAPTER 1

FACING REALITY

"We have forgotten that the economy is a tool to serve the needs of society and not the reverse. The ultimate purpose of the economy is to create prosperity with stability."[1]

SIR JAMES GOLDSMITH,
CEO, the Goldsmith Foundation, 1994

"While America's super-rich congratulate themselves on donating billions to charity, the rest of the country is worse off than ever. . . . Millions of Americans are struggling to survive. The gap between rich and poor is wider than ever and the middle class is disappearing."[2]

THOMAS SCHULZ,
***Der Spiegel*, August 19, 2010**

"That was the old curve. Then I drew the new one. It curves down: wages don't rise; you can't get on the property ladder. Fiscal austerity eats into your disposable income. You are locked out of your firm's pension scheme; you will wait until your late 60s for retirement. . . . This generation of young, educated people is unique—at least in the post-1945 period: a cohort who can expect to grow up poorer than their parents."[3]

PAUL MASON,
***The Guardian*, July 2012**

Americans have long been proud of their economy. And why shouldn't we be? From the time we were children, we've been told that we live in the best country in the world, with the most expanding and dynamic economy. We've been told that our economy allows Americans to enjoy a lifestyle that is the envy of the world. And we've been told that we live in the home of the American dream, a country that—more than any other—allows people to rise up from poverty into the ranks of the rich. But is it really true?

Unfortunately, the answer is no. These things haven't been true for a long time. But they used to be true.

In the period from 1946 to 1972, America experienced the longest and most robust period of wealth creation the nation has ever experienced.

Year after year, the economy grew substantially. Productivity growth was equally dramatic. Businesses experienced strong profits, and employees experienced steady growth in wages. It was a golden age for America, and, throughout this book, I'll refer to this period of time as the golden age.

Most of the major industrialized countries experienced similar growth. Because of the rebuilding after World War II, and the aid afforded by the Marshall Plan, many European countries grew even faster than the United States. Every country's experience was unique, driven by their particular circumstances, but, overall, the trend was up. Economies grew, businesses thrived, and wages expanded.

Moving into the mid-1970s, America's economic performance suffered. Stagflation—inflation combined with minimal economic growth—eroded wages and profits, weakening business and consumer confidence. Escalating energy prices and an overly loose monetary policy were the major causes. In August 1979, President Jimmy Carter appointed Paul Volcker as Chairman of the Board of Governors for the Federal Reserve System. Volcker is widely credited with ending stagflation by tightening credit, and by 1983 inflation was back to a relatively healthy 3.2 percent. In November 1980, Ronald Reagan was elected president and took the economy in a dramatic new direction, a direction that, with some twists and turns, has continued to this day. Throughout this book, I call this new direction Reaganomics, in honor of the man identified most closely with this new economic direction. But Reagan isn't alone. As we'll see, Presidents George H.W. Bush and Bill Clinton did very little to change this direction. President George W. Bush doubled down on Reaganomics, and President Barack Obama, amid a gridlocked Washington, has been stymied in efforts to change it.

We've been living under Reaganomics since the 1980s, a span I call the Reagan era. Please be clear that I'm referring to the entire period from 1980 until now, and not just the duration of Reagan's presidency.

I'll define Reaganomics in detail later in the book, but for now, this brief description will suffice. Reaganomics is a version of *laissez-faire* capitalism that emphasizes a minimum of regulation, especially in the financial sector; a lowering of taxes, especially on the wealthiest individuals; rapid growth in government spending, especially on national defense; and an indulgent attitude toward the business community.

The Impact of Reaganomics

Economists are critical of the overall impact of Reaganomics on productivity and family prosperity. Yet millions of ordinary Americans believe it has been a positive recipe for the country, a perspective I believe ignores the big picture. As we shall see throughout this book, Reaganomics has been unkind to most Americans.

The failure of Reaganomics is not limited to income erosion. The growth in American productivity dropped precipitously over the Reagan era. Productivity growth is not discussed much in the United States (it is in some other countries, as we shall see), but it's the single most important measure of economic performance. Productivity is commonly defined as total production divided by the number of labor hours. Raising productivity is the only way that inflation-adjusted salaries can increase on a per capita basis. During the golden age, productivity grew an average of 2.8 percent per annum; it slumped during the stagflation of the 1970s and then averaged a third lower, at 1.9 percent through 2011.

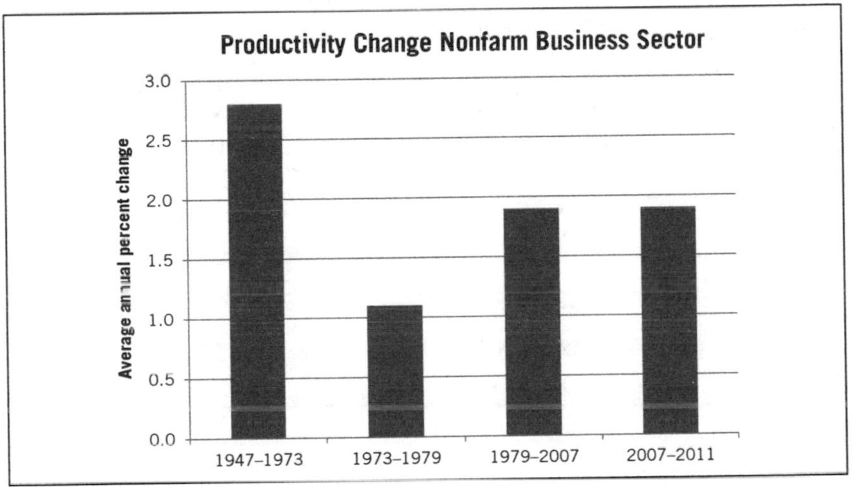

Chart 1.1.
Source: "Productivity Change in nonfarm business sector, 1947–2012, Bureau of Labor Statistics, Washington. http://data.bls.gov/cgi-bin/print.pl/lpc/prodybar.htm.

Despite the slowdown in productivity growth during the Reagan era, there was still room for both wages and profits to grow, although at more modest levels than in previous years. But that didn't happen; average wages went flat or worse in the Reagan era. So where did the gains from rising productivity growth go? Virtually all of the gains flowed into corporate profits and into earnings at the very top of the income pyramid. To be precise, economists Emmanuel Saez and Thomas Piketty have concluded that only 5 percent of earners enjoyed income gains exceeding inflation during the Reagan era, and most of that was concentrated in the earnings of the top 1 percent. That is why income disparities widened noticeably.[4,5]

Such a skewing of incomes over a span measured in decades is unlikely to be a chance event. Rather, it was the outcome of Reaganomics, a replay of the Gilded Age of the 1920s when the business community was also weakly regulated. Here is how Harvard professor Alexander Keyssar summarized Reaganomics:

> "It's difficult not to see a determined campaign to dismantle a broad societal bargain that served much of the nation well for decades. To a historian, the agenda of today's conservatives looks like a bizarre effort to return to the Gilded Age, an era of little regulation of business, no social insurance and no legal protections for workers."[6]

Pundits have come up with explanations for the economic outcomes of the Reagan era, including technological change and globalization. But these explanations make little sense when we consider that labor compensation in other rich democracies rose briskly.

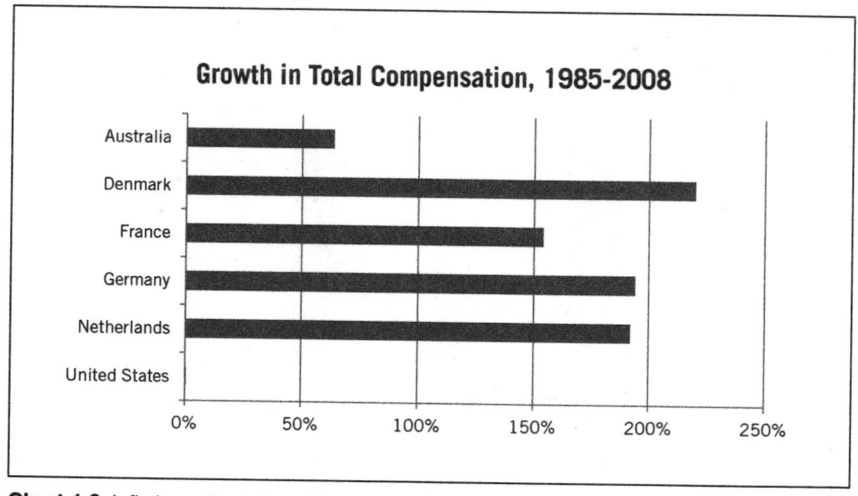

Chart 1.2. Inflation-adjusted total labor costs per hour in dollars.
Source: "International Hourly Compensation Costs for Production Workers in Manufacturing (wages, all benefits, social insurance expenditures and labor-related taxes)," Department of Labor, Bureau of Labor Statistics, Washington, http://www.bls.gov/fls/pw/ichcc_pwmfg1_2.txt, and "Private Consumption Deflators," Economic Outlook No. 90, December 2011. OECD, Paris, http://stats.oecd.org/Index.aspx?QueryId=32463#.

The problem with this line of reasoning is that other countries were also affected by these phenomena. Technology change impacted Australia. Germany, France, and Denmark are far more exposed to globalization than America is. Yet none of these countries experienced the stagnant wages that America is still facing.

The lesson is that the different outcome in America has nothing to do with these various economic forces like globalization. Instead, it has everything to do with the economic choices America's leaders in Washington made in responding to these forces. They made different choices than leaders abroad, and so the outcomes were different. The experience abroad confirms that there is an alternative to Reaganomics. I call it "family capitalism," and it's what America practiced with great success in the decades following World War II.

The Alternative: Family Capitalism

Family capitalism, like Reaganomics, is based on free-market economics. But it recognizes that the market isn't perfect. In particular, family capitalism:

- Understands the importance of selective government regulation, particularly in the financial sector.
- Puts a premium on long-term productivity growth.
- Recognizes and modulates the dangers of corporate influence on government.
- Puts a priority on long-term growth in wages as the key to family prosperity.

Based on the above principles, there are more than a dozen rich democracies around the globe practicing family capitalism. Because of data availability, I focus on eight of them: Austria, Australia, Belgium, Denmark, France, Germany, the Netherlands, and Sweden. Throughout this book, we'll compare the Reagan-era performance and practices of these eight countries with those of the United States. The results, I warn you, won't be pretty.

I don't claim that these eight countries all follow the same practices. They don't. There are distinct difference in their economies and their politics, ranging from Sweden, where the government plays a very large role in the economy, to small-government Australia, which the conservative Heritage Foundation rates as "more free" than the United States.[7] Even so, there is a similarity in economic policies and outcomes, which allows me to classify them all as Family Capitalist countries.

Further, I don't claim that these eight countries get everything right. For example, all but Australia belong to the free trade zone embodied in the European Union, an alluring but incomplete concept that jeopardizes the future of the northern European economies. The lessons reviewed in this book are not related to these macroeconomic troubles, however, but are drawn from the internal mechanisms that Australia, Germany, and others successfully utilize to broadcast the gains from growth broadly among families within national borders. There are definitely things each of them can learn from American approaches. But, overall, the data on wage growth forces me to conclude that they get it right more often than we do. Once you review the data, I think you'll agree.

Because most of the Family Capitalist countries are European, it's easy to conclude this is a review of the big government aspects of northern Europe. Certainly, conservative politicians frequently caution Americans of the danger posed by the European social welfare state, and delight in accusing political targets of harboring secret ambitions to transplant that model to America. I am advocating no such thing, as the inclusion of low-tax Australia evidences. With the world's highest median wealth, it shows that economic outcomes rather than the size of government are determinant in this book.[8] As you will see, the lessons they offer have nothing to do with high or low tax rates or big or small public sectors. Moreover, family capitalism is as American as apple pie. It's the system we practiced from the end of World War II until the 1970s, the most prosperous period of our nation's history. If not invented here, America's golden age certainly put wind beneath its wings as a goal eagerly adopted overseas.

How I Got Here

I bring a practical amalgam of training, background, and experience to the analyses of national economic goals and structure in *What Went Wrong*. My insight about the different outcomes in the United States and abroad was reached partly as a byproduct of helping establish a nonprofit organization in Europe to conduct medical research. Despite the ease of travel, few Americans beyond a tiny number of executives at multinational firms and banks have reason to develop familiarity with the Australian or northern European economies. And even fewer American scholars bother since the demise of the Cold War demoted the US study of comparative economic systems to an academic backwater.

My experiences over more than a decade of travel and consultation in Europe have provided a rare opportunity for a seasoned American economist with a background in international economic issues. I became immersed over this period in the structure, nuances, and current operation of the northern Europe economies, particularly their wage mechanisms, corporate governance, and labor market policies. I began applying typical professional standards of observation and analysis in gathering and synthesizing the information about the European economies presented here, later adding the Australian economy as well.

My career provided me a leg up in this analysis, beginning with several decades as an economist in the US Senate working for the admired Hubert Humphrey toward the end of his fruitful life. Later I joined Senator and then Treasury Secretary Lloyd Bentsen, a trade and tax expert. My work involved analysis of a wide variety of issues ranging from budgets to energy policy, taxes, and trade policy. And that experience broadened further during my several years early in the Clinton Administration at the Treasury Department. I worked primarily on budget issues involving international financial institutions including the International Monetary Fund (IMF); the development banks for Eastern Europe, Latin America, and Asia; and on international trade legislation (the North American Free Trade Agreement, or NAFTA). The months of work on NAFTA, in particular, sparked my interest in wages and outsourcing issues, which continued during my subsequent work at the World Bank. Work with the development banks provided me with an intensely useful education in the various models of capitalism across the globe.

After developing real estate projects for some years, I collaborated in 1998 with a senior official at the Institute of Medicine, in crafting an innovative concept to stimulate the development of medicines for neglected tropical diseases. That process included a period of conferences and meetings abroad, with the concept eventually being embraced in 1999 by the international aid group Doctors Without Borders.[9] Several years of collaboration followed as the *Drugs for Neglected Diseases* initiative took shape.

Helping establish a nonprofit in Geneva with a €15 million budget and serving over the last decade on its audit committee involved considerable research of and exposure to uniquely European wage and business practices. I learned firsthand the nuts and bolts of European capitalism, an education that took on a life of its own. It has become enriched in the years since with serious scholarship, a heavy dose of statistics, and interaction with international financial and labor economists. That has enabled me to take the full professional measure of the starkly different economic goals and wage determination schemes in Reagan-era America and in the family capitalism countries.

The bottom line is this: Voters in nations such as Germany, the Netherlands, or Australia expect everyone—from the corner grocer to government officials and corporate CEOs—to prioritize family prosperity. They demand government standards and rules that prioritize rising wages nationwide, quality education and upskilling opportunities, and the creation and maintenance of high-quality jobs. Enterprise serves families—not the other way around. The three most important topics on voters' minds are: wages, productivity, and how much of the rise in labor productivity growth flows to families.

While the family capitalism countries are rich democracies like the United States, their goals and outcomes are so dissimilar from America since the 1980s that they seem to be operating on different planets, as you will see.

Can This Be Right?

This book argues that, beginning in the 1980s, America took a wrong turn. That is why, over the next thirty years, our economy has delivered substantially less to its citizens than the eight family capitalism countries that avoided the pitfalls of Reaganomics.

That may be difficult to accept. Virtually every American has grown up believing in the superiority of our economy. We've felt almost contemptuous of "old Europe" and its sclerotic economic system. Surely these countries cannot be delivering what America has not—higher wage growth, higher productivity growth, and more economic opportunity?

I'll begin making this case by addressing several issues.

First, the statistics I use are publicly available through US and foreign government agencies, including: the Organization for Economic Cooperation and Development, the IMF, United Nation agencies, peer review professional journals, and books by respected economists from Niall Ferguson to Paul Krugman.

Second, I conclude that families in the family capitalism countries have economically overtaken American ones, a puzzling assertion since American Gross Domestic Product (GDP) per capita is higher. Like oil-rich Norway or banking center Luxembourg, US GDP per capita is higher than the family capitalism countries, but that reveals nothing about whether that output translates into compensation for ordinary employees and families. Indeed, all nonpartisan economists acknowledge that growth in the economy since the 1980s has gone almost entirely into corporate profits and the incomes of the very richest Americans. Having relatively large energy and banking sectors adds to US GDP, but only a portion is translated into wages.

Third, some might argue that this skewed allocation of the gains from growth is temporary. The major principle of Reaganomics is that by freeing up business to maximize profitability, wealth will be created, which—ultimately—will benefit all. If you are old enough to remember the beginning of the Reagan era, you'll recall that this was once called "trickle-down economics." Well, thirty years on, most families are still waiting for trickle down to deliver.

It's Not Reaganomics, It's Globalization

Another argument is that globalization and outsourcing of jobs, not Reaganomics, are responsible for weak wages. But as I noted previously, this argument is belied by the experience of the family capitalism countries. In fact, globalization strengthens my argument. Due to the relatively high international trade intensity of the family capitalism countries, globalization has impacted them much more severely than the United States. So the difference must not be in globalization itself, but in the policies crafted in reaction to it.

The unfettered international flows of capital, technology, and goods characteristic of global integration have dramatically improved global economic efficiency. Overall, this is a good thing. But the American experience demonstrates that those same forces pose an existential threat to the high wages and living standards of the rich democracies if not remediated. This book reveals that policies to ameliorate the dangers of globalization and to maximize its benefits can succeed. And the evidence is provided by the different outcomes of policies pursued during the Reagan era by an indifferent Washington in contrast to policies by leaders in cities like Berlin, Canberra, Copenhagen, Paris, and Vienna.

Washington officials in the throes of Reaganomics refused to ameliorate the forces of global integration, leaving families like deer in the headlights; they abandoned American families to become mere commodities in hostile labor markets. Washington rejected intervention, such as reformed corporate governance or upskilling of workforces, to instead honor the dictates of the marketplace as interpreted by US multinationals and Wall Street. The impact on virtually all Americans was severe.

The erosion in US wages is mostly a consequence of quite profitable firms across America demanding large-scale wage and benefit concessions across the board, freezing total employee costs in real terms, adjusted for inflation. Nearly unique among rich democracies, American executives have been on a tear for decades, aggressively capping employee costs because—well, because they can. For a while, rising outlays for health care and other fringe benefits offset some of the wage erosion, but that ceased to be true nearly a decade ago. In contrast, overseas in the family capitalism countries (and during the golden age in America) there is an aversion by healthy companies to arbitrarily freezing or lowering the compensation of good employees.

For example, the beverage conglomerate Dr. Pepper Snapple Group in 2010 demanded $3,000 wage concessions, froze pensions, and reduced fringe and health care benefits at its Mott plant in Williamson, NY. These givebacks were demanded despite Dr. Pepper Snapple earning profits of $555 million in 2009 on sales of $5.5 billion, an enviable 10 percent profit margin during a soft year.

Like many other US employers now, Dr. Pepper Snapple didn't bother even to intimidate employees by threatening to export jobs. Instead, the company warned of hiring replacement workers for as much as one-third less from the same Williamson area. The message was take it or leave it. What happened to the costs savings from these lower wages? Dr. Pepper Snapple increased its dividend by 67 percent in May 2010.[10] Indeed, the profits of Dr. Pepper Snapple are indicative of a remarkable aspect to this dispiriting wage trend of the Reagan era. Families have experienced falling wage offers from profitable firms for the first sustained period ever in American history; yet voters, and thus Washington officials, appear indifferent to highly profitable firms like Mercury Marine or Harley-Davidson cutting wages to bolster profits.[11]

With little public debate, Washington policy allowed American jobs to become disposable, which allowed family prosperity to become vulnerable. Iconic firms like Apple shifted millions of jobs to cheap and subservient labor forces abroad willing to work 12-hour, six-day-a-week schedules, the ideal docile and disposable labor force in the eyes of Reagan-era American executives. This outcome was facilitated by the pecuniary foundation of US politics and an increasingly marginalized trade union movement.

When challenged, firms that have exported jobs obfuscate the facts. When the impact of offshoring jobs is pointed out, executives frequently blame the victims. They blame American employees. As an example, one Apple executive mendaciously justified his Chinese labor force this way: "The US has stopped producing people with the skills we need."[12] Well, it's theoretically possible that Apple is really responding to the superior training of Chinese workers, rather than their $145 per month salaries, but I seriously doubt it.

In contrast, the family capitalism countries were proactive, prospering despite the tumult of global integration. They rejected trade controls, the commoditization of workers, and market fundamentalism in favor of canny mechanisms to maximize productivity and family income growth. Unhampered by ideology and buttressed with centuries of vigorous economic debate between the likes of Adam Smith and Friedrich Hayek, they focused on meeting election mandates demanding family prosperity.

It wasn't that difficult to accomplish, because these rich democracies came armed to the existential struggle with better tools than America. They have political systems dominated by voters instead of donors, a superior hyper-competitive corporate governance structure, and an electorate strongly appreciative of the wealth free trade creates and keenly sensitive to the role of wages in driving the prosperity of the family.

Leaders in these nations reacted with dispatch, transforming the dangers of global integration into broadly based prosperity. Protectionism was avoided and even aggressively attacked when identified abroad. These nations didn't experience an American-style stagnation of wages and offshoring of jobs. Instead, Australia and northern Europe pursued policies informed by the best and brightest trade economists of our age.

Drawing on the theories of David Ricardo, for example, economists Paul Samuelson and Wolfgang F. Stolper had concluded as early as 1941 that international trade creates long-term losers as well as winners. So leaders abroad crafted remediation: a balance of clever mechanisms maximizing the gains from globalization and broadcasting those gains to families, while minimizing its harm to jobs and wages.

This reality reveals the hollowness of complaints by American firms such as Apple that routinely warn about high American labor costs and mediocre skill levels. Adam Smith, whose book, *The Wealth of Nations*, marked him as the father of capitalism, had heard the same thing when writing back in the eighteenth century. Like today, profits were high, but British business leaders in 1776 nonetheless vented about high wages harming sales. Smith would have none of it.

"Our merchants and master-manufacturers complain much of the bad effects of high wages in raising the price, and thereby lessening the sale of their goods both at home and abroad. They say nothing concerning the bad effects of high profits. They are silent with regard to the pernicious effects of their own gains. They complain only of those of other people."[13]

In the end, we are forced to conclude that the gap between US outcomes and those of the family capitalism countries is real. It isn't an artifact of the data. It isn't a sensible tradeoff between conflicting beliefs. It's not a short-term problem that will go away. And it's not an inevitable result of globalization. The United States simply made a fundamentally wrong turn. What could have been a temporary sidetrack became the main track—and American families are still paying the price decades later.

CHAPTER 2

WHAT IS REAGANOMICS?

"We are a low-wage country compared to Germany."[1]

KRISTIN DZICZEK,
Director, Center for Automotive Research, Detroit

"In the great days of the USA, Henry Ford stated that he wanted to pay high wages to his employees so that they could become his customers and buy his cars. Today, we are proud of the fact that we pay low wages."[2]

SIR JAMES GOLDSMITH,
CEO, the Goldsmith Foundation, 1994

"The idea that markets are self-regulating received a mortal blow in the recent financial crisis and should be buried once and for all. . . . Markets require other social institutions to support them. They rely on courts and legal arrangements to enforce property rights and on regulators to rein in abuse and fix market failures. . . . In other words, markets do not create, regulate, stabilize or sustain themselves. This history of capitalism has been a process of learning and relearning this lesson."[3]

DANI RODRIK,
Harvard University, *The Globalization Paradox,* 2011

The period from 1946 to 1972 created the great American middle class. Breadwinners returned from World War II to a vibrant economy. The boom extended for decades, creating good jobs for farmers' sons like Augustine Powell, profiled by Jonathan Mahler in the June 2009 *New York Times Magazine*.[4] Augustine and his wife, Marva, arrived in Detroit in the 1960s; they were fresh off the farm and Augustine eventually ended up on the assembly line at General Motors.

Wages rose steadily, thanks to laws like the Wagner Act that helped open the door wide to solid union jobs for millions of men and women. As in Australia today, the United Auto Workers (UAW) and other trade unions had taken care of the rest—winning regular wage hikes that matched rising productivity and kept pace with profits—while also providing health insurance and the promise of a secure retirement.

Moreover, heavy manufacturing—autos, for example—set the standard across America's industrial heartland for livable wages, enabling tens of millions of hardworking Americans like Augustine to earn their way into the middle class.

A few years before coming to Detroit, Augustine and Marva had married. Two sons soon followed, joining millions of others in the post-war baby boom that became the largest cohort in American history. Almost all of these families rented for a while and remained careful with their spending as they held onto their hardscrabble habits from the Great Depression. But with wages rising faster than inflation, most could soon afford the down payment on a home like the one Augustine and Marva bought on Curtis Street, in a good school district with stores close by. Fishing boats rested on trailers and nearly new cars sparkled in carports. They were living the dream envisioned by Adam Smith and Henry Ford.

Your parents or grandparents were probably raised in homes on streets just like Curtis and, perhaps like Augustine, went vacationing to visit relatives all over the South and Midwest, or perhaps as far away as Niagara Falls or even exotic California. And the best part was the future for their children: college was affordable and the sky was the limit. It was a period your parents or grandparents cherish, and for good reason: it was the most miraculous period of broadly rising prosperity in American history.

Perhaps the best part of this magical era was that Augustine's grit and determination paid off back then, with regular wage increases arriving like clockwork. He—and millions of others—gave their hearts to corporations and most received a piece of the American Dream in return, creating a golden age for aspiring men and women from even the meanest roots. And, importantly, executive suites saw men like Augustine as their partners in that prosperity, critical to driving firms forward. CEOs viewed themselves as collaborators in the footsteps of Henry Ford in creating prosperity and the best America possible, investing heavily in new plants and in upskilling, and paying rising wages, because higher productivity meant even higher profits in the future. American income distribution grew more equal than ever in history.

Importantly, banks were corralled. Federal Reserve System chiefs William McChesney Martin, who retired in 1970, and later, Paul Volcker, had taken the lessons of the Great Depression to heart. Regulations were tough. Wall Street and local bankers were forced to be cautious and methodical, careful with your money, not jittery financial entrepreneurs seeking windfalls, eager and able to gamble with your deposits. And they earned far less than executives at firms such as GM, which actually generated real wealth. Manufacturing careers were the ticket to a bright future back then, rather than the financial engineering jobs of today, conjuring opaque securities. That same prudent mentality carried over to the government, where federal budget deficits were tiny, with taxes and spending nearly in balance and the national debt from World War II shrinking steadily under both Democratic and Republican presidents.

Not all Americans benefited, though. There was plenty of poverty, especially among discriminated minorities. Poll taxes and literacy tests restricted the right to vote across the South until 1964. Too many schools were poor and the economic safety net was weak. Michael Harrington's 1962 book *The Other America* provides a sober and accurate portrayal of desperation amid the rising plenty back then. Yet, with the gains from trade and growth being broadly enjoyed, the economic life for virtually every American improved. Income wasn't being redistributed by government, but instead simply flowed to those like Augustine who increased productivity, rewarding hard work. It was a slow grind, with real incomes inching ahead 1 percent or so year after year—the only way vast middle class prosperity can improve. It was a wondrous time in America, where the system of wage settlements enabled hardworking families to realistically aspire to the middle class and expect prosperity as an American birthright. Here is how *Harper's Magazine* writer Ben Austen described the roots of the golden age:

> "The auto industry came to symbolize blue-collar upward mobility and empowerment. The real incomes of autoworkers doubled from 1947 to 1973; and because many other unions as well as nonunion firms adopted auto-industry pay rates, the bottom half of American earners saw their incomes increase during this period at the same pace as that of the top 10 percent of wage earners."[5]

By 1972, rising prosperity had increased weekly wages to an annual average of $7,300 per employee. That paycheck was certainly worth more than the 3,360 francs averaged in France, which translated to about $4,500 that year. That year—1972—was the high-water mark for the American middle class. With inflation, that $7,300 paycheck was equal to $40,200 in 2012, an above average wage today.

The Fairytale Ends

It must all sound like a fairytale to you.

Twenty-first century America is something altogether different from the golden age. The experience of your parents or grandparents and men like Augustine doesn't remotely resemble experience since. The common outcome instead is the experience of folks like Tim Slaughter, a friend of Augustine's son. Along with nearly all of America's 150 million employees, he's been caught up in the disappearance of good jobs in Detroit and across the nation. Tim became flotsam, reeducating himself to be a computer technician, but at $20,000 less than he earned at Ford, as rising middle-class prosperity ground to a standstill in an America evolving to a low-wage nation.

The American economy since then has morphed into a repetition of the Gilded Age of the Roaring Twenties, a transformation that would startle and repel our parents or grandparents from the golden age. It has left folks like Tim Slaughter on the crack end of a whip powered by dimly understood forces in the wake of the collapse of rules and expectations that crafted the golden age. Stagnant and declining wages are the new reality that makes Tim's experience a common one, including surprisingly low wages, even in union shops or for higher technology jobs requiring college degrees and intensive training.

Unionization has been integral to higher wages, and still is; in 2010, for example, unionized manufacturing workers in Indiana earned 16 percent more than nonunion employees. Union membership began eroding in 1965. But the benefits to the middle class of collective bargaining began to fall most sharply after 1980 as a new breed of executives began utilizing the Taft-Hartley Act to weaken unions and wages while stepping up the offshoring of high-value manufacturing jobs.[6] Desperate to attract new jobs amid recession and rising imports, the UAW and other industrial unions reluctantly began to accept two-tier wage structures during the 1980s. That trend ended temporarily as these labor contracts expired in the robust 1990s amid tight labor markets and rising wages. But two-tier reemerged in contracts during the jobless recovery of the George W. Bush years. The UAW accepted them again beginning in 2003, with new hires earning $14–$19 per hour. Including benefits, that was not much above one-half the wages and benefit cost of grandfathered employees.[7] And real longtimers like Augustine made even more.

Even so, these auto firms are the premier employers for Americans lacking college degrees. Starting wages are one-third lower still in most of the rest of the United States, including Walmart or McDonald's, the largest employers. For example, production jobs at the Suarez Corporation Industries plant in North Canton, Ohio, pay no more than the Ohio minimum wage of $7.70 per hour, in contrast to the former $20-an-hour jobs there that Hoover long ago offshored to China.[8] Even worse, firms like Suarez are increasingly refusing to pay fringe benefits such as health insurance and pensions, insisting that employees technically work for outside contractors. This also shifts the full cost of Social Security and Medicare payroll taxes onto employees while saving the firm other taxes as well, such as unemployment insurance.

New jobs at hotels or factories promising something better than minimal wages attract thousands upon thousands of hopefuls drawn from the shadows of the American economy, little realizing the odds are far better of being accepted at Harvard than landing a $15-an-hour job. And leading the wage compression are blue chip firms like GE and Caterpillar. When Toyota opened its Georgetown, Kentucky, plant over twenty years ago, it was deluged with 142,000 applicants for the 3,000 openings—most lured by wages about double those in a state where industrial pay averages $8 per hour.[9] It is the same today. VW was overwhelmed with 83,000 applicants for 2,500 jobs paying around $15 an hour in Chattanooga in 2011.[10]

Down the way a bit in one of the most beautiful spots in the South, in the Chattahoochee Valley, 43,000 Georgians applied for 2,600 jobs in the new Kia auto plant at West Point paying no better.[11] In Indiana, the C.R. England trucking company received 500 applications in the summer of 2009 for a single clerical job paying even less, rejecting many for being vastly overqualified.[12] And over in Danville, Virginia, new employees at the IKEA plant receive $8 per hour, far lower than wages paid by the same company in Scandinavia.[13] In all these plants, employees will top out many years from now at wages about equal to the inflation-adjusted starting wage for their parents or grandparents during the golden age. And the retirement of senior, higher-wage employees will exacerbate the deterioration in wages. For example, Chrysler is projecting that the share of its lower-tier employees will quickly double from 13 percent in 2011, to at least 25 percent by 2015.[14]

The golden-age American wage structure where pay rose with productivity is in tatters. American firms have become so fixated on compressing the incomes of employees and their families that higher wages are no longer even an option in addressing worksite issues. In 2007, for example, a survey of employee retention programs by the US staffing firm Spherion found that workers predictably prioritized issues like growth and earning potential, higher salaries, and better health insurance. Yet American managers didn't even rank wages among their top five retention tools; instead, they prioritize ephemeral steps such as enriched "supervisor relationships" and improved "workplace culture."[15]

Similar findings are noted in the Society for Human Resource Management's 2007 Job Satisfaction Survey Report.[16]

The American judiciary has added to the downward spiral of wages, indifferent to enforcing employee protections or the right to organize and refusing even to establish guidelines on burgeoning issues including independent contractors. Among others, Nissan and SuperShuttle exploit the resulting gray area to routinely misclassify employees as contractors or franchisees. SuperShuttle, for example, shifts traditional routine firm costs (equipment purchases, fringe benefits, and Social Security/Medicare fees) to employees, while also dodging traditional obligations (minimum wages, overtime pay, and workers' compensation fees). Emma Schwartz with the Center for Public Integrity in Washington quotes SuperShuttle's stated goal of shifting "hard to manage variable costs from the company" to the drivers.[17]

Nissan pursues the same strategy. Most new jobs at Nissan's Smyrna plant in Tennessee are temporary, low-wage positions working for an entity called Yates Services. Yates contractors comprise up to 60 percent of shop-floor employees in some sections of the plant and perform the same work as ordinary Nissan employees.[18] The difference besides lower pay and benefits? While performing identical tasks, they're the ones wearing brown, not Nissan blue or gray.

This downward spiral in wages has caused many reliable employees with solid job skills, but without college educations, to fall from the middle class to the ranks of the working poor. As labor economist Harley Shaiken at the University of California, Berkeley noted, family incomes for many now hover around the eligibility level for food stamps.[19] Eroding wages has made this cohort of working poor enormous, as described by MIT economist Paul Osterman in August 2011:

> "Last year, one in five American adults worked in jobs that paid poverty-level wages. Worker displacement contributes to the problem. People who are laid off from previous stable employment, if they are lucky enough to find work, take a median wage hit of over 20 percent."[20]

The plight of today's generation of Americans is defined by such wage compression. Every downturn sees fewer good jobs emerge in the subsequent recovery.[21] Some 79 percent of the six million jobs lost in the deep recession of 2008–2009 paid more than $13.84 an hour, for example, but barely half that share (42 percent) of the four million jobs created in 2010–2012 paid as well. The rest—mostly service jobs—paid less.

This wage compression has deeply affected the morale of America. Polling by the Pew Global Attitudes Project in 2011 delivered this shocker: Fewer than one-half of Americans still believe the US culture is superior to others; that's down from 60 percent in 2002, meaning the decline has been precipitous.[22] And other polling fingers economics as the culprit. The survey firm Gallup, for example, found that a majority of Americans in April 2011 agreed—for the first time—that it was unlikely their children would ever live as well as themselves. Their pessimism is justified, because the youngest members of the American workforce are bearing the heaviest burden of the Reagan era: while overall unemployment (including labor force dropouts) was around 15 percent in 2010, 37 percent of working men and women between 18 and 29 were either unemployed or labor force dropouts—a rate reminiscent of the Great Depression. A third lack health insurance and many continue living at home after schooling, cursed to come of working age amid a recession. On top of that, the cost of college continues to climb, leaving many with crippling student loan debts.

America has had blighted generations before, like those born in the decade after 1835 and especially the decade after 1905, which was cursed by both war and the Great Depression. The children of today's baby boomer generation have joined that discouraging list, beset by weak wages and wealth erosion.

Worse, they are poised to become the template for future generations. Like baby boomers, today's youth will become another generation destined to squander decades of toil and savings to retire with little more than their parents or grandparents. How severe is it? Their wages are flat. And good jobs are dwindling: Indeed, too many youths are being outmuscled for scarce job openings by their economically anxious grandparents, who are forced into working retirements at Walmart or laboring under the golden arches of McDonald's in their golden years. Despite the recession, the number of seniors working rose by 700,000 between 2007 and 2009, while the number of youths sixteen- to twenty-four-years-old working fell by 2 million.

Unsurprisingly, these trends have elicited a sober reappraisal of American capitalism among eighteen- to twenty-nine-year olds. Pew found that fewer American youths believe in the superiority of the US culture (37 percent) than youths in Germany, Spain, or Britain who view their own cultures as superior, even amid the European sovereign debt turmoil.[23] Reaganomics has caused America's children to conclude that their nation is no longer the exceptional land of opportunity it was for their grandparents.

It has also sparked a much more dramatic reappraisal. Extrapolating these trends, political scientist and author Francis Fukuyama has grown alarmed that the decline of the American middle class poses an existential threat to democracy itself. By widening income disparities and shrinking the middle class that anchors societies, he frets that global integration threatens the very foundation of Western democratic institutions and practices. Frustrated and angry voters from the devolving middle class might well demand that leaders emulate Chinese state capitalism—or worse. This ignores the lessons provided by the family capitalism countries. But American-centric Fukuyama is certainly correct about one thing: the three decades of the Reagan era darkened the American Dream for most Americans.

The discouraging economics of young workers today means they frequently turn to their parents for help against the backdrop of stagnant wages. Fully one-half of all first-time buyers can afford a home of their own only with parental loans. Parents would like to do even more, but baby boomers are too hard-pressed themselves, confronting delayed retirements and the prospect of having to help their children, instead of the other way around.

At one level, this anxiety reflects a perceived rupture in the social pact that many Americans feel had bound them firmly to the nation's fabric. That pact now seems tattered: debt-free corporations juxtaposed with a record amount of household and national debt. Corporate profits and Wall Street bonuses are measured in the hundreds of billions of dollars, while wages remain stagnant. The image of the middle class as a sanctuary that inspired our parents' love of American capitalism, along with the expectation of steadily rising wages and a comfortable retirement, has proven to be a mirage for baby boomers and their children. Unlike their parents who prospered with age, baby boomers will be fortunate to pass away in a home nicer than the one in which they grew up. As columnist Harold Meyerson of the *Washington Post* concluded in 2009, "What emerges is a picture of a nation in decline. The first nation in human history to create a middle class majority looks increasingly to be losing it."[24]

In contrast to the fortunate few atop the income pyramid, the net wealth of most other households in America has dwindled in recent years. Different groups compile different statistics. But their conclusions mirror research by the dean of American economists on wealth issues, Edward N. Wolff of New York University. Wolff has concluded that median household net worth in 2009, adjusted for inflation, was lower than in 1983; American families have less wealth today than their parents or grandparents a quarter of a century ago. Median wealth is the net value of assets including homes, financial assets, and so forth owned by the household in the precise middle of the asset distribution. This outcome, depicted in Chart 3, was derived by Wolff from Federal Reserve Board survey data.

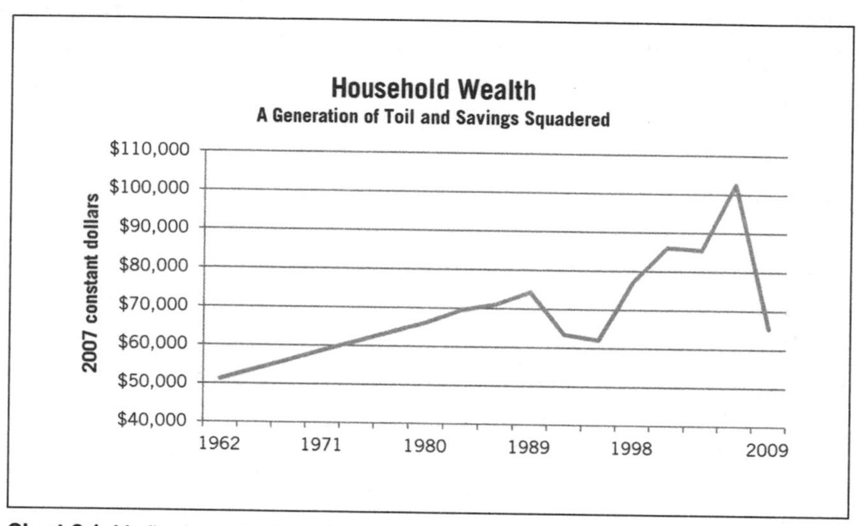

Chart 2.1. Median household wealth.
Source: Edward N. Wolff, "Top Heavy," p. 11, The New Press, NY, 20012; Edward N. Wolff, "Recent Trends in Household Wealth in the United States: Rising Debt and the Middle Class Squeeze," Levy Economics Institute at Bard College, March 2010, and Survey of Consumer Finances, Federal Reserve Board, Washington, various issues. 1965–1980 smoothed trend.

Wolff believes that almost all families are worse off, and rising stock prices has not altered that conclusion. Homes comprised 65 percent of assets held by the three middle income quintiles in 2007, while mutual funds, stocks, and the like comprised only 3.6 percent. The sobering conclusion is that American families have seen three long decades of work and savings squandered, lost forever.

Not Everyone Suffered in the Reagan era

Not all suffered, however, which is why Virginia Commonwealth University economists Robert Trumble and Angela DeLowell term the income shifts during the Reagan era "the largest peacetime transfer of wealth in history."[25] Employees at every income level—except the pinnacle—felt the deterioration. Judith Warner captures the feeling in her evocative book, *Perfect Madness: Motherhood in the Age of Anxiety*:

> "In the 1970s, even in New York, it had been financially possible for a middle-class family to survive if parents—even one parent—built

a professional life around something other than purely making money. . . . But by the late 1990s, in New York, if you weren't in the financial industry, it was hard to survive. As so it went in a more general way, throughout the country, in the whole winner-take-all era . . . life got harder and scarier and more confusing. The feeling of injustice wasn't just about money, though it was partly about being more than solidly middle class and still struggling to pay the bills. . . . It was rather that the wrong people had inherited the earth. Many of us who'd proudly decided to pursue edifying or creative or 'helping' professions, woke up to realize, once we had families, that we'd perhaps been irresponsible. We couldn't save for college. We could barely save for retirement . . . so like just about everyone, we worked hard and treaded water, but felt we were entitled to do better. And if we lived in the New York area, or another wealthy place where the spoils of the new Gilded Age were constantly thrust in our faces, we felt a little something more: we knew that we were losers."

The winners in the American wealth derby during the Reagan era have been corporations and a thin slice of American families, the oft-referenced 1 percent. While American firms fret about regulation, labor costs, and taxes, globalization opened profitable new horizons for many since 1980. That was especially true when executives proved willing to delink productivity and wages by capping labor costs. That decision enabled most of the rise in productivity to flow through to enterprise bottom lines, causing profit margins to rise from 27 percent in 1980 to 35 percent in 2009; corporate profits as a share of GDP increased from 6 percent in 1982 to 14 percent of GDP in 2006 and 2007.[26] Little wonder the Swiss investment bank UBS described the Reagan era as America's "golden era of profitability."[27] These trends made executives and shareholders the big winners.

I noted earlier that economists Piketty and Saez determined only 5 percent of Americans beat inflation during the Reagan era, but economists have parsed that figure further. And it turns out that the real winners were folks in that top 1 percent, composed of people like legacy wealth holders, entrepreneurs, athletes, Hollywood stars, and especially those like hedge fund managers or senior firm officials connected to American enterprise. This 1 percent received nearly one-half of all the economic growth in the 1990s and its share has risen sharply since then, as noted in Chart 2.2. An update in 2013 by Saez found that they received all of the gains from growth 2009–2011.[28]

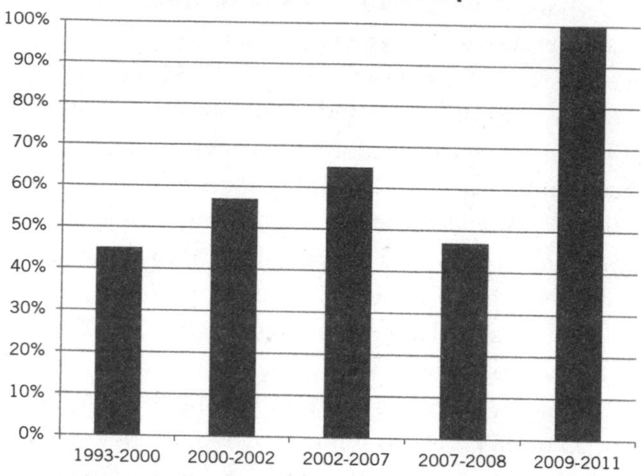

Chart 2.2.
Source: Emmanuel Saez, "Striking it Richer: the evolution of Top Incomes in the United States (updated with 2011 Estimates)," University of California, Berkeley, Jan. 23, 2013. http://elsa.berkeley.edu/~saez/saez-UStopincomes-2011.pdf. See also Robert Frank, "The 1 % Captures most Growth from recovery," Wall Street Journal blog, The Wealth Report, 3-6-12, http://blogs.wsj.com/wealth/2012/03/06/the-1-captures-most-growth -from-recovery/.

The gains from growth were far more widely enjoyed before the Reagan era. Based on data from Saez and Piketty, tax expert and former journalist David Cay Johnston determined that during the golden age until 1975, $4 of income accrued to each of the top 1 percent of earners for every $1 that reached each American in the bottom 90 percent. Yet, between 1981 and 2005 during the Reagan era, nearly $5,000 of additional income flowed to each member of the elite 1 percent for every $1 going to each of the bottom 90 percent of American earners.[29] Even within that elite group, income flowed still higher; the real winners in recent decades have been the 13,400 families comprising the top 1/100th of the 1 percent at the tip of America's income pyramid. Johnston concluded that for every $1 of additional income earned by the bottom 99 percent of Americans since 1970, each member of these dynastic families received $7,500 additional; collectively, in 2000, these families received as much income as the poorest 96 million Americans.[30]

How We Got Here

America arrived here as a result of choices made at the polls; specifically the elections of Presidents Ronald Reagan, George H.W. Bush, George W. Bush, and (to a lesser degree) Bill Clinton. Not until the election of President Obama was an effort made to address at least some symptoms of Reaganomics like financial deregulation. But why would Americans make these earlier economically harmful choices?

Part of the answer rests with the nature of economic information. Economic results are slow to accumulate in the mind's eye of voters. Excepting recessions, it takes many years before hindsight can actually distill fiction from facts about the quality of economic leadership.

And when the facts become clear sometimes years later, even well-informed voters have difficulty linking their plight to seminal trends such as the regulatory capture of Washington by the business community, or the devolution of the American executive suite culture. The fog of busy, complex, and immediate lives is too enveloping for most to discern responsibility amid the cacophony of contradictory political narratives. That is especially true in America recently when a pronounced external event—globalization or technological change—can credibly be blamed for their plight. Finally, American voters have lacked information about the continued economic success of families in Australia and northern Europe or choices at the polls based on that success.

In retrospect, Reaganomics has been an enormous gift to corporations and the wealthiest Americans—a gift from the other 95 percent of Americans. The greatest redistribution of income ever in peacetime. But voters didn't knowingly vote to give this gift. Weary of stagflation, they accepted the assurance of President Reagan and his team in 1980 that Reaganomics would lead to prosperity. And the two most important figures behind this narrative were economist Milton Freidman and philosopher and novelist Ayn Rand.

Milton Friedman and the Chicago School

The late Milton Friedman is rightfully considered one of America's leading monetary economists. Drawing on Irving Fisher's influential work, University of Chicago economists Friedman and Anna Schwartz popularized the role of money in creating and establishing price stability as an important precondition for economic growth. Their 1963 book, *A Monetary History of the United States 1867–1960,* is considered a seminal work of economics, even though Friedman's monetarism theory was hopeless as a practical guide to action.[31]

But Friedman didn't stop with economic theory. He blended ideology with his economic research to emerge as a persuasive architect who credentialed Reaganomics. In doing so, he veered into the ideological realm far beyond what his research could support.

It's worth acknowledging a bit of background information here. Milton Friedman was a vociferous opponent of regulating the business community. Yet, economists have long believed that some measure of market regulation is essential to sustain a productive, stable economy. Regulation prevents business interests from combining to create exploitative monopolies. Regulation ensures that externalities such as pollution are managed. Regulation creates minimum worksite standards for employees. Regulation avoids the problem of financial speculation by banks, a problem ever since credit was conceived centuries ago. And regulation enforces a basic level of honesty and integrity on the part of business interests. Regulations are appropriate, because the business community will not only adopt policies in conflict with the public good; centuries of experience teach that it will seek to capture and bend government regulations to its parochial goals.

The Economic Basis of Democracy

Justification for regulating the business community is most strongly identified with Adam Smith, but its roots stretch back 2,300 years to Aristotle, where the nexus of democracy and economics was formed. We look to ancient Greece as a governance touchstone, because the philosophers Socrates, Plato, and his pupil, Aristotle, pioneered exploring the nuances of secular governance and were the first to lift mankind with dreams of societies that would enrich all. In an era when slavery was widespread and tyrants touted their relationships to the gods, Aristotle's vision of a democracy pooling the wisdom of many to manage society was revolutionary. It took two centuries of darkness, the Renaissance, and the Reformation, however, for philosophers like Thomas Hobbes, John Locke, and Jean-Jacques Rousseau to fully resuscitate the classical Greek ideal of collective governance. The inspirations they drew on were Plato's *Republic* and especially Aristotle's *Politics* and his humanistic *Ethics*.[32]

Economics was considered central to the creation and preservation of democracy, making Aristotle one of the first economists two thousand years before Adam Smith. They both were market *aficionados* favoring competition; when it was limited through collusion by those whom Aristotle or Smith viewed as special interests—large land owners or dominant merchants in their day—the collusion always came at the expense of small business, farmers, and families. Here is how the Canadian economist Thomas J. Lewis explained Aristotle's concern in 240 BC:

> "If the number of producers of a given type of commodity is small, they can be expected to engage in familiar oligopolistic behavior; that is, to attempt to extract a maximum return through hard bargaining,

strengthen their bargaining position through collusion to restrict supply, and restrict the entry of new producers into the market."[33]

Responsible for Aristotle's great interest in economics was the realization that such collusion produced dangerous economic and political elites he called "oligarchs," whose self-aggrandizing behavior subverted democracy. The stark outcome he described, and which remains relevant today, is that a society achieves stability only once it evolves to become either a democracy or a tyranny of a rich elite. After much contemplation, in fact, Aristotle eventually settled on the degree of economic power held by what he called the "unpropertied" as a seminal measure of political freedom.

> "What differentiates oligarchy and democracy is wealth or the lack of it. The essential point is that where the possession of political power is due to the possession of economic power or wealth, whether the number of persons be large or small, that is oligarchy, and when the unpropertied class have power, that is democracy."[34, 35]

Aristotle established a bright-line for whether democracy exists: Do law and regulation constrain the economically powerful and thus enable the broad diffusion of economic gains? Adam Smith, ironically championed by conservatives as the conceptualizer of free market capitalism, understood this clearly. Perhaps his single most evocative conclusion emphasized his distrust of the business community for chronically placing their own interest above all others.

> People of the same trade seldom meet together, even for merriment and diversion, but the conversation ends in a conspiracy against the publick, or in some contrivance to raise prices.[36]

Drawing on the example of Bengali-based East India Company factotums, Smith explained at length in book IV of *The Wealth of Nations* how the business community's motivation chronically and directly contravenes sound government policy. They aren't amoral folks necessarily—just greedy. His writings make clear that Smith was fashioning the seminal philosophy and goals of family capitalism, not *laissez-faire* Reaganomics. He believed that improving consumer and family prosperity through lower prices and a greater variety of goods was the goal of economics. Smith explicitly rejected the *laissez-faire* deregulation version of capitalism popular during his day and during the Reagan era that prioritizes the prosperity of the business community. He endorsed placing the prosperity of families above the interests of the self-absorbed business community in the clearest possible language, explaining that "the welfare of the producer ought to be attended to, only so far as it may be necessary for promoting that of the consumer."[37]

As much as we identify the concept of the invisible hand with capitalism, Smith's most seminal contribution to economics was to channel Aristotle in clarifying that the goal of market capitalism is to enrich families at the expense of the business community. And one of the sharpest lessons offered by this book is that Reaganomics abandoned Smith's goal, even as the family capitalism countries tightened their embrace of it.

Excessive regulation can, of course, be an economic problem as well. That is why mainstream economists today seek to strike the right balance: a degree of regulation that ensures stability and fairness while allowing businesses freedom to innovate, invest, and flourish. Achieving those goals demands that government practice a carefully monitored capitalism where competition is kept vibrant by being free from regulatory capture by any economic interest.

Friedman would have none of it. Distrustful of government, he disagreed with Adam Smith, the Englishman John Maynard Keynes, and most mainstream economists on the appropriate scope of regulation in the economy. His suspicions of government regulation obligated him to conjure a sufficiently orderly economic world, where government regulation is virtually unneeded.

Appointed by President Reagan to be chairman of the Federal Reserve System in 1987, Alan Greenspan joined Milton Friedman and other advisors in minimizing the lessons drawn by Keynes from the Great Depression regarding the dangers lurking in mankind's animal spirits. Indeed, their rejection of mainstream economics was more far-reaching than just ignoring greed; it went to the heart of how gains from growth should be allocated within capitalism. I suspect President Reagan never actually understood this point. In the place of the carefully regulated market capitalism envisioned by Adam Smith and Keynes, his advisors urged with fervor a return to nineteenth-century market fundamentalism. That appeal was politically alluring to conservatives, including Ronald Reagan, who coalesced in the 1960s around the late Senator Barry Goldwater of Arizona and his inspiring themes of small government, low taxes, and self-regulation of industries. Their notion was that history was wrong and markets don't require adult supervision, after all.

Famously, in President Reagan's resurrection of Gilded Age deregulation, government became the problem—not the solution. And too many American macroeconomists at least temporarily and often to their later regret, supported an economic theory that didn't comport with reality.

As Wall Street economist Robert J. Barbera explained in his book, *The Cost of Capitalism*,

> "We embraced the wrong paradigm. The events of 2008 revealed that using simple-minded free-market rhetoric as a policy guide is a recipe for disaster."

The imperfectability of markets and man means that deregulated Reaganomics has feet of clay. It seems that the president's advisors came to believe that Reaganomics somehow suspended the laws of human behavior, that this time was different. It wasn't. It never is. The outcome was 2008. Whether its tulips or South Sea shares in seventeenth- and eighteenth-century Europe or Wall Street in the Roaring Twenties, deregulation always fails spectacularly.

Reaganomics ignores the fact that markets, especially financial ones, are beset by imperfections ranging from the impact of leverage to central bank manipulation to front running by intermediaries to woeful information discontinuities, and many other flaws. It assumes that people behave with perfect rationality, which is an absurd notion. As has long been recognized by most economists and by the psychology profession, people chronically suffer from irrationalities including: the confirmation bias (we give more credence to information that reinforces our viewpoint); the availability bias (we act inordinately on the latest if not necessarily the most accurate information); the herd instinct; thinking the future will be like the present; or overrating our abilities on a broad range of activities.[38]

None of the key assumptions undergirding Reaganomics are valid in the real world, and the irrational behavior that Smith and Keynes warned about is omnipresent. We know this deregulation spasm turned out badly just like the Gilded Age before it, and the signals were evident even as President Reagan's term ended, with the Savings and Loan crisis erupting and the 1987 market crash. Here is how *Financial Times* columnist John Kay put it:

> "Much of what . . . causes instability in the global economy results from the failure of these assumptions. Herd behavior, asset mispricing, and grossly imperfect information have led us to where we are today."[39]

Columbia University economist Joseph Stiglitz, the 2001 recipient of the Nobel prize in economics, noted in September 2007, that the self-regulation policies of Reaganomics:

"were never based on a solid empirical and theoretical foundation, and even as these policies were being pushed, academic economists were explaining the limitations of markets—for instance, whenever information is imperfect, which is to say always."[40]

Deregulation flourished after 1980 and, unsurprisingly, the consequence has been serial speculative credit bubbles in a reprise of the Roaring Twenties or eighteenth-century London, Paris, or Edinburgh. What were the Bush I and II and Clinton Administrations thinking when they deregulated finance? And what were officials like Alan Greenspan, N. Gregory Mankiw, or Glenn Hubbard thinking as the housing bubble inflated during the 2000s, when they permitted fully half of the American banking sector to go unregulated—while allowing leverage at investment banks to double? Here is how Michael Lewitt, an American money manager, explained the consequence of their regulatory lapse to John Plender of the *Financial Times* in September 2008:

> "Allowing investment banks to be leveraged to the tune of 30 to 1 is the equivalent of playing Russian roulette with five of the six chambers of the gun loaded. If one adds the off-balance-sheet liabilities to this leverage, you might as well fill the sixth chamber with a bullet and pull the trigger."[41]

The outcome was that officials and families relearned the age-old lessons first clarified by Adam Smith. New York University professor Nouriel Roubini—one of the few who predicted the Wall Street meltdown—concluded that:

> ". . . the Anglo-Saxon model of supervision and regulation of the financial system has failed. . . . [it] "relied on self-regulation that, in effect, meant no regulation; on market discipline that does not exist when there is euphoria and irrational exuberance; on internal risk management models that fail. . . ."[42]

Behind Friedman's Influence

Market fundamentalism was pretty thin gruel for economists schooled in history. It quickly attracted as sharp critics the British economist Andrew Smithers and Yale economist Robert J. Shiller, who as early as 1984 judged the underlying theory "one of the most remarkable errors in the history of economic thought."[43] It actually faded in popularity quickly as the profession came to terms with its unreal assumptions. So an obvious question is this: How did *laissez-faire* economics, discredited as recently as the 1930s and lacking any theoretical basis, actually re-emerge as American economic dogma?

The answer is that the business community, as early as the 1970s, grasped the implications of deregulation and the profits to be gleaned from a return to Gilded Age economics. All they needed to do was expand the tiny circle around Senator Goldwater and then Governor Reagan to convince Washington and voters that supporting a reintroduction of *laissez-faire* economics was somehow in the interest of families. That challenge was captured in a remarkably candid, if indelicate, comment by *Business Week* in 1974:

> "It will be a hard pill for many Americans to swallow—the idea of doing with less so that big business can have more. Nothing that this nation, or any other nation, has done in modern economic history compares in difficulty with the selling job that must now be done to make people accept the new reality."[44]

A showman of extraordinary ability, ideally unschooled in economic history, was required if families were to be convinced to vote against their own economic interest. That leadership was provided by the charismatic and trusted Ronald Reagan. Much of the subsequent success in stripping economic sovereignty from families that we discuss shortly lies with the advocacy role of Friedman and his powerful ability to appeal to wealthy executive suites and, through them, to Ronald Reagan. Similar to prominent twentieth-century scientists such as Francis Crick or Linus Pauling, Friedman's professional accomplishments lent undue weight to his personal philosophical musings. With the test of time, however, his Reaganomics has proven no more credible than Crick's flirtation with eugenics or Pauling's belief in megadoses of vitamin C.

The courtship of the economic neophyte Reagan beginning in the 1970s was built on three elements:

- First, Milton Friedman's philosophy was appealing to Reagan in his role as General Electric's corporate spokesman to generally affluent shareholders. The notions of deregulation and the demonization of government were alluring to upwardly mobile Americans like Reagan and to major Republican Party business contributors like the ITT Corporation.

- Second, supporters conflated the cause of Reaganomics with that of democracy during the Cold War era, arguing powerfully that only laissez-faire economics was consistent with the American ideals of capitalism and democracy. They exploited the Cold War to toss mainstream economics and Aristotle under the bus.

- Third, it was argued that Reaganomics was an aspect of American exceptionalism reflecting individualism and the nation's frontier spirit. Exceptionalism was originally conceived by Alexis de Tocqueville who argued (erroneously, as it turned out) that the melting pot of America without class or religious distinctions would enable it to soar and avoid internal strife. In economics, that has morphed into a truth that optimism, risk-taking, and the courage to challenge the present are features of America's DNA. A revolutionary democracy, the United States was created by the daring and bold, and our open society fortunately has continually been replenished over the centuries with some of the most clever and bold from across the globe. Yet, as we will see, the outcome of Reaganomics has been to erode—rather than enhance—opportunity and diminish American exceptionalism.

The Role of Pecuniary Politics in the Rise of Reaganomics

Wealthy businessman and Senator Mark Hanna defined the pivotal role of corporate funding of politicians and political parties a century ago. You may recall his comment that three things are important in politics; the first is money—and he couldn't recall the others. Money has always played a relatively large role in our nation's politics. Donations from executives were helpful in the political career of Ronald Reagan and contributed to the Chicago School's success in promoting deregulation. Friedman allowed his ideology to be exploited by executive suites, providing a fig leaf of respectability for their emerging narcissism. Writer Naomi Klein explains Friedman's role in resurrecting *laissez-faire* economics this way:

> "If Friedman's close friend Walter Wriston, head of Citibank, had come forward and argued that the minimum wage and corporate taxes should be abolished, he naturally would have been accused of being a robber baron. And that's where the Chicago School came in. It quickly became clear that when Friedman, a brilliant mathematician and skilled debater, made those same arguments, they took on an entirely different quality. They might be dismissed as wrong-headed, but they were imbued with an aura of scientific impartiality. The enormous benefit to having corporate views funneled through

academic, or quasi-academic, institutions not only kept the Chicago School flush with donations, but, in short order, spawned the global network of right-wing think tanks to churn out Reaganesque propaganda."[45]

President Reagan was an American success story of the first order, a self-made man who harbored strong sentiments for working class families by drawing on his own troubled childhood. The idealistic Ronald Reagan was ill-served by his trusted advisors. Even though he presented himself as president-turned-pitchman for a resurrected Gilded Age, the popular and charismatic Reagan was a complex figure. He was perhaps the most powerful politician of his time. Yet his was a thematic personality, inattentive with details, leaving the implementation of Reaganomics to underlings. He practiced what historian David E. Hoffman describes as a "passive management style, often more focused on performing than the details of governing."[46]

The engaging Reagan was inclined to swapping stories during business meetings with folks like one of my employers, the late Texas Senator and Treasury Secretary Lloyd M. Bentsen. Like most folks of every political persuasion, Bentsen found the garrulous President Reagan extraordinarily likeable. Handing me a card with Reagan's talking points after one White House meeting, the Senator noted that it contained the Administration's position, but most of the meeting was spent swapping stories, he said.

Reagan's unfocused intellect has dimmed his luster a bit, as noted by President George W. Bush's speechwriter David Frum: "The most dangerous legacy Reagan bequeathed his party was his legacy of cheerful indifference to detail."[47] Yet detail is vital in the zero-sum game of economics.

Reagan's failures are significant, but so are his successes. Ronald Reagan was an admired president, a genuine American success story who adroitly maximized his skill set to become leader of the Free World. He indexed income tax rates, which ceased drawing the middle class into higher and higher brackets. He simplified the tax code, an extraordinarily difficult chore. And he was a master at compromise, which is a skill in short supply nowadays among his party's officials in Washington. Few Americans would disagree that the nation would be better off if he still championed the conservative cause. Additionally, he proved as committed as any Democratic president to world peace.

But he was dazzled by articulate economists like Friedman, Secretary of State George Schultz, and Martin Feldstein, chairman of the Council of Economic Advisors, who married Reagan's distaste for taxes and regulation with his indifference toward deficits and disinterest in details. Reaganomics was subsequently nurtured by ideological think tanks, such as the Washington-based Heritage Foundation, attuned to the profits to be gleaned by fronting for firms and wealthy conservatives in advocating deregulation. They provided a gloss of *faux gravitas* in classic Madison Avenue style: Reaganomics was sold to Americans as some sort of gauzy new-age economic *wunderkind* discovery of untold promise, when it was nothing more than Gilded Age *laissez-faire* economics repackaged with new lipstick and a glossy wig.

For their part, always thinking about money gives economists finely tuned financial antennae, and some from prominent universities wasted little time in seizing the opportunity to moonlight as advocates of deregulation. Milton Friedman and Alan Greenspan were not the only prominent economists whose reputation suffered greatly from the notion of market perfection. The bankruptcy of the hedge fund Long Term Capital Management in 1994 humiliated Myron Scholes and Robert Merton, both Nobel laureates and champions of flawed economic theory. Other academicians closely identified with Reaganomics, including Hubbard, Mankiw, and Martin Feldstein, became controversial as well.[48] Europeans even have a name for them, calling such American economists "the secret lobbyists."[49]

The economics profession owes you an apology for permitting Reagan and George W. Bush to be misled by a key subset of our colleagues, who at least in some instances too readily blended self-interest with ideology.

The business community's lavish support of Reagan also linked it firmly to his political party, a marriage that has persisted for decades. Research by Cornell University economist Jin-Hyuk Kim, for example, found that donations by the most powerful and largest American firms markedly favor Republican politicians. Using a panel data set comprised of companies from the Standard & Poor's 500 Index from all sectors of the economy, covering the period 1998–2004, Kim found that one-quarter of the firms donated little to politics and 10 percent favored neither political party, while 6 percent favored Democrats and ten times as many, or 60 percent, favored Republicans.[50]

Do corporate donations pay off? There is some disagreement about this, but the weight of scholarly evidence is that Hanna had it right.[51] Kim found that by doubling donations, firms on average boosted equity returns by 2.4 percent compared to all firms, and by 1.3 percent compared even to peers in the same industry. These sorts of returns translate to serious profits for firms with equity measured in the billions for the investment of a few million dollars. Steven Brill, writing in *Time Magazine* in July 2010, calculated that hedge fund and other money managers invested perhaps $15 million, successfully diluting the Obama Administration's Wall Street reform legislation known as Dodd-Frank. That saved their industry an estimated $10 billion in taxes annually—an astronomical return of about 660 percent.[52] And a study by researchers at the University of Kansas identified a tax loophole crafted by lobbyists during the George W. Bush administration that involved the repatriation of profits sequested in foreign tax havens, which returned $220 for every lobbying dollar spent.[53] With such returns attainable, only a remarkably tin-eared CEO would forgo having an effective lobbying shop in Washington. Exploiting the pay-to-play American system to seek a specific policy change affecting profits is perhaps the single best investment an American corporation can make. Yet, as the 2012 Presidential outcome indicates, benefits from direct lobbying of Congress are not necessarily reproducible for national elections.

The Rise of Ayn Rand

President Reagan and his advisors—notably, Alan Greenspan—drew much of their staunch commitment and faith in deregulation from the Russian émigré and novelist Alisa Rosenbaum, better known to her fans as Ayn Rand. She authored best-sellers like *Atlas Shrugged* and *The Fountainhead* in the period during and after World War II that were paeans to individualism, self-regulating Reaganomics, and above all, self-absorption.

Her protagonists were Nietzschean superheroes—smart and strong entrepreneurs dismayed by civil servant Lilliputians constraining innovative American capitalism. These formulaic novels are great reads even today. In them, Rand popularized and legitimized the demonization of government which appealed so strongly to Ronald Reagan and became a seminal element of the era that later took his name.

Moreover, Rand vigorously rejected religious piety and the teachings of Christian charity in her personal life and extrapolated that to society—urging rejection of the wisdom of altruism and self-sacrifice for the greater good. Referring to altruism, Rand argued, as Kim Phillips-Fein explained in the December 2009 *Harper's Magazine*, that Christianity mistakenly, "had taught people to sacrifice themselves in the name of a false ideal."

As an alternative, she fabricated objectivism, a made-up ethical structure based on what she labeled rational selfishness, which exalted the selfish pursuit of individual satisfaction.[54] In essence, she promoted what the early twentieth-century American sociologist Thorstein Veblen would have termed a culture of exploitation where riches are "the basis of conventional esteem." Altruism was dismissed, replaced with the primacy of narcissism and self-absorption.[55]

Ayn Rand's contribution to American economics was to mute the traditional national guilt toward greed. If the market rewarded behavior, it was morally acceptable, even if it violated community norms or one's conscience formed by parents, biblical teachings, and society at large. This made-up philosophical construct provided psychological support for *laissez-faire* economics and justified the greed undergirding Reaganomics. Rand urged acolytes to reject as immoral any religious or ethical discomfort they might feel from the ensuing growing disparities in wealth or the human condition, certain to follow from the abandonment of altruism in executive suites or in the public square. Phillips-Fein concludes:

> "Her work offers a way of making sense of a profoundly unequal society, of making it tolerable, even virtuous."

Ayn Rand's philosophy spread throughout much of the financial and political elite in the Reagan era. Even many who never heard of Rand came to hear of and embrace her philosophy, as embodied by Gordon Gekko, a character in Oliver Stone's 1987 film, *Wall Street*:

> "The point is, ladies and gentleman, that greed, for lack of a better word, is good. Greed is right, greed works. Greed clarifies, cuts through, and captures the essence of the evolutionary spirit. Greed, in all of its forms; greed for life, for money, for love, knowledge, has marked the upward surge of mankind. And greed, you mark my words, will not only save Teldar Paper, but that other malfunctioning corporation called the USA."

Ayn Rand's associate during this period was Alan Greenspan, then a neophyte learning the ways of Wall Street. His deregulatory ethos, drawn from Ayn Rand's philosophy, led to the serial credit bubbles, the 2008 credit crisis, and the biggest economic calamity in three generations. The system he crafted is described in these terms by *Washington Post* columnist Steven Pearlstein:

> "It rewards manipulation over innovation and speculation over genuine value creation, resulting in massive misallocation of capital and the accumulation of unheard-of wealth in the hands of money managers and top corporate executives who are more lucky than they are skilled."[56]

The Elements of Reaganomics

The Reaganomics described by Pearlstein has eleven characteristics, each of which represents a departure from the political, cultural, and economic thinking of the golden age.

A Culture of Selfishness

Beginning in the 1980s, Ayn Rand's philosophy of self-absorption was increasingly adopted in the management and financial communities; greed was no longer embarrassing. There was a feeling of contempt for those who were unwilling or unable to enrich themselves or for the trusting souls fleeced by the market—men and women like you that Goldman Sachs financiers began calling "muppets."[57]

Government Is Invariably Dangerous

Americans have always been relatively independent and self-reliant, suspicious of both Big Business and Big Government. With Reaganomics, the notion took root that big government needed to be starved of resources with tax cuts. Simultaneously, the business community was transformed into a victim needing to be set free from government regulation. As Reagan said many times, "Government is not the solution to our problems; government is the problem."

An important economic debate on the role of government regulation in the early twentieth century involved the Austrian economist and philosopher Friedrich Hayek, author of *The Road to Serfdom*, who famously wanted dangerous government constrained.[58] His opponent was John Maynard Keynes, who was in "deeply moved agreement" with Hayek's concern, argues economic historian Sylvia Nasar, although much more willing to endorse careful government initiatives and regulation of business.[59] Hayek's concern was not targeted just at the collectivists, among them Karl Marx, but more broadly at the dangers posed by regulatory capture of the sort which emerged later in the Reagan era. He and Keynes feared the economically powerful of any persuasion including communists or the merchant class seizing the apparatus of the state to insulate themselves from market forces and competition.[60]

Their fears played out during the Reagan era; the regulatory machinery of Washington was utilized by executive suites to redirect the nation's income stream upward, upsetting the careful regulatory balance marking the golden age. Here is the *New York Times'* stark editorial assessment after a generation of deregulation delivered in January 2009:

> "The decades-old ways—in which . . . federal regulators have relied less on rules and enforcement and more on faith in market discipline to limit risk to the system—have been a manifest failure."[61]

Regulatory Capture

Regulatory capture describes a seizure of the tools of government by special interests; in this period, by the business community. As Adam Smith had concluded, the business community always seeks to influence government, and there was remarkable progress toward that goal during the Reagan era. The tone of government shifted; government was no longer supposed to be a check on the power of big business. Instead, it was supposed to get out of the way, or—even better—facilitate the goals of that community.

Senior government officials whose job it was to regulate industry became increasingly drawn from the ranks of industry itself, with plans to return when their stint in government was complete. These circumstances were rife with conflicts of interest as regulatory oversight weakened, especially in finance. Longtime civil servants were on the defensive, now considered to be part of the problem. And self-regulation prevailed whose inevitable outcome was described by Martin Wolf, chief economic columnist for the *Financial Times*, in December 2007:

> "What is happening in credit markets today is a huge blow to the credibility of the Anglo-Saxon model of transactions-oriented financial capitalism. A mixture of crony capitalism and gross incompetence has been on display in the core financial markets of New York and London. From . . . subprime lending to the placing (and favourable rating) of assets that turn out to be almost impossible to understand, value or sell, these activities have been riddled with conflicts of interest and incompetence."[62]

The rather dire consequences for the real economy of regulatory capture were also noticed in Asia. Kishore Mahbubani, dean of Singapore's Lee Kuan Yew School of Public Policy, argues that the lessons taught by history were cast aside after 1980: "Do not liberalize the financial sector too quickly, borrow in moderation, save in earnest, take care of the real economy, invest in productivity, focus on education. . . . While America was busy creating a financial house of cards, Asians focused on their real economies."[63]

Shareholder Capitalism

There are two general goals that enterprise managers can pursue. In stakeholder capitalism, executives balance the needs of shareholders with that of employees and other stakeholders: customers and debtors, even job seekers, and the national prosperity. They considered themselves duty bound not only to their shareholders, but to the community at large. Stakeholder capitalism flourished during the golden age in America, featuring steadily rising wages and job creation that translated to improving family prosperity. Think Henry Ford paying double or more the prevailing wage. Stakeholder capitalism is practiced in the family capitalism countries today.

In contrast, one of the hallmarks of Reaganomics was a transition from stakeholder capitalism to shareholder capitalism since the 1980s, in which executive suites nominally seek to maximize shareholder value. Here is how economists Isil Erel, René Stulz, Reena Aggarwal, and Rohan Williamson explained the difference:

> "Corporate governance differs across countries. In some countries, many view the objective of corporations to maximize the welfare of a collection of stakeholders, while in others, especially the UK and US, it is more commonly believed that corporations should be run to maximize the wealth of shareholders."[64]

The pursuit of these different goals produced the profoundly different outcomes we are exploring. To crystallize the transition in corporate goals wrought by Reaganomics, I compare two mission statements from the Washington-based corporate lobby called the Business Roundtable; its membership is CEOs of the largest American firms. The golden age orientation is reflected in its October 1981 mission statement, promulgated still early in the Reagan presidency:

> "Balancing the shareholder's expectations of maximum return against other priorities is one of the fundamental problems confronting corporate management. The shareholders must receive a good return, but the legitimate concerns of other constituencies also must have appropriate attention. Striking the appropriate balance, some leading managers have come to believe that the primary role of corporations is to help meet society's legitimate needs for goods and services and to earn a reasonable return for the shareholders in the process. They are aware that this must be done in a socially acceptable manner. They believe that by giving enlightened consideration to balancing the legitimate claims of all its constituents, a corporation will best serve the interest of the shareholders."[65]

That statement in support of stakeholder capitalism sounds hopelessly out of tune with the Randian narcissism and self-absorption fashionable today, exemplified by its 1997 mission statement:

> "In the Business Roundtable's view, the paramount duty of management and of boards of directors is to the corporation's stockholders; the interests of other stakeholders are relevant as a derivative of the duty to stockholders. The notion that the board must somehow balance the interests of stockholders against the interests of other stakeholders fundamentally misconstrues the role of directors."[66]

Weak Corporate Governance

Shareholder capitalism reduces a nation's competitiveness. Despite its name, shareholder capitalism disproportionately empowers management to prosper at the expense of everyone else. That is a problem because, in combination with stock options, it incentivizes what economists call *short-termism* in executive suites. Eyeing windfalls from stock options should stock prices rise, managers prioritize policies such as unwise mergers to spike stock prices and cuts in overhead to boost profits. That means wage compression, but it also means less research and development (R&D), lower investment, less workforce upskilling, and the offshoring of production to cheaper locales. Each of these behaviors weakens attributes that are vital to long-term firm success and to productivity growth. They incentivize precisely the wrong corporate strategy. In a climate of self-absorption and a focus on growing personal wealth, too little responsibility to the distant future (anytime beyond the end of the current quarter) has been evident in executive suites.

Short-termism is an anchor slowing the American economy. As the powerhouse German economy exemplifies, one of the most important advantages a nation can muster in this fiercely competitive era of globalization is the quality of enterprise governance. Weak corporate governance is America's Achilles heel.

Tax Cut Cultists

The Republican Party has rebranded itself in recent decades to emphasize tax cuts over its traditional focus on fiscal probity. Such cuts are now routinely posed as a solution to every problem, causing budget deficits and the national debt to soar. Moreover, this transformation has featured abandonment by that Party of the age-old tax principle of ability-to-pay, where those of similar incomes are treated similarly and higher incomes have higher tax rates.

Political scientists Jacob Hacker and Paul Pierson explain how this emphasis on lower taxes, especially on the wealthy, has changed the American socioeconomic landscape:

> "A generation ago, the United States was a recognizable, if somewhat more unequal, member of the cluster of affluent democracies known as mixed economies, where fast growth was widely shared. No more. Since around 1980, we have drifted away from the mixed-economy cluster, and traveled a considerable distance toward another: the capitalist oligarchies, like Brazil, Mexico, and Russia, with their much greater concentration of economic bounty."[67]

"Deficits Don't Matter"

With economic growth underperforming, Presidents Reagan, George H.W. Bush, and George W. Bush, resorted to traditional monetary and fiscal policies to spur growth. In so doing, they abandoned prudence in government finance, ushering in decades of big government spending resulting in unprecedented peacetime budget deficits. (The Democratic President Bill Clinton added little to the national debt.) They increased the national debt a startling tenfold; that caused each family's portion of the national debt to rise from about $4,000, when Ronald Reagan was elected, to $34,750 by the end of the second Bush Administration in 2008—a stunning increase engineered by Republican presidents promising balanced budgets. The ensuing jump in national debt left the Obama Administration poorly positioned to respond to the economic downturn it inherited, the worst since the Great Depression. Among the harshest critics of the Reagan-era debt splurge from 1981 to 2008 have been Republican debt scolds. President Nixon's Secretary of Commerce, Peter G. Peterson, billionaire cofounder of Blackstone private equity and a prominent Republican, pulls no punches about his party's leaders:

> "The conservative stewards of Reaganomics, ironically, have themselves created the Keynesian nightmare—large and permanent deficits—they so much feared. . . . To find the proper historical parallel for the United States in the 1980s, we . . . must look to those rare historical occasions when an economy's large size, its world class currency, and its open capital markets have allowed it to borrow immense sums primarily for the purpose of consumption and without regard to productive return. The illustration of lumbering, deficit-hobbled, low-growth economies that come most easily to mind are Spain's in the late sixteenth century, France's in the 1780s, and Britain's in the 1920s."[68]

Reagan-era America fits readily into this group of feckless spendthrifts brought low by credit binges. But America isn't alone: other far smaller democracies have also borrowed excessively in recent decades, mostly nations around the Mediterranean, the UK, and Ireland. Like the US, all faced serious sovereign debt challenges and years of slow growth. These nations were perhaps following the example of President Reagan who nearly tripled the national debt himself. But maybe not: Politicians scarcely need role models from abroad to spend more than they collect in taxes.

Illusory Prosperity

As the budget deficits document, America embarked on an unprecedented credit binge during the Reagan era. Easy credit was adopted, featuring financial sector deregulation and expansive central bank monetary policy. When combined with rising corporate debt, rising household debt (to sustain living standards amid stagnant wages), and rising national debt, American credit outstanding grew from $5 trillion, when President Carter left office, to $53 trillion when President George W. Bush departed, easily the worst credit blowout in world history. It was possible only because President Nixon abandoned the gold standard and because investors abroad viewed the dollar as a key currency and proved willing to hold American debt as a precautionary reserve against their own economic troubles.

Little of this splurge benefited American families, however, and it certainly didn't bolster productivity or investment, either. Mindful of the slump in American productivity and stagnant wages characterizing the Reagan era, Michael Pascoe, a business editor at the *Sydney Morning Herald*, put the credit blowout in perspective:

> "It wasn't the subprime crisis and the subsequent GFC [Global Financial Crisis] that flat-lined the US—it was already going nowhere but no one noticed because the stagnation was papered over by its debt explosion. The World's biggest economy was like an individual on a fixed income who runs up a big credit card debt buying the new car, the new boat, and a flash holiday. The individual looks richer and has more stuff, but in reality is not richer. . . . Much of America's middle and working classes didn't even get to share in the illusion while it lasted—their incomes have grown little and the debt-fueled jobs growth proved as illusionary as George Bush's 'mission accomplished' and Fannie Mae's balance sheet."[69]

Rising Income Disparity

By compressing wages and seeing that virtually all the gains from growth are being redistributed upward, Reaganomics has caused income disparities to widen to levels not seen since the Roaring Twenties. Some of the best scholarly research on American income inequality was performed by economist Larry Bartels of Vanderbilt University. During the decades of the golden age, incomes at the top of the middle class were about three times greater than at the bottom of the middle class. It takes a dramatic shift over many years to change income disparities, but events during the Reagan era proved sufficiently powerful that Bartels has determined the ratio is now close to four times larger.[70] A poster child for this new Gilded Age is former Walmart CEO Lee Scott, Jr. who in 2005 received 900 times the paycheck of his typical employee. He earned in two weeks what an average Walmart employee will earn in a lifetime.[71]

The speed, enormity, and perseverance of this jump in income disparity has fascinated observers in the family capitalism countries. Here is German journalist Thomas Schulz, writing in Hamburg-based *Der Spiegel* in August 2010:

> "One in eight American adults and one in four children now survive on government food stamps. These are unbelievable numbers for the world's richest nation. . . . They face a bitter reality of fewer and fewer jobs, decades of stagnating wages, and dramatic increases in inequality. . . . Income inequality in the United States is greater today than it has been since the 1920s."[72]

This reads as though Schulz is writing about some misfiring society in a far-off land. America today has by far the most severe income disparity of any rich democracy, nearly identical to the income disparity in Turkey and more than twice as skewed as other rich democracies like Australia. How severe is it? Well, the wealthiest 400 have come to own more than the poorest 150 million Americans, marking a resurrection of the Gilded Age. It's no wonder that foreign media, *Der Spiegel*, for example, regularly feature such headlines as "Has America become an Oligarchy?"[73]

Reducing Opportunity

America is the land of opportunity, the land of Horatio Alger, where pluck, education, and ability are a certain ticket to prosperity. Stout advocates invoked that promise repeatedly during the Reagan era, like President George W. Bush in November 2008: "Free market capitalism is . . . the engine of social mobility, the highway to the American Dream."[74]

And it used to be that way, as your ambitious ancestors, along with millions of other immigrants, made their way to American shores and prosperity. That magical epoch was brought to an end by Reaganomics. Wage compression, shareholder capitalism, job offshoring, tax changes, and sharply rising incomes at the top have knocked the props from beneath the opportunity society. Here is MIT professor Paul Osterman:

> "One objection we hear is that these bad, low-wage jobs are transitory, that people just move through them on their way up. But that's not true. Overwhelmingly, adults stay in these jobs for years and years. It's not Horatio Alger."[75]

With quality jobs drying up, economic mobility since the 1980s has diminished by about one-third. It is now so weak that America has become distinguished for having the worst—rather than the best—opportunity among rich democracies. Analyses have concluded that 42 percent of sons in poor families (in the bottom 20 percent of families by income) will be poor themselves as adults a generation later, while 40 percent of sons from rich families will themselves be rich as adults. That means the most important economic decision any American makes is to pick parents very, very carefully. Rags to riches? It still happens, but the odds are vanishingly small for sons from poor families, where only 6 percent manage to become rich. That means your odds of being rich are almost seven times better if born rich than poor. The America of Horatio Alger has devolved to become the best rich democracy in which to be born rich, but the worst in which to be poor. Opportunity in America resembles that in struggling Third World nations, not Australia or Germany.

Economic Mythmaking

The consequences we are exploring make Reaganomics an economic disappointment for families and voters. Economic myths have been important in sustaining it. Three of them are noted above, including the canards that government is inevitably dangerous, that deficits don't matter, and that Reaganomics has enhanced American economic opportunity. But other important myths have also been nurtured during the Reagan era, including erroneously blaming wage compression on globalization.

Another myth is that education and pluck are the answers to wage stagnation. In reality, real wages for college graduates are lower today than a generation or more ago. Education and pluck are obviously not sufficient keys to riches; if they were, computer scientists and other engineers, mathematicians, and Harvard professors would be reaping millions of dollars a year rather than financial engineers and corporate executives.

Another myth is that the economies of northern Europe are misfiring and sclerotic. Yet, these are economies where productivity has grown one-third faster than America's for three decades. In fact, those in the best position to know—American corporations—are enthralled with rich old Europe, where they have created many thousands of jobs paying $10 an hour more than at home.

The Shift

While the shift in political, cultural, and economic directions embodied by Reaganomics was profound and dramatic, it failed to improve middle class living standards. In fact, one study by the nonpartisan Pew Research Center concluded that eroding wages caused the middle class to shrink in size from 61 percent of adults in 1971 to 51 percent in 2011.[76] In contrast, the middle class has continued to prosper in those nations such as Australia and Germany under family capitalism, as we see in the next chapter.

CHAPTER 3

THE TRIUMPH OF FAMILY CAPITALISM

"There are important lessons to be learnt from the Netherlands and Germany, and the effective collaboration between . . . employers and the workers—that actually allowed companies to find the best way to respond to what was a very large shock."[1]

STEFANO SCARPETTA,
OECD, *Financial Times*, August 2011

"The Findings set out in this report suggest that rapid deterioration in the face of global economic forces is not inevitable, and that states, firms and workers have some ability to influence and affect this relationship."[2]

JESS BAILEY, JOE COWARD, and MATTHEW WHITTAKER,
***Painful Separation*,**
Resolution Foundation, London, October 2011

Family capitalism draws its sharpest distinctions with Reaganomics in five areas:

REAGANOMICS	**FAMILY CAPITALISM**
Shareholder Capitalism	Stakeholder Capitalism
A Culture of Selfishness	A Culture of Responsibility
Regulatory Capture	Wariness of Corporate Influence
Weak Corporate Governance	Codetermination
Illusory Prosperity	Genuine Wealth Creation

Let's consider each in turn.

Shareholder vs. Stakeholder Capitalism

The stakeholder capitalism practiced in the family capitalism countries has more beneficial outcomes for families than American shareholder capitalism. It symbolizes that the rules and procedures in such nations are intended to maximize wages and the number of high-quality jobs that justify those high wages. Family prosperity is the covenant in these nations, with voters demanding that enterprise management hew to it. In contrast to Reaganomics, real wages rise, domestic production rather than imports are emphasized, and few quality jobs are offshored while executive suites adopt a host of practices such as R&D, workforce upskilling, and investment to nurture productivity growth. It is the same orientation common in the golden age where, for example, the pay of US CEOs rose less than 1 percent annually, which meant their wages about kept pace with employee real wages. The top three executives at America's largest firms back then earned about 30 times more than the average of their employees.

Under shareholder capitalism today, they earn about 300 times more than the average employee. That contrast symbolizes how American voters in recent decades have *de facto* prioritized the prosperity of the business community rather than families. Executives have been exploiting this notion, combining supine corporate boards and stock options to game shareholders and seize most of the gains from growth. At the same time, pay-for-performance in executive suites has collapsed, as noted by columnist Gideon Rachman of the *Financial Times*:

> ". . . a link between virtuous effort and just reward has been effectively destroyed by the spectacle of bankers driving their institutions into bankruptcy while being rewarded with million-pound bonuses and munificent pensions."[3]

Worse, as noted a moment ago, shareholder capitalism incentivizes a set of lushly remunerative behaviors by executives quite destructive to broader American economic progress. Shareholder capitalism promotes management over shareholders, management over the firm, and the firm over employees, families, and society. Dismayed by Milton Friedman's harmful vision, criticism of shareholder capitalism has become sharp, exemplified by Cornell law professor Lynn A. Stout, author of *The Shareholder Value Myth: How Putting Shareholders First Harms Investors, Corporations, and the Public:*

> "In the quest to 'unlock shareholder value,' they sell key assets, fire loyal employees, and ruthlessly squeeze the workforce that remains; cut back on product support, customer assistance, and research and development; delay replacing outworn, outmoded, and unsafe equipment; shower CEOs with stock options and expensive pay packages to 'incentivize' them; drain cash reserves to pay large dividends and

> repurchase company shares, leveraging firms until they teeter on the brink of insolvency; and lobby regulators and Congress to change the law so they can chase short-term profits speculating in high-risk financial derivatives."[4]

Little wonder American productivity growth is so weak.

A Culture of Responsibility

While Reaganomics endorses a culture of self-absorption, executives and financial leaders in the family capitalism countries reflect a culture of responsibility. As we shall see, Reagan-era America features executive suites receiving the grandest remuneration in the world despite mediocre productivity performances, with pay-for-performance all but abandoned. The American market for executive compensation is a classic example of market failure.

In contrast, voters in the family capitalism countries expect executives to strike a balance between their own compensation, employee compensation, growing productivity, and nurturing long-term enterprise success with investment and research. Additionally, they expect that government officials will carefully monitor and reinforce those expectations. Nowhere is this vastly different perspective more evident than in wage outcomes. For example, the highest US industrial wages are in the auto industry, where wage and benefit costs averaged $36.34 per hour in 2008 before the recession.[5]

These wages became a flash point when GM was poised in 2009 on the brink of bankruptcy, with Republican politicians withholding succor and demanding wage cuts. Executives in family capitalism countries must have found that focus on wages baffling. American autos face their toughest competition from German firms, BMW, VW, and others, where employee costs are considerably higher.

Moreover, American firms in northern Europe pay those same high wages to their employees there. In 2009, for example, Ford's German employees at the giant Saarlouis complex had a comprehensive cost of about $62 per hour, according to Barclays Capital.[6] And despite the slowdown in Europe, Ford continues to prosper. "It has done very well to contain costs, and the products are pretty good," explained Peter Wells, codirector of the Center for Automotive Industry Research at Cardiff University in Wales, in April 2012.[7] Indeed, tens of thousands of German autoworkers at Daimler/Mercedes, VW, Ford, and other firms earn more than unionized US autoworkers, which indicates that wages and benefits had nothing to do with GM's threatened bankruptcy. Firms like Daimler can pay higher wages and benefits because German executives in a number of sectors simply have outperformed American management in recent decades.[8]

Regulatory Capture: The Relationship of the Business Community with Government

Like Americans, voters in the family capitalism countries are dubious of government. In contrast, however, that wariness also extends to its relationship with the business community; voters expect their politicians to prevent regulatory capture and to move aggressively when abuses become evident. In America, for example, during the housing bubble, Goldman Sachs and other firms sold financial instruments to customers, while betting at the same time that those instruments would fail. They made billions of dollars betting against their own clients in that fashion, yet few if any sanctions followed. The same abuse occurred to a lesser degree in Germany, but the outcome has been remarkably different, and informative.

Like Goldman Sachs, Deutsche Bank sold complex financial instruments to its customers such as the Ille paper firm in Hesse, while simultaneously taking positions against them. Deutsche Bank's self-dealing was contrary to German voter expectations of morality in commerce, however, and the courts agreed. In March 2011, the highest German court for civil cases ruled against Deutsche Bank's practice and imposed harsh penalties. Even worse for this giant bank, their behavior shocked enough people sufficiently to induce broad remedial legal action by the German political system, creating legislation similar to the original Dodd-Frank in the United States, but with teeth and without loopholes.

Such self-dealing is now illegal in Germany, and banks must clearly and explicitly warn potential investors and customers about risks or when institutions take positions designed to profit when customers incur losses. *Die Welt* explained:

> "This ruling has far-reaching consequences. After all, it does not only apply to Deutsche Bank. . . . This verdict contributes more to investor protection in this country than many of the well-intentioned laws that have been introduced by the Germany government since the financial crisis. . . . The new requirement, laid down by the court in its ruling, [is] that customers have to have the same level of knowledge as the bank. . . ."[9]

Australian officials react similarly to their own instances of corporate abuse. In a 2011 guilty verdict, a court concluded that the giant Centro

Properties' board of directors had breached the national Corporation Act by rubber stamping incorrect financials, thus misleading investors. As evidence unfolded in court, it turned out that directors had approved misleading accounts which did not disclose the imminent maturation of billions in short-term debt that would require expensive refinancing. An ensuing class action suit flowing from the verdict against the shopping center owner wiped out eighteen months of earnings.[10] The presiding Judge John Middleton explained the Australian expectation that corporations will behave responsibly, noting that boards of directors "have a profound effect on the community and not just shareholders, employees, and creditors." He elaborated:

> "The whole purpose of the directors' involvement in the adoption and approval of the accounts is to have the directors involved in the process at a level and responsibility commensurate with their role."[11, 12, 13, 14]

The Australian judicial system is more protective of the public interest than US courts, which tend to view economic issues through the lens of the business community. In that sense, the Australian legal system more accurately reflects Adam Smith's skepticism toward that community. While the marketing of addictive nicotine is legal in both, for example, the tobacco industry there is corralled; unlike in the United States, cigarettes can only be packaged in drab brown wrapping without brand logos, and they are dominated by vivid pictures of oral cancer victims and the caution that smoking causes mouth and throat cancer.[15] US courts rejected similar steps in August 2012.

Voters and the Australian government demand corporate accountability, with courts routinely pinning blame and punishment for ineptness, fraud, or mendacity at the very top, on CEOs and directors. The builder conglomerate James Hardie, for example, was a significant and profitable purveyor of asbestos-heavy products since the 1930s. Liability claims have risen sharply with improved science in recent decades, and Hardie's board and CEO faced an ethical dilemma. Looming accounting law reforms would saddle the firm with well more than a billion dollars in compensation costs over two decades. The board in 2001 had a choice: put up the money or decamp abroad. Members chose Plan B and announced a corporate relocation to the Netherlands, claiming the pursuit of lower taxes. To placate public opinion, it spun off a (severely underfunded) foundation intended to address victims of asbestos and related diseases.

But this strategy unraveled under investigation by the Australian Securities and Investment Commission (ASIC). For one thing, it seems taxes were higher in Holland than in Australia (Hardie has since relocated to the tax haven of Ireland). Moreover, the compensation fund quickly became threadbare, funded with A$293 million ($300 million) intended to cover claims now exceeding $1.5 billion.

The national press has excoriated Hardie for "leaving a rapidly-emptying pot for the victims of asbestos disease," according to *Sydney Morning Herald* reporter Leonie Lamont. "Public sentiment turned on what was seen as an act of corporate bastardry," added Lamont with Australian color; the supreme High Court and ASIC agreed. Hardie's CEO and board members were banned from other boards for as long as fifteen years and heavily fined.[16]

The contrast with Wall Street CEOs guilty of comparable amorality clarifies the higher expectations for responsible firm leadership in the family capitalism countries. Further, the public sector reaction to Deutsche Bank, Centro, and Hardie are indicative of a generalized wariness toward regulatory capture. And when it becomes an issue, voters respond quickly, as demonstrated by the plight these days of the Free Democratic Party (FDP) in Germany.

An excited FDP received 15 percent of the vote in September 2009, enough to join Angela Merkel's Christian Democratic (CDU) governing coalition as a junior partner. Its leaders became the German Foreign Minister and the Environmental Minister. Without missing a step, the FDP exploited its pivotal position in the new government to force through a significant tax cut for hoteliers, only later to admit the loophole was a *quid pro quo* for donations from the Mövenpick hotel magnate.

Sordidly, it turns out that the donor, Baron von Finck, Germany's richest man, is a tax dodger closeted in a Swiss castle.[17] That revelation quickly proved toxic in a sober Germany scandalized by this home-grown version of pay-to-play US politics. The reaction was swift and severe. Since 2010, the FDP has been on life support. It may even fall below the 5 percent threshold required to hold any parliamentary seats in the 2013 elections.[18]

Corporate Governance: Codetermination

The differences between the family capitalism countries and Reagan-era America is not just seen in attitude, voter expectations, outcomes, or executive morality. There are quite significant structural differences as well. The most important is the device at the center of the black box of corporate governance in northern Europe, which accounts for Germany in particular being the globe's most competitive economy. I mentioned earlier that shareholder capitalism places America at a competitive disadvantage, in part because it empowers short-termism. Germany avoids short-termism with *codetermination*, an accident of history that emerged in the wake of World War II, with employees holding a minority of seats on corporate boards. As we learn in later chapters, this device affords a considerable competitive advantage to German and northern European enterprises and certainly accounts for some of the outcomes we are reviewing.

In the family capitalism countries of northern Europe, voters insist that employers prioritize family prosperity. That expectation is enforced with codetermination. It produces long-term horizons featuring innovation, investment, rising real wages, and workplace upskilling. Voters have insisted that codetermination be complemented and reinforced with public policies that include quality education, extensive school to work transition, and intensive career-long upskilling, all proven to drive productivity and economic growth. The combination of such public policies and codetermination has yielded superior private sector innovation, investment, and entrepreneurship, and enabled the family capitalism countries of northern Europe to increase productivity for the past thirty years one-third faster than Reagan-era America. Broadly based and rising prosperity has been the consequence, exemplified by nations paying the world's highest real wages even as America devolved to be a low-wage nation.

Illusionary or Real Wealth Creation

Americans have come through an era in which decades of toil and savings produced what has turned out to be only illusionary wealth, built on a breathtaking $48 trillion credit expansion. The history during this era of wage stagnation is no better. In contrast, as we've discussed, real wages have multiplied smartly for decades in the family capitalism countries. Certainly, some segments of these societies have done better than others, but, as we'll see later, economists have documented that these income gains have been broadly based. America may be the best nation on earth in which to be born rich, but the best nations on earth to be born poor are Australia and France. They and the other family capitalism countries explicitly operate a version of capitalism that successfully treats an impoverished birth as a temporary condition to be cleverly remediated, not a lifelong curse that it too often is in America.

As a result of these trends, America has become a low-wage nation, where both wages and total employer costs for labor, once the highest in the world, have been surpassed by many other rich democracies.

As we see depicted in Chart 3.1, comprehensive costs for all private sector workers, including benefits paid by employers in shops, offices, and plants across northern Europe, are about 30 percent higher than in America.

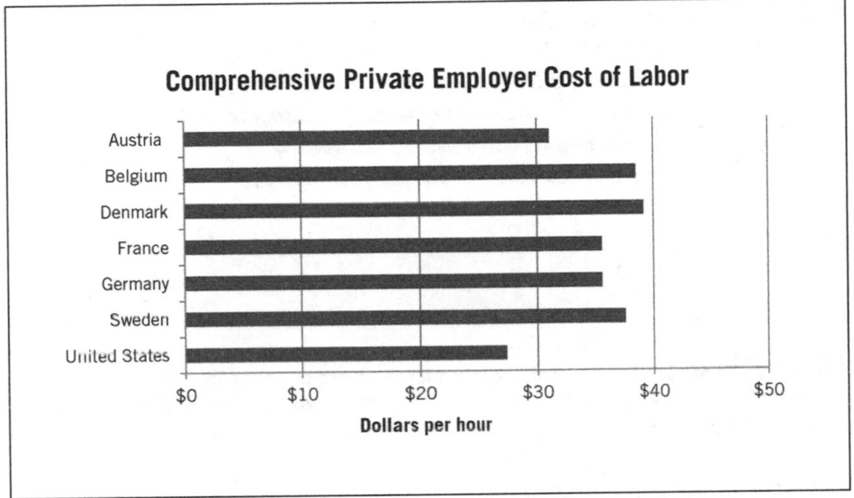

Chart 3.1. 2008, cost adjusted for purchase power parity. All private sectors including non-farm business industry, construction, and services. European data includes part time and employees at firms > 10 employers, but excludes annual bonuses generally equal to one month pay. Germany includes the former German Democratic Republic.

Source: Hourly Labor Costs, Eurostat 2011, Marie Visot, "The Debate on Labor Costs Revived," Le Figaro, February 28, 2011, OECD.StatExtracts, "Employer Costs for Employee Compensation, Bureau of Labor Statistics Historic listing (December 2008), and "The Cost of Labor Divides Senators," Le Monde, March 9, 2011.

The slowdown of recent years has not affected this pattern. In Germany, for example, the Düsseldorf-based Macroeconomic Policy Institute determined that employers incurred a gross cost per private sector employee in 2010 of €29.10 ($35.80) per hour, including fringe benefits and contributions to social security and other taxes.[19] And costs in Belgium, Denmark, France, and Sweden were higher still and higher than in the US. Domino's, for example, pays its drivers in Australia three times what it pays in America, but still manages record profits year after year.[20] Writing about Long Beach, California, port truckers, *Sydney Morning Herald* columnist Malcolm Maiden explains, "By our standards, they get a pittance."[21]

That disparity is emphasized by comprehensive employer cost data from the key manufacturing sector, reproduced in Chart 3.2. That sector is the fount of most productivity growth, typically pays the highest wages aside from finance, and is the sector most stressed by globalization. The actual wage component of these figures ranges from about one-half in Belgium to two-thirds or so in Australia and the US.

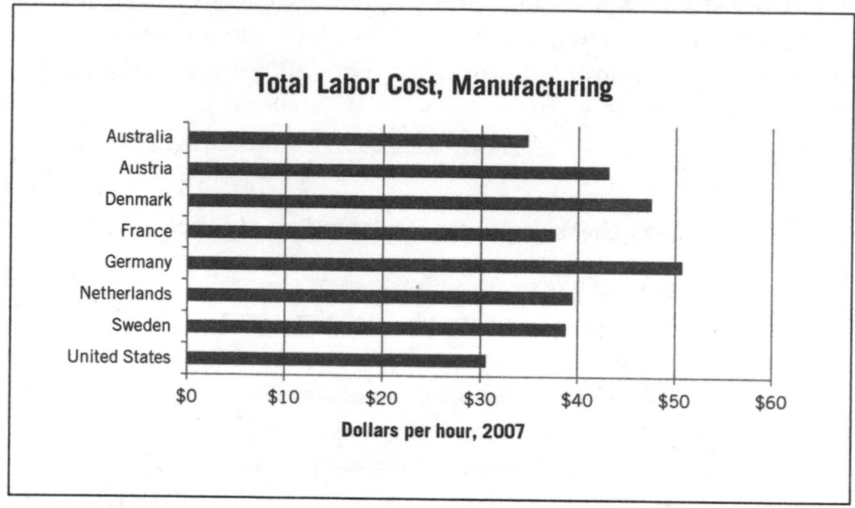

Chart 3.2. Private sector, US dollars adjusted for purchase power parity, 2007.
Source: Hourly Compensation Costs, Competitiveness in Manufacturing, Bureau of Labor Statistics, Department of Labor, 2010, Washington, table 3.1.

These high wages are the consequence of the family capitalism countries achieving steadily rising real wages. That means workers have received a notable portion of the gains from growth for decades. Americans are justly proud of the nation's genuine entrepreneurial and innovative culture and presume that the US economy remains fundamentally potent. The key measure of economic prowess is the growth rate of productivity, the value of output for each hour of work. America certainly enjoyed superior performance in the post-war golden age, when labor productivity growth averaged 2.8 percent annually. But, as we learned earlier, since 1979, productivity growth has averaged nearly a percentage point less per year. In contrast, international statistics show that productivity growth in northern European nations like France and Germany, for that same sustained period of three decades, has averaged one-third higher than America. Wages have risen to overtake America, because employees in the family capitalism countries have been receiving 30 percent or more of the gains year in and year out from that growth in productivity, while all but a few Americans received none. That is why European multinationals now view America as a low-wage nation and Americans as low-wage workers.

Family Capitalist Firms Abroad

Enterprises in the family capitalism countries face a community expectation that families will share in their success and obviously, they have pursued wage and other policies to meet those expectations—at home, anyway. But those same firms readily abandon domestic standards—particularly on wages—when investing abroad. They unabashedly pay local scale overseas, which is always lower than at home. Indeed, they are so aggressive in compressing wages to the extent permitted by foreign rules that they occasionally are targets of criticism.

For example, on September 2, 2010, Human Rights Watch fingered ten of the largest northern Europe firms, including Siemens, Deutsch Telekom, Gamma, Kongsberg, and Sodexo, for exploiting workers in a foreign market, where voters endorse weak local laws that were "less protective of freedom of association of employees." Human Rights Watch highlighted that these firms in the foreign market were "adopting practices common [there] but banned in Europe." Their goal was to maximize profits by suppressing wages, and they were duplicitous about it, as Human Rights Watch pointed out:

> "These companies proudly state their commitment to international labour standards, but in practice they have taken steps to create a culture of fear about organizing. . . ."[22]

The European firms, viewing employee activists urging wage hikes as threats, were guilty of a variety of practices not permitted in northern Europe. They included: intimidating employee organizers with "interviews akin to interrogation," firing labor organizers, refusing to negotiate with unions, changing job classifications to deprive employees of organizing rights, deploying misinformation, and hiring replacements for striking workers. Deutsche Telekom demurred, noting accurately: "We respect all [local] rules and laws. . . . It's baffling that we are named in this context and firmly reject all the allegations." As it transpired, the firms could legally commit these abuses because laws in this low-wage nation permitted it; their American, Japanese, and Korean competitors were doing precisely the same thing.

Families in what nation were being victimized by this employee abuse? Was it Cambodia, Nigeria, China, or perhaps Tajikistan?

It was being done in . . . America.

Low-wage America. The *Financial Times* reports that Daimler had settled on a new location to shift some C-Class sedan production from Sindelfingen, Germany, in order to exploit cheap foreign wages:

> "The Tuscaloosa plan was a blow to the 94-year-old Sindelfingen plant and underscored how managers are looking to expand plans in regions with low labour costs and weak currencies."[23]

European firms have eagerly taken advantage of the low-wage culture empowered by Reaganomics. Corporations content to pay the world's highest wages at home ruthlessly exploit the low wages permitted in the US. Volkswagen, for example, offered jobs at $14.50 per hour at its new Chattanooga plant—one-quarter its labor costs in lower Saxony.[24]

Richard Voorberg, director of projects for Siemens Energy, explained to reporter Joe Nocera of the *New York Times* that his firm is locating a new plant in North Carolina rather than China in part because "the labor cost differential wasn't very big."[25]

Here is how former Federal Reserve Board chairman Paul Volcker described the situation in December 2009 to *Der Spiegel*: "I think the labor cost is higher in Germany than it is in the United States, but you can somehow maintain that export edge. Tell me the secret of how the Germans keep this going."[26] The secret is hidden in plain view: superior corporate governance from codetermination that incentivizes corporate management to focus on productivity growth and the long-term prosperity of the firm.

Critically, European firms can afford to pay higher wages domestically because the labor component of most industrial goods across the globe is small, less than 20 percent. "Wages and benefits account for 15 to 20 percent of our costs," explained John Surma, CEO of United States Steel.[27] In autos, labor costs comprise 10 percent or even less in America.[28, 29] A host of other factors, including materials and energy costs, management competence, product styling, efficiency and customer service, are significantly more determinant than labor costs to enterprise success. Labor cost in many emerging industries, high-tech batteries, for example, is so insignificant that Korean LG Chem Power invested in a Michigan plant despite wages far above Asian levels. "Only 5 to 10 percent of the cost of a battery cell comes from labor; materials account for the bulk of expenses," explained CEO Prabhakar Patil in August 2011, to reporter Jon Gertner of the *New York Times Magazine*.[30] Moreover, as noted, annual productivity growth in a number of other rich democracies has averaged one-third higher than the US since President Reagan's election, enabling European enterprises to raise wages year after year without impinging on profits, dividends, or investment needs.

It was perhaps the Germans who first noticed that the US had become a low-wage nation and what had consequently happened to Americans. Here is Gabor Steingart, editor of the Dusseldorf-based business newspaper *Handelsblatt*, writing about baby boomers in 2006:

> "For many blue- and white-collar workers, this decline is already absolute because they have less of everything than they used to. . . . They're the losers in the world war for wealth."[31]

Australian Family Capitalism

American conservatives consistently list Australia among the most admired capitalist economies. The Heritage Foundation's *2012 Index of Economic Freedom* placed it third, behind the city-states of Hong Kong and Singapore and just ahead of egalitarian New Zealand.[32] America is tenth. It's conceivable that American conservatives are infatuated by solidly rising Australian wages and the high voter expectations for responsible corporate behavior, but more likely they are poorly informed. Australia pursues the same family capitalism model as Northern Europe, and, in some instances, is the country of origin of its important elements, like their highly effective national wage setting mechanisms.

American conservatives may be surprised by how dramatically the Australian economy differs from Reaganomics, despite the many superficial similarities between the two nations. Both were settled by British colonists intent on seizing land and wealth and making a better life, regardless of the cost to indigenous populations whose rights were homicidally flouted. Each featured vast frontiers rich in natural resources to be won by force of arms and grit, which nurtured individualism, a strong sense of community, and distrust of central authority. Each subsequently exhibited a frontier legacy of communal effort and, over time, a reliance on government to temper emergent corporate excesses.

In the United States, Washington took a number of steps to manage and regulate corporate abuses beginning in the Teddy Roosevelt period a century ago and again during the New Deal, but the outcome has been mixed. The reforms reached a strikingly greater maturity in Australia, which, along with New Zealand, proved to be a major incubator of family capitalism. New Zealanders conceptualized the minimum wage in 1894, for example.

In 1907, the first conceived minimum standard of living, or a livable wage, was institutionalized by Australia's Harvester Judgment . The reverence for this historic role in the evolution of capitalism is captured by a June 2010, editorial in the *Sydney Morning Herald*:

> "Australia pioneered the living wage, the principle that pay should sustain a standard of living that was reasonable for 'a human being in a civilized community.' That principle has underpinned the nation's prosperity and stability for a century."[33, 34, 35]

The spread to near-universal appreciation of the concept of livable wages accounts for voter determination there and in the other family capitalism countries that all economic actors should strive for ever-rising family prosperity. Prioritizing family prosperity also drives the

Australian focus on education and upskilling. Here is how Australian Treasury Secretary Martin Parkinson explained it:

> "As competition intensifies globally, as the global economy transforms and as our population ages, we are going to only be able to deliver rising living standards if we are going to be able to deliver greater productivity. . . . Productivity is not about working harder or working longer, it's actually about working smarter. This requires . . . top-notch management skills that would innovate and capture opportunities."[36]

The urgency of upskilling drives an inclusive education system where "every Australian is offered the opportunity to succeed and reach their full potential," explained Chris Evans, Australian Minister for Tertiary Education, Skills, Jobs and Workplace Relations in November 2010. And it drives a business culture in which expectations are a "fair day's work for a fair day's pay, the right of employees to collectively bargain with their employer and the right to safe and fair working conditions."[37]

For nearly a century, Australian voters have repeatedly made clear they want those expectations to be met by the business community and to be monitored by an alert trade union network and public sector. They demand that conservative and liberal governments alike implement those expectations, with a nationwide comprehensive bargaining and wage system overseen by the federal government as the day-to-day guarantor of Australian family prosperity. Voters understand the role of the market in facilitating this system, but would view an American-style transfer of economic sovereignty from families to firms as a betrayal of their most sacred economic principle: family prosperity.

In contrast to US voters, Ross Garnaut, Vice-Chancellor's Fellow at the University of Melbourne, explains that Australians reject "the treatment of labor as a commodity." In the most fundamental way economies can differ, Australia is the polar opposite of Reagan-era America. Its family capitalism model has ensured that productivity gains are shared by employees and employers alike in annual wage agreements. That goal is not attained mystically, but through a collaborative effort by business, government, and employees using a mechanism adopted in most other rich democracies.

Trade union activism has been important to achieving that goal. That activism led to paid four-week vacations, paid holiday leave, a cap on maximum working hours, and other worksite protections such as higher pay for evenings, nights, and weekends. Supported traditionally by both major parties, but initiated by the Labour Party, what emerged many decades ago is a national consensus: noninflationary wages are best achieved by a blend of trade federation and employer negotiations carefully monitored by the public sector. The Australian Bureau of Statistics describes the widely emulated mechanism this way:

> "In Australia, the 1983 Wage Accord established a centralized wage-fixing system that took into account economic policies and the Consumer Price Index. By 1987, the replacement was a two-tier system that distributed a flat increase to all workers and made further increase provisional on improvement in efficiencies. In 1988 and 1989, efficiency provisions were replaced by award restructuring and training provisions."[38]

In exchange for certainty in real wage growth linked to productivity, the 1983 Accord removed some labor protections in order to strengthen employer flexibility. This centralized wage determination structure is responsible for Australians enjoying real wage growth for decades, while Americans received none. Two quasi-independent entities comprise this structure, Fair Work Australia and the Australian Productivity Commission; similar institutional arrangements exist in the other family capitalism countries.[39]

These institutions enjoy powerful support from voters and enforce government rules supporting broadly based prosperity. On a spectrum of income disparity, the Reagan-era US income distribution leans toward the crony capitalism of nations such as China, with wide disparities. At the other end of the spectrum are Australia and the other family capitalism countries, where families broadly enjoy economic sovereignty and garner a considerable portion of the gains from growth. As I have emphasized, it's not the quantity of government regulations, taxes, or the size of government that distinguish Australia or Germany from the US, but whether government rules broadcast the gains from growth widely or narrowly. In Australia, this evolution to contemporary family capitalism occurred gradually with relatively modest conflict over nearly a century. Not so in Europe, as we see now.

Evolution of the Grand Bargain Undergirding Family Capitalism

The eighteenth-century industrial revolution launched an unprecedented wave of productivity growth and increases in wealth. But the ensuing income disparity provoked bitter debate. As Jeremy Rifkin noted, "Although Europe was the seedbed for advancing a private property regime, there was opposition from the start," mostly farmers and the urban working class—subsisting in such squalor that they fled the dreadful conditions of the early Industrial Revolution by the millions for opportunity offered by new lands in the Americas, Australia, South Africa, and Canada.[40]

Dickensian eighteenth- and nineteenth-century societies demonstrated that joint stock entities and the rising merchant bourgeois class could easily outmuscle families to seize economic sovereignty. Rising income disparities gave voice to collectivists; Jean-Jacques Rousseau, for example, who published *Discourse on the Origin of Inequality* in 1755, and Karl Marx, whose dense *Communist Manifesto* was published nearly a century later.

Mainstream critics sought to temper the increasingly evident excesses of poverty, wage suppression, and the amorality endemic with *laissez-faire* capitalism, as popularized by Charles Dickens and others, and later, by American writers such as Upton Sinclair and John Steinbeck. It was a battle first waged in England, featuring the Chartist laborers' uprisings in 1838–1848 promising class warfare.[41] Forced by public opinion to acknowledge the validity of long-suppressed employee grievances, Parliament launched study commissions and soon crafted a middle ground between conservatives like Thomas Carlyle and socialists like John Stuart Mill that became a continent-wide template. The Parliament's Factory Acts of 1844 addressed a host of issues—industrial accidents, hours of work for women and children, and child labor—and was a milestone amid the long grind to family capitalism.[42]

The philosophy undergirding these reformers evolved and spread from the first industrial states of England, the Low Countries, and Germany. It included contributions from socialists and compromises from powerful market advocates; even the stoutest market defender accepted the principle espoused by philosopher Jeremy Bentham and others, for example, that capitalism should not abandon the poor.[43] It drew on capitalist writings from Adam Smith, well aware of the flaws of unfettered *laissez-faire* enterprise and deeply suspicious of the merchant class. It was Smith, for example, who publicized that the East India Company had profited by harming its own farmers. The EIC restricted supply and raised food prices during the Bengali famine—a famine that played such a pivotal role in the 1773 Boston Tea Party.[44,45] And it was Smith more than any other economist, who gave lift to the remarkable concept that the brutal hand-to-mouth conditions of mankind throughout history weren't immutable. He believed they were amenable to reform and human intervention and improvement, through the careful exploitation of the ancient concept of markets and the human impulse of greed. That made him a great admirer of the grand experiment unfolding in the American colonies, especially in New England, which he praised in *The Wealth of Nations*:

"There is more equality, therefore, among the English colonists than among the inhabitants of the mother country. Their manners are more republican, and their governments, those of three of the provinces of New England in particular, have hitherto been more republican, too."[46]

Led by the German Chancellor Bismarck and other crafty politicians, European nations devised the clever bargain that still attains today: purchasing the support of employees and the landless for open trade, for free enterprise, and for capital accumulation by ensuring that families prospered as well as traders, capitalists, and entrepreneurs. Vital elements were publicly funded economic safety nets, workplace cooperative agreements, and labor unions that mobilized and coalesced public opinion in support of job and wage stability. As the Industrial Revolution matured, this grand bargain emerged as a family-focused market economy. It is impossible to overestimate its importance, for the evolution of that *de facto* bargain enabled the free-market concept to become the seminal feature of European economies and, eventually, the American economy, driving global prosperity. Here is how Rifkin describes it:

"It was a grand compromise, a way to appease the rising *bourgeois* class and the remaining aristocracy on the one hand, and Europe's working class and poor on the other hand. The idea of a private property regime would be upheld in return for a promise that some of the excesses of unbridled market capitalism would be redistributed, in the form of government social benefits. The welfare state would become a way to balance the books and prevent class divisions from turning into open warfare and revolution in the streets. For the most part, the great European compromise succeeded."[47]

But the default setting remained dictatorship and disrupted commerce, which reemerged in the wake of World War I as inflation, starvation, and the bloody flag of revolution stalked Europe, especially Germany.[48] During the disastrous Weimar inflation of the early 1920s, a streetcar ride that had cost a single mark before the war became priced at 15 billion.[49] Germany was the world's third largest economy at the time, and the failure of capitalism there in the early Bolshevik era would have had profound implications, irresistibly thrusting Lenin and later Stalin into the heart of an enfeebled Europe.

The armed Bolshevik threat Europe faced down in the tumult following World War I was an existential tipping point for capitalism. There was a pitched uprising in Berlin, bloody insurrections featuring a homegrown

Red army occupying the Ruhr in 1920, Saxony, and Thuringia under Bolshevik governments in 1923, and an attempted Communist revolution in conservative Bavaria.[50] The westward march of the Red Army itself stalled at the Vistula, thanks to Józef Pilsudski, and southward at the Caucasus, thanks to Kemal Atatürk.[51] The weapons were bullets and social reforms, including laws like the eight-hour workday (France 1919) and mandated corporate work councils in 1920, along with unemployment insurance, health, and welfare subsidies. Professor François Furstenburg of the Université de Montréal explains:

> "The Gilded Age plutocrats who first acceded to a social welfare system and state regulations did not do so from the goodness of their hearts. They did so because the alternatives seemed so much more terrifying."[52]

Europe was the battleground against collectivist ideology. Among others, Englishmen John Maynard Keynes and the journalist George Orwell, who authored *Animal Farm*, were passionate critics of collectivism. Yet deregulated capitalism was its own worst enemy. Washington officials, for example, proved unwilling to regulate bankers in the Roaring Twenties with strict caps on loans for stock speculation. Weak regulation and mismanaged credit causing the Great Depression deeply besmirched capitalism.

Staggering losses from panic selling beginning on Black Thursday, October 24, 1929, nearly equaled 50 percent of GDP. Even leaders like Winston Churchill were nearly wiped out personally; his home, Chartwell, had to be sold in 1929.[53] Tribally bound to honor the terms of the gold standard, central bankers took leave of their senses: despite deflation of 7 percent, the Fed doubled interest rates to 3.5 percent (to lure capital from abroad)—raising real rates into double digits even as industrial output was collapsing at a 25 percent rate. Less than one year later, national income was down 45 percent and nearly 30 percent of all Americans had no apparent source of income.* And the need for cash under the gold standard was so severe abroad that the Bundesbank

*Contrary to popular legend, it was not the Smoot-Hawley tariffs that caused the Great Depression, but the evaporation of credit. In fact, American import taxes redirected domestic consumption to domestic producers, stimulating demand and offsetting the loss of exports. Liaquat Ahamed explained it this way: "Far more damaging that the effect of the protectionist Smoot-Hawley Act was the collapse in capital flows. . . . It was the hoarding of gold by the United States and France and the resulting shortage in the rest of the world that had brought on the Depression." *Lords of Finance*, pp. 375, 431, 436, and 448.

officials also amazingly raised interest rates, hoping to lure capital home from America despite double-digit unemployment.

The Great Depression presumably forever tattooed *laissez-faire* economics a failure, with Keynes among the visionaries crafting the emerging European family-market capitalism in the 1930s. They realized that it was bad rules and inept management, rather than inherent fatal flaws, that had discredited capitalism. And they planned for a rebirth of family capitalism even as World War II raged, drawing inspiration from Franklin Roosevelt. His January 1944 fireside chat encapsulated the wisdom that human fulfillment has an inescapable economic component: "True individual freedom cannot exist without economic security and independence. People who are hungry and out of a job are the stuff of which dictatorships are made."[55] Drawing on Adam Smith, their alternative was to remediate the flaws of *laissez-faire* capitalism with careful regulation, creating a twentieth-century grand bargain, with government maintaining prudent regulations on commerce and labor markets and expanding the safety net with retirement and unemployment support.

As explained by his biographer, Robert Skidelsky, Keynes supported regulation to "redress the failings of society not because he loved it, but because he saw it, in the last resort, as the savior of capitalism from the temptations of collectivism or worse."[56,57] In clarifying a capitalism that sanctified family prosperity, Keynes and others fended off the Bolsheviks and provided the intellectual heft and insights vital to victory later during the Cold War. As much as Adam Smith, Keynes created the moral high ground enjoyed by free-market capitalism today by explaining how the abusive greed of markets could be ameliorated and corralled to avoid the unemployment and periodic financial panics of *laissez-faire* Reaganomics. As Yale economist Robert Shiller explained, Keynes'

> ". . . General Theory also had a deeper, more fundamental message about how capitalism worked, if only briefly spelled out. It explained why capitalist economies, left to their own devices, without the balancing of government, were essentially unstable. And it explained why, for capitalist economies to work well, the government should serve as a counterbalance. . . . Its role is to ensure a 'wise *laissez-faire*.'"[58]

Family capitalism was born in the wake of World War II, as western European officials clarified the role that enterprises should play in marshaling and deploying the risk capital needed for productivity growth and production. The vision of Smith, with his jaundiced eye on the merchant class, inspired European officials determining how best to prioritize family prosperity. They combined Adam Smith with mainstream Biblical verities drawn from the Catholic communitarian theology and the Protestant Social Gospel to alleviate poverty, hunger, and economic injustice. That is why some of the least religiously observant nations on earth have the most religiously grounded capitalism.[59]

The consensus was that the artifice of corporations shouldn't be imbued with the rights of man; there would be no American-style cult of the corporation in Europe. Paul Rayment, former Director of Economic Analysis at the United Nation's Economic Commission for Europe, explained the philosophy governing the role of business in Europe this way: "In a democratic political system, the activities and institutions of the corporate sector derive their legitimacy from the political sphere, not the reverse."[60] Firms are mere devices to efficiently marshal resources, spread investment risks, and create wealth, not entities capable of self-regulation, much less endowed with constitutional rights mimicking those enjoyed by genuine citizens. They are a subservient contrivance yoked by the counterbalancing rules of government to empower broad societal prosperity and enrich families, tools to be modified or even discarded when no longer useful to society.

In America, a European-style safety net was also gradually crafted beginning in the nineteenth century, inspired by worker activism including the Molly Maguires, the national railroad strike of 1877, the Haymarket affair in 1886, and the murderous Homestead strike in 1892. The safety net was weak, however, an outcome of the pecuniary nature of American politics, which—then, as now—bestows outsized influence on the affluent donor class including the business community.

And so we arrive at 1981. A wave of new politicians crowded into Washington, determined to unravel this grand agreement so painfully and thoughtfully pieced together in the 1930s and 1940s. Suffering with cognitive dissonance toward economic history, unwilling to learn from the Great Depression, and enthralled by the certitude of powerful personalities pursuing an ideological agenda, they launched the Reagan era. What was their biggest mistake? They threw Adam Smith under the bus, ignoring his warning that "The government of an exclusive company of merchants is, perhaps, the worst of all governments for any country whatever."

Section Two

THE SHIFT

Greed is hardwired into human DNA, and the reintroduction of *laissez-faire capitalism* sixty years after the Roaring Twenties gave it free rein. Reaganomics also gave free rein to historically unprecedented big government tax and spending policies. The late conservative Murray N. Rothbard of the Austrian School of Economics once explained that Reaganomics is a blend of three inconsistent schools of economic thought: policies drawn from big government conservatives like President Reagan, from monetarists, and from supply-siders.[1] While the second and third schools quickly proved theoretically deficient, the outcome of these three threads has been decades of big government spending, large tax cuts, and credit expansion unparalleled in US economic history.

But Reaganomics is more than just the economic elements highlighted by Rothbard. It also consists of political elements like deregulation and cultural elements, with the self-centered focus of Ayn Rand supplanting the community spirit of the golden age. Those elements gave the American business community both the means and the incentive to capture Washington regulators and pursue payday windfalls. The outcome has sidetracked America's evolution to family capitalism; the national goal became the prosperity of business rather than families. Shareholder capitalism replaced stakeholder capitalism.

This transformation was never presented for voter approval—for the very good reason that it would have been rejected. Few voters would have countenanced an end to the golden age and even fewer would have endorsed the adoption of the author Ayn Rand as the Reagan era's philosophical touchstone. Indeed, many voted for Ronald Reagan precisely because he promised to *restore* family prosperity, not derail it.

This section examines the elements of Reaganomics, beginning with its hallmark feature: deregulation. This resulted in dramatically reduced public oversight of corporations and regulatory capture, causing Washington to support the emergence of shareholder capitalism and ignore the impact of globalization on families. The most familiar consequences have been wage stagnation and widening income disparities. But as we will see, shareholder capitalism didn't work even on its own terms. Weakly governed firms came to be run for the interests of managers rather than shareholders. Short-termism and weak productivity emerged as executives became inattentive to the long-run success of corporations, minimizing shareholder value.

The most potent threat to shareholder capitalism is more public oversight. To reduce that risk, the business community has aggressively argued that government Is invariably dangerous, and engineered government gridlock to thwart reregulation. With the gains from growth mostly flowing to the 1 percent, another threat was higher taxes. Thus, the business community's solution to every problem is lower taxes—especially on the richest Americans. Spending cuts proved difficult and the combination produced large government deficits.

The first element of Reaganomics we examine unfolds in the next chapter, the regulatory capture of Washington.

CHAPTER 4

REGULATORY CAPTURE

"After fifty years without a financial crisis—the longest stretch in the nation's history—financial firms and policymakers began to see regulation as a barrier to efficient functioning of the capital markets rather than a necessary precondition for success."[2]

Congressional Oversight Panel,
Troubled Assets Relief Program (TARP)

"They took 50 sheriffs off the beat at a time when lending was becoming the Wild West."[3]

ROY COOPER,
Attorney General, North Carolina

"The idea that markets are self-regulating received a mortal blow in the recent financial crisis and should be buried once and for all. . . . Markets require other social institutions to support them. They rely on courts and legal arrangements to enforce property rights and on regulators to rein in abuse and fix market failures. . . . In other words, markets do not create, regulate, stabilize, or sustain themselves. The history of capitalism has been a process of learning and relearning this lesson."[4]

DANI RODRIK,
Harvard University, 2011

"Take it from a conservative economist who prefers less to more government: if markets are not competitive, or if they are otherwise failing to function properly, it takes the long arm of government to protect the invisible hand."[5]

IRWIN STELZER,
Director, Economic Policy, Hudson Institute

It was the most extraordinary departures in memory from the genteel and courteous language at the hushed senior level of America's central bank. Perhaps because it was delivered in Atlanta during the New Year's holiday in 2010, away from the spotlight in Washington, the accusation attracted little attention. It should have, because the message was distinct: Federal Reserve Chairman Ben S. Bernanke blamed the deregulation policies of his predecessor, Alan Greenspan, for the Wall Street meltdown. In a message that just as accurately could have been delivered during the Great Depression in 1932, Bernanke was blunt:

> "Stronger regulation and supervision aimed at problems with underwriting practices and lenders' risk management would have been a more effective and surgical approach to constraining the housing bubble than a general increase in interest rates."[6]

Bernanke has good reason to be angry with this regulatory capture of Washington by market fundamentalists over the last three decades. But you have even more reason than he does to be angry because regulatory capture very likely stymied your earning prospects during the entire Reagan era and is darkening prospects for your children as well.

How do we know regulatory capture occurred?

The answer is simple: it is designed to redistribute money from families to firms, so just follow the money. The great shift that occurred during the Reagan era saw most of the gains from growth redirected from employees to elite earners and the business community. And it occurred because officials in Washington placed their thumbs on the regulatory scales, deregulating finance and other sectors.

What does regulatory capture look like? In finance, it is exemplified by rising profit streams and bursting bubbles. Inadequate regulation was responsible for panics and credit bubbles in 1837 and 1858; the collapse of Jay Cooke and Company that bankrupted railroads during the Panic of 1873; and other panics in 1893 and 1907. Almost like clockwork, several decades after 1907, it occurred again: irrational animal spirits seized the usually sober family breadwinners who flocked to unregulated stock-gambling dens called bucket shops to gamble on penny stocks and investments touted by schemers, setting the stage for the Great Depression.

It happened all over again in the 1980s. Deregulation of commerce this time around featured rampant insider loans at savings and loan associations and later so-called subprime home mortgages available for the penniless and jobless, with cunning Wall Street firms such as Goldman Sachs calling their loyal customers "muppets."[7] "What Milton Friedman said was that government should not interfere." That's how Allen Sinai, chief global economist for Decisions Economics, Inc., described the ideology that resurfaced with Ronald Reagan. "It didn't work. We are now looking at one of the greatest real estate busts of all time."[8] History teaches that such deregulation invariably creates speculative bubbles that just as inevitably burst—whether in medieval

Barcelona, eighteenth-century Paris and Scotland, or Wall Street in 1932 or 2008, destroying the savings of thousands or millions.

The American Tradition: Don't Trust Corporations

The danger posed by regulatory capture was a great concern of our Founding Fathers and influenced their attitude toward corporations.

Continental Europe was the site of all three pivotal elements comprising modern financial economics: joint stock companies, banks conducting fractional reserve lending, and stock exchanges. Each was essentially in place around the time settlers reached Jamestown. That allowed greedy sovereigns and schemers during the Colonial era to profit on a mass scale from the opportunities offered by credit. Perhaps the most famous bubble was the 1636 Tulip Mania that caused the Dutch to wildly bid up prices—some writers suggest even so high that the value of one bulb could feed a merchant ship's crew for one year; woe the unfortunate sailor who munched one, mistaking it for an onion.[9]

In the eighteenth century, the Mississippi Scheme in France and the South Sea Bubble in England caused 1720 to be a particularly bad year for deregulation—worse even than the Great Depression. In the first case, a financial engineer John Law snookered the French aristocracy, selling them shares in bogus Louisiana gold deposits. Share speculation in the riches to be had—never mind the Indians and malarial mosquitoes or the absence of gold—reached a fever pitch in 1720 when shares soared 36-fold before the bubble burst.[10] The impact devastated Continental commerce and entered national lore so forcefully that the French remain leery of stock speculation to this day.

Across the channel in England a few years earlier, a chiseler named John Blunt bribed his way into a government trade monopoly involving the fabled riches of Spain's South American colonies. Bidding on Blunt's newly issued South Sea ownership shares became spectacular, with prices rising until July 1720, when the original investors cashed out, bursting the bubble. Thousands were bankrupted; corrupt crown officials and others were jailed; in the end, the venture's only profitable element turned out to be the slave trade.[11] These financial calamities inexorably linked joint stock ventures with calamity in the minds of many Americans in the late eighteenth century, as the American Revolution was taking root.

Even more eventful in forming attitudes was colonial experience with the infamous British East India Company (EIC), a monopoly importer. The EIC suffered from widespread flooding and crop failures in 1769 and 1770 in India that killed a mind-numbing 3 million Bengalis. The company was bankrupt, its speculation in Bengal gone woefully bad.[12]

Members of the English Parliament, however, who were important East India stockholders, enacted the 1773 Tea Act to bolster its fortune with higher commodity prices created by new tariffs on American tea.[13] That provided the Founding Fathers with a memorable lesson in monopoly power and regulatory capture.

America's Founding Fathers were economic sophisticates. Some were involved in the Stamp Act Congress in 1765 that first raised the idea of bearding the English lion. They were tough, brave characters who risked their lives and fortunes in rebellion against a greedy global military and economic superpower. Opinionated, anxious, and visionary, they had difficulty reaching agreements. But one thing they certainly united behind was disgust with the EIC, which is why any rights for corporations were explicitly written out of the Constitution and other founding documents.

The founders' deep reservation was based on hard evidence, with the success of the EIC unmatched by any other corporation in history. Its equal will likely never reappear. Its political influence was founded firmly on its trading, especially opium wealth, and job creation that helped fund the entire British Empire for centuries—and I mean centuries. The world's mightiest multinational ever, it is the only firm in world history to generate one-half of all world trade and to employ one-third of the entire non-farm UK workforce. Americans despised it as much as the British public admired it for its ability to extract wealth from colonists. Here is how *The Times* of London lamented its disappearance in 1874: "It accomplished a work such as in the whole history of the human race no other company every attempted and as such is likely to attempt in the years to come."[14]

Informed by this flagrant example of corporate excess, the historical record suggests that distrust of joint stock companies is why founding documents excluded the concept. Indeed, it was Thomas Jefferson's hope that the collective wisdom and power of representative government would prove able to eliminate "the excesses of the monied interests."[15] His hope was dashed as early as 1816. With the corrupting influence on the young Republic of joint stock firms already evident, Jefferson declared,

> "I hope we shall . . . crush in its birth the aristocracy of monied corporations which dare already to challenge our government to a trial by strength, and bid defiance to the laws of our country."[16]

The Founders were so distrustful of corporations that the only notion of collective risk they endorsed was that of public entities pursuing purely public goals, as explained by Baruch College historian Brian Murphy:

"Americans inherited the legal form of the corporation from Britain, where it was bestowed as a royal privilege on certain institutions, or more often, used to organize municipal governments. Just after the Revolution, new state legislators had to decide what to do about these charters. They could abolish them entirely, or find a way to democratize them and make them compatible with the spirit of independence and the structure of the federal republic. They chose the latter. So the first American corporations end up being cities and schools, along with some charitable organizations."[17]

Cities, schools, charities? Corporations like Goldman Sachs and Enron, and the rising domination of American politics by men and women grown wealthy from joint stock enterprises, such as the Koch brothers, are a far cry from that original American concept. Time and again since the Colonial era, weak regulation has been exploited by the well-connected, and the outcome is inevitably regulatory capture, as columnist John Kay of the *Financial Times* explained in the wake of the 2008 credit crisis.

"The effect is to enhance that wealth and power. This process is likely to end in political and economic crisis. That was the history of royal courts across Europe, from Versailles to St. Petersburg. More recently, it has been the experience of many developing countries and transitional economies. In the three decades since Margaret Thatcher and Ronald Reagan inaugurated the market revolution, it appears that Britain and the US have joined their ranks."[18]

Perhaps the most pronounced example of regulatory capture during nineteenth-century America were the railroads. Shopkeeper Leland Stanford became a rich railroad mogul not by driving spikes but by representing a few California merchants in Washington just as the nascent transcontinental railroad system began to take shape. More than two decades later, in 1887, the Interstate Commerce Commission was established to corral railroad barons like him, who routinely exploited employees with low wages while cheating farmers with collusively high rates. In a lesson for the ages, however, the ICC quickly fell under the sway of those very same railroaders. The pay-to-play politics of the day caused Washington to fill the ICC with railroad attorneys. One railroad attorney, Richard Olney, became head of the Justice Department during that era; he cynically described the nineteenth-century regulatory capture by railroaders this way:

"It satisfies the popular clamor for a government supervision of railroads at the same time that that supervision is almost entirely nominal. Further, the older such a commission gets to be, the more inclined it will be found to take the business and railroad view of things. It thus becomes a sort of barrier between the railroad corporations and the people and a sort of protection against hasty and crude legislation hostile to railroad interests."[19]

Regulatory Capture Returns

Oversight was improved during the Teddy Roosevelt era and again during the New Deal, but Reagan era ideologues brought a return of nineteenth-century regulatory capture (and income redistribution upward) to Washington. As Hedrick Smith has noted, the trend toward redistribution/deregulation began in the late 1970s when bankruptcy laws were changed to allow troubled firms to abrogate union contracts. Tax laws were modified to create 401(k) retirement accounts, enabling firms to shed expensive defined-benefit pension program for employees with cheaper defined-contribution plans. And 1978 also saw the lifting of interest rate caps on consumer loans, which contributed to the housing bubble.[20]

The new Reagan administration greatly accelerated deregulation. For most households, the bellwether wasn't deregulation of railroads this time around, but deregulation of electricity generation, a process that made Enron a household name. Under deregulation, power plants and distribution systems became board pieces in a giant game of Monopoly, with firms like Enron deploying every stratagem to conduct mergers and gain market share. The firm also proved eager to exploit deregulation to spike stock prices, much like 1920s swindlers issuing penny stocks. Enron's executives crowed about investing $90 billion in exploration after 2002, as noted by reporter Charles Morris of the *Washington Post* in November 2008. Yet it paid out even more just to spike stock prices—some $120 billion paid in dividends over the same span.[21] Enron was producing executive windfalls—not electricity.

And consumers paid the price. The federal deregulation of electricity split states into two categories. Most continued to regulate utilities and cap rates on behalf of consumers. But twelve states and Washington, DC, decided to deregulate, setting up an instructive economic experiment. (Montana has since reregulated.) By the end of the Reagan administration, notable price differences for electricity had already emerged. And today, residential, industrial, and commerce electric retail prices in deregulated states are about 50 percent higher than in regulated states.[22] Deregulation forced customers to pay about $50 billion more annually for electricity in 2007, for example, than their neighbors in regulated states.

Enron self-immolated later, but it was a big winner early on, netting gains from running one of the most brazen and profitable consumer scams in American history. The most egregious example was the West Coast electricity shortage over the winter of 2000–2001 engineered by a handful of newly emergent power conglomerates, including Enron, which collusively manipulated markets. It was a textbook consumer squeeze: power firms maliciously closed 13 gigawatts of generating capacity throughout the western United States that winter—decreasing production nearly three times more than typical winter-plant-maintenance shutdowns. Enron was introduced to Americans for the first time as contrived shutdowns by the company and its confederates caused a number of rolling blackouts in California—in a nation that rarely suffers blackouts unless weather-related. Niall Ferguson counted thirty-eight California blackouts in the span of just six months.[23] Deregulated interstate prices and profits soared.

Deregulation became widespread. Most consumers were directly harmed by deregulation of banking, for example, as explained by Senator and former Harvard Law professor Elizabeth Warren; she is an American bankruptcy expert who went on to establish the US Consumer Financial Protection Bureau:

> "Since the early 1980s, the credit industry has rewritten the rules of lending to families. Congress has turned the industry loose to charge whatever it can get and to bury tricks and traps through credit agreements. Credit-card contracts that were less than a page long in the early 1980s now number thirty or more pages of small-print legalese."[24]

Julie L. Williams, chief counsel at the Comptroller of the Currency, explained this new business model in 2005: "Today the focus for lenders is not so much on consumer loans being repaid, but on the loan as a perpetual earning asset."[25]

Regulatory capture has long been criticized by economists across the political spectrum, ranging from Friedrich Hayek, Mancur Olson, and Lawrence Summers, former Secretary of the US Treasury, to Simon Johnson and Paul Krugman.[26] The characteristic of regulatory capture in which the intense will of a few (say, producers) can overwhelm the slight and diffused will of many (consumers or families) made Mancur Olson and George Stigler justifiably famous among economists. Stigler won a Nobel Prize describing it.[27]

Some conservatives share the frustration of economists with the inefficiencies and redistribution of income characteristic of regulatory capture, including the conservative author and blogger Ross Douthat, writing in 2010:

> "In case after case, Washington's web of subsidies and tax breaks effectively takes money out of the middle class and hands it out to speculators and have-mores. . . . We give tax breaks to immensely profitable corporations that don't need the money and boondoggles that wouldn't exist without government favoritism."[28]

And here is the author and *New York Times* columnist David Brooks:

> "The legitimacy of American capitalism has rested on the fact that many people, like Warren Buffett and Bill Gates, got rich on the basis of what they did, not on the basis of government connections. But over the years, business and government have become more intertwined. The results have been bad for both capitalism and government. The banks' growing political clout led to the rule changes that helped create the financial crisis. . . . Can the state do anything to effectively promote virtuous behavior? Because when you get into the core problems, whether in Washington, California, or on Wall Street, you keep seeing the same moral deficiencies: self-indulgence, irresponsibility, and imprudence."[29]

The Revolving Door of Regulatory Capture

A prominent characteristic of regulatory capture is the revolving door, with industry officials morphing into Washington officials and then into lobbyists or back into industry officials—their personal gain blending seamlessly into fervor for shielding the business community from regulation. They comprise what George Packer describes as permanent "money power" in Washington, devoted to ensuring that economic sovereignty remains with firms rather than families.[30]

One example is Wendy Gramm, wife of former Republican Senator Phil Gramm. She was chair of the Commodity Futures Trading Commission (CFTC) under President George H.W. Bush in the early 1990s. (The CFTC regulates financial derivatives as well as commodities such as oil, gold, and cotton.) There, she successfully led efforts to deregulate derivatives in the period of time before she joined the board of Enron, netting herself a million-dollar payday. CFTC deregulation permitted Enron to profit handsomely in the years before its speculative collapse. Enron got a real bargain because Gramm, it turned out, had left a "Manchurian regulator" behind—a sleeper only revealed decades later by CFTC administrative law judge George H. Painter. Painter presided over cases of firms charged with abusing investors and when he retired in 2010, he asked that none of his pending cases be transferred to an obscure fellow judge named Bruce Levine. He explained that odd request in writing this way:

"On Judge Levine's first week on the job, nearly twenty years ago, he came into my office and stated that he had promised Wendy Gramm, then Chairwoman of the Commission, that he would never rule in a complainant's favor. A review of his rulings will confirm that he fulfilled his vow. Judge Levine, in the cynical guise of enforcing the rules, forces *pro se* complainants to run a hostile procedural gauntlet until they lose hope, and either withdraw their complaint or settle for a pittance, regardless of the merits of the case."[31]

The revolving door also incentivizes lawmakers themselves to weaken regulation, because they have their own subsequent careers to consider. The purchase of obliging legislators is a well-established tradition of American pay-to-play politics, particularly prominent in the Reagan administration. A financial crisis began in 1987 following the deregulation of savings and loan banks (S&Ls), where bad loans to board members and other officers eventually bankrupted 747 institutions. When subsequently asked by Congressional investigators if the $1.5 million he had donated to a handful of legislators was to buy influence, industry leader Charles Keating replied, "I certainly hope so."[32] Lucrative second careers weren't much on the minds of legislators during the golden age before 1980, but that changed after 1980, as former US Secretary of Labor Robert Reich and now public policy professor at the University of California, Berkeley, explains:

"In the 1970s, only about 3 percent of retiring members of Congress went on to become Washington lobbyists. But by 2009, more than 30 percent did, because the financial incentives for lobbying had become so large. . . . Former members who were committee or subcommittee chairs commanded $2 million."[33]

The door revolved particularly fast at the Pentagon. By 1985, midway through President Reagan's two terms, for example, about five times as many Defense Department officials were taking jobs in private industry than in 1975 under the previous Republican President, Gerald Ford.[34]

The Revolving Door Is Bipartisan

Americans identify the Republican Party as more attuned to corporate America, and for good reason. For example, Congressional Republicans in July 2011 voted to defund the Securities and Exchange Commission and to derail new regulations implementing the Democratic Party's Dodd-Frank financial reforms.[35] Yet pay-to-play politics leaves both major parties vitally dependent on special pleaders for campaign donations; the biggest donors tend to be from the business community, especially firms with business before Washington lawmakers and regulators. Democrats listen to their concerns, too. For example, the Clinton administration returned fiscal prudence and balanced budgets to Washington, a remarkable accomplishment. Yet too many officials supported Reagan era deregulation, especially in finance. Tossed under the bus were restraints on bank size and activities imposed during the Depression by the Glass-Steagall Act. The Clinton administration also endorsed offshoring (exporting jobs), and dragged its heels on minimum wages and labor law enforcement.

Moreover, like the Republican Party, Democrats have their share of prominent members who have walked through the revolving door, including Robert Rubin, the former Goldman Sachs banker and US Secretary of the Treasury in the Clinton administration. An elegant and genial man of great intelligence, he headed Citigroup that was bailed out during the financial crisis, even though the company was more bankrupt than Lehman Brothers.[36]

Deregulation Can Improve Efficiency

Despite the sordid history of deregulation, economists remain committed to the concept of lightly regulating business. Deregulation, when done carefully, can improve economic efficiency, expand consumer choice, and lower consumer prices. In the years immediately before the Reagan era, for example, the Carter administration provided a textbook example of positive deregulation in a cross section of over-regulated industries. Careful cost/benefit analyses were used by that administration to free industries such as trucking and telecommunications from regulatory capture. In these instances, deregulation with a scalpel worked well, opening entry to new firms and spurring innovation, lowering prices, and raising competition. Murray N. Rothbard, who was no friend of Democrats, described the Carter reforms this way: "The most conspicuous examples of deregulation, the ending of oil and gasoline price controls and rationing, the self-regulation of trucks and airlines, were all launched by the Carter administration, and completed just in time for the Reagan administration to claim the credit."[37]

The goal of regulation is to corral mankind's greed, protect against mankind's cognitive limitations, such as the herd instinct and myopia, and also prevent collusion. The challenge is to find a balance: the proper measure of oversight that promotes entrepreneurial risk taking while preventing regulatory capture. As a consequence of the Great Depression, America eventually settled on a set of prudent government rules that prevented regulatory capture and enabled the business community to prosper, while also benefiting families and employees. Prudent regulations, for example, constrained the financial sector back then, making banking boring, enabling the United States to focus on manufacturing, high-end services, and innovation—skills vital in winning a world war, demonstrating the superiority of stakeholder capitalism and democracy during the Cold War and in creating the middle class during the golden age. Augustine Powell and his postwar generation were the winners of that goldilocks balance in regulation.

Arrival of the Reagan administration upset that balance and also weakened the foundation of American capitalism, with financial engineering supplanting genuine engineering and high-value services as the primary engine of US growth.

The Regulatory Capture of Washington

The Reagan era arrived like a whirlwind in Washington, as explained by Richard V. Allen, President Reagan's new national security advisor:

> "Reagan's was one of the most carefully planned Presidential transitions in modern political history, replete with teams of 'Reaganauts' dispatched to each department and agency in the days following the election. Staffing lists were compiled and Presidential and sub-cabinet appointments were made swiftly, background and vetting checks completed and requisite Senate hearings scheduled."[38]

A number of President Reagan's political appointees, such as US Secretary of the Interior James G. Watt, were former industry officials determined to deregulate and convert public goods to private gain. A lumber executive ran the US Forest Service during the Reagan era. And a coal executive ran the US Department of the Interior's strip mining office.[39] They weren't just wobbly on regulation; they staged a transformation: the regulated came to dominate erstwhile regulators. It was the nineteenth-century Interstate Commerce Commission all over again—magnified across the entirety of Washington.

An aspect of the administration's deregulation initiative was marginalizing civil servants, mostly highly educated officials dedicated to improving the functioning of American society. These conscientious men and women were demonized and shunted to the side across the federal bureaucracy after 1980, supplanted or overruled by political appointees from an administration that, oddly, drew its strategy from Soviet revolutionaries. Here is how Reagan White House staffer and now tax cut cultist Grover Norquist described events midway through the administration:

> "First, we want to remove liberal personnel from the political process. Then we want to capture those positions of power and influence for conservatives. Stalin taught the importance of this principle. He was running the personnel department, while Trotsky was fighting the White Army. When push came to shove for control of the Soviet Union, Stalin won. His people were in place and Trotsky's were not.... With this principle in mind, conservatives must do all they can to make sure that they get jobs in Washington."[40]

Demeaning civil servants has a long history in the business community, as indicated by this complaint from 1928 by Homer Ferguson, President of the US Chamber of Commerce:

> A thoroughly first-rate man in public service is corrosive. He eats holes in our liberties. The better he is and the longer he stays, the greater the danger. If he is an enthusiast—a bright-eyed madman who is frantic to make this the finest government in the world—the black plague is a house pet by comparison.[41]

The kneecapping of civil servants by the administration is described by Irene S. Rubin, professor emeritus at Northern Illinois University: "The offices they supervised were stripped of functions, or they were sent on assignment to a US trust territory or given an office in an empty suite with nothing to do."[42] The adverse consequences have been especially evident in the banking and energy sectors. My former colleague and University of Texas economist James K. Galbraith explains:

> "The deregulation of the savings and loans was the work, in substantial part, of a task force in the early 1980s headed by Vice President George H.W. Bush; the beneficiaries were people like Charles Keating, head of Lincoln Savings and Loan, the largest fraudulent S&L, who could hire Alan Greenspan, then in private consulting

practice, to shill for his company with federal regulators. The self-regulation of electricity in California, which so favored Enron (a company headed by George W. Bush's largest campaign contributor), was facilitated by an energy task force in the early 2000s headed by Vice President Richard W. Cheney. The mode of operation and the results were entirely parallel in the two cases."[43]

Harmful Regulatory Capture of Banking

Credit can be a positive force for prosperity, but it can also be abused, destabilizing capitalism. The issue emerged in 1657 when a milestone in the history of credit creation—formally creating money out of thin air—originated with the Stockholm Banco.[44] Banks simply started lending more money than the size of their deposits. To the chagrin of Friedrich Hayek and the Austrian School of prudent economists, economics has never recovered from conjuring up credit out of thin air.

In the centuries since, governments have wrestled—not always successfully—with attaining balanced regulation of banking to limit credit expansion. Indeed, all major nations like the United States, France, and the United Kingdom have suffered from regulatory capture of their banking systems which eventually ended in recession. The Reagan era was just one among many such episodes.[45] Balance in banking regulation was knocked askew, reflecting hostile sentiments like this from William Isaac, President Reagan's first chairman of the Federal Deposit Insurance Corporation: "I believe there is such a thing as too much [reserve] capital."[46] Economist Paul Krugman notes in explaining the roots of the 2008 Wall Street collapse:

> "There's plenty of blame to go around these days. But the prime villains behind the mess we're in were Reagan and his circle of advisors—men who forgot the lessons of American's last great financial crisis and condemned the rest of us to repeat it."[47]

Make no mistake: large banks dominated Washington regulators. Here is Neil Barofsky, Special United States Treasury Department Inspector General for the TARP program that bailed out Wall Street during the waning days of the George W. Bush administration:

> "The suspicions that the system is rigged in favor of the largest banks and their elites, so they play by their own set of rules to the disfavor of the taxpayers who funded their bailout, are true. It really happened. These suspicions are valid."[48]

Evidence of regulatory capture emerged not long after the 1981 transition. In 1982, for example, President Reagan signed the Garn–St. Germain Depository Institutions Act, declaring,

> "This bill is the most important legislation for financial institutions in the last 50 years. It provides a long-term solution for troubled thrift institutions. . . . All in all, I think we hit the jackpot."[49]

President Reagan had no idea of the irony of his comment. S&L officials certainly hit the jackpot quickly, because Garn–St. Germain freed industry insiders from oversight, precipitating self-dealing and featuring improvident loans to themselves, their wives, and their cronies. Here is how economic historian Kevin Phillips describes events:

> "These once-solid institutions had been deregulated at the urging of the Reagan administration in 1981 and given effective *carte blanche* to borrow and invest (read: wheel and deal) in commercial real estate, junk bonds, and other temptations. Edwin Gray, the California Republican who headed the Federal Home Loan Bank Board (FHLBB) under Reagan, agreed that self-regulation was culpable because oversight was so badly neglected. 'The White House was full of ideologues, particularly free-market types.' They'd say, 'The way to solve the problem is more deregulation'—and by the way, self-regulation means fewer bank examiners."[50]

Reimbursing customers for deposits looted by S&L executives such as Charles Keating in the 1980s eventually cost taxpayers $256 billion (in 2008 dollars). In a precursor to the Wall Street bubble and 2007/2008 meltdown, taxpayers ended up on the hook for the equivalent of 2 percent of GDP.[51] And it all happened again eighteen years later because President Reagan had appointed Alan Greenspan head of the Federal Reserve Banking system in 1986, making him the nation's top bank regulator. He replaced Paul Volcker, a sober banker schooled in lessons of the Great Depression, who had just cured stagflation. Volcker believed in balanced budgets and balanced regulations—and so President Reagan replaced him with Alan Greenspan.

Reagan's economic advisors were hard-core ideologues. Milton Friedman himself, for example, believed insider trading should be *legal* because rules curtailing it would be too intrusive. That is a true story, and if Friedman had gotten his way, it would have fundamentally transformed American-style capitalism. It would have changed shareholder capitalism into an even more harmful version of today's managerial capitalism, a position too extreme even for some of the business media like the *Financial Times*, which harshly criticized Friedman's position in a 2010 editorial:

> "These arguments completely fail to justify what amounts to corporate corruption. If executives—and the bankers, consultants, and lawyers who advise them—are permitted to profit from inside information in this way, it makes a mockery of fairness and undermines the legitimacy of financial markets."[52]

Alan Greenspan's equally uninformed and obsessive distrust of regulation featured odd beliefs, especially that men and women in business are concerned foremost with preserving their own good reputations. The self-discipline imposed by these concerns rendered regulations unnecessary; indeed, regulation disrupted the smooth functioning of markets. Greenspan's mantra that regulation is superfluous first surfaced in his 1963 essay in Ayn Rand's newsletter: "It is in the self-interest of every businessman to have a reputation for honest dealings and a quality product."[53] Unlike Friedman, however, Alan Greenspan actually controlled banking regulators, and was absurdly unrealistic about the benefits of banking deregulation, as reflected in this 2003 speech:

> "The use of a growing array of derivatives and the related application of more sophisticated methods for measuring and managing risk are key factors underpinning the enhanced resilience of our largest financial institutions. . . . As a result, not only have individual financial institutions become less vulnerable to shocks from underlying risk factors, but also the financial system as a whole has become more resilient."[54]

We know how that turned out.

Indifferent to the lessons of the S&L fiasco, Greenspan made up facts like this one in 2005: "Private regulation generally has proved far better at constraining excessive risk-taking than has government regulation."[55] During much of the Reagan era, he dominated discussions in Congress and the White House as few Fed chairmen before him had. And he insisted that like-minded deregulators—former Congressman Christopher Cox, for example—fill important slots in Washington. Shortly after Cox was appointed to head the SEC in 2005, his actions sparked investigations, including one by the US Government Accountability Office, which concluded that Cox had disrupted investigations of stock manipulation, weakened enforcement, and minimized fines.[56] According to an investigation by the *Washington Post's* Zachary Goldfarb in June 2009, "He adopted practices that undermined the enforcement division's efforts to investigate cases of corporate wrongdoing and punish those involved, according to interviews with nineteen current and former SEC officials." Moreover, Cox weakened proposed fines and sanctions that in some instances had already been agreed to by firms. In one instance, Cox set penalties on JP Morgan at $2 million for behavior that had lost investors $2.6 billion. SEC penalties fell 84 percent during his tenure.[57]

Harvard economist and Nobel Laureate Amartya Sen summarized the consequence of Greenspan's stewardship:

> "The need for supervision and regulation has become much stronger over recent years. And yet, the supervisory role of the government in the United States in particular has been, over the same period, sharply curtailed, fed by an increasing belief in the self-regulatory nature of the market economy. Precisely as the need for state surveillance has grown, the provision of the needed supervision has shrunk."[58]

Now you understand why Bernanke was so frustrated with Greenspan and his acolytes. He rolled back regulation. He rejected warnings from private economists like Robert Shiller of Yale.[59] He even overruled more insightful colleagues hoping to bolster regulation by enlisting the forces of the marketplace itself. And that brings us to Arthur Levitt, Jr.

Greenspan faced a few courageous opponents in Washington who favored tighter regulation, but he succeeded in either chasing them from Washington (Brooksley Born, chairperson of the Commodities Futures Trading Commission from 1996–1999) or marginalizing them (Arthur Levitt, Jr.). One modest rulemaking in the 1990s might have prevented the catastrophic 2007/2008 credit crisis, preserving trillions of dollars in wealth and millions of jobs; even better, there was a Horatius up to the challenge. Appointed SEC chairman by President Clinton, Arthur Levitt, Jr. was no foolish ideologue channeling Ayn Rand. Savvy from a career running the American Stock Exchange, Levitt, like Adam Smith, understood that competition must be nurtured by prudent regulation. His solution to Greenspan's ideological deregulation was simple: exploit the unparalleled expertise of the Big Five (now Four) accounting firms to more effectively police Wall Street.

Levitt's years on Wall Street had taught him that accounting firms were negligent policemen. Accounting firms should be the alarm system on Wall Street, yet their lucrative consulting practices in firms they also audit creates a conflict of interest, disincentivizing effective oversight.

Levitt concluded that prohibiting auditors from also consulting for the same firm would free them to blow the whistle on customers such as Lehman Brothers. Rather than being paid to overlook problems, they would be paid to spotlight firms mispricing risk, holding inadequate reserves, or hiding liabilities on off-balance-sheet affiliates. Using market expertise to enhance market operations made eminent sense to economists, too, but there was a problem, a big problem: objections from the Big Five worried about lost profits. Like the Japanese Nikkō monkeys, they just wanted to "see no evil, hear no evil, speak no evil" while profiting from cozy auditing arrangements.

Levitt needed firm-specific statistics with which to conduct a required cost-benefit analysis of his idea. Naturally, the accounting firms refused to release the data. Levitt needed muscle, but neither Greenspan nor Congress supported his attempts to extract it. The proposal died, and so did perhaps the best opportunity to prevent the worst economic crisis to hit America since the Great Depression. Years later, in August 2011, Levitt explained why the statistics were critical: "Such analysis, however, is highly judgmental, and its outcome depends on the support it has from Congress to get the data it needs. Problem was, the big audit firms alone held the cost data. We asked them for those data, which they declined to provide."[60]

Regulatory Capture Reduced Antitrust Enforcement

Antitrust enforcement was dialed down significantly during the Reagan era. This is most evident in the case of banks grown too big to fail. But the problem is general. When combined with deregulation, lax antitrust enforcement is an invitation to collusion. It's as though control over bed nets, mosquito repellant, and antimalarial medicines in Africa was abruptly turned over to malaria parasites. As *Washington Post* columnist Steven Pearlstein summarized: "For years now, the courts and regulators have turned a blind eye as industry after industry consolidates into two or three dominant firms."[61]

The need for vigorous antitrust enforcement was one of the clearest lessons drawn by economists from the early days of capitalism. Adam Smith was not a starry-eyed idealist. He was certainly a moral philosopher and the greatest economic revolutionary in history, envisioning capitalism as a scheme to provide the greatest prosperity for all. He wrote in 1776 during the East India Company era, when exploitative mercantilism and *laissez-faire* prevailed. That era provided the evidence that Smith utilized in arguing that the business community readily colludes against consumers, employees, and the public interest, resulting in higher prices, less innovation, and a reduced variety of goods. That sentiment also informed the works of political scientist Joseph Schumpeter. He fathered the concept of "creative destruction," which describes the capitalist process: new, innovative competitors—Apple or Google, for example—arise to challenge established giants such as Microsoft or IBM. The level of such enterprise destruction runs about 10 percent annually in the United States; between 1989 and 1997 an average of 611,000 US firms disappeared each year, out of about 5.7 million.[62]

Antitrust policy is designed explicitly to promote and nurture this creative destruction process by limiting the ability of aging dinosaur firms to metamorphose into conglomerates that restrict competition; without it, capitalism stagnates as dinosaurs stagger on, dominating weaker innovators. The consequence becomes what Mario Monti, sometime Prime Minister of Italy and former President of Milan's Bocconi University, an antitrust expert, derisively terms, "destruction conservation."[63] Families are harmed by less innovation and also lower living standards, because cartels impose price penalties of 20–25 percent or even higher.[64] The Reagan era deregulation of antitrust enforcement derailed Schumpeter's creative destruction process, with investigations and prosecutions rolled back. For example, there are almost 8,000 banks in America, yet the largest 20 came during this period to control 90 percent of the market, and the top three control 44 percent.[65] In the 1980s, the ten biggest banks held fewer than 30 percent of total deposits, but held 54 percent of them in 2012. This anticompetitive outcome was described editorially by the *Financial Times* in 2009:

> "Weak competition is obvious to customers: financial companies demand high fees that are often calculated according to illogical tariffs. Fund manager charges, for example, are usually large and often not linked to the quality, or the real cost of their services. The lack of competition shows up to economists in the sector's staggering profitability."[66]

This trend is exemplified by financial firms such as Goldman Sachs or Morgan Stanley. They were permitted in recent decades to grow too big to fail, Red Queens as in the Land of Oz—reality is what they say it is. Rich democracies police capitalism by holding firms accountable either to voters or to the marketplace, but Red Queens are accountable to neither. The best description of these banking creatures created by the weak antitrust policies of the Reagan era is from David Stockman in August 2010:

"The trillion-dollar conglomerates that inhabit this new financial world are not free enterprises. They are rather wards of the state, extracting billions from the economy with a lot of pointless speculation in stocks, bonds, commodities, and derivatives. They could never have survived, much less thrived, if their deposits had not been government guaranteed and if they hadn't been able to obtain virtually free money from the Fed's discount window to cover their bad bets."[67]

The genesis of too big to fail occurred on Monday, October 19, 1987, when Wall Street share prices fell sharply and Fed Chairman Alan Greenspan overreacted by cutting interest rates sharply. As University of Chicago economists Douglas W. Diamond and Raghuram G. Rajan explained in a May 2012 analysis, that step to protect banks created the famous "Greenspan Put," a hallmark of the Reagan era. If sufficiently large, bankers making risky speculations that sour will be bailed out by taxpayers. It's called corporate socialism.[68] *Handelsbatt* reporter Olaf Storbeck in February 2011 explained the new banking industry incentive structure created by deregulation and the Greenspan Put:

"State protection is also so attractive that banks have systematically attempted to reach the 'too big to fail' status—the implied government guarantees were a key engine for the many mergers and acquisitions in the industry since the 1990s."[69]

The rest, as they say, is history. To seize perpetual life, quick-witted entrepreneurs on Wall Street created Red Queens. They paid premiums estimated by economists at $14 to $17 billion apiece for mid-sized banks in order to become behemoths impervious to the existential dangers normally posed by competition.[70] The acquiring bank can afford to pay higher prices because attaining "too-big-to-fail" stature translates to lower deposit costs and adds an average $4.7 billion to their return annually, according to research by economists Priyank Gandhi and Hanno Lustig at the University of California, Los Angeles.[71]

Like investing in lobbying, any banking executive would be foolish indeed not to exploit Reaganomics to become an immortal behemoth—which is about as bizarre a concept as an economist can imagine occurring in Schumpeterian capitalism. This business model is distilled in an advertisement by Interactive Brokers: "It is our belief that the US government would do everything within its power to prevent the failure of any of the major money-center banks with whom IB maintains deposits."[72] Used as an inducement in late 2010 to place capital with that

Wall Street firm, moral hazard has come to profitably permeate Reagan-era banking.

The Red Queen problem is general across the economy. President George W. Bush permitted the Federal Trade Commission to bring only one antitrust case, for example, an insignificant one involving several newspapers in West Virginia. In November 2010, *New York Times* reporter Heidi N. Moore explained:

> "The FTC, in particular, was frequently derided during the Bush administration for being a rubber-stamp agency, unwilling to block giant mergers and essentially defanged."[73]

The other antitrust agency, the Justice Department, received equally poor marks; since 2004, when it sued to block Oracle's purchase of PeopleSoft, it has not challenged any sizable merger. Writing about the Justice Department, a November 2009 editorial in the *New York Times* concluded:

> "Throughout the entire Bush administration, it has not brought a single case against a dominant firm for anti-competitive behavior. And, it has argued enthusiastically on behalf of monopolists before the Supreme Court."[74]

One final blow against competition was struck in the end of days of the Bush administration in September 2008, when it issued watered-down nationwide anti-monopoly guidelines. A firestorm followed. Amazingly, in a Washington grown increasingly partisan, three FTC Commissioners—an Independent, a Republican, and a Democrat—came to agree that the guidelines placed "a thumb on the scales in favor of firms with monopoly or near-monopoly power and against other equally significant stakeholders." The guidelines were "a blueprint for radically weakening enforcement" against monopolies that would consequently be permitted to manipulate prices "with impunity," and "make it nearly impossible to prosecute a case."[75]

The *de minimus* antitrust profile of the Reagan era is ridiculed by European antitrust officials such as Mario Monti.[76] Inventive Silicon Valley entrepreneurs agree. They are by nature impatient, not inclined to sit idly by and passively allow government officials to slow innovation and dictate their fortunes. Silicon Valley tackles challenges aggressively, and has come to rely on assertive European trustbusters to promote competition, especially in high technology. And their faith is justified: EU officials outright rejected the merger of General Electric and Honeywell *after* it was approved by the Bush administration.[77] And overall, they imposed three times more price-fixing fines than the United States during the decade of the 2000s, according to reporter Mathilde Visseyrias in *Le Figaro*.[78] European officials are more feared by colluding firms than US officials, because penalties can be imposed immediately on administrative fact finding, instead of being delayed by the judicial process. They also assign a far higher priority to improving competition than America, as attorney Peter Alexiadis with the Brussels law firm Gidson, Dunn & Crutcher noted in mid-2009:

> "Europeans still have a lot more concerns than Americans about companies using strong or dominant positions to create bottlenecks for competitors in the information and technology sectors."[79]

The Bush administration's hostility to competition policy has been reversed by the Obama administration and its antitrust chief, Christine Varney. As noted by *New York Times* journalist Steven Labaton, "Ms. Varney scrapped the Bush administration's monopoly guidelines, which had sharply limited the government's ability to prosecute large corporations that used their market dominance to elbow out competitors."[80] As in other areas, the antitrust policies of the Reagan era enabled northern Europe to leapfrog over the United States. As explained in a *Financial Times* editorial in May 2009: "Although her approach is rooted in the rich American trust-busting tradition, Ms. Varney is now racing to catch up with Europe. In the past eight years, weak US enforcement has made the Brussels authorities leaders in the field. . . ."[81]

Failure to Punish Wall Street Fraud

Another consequence of regulatory capture: federal prosecution of bank fraud was sharply rolled back during the George W. Bush administration, according to statistics from the Transactional Records Access Clearinghouse at Syracuse University.[82] This pullback is also evident in the adoption of the practice of deferred prosecutions. Instead of suspect executives facing contempt charges and jail, fines are imposed on violating firms. This occurs even for repetitive frauds involving the same Wall Street firms. For example, the SEC collected multimillion-dollar fines for financial fraud in 51 instances from 19 firms between 1995 and 2010, with major Wall Street firms repeat offenders. Yet contempt charges were not filed. Instead, Goldman Sachs, Morgan Stanley, and JP Morgan Chase, among others, paid fines and agreed to abandon fraudulent practices—only to reemploy them just a few years hence.

The SEC has punished Citigroup *four* times for repetitive frauds in the last decade, for example. Yet, despite the firm's serial recidivism, when it negotiated a fifth penalty in 2011, this time with the Obama administration, the SEC refused to seek contempt charges.[83]

Defrauding the public by the financial sector has been converted from an existential threat to a mere operating expense. Indeed, the practice of resolving illegalities without incarcerating executives, especially CEOs, incentivizes more egregious behavior, because the rewards are higher and certain while punishment is rare and mild. The late Senator Arlen Specter explained it this way:

> "Criminal fines are added to the cost of doing business. Going to jail is what works to deter crime."[84]

Moreover, on occasion, fines were set too low and bore no relation to victim losses; for example, the SEC agreed to a $285 million settlement with Citigroup in 2011, even though the fraud cost consumers $700 million.[85]

How can the financial sector be so weakly regulated in light of recent history? The problem rests with a gridlocked Congress, which has constrained resources available to the SEC and Justice Department. Exemplified by their different positions on the Dodd-Frank financial reregulation law, this is one of many regulatory issues where the two political parties are sharply divided. Congressional Democrats seeking to increase enforcement budgets have been unable to overcome Republican Party opposition united against enhanced enforcement of Wall Street.

It seems, however, that such tactics do not enjoy universal support among Republicans or conservatives. University of Chicago jurist Richard A. Posner, for example, argued in January 2010: "We need a more active and intelligent government to keep our model of a capitalist economy from running off the rails."[86] And conservative journalist David Brooks compared the need to achieve balanced regulation to that of fire: "a useful tool when used judiciously and a dangerous menace when it gets out of control."[87]

Deferred Prosecution Windfalls for Republican Insiders

The Reagan era's use of fines and deferred prosecutions also saw the creation of a new tactic that rewarded well-connected Republicans. It worked this way: rather than prosecute antitrust and other violators, the Bush administration negotiated punishment where violators agreed to end illegalities and accept outside monitoring. This scheme turned out to produce some big windfalls among more than a score of well-connected Bush officials appointed monitors. John Ashcroft, a former Senator, Presidential Candidate, and US Attorney General, earned little during a career of public service before retiring in 2005. His net worth was dramatically enhanced, however, when his former Justice Department subordinate (and currently New Jersey Governor) Chris Christie appointed Ashcroft as monitor of a remedial agreement involving illegal kickbacks to physicians. Zimmer Orthopedics avoided prosecution by agreeing to a Justice Department bargain including paying Ashcroft at least $29 million for 18 months of work as monitor. Worse, the firm wasn't required to pay fines to the federal government, apparently because the monitor fees were considered sufficient punishment—even though they enriched Ashcroft's law firm rather than reimburse victimized patients or taxpayers.[88]

Indeed, such monitoring windfalls became a flood in the last few years of the Bush administration. Others monitors included James Doty, a lawyer for George W. Bush's family, and former FBI director Louis Freeh in 2010 who investigated corruption at automaker Daimler.[89] In one instance, for example, as part of a deal to avoid prosecution, the pharmaceutical firm Bristol-Myers Squibb agreed, among other conditions, to endow a chair—in "Business Ethics," no less—at a Bush appointee's *alma mater*, Seton Hall law school. Mike McDonald, a former investigator for the Internal Revenue Service, noted: "It looks too much like the boys are taking care of buddies, because these are lucrative contracts."[90] Overall, at least 30 politically connected Republican officials were lavishly reimbursed as enterprise monitors after they retired.

Regulatory capture figured prominently in the European economies in the past. But their postwar history reflects success in finding a Goldilocks balance—not too much, not too little—in regulation resembling the one that prevailed during the American golden age. And they have sustained that balance, even as it was lost during the Reagan era that followed, as we now see.

Europeans Are Alert to the Dangers of Regulatory Capture

The obscure French agency carries a grandiose name, the Committee on Public Standards. But it's the real deal, a tiny safeguard that more than fulfills the promise of its elegant name.

American executive suites and many politicians would loathe it.

Can you imagine a handful of judges telling Wendy Gramm, commissioner of the Commodities Futures Trading Commission, that she couldn't join Enron's board only months after deregulating the derivatives the company favored? Or that Meredith A. Baker, a retiring Federal Communications Commissioner, couldn't join Comcast in 2011, also just months after approving its acquisition of NBC Universal? Or that Kayla Gillan couldn't join PricewaterhouseCoopers, a firm she regulated as deputy chief of staff at the Securities and Exchange Commission?

Yet, that is precisely what the French Committee on Public Standards did in December 2010, rejecting a lucrative move by Alexandre de Juniac, chief of staff to then-Economic Minister Christine Lagarde, to the nuclear power giant Areva.[91] That Committee prevents narrow commercial interests from gaining undue influence on government policy, thus allowing the public interest to be more carefully nurtured than in America. And it does so by standing astride the revolving door, clarifying that the regulatory capture which Nobel prize–winning economists such as the late George Stigler warned about is not acceptable in that rich democracy. Officials like de Juniac must cool off for some period, as he did before later becoming a senior executive at Air France in October 2011.

This committee, and the commitment it reflects, is the culmination of centuries of efforts across northern Europe to attain a balance in regulation, some with serious consequences. In 1360, for example, a banker was executed in front of his failed Barcelona bank, in order to discourage others from gambling with depositors' funds.[92] In striving for that balance, Australia and northern Europe have looked to Adam Smith as their touchstone on the proper role of regulation.

Adam Smith: The Father of Regulated Capitalism

Adam Smith was the Father of Capitalism, and argued in his first book, *The Theory of Moral Sentiments,* published in 1759, that broadly improving family prosperity is the goal of economics. Recall that he explained, "The interest of the producer ought to be attended to, only so far as it may be necessary for promoting that of the consumer."[93]

That is the clearest statement in all of economics—by the father of market capitalism, no less: family sovereignty should prevail over enterprise sovereignty.

The subservient role he envisaged for producers explains Smith's strong advocacy of government rules to prevent abuse of the free-market concept, in order to maximize its potential to generate broadly enjoyed wealth. He explicitly endorsed regulation to achieve what we now recognize as an Aristotelian balance that rejects the market fundamentalism of *laissez-faire* Reaganomics. For us today in interpreting Adam Smith, an especially important bubble arose in 1772 in Scotland, when the giant Ayr Bank and others collapsed, impoverishing Scotland for years. P.J. O'Rourke explained the environment in which Smith wrote the Wealth of Nations in a February 2009 column in the *Financial Times*:

> "The Mississippi Scheme and the South Sea Bubble had both collapsed in 1720, three years before his (Smith's) birth. In 1772, while Smith was writing *The Wealth of Nations*, a bank run occurred in Scotland. Only three of Edinburgh's 30 private banks survived."[94]

As he looked out his study window, Adam Smith could scarcely avoid the financial news of the day, and realized the barrier such abuses posed to his hopes for advancing the condition of his day.[95*] That accounts for his abiding support for prudent government regulation to channel the business community's greed into competition. In 1705, the fraud John Law had proposed establishing a Scottish bank to issue vast credits. Dodging a bullet, cautious government regulators of the day killed that scheme, sending him packing (to the misfortune of France). P.J. O'Rourke notes that Adam Smith approvingly wrote that the Scottish parliament "did not think proper to adopt it."[95]

Smith was too keen an observer of history and human nature to be a market fundamentalist. Now you understand why he wrote that business executives from the same industry rarely meet, "even at festivals and amusements together, without ending the conversation in a conspiracy against the public."[96]

This is the man America's business community seems to believe would be pleased with deregulation of Wall Street?

The classicist and sober Smith knew that his invisible hand concept describing the self-regulating behavior of the marketplace came with an enormous asterisk: careful regulation was critical to the success of capitalism. That's why Smith's support of regulation was unqualified:

> "Such regulations may, no doubt, be considered as in some respects a violation of natural liberty. But these exertions of the natural

---

*Smith's free market enterprise concept was the antithesis of socialism, because he saw a carefully-regulated capitalism as far more capable of delivering broadly-based prosperity. The typical Englishman of his day lived little better than a Roman tenant farmer, tied to the land, cohabiting with animals, and subsisting on 1,500 calories a day of coarse wheat and barley, with periodic starvation common, as had been the human condition for time immemorial. Child labor was *de rigueur*. Girls and boys, Charles Dickens among them, labored in rat-infested shoe polish warehouses, a world away from the life of the wealthy early industrialists. See Sylvia Nasar, *Grand Pursuit*, 12–13.

liberty of a few individuals, which might endanger the security of the whole society, are, and ought to be, restrained by the laws of all governments."[97]

Yet Smith was no fan of government. Like John Locke and Thomas Jefferson, Smith viewed state authority as dangerous, an existential threat to individual liberty and to markets. But it was also the only counterbalance to the normal behavior of the business community, as Finance Minister Trevor Manuel of South Africa explained in 2009:

> "Political economists since Thomas Hobbes and Adam Smith have understood that capitalism relies on state power to impose instrumental checks on greed and the abuse of influence."[98]

Thus, in the end, Smith supported balanced and prudent regulation, a belief philosophically inspired by his background as a moral philosopher, as explained by biographers such as Nicholas Phillipson.[99] Like America's Founding Fathers, he was informed by the Enlightenment and Reformation and was the intellectual inheritor of Voltaire, Locke, and the Scot David Hume, his friend and colleague. Today his European heirs reflect Smith's trenchant sensitivity to the need for regulation. It is they—not market fundamentalists in the mold of Ayn Rand or Milton Friedman—who are true to Smith nearly three centuries later. Smith wrote to exploit markets—not to glorify them. Surely a student of Aristotle, Smith saw capitalism as a means of fulfilling the human potential in each of us.

Finding Regulatory Balance in Family Capitalism

Corralling garden-variety greed certainly justifies careful regulation. But officials in family capitalism countries appear to realize that success in attaining a handful of other important goals, such as incentivizing economic and productivity growth, hinge on a nation's regulatory framework as well.

First, they realize there are many markets where regulation is scarcely warranted. University of Texas economist James K. Galbraith explains:

> "This is the case in many instances of daily life, where the product transacted is transparent to both buyer and seller. . . . Barbershops, landscaping services, bowling alleys, cinemas, and outdoor concerts are similar: what you see is what you get, potential losses are small, and there is little apparent need to validate that the service provided is in fact the one represented."[100]

Second, competition is promoted by tough antitrust regulations in the family capitalism countries, but also by careful regulation of industries subject to economies of scale. There are a handful of industries, communications and utilities, for example, where economies of scale favor gargantuan size. Economists long ago learned that the only effective means to mimic the outcome of competition in such settings is through careful public regulation. The *Financial Times* acknowledged the case for such regulation in a December 2009 editorial:

> "Well-run countries limit the prices monopolies (such as utilities) may charge, in effect transferring profits to consumers. Characteristic of such sectors is economic 'rent' that springs from legally sanctioned market power. Rent corrodes the market's fairness and efficiency by rewarding those lucky or powerful enough to capture it, not those whose effort, initiative, or talent benefit society. To make markets work, which the FT believes is the right aim for economic policy, the state may, and sometimes must, tax high-rent activities aggressively."[101]

Third, regulations are justified that enhance the quality of society and improve health to the benefit of consumers and families. Regulations on food safety, abuse of consumers, occupation and transportation safety, smoking, building codes, medical safety, and the like come to mind. Cost-efficient regulation in these fields is achievable; since the Food and Drug Administration labeling requirements were instituted in 2003, the trans fats in the bloodstream of Americans have declined by 50 percent.[102] The same logic is seen in Australia, where the government took the global lead in restricting cigarette packaging to plain wrappers, complete with photos of cancer victims as a warning.

Regulatory Balance Aids Job and Economic Growth

There is evidence that prudent regulations can promote economic and job growth. Indeed, there are strategic economic development factors that justify regulation, articulated persuasively over the years by Harvard business professor Michael E. Porter. For decades, he has been documenting how regulation can stimulate industry to innovate, creating global-leading entrepreneurship that yields export prowess and new jobs. Back in 1991, for example, Porter noted that German and other foreign firms controlled 70 percent of the air-pollution-abatement industry in America—thanks to more rigorous air-quality standards in Europe. "Tough standards trigger innovation and upgrading," he concluded. Another example: the global advantage gained by firms a decade ago when the US was among the leaders in phasing out atmosphere-destroying chlorofluorocarbons (CFCs), giving American firms such as DuPont a vital jump ahead in devising less harmful substitutes.[103]

Environmental regulations like those imposed on CFCs point up a myth, promoted by deregulators during the Reagan era, that environmental rules reduce employment. In fact, they create jobs in many cases, like the Clean Air Act. The independent Washington-based Economic Policy Institute examined the jobs' impact of the Clean Air Act in June 2011 and concluded it had created employment on a net basis. The Environmental Protection Agency's own analyses confirmed this outside study. More broadly, Josh Feinman, global chief economist at Deutsche Bank Advisors, and other independent economists, have concluded there is not even the most general evidence that regulation actually costs jobs.[104]

Moreover, regulation can prevent economic harm. Deregulation spread financial bubbles and recession across the United Kingdom, Ireland, Spain, and the United States, but careful and prudent regulation of the finance and housing sectors prevented those events from happening in Canada, Australia, or northern Europe.

The value of preventive financial regulation of the sort adopted in Canada and the family capitalism countries is documented in an elaborate analysis involving 102 nations. Three economists, led by London Business School professor and former research director at the European Central Bank, Lucrezia Reichlin, concluded that capitalist countries with more regulated financial markets—Brazil, for example—sustained economic growth better during the credit crisis than poorly regulated nations like the United States, Spain, or Iceland.[105] In fact, the secret to Australia becoming the world's wealthiest nation measured by median wealth per capita has been broadly spread wage growth year after year for decades, while using strict regulation to avoid banking crises.

How valuable is the prudent regulation model prioritized by the family capitalism countries? Had Brazil been among the least-regulated nations (such as the United States) that fact alone would have caused its GDP to decline by a projected 3.2 percent during the recent recession rather than rise by the 2.21 percent actually recorded, Reichlin determined. That is a deregulation, or regulatory capture, penalty of more than 5 percentage points of GDP during one year alone.

Regulatory Capture Is Punished by Voters in Germany

The Free Democratic Party (FDP) in Germany is the political party in northern Europe most closely resembling the Republican Party in the United States; its agenda disproportionately reflects the concerns of affluent households. Internal FDP documents from 1994 even acknowledged it is "the party of higher earners."[106] Its showing in the 2009 election enabled it to join the government of Chancellor Angela Merkel as a junior partner. The FDP exploited its new position to force through significant business tax cuts. One was given to hoteliers that it later admitted was a *quid pro quo* for donations from the Mövenpick hotel magnate, Baron von Finck, Germany's richest man and a tax dodger closeted in a Swiss castle at Weinfelden.[107] The party's relentless pursuit of lower taxes and deregulation is why even the sober-minded *Der Spiegel* occasionally terms the FDP as the "client party," the "millionaire party," or the "party of the wealthy."[108]

Von Finck practiced American pay-to-play politics during the German elections, contributing €1.4 million to the FDP, a gargantuan donation in Europe. The tax cut saved hoteliers at least €1 billion annually, a spectacular return for such a tiny bribe—far better than the payoff typically delivered by Washington officials in exchange for campaign donations. *Der Spiegel* described the FDP's postelection legislative handouts to German business donors this way: "Since then, hardly a week has passed without some new giveaway being handed to the party's base, triggering a festive mood among German tax accountants, pharmacies, hotel owners, and asset management companies."[109]

The revelations have proven toxic; voters were scandalized by this episode of US-style pay-to-play politics, especially after an FDP official serving as German Justice Minister subsequently defended the use of hidden Swiss bank accounts by wealthy Germans. The opposition, the Social Democrat Party (SPD), labeled the FDP the "tax evaders' patron party, "and "a lobbyist for criminal tax evaders." The SPD vice chairman concluded that ". . . the FDP must have big fears for their tax-evading clients."[110]

This and similar examples of American-style pay-to-play politics proved too much for Chancellor Merkel and German voters. An exasperated and embarrassed Michael Fuchs, Merkel's political party's Vice Chairman, urged eliminating the FDP's billion-Euro hotel tax loophole, but it was too late.[111] The party was polling a bare 2 percent as the 2013 campaigning season got underway, facing legal extinction.[112]

CHAPTER 5

SHAREHOLDER CAPITALISM

"Market fundamentalists never really appreciated the institutions required to make an economy function well, let alone the broader social fabric that civilizations require to prosper and flourish."[1]

Nobel Laureate JOSEPH STIGLITZ,
September 2007

"Workers have learned to internalize and mask powerlessness, but the internal frustration and struggle remain. . . . Today, the concerns of the working class have less space in our civic imagination than at any time since the Industrial Revolution."[2]

JEFFERSON COWIE,
Historian, Cornell University,
"That '70s Feeling," the *New York Times*, September 5, 2012

"Less loyalty and trust. . . . In the United States, this trend has emerged over the past three decades. The relationship between employers and employees here became more distant, transactional . . . employment security has substantially decreased since the 1980s, when downsizing, restructuring and outsourcing costs many jobs. . . . Employers broke implicit contracts with employees who had been willing to invest in firm-specific human capital. . . . Thus, firms lose one of their most valuable and distinguishing resources."[3]

SUSANNE ROYER, JENNIFER WATERHOUSE,
KERRY BROWN, AND MARION FESTING,
***European Management Journal*, August 2008**

What most importantly differentiates Reagan-era America from the family capitalism countries? In those foreign nations, the national covenant is maximizing the prosperity of families. That's the standard used by voters to evaluate public policy options and candidates. In contrast, lacking clear options at the polls, Americans have repeatedly voted since 1980 to abandon family prosperity, to prioritize enterprise prosperity over family prosperity. They have voted to become the first rich democracy where enterprise autonomy is the national covenant, the standard against which all public policy proposals are measured. They are the first ever to vote to transfer economic sovereignty from families to firms and install shareholder capitalism.

The Evolution of Shareholder Capitalism

Economic historians such as Robert S. McElvaine argue that the shocks of the Great Depression produced a return to the shared values and community spirit of the Colonial era and of small town America. In the golden age that followed, that return was characterized by:

> "A generous expansion of values: a regrowth of the more traditional, community–oriented values that have generally been in decline since the early twentieth century. . . . It was a cooperative individualism that placed the individual within the context of a community and was distinct from the acquisitive individualism of the new industry economy. People were seen as citizens and neighbors, not merely consumers."[4]

Economists call this stakeholder capitalism, because the business community is concerned with issues such as wages, the environment, and poverty as well as profits. McElvaine explained how Franklin D. Roosevelt helped guide this rejuvenation of traditional American values and thereby became a transformational president:

> "Franklin Roosevelt was one of those rare individuals who had a significant impact on history, but his leadership explains less about the changes the United States underwent in the 1930s than does a fundamental shift in the values of the American people."[5]

Building on reformers including President Theodore Roosevelt, Ida Tarbell, and Upton Sinclair, the recrafting of American capitalism by Franklin D. Roosevelt placed the US economy on a trajectory toward family capitalism. In calling on the "angels" in each of us, Roosevelt reawakened the frontier mindset of Americans to look beyond their own lives to broader concerns, such as the value added to society by expansive public education. A few years later, this spirit sustained those 420,000 of The Greatest Generation, who made the ultimate sacrifice in World War II to nurture the freedom and prosperity of those back home.

Reinforcing this cultural transformation was a synthesis of political sentiment, with Republican politicians joining Democrats in policies to promote family prosperity. Republicans of that era—Dwight

Eisenhower, Nelson Rockefeller, Everett Dirksen, Howard Baker, and Charles Percy—reflected what historians such as Sean Wilentz and Douglas Brinkley term the socially progressive "heart and soul" of the pre-Reagan-era Republican Party.[6] They joined Harry Truman, John Kennedy, and Lyndon Johnson in expanding the American social safety net. Community-focused Democrats like Hubert H. Humphrey were supported by centrist politicians such as Percy and Dirksen who represented the Republican Party in Washington.

President Nixon, for example, supported: affirmative action and wilderness preservation; Indian tribal autonomy; Supplemental Security Income for the disabled and elderly poor; and the antipoverty Family Assistance Plan. He also quadrupled the staff of the Occupational Safety and Health Administration and established the Environmental Protection Agency and the Consumer Product Safety Commission. Drawing on his hardscrabble youth, Nixon also aggressively supported racial equality, expanded food stamps, proposed comprehensive health care, and made Social Security cost-of-living adjustments automatic.[7] Both Democratic and Republican presidents increased the minimum wage, which reached $10.11 per hour in 1968 and then hovered around $9 per hour until plunging in the Reagan era (all measured in 2008 dollars).

Family or stakeholder capitalism in America was also evident in tax policy during these decades. President Eisenhower, for example, opposed lowering the top marginal income tax rate of 91 percent for millionaires, who were mostly movie actors, athletes, and corporate leaders. And the American tax system was progressive, with the top 1 percent paying an average federal income tax rate about three times higher than the working poor. Moreover, Richard Nixon in 1971 signed legislation that placed a higher top marginal tax rate on unearned income such as dividends (70 percent) than on wages earned from work (50 percent).[8]

Also reinforcing this cultural transformation to stakeholder capitalism was a synthesis of sentiment in executive suites that emerged from the Great Depression and a world war. From the 1940s through most of the 1970s, the cultural norms featured altruistic concerns by executives, including the well-being of employees and the prudent nurturing of corporate assets for the long term. Typical of CEOs of the day, Kenneth J. Douglas of Dean Foods, the family owners of Marvin Windows in Warroad, Minnesota, and Robert Wood Johnson of Johnson & Johnson, acknowledged the debt owed by the business community. This expansive, even paternalistic, mindset formed the foundation of the halcyon golden age: it encouraged executive suites to collaborate with trade unions and employees and to manage with a long-term horizon, which created an environment of quickening innovation amid toughening foreign competition from Japan and elsewhere. Executives like General Motors' Charles E. Wilson or Kenneth Douglas channeled Henry Ford, pleased by the resulting boom in middle class prosperity. And they did it while resisting outsized paydays.

Union agreements in the 1940s at firms like General Motors came to feature steadily rising real wages. These accords subsequently taught American management that it could prosper by collaborating—rather than colliding—with employees. These agreements were a cathartic moment in American economic history; for the first time, political and business leaders agreed to explicitly give lift and life to the spirit of Adam Smith and of family capitalism. The richness of the collaboration and collusion that defined the golden age enshrined for decades the concept that wage hikes should include both cost-of-living and productivity-growth components.[9] The greatest middle class in history began to coalesce behind rising real wages. What was good for GM back then was actually good for America, too.

I encountered one of these stakeholder managers in my first college teaching job. Harry C. Gravely had been entrusted upon his father's death with management of a furniture factory in the small hamlet of Ridgeway, Virginia. Ridgeway Furniture combined German clockworks with American carpentry to produce grandfather clocks, a handsome product and a sound family business. One of my students intended to return home to Ridgeway after graduation and had applied to Gravely, referencing me. I was surprised to receive a call from the CEO himself, but management ranks are thin in family firms and a white-collar hiring mistake can be costly. My student's perceived analytical skill, diligence, and ability were important, but what most concerned Gravely was his ability to interact in a constructive and respectful fashion with the blue-collar workforce there. Gravely knew the success of his family enterprise was intimately linked with the performance of his skilled cabinetmakers, whose cooperation transcended issues of wages and management hierarchies. He needed managers who would listen as well as talk. Like most southern management, Gravely distrusted trade unions, but felt an abiding obligation to respect and regularly reward employees.

This communitarian spirit and attitude was common with managers of many family owned, as well as larger, professionally managed firms, such as General Electric and GM. And it was reinforced by laws—the Wagner Act, for example—that provided some legal rights for unions and employees, adding to their negotiating power, nurturing family economic sovereignty, and nudging managers like Gravely toward flexibility. Such laws were important, but they did not, and cannot alone, create the community spirit exemplified by that greatest generation of American management. CEOs could scarcely abuse employees after going through basic training, sharing a foxhole, or navigating a B-17 they piloted. It was that culture of stakeholder capitalism more than any other single factor that accounted for the golden age creating America's great middle class.

That culture was also reflected in executive compensation. Economists Carola Frydman of the Massachusetts Institute of Technology and Raven Sakes of the Federal Reserve System found that inflation-adjusted compensation for CEOs remained stable. Their salaries were about $1 million in today's dollars from the mid-1930s to the mid-1970s.[10]

Here is how the late Frank W. Abrams, chairman of Standard Oil of New Jersey during the golden age explained his job:

> "The job of management is to maintain an equitable and working balance among the claims of the various directly affected interest groups . . . stockholders, employees, customers, and the public at large."[11]

The prevailing stakeholder culture is also explained by Leo Hindery, former chief executive of AT&T Broadband:

> "In 1972, Reginald Jones, Jack Welch's predecessor at General Electric . . . said in his maiden speech as chief executive that while he fully respected the fact that his job was to keep GE successful on behalf of its shareholders, he had equal responsibility to employees, customers, communities, and the nation. . . . For the 35 years following the end of the Second World War, executives such as Reg Jones viewed responsibility and fair business behavior as a critical component of the American Dream."[12]

And former Congressional aide and writer Ken Jacobson quotes the wartime CEO of GE, Owen D. Young, speaking some years earlier at the Harvard Business School:

> "No man with an inadequate wage is free. He is unable to meet his obligations to his family, to society, and to himself. No man is free who can provide only for physical needs. He must also be in a position to take advantage of cultural opportunities. Business, as the process of coordinating men's capital and effort in all fields of activity, will not have accomplished its full service until it shall have provided the opportunity for all men to be economically free."[13]

Another example is Robert Wood Johnson of Johnson & Johnson, who noted in the 1940s that his firm's first obligation was to its customers, then to employees and management, followed by the broader community—with shareholders in the last spot.[14]And recall that even the Business Roundtable, representing CEOs of the largest US firms, espoused stakeholder capitalism into the 1980s. Stakeholder capitalism was *de rigueur* across America, with blue chip firms leading the way.

The Emergence of Shareholder Capitalism

President Reagan would have none of it.

Stakeholder or family capitalism prevailed broadly in executive suites until the early 1980s, when the Reagan administration resurrected the culture of corporate dominance last seen during the Roaring Twenties. The communitarian spirit of small-town America savored by the Founding Fathers was ejected from the public square.

A series of films critical of Roaring Twenties amorality were made in the early Depression years. *Corsair*, in 1931, aptly captured the essence of resurgent *laissez-faire* Reaganomics after 1980. Chester Morris sets out to prove to his girlfriend that he can be as successful a businessman as her father, so he becomes a pirate. "It doesn't matter how you make your money; it's how much you have when you quit," he explains in language that aptly describes values of the Reagan era.[15]

The Reagan era put stakeholder capitalism in deep freeze. A different breed of executive came to command enterprises whose management imperative was adopted from folks like Alfred Rappaport, professor emeritus at Northwestern. In *Creating Shareholder Value*, he argued that "the ultimate test of corporate strategy, the only reliable measure, is whether it creates economic value for shareholders."[16]

Only a few executive suites, such as Marvin Windows, resisted.[17] Self-absorption became acceptable and, eventually, admired in business. Only a few executives today—the former CEO of Costco, Jim Sinegal, is an example—have resisted, still managing as executives did during the golden age. Before retiring in January 2012, Sinegal received remuneration only about one-third the US average for comparable firms.[18]

The election of 1980 ignited the transition from stakeholder to shareholder capitalism. It was an unacknowledged transfer for certain, its beginning marked by the 1981 air traffic controllers' strike, which cost the government billions of dollars more than the strikers had demanded.[19] Executives watched carefully, and the administration's actions resulted in devolution of employee-employer relations, as noted by Georgetown University economist Joseph A. McCartin:

"Reagan's unprecedented dismissal of skilled strikers encouraged private employers to do likewise. Phelps Dodge and International Paper were among the companies that imitated Reagan by replacing strikers rather than negotiate with them. Many other employers followed suit."[20]

The administration's trumpeting of shareholder capitalism, implemented by deregulation, regulatory capture, and reconfigured tax and budget priorities, began the transfer of economic sovereignty from families to the business community. And in the years since, it has become deeply ingrained Washington policy by Republicans, and too many Democrats, to ensure that the American workforce is docile, disposable, rarely upskilled, priced at market wages, and forced to compete *mano a mano* with the rest of the world. This transition has made for the juxtaposition of world-class technology, competitive capital markets, and incentives for cleverness, imagination, and fraud, with domestic labor markets reminiscent of the Third World, as exemplified by disposable employees at the Mott plant in Williamson.

The Disparagement of Socially Responsible Stakeholder Capitalism

The emergence of shareholder capitalism has its roots in the philosophy espoused by Milton Friedman in *Capitalism and Freedom*, which drew on the notions embodied in Ayn Rand's rational selfishness theology.* In a 1970 *New York Times Magazine* article entitled "The Social

*In the modern era, the debate over the scope of corporate responsibility began in America in 1932 during the Depression; economists argued whether socially responsible behavior (e.g., rising real wages) was a suitable enterprise priority. Advocates taking a broad view of business obligations such as Harvard dean Donald K. David, Howard R. Bowen, and Frank Abrams were criticized by others including Theodore Levitt and later Milton Friedman. There is a rich literature on this topic from Forest L. Reinhardt, Robert N. Stavins, and Richard H.K. Vietor, among others. "Corporate Social Responsibility Through an Economic Lens," *Review of Environmental Economics and Policy*, vol. 2, issue 2, Summer 2008. Archie B. Carroll and Kareem M. Shabana, "The Business Case for Corporate Social Responsibility: A Review of Concepts, Research and Practices," *International Journal of Management Reviews*, British Academy of Management, 2010. E. Merrick Dodd, Jr., "For Whom Are Corporate Managers Trustees?," *Harvard Law Review*, vol. 45, no. 7, May 1932, 1145–1163. Adolf A. Berle, "Corporate Powers as Powers in Trust," *Harvard Law Review*, 1931, 44:1049–1074. H. Bowen, *Social Responsibility of the Businessman* (New York: Harper and Row, 1953). Archie B. Carroll, *A History of Corporate Social Responsibility: Concepts and Practices. The Oxford Handbook of Corporate Social Responsibility*, A. Crane, A. McWillliams, D. Matten, J. Moon, and D. Siegel, editors (Oxford Handbooks online, Feb. 14, 2008).

Responsibility of Business Is to Increase Its Profits," Friedman famously criticized the altruistic and socially accountable stakeholder capitalism practices then widespread in American business as reflecting ". . . a fundamentally subversive doctrine."

> "There is one and only one social responsibility of business—to use its resources and engage in activities designed to increase its profits. . . ."[21]

He repeatedly and loudly disparaged management of any firm that:

> "takes seriously its responsibilities for providing employment, eliminating discrimination, avoiding pollution, or whatever else may be the catchwords of the contemporary crop of reformers. In fact they are—or would be if they or anyone else took them seriously—preaching pure and unadulterated socialism. Businessmen who talk this way are unwitting puppets of the intellectual forces that have been undermining the basis of a free society these past decades."[22]

Further academic veneer for shareholder capitalism was provided by the economist Michael Jensen of Harvard and the late William Meckling of the University of Rochester in a 1976 article, who argued that this new focus on share prices would resolve the "agency problem."[23] First identified by Columbia University professors Gardiner Means and Adolf Berle in the 1930s, the agency problem refers to the disconnect in goals between shareholders and their agents managing a firm; a disconnect presumably resolved by the new executive focus on share price appreciation.[24] In reality, as we see in the next chapter, shareholder capitalism has exacerbated the agency problem by empowering a narcissistic focus on short-term goals and their own remuneration by management.

Friedman's apotheosis came in a subsequent speech by General Electric CEO John F. Welch, Jr. Dubious CEOs, Gravely of Ridgeway Furniture among them, might easily ignore the arguments of academic gadflies or an émigré Russian such as Ayn Rand, who abandoned Communism in her first exposure to lush southern California capitalism. But ignoring the successful Jack Welch was something else entirely. *Fortune* magazine named him corporate manager of the *century*.* Welch famously argued in 1981 that the sole goal of a firm is to maximize shareholder value,

*Floyd Norris, "Inside GE, a Little Bit of Enron," the *New York Times*, August 7, 2009. Batting 0-2, Fortune also named Enron America's most innovative firm for six consecutive years from 1996–2001. Enron at the time was distributing more in dividends than spending on energy exploration, while collusively cheating West Coast electricity consumers. See also Niall Ferguson, *The Ascent of Money* (New York: Penguin, 2008), 169.

to push share prices ever skyward.[25] With his imprimatur, the market measurement of share prices became a mantra.

This new philosophy, which rejected stakeholder capitalism, meant that "management had ceased to be a profession," explained Harvard business school Dean Nitin Nohria in 2008. Even though corporations are the device licensed ultimately by voters to generate prosperity, managing corporate resources to generate weath beyond shareholders (and management) was abruptly *passé*. Executives became simply the agents of owners. And students were taught the new ethos.

> "As concepts such as efficient market theory moved into the classroom in the 1980s, the system of manager-dominated capitalism was collapsing. . . . MBA students were being taught that they were bound by contractual relationships to clients and shareholders. Managerial incentives, such as stock options, redefined managerial self-interest from fallibility to a virtue."[26]

The business community reverted to the Roaring Twenties and nineteenth-century practice of regulatory capture, in which the executives of Adam Smith's era had viewed government as "an appendix to that of the merchant, as something which ought to be made subservient to it . . ."[27] *New York Times* reporter Joe Nocera highlighted the obsessive new focus of executives this way: "To ask them to put aside the profit motive, even temporarily, for the good of the country—it's not even in the frame of reference."[28]

Advocating for this robber baron philosophy became a lifelong crusade for acolytes such as Friedman. Of course, the golden age management philosophy Friedman demonized had powered America out of the Great Depression, was vital to winning World War II, created the largest middle class in world history, and produced the greatest age ever of American research and development (R&D), investment, and prosperity.

Friedman's writings and name calling give a sense of the churlish intensity and certitude of those advocating for shareholder capitalism and Ayn Rand's philosophy. Her self-absorptive objectivist culture was essentially a rewrite of Spencer's nineteenth-century, pseudoscientific social Darwinism: markets infallibly know best, and those executives who profit best warrant superior standing. This Randian narcissism, which marks the Reagan era, is a stark rejection of Adam Smith's capitalism, which places the interest of consumers above that of corporations. About the dangers of unbridled capitalism, where individuals can personally prosper by subverting competition, Smith observed:

> "To narrow the competition . . . comes from an order of men, whose interest is never exactly the same as that of the public, who have generally an interest to deceive and even to oppress the public, and who accordingly have, upon many occasions, both deceived and oppressed it."[29]

Friedman remained remarkably steadfast in opposition to Smith, despite mounting evidence of his error. In 2005, after decades of bursting credit bubbles and income disparities that widened in the Reagan era, Friedman still condemned the practice of Whole Foods' CEO, John Mackey, who donated 5 percent of net profits to charity. "I believe Mackey's flat statement that 'corporate philanthropy is a good thing' is flatly wrong."[30]

"Us *vs.* Them"

The logic of shareholder capitalism demands steps to spike stock prices, and rewards a laser-like focus on near-term profits by corporate managers. The path to success is extreme cost cutting in order to exceed Wall Street quarterly profit expectations, and anything—or anyone—who stood in the way became the enemy. GE's CEO Jeffrey Immelt described this new "Us vs. Them" culture in a December 2009 speech at West Point, explaining that "tough-mindedness, a good trait—was replaced by meanness and greed—both terrible traits."[31]

Aside from a few loyal lieutenants, everyone became the CEO's enemy. In this new environment, "them" were R&D budgets, Wall Street analysts, employees and their unions, truculent shareholders, long-term investment (it always drains next quarter's profit), the bond market, foreign and domestic competitors, Washington regulators, bond holders, and quarrelsome board members.

A major threat to this new dynamic was labor unions that naturally resisted wage cuts and layoffs, but the truly existential threat was posed by government laws and regulations. That made regulatory capture of Washington an imperative and a key feature of this era. With an appealing ideology credentialed by the charismatic President Reagan, and made even more appealing by campaign donations, Ayn Rand's Washington men found ready acolytes to Reaganomics among members of Congress. And their outmanned opponents in unions and other groups quickly learned the truth of the Upton Sinclair proverb: "It is difficult to get a man to understand something when his salary depends upon his not understanding it."

The New Norm: "Savage Cost Cutting"

> "It is a good time to be a corporate insider, particularly at major financial companies. First you report productivity gains and 'operating profits'—not by making smart investments in productive assets, but instead . . . at industrial firms, by cutting the number of workers per unit of capital."[32]

That was mutual fund manager John P. Hussman writing in July 2010, explaining the source of *animus* that has emerged at American worksites since 1980. In the golden age, executive suites tended to be protective of skilled employees, nurturing, rather than disposing of them in downturns. If demand for a corporate product fell 3 percent below long-term trends, for example, firms in the golden age would typically not reduce employment commensurately, retaining some unneeded, but skilled, employees temporarily for the better days ahead. This behavior was so persistent for decades that it became enshrined in economics as "Okun's Law," named for the late Yale economist Arthur M. Okun, and chairman of President Lyndon Johnson's Council of Economic Advisors.

Times are different now. By the mid-1980s, with Us vs. Them spreading, CEOs had developed a fast trigger-finger, firing employees at the first hint of gunsmoke. Okun's Law became an artifact. Today's era of precarious employment featuring suddenly disposable employees was arriving, as explained in detail by economists such as Truman Bewley of Yale University.[33] Firms became increasingly inclined in slowdowns to reduce employment rather than to hoard skilled employees. In fact, Northwestern University economist Robert Gordon concluded companies utilize downturns to boost profits by cutting 1.27 times *more* employees than justified by the decline in demand. Here is how Gordon described this new environment of what he termed "savage cost cutting":

> "The intensity of cost-cutting reflected the interplay between executive compensation, the stock market, and corporate profits. . . . During the 1990s, corporate compensation has shifted to relying substantially on stock options . . . leading first to the temptation to engage in accounting tricks during 1998–2000 to maintain the momentum of earnings growth, and then sheer desperation to cut costs in response to the post-2000 collapse in reported S&P earnings and in the stock market."[34]

This new pattern explains why employment fell more than the GDP during the credit crisis and recession, and why job growth has been anemic during the rebound. The outcome is a new Reagan-era paradigm, where jobs gyrate more than the economy. It also means weak recoveries with unwarranted job cuts slowing consumer spending.

This pattern is a direct outgrowth of shareholder capitalism: with employment and wages lagging GDP growth, much of the gain from a rebounding economy now flows to the business community. Economists Andrew Sum, Ishwar Khatiwada, Joseph McLaughlin, and Sheila Palma at Northeastern University found that in the first eighteen months since the recovery began in mid-2009, "Corporate profits captured a lopsided 88 percent of the growth in real income, while aggregate wages and salaries accounted for only slightly more than 1 percent."[35] And recall we learned earlier that the wages of jobs lost during the 2008–2009 recession were well above wages for new jobs created during the recovery in 2010–2012.[36] In contrast, during the recovery in the early 1980s in the first days of the Reagan era, profits and wages both increased, with the portion going to higher profits representing only 10 percent of the combined increase. Those rising wages spreading broadly across America helped fuel a powerful recovery in the early 1980s, very much unlike the current one. Gordon summarized the reasons for the difference:

> "The declining minimum wage, the decline in unionization, the increase in imported goods, and the increased immigration of unskilled labor have undermined the bargaining power of American workers. As a result, employers can reduce labor hours with impunity and without restraint in response to a decrease in the output gap, in contrast to the period before 1986 when their behavior was more constrained by the countervailing power of labor."[37]

Employees Have Become Commodities

The outcome is an insecure labor market, with men and women treated like disposable commodities resembling employees in developing African or Asian nations. It also means efforts by employees to upskill and acquire more marketable skills is no guarantee of higher wages. Following all the rules as Tim Slaughter did by upskilling to become better educated or computer savvy is a smart thing to do. Innovative technology has produced robust job growth in new industries and some workers certainly prosper by moving into nascent technology fields. That's what Tim did in Detroit, with a union contract requiring that Ford foot his $30,000 tuition cost for two years of upskilling. Yet, after graduation, Tim discovered that salaries for new computer hires were barely one-half traditional UAW wages.

That happens not only in the computer field. Many Americans who return to education mid-career find that wages may not reward their initiative much, if at all. Even the college-educated and white-collar workforce in America is now vulnerable to wage stagnation linked to outsourcing, offshoring, Us vs. Them, and the other characteristics of Reaganomics. College remains a good investment at an individual level, with wages higher than for those lacking degrees. But it is not a panacea for wage stagnation, because wages on average have not grown for the college educated during the Reagan era; statistics reveal that the only certain way to out-earn your parents is with a graduate or a professional degree.

With or without a college degree, America has become a meaner nation, where estrangement between employees and employers is commonplace, as described by New York University sociologist Richard Sennett.[38] Today, neither employers nor employees owe particular loyalty to the other. Employers renew work contracts at two-week intervals, but are free to fire. And for their part, employees reenlist every two weeks for another stint at the worksite, all the while scanning the horizon for something better.

The shareholder capitalism of the Reagan era has devolved to a free-fire zone with employers—rather than families—holding all the heavy weaponry. No matter how diligent or valuable an employee, cost-cutting dominates worksites. The glitter of quarterly profits trumps traditions of loyalty and has sent to the dustbin of history the traditional American exchange of good pay for hard effort. This robber baron culture has become so pronounced as to become a badge of honor among executives wanting to be seen as ruthless, although the preferred Wall Street term is "disciplined." In what is a chilling and revealing quote documenting the devolution of the America business culture, Peter Cappelli, a professor at the University of Pennsylvania's Wharton School of Business, noted,

> "Today, a CEO would be embarrassed to admit he sacrificed profits to protect employees or a community."[39]

An important consequence of the Us vs. Them culture of Reaganomics has been deterioration in the broader American culture. Main Street America has morphed into Mean Street America, with good jobs and good wages increasingly scarce. This culture offends Democrats, as one would expect, but also a number of conservatives, such as David Brooks writing in June 2008:

> "The United States. . . . For centuries, it remained industrious, ambitious and frugal. Over the past 30 years, much of that has been shredded. The social norms and institutions that encouraged

> frugality and spending what you earn have been undermined. The country's moral guardians are forever looking for decadence out of Hollywood and reality TV. But the most rampant decadence today is financial decadence, the trampling of decent norms about how to use and harness money."[40]

The devolution of traditional American culture is most evident in the business community, now featuring narcissistic self-absorption. Americans deserve a corporate governance structure that reinforces traditional marketplace values such as individual responsibility, morality, and the work ethic. Another conservative who has come to express doubts about the betrayal of traditional American values under shareholder capitalism is the conservative *Washington Post* columnist Robert J. Samuelson:

> "Everyday Americans will conclude rightly that this brand of capitalism is rigged in favor of the privileged few. . . . Wall Street's pay practices perversely encourage extreme risk-taking that can destabilize the economy. . . . Just why investment bankers and traders out-earn, say, doctors or computer engineers is a question I've never heard convincingly answered. . . . Indeed, many Americans may conclude that capitalism has run amok."[41]

Count me as one of those many Americans.

Shareholder Capitalism Has Diminished Corporate Morality

Erosion of business community morality has made for some mighty awkward moments in the Reagan era.

CEO John Thain bankrupted the investment bank Merrill Lynch, yet as he was leaving in 2008 surreptitiously diverted taxpayer bailout funds to pay $3.6 billion in parting bonuses to his colleagues. Moreover, he spent $1.22 million redecorating the office he was soon to vacate. "Surreptitious" in this instance means Thain rushed out the unwarranted bonuses in the lawless three-day *interregnum* following bankruptcy, but before Merrill was taken over by (a displeased) Bank of America.[42]

A broker named Chris Ricciardi pioneered the sale of opaque Collateralized Debt Obligations (CDOs) at Credit Suisse First Boston and then greatly expanded their marketing by Merrill Lynch, which sold $28 billion alone in the first six months of 2007. CDOs are securities whose return is dependent on another asset, such as mortgages, and their risk level can be impossible to accurately assess. He pocketed his $8 million paycheck and skipped out—just before the meltdown hit Merrill, technically bankrupt from his toxic CDOs issued with grossly inadequate reserves.[43] Ricciardi kept his money.

A mortgage banker named Stanford Kurland was the No. 2 official at America's largest subprime mortgage lender, Countrywide Financial. He directed the vast expansion of toxic subprime mortgage products there, including ones issued to jobless borrowers with poor credit. Kurland left with $140 million from the exercise of options before Countrywide went bankrupt.[44]

After the Deepwater Horizon disaster tragically killed 11 drilling-rig employees in the Gulf of Mexico, British Petroleum CEO Tony Hayward complained about his busy schedule, saying, "I'd like my life back."[45]

Don Blankenship, CEO of Massey Energy, insisted his West Virginia coal company surreptitiously keep two sets of books to hide hazardous conditions from regulators.[46] He succeeded in avoiding expensive safety upgrades. After 29 employees died in a mining accident in April 2010, Blankenship argued that *excessive* mine regulation was responsible for the tragedy. To prevent the deaths, he suggested, "I probably should've sued MSHA." MSHA is the Federal Mine Safety and Health Administration whose inspectors were misled by Massey. West Virginia investigators subsequently determined that Massey had operated "its mines in a profoundly reckless manner, and 29 coal miners paid with their lives for the corporate risk-taking."[47]

Shareholder Capitalism: Chiseling the European Union

One of the world's most indebted nations is Greece, whose government deficits jeopardize the Eurozone currency union. Greece would never have been permitted to join the European Union over a decade ago had its actual fiscal condition been known at the time. Investigators from Eurostat, the EU statistical agency, concluded in September 2011 that Greece obfuscated its budget data to gain EU admission, despite having a deficit well in excess of the strict EU upper limit of 3 percent of GDP. And the deceit was severe and of long standing, with information about chronically large budget deficits fudged for years. The whitewash involved the tiny board of the Greek statistical agency Elstat and a handful of secretive senior central bank and treasury officials who conjured inaccurate statistics for years to meet strict EU accounting goals.

The remarkable fraud was only revealed in October 2009 by stunned officials from a newly elected government.[48] That revelation and the nation's desperate current financial straits precipitated the European sovereign debt crisis. How did a handful of Greek politicians and bureaucrats managed to carry off this charade for nearly a decade? Well, we need only ask the American firm Goldman Sachs. It seems that firm displayed the same lack of ethics abroad that it displayed over the last decade in America. For tens of millions of dollars in fees, it engineered a scheme in 2000 to defraud the EU on behalf of Greece, according to *New York Times*' journalists Nelson D. Schwartz and Sewell Chan:

> "As far back as 2000 and 2001, Goldman helped Athens quietly borrow billons to mask its poor finances by creating derivatives that essentially transformed loans into currency trades that Greece did not have to disclose under European rules."[49]

Snookered EU officials were incensed at vital information being hidden from view with financial technicalities engineered by Americans. German Chancellor Angela Merkel is a debt scold, and fingered the Goldman Sachs frauds in February 2010:

> "It would be a disgrace if it turned out to be true that banks that already pushed the US to the edge of the abyss were also a party to falsifying Greek statistics."[50]

It *is* a disgrace and dramatizes the different perspectives and outcomes between shareholder capitalism and the stakeholder capitalism envisaged by Adam Smith.

Adam Smith the Revolutionary: The Father of Stakeholder Capitalism

Recall Adam Smith believed that producers should be subservient to the greater goal of serving consumers. That makes Adam Smith the antithesis of Ayn Rand. While Rand exalted and credentialed the selfish aspects of man, Adam Smith glorified the potential for mankind's generosity, our capacity for innovation, and justice to improve everyone's living standards. The single most important aspect of Adam Smith is this: he intended that the beneficiaries of capitalism be every family across the globe.

He rejected the prevailing mercantilism of the day where domestic manufacturers in Colonial powers such as the United Kingdom prospered by exploiting Bengali farmers and Boston tea drinkers. It was the quality and quantity of innovation, and work and goods—not gold or silver—that measure a nation's worth. His goal was to divine the best scheme possible for creating broadly based prosperity. We know that because Smith's other, earlier remarkable book *The Theory of Moral*

Sentiments outlined his sympathies and engagement with mankind.[51] Smith's regulated capitalism, fired by competition and greed, is the scheme he designed to avail the fullness of life to those of even the meanest of birth by broadly expanding prosperity and opportunity. In the intent to improve living standards for everyone regardless of birth, Smith's *Wealth of Nations* is easily the most revolutionary writing in economics amid the most wondrous revolutionary century in the history of mankind.

In making family prosperity their economic covenant, Australia and northern Europe hew closely to the dream of Adam Smith. The catastrophic Ayr Bank bankruptcy taught him firsthand the destructive effects of *laissez-faire* economics. Smith admonished readers to guard against such abuses and strive for broadly based prosperity:

> "Servers, labourers, and workmen of different kinds make up the far greater part of every great political society. But what improves the circumstances of the greater part can never be regarded as an inconvenience to the whole. No society can be flourishing and happy, of which the far greater part of its members are poor and miserable. It is but equity, besides, that they who feed, clothe, and lodge the whole body of the people, should have such a share of the produce of their own labour as to be themselves tolerably well fed, clothed, and lodged."[52]

Well-regulated markets were necessary to achieve these goals, but Adam Smith argued they needed to be buttressed with public institutions to achieve the measure of generosity and broad prosperity he envisioned. Smith was a firm believer that governments craft institutions like public education to address seminal economic challenges, such as poverty and its remediation, which Ayn Rand dismissed. As Amartya Sen explained:

> "Despite all Smith did to explain and defend the constructive role of the market, he was deeply concerned about poverty, illiteracy, and relative deprivation. . . . Smith was not only a defender of the role of the state in doing things that the market might fail to do, such as universal education and poverty relief; he argued, in general, for institutional choices to fit the problems that arise rather than . . . leaving things to the market."[53]

Different Goals of Stakeholder and Shareholder Capitalism

 The former CEO of Siemens, Klaus Kleinfeld, explained that the key to German success is, ". . . the social contract: the willingness of business, labor, and political leaders to put aside some of their differences and make agreements in the national interest."[54] You have just read why German families are living the American Dream and you are not.

The goal of stakeholder capitalism is to nurture the prosperity of families. And that sentiment in the family capitalism countries is quite broad, ranging across the political spectrum, the media, academia, and even corporate boardrooms. Implementing that family prosperity covenant relies on a commonality of interests, religious perspectives, and shared goals between families, corporate leaders, and public officials, stretching back, in the case of Australia, for more than a century.

Elements of family capitalism were first crafted 117 years ago by visionary Australians who instituted a minimum wage in the bread-making, clothing, and furniture industries in 1896.[55] There and in the other family capitalism countries, the public culture has come to reflect the need for balancing the interests of free market capitalism with the social imperative to nurture family prosperity. This symbiotic culture is maintained by public officials and monitored by vigilant public opinion—the ultimate arbiters in rich democracies. And it starts at the top. Here is Germany's chancellor, Angela Merkel, and leader of the ruling Christian Democratic Union political party, in June 2008:

> "It is a system that had and still has social cohesion and equality at its core. It tries to forge alliances. . . . In a way, we will perhaps always insist on a higher degree of equality than in Anglo-Saxon societies."[56]

Their institutions, goals, and incentive structures include clear expectations involving the role of the business community. Journalists at the *Financial Times* described Merkel's philosophy this way: "Echoing a widespread sentiment in Germany, she insists on the social responsibility of business."[57] And she's the leading *conservative* in German politics!

The former German president, Horst Köhler, another conservative, argued in 2008, that "business leaders must be an example to society."[58] Support for family capitalism is widespread in German executive suites, too. In early 2009, for example, executives joined unions in asking Berlin to explicitly target economic stimulus to reduce job loss. Michael Sommer, chairman of the Germany Confederations of Trade Unions, described one meeting: German executives "were saying: 'We need a state investment programme. We need short-time working; we don't want the people ending up on the street.' I thought I was at the wrong meeting."[59]

This attitude applies to tax policy as well. Back in 2009, Chancellor Merkel had proposed sweeping tax cuts for firms and households to help the recovery. But when the Greek debt crisis erupted, and the focus in northern Europe turned more to austerity, German executives rejected corporate tax cuts as imprudent. Hans-Peter Keitel, president of the German business association BDI, told *Focus* magazine in late 2009 that corporate tax cuts financed with budget deficits would just worsen the larger problem:

> "Ever more billions in borrowings also mean higher interest payments, and the financial room for maneuver for politicians becomes ever narrower. For that reason, our priority is: budget consolidation. That is more important than comprehensive tax cuts."[60]

Expectations and attitudes are similar in Australia. Guess what happened there when a new 18-week paid parental leave policy threatened to create budget deficits? During the 2010 campaign, conservative party leader Tony Abbott criticized the leave policy as *insufficient*, and proposed a more generous one, but funded by a new 1.5 percent tax on larger firms: "Larger businesses have the capacity to pay. As an Australian, you should want to see a better deal for families, a better deal for families with kids and that's what this is all about."[61] And he's the leading conservative in Australia!

These quotes capture the vast gulf between the culture and perspective of corporate governance in the family capitalism countries and Reagan-era America. It is unimaginable that the US Chamber of Commerce would reject corporate tax cuts in order to avoid deeper budget deficits or to urge higher corporate taxes to fund benefits for employees. Indeed, their prescription for all real or perceived ills is further tax cuts.

Enterprise relations with employees and their unions in the family capitalism countries are collaborative rather than confrontational. Here is GM-Holden's personnel director in Australia, Mark Polglaze, explaining that his firm had successfully maneuvered through the recent recession with "the creative and collaborative approach of our unions and other stakeholders that allowed us to find some mutually beneficial solutions."[62] Mutually beneficial solutions are no longer in the US business lexicon. The behavior of Australians reflects a much different culture from the US, as noted by columnist Michael Pascoe of *Western Australia Today:*

> "We go to work and earn our money and pay our taxes. . . . We generally try to pick the lesser evil when we vote. Collectively, we help our neighbors. . . . We somewhat instinctively know that unrestrained selfishness is not the best policy."[63]

And the Australian judiciary goes to considerable lengths to enforce demanding community expectations about the morality and behavior of the business community. For example, former Hanlong Mining managing director Steven Xiao, under investigation for insider trading, absconded to China and deserted his family. Displeased investigators insist that his wife Xike Hu remain in country until her husband returns to face authorities; that was in November 2011. As of this writing, she remains in Australia at the insistence of the Supreme Court.[64]

Attitudes Toward Employees in Stakeholder and Shareholder Capitalism

Firms in America feel empowered to chisel employees. While worksite relations have deteriorated, jobs offshored, and wages flattened for most employees, the most severely impacted may be the most vulnerable: Working poor men and women victimized by employers violating national wage and hour laws. An authoritative analysis of employer wage embezzlement was jointly conducted in 2009 by the University of California at Los Angeles, the Center for Urban Economic Development, and the National Employment Law Project. Their analysis focused on the working poor, that 20 percent of adults earning around the minimum wage. These employees tend to be the least assertive and informed and consequently more subject potentially to employer abuse. Indeed, researchers found that employers routinely and illegally retained an average of $51 from paychecks averaging $339 per week during the analysis period.[65] That $2,500 or so over the course of a year is an important amount for these Americans with few cash reserves, living paycheck to paycheck.

The most egregious specific violation involved overtime calculations, with some 76 percent of employees underpaid. Researchers also discovered that 26 percent of workers had illegally been paid less than the minimum wage, usually by more than $1 per hour. And 12 percent of workers were found to have had tips stolen by employers. As we see in a moment, such swindling sparks headlines, perp walks, and jail time in most other rich democracies, but US employers are just following the example set by Walmart.

America's largest employer, Walmart, exploited weak enforcement of wage and hour regulations during the administration of George W. Bush to repeatedly defraud employees. Employees complained, but the US Department of Labor's policy during these years was to drag out investigations for years until most complaints by employees were dropped. In contrast, the Obama administration campaigned in 2008 on the promise to uphold Labor Department standards. The outcome of that election caused a stampede by Walmart and other firms in the last months of the Bush administration, rushing to confess to illegal practices in order to avoid potential larger fines from the incoming administration. For example, Walmart admitted guilt in a 2008 Christmas Eve announcement, agreeing to pay as much as $640 million in fines to settle long-standing complaints involving thousands of employees nationwide.[66]

By permitting such cases to languish for years, the Bush administration proved a dead end for families expecting fairness from Washington. Created to protect against employment abuse, the Department of Labor perversely protected *employers* from aggrieved employees, a classic regulatory capture outcome. A Congressional investigation in 2008, for example, found that an amazing 90 percent of serious complaints to the Labor Department's Wage and Hour Division were mishandled, many simply gone missing. Moreover, caseworkers at the Department were discovered to be discouraging the filing of complaints, instead urging aggrieved employees to seek personal legal action at their own expense against employers. That is an unrealistic alternative for most Americans: time consuming, expensive, and almost certain to lead to firing. The researchers concluded:

> "This investigation clearly shows that Labor has left thousands of actual victims of wage theft who sought federal government assistance with nowhere to turn. Unfortunately, far too often the result is unscrupulous employers' taking advantage of our country's low-wage workers."[67]

Such hostility is in stark contrast with Government agencies in the family capitalism countries that very actively monitor and promptly adjudicate worksite disagreements. Fair Work Australia (FWA) meets public accountability expectations by publicizing its dispute settlement agreements, and operates with short timelines to settle contract disagreements. By mid-2013, it will have an online dispute and compliant lodgment system, with detailed instructions to facilitate the filing of unfair dismissal complaints by individual employees representing themselves. It is determined to be user-friendly for employees. FWA President Justice Lain Ross explained the logic: "For those unfamiliar with the tribunal's processes and how a hearing is conducted, the experience can be daunting. The information and assistance provided can be a significant benefit to parties."[68]

Active public sector monitoring of worksite practices is matched by voter attention to worksite fairness issues. Remember the antics involving its plant in Williamson, New York, where Dr. Pepper Snapple threatened to hire replacement workers for as much as one-third less pay? Such wage dumping is so commonplace as to be unworthy of media coverage in America, much less boycotts. Not so in northern Europe or especially in Australia, where wage abuse is so rare that even modest infractions induce attention-grabbing headlines nationwide. The behavior of Dr. Pepper Snapple management would have been scandalizing front-page news in *Der Spiegel*, *Le Monde*, or *Western Australia* for weeks, because voters abroad expect firms to enhance—rather than erode—family prosperity. Few employers in these rich democracies have proven sufficiently tin-eared to risk public opprobrium by running afoul of community standards, because violators suffer humiliation, legal sanctions, and almost certain consumer boycotts.

For the same reason, minimum-wage violations are so rare as to be novelties in Australia. How rare? Well, the press there extensively reported on a November 2010 prosecution by the Fair Work ombudsman of wage dumping by an enterprise in the state of Queensland. A court magistrate determined that wages had been shorted by one-third, and imposed fines on the owner personally. Who was the scoundrel? The giant retailer Woolworths or Coles Supermarkets? Nope. It was a tiny fruit and vegetable shop fined A$67,650 (US$70,000).[69] Another incident produced a September 2011 headline in the *Sydney Morning Herald* reading, "Student paid 'just $3.30 an hour.'" A businessman exploited an ambitious immigrant by paying far less than the legal minimum (above US$10 per hour) over the course of a year. The scoundrel? Ali Baba Kabobs and Wraps at Southland Shopping Centre in Cheltenham.[70]

The value of public opinion has been especially important in Germany, where the absence of a comprehensive minimum wage tempts an occasional employer to practice US-style wage dumping. For example, public opinion in 2009 was instrumental in ending the low-wage practice of the large Kik discount retailer. Termed a wage "pariah" in a *Berliner Zeitung* headline, Kik in 2010 agreed to boost pay by almost 40 percent, to at least €7.50 per hour (more than $9.00).[71]

Wage dumping also became a huge marketing, and eventually legal and financial problem for Walmart in Germany, as we will learn in a later chapter. Both Walmart and what was then the largest German drugstore chain, Schlecker, were punished for wage dumping by consumer boycotts. It ended badly for both. In early 2010, Schlecker began closing 500 smaller outlets and opening rebranded "XL" megastores. It turned out that Schlecker's leadership was conducting a corporate wage-suppression strategy behind the veil of this store upgrade program. The scheme turned into a marketing disaster when the firm was discovered rehiring seasoned employees for the new megastores at much lower wages, as well as replacing hundreds of experienced sales staff with cheap temporary workers. The new hires and rehires were paid about one-half old wages, some as low as €6.50 ($8.00) per hour, among the lowest wages anywhere in northern Europe.

As adverse publicity mounted, management was subject to what the *Berliner Zeitung* termed "massive public criticism for the reconstruction of Schlecker branches."[72] *De facto* community standards were not being met, and customer traffic fell by double-digits; amazingly (to an American, anyway) Schlecker management was even criticized by other employer groups, including the retail association HDE and even the FDP, the "millionaires" political party. Schlecker reversed course, restoring pay of at least €12.27 per hour and giving hiring priority to its experienced employees.[73] But the falloff in traffic was too severe, and the firm fell into bankruptcy.

In fact, Schlecker management was fortunate to escape jail because wage dumping is subject to judicial remedies in Germany. For example, a Dusseldorf court in 2010 sentenced eight executives in the meatpacking industry to as much as five-and-a-half years in jail for underpayment of wages and defrauding the Social Security system.[74]

A similar attempt at wage dumping occurred in Leiden, in the Netherlands. After the brewer Heineken outsourced cafeteria services, the winning contractor promptly cut wages for existing employees by more than one-half, from €46,000 to €20,000 per year for the same work. The European Court of Justice prosecuted Heineken, with the Amsterdam paper *De Volkskrant* headlining, "Employer Court Puts Stop to Employer's Trick Move."[75]

The wage-dumping strategy tried by Schlecker is also illegal in France. The optical Group Metaleurop SA, for example, closed outlets and fired 482 employees in June 2003 "without real and serious cause," according to reports in *Le Figaro*. They were reopened later, paying lower wages under the new name of Lens Recylex. A trial resulted; the firm was sentenced to pay former employees up to €30,000 apiece.[76]

The use of temporary employees is widespread in America as employers seek lower wage and benefit costs, and can perhaps dodge paying any payroll taxes. The same wage compression strategy has appeared in northern Europe, and can result in significant savings to employers there, too, because temps are paid €5.06 per hour less than regular staff, according to trade union researchers. The European press has publicized the issue, with the *Berliner Zeitung* and Agency France-Presse calling temps "slaves." Frustrated with this new subterfuge threatening wages, Europeans demanded legal remediation. Unlike America, the political system produced a remedy in short order.

In October 2011, EU officials mandated that after twelve weeks of employment, employers must extend the same wages, holiday, and maternity leave rights to temporary workers that are enjoyed by full-time employees.[77] Not all EU members were pleased. The United Kingdom was one of the few EU nations, along with Iceland, Ireland, and Spain that enthusiastically adopted Reaganomic deregulation; the Tory government of Prime Minister David Cameron there retains a finely tuned antenna to business concerns. This EU directive to police the exploitation of temporary workers was greeted with dismay by Cameron's government; the Tory *Daily Telegraph* fumed it could cost firms almost £2 billion a year, which "could derail Britain's fragile recovery."[78] Every economist in the world would disagree. In reality, *boosting* wages of lower-income households with high marginal propensities to spend is about the very best step to strengthen—rather than derail—a recovery.

Attitudes Toward Investors in Stakeholder and Shareholder Capitalism

Deregulation harmed investors across the globe. Unlike America, the family capitalism countries took steps in the wake of the credit crisis to prevent a recurrence. The harm can be traced to executive suite narcissism during the Reagan era that caused a decline in ethics of the business community, never terribly high in any case, if one believes Adam Smith. In particular, financial fraud has risen sharply since the 1980s, exemplified by the epidemic of insider loans by deregulated S&L executives during the Reagan administration.

Economists know such malfeasance is widespread, thanks to documentation developed by researchers including Professors Lauren Cohen and Christopher Malloy of the Harvard Business School; Lukasz Pomorski of the University of Toronto; Karl A. Muller, III of Penn State; Monica Neamtaiu of the University of Arizona; and Edward J. Riedl with the Harvard Business School.[79] And victims include small investors and families harmed by the 2007/2008 credit crisis as well as large sophisticated investors like hedge funds as evidenced by the recent Dark Pools saga. In recent years, rampant front-running induced mutual, hedge, insurance, and pension funds seeking optimum prices to utilize Dark Pools, where their large block trades were presumably obfuscated and anonymous, allowing for more competitive pricing. Yet the certainty of trading gain proved too alluring; the Dark Pool exchange platform Pipeline Trading Systems was discovered front-running its own block traders and was fined by the SEC in 2011.[80]

The reality is that the discipline of market forces has proven no match for the practices that have proliferated in the wake of financial deregulation. Alan Greenspan called Wall Street bankers who exploited deregulation to conjure new financial products like subprime mortgages "pollinating bees" in his 2009 book, *Age of Turbulence.* Some of his pollinators' products proved toxic to investors, who unfortunately still today have only modest recourse under the *caveat emptor* rules of American law, even in instances when they were denied critical information by broker-dealers or by rating agencies.

In contrast, as we see now, recent reforms have imposed much higher standards of honesty and fiduciary responsibility on financial market participants in some stakeholder capitalism nations like Australia.

With American financiers balking at buying risky bundles of subprime mortgages, Greenspan's pollinators went international, hawking the toxic instruments to trusting folks from tiny Norwegian towns such as Narvik to the Australian Outback.[81] Laughed out of institutional investor offices across Sydney, for example, Lehman Brothers subsequently purchased a local brokerage house, Grange Securities, to more readily move subprime mortgages off their own books, trolling down-market in unsophisticated towns like Parkes. Investors like Parkes subsequently suffered grievous losses when the credit crisis unfolded. A report in *Euromoney* magazine said that Parkes was "among some of the 150-odd Australian councils, churches, universities, charities, hospitals, and community groups nursing a $2-billion black eye after buying now-toxic collateralized debt obligations from Grange . . . wasting years of rural thrift at the worst possible time in Australian agricultural history as the country copes with a crippling decade-long drought."[82]

Only belatedly did these trusting souls realize they were dealing with reincarnations of Albert Wiggins, the Depression-era president of Chase National Bank who shorted his own bank stock to reap millions at the expense of his shareholders. Lehman Brothers and other pollinators bet against their trusting investors, pocketed their fees and profits, and stole away before the roulette wheel finished rotating.

It was a sweet time to be on Wall Street if you chose to channel Wiggins.

Defrauded Australians grew angry enough to sue all financial intermediaries involved, including the rating firm S&P for anointing risky assets with AAA ratings. In the United States, S&P is fending off similar suits by arguing that its made-up ratings are some variation or other of free speech shielded by the First Amendment. That is an odd claim to make for a business product—and also a dubious claim, since the ratings in question in 2006 and 2007 were just shared with a few—rather than all—investors.

That argument certainly fell on deaf ears in Australian courts, where S&P's first fraud suit went to trial in October 2011. Twelve Australian communities relied on its bogus AAA ratings in 2007 and lost 93 percent of their capital in a structured financial asset called Rembrandt.

The original issuing bank ABM Amro prepared marketing claims about Rembrandt, which S&P merely cut and pasted into its own ratings documents without conducting its own due diligence. That obviously pleased officials from ABM Amro, even as they acknowledged such incompetence was "highly weird. An opportunity, however."

In the end, other analysts within S&P itself became too embarrassed and vented against the inept colleagues, as revealed in another Australian court document:

> "You are the wuss for bending over in front of [ABM Amro] bankers and taking it . . . you rate something AAA when it is really A-? You proud of that little mistake? It's nothing about growing up, it's about doing your job to a high standard."[83]

With a clear sense of right and wrong, a decision was rendered by an Australian court in November 2012; it found all parties to the derivative Rembrandt guilty. ABM Amro, the rating agency S&P, and the broker-dealer Lehman Brothers/Grange had "deceived" and "misled" clients. The court awarded full restitution, damages, legal fees, and interest to the local communities.

This decision went against the Reagan-era American business ethos in three ways. First, the issuing bank was held responsible for marketing a financial product despite knowing it was unsound. Second, Lehman Brothers was found guilty of marketing a product without providing full disclosure to customers. But perhaps the biggest difference was the Australian legal rejection of S&P's First Amendment defense. While a few US courts have disagreed, that defense is largely the reason some 40 suits against rating agencies have been dismissed in the US.[84] As reporter Michael West of the *Sydney Morning Herald* concluded,

> "The court's finding this morning acknowledges that investors are entitled to and indeed do rely on credit ratings and can expect them to be based on reasonable grounds. S&P cannot express its opinion, knowing that investors rely upon it, get paid for that opinion and then disclaim liability."[85]

A *Financial Times* editorially made the same point about S&P: "It is precisely their role as gatekeepers to the capital markets that means they should be responsible for the ratings they give."[86] Similar to the decision mentioned earlier by German courts in the Deutsche Bank instance, Australia has now clearly specified the responsibility of issuing institutions, broker-dealers, and rating agencies to act as faithful fiduciaries for customers.

CHAPTER 6

A CULTURE OF SELFISHNESS

"Stock-based compensation plans are often nothing more than legalized front-running, insider trading, and stock-watering all wrapped up in one package."[1]

ALBERT MEYER,
Founder, Bastiat Capital

"If a worker's rewards are based on only some of her tasks, that is where she will concentrate her effort. For example, a CEO whose compensation depends on the current stock price will try to run up the current stock price, but will ignore the long-term consequences."[2]

GEORGE AKERLOF and RACHEL E. KRANTON,
***Identity Economics*, 2010**

"If the absolute value of every top earner's take-home pay were to fall by half, the same executives would end up in the same jobs as before."[3]

ROBERT H. FRANK,
Cornell University

"Management has become obsessed with share price. By focusing on short-term moves in stock prices, managers are eroding the long-term value of their franchises."[4]

JESSE EISINGER,
***New York Times*, June 28, 2012**

There are two secrets about shareholder capitalism:

First, shareholder capitalism presumes that firms maximize profits. The truth is, it seems that relatively few firms do that. Many CEOs actually have only vague notions of exactly how to maximize profits.

Second, it turns out not to matter because of the next secret: the real goal of management is maximizing executive compensation.

I'll let Justin Fox of the *Harvard Business Review* and Harvard professor Jay Lorsch explain:

"Conflict between shareholders and managers is asymmetric warfare, with shareholders in no position to prevail."[5]

Because of management's ability to control information, it was inevitable that shareholder capitalism would devolve to managerial capitalism, where enterprises in Reagan-era America neither maximize profits nor maximize shareholder returns. That has made shareholder capitalism useless as an operational philosophy.

The Myth of Profit-Maximizing Enterprises

During the golden age, US executives were paid modestly, with the rare outstanding performance rewarded with bonuses or higher salaries. Compensation was important, but so were other issues. That changed in the Reagan era. Firms nominally became profit maximizers, ostensibly managed solely for the benefit of shareholder-owners. And that outcome was to be accomplished by linking executive compensation to profits. This conceptualization of shareholder capitalism argued that management should pivot from the golden age ethos of prioritizing profits along with community and employee goals to a sole focus on profits. And it is certainly true that profits have risen sharply. But one of the first rules of economics is to follow the money. And that trail teaches us that profits and share prices have risen much less than executive compensation. Management—not shareholders—has been the big winner in Reaganomics. Indeed, economists have determined that executives don't even bother to maximize firm profits.

The extensive research documenting this reality has been unkind to Milton Friedman's 1953 dictate that profit maximization should drive executive suite behavior:

> "Whenever this determinant happens to lead to behavior consistent with rational and informed maximization of returns, the business will prosper and acquire resources with which to expand; when it does not, the business will tend to lose resources and can be kept in existence only by the addition of resources from outside."[6]

Friedman's market determinism has been discredited. Indeed, it's unlikely that executives could manage to maximize profits instead of executive compensation even if actually interested in doing so. A large body of management and behavioral economics research has documented that, lack of motivation aside, guiding firms turns out to be too nuanced and demanding for managers to behave ideally and consistently, as Friedman suggests. Economists Mark Armstrong and Steffen Huck of University College London, for example, concluded in 2010 that executives are little better than consumers at resisting herding and other economically irrational human tendencies.

"We present evidence—both real world and experimental—that firms . . . sometime depart from the profit-maximizing paradigm. For instance, firms may be content to achieve 'satisfactory' rather than optimal profits, firms might rely on old patterns—such as imitating the strategies of well-performing rivals, or continuing with strategies which have performed reasonably well in the past—rather than on explicit calculations of complex optimal strategies. . . ."[7]

Maximizing short-term executive pay, reputational preservation, maintenance of market share, fear of hostile takeovers, friendship or annoyance with peers, or a fiercely competitive streak: all these concerns and behaviors produce suboptimal profits. That occurs also when management adopts the goal of Wall Street analysts and targets profit growth rates relative to rivals rather than to absolute profits. Or they may pointlessly price too aggressively, perhaps signaling an eagerness to discourage potential competitors from entering their market. Suboptimal outcomes are also common because management resorts to shortcuts and rules-of-thumb in dealing with their highly complex and uncertain environment. Moreover, it is simply too time consuming to determine where the profit-maximizing intersections of marginal costs and marginal revenues rest for hundreds of products in hundreds of overlapping markets, each with unique dynamics.

Far worse, it turns out that even the most informed, analytical, and competent American executives have not even bothered to clarify the proper data set required for profit-maximizing production and pricing. CEOs tend to base pricing decisions on sunk or fixed costs, even though economists have long taught MBA students that profit-maximizing price and output decisions should be dictated by marginal revenues and costs. As early as 1939, it was realized that this seminal rule is broadly flouted and may not even be known by many executives. The shift to shareholder capitalism should easily have rectified the problem, but did not. Studies as recent as 2008 confirm that this same suboptimal behavior persists, with pricing decisions by a majority of managers including considerations of fixed or sunk costs.[8]

Ignorance and inadequate information aside, the existential fallacy in Friedman's philosophy is that enterprise executives are the major beneficiaries of the shift to market fundamentalism in recent decades, not shareholders or anyone else, especially not the firms they manage. Management maximizes enterprise profits beyond the immediate quarter almost by happenstance. And it is not at all unusual for enterprise leaders to mismanage firm assets, diminishing rather than enhancing longer-term firm profit prospects. These suboptimal outcomes have been most commonly identified with undue self-confidence, a typical behavioral trait of survivors in the US executive-suite derby; it makes CEOs too quick to launch ill-fated takeovers or mergers, for example, simply because they view them as likely to spike quarterly results.

Perhaps the most prominent research on this and other aspects of contemporary managerial irrationality dates from 1986, when economist Richard Roll linked such excessive merger behavior with executive suite overconfidence.[9] Other researchers agreed. Over-projecting the synergistic benefits of acquisitions "could therefore be one explanation for why companies which undertake mergers seem to underperform," noted the University College London economists Armstrong and Huck. Indeed, they concluded that there were a number of similar factors causing underperformance: "We see there are several situations in which Friedman's (1953) critique of non-profit maximizing behavior appears to fail."[10]

Managerial Capitalism

Walmart CEO Michael T. Duke is in a great hurry to open new stores. You see, his bonus is in jeopardy. In the past, the bonus was tied to same-store sales, which is the only accurate way to measure firm and management performance. But sales at existing stores are slumping. Duke's solution? Insist that his board of directors put their thumbs on the scale: replace Duke's bonus plan with one linked to total companywide sales, helpfully bloated by opening new stores in nations like Mexico.[11]

Despite being quite capable, American executives get a lot wrong today, as we are about to learn. But one thing all of them get right is superbly gaming the dysfunctional American system of corporate governance to enhance compensation while compressing wages, R&D, and investment.

We know that from sentiments of corporate leaders like GE CEO Jeff Immelt. By July 2009, he had grown embarrassed by the narcissism of American executives: "I would hate to think that the lasting impression of this generation of American business is the one that exists today."

Former *New York Times* reporter David Cay Johnston noted that the new pattern of compensation that emerged with the Reagan administration is exemplified by the earlier GE CEO Welch, "whose way was to squeeze the pay and numbers of the rank and file and then richly reward executives." Welch mentored many executives, such as John M. Trani, who subsequently endeavored to move the Connecticut firm Stanley Tools from New Britain to Bermuda to avoid paying US taxes. Johnston described the archetypal new manager Trani this way:

"He was part of a new era of corporate managers, many of them Welch acolytes, who never shook hands with anyone who got grease on theirs, even if they had wiped them clean when their one big chance came to meet the boss. They neither mingled with the people who made their company products nor did they appear to think much about their lives."[12]

Was the Creation of Managerial Capitalism a Conspiracy?

A conspiracy?

It's tempting to ascribe rising executive pay and US income redistribution since 1980 to a vast conspiracy, but it is not. Rather, it is the outcome of the business community becoming intellectually willing and politically able as Reaganomics unfolded to pursue narcissistic self-absorption in the best traditions of nineteenth-century robber barons. And no one, especially shareholders or employees, was permitted to stand in its way.

History records that the Reagan era was just the latest of America's Gilded Ages. The first episode occurred in the three decades after 1880, when entrepreneurs such as Pierpont Morgan, Andrew Carnegie, and John Jacob Astor emerged. They seized upon the quack pseudoscience offered by Yale professor William Graham Sumner, Herbert Spencer (*Social Statics*, 1851), and others in the afterglow of Darwinism to justify widening income disparities. Great wealth is the imprimatur of mankind's most evolutionary fit, and the means for such evolutionary superiority to be perpetuated. This pseudoscientific logic helped assuage any guilt and deflected brickbats from critics such as Mark Twain.

During the Reagan era, similar pseudoscientific rationale was provided by the themes of shareholder capitalism, and especially by Ayn Rand. The outcome is that business leaders are constantly driving one another to garner more income. As Diane Coyle, visiting professor at the University of Manchester, wrote:

"[The] banking bonus culture validated making a lot of money as a life and career goal. . . . Remuneration consultants . . . helped ratchet up the pay and bonus levels throughout the economy."[13]

"Too much" became "never enough." In hindsight, it's clear that CEOs pursuing their own magnified self-interest within this new environment enabled business leaders to engage in *de facto* class warfare as they strove to seize a larger share of the gains from growth. But class warfare was the last thing on their minds. Like the John Laws of yesteryear, their motivation was simply to increase their incomes at anyone else's expense.

They succeeded in stagnating wages, lowering taxes, slowing investment, and weakening the social safety net—never mind the long-term interest of shareholders, the urgency of driving productivity, or the tens of millions including children lacking health care or bedding down hungry every night in their own cities. Most seem indifferent to the reality that one of every two American children will need food stamps at some point or that tens of millions live on the margins in a shadowy economic netherworld, much like subsistence farmers in some far-off, developing nation. The business community looks right through those Americans.

This pattern is sufficiently stark that the psychological framework supporting such callous behavior in robber baron periods has become a fascination for social scientists parsing the relationship of socioeconomic class and unethical behaviors. This includes researchers like Paul K. Piff at the University of California, Berkeley, lead author of a study published in the February 2012 *Proceedings of the National Academy of Sciences*.[14] In a series of elaborate experiments, Piff and his colleagues found a consistent difference in the reaction to ethical situations between middle- and working-class participants and upper-class participants; upper-class subjects routinely exhibited greater selfishness and unethical behavior. Displaying a sense of entitlement, upper-class folks proved more likely to lie and cheat, among other pathologies; they stole twice as much candy from children; readily deceived job candidates by withholding important information (e.g., the job was only temporary); and cheated by embellishing their scores in self-reporting competitions.

"The increased unethical tendencies of upper-class individuals are driven, in part, by their more favorable attitudes toward greed," concluded Piff. Relatively indifferent to community standards, "Upper-class individuals are more self-focused, they privilege themselves over others, and they engage in self-interested patterns of behavior." Sound like anyone you know or have read about?

Dysfunctional Corporate Boards of Directors

Recall the imagery of the pigs greedily exploiting the effort of others in George Orwell's *Animal Farm*? A genuine and faithful incarnation is the behavior in recent decades of American executives colluding with colleagues on corporate boards of directors.

Supervisory oversight of CEOs has historically been weak in America, where boards have traditionally been widely held to be ineffective.[15] But the opportunity for windfalls during the Reagan era caused traditional supine board governance to deteriorate even further. Too many CEOs are able to pick their own boards: board elections feature a management-selected list of candidates, with critics facing daunting expense and administrative barriers to landing positions on the ballot. Only rich corporate raiders like William A. Ackman of Pershing Square Capital Management can compete. Journalist Ian Austen explains:

> "We forget how unusual the corporate election system is in a democracy. Ninety-nine percent of the time, shareholders are not given a choice as to who they wish to represent them on the board of directors."[16]

Firm performance would benefit from visionary and even contentious boards rather than incurious ones. Instead, CEO friends and cronies are appointed to boards. CEOs also tend to join other boards, readily approving handsome compensation packages, using a practice economists term peer-benchmarking. CEO compensation is routinely set at the 90th percentile of peer firms for CEOs like Angelo Mozilo at (bankrupt) Countrywide Financial. That scheme creates an automatic escalator in executive pay.

How incestuous are board-CEO relationships? Well, a survey involving 350 of the firms comprising the S&P stock indices over 15 years by University of Michigan business professor James Westphal found that nearly 50 percent of compensation committee board members were identified by CEOs as "friends" rather than acquaintances.[17] Such custom-crafted boards routinely tolerate mediocre or worse performance. Examples abound.

Amgen CEO Kevin W. Sharer finally resigned in May 2012, but his annual compensation had increased 37 percent to $21 million over his years of service—despite shareholders losing 7 percent. One of the firm's largest shareholders, Steve Silverman, complained to Peter Whoriskey of the *Washington Post* in 2011:

> "Members of the Amgen board are basically just rubber-stampers. Kevin put most of them on the board himself. If he's getting paid too much—and he certainly is—they're not going to say so."[18]

A particularly egregious example was the antics of board members at Merrill Lynch in 2007. Bankrupt and headed for a fire sale at pennies on the dollar, they inexplicably decided to let the incompetent CEO, E.

Stanley O'Neal, resign instead of firing him. In doing so, they dinged shareholders for $131 million in stock options O'Neal would otherwise have forfeited.[19]

Another example is reported by David Cay Johnston in his book *Perfectly Legal*, involving Eugene M. Isenberg of Nabors Industries, a large oil-drilling firm. In 2000, that firm reported sales of $1.3 billion. Amazingly, through a combination of stock options and a well-crafted compensation agreement, Isenberg received $127 million of that cash flow, or nearly 10 percent of gross revenue.[20]

And, there is Craig Dubow. Dubow was CEO of the media giant Gannett for six years, which ended with his resignation in 2011. It was a lush run for him: Dubow received a golden parachute worth $37.1 million, plus $16 million in cash during just his last two years. Yet, Dubow's record was poor, with share price falling from $75, when he arrived, to $10.[21]

Board members supporting CEOs like these covet the relationships, perks, and pay; median remuneration for nonexecutive board members at Fortune 500 firms was $199,949 in 2008, according to the compensation firm Towers Perrin.[22] Moreover, most are incurious, because few have significant personal wealth linked to their companies, while opaque board proceedings, and directors- and officers-insurance shield them from personal liability, even in bankruptcy. Compensation experts John Gillespie and David Zweig, authors of *Money for Nothing*, note that there were a bare 13 instances between 1980 and 2006 when outside directors settled suits with their own personal resources. Even then, punishment was mild: Enron directors "paid only 10 percent of their prior net gains from selling Enron stock."[23] Remarkably, their careers also seem unaffected by the Enron connection; four served on other boards, one taught at Stanford, and another became Chancellor at London's Brunel University. Wendy Gramm? Well, she has resided at George Mason University's Mercatus Center, supported in part by donations from the Koch brothers (who preach there should be penalties for market failure).[24]

CEOs enjoy celebrities and so have tended to appoint them to boards. That's why boards too often look like an American version of *Debrett's Peerage* or at least *Dancing with the Stars*. The list of board members has included Lance Armstrong, skier Jean-Claude Killy, Tommy Lasorda, Fran Tarkington, and even Priscilla Presley and O.J. Simpson (on the *audit* committee at Infinity Broadcasting). The Lehman Brothers board included actresses, theater producers, and a retired admiral. This trend has abated in recent years with boards under more scrutiny. Yet, the innate collegiality of US board members limits contention. As Gillespie and Zweig note, board members:

"... don't want to appear foolish by asking questions. Others don't want to rock the board for fear of ostracism. Sometimes the desire for collegiality seems much more immediate than the need to represent shareholders who are not in the room."[25]

One problem is that too many members are unqualified, lacking industry, financial, or investment expertise. Folks with excellent people skills, but lacking skill in complex financial matrices, are particularly ill-suited members. A second problem is conflicts of interest. A common technique to ensure deferential boards is for CEOs to flout the intent of NASDAQ rules that require a majority of members to have limited or no company ties. A designated "independent" member of Rupert Murdock's News Corporation's board, for example, is the former CEO of Murdock's Australian subsidiary, News Limited. Another is a godfather to a Murdock grandchild. And virtually all of his board members owe careers or wealth to Murdock's enterprises.[26]

The independence of such boards is nominal. Experts such as Harvard law professor Lucian Bebchuk (also director of the Harvard Program on Corporate Governance) and economist Jesse Fried are highly critical of boards for their routine endorsement of lush compensation packages for CEOs. In a 2010 analysis, for example, they concluded compensation is not set at arm's length by such boards, but instead that CEOs essentially manipulate boards to set their own pay:

"Directors have had various economic incentives to support, or at least go along with, arrangements favorable to the company's top executives. Collegiality, team spirit, a natural desire to avoid conflict within the board, and sometimes friendship and loyalty has also pulled board members in that direction. . . . Indeed, there is a substantial body of evidence indicating that pay has been higher, or less sensitive to performance, when executives have more power over directors. . . . Executive pay is also higher when the compensation committee chair has been appointed under the current CEO . . ."[27]

Here is a February 2010 editorial by the feisty *Financial Times* discussing the result of high pay:

"There is no evidence that such packages promote exceptional performance—and much to suggest they destroy the social fabric of companies as the gap between chief executives and workers soars. The clubby remuneration committees behind these preposterous packages deserve to be slung out on the street."[28]

Why has the American system of supine boards persisted? An important factor is they have been credentialed by academics such as Harvard business professor Michael C. Jensen. Like Milton Friedman, who provided a veneer of intellectual *gravitas* for Reaganomics, Jensen's musings on Harvard stationery have lent a patina of respectability to a compensation system riddled with conflicts of interest and market failure, with pay disconnected from performance. He wrote several academic papers in the 1980s credentialing stock options and the extremely high executive compensation they produced. Some academic colleagues disagreed, and so Jensen and a coauthor, University of Southern California professor Kevin J. Murphy, wrote in the *New York Times* in May 1984:

> [Readers] ". . . must be wary of wolves dressed in sheepskin currently attacking executive compensation to achieve their own ends. Many assert that executives are overpaid and paid in a way that is independent of performance."[29]

The embarrassment for Jensen and Murphy is that their academic critics have been proven correct. (To their credit, they had come by 1990 to agree with critics.) The consensus is explained by Gillespie and Zweig:

> "Our initial inquiry into why so many boards seem to have failed led us quickly to this realization: . . . It is as if the American economy has been driving a race car without having the slightest idea of how a steering wheel works—not to mention the brakes. . . . Although it's not supposed to be the case, most CEOs exercise powerful control over their boards. They dictate or greatly influence the directors' selection and compensation, they set the boards' agendas and committee assignments, and they control access to information. Thus, many boards come to represent executives' interests rather than those of the shareholders."[30]

Critics of board governance also included prominent conservatives such as Richard A. Posner, the federal appeals court judge quoted earlier, who has acknowledged that the market for executive compensation is dysfunctional. Writing in a 2008 dissent to a decision by the Seventh Circuit Court of Appeals in *Jones v. Harris Associates*, Posner concluded, "Executive compensation in large publicly traded firms often is excessive because of the feeble incentives of boards of directors to police compensation."[31]

Think of the scope of the problem in weak corporate governance this way: behind every single report in the media of CEO pay not reflecting performance is a dysfunctional board. An apt analogy is the cozy search conducted by Richard Cheney for a vice presidential candidate to join Governor George W. Bush's ticket in 2000. The outcome resembled events surrounding the antics of the board in recent years of the giant computer company Hewlett-Packard. Meg Whitman's selection as the new CEO in 2011 was "secretly engineered" by a single board member "without putting the board or the company through the time and expense of conducting a proper search or seriously considering other candidates," explained economics reporter Steven Pearlstein of the *Washington Post*.[32] As Stanford law professor Donohue subsequently noted, "After what HP had gone through, you'd think the board would have been on their toes rather than asleep at the switch again."[33]

Bonuses and Stock Options Are Accelerants in Rising Executive Pay

Since the 1980s, stock options have offered management the prospect of bountiful windfalls. But despite the whiff of greenbacks in the air, there was an asterisk. Those windfalls hinged on constantly improving earnings per share from one quarter to the next. It took only a New York minute for CEOs to figure it all out at the dawn of the Reagan era: management should ignore what they had been taught in business schools about focusing on productivity growth and longer-term investment, and abandon the principles that had guided American enterprise and economy in the wondrous decades after World War II. Instead, to personally strike gold, they needed to spike earnings per share over the next 90 days.

The easiest way was to switch corporate outlays from expenses (such as wages and R&D) to share buybacks and risky mergers. For American executives, the long term abruptly crystallized at three months. At the same time, management quickly mastered the trick of obfuscating and rendering opaque the system of option awards and bonuses. Australian journalist Ian Verrender explained the conjury this way:

> "From an executive point of view, the brilliance of the bonus system is its sheer complexity. Each company employs different systems, imposes different hurdles, and arbitrarily alters them when conditions require."[34]

Recall that senior American executives during the golden age earned about 30 times the average pay of their employees. Management pay was stable for decades before accelerating as the Reagan era unfolded, with that multiple rising to more than 300 times average employee wages now.

In inflation-adjusted dollars, as depicted in Chart 6.1, compensation for the top three executives has increased fivefold since the 1980s, while real employee compensation went flat. It is now typical for a handful of senior executives at sizable firms to *each* average $5 million in annual pay, including bonuses and the value of stock options. Here is a startling statistic: CEOs now receive 10 percent of all corporate profits, according to Gillespie and Zweig.[35]

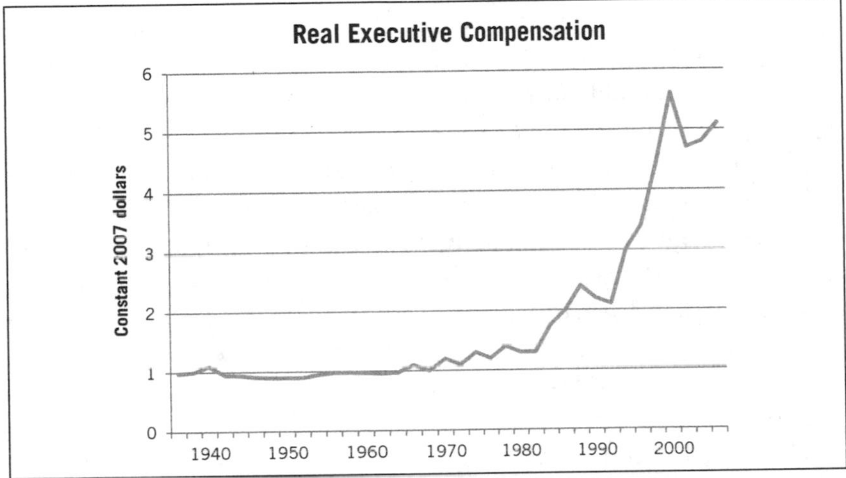

Chart 6.1. Median executive compensation received by the top three officials at the fifty largest US firms. Compensation includes salary, bonuses, long-term pay, and stock options based on the Black-Scholes value calculation of option grants.

Source: Carola Frydman and Raven E. Saks, "Executive Compensation: a New View from a Long-Term Perspective, 1936-2005," Figure 1. Ron Haskins and Isabel Sawhill, Creating an Opportunity Society, Brookings Institution Press, 2009, Figure 3-10.

This new breed of American executive was quickly fingered by observers in the family capitalism countries. Here is columnist John Kay of the *Financial Times* in November 2009 looking back on this era:

> "America has a new generation of rent-seekers. The modern equivalents of castles on the Rhine are first-class lounges and corporate jets. Their occupants are investment bankers and corporate executives. . . . The scale of corporate rent-seeking activities by business and personal rent-seeking by senior individuals in business and finance has increased sharply. The outcome can be seen in the growth of Capitol Hill lobbying and the crowded restaurants of Brussels; in the structure of industries such as pharmaceuticals, media, defense equipment, and, of course, financial services; and in the explosion of executive remuneration."[36]

Exploding American executive pay is sharply at odds with pay patterns in any other rich democracy. Executive pay in most democracies, such as Germany, has risen far less during the Reagan era. Even in the Anglo-Saxon countries of Canada, the United Kingdom, and Australia, increases are dwarfed by the American experience.

The closest pay scale to America appears to be CEOs at the 100 largest firms on the United Kingdom's major stock exchange (FTSE 100), where pay averaged 88 times employee wages in 2009.[37] Elsewhere, Australian journalist Verrender notes that *altogether*, the top 14 executives of Japan's biggest bank, Mitsubishi UFJ, were paid a total of $8.1 million in 2008—while Morgan Stanley CEO John Mack *alone* received $41.4 million in 2007 (Mitsubishi owns 21 percent of Morgan Stanley).[38] Even at the most profitable firms in the world such as VW-Audi-Porsche in Europe, compensation is well below America.

The pattern is the same all across northern Europe. The CEO of Statoil, the giant Norwegian oil company, Helge Lund, for example, was paid about $1.8 million in 2010, with no share options, while Rex W. Tillerson, CEO at Exxon Mobil, received $21.7 million in 2009, including options. Tillerson's pay alone is more than double the top nine Statoil executives combined, but is certainly not justified on pay-for-performance criteria. Statoil's annual stock appreciation has averaged twice that of Exxon Mobil for the last decade.[39]

Overall CEO compensation levels in the family capitalism countries are a bit less than one-half American levels. Data gathered by the management consulting firm Hewitt Associates on remuneration for the year 2008 is reproduced in Chart 6.2.

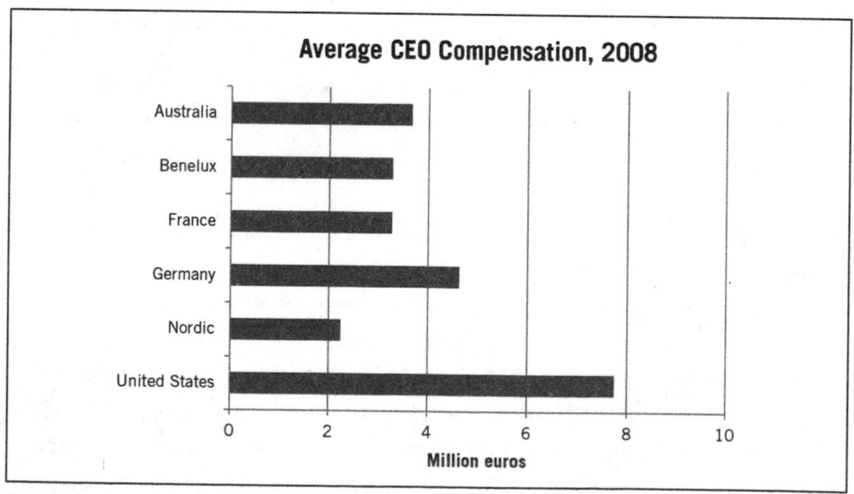

Chart 6.2. 2010 Australia.

Source: Yann Le Gales, "French Officials Are Paid Less Than Others," Le Figaro, March 5, 2010, and "Laws to Curb Executive Pay Soon," Sydney Morning Herald, November 26, 2011.

Remuneration figures like these have captured voter attention abroad in nations including the United Kingdom and Australia. The concern is both with the level of pay and with the apparent disconnect between pay and performance. Even the silk-hat British Institute of Directors concluded in 2011 that "the legitimacy of UK business in the eyes of wider society is significantly damaged by pay packages that are not clearly linked to company performance."[40]

The reaction to rising paydays has been stronger in Australia, where aggressive voters pushed back against large pay awards and succeeded; a 2011 law provides shareholders with the ability to readily spill or fire offending boards over executive pay. Voter attitudes there are exemplified by the journalist Verrender, writing in the *Sydney Morning Herald*:

> "The idea that the exponential growth of corporate salaries is a global phenomenon, and that Australia has no option but to keep pace or lose top management talent, is a myth. It is an outright distortion of facts. The corporate salary race is a purely Anglo phenomenon, confined to North America, Britain, and Australia. European and Asian executives, even those running multinational corporations, are paid a fraction of the salaries paid in the Anglo sphere."[41]

CEO Lemons: The Collapse of Pay-for-Performance in America

Foreign scholars describe American firms as providing "pathological overcompensation of fair-weather captains."[42] They are correct: the rise in US executive compensation of recent decades is unjustified by any performance metric, vastly outstripping indices like sales, profits, or returns to shareholders. The Clinton administration's Secretary of Labor, Robert Reich, unearthed the smoking gun evidence:

> "By 2006, CEOs were earning, on average, eight times as much per dollar of corporate profits as they did in the 1980s."[43]

A vast disparity like this in trend lines is powerful evidence that executive pay suffers from market failure. There are many instances where genuine value for shareholders has been produced by well-run or visionary executive suites, justifying higher compensation. But examples abound, especially of late on Wall Street, where weak executives have also received lush compensation. *Financial Times* columnist Martin Wolf discussed this failure, focusing on the financial sectors in the United States and the United Kingdom, where investment management presents

> ". . . a huge 'lemons' problem: in this business it is really hard to distinguish talented managers from untalented ones. For this reason, the business is bound to attract the unscrupulous and unskilled, just as such people are attracted to dealing in used cars (which was the original example of a market in lemons). . . . Now consider the financial sector as a whole: it is again hard either to distinguish skill from luck or to align the interests of management, staff, shareholders, and the public. It is in the interests of insiders to game the system by exploiting the returns from higher probability events. This means that businesses will suddenly blow up when the low probability disaster occurs, as happened spectacularly at Northern Rock and Bear Stearns."[44]

The syndrome is generalized across the entire American economy, and certainly not restricted to the financial sector. Indeed, a host of studies have caused compensation experts to conclude that much of the rise in executive pay across all sectors in recent decades is unjustified by performance. Their conclusions are encapsulated in this April 2011 editorial in the *Financial Times*:

> "'Pay for performance' often turns into pay without performance. Incentives are easy to game and can undermine people's intrinsic motives for doing a good job."[45]

Scholars examining the failure of pay-for-performance include Virginia Commonwealth University economists Robert R. Trumble and Angela DeLowell:

> "There is an inherent problem with this reward structure, though, as stock value may rise and fall independently of CEO influence. . . . In fact, no consistent connection has yet been made between CEO pay and corporate performance levels as measured by financial indicators such as stock price, profits, and sales."[46]

Professors Alex Edmans from the Wharton School of Business at the University of Pennsylvania and Xavier Gabaix from the Stern School of Business at New York University concluded similar research in 2010 by noting, "Many CEOs are richly paid, even if their performance has been poor."[47] The iconic compensation expert Graef Crystal in 2009 examined the pay of 271 CEOs, using formulas he devised during his 30 years as compensation consultant to Fortune 500 firms like CBS and Coca-Cola. "Simply put, companies don't pay for performance."[48]

University of Southern California economist Murphy reached the same conclusion. While at the University of Rochester in 1990, Murphy and Jensen of Harvard parsed a database of 2,505 CEOs at 1,400 large firms over the period 1974 to 1988; they found that "in most publicly held companies, the compensation of top executives is virtually independent of performance. . . . Annual changes in executive compensation do not reflect changes in corporate performance." For every $1,000 rise or fall in company value, for example, they found that CEOs received or lost a scant $3.25—a tiny 0.00325 percent equity link.[49]

Murphy recently updated his analysis by evaluating pay-for-performance of the top-earning 25 CEOs from 2000 to 2010 for the *Wall Street Journal*. Based on data drawn from company SEC filings that include all compensation, such as stock options, Murphy noted in July 2010 that performance of these lavishly paid CEOs was entirely unrelated to shareholder returns. Pay was utterly random, judged by relative or absolute share price movement. Only five ran firms that outperformed the Dow Jones stock index and four of them ran firms—AC/Interactive, Countrywide, Capital One, and Cendant—whose shareholders lost money during their tenure. And that list doesn't include infamous losers like Michael Dell, paid $454 million while shareholders lost 66 percent of their value in recent years—much less Richard S. Fuld, who received $457 million driving Lehman Brothers bankrupt in 2008.[50] Shareholders in these firms and hundreds, if not thousands, of others burdened with mediocre management endorsed by weak boards would have done better to stick their money under a mattress.

Market Failure in Executive Pay

American executives are overpaid by international standards and far too many are paid without regard to performance, benefiting from market failure in American executive pay. The statistics are persuasive. US compensation levels have been found by academic researchers such as Harvard Business professor Rakesh Khurana to exceed what would be obtainable by executives under the normal conditions of a competitive free market.[51] And New York University economist Thomas Philippon and Ariell Reshef, an economist at the University of Virginia, examined banking industry data over the last century since 1909.[52] They concluded that Wall Street pay between the mid-1990s and 2006 ranged from 30 percent to 50 percent higher than if compensation had been determined solely by the normal forces of competition.

Indeed, Professors Edmans and Gabaix found that the *250th* best-paid American CEO in 2008 received $9 million—a compensation level only exceeded by a tiny few executives in any other rich democracy.[53] It is inconceivable that the most richly compensated 250 American CEOs outperform almost all executives anywhere in the world. Indeed, in light of the weak US productivity and investment performance of the Reagan era, never in history has so much been paid so many for so little. The same market failure exists in the United Kingdom. Pay there, too, is disconnected from performance. A far-ranging study in 2011 by the independent blue-ribbon High Pay Commission "found little evidence that executives' compensation is correlated with firms' performance," as summarized in an editorial by the *Financial Times*.[54]

The market failure in executive compensation has dulled American capitalism. Here is Stanford law professor John J. Donohue, president of the American Law and Economics Association:

> "It is a terrible mistake to set up a structure where the top person walks away with millions even if the company is laid waste by their poor decision making, yet this is what's happening. It's a shocking departure from capitalist incentives if you lavish riches on the losers."[55]

How exactly have executives been able to thwart market forces? Certainly, dysfunctional boards are a big factor along with peer benchmarking. But three other factors also appear to be responsible for even the most conscientious and shareholder-friendly boards failing to link pay with performance.[56] They are why corporate governance experts Gillespie and Zweig have concluded:

> "The bigger problem is the culture of boards, which doesn't allow directors to do an effective job even if they wanted to."[57]

First, Cornell economists Robert H. Frank and Philip Cook found that competition for top business talent has intensified in America in recent decades. Very minor differences in executive performance can have an enormous impact on corporate profits and share prices at large firms. Frank cites the example of a talented CEO heading a multibillion dollar firm whose "handful of better decisions each year" than his competitors can produce hundreds of millions in added profits.[58] Shareholders can be convinced to offer excessive compensation in that scenario when bidding for new talent.

Second, the "anti-raiding norms" that discouraged CEO-poaching by competitors during the golden age have "all but completely unraveled," argue Frank and Cook, producing a winner-take-all competition for top talent akin to Hollywood or the advent of free agency in baseball some years ago.[59]

Third, stock options became commonplace.

Stock Options

Around for many decades, stock options were rarely utilized by firms until the Reagan era. By the end of that president's two terms, however, they dominated executive-suite compensation and represent two-thirds of remuneration, as noted in Chart 6.3. The use of options is even higher in instances of gargantuan paychecks: Murphy's July 2010 *Wall Street Journal* analysis found that options accounted for 78 percent of the pay of the top 25 bankers he examined.[60] The family capitalism countries rely notably less on options.

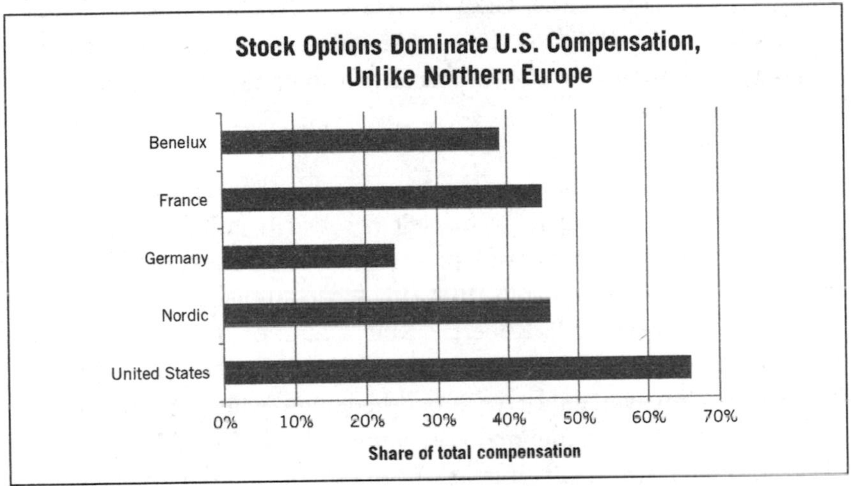

Chart 6.3. Total compensation is salary, bonuses, and stock options, 2008.
Source: Yann Le Gales, "French Officials Are Paid Less Than Others," Le Figaro, March 5, 2010.

Stock options were originally envisaged as a solution to the agency problem mentioned earlier, where managers prioritize their own interest, not shareholders'. Adam Smith recognized this disconnect centuries ago, writing critically of enterprise managers:

> "Directors . . . being the managers rather of other people's money than of their own, it cannot well be expected that they would watch over it with the same anxious vigilance."[61]

The weight of evidence is that shareholder capitalism fails to resolve the agency problem, and stock options exacerbate the failure. Indeed, options have been determined to have no persistent impact on shareholder value according to research conducted at the University of Hong Kong School of Business by Liu Zheng and Xianming Zhou. Using statistics from the Computstat® ExecuComp database, they examined the correlation between share prices and 1,337 CEO retirements; these are events when options must be exercised, but whose timing in the preceding years or months is discretionary. The control was the share price of firms headed by retiring CEOs with few option holdings. Zheng and Zhou found that share prices at firms where CEOs held large option positions exhibited abnormal spikes during the retirement period. Unfortunately for shareholders, however, the price spikes were not sustained:

> "We find significant abnormal stock returns in the months surrounding CEO departure for those with high option holdings, which are reversed shortly after CEO departure. . . .Without any persistent effect of stock options on shareholder value, our results do not support the presumed role of options in providing managerial working incentives."[62]

Options misalign managerial interests with shareholder interests in two ways. First, management doesn't necessarily suffer economic loss from poor performance because payouts are nonetheless required under most employment agreements. In 2011, for example, corporate failures like Leo Apotheker (HP), Robert P. Kelly (Bank of New York Mellon), and Carol A. Bartz (Yahoo) received nearly $10 million in severance.[63] Moreover, the availability of stock-hedging—where executives can obtain insurance at a minimal cost against losses should the price of their optioned stock fall—further negates individual blowback from negative job performances. *New York Times* reporter Eric Dash in February 2011 wrote that over 100 Goldman Sachs executives used such hedges to protect against losses during the meltdown and recession, including one whose hedges avoided $7 million in losses.[64] Here is how corporate governance expert Patrick McGurn of RiskMetrics explained the conceptual breakdown to Dash:

> "Many of these hedging activities can create situations when the executives' interests run counter to the company. I think a lot of people feel this doesn't have a place in compensation structure."[65]

Second, pay-for-performance is rendered ineffective by the absence of meaningful clawback provisions in executive compensation agreements, and by the inclination of corporate boards to reprice options that go underwater from poor performance. Repricing has occurred in recent years by boards at Starbucks, Google, and Composite Technologies, and frequently reflect abuse of shareholders with management being rewarded regardless of performance. The smoking-gun evidence is provided by professors such as Erik Lie of the University of Iowa and Randall Heron of the University of Indiana. They examined a huge database of nearly 39,000 options granted by 7,700 companies over a ten-year period, finding a pattern of firms listing option grants on dates where share prices are at cyclical lows.[66] They discovered, as David Cay Johnston explained: "Executives had an uncanny ability to have options granted to them on the days when the stock price was at its low point during each period. The timing was too perfect to be possible were the rules being followed."[67]

Such perfect market timing is extremely unlikely to be random, of course; it reflects backdating, or the equally pernicious insider practice of pricing options on days when adverse corporate performance information is being released to the public. Such practices are apparently legal in most instances.[68]

Even worse, the prospect of giant rewards from options incentivizes fraud in a US business community already struggling mightily with ethical issues. Drawing on the sociologist Max Weber's work on the theory of the firm as a collective that reacts rationally to prevailing systems, Nobel Laureate behavioral economist George A. Akerlof and Rachel E. Kranton explained it this way:

> "The more a CEO's compensation is based on stock options, for example, the greater is the incentive to maximize the price at which to cash in. There are at least two ways to do this: one is by increasing the firm's true value; another is by creatively managing the firm's books. Recent evidence shows that executives have understood and embraced the second possibility."[69]

Yet boards seem unfazed, even routinely writing employment contracts enabling CEOs to receive millions when defrauding their firms. Michael Jensen and coauthor Kevin Murphy have documented the get-out-of-jail cards issued by boards to CEOs who embezzle from their corporations and shareholders. Some 44 percent of all CEO employment contracts they examined required severance payments to CEOs even if convicted and fired for cause.[70]

One of the most dramatic ways options delink executive reward from shareholder returns in today's managerial capitalism is by incentivizing risky and economically dubious mergers, which produce suboptimal firm performance. American and foreign research drawing on behavioral economics provides such evidence, portraying stock-optioned American CEOs as jittery children around a candy jar, constantly calculating the prize to the exclusion of shareholder returns or much else. Research by professors Donald C. Hambrick of Penn State University, and William Gerard Sanders of Brigham Young University, for example, caused them to conclude that:

> "The more that a CEO is paid in stock options, the more extreme the firm's subsequent performance, and the greater the likelihood that the extreme performance will be a big loss rather than a big gain."[71]

And the biggest losses occur when mergers go bad.

Value-Destroying Mergers Belie Shareholder Capitalism

Milton Friedman insisted in 1953 that a given pattern of managerial behavior will persist only if it is profit maximizing. That is a central dictum of what came to be shareholder capitalism. Yet Friedman's principle does not align with facts or experience in the real world, as noted by University College London economists Armstrong and Huck. That dictum is belied by the wave of value-destroying mergers characterizing American enterprise in recent decades. Shareholder capitalism incentivizes mergers that destroy shareholder value.

It works this way: managers are rewarded for spiking share values in the current reporting quarter, affording them the opportunity to cash out options. And nothing spikes earnings per share better than a merger that dramatically enhances revenues. But what happens to shareholders, particularly those who have adopted the Wall Street mantra of "buy and hold?"

Economists Ulrike Malmendier, Enrico Moretti, and Florian Peters of the University of California, Berkeley, examined *all* contested US mergers between 1985 and 2009 where at least two suitors vied. Published in April 2012 by the National Bureau of Economic Research, their analysis examined market evaluations of the successful suitors (acquirors) and losing bidders before and after mergers. Their results were startling:

> "After the merger, however, losers significantly outperform winners. Depending on the measure of abnormal performance, the difference amounts to 49–54 percent over the three years following the merger. . . . We also show that the underperformance of winners does not reflect differences between hostile and friendly acquisitions, variations in acquiror [Tobin] Q, the number of bidders, differences between diversifying and concentrating mergers, variation in targets size or acquiror size, or differences in the method of payment."[72]

That is simply an enormous stock price penalty on shareholders of successful suitors. What accounts for the striking underperformance of successful suitors? The culprit was the debt taken on to effect the merger: "Specifically, winners have significantly higher leverage ratios than losers, which the market may view as potentially harmful to the long term health of the company."

Sharply higher debt as a consequence of mergers was also fingered by University of Richmond economist Jeffrey S. Harrison and Derek K. Oler of Indiana University, who explained the consequences. They examined over 3,000 mergers and determined that enterprise debt leverage concurrently rose an average 45 percent, sufficient to require what economists call risk balancing. That means cutting spending elsewhere in the firm on expenses like R&D and wages; acquirors took on considerable new risk and were forced to pare back other investments and initiatives. Harrison and Oler concluded that management responded "to higher financial risk by reducing risk in other areas, such as new investments."[73]

Such as new investments? What? You should have sat up at that, because investment is crucial to productivity growth and to raising incomes. And we will examine the quite serious implications of the Malmendier, Moretti, Peters and Harrison, and Oler's conclusions in the next chapter.

But to conclude this chapter, let's see how a more proactively Australia has addressed the issue of rising executive pay.

Australia: Occupy Wall Street Writ Large—with Teeth

By 2010, Australians came to realize that CEO compensation had risen excessively, approaching one-half of American levels. Worse, executive pay had become disassociated from performance. Share prices rose 31 percent on the Australian big board (the S&P/Australian 100 exchange) from 2001 to 2010, but median CEO salaries rose 131 percent and bonuses were up 190 percent. Australian executives reaped four to six times more than shareholders, a broken system just like America.

Voters became aware because the local press began highlighting abusers, such as former CEO Sue Morphet of clothing firm Pacific Brands. The firm lost A$132 million (US$135 million) in 2010 and also the valuable Kmart account; regardless, the directors granted Morphet a bonus of A$910,000 in cash atop her million-dollar salary. BlueScope Steel lost A$1 billion and announced 1,000 layoffs the same day in late 2011 that managing director Paul O'Malley and colleagues shared A$3 million in bonuses.

Over at Commonwealth Bank, a pool of A$36.1 million had been set aside for top executives if specific performance goals like superior customer service ratings *vis-à-vis* other banks were met. The goals and rules were clear: "In the absence of substantial and sustained improvement [in customer service], no vesting will occur at all," read the bonus arrangement in 2008 approved by shareholders. The bank fell short, but the board ignored the restrictive language and allowed executive options to vest in 2011 anyway, including A$2.89 million to the CEO Ralph Norris. The same thing happened at giant Downer EDI engineering, and at Boart Longyear, the world's leading mineral exploration and drilling firm where executives received pay they hadn't earned. At each of these Big End firms, pay was disconnected from performance.[74]

And pay abuse was widespread: CGI Glass, an executive pay consultancy that advises investors, pinpointed as lavish the remuneration packets at 52 percent of the 700-plus firms it examined in 2009.[75] Australians could have shrugged off this market failure like most Americans do. But Australia has perhaps the globe's richest tradition of stakeholder capitalism, which includes finely tuned antennae to corporate misbehavior. I have yet to meet a docile Australian—conservative or liberal—when it comes to unwarranted executive pay. Here is how business editor Michael Pascoe of the *Sydney Morning Herald* described this national intolerance of abusive pay:

> "Quantas's sorry history of overpaying its CEO is as good an example as any on how out of touch Big End boards have become. . . . The boards genuinely can't comprehend that they're responsible for the obscene blowout in executive remuneration, that our society—their employees, their customers, their shareholders—are increasingly jack of it and that their remuneration committees' excuses simply don't hold water, let alone multimillion-dollar pay packets. . . . The defensive attitude of the directors' club is understandable, though—members don't want to consider that they've been incompetent, that they've stuffed up, that the American model of competitive overcompensation is simply wrong."[76]

And that explains how David Bradbury came to implement the Occupy Wall Street agenda.

Mr. Bradbury, you see, is the powerful Assistant Treasurer and former Parliamentary Secretary to the Treasurer in Canberra; in November 2010, he echoed public opinion, warning boards that executive compensation was "out of step with community expectations."[77] Pressured by voters, the newly elected Australian Labor government of Julia Gillard responded by adding muscle to shareholder rights' laws.

Real muscle. Bradbury demanded tighter accountability from corporate boards, because "many institutional investors are taking even greater note of how a company's reputation is playing out in the wider community and how that contributes to value." Australians had expectations that local corporations would reform to "lead the world in defining a new brand of corporate leadership."

And Gillard's government matched his tough language with an iron fist, enacting the two-strikes pay law in July 2011, which automatically jeopardizes deaf boards ignoring these expectations. If a quarter of shareholders vote against executive pay packages two years running, the board suffers the embarrassment of a mandatory resolution being automatically brought before shareholders to dissolve the board. And if a majority of shareholders then vote for dissolution, the board is spilled; firms have 90 days to conduct elections for a new board.*

With executives and directors accountable to shareholders for compensation decisions, this new law had an immediate impact. In early October 2011, the remuneration package of the first major firm, Sunbeam Appliance GUD Holdings, was rejected; more than one-quarter of shareholders were annoyed that its board had granted CEO Ian Campbell a 33 percent pay hike despite a 14 percent decline in profits. Campbell subsequently told the *Sydney Morning Herald*, "The board now has no option but to consult with constituents because the shareholders had redrawn the boundaries."[78] The remuneration packages at a number of other firms, including Pacific Brands and Cabcharge, were also rejected by a quarter of shareholders in the following weeks. In total some 108 companies suffered a first strike, a no vote of 25 per cent or more, against their remuneration reports in 2011.[79] Australian corporate leaders, as headlined by a local paper, began acting like cats on a hot tin roof. JP Morgan analyst Gerry Sherriff put it this way: "The two-strikes rule puts greater scrutiny on boards to devise executive remuneration structures better aligned with the performance of the company."†

---

*Bradbury later in 2011 initiated other steps to enhance the quality of Australian corporate governance, including reforms such as electronic voting to replace opaque manual voting and the practice of leaving votes at annual meetings open for several weeks to allow shareholders to mull over issues discussed at the meeting before voting. See Ruth Williams "Boardroom Boredom Set for a Radical Overhaul," *Sydney Morning Herald*, Dec. 7, 2011.

†Eric Johnston, "Two-Strikes Policy Hits Home," *Sydney Morning Herald*, Oct. 21, 2011. Two Strikes has two shortcomings: First, as in America, many, if not most, shares in Australian firms are held by institutional investors. Some fund managers unhappy with compensation schedules report being blackmailed to support dubious board pay packets on pain of being denied timely firm information. *Second*, an important safeguard in Two Strikes precludes top management and nonexecutive directors voting their personal shares on pay packages. That creates a conundrum should

In most instances, the scrutiny produced the desired moderation, with only a few firms in 2012 like Globe International actually suffering a second strike on remuneration reports, with boards being spilled and new elections required.[80]

Two strikes is indicative of just how seriously voters in the family capitalism countries take responsibility for their own prosperity. Australian voter expectations regarding the behavior of corporate leadership are demanding. And their goal in this episode was broader than just returning executive pay to earth; it included incentivizing management to adopt longer time horizons and eradicate the American plague of short-termism we discuss shortly. Here is how *Sydney Morning Herald* journalist Malcolm Maiden describes the three bottom lines of "shareholders, employees, and the community at large" that voters expect corporate boards there to meet:

> "A company's best interests are protected and advanced when the best interests of all stakeholders—including employees, customers, investors, lenders, and suppliers—are taken into account."[81]

The two-strikes pay law surely makes American management uneasy. But there's a lot worse for them ahead. It is time to explore in detail the greatest danger posed by Reaganomics, which is short-termism, and how the family capitalism countries in northern Europe have eradicated that danger. That remedy is also the most frightening nightmare lurking in the sleep of American executives: a black-box corporate governance structure that avoids value-destroying mergers, eliminates short-termism, mitigates CEO narcissism, incentivizes higher investment and productivity growth, and has produced steadily rising real wages across entire economies for decades while creating the most competitive economies on earth.

You are about to learn why America's best economists, such as Nobel Laureate Edmund S. Phelps of Columbia University, find Reaganomics so maddening—and the real reason why a narcissistic American business community relentlessly demonizes northern Europe.

---

the board be dumped. For example, the remuneration packet of Crown Ltd was rejected in October 2012 by shareholders, only because gambling billionaire and Crown executive chairman James Packer could not vote his 45.6 percent ownership share. Even if a second vote in 2012 spills the board, an uncowed Packer vowed to reelect his hand-picked board.

CHAPTER 7

SHORT-TERMISM

"Employees and customers often know more about and have more of a long-term commitment to a company than shareholders do. . . . The argument here isn't that managers and boards always know best. It's simply that widely-dispersed, short-term shareholders are unlikely to know better—and a governance system that relies on them to keep corporations on the straight and narrow is doomed to fail."[1]

JUSTIN FOX and JAY W. LORSCH
***Harvard Business Review*, July–August 2012**

"Short-termism is a market failure of a sort that . . . leads to investment too low, especially in those long term infrastructure and high-tech projects on which future growth depends."[2]

RICHARD LAMBERT,
Chancellor, University of Warwick

"While companies always talk about the need to invest in 'human capital,' they do not because, if the cost of such an investment is immediate, its benefits can be seen in the long term."[3]

ALEX EDMANS,
Wharton School, University of Pennsylvania

"German unions have long practiced 'codetermination' with management on corporate boards, but their approach differs dramatically from American counterparts. They are committed to ensuring that their companies do well, produce superior products, and are cost-competitive. Work rules are flexible. Strikes are rare. They focus on collaborative relationships to make their enterprises competitive on a world scale."[4]

BILL GEORGE,
Harvard Business School and former CEO, Medtronics

Quail hunting is the sport *du jour* of American executives, even though their behavior in recent decades more resembles eighteenth-century Swiss philosopher Jean-Jacques Rousseau's narcissistic deer hunters:

"If a deer is to be taken, everyone saw that, in order to succeed, he must abide faithfully by his post: but if a hare happened to come within the reach of any one of them, it is not to be doubted that he pursued it without scruple, and having seized his prey, cared very little, if by so doing he caused his companions to miss theirs."[5]

The philosopher Thomas Hobbes famously perceived mankind's natural state as "nasty, brutish, and short," where magnified self-interest produces "a condition of war of every one against every one, in which case everyone is governed by his own reason. . . ." This Darwinian internecine war is only to be relieved, concluded Hobbes, by each sacrificing some individual rights to a higher community authority, his Leviathan.[6] Rousseau's deer hunters may have rubbed the harsh edge off of Hobbes, but he similarly argued that magnified self-interest would not benefit all, especially in complex economic settings featuring a division of labor and capital accumulation.

Adam Smith agreed, sharing many of the same worries about markets, and his support for market regulation discussed earlier was strongly influenced by the insights of his contemporary Rousseau. The *Financial Times*' John Kay explained the philosophical consensus that finally emerged in the very earliest days of capitalism:

"If the hunt was to catch a deer, it would need to establish shared values, and probably impose them through some sort of hierarchy. Without such a structure, there would be no more for supper than the occasional hare."[7]

This philosophical debate occurred against the backdrop of the miraculous Industrial Revolution then creating the first sustained period in human history where notable economic surpluses were being created as productivity rose. An important issue soon emerged: How much to rely on markets to divide the surplus produced by entrepreneurs, employees, and capitalists. Spoils in the past were claimed by brute force, but that began to change in the eighteenth century, and the gains of capitalism today are divided according to the rules each society crafts.

But those domestic rules, which are the focus of this book, are only so helpful because global integration has created new frontiers, and domestic cooperation only goes so far internationally. The competition each country confronts today isn't for deer or hare, but the global war for wealth. And it's won by those nations that conjure the best domestic set of rules and regulations; that is, shared values that yield a high rate of investment and upskilling leading to robust labor productivity growth. It is that growth and that growth alone that creates opportunities for their domestic economies to flourish.

In this setting, critics of Reaganomics have a target-rich environment. A number of Reagan-era politicians have fashioned themselves market *aficionados* and conservatives. By the standards of history, they are neither. They adopted Ayn Rand and threw Adam Smith under the bus, endorsing deregulation, the emergence of Red Queens and managerial capitalism characterized by stagnant wages, market failure in executive compensation, and widening income disparities. They adopted a version of capitalism enabling management to prioritize executive compensation while deemphasizing the prosperity of shareholders and the firm itself.

Big problems all.

But most critics neglect perhaps its single most dangerous consequence, which guarantees that American families and the American economy are a sure bet to fare poorly in the relentless Hobbesian global war. Edmund Phelps terms it "short-termism."[8] And its major characteristic was mentioned by Harrison and Oler in the previous chapter: taking steps like mergers to maximize their own pay had management "reducing risk in other areas, such as new investments."[9]

Reaganomics deincentivizes research and development and demotes human capital and other long-term investments critical to productivity growth. Ayn Rand's rational selfishness has gutted America of executives willing to manage or invest for the long term.

Most dangerous, among the rich democracies, this affliction is very nearly uniquely American, as noted by Phelps in August 2010:

> "In established businesses, short-termism has become rampant. Executives avoid farsighted projects, no matter how promising, out of concern that lower short-term profits will cause share prices to drop. . . . Timid and complacent, our big companies are showing the same tendencies that turned traditional utilities into dinosaurs. Meanwhile, many of the factors that have long driven American innovation have dried up."[10]

This chapter will examine the evidence for the short-termism identified by Phelps and others such as Michael Clowes, and then explore how the corporate governance structure of the family capitalism countries in northern Europe has been refined over many decades to avoid this precise problem.

Short-Termism

One tip-off is hidden in plain sight. Apprentices are the seed corn of any enterprise; one of the vital guarantors of future prosperity. Well-managed firms never neglect the future, which is why German enterprises have evolved some 350 or so specific apprentice tracks. American firms have only about one-half the number of apprentices proportionately as other rich democracies, including Germany. That's puzzling behavior because the United States is filled with community colleges eager to collaborate. Why so few apprentices? The answer comes from Siemens, which spends about $220 million annually on apprenticeships. It turns out that the productive work done by its trainees covers only one-third of their cost and the net drain can persist for two or three years.[11] Apprentices reduce profits in the short term and so American CEOs do without, yet Siemens and other firms in family capitalism countries can't find enough of them.

Unlike Siemens, managerial capitalism precludes many American executives from even thinking longer term. Evidence that short-termism originated with the Reagan era is found in the analyses of economists such as Robert J. Gordon. Recall our earlier conversation about Okun's Law? American firms prior to the 1980s tended to hoard workers in downturns. That changed with Reaganomics, with firms conducting savage cost cutting to shield short-term profits in any and all environments.[12]

The problem of short-termism isn't the quality of American management; they are as capable as any on earth. But they represent the same problem that Adam Smith perceived in the East India Company officials of his day. Smith criticized these far-off officials in India and elsewhere, but took care to explain that the problem was the incentive structure they confronted, including the prevailing ethos of mercantilism. They could grow rich by acting *against* the best interest of the East India Company.[13]

Similarly, America's challenge isn't the quality of its business community, but Reagan-era managerial capitalism in which executives can seize windfalls by shortchanging R&D, productivity, innovation, and investment. And they have done so relentlessly in the pursuit of quarterly earnings targets, operating on a different astral plane from the previous generation of executives who created the greatest middle class in history. Too many American managers today behave like their Greek counterparts, as described by reporter Claire Gatinois for *Le Monde* in May 2012:

> "The [Greek] business community . . . is better schooled in the art of offshoring and tax evasion than it is in research and development. . . ."[14]

The danger of short-termism was acknowledged more than a century ago by the great classical economist Alfred Marshall, who noted that managers, investors, and others behave like "children who pluck the plums out of their pudding to eat them at once."[15] Today, the plums are executive stock options linked to quarterly and annual share performance. A modern-day restatement of Marshall is provided by Jeffrey Sonnenfeld, Dean of Yale's School of Management, who criticizes Reaganomics:

> "Immediate shareholder value maximization, by itself, was always too short-term in nature. It created a fleeting illusion of value creation by emphasizing immediate goals over long-term strategies."[16]

Managerial capitalism has reduced investment time horizons dramatically. The visionary CEOs of old, Robert Wood Johnson or even Henry Ford, are no longer role models. James Surowiecki of the *New Yorker* magazine conceptualized what happened this way: During Johnson's day in the golden age, American management "faced less short-term pressure from shareholders; they could invest heavily in work that didn't yield an immediate return. Those days are gone, and American companies now do less basic research."[17] The opportunity to score outsized compensation by spiking quarterly earnings discourages long-term investment in favor of mergers, share buybacks, and other "short-termisms," explains Phelps.[18]

Reaganomics has mutated the traditional executive-suite ethos taught in academia, bringing to the fore managers who are experts at the short term because it wildly overcompensates for stock price manipulation. Expectations by shareholders and board members during the golden age prevented most executive suites from plucking the plums prematurely and facilitated longer-term projects not necessarily adding to profits until years in the future. Visceral disdain by colleagues and competitors alike would have been the reaction to expedient steps such as cutting R&D, unwise mergers, or wasteful stock buybacks intended to temporarily spike share prices.*

---

*That would especially apply to buybacks involving insider self-dealing, such as this example: In early 2011, a small Internet content firm, Demand Media, obtained $71 million for product development and marketing in an Initial Public Offering. Yet profits proved elusive in the months that followed, mostly because Google altered its search engines to strip out low-quality content from firms such as Demand Media. So the Demand Media board decided in mid-2011 to divert one-third of the IPO proceeds to share buybacks. The buybacks were timed to nicely spike slumping share prices just as post-offering six-month lockups for the executive suite were unwinding. John Foley and Robert Cyran, "Shameful Buyback," *The New York Times*, August 29, 2011.

Here is how Sheila Bair, the former chief of the Federal Deposit Insurance Corporation, describes this new Reagan-era culture:

> "Business executives squeeze expenses of all types to meet their quarterly earnings targets, even cutting research and development that could create a competitive advantage down the road. This market failure leads to under-investment in projects with long payoff periods. 'Patient capital' has become almost quaint."[19]

Short-Termism Has Spread to Investors

This psychology has spread to stock market investors, many of whom now seek to maximize short-term returns, reinforcing the short-term focus of management. As Jay Lorsch and Justin Fox at Harvard noted, "And short-termers have been taking over the stock market."[20] That trend was documented in an extensive study by Andrew Haldane and Richard Davies, economists at the Bank of England. In a 2011 analysis, they determined that investors by the mid-1990s had begun inappropriately discounting anticipated profits from longer-term projects such as R&D:

> "Some projects with positive net present value might be rejected because future cash flows are discounted too heavily, reducing investment and ultimately growth. . . . Cash flows five years ahead are discounted at rates more appropriate eight or more years hence."[21]

Spreading in the 1980s and 1990s among American CEOs, the plague of short-termism has come to dominate capital markets. Prior to 1980, for example, annual turnover on the New York Stock Exchange averaged around 20 percent. Now, even annual pension fund turnover exceeds 90 percent. The average holding period has declined from seven years in the 1950s to six months today.[22] And Jesse Eisinger of the investigative journal *ProPublica* has written that in 2012, shares were being held an average of only four months.[23]

A major accelerant of investor short-termism is the shift in composition of exchange participants toward money managers anxious to show quarterly gains; impatient money managers now hold 70 percent of all shares of American corporations, compared to just 8 percent in the 1950s, outweighing traditional buy and hold investors. Thus, the vast majority of share traders have become a Greek chorus for quarterly capitalism and the short-termism of CEOs, with little interest and even less incentive to follow more detailed elements of corporate decision making. It's as though America is competing in the Super Bowl (against Japanese and northern Europe competitors), with our guy Tom Brady limited to three-yard dump-off passes.

An accelerant in the focus of money managers like mutual funds on the short term has been explored by Michael Clowes. In *The Money Flood*, he concludes that the transition from defined benefit to defined contribution retirement plans by US firms during the Reagan era dramatically altered the behavior of pension managers. The gargantuan pool of US pension capital in 401(k)s became impatient capital, eagerly seeking short-term gains, especially in the equities market. Money managers had no choice but to respond, eschewing longer-term investments in the relentless search for quick scores.[24]

This transformation in the attitude of investors has magnified and reinforced the short-termism of executives. Their jobs—as well as big paydays—now hinge on the imperative of limiting R&D, wages, investment, and upskilling. Let's get to the statistics.

Short-Termism Hobbles R&D and Investment

Haldane and Davies in their study just noted concluded that American (and British) executives now require investments to pay off in from 4.5 to six years rather than in ten years. Arbitrarily raising the threshold investment cash payback in this manner shrinks the universe of acceptably profitable investments and thus investment rates. Routinely rejected today are many viable R&D and other longer-term investments profitworthy under conventional golden age analytical standards based on inflation, risk assessments, and the cost of capital. The ensuing investment paucity shows up vividly in R&D statistics, which document that American executives bunch whatever research projects they still fund in the near term, focusing on those yielding immediate payoffs, and ignoring many other economically sound projects.

That shamble stands in sharp contrast to practices at firms in northern Europe where R&D is concentrated in longer-term projects. Harvard economist James M. Poterba and Harvard president *emeritus* and former US Treasury Secretary Lawrence H. Summers, for example, have documented that German firms "devote much larger shares of their R&D budgets to longer term projects than their US competitors do."[25] Their research findings are reproduced in Chart 7.1. Poterba and Summers found that US investment had suffered during the Reagan era because CEOs established a return threshold averaging 12.2 percent. That is far above the rate of inflation or the cost of acquiring capital to use for such projects, which averaged 5.6 percent on long-term corporate bonds over their study period.

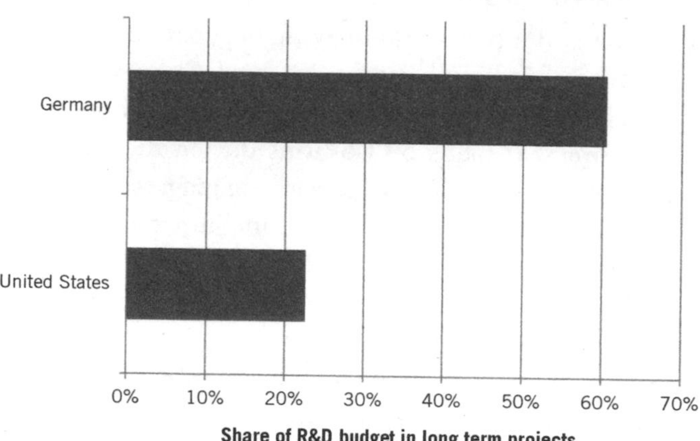

Chart 7.1.

Source: James M. Poterba and Lawrence H. Summers, "A CEO Survey of US Companies' Time Horizons and Hurdle Rates," Sloan Management Review, Fall 1995, Table 4.

Moreover, American executives appear to be in denial about their behavior. Poterba and Summers determined that American executives underestimate their competitors' investment and R&D time horizons. Supporting documentation comes from *Der Spiegel* reporter Thomas Schulz who writes that Rob Atkinson, president of the Washington-based Information Technology and Innovation Foundation, believes Germany now invests an astronomical 20 times as much as the United States (as a share of GDP) in industry-related R&D at small and medium-sized firms.[26]

Foregoing profitable investments being made by your most ferocious competitors is irrational behavior from the perspective of long-term firm survival and prosperity. Even so, weak investment behavior is widespread in American enterprise. A good example of executive suite short-termism can be found at the iconic high technology firm Hewlett-Packard. You may recall the discussion in the previous chapter of the important analysis by Malmendier, Moretti, and Peters, which concluded that mergers tend to prove toxic for winning suitors; larded down with excessive debt, management shortchanges investment to finance mergers.[27]

A poster child for such widespread antics is Mark V. Hurd, HPs CEO for five years, retiring under fire in mid-2010. He reduced new-product R&D by about 20 percent; research spending dropped from 9 percent of sales to about 2.5 percent during his term—compared to 6 percent at rivals like Apple, Cisco, Dell, and IBM. Charles House, a Stanford University researcher and long-time HP engineer, provided this detail about his R&D spending: "In the personal computing group, it is seven-tenths of 1 percent. That's why HP had no response to the iPad."[28]

What did Hurd do with the money freed by the R&D cutbacks? Well, he conducted more than 30 acquisitions to spike share prices. And his personal goals were met, with earnings per share rising a handsome 22.5 percent annually and stock prices rising apace, providing Hurd with a huge compensation package.[29] But a careful parsing of performance parameters and analysis led CNBC journalist Herb Greenberg to conclude these returns were illusory: "The numbers suggest the stock did considerably better than the underlying company." Regarding the earnings figure, he explained:

> ". . . a chunk of that is related to merger-related cost cutting, a decline in shares outstanding, thanks largely to buybacks and an 18 percent drop in research and development spending, not necessarily an admirable trend for a tech company."[30]

Some of the mergers were fruitful, but many—including that of Palm and Electronic Data Services (EDS)—were not. For example, the current CEO, Meg Whitman, in August 2012 was forced to write off $8 billion of the $13.9 billion EDS purchase price.[31] And she admitted in October 2012 to Wall Street analysts that a recovery will take until 2016.[32] By 2010, HP's R&D was weakening and stock price falling; the reaction of HP's directors exemplified another harmful widespread trend of the Reagan era. Did they divert billions to new R&D? Well, no. They reacted as most US managers have done in recent decades, diverting cash needed for R&D to a $10 billion stock buyback; HP's board devoted an entire year's worth of free cash flow to spike share prices.

The mergers and this buyback strategy explain why HP remains today on its back foot, playing catch-up with more adept and faster-moving competitors in the dynamic technology landscape of smartphones and tablets. Hurd prospered at the expense of shareholders and HP. "We lost a product cycle—no doubt about that," acknowledged Jon Rubinstein, former Palm CEO and an HP vice president.[33] Here is how reporter Quentin Hardy of the *New York Times* described the final outcome of Hurd's tactics, commonplace across the American economy:

> "At one time, HP also had a vaunted reputation for advanced research at its HP Labs division, which underwent such drastic cuts under Mr. Hurd that, according to one insider, scientists were relying on pirated software to run their computers."[34]

Hurd's choices and that of HP's board resemble too many firms across the nation. Here is how the situation is described by economists and financial advisors Yves Smith and Rob Parenteau in mid-2010:

> ". . . public companies have become obsessed with quarterly earnings. To show short-term profits, they avoid investing in future economic growth. To develop new products, buy new equipment, or expand geographically, an enterprise has to spend money. . . . Rather than incur such expenses, companies increasingly prefer to pay their executives exorbitant bonuses, or issue special dividends to shareholders, or engage in purely financial speculation. But that means they also short-circuit a major driver of economic growth."[35]

Economists know this Hurd-like behavior is the rule, rather than the exception, because of extensive research by a host of economists such as Marianne Bertrand and Antoinette Schoar. They examined over 600 American firms in documenting serial acquisitions at the expense of vital investment: "Managers that engage in more external acquisitions and diversification also display lower levels of capital expenditures and R&D," they concluded.[36] Analyses by economist Nancy Folbre and separately by Lucian Bebchuk have documented the same phenomenon. Folbre concluded that the structure of American corporate governance "emphasizes the incentives to pursue short-run rather than long-run gains."[37]

The choice of American CEOs and boards to short-change investment in pursuit of quarterly capitalism is also revealed in an analysis by John R. Graham, Campbell R. Harvey, and Shiva Rajgopal. They surveyed 401 financial industry leaders in 2004, and found that most executives routinely cut investments, even those viewed as "very valuable," to attain a smoothly rising earnings record. They explained their conclusions, depicted in Chart 7.2, this way:

> "The majority of firms view earnings, especially Earnings Per Share, as the key metric for outsiders, even more so than cash flows. Because of the severe market reaction to missing an earnings target, we find that firms are willing to sacrifice economic value in order to meet a short-run earnings target."[38]

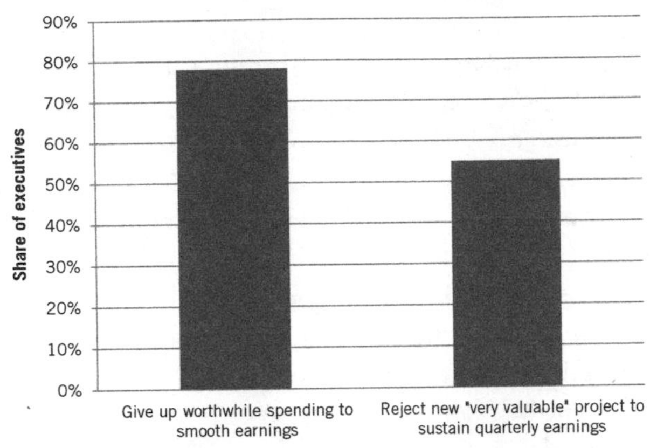

Chart 7.2. 2004.

Source: John R. Graham, Campbell R. Harvey, and Shiva Rajgopal, "The Economic Implications of Corporate Financial Reporting," Journal of Accounting and Economics, 2005, vol. 40 (1-3 Dec), 3–73.

Short-Termism Encourages Inappropriate Stock Buybacks

The longer-term imperative of firm prosperity dictates that enterprises should be investing first and spiking share prices last, but the perverse incentive structure of the Reagan era leads too many executives to do the reverse. And the tools of choice are mergers and especially buybacks, such as those conducted by HP.

Recall Zimmer Orthopedics, the firm that paid former US Attorney General John Ashcroft's law firm tens of millions of dollars to avoid prosecution for antitrust violations? Its CEO in 2010 was David C. Dvorak. Fully 50 percent of Mr. Dvorak's $1.03 million cash bonus in 2010 hinged on topping corporate earnings of $4.28 per share. Fortunately for Dvorak, Zimmer squeaked by, earning $4.33. Those earnings resulted from a carefully calculated, $500-million buyback that reduced shares outstanding; without it, earnings would have been no higher than $4.10 per share. Moreover, despite revenues increasing less than 5 percent, Dvorak's buyback goosed Zimmer's earnings per share in 2010 by 10 percent, triggering his bonus. Oh, and that $500 million in cash diverted to the buyback? It was more than *twice* what Zimmer (a medical device research firm) spent on R&D that year.[39]

Buybacks are "totally wasted money. It does not do anything long term for companies," explains economist William Lazonick, Director of the University of Massachusetts (Lowell) Center for Industrial Competitiveness.[40] Pfizer is another poster child for this syndrome, as highlighted by journalist Andrew Jack of the *Financial Times* in February 2011:

> "The US pharmaceutical giant is trimming up to $3 billion a year from its $9-billion research budget, while buying back $5 billion of its own shares. . . ."[41]

Despite expiration of its lucrative Lipitor patent and R&D costs of developing new substitute pharmaceuticals in the many hundreds of millions, Pfizer spent $20 billion on share buybacks between 2005 and 2010 before the further $5 billion announced in 2011. If devoted instead to R&D, that funding might have brought new blockbusters to market, and investors know it. Disenchanted investors voted with their wallets, with the share price dropping 30 percent between 2005 and 2010.[42]

Short-termism has hobbled investment generally, not just R&D. And law professor Lawrence Mitchell has produced a smoking gun, documenting how Reaganomics has shortchanged investment. In the three boom years preceding the credit crisis, the amount of stock buybacks by S&P 500 firms exceeded their investment in new production capacity.[43] Even the very best do it: in September 2009, with shares slumping amid the recession, Microsoft raised dividends 18 percent and began a $40 billion, stock buyback program spread over five years.[44]

Short-Termism Has Hobbled Human Capital Investment

With labor becoming a mere commodity under Reaganomics, American firms have evolved to be quite hierarchical, with top-down management structures that are unusual compared with the family capitalism countries, especially in northern Europe. The US collaborative management style of the golden age has been replaced by a command style that discourages loyalty. Employee loyalty now comes in two-week segments until the next paycheck, with longer-term upskilling and the concept of employee commitment to the firm hollowed out. By deincentivizing human capital investment, hierarchical management schemes deny America the productivity edge reaped by firms in the family capitalism countries that feature management-employee collaboration and expansive two-way information flow. Here is how MIT's Paul Osterman explained the consequence on human capital of Reaganomics, as quoted by Steven Greenhouse of the *New York Times*:

> "The path of least resistance is not to invest in your workforce, not to invest in a career ladder, to squeeze on wages and benefits, to make your work force more contingent and flexible."[45]

This lack of collaboration harms productivity growth. The reaction of those American managers who grow concerned is to apply a bit more capital, ascribing to the outdated simplicity that solving sagging productivity means applying more capital. Economists such as J. Morris McInnes of MIT have been discrediting this approach since the early 1980s:

> "The application of relatively greater amounts of financial capital, without attendant progress in the technical quality of assets, is ultimately self-defeating as a path to sustained productivity growth. A few authors . . . propose a broad, total-system approach to the management of productivity. This begins from the precept that productivity is an outcome of the total design of an organization, its technologies, and its operating environment."[46]

McInnes and others emphasize the total design of an organization combining upskilling, employee utilization, and more capital. This approach is rooted in postwar Japanese firms, the first ones that began to focus broadly and proactively on productivity bottlenecks and adopt solutions comprehensively involving management, employees, and technology. They went beyond the quasi-collaborative golden age American model of the day in seeking to aggressively harness the skills and capture the innovation of employees with cooperative and collaborative management and process design to bring all brains to bear. Their practices embody the insight that longer-term research and sustained investment in human capital and innovation are all required to maximize productivity growth. McInnes termed it "a powerful managerial prescription" for driving productivity, and he is right.

Observant management in northern Europe came to adopt these same techniques, as did higher technology US firms and multinationals such as Boeing and Google. The outcome is that such farsighted US multinationals have continued to drive productivity more effectively than domestic enterprises in the many US nontradeable goods sectors. Research published in the *American Economic Review* in February 2003, for example, by Andrew Bernard[47] and others found US exporters have a 33 percent higher productivity level than other domestic firms; they also have a 15 percent advantage over nonexporters in their same industry.*

*This study by Andrew Bernard, Jonathan Eaton, J. Bradford Jensen, and Samuel Kortum discovered that US firms in the nontradable goods sectors producing the same commoditized products such as carbon black or milk exhibited a wide range of company-specific productivity levels, varying from 25 percent to 200 percent of industry averages. This broad variation provides insight into the lackluster US performance of recent decades. But how can such a wide variation, particularly on the

The decline in productivity growth rates during the Reagan era has economists "concluding that productivity is not a matter which has been addressed seriously and purposefully by senior corporate executives," McInnes explained. In contrast, "the Japanese are significantly more likely to hold managers explicitly and tightly accountable for the attainment of productivity improvements." McInnes expressed frank dismay at the "reactive" performance of at least those US executive suites in the nontradeable goods sectors:

> "There is a sense that strategic direction is lacking in the US response to lagging productivity growth. . . . The overall findings of the research . . . present a provocative and challenging picture. Particularly compared with the proactive, strategic response to productivity exhibited by the Japanese, American management seems tentative in their approach. The conclusions of the study are . . . disquieting."[48]

McInnes concludes that "these observations do not provide a basis for great optimism that cooperative efforts, as advocated by the authors referenced earlier in this paper, are likely to meet with any rapid success." The persistent weakness in productivity growth since 1983 when his research appeared indicates how harmful the short-termism of Reaganomics has proven over time to be. Indeed, American executives appear somewhat delusional about the productivity issue, with an inflated sense of their knowledge of management science, believing they're following best practices, all evidence to the contrary. That's the prospect raised by some of the very best analytical management research in recent years, conducted by Nicholas Bloom and other colleagues at Stanford, the University of California, Berkeley, and at the World Bank under the auspices of the National Bureau of Economic Research. Their seminal 2011 analysis "provides the first experimental evidence on the importance of management practices in large firms." Like McInnes and others,

---

low end, for essentially identical commodity goods, exist in capitalism? Put another way: How have US firms prospered during the Reagan era despite weak productivity growth? The answer appeared in 2008 in that same journal with research by Lucia Foster, John Haltiwanger, and Chad Syverson; they concluded that productivity levels are less important to actual firm profits than a variety of idiosyncratic marketing and other factors like long-term firm relations with customers or favorable transportation costs. The sizable US internal market helps as well, providing niches. These analyses explain how (at least domestic) American firms could treat employees as disposable without incurring much of a competitive penalty. See Lucia Foster, John Haltiwanger, and Chad Syverson, "Reallocation, Firm Turnover, and Efficiency: Selection on Productivity or Profitability?," *American Economic Review*, 2008, 98:1, 394–425.

Bloom and his colleagues found management inattention to productivity concerns to be widespread in the United States. Indeed, intensive management training over just five months conducted as part of their research protocol produced an average productivity gain of 11 percent among their target firms. These researchers concluded:

> "The natural question is why firms had not previously adopted these practices. Our evidence suggests that information constraints were an important factor. Firms were often not aware of the existence of many modern management practices, like inventory norms . . . or did not appreciate how these could improve performance. For example, many firms claimed their quality was as good as other firms and so did not need to introduce a quality control process."[49]

This very current research explaining the weak US productivity performance is dismaying. Firms in the family capitalism countries have drawn quite heavily on Japanese practices in recent decades to outperform the United States. These practices are not complex, opaque, or obtuse. The reality is that too many American firms have simply been indifferent to the issue even though US economists readily parsed the collaborative Japanese and family capitalism models and determined why they produce superior worksite outcomes. Bradley Staats, Francesca Gino, and Gary Pisano, for example, documented in 2010 that job satisfaction and respect from supervisors willing to accept criticism are vital for firms hoping to maximize employee contributions to productivity. The psychological security associated with genuine team spirit and a two-way information flow causes employees to be more willing to introduce their own ideas and spar with colleagues and supervisors, elements simply indispensable in maximizing productivity.[50]

One way that collaboration enhances productivity is by incentivizing work effort. Economists know the importance of such measurables as investment, upskilling, and education to productivity growth, but acknowledge difficulty in quantifying another element: work effort. Workplace disaffection may have a particular impact in the instance of highly skilled employees whose performance expectations include taking initiative. In the past, these were the type of employees that US management typically thought would respond to financial incentives.

That assumption is being questioned. First, research by German economists at the Universities of Bonn, Erfurt, and Magdeburg determined that even a strategy of paying higher wages to motivate key employees can fail if firm management is viewed as uncommunicative.[51] Moreover, Samuel Bowles at the Sante Fe Institute has found that one factor accounting for the American productivity slowdown since the 1970s was the loss of employee "hearts and minds" by enterprises. Bowles elaborated on this theme in a series of Castle lectures at Yale University in the winter of 2009–2010, questioning whether employees operating essentially at the technology frontier can be sufficiently incentivized with monetary appeals. He cautioned American management against overreliance on financial incentives.[52] An extreme example is the military where the best performing units are not mercenaries, but those who identify with their cause and colleagues. As Robert J. Shiller notes:

> "a relatively uninterested, insecure work force is unlikely to bring about a vigorous recovery. Solutions for the economy must address not only the structural instability of our financial institutions, but also these problems in the hearts and minds of workers."[53]

Short-Termism Has Weakened American Innovation

With short-termism hobbling R&D and other forms of investment, it is unsurprising that it has weakened innovation and technology prowess as well. Productivity growth is the consequence of labor, capital, and innovation coming together, with economists utilizing the concept of multifactor productivity (MFP) as a proxy for innovation performance. MFP is measured by the Bureau of Labor statistics. As reproduced in Chart 7.3 from such data, the pace of American innovation and technology progress during the Reagan era has been one-third lower than during the golden age.

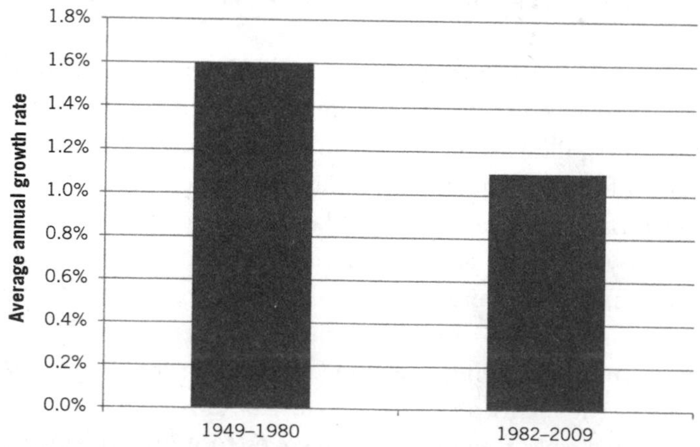

Chart 7.3. Annual average growth rate (MFP was negative during the 1980–1982 recession). *Source: Bureau of Labor statistics and Organization for Economic Cooperation and Development. OECD, "Economic Surveys: United States 2012," Paris, 2012, Figure 15.*

Weak R&D, productivity growth, and lower innovation provide evidence that Reaganomics is anti-growth. That explains the judgment rendered on shareholder capitalism by Lynn Stout, Cornell University professor of corporate and business law at the June 2012 Harvard Law School Forum on Corporate Governance and Financial Regulation:

> "Worse, when we look at macroeconomic data—overall investment returns, numbers of firms choosing to go or remain public, relative economic performance of 'shareholder-friendly' jurisdictions—it suggests the shareholder value dogma may be economically counterproductive."[54]

How Family Capitalism Avoids Weak Corporate Governance

Cutting R&D or human capital investment is scarcely the prescription for firm and shareholder prosperity. That's why economists like Edmund Phelps have argued that sustained new longer-term investment by US firms is needed, in innovation, in cutting-edge products, and in business methods, to boost employment and productivity.[55]

But refocusing the US corporation takes an attribute in scant supply among jittery American executives: a willingness to explain to boards, colleagues, and investors that a long-term perspective will be more profitable for shareholders. Instead, the easiest course is to emulate Hurd: inflate threshold discount rates on investment and R&D opportunities to immediately boost profits, cut upskilling, cut research, and spike stock prices with stock buybacks and dubious mergers. Tomorrow can fend for itself.

The Reagan-era culture has raised the price of responsible, traditional old school long-horizon CEO behavior to an impossibly high level. In both the executive suite and the workplace, it has weakened the traditional values of thrift, prudence, individual responsibility, and the ethic of a good day's pay for a hard day's work that informed the postwar stakeholder culture of America and still informs the economic life of the family capitalism countries. What is the mechanism that causes firms there to emphasize the long-term and productivity growth?

Remember how the German firm Siemens invests heavily in apprenticeships, unlike many American firms? The German model yields a more competitive, higher-wage economy because firms like Siemens have a radically different perspective. The answer is codetermination, the explanation why firms in Germany, in particular, and northern Europe generally have a longer-term and more competitive perspective than American firms.

Codetermination Makes Corporate Governance Accountable to Families

The key to resuscitating the American Dream is hidden in plain sight in every elegant German corporate boardroom.

A scenario crafted by journalist William D. Cohen dramatizes the differences between the American and northern European corporate cultures. He fictionalized a scenario in which Senator Elizabeth Warren became a board member on Wall Street. As a Harvard professor in the past, Warren has written that, "Middle-class families have been chipped at, hacked at, squeezed, and hammered for a generation now. . . . Washington is rigged for big corporations that hire armies of lobbyists." Warren may never sit on Goldman Sachs' Board.[56]

Yet, she could readily sit on German corporate boards today.

Cohen had the right concept, realizing that Wall Street, and by implication, American enterprise, can best be reformed from within. And Senator Warren is the perfect example: she is the godmother of the US Consumer Financial Protection Bureau created by the Dodd-Frank financial reforms law.

While far-fetched in the United States, this scenario is commonplace in northern Europe, where nonmanagement routinely sits on hundreds of boards of all the most important banks and corporations. Overall, some 27 percent of European firms, including all the large ones, have employee representatives on their boards of directors. The more important the enterprise, the greater the likelihood that these representatives have instrumental roles in determining corporate board policy in partnership with shareholders. Codetermination is why firms in the family capitalism countries have long-term perspectives, and put shareholders, employees, and the broader community ahead of executive compensation.

Evolved family capitalism featuring codetermination is the antithesis of socialism. Are predatory innovative giants such as BMW or Siemens socialist tools? Do you think socialist enterprises have produced $200 billion trade *surpluses* and positive trade balances with China, Japan, India, and the rest of Europe? Employers and shareholders there, and at firms such as Adidas or VW-Audi-Porsche, would snicker at the notion. Codetermination is the innovation that has had the most impact on corporate governance since World War II—the black box at the economic core of the most competitive high-wage democracies in the world.

And codetermination is the only proven option for creating the American Dream for your children.

As the home of the Reformation, the Renaissance, John Calvin, John Locke, Rousseau, Voltaire, Adam Smith, and Friedrich Hayek, it is no surprise that northern Europe also became the center over the last century of reforms to strengthen capitalism. The explanation for that outcome is straightforward: voters have expectations of superior corporate governance. Enterprises are the device rich democracies have crafted to create rising living standards for all; maximizing that goal requires high-quality management committed to productivity growth and amenable to broadcasting the gains from such growth throughout society.

Codetermination is the black box that achieves that duality, and it's gone viral across northern Europe since World War II, spreading from its German roots. Firm for firm, that nation enjoys the world's most competitive capitalist base, and is the world's second-greatest exporter after China from an economic base barely one-fifteenth as large. Its economic superiority is globally acknowledged by those with the most at stake: the Edelman Trust Barometer survey of five thousand wealthy investors taken at the 2011 Davos conclave ranked German firms over all others for their sound management and "innovativeness" as the world's best.[57]

And one-half of German firm board members are employees.

It is the best-performing economy on the face of the globe, because codetermination conjures vigorous competition and a long-term perspective at the pivot point of capitalism, at the pinnacle of corporate control in corporate boardrooms.*

Codetermination Succeeds by Maximizing Competition in Board Deliberations

Competition! Competition is the wellspring of invention, rising efficiency, and economic growth. That paradigm is as applicable to the seats of power in corporate boardrooms as to the macroeconomy. The secret to the superior outcomes of German enterprises is greatly enhanced competition in board deliberations, complemented by another

*A recent Siemens annual report includes this statement: "The Supervisory Board of Siemens AG has twenty members. As stipulated by the German Codetermination Act, half of the members represent Company shareholders, and half represent Company employees. The shareholder representatives were elected at the Annual Shareholders' Meeting on January 24, 2008, and the employee representatives, whose names are marked with an asterisk (*), were either elected by an assembly of employee delegates on September 27, 2007, effective as of the end of the Annual Shareholders Meeting on January 24, 2008, or replaced an employee representative who had resigned from the Supervisory Board."

European innovation: work councils.* The high-efficiency combination of codetermination at the board level and joint employee-employer deliberation at the mid-management level is called *Mitbestimmung.*[58]

The ensuing stakeholder oversight and competition provided by these two entities reduces the likelihood that management will behave stupidly or with venality. By forcing executives to manage for the long term, employee representatives solve the agency problem while inoculating enterprises against short-termism. And some of America's best entrepreneurs and managers, like the former CEO of Medtronics now at Harvard, Bill George, know it works.[59]

Surprisingly, the most comprehensive, compelling evidence of the potency of the concept of board competition central to codetermination is found in recent analyses by American economists. One is Yale business school dean Jeffrey Sonnenfeld, who concluded in the *Harvard Business Review* that "The highest performing companies have extremely contentious boards that regard dissent as an obligation and treat no subject as undiscussable."[60]

Western Allies Impose Codetermination

The late Mancur Olson was perhaps the American economist who best framed the momentous events in Germany in the wake of World War II. Better known for his 1965 seminal analysis of regulatory capture, Olson also explained that the ensuing web of vested interests passing for the economic *status quo* is difficult to unravel or corral in the absence of calamity. The economic postscript to World War II proves his point: "In Germany and Japan, the fierce cataclysm cleared away the *detritus* of stability,"[61] clearing the way for codetermination to be born.

It emerged in the immediate postwar era from British and American concern with weakening the 1930s industrial cartels that empowered Adolph Hitler's National Socialism, known as Nazism. Hitler's nascent political party was an also-ran, receiving only one-third of the 1932 vote. It was the financial muscle and visible support from the wealthy conservatives and influential industrialists running these cartels that enabled his subsequent rise and takeover of Germany.[62]

Americans in postwar Germany abhorred the cartels, as did domestic German leaders. Occupation officials despised them, but the Cold War necessitated a resurgent German economy, with industrialists who had formed the base of Hitler's movement corralled rather than garroted.

* Established nearly a century ago in part to help fend off Bolsheviks, work councils are management and employees who collaboratively perform the duties done in the US by mid-management.

The many thousands of white-collar Nazi sympathizers at firms such as Krupp or I. G. Farben—a fearsome and gigantic innovative brute of a cartel and the world's fourth-largest firm before World War II—had to be harnessed rather than banished.

Allied and German officials faced a devilish dilemma unique in economic history as they pondered how to recraft postwar German capitalism. It forced German reformers such as Chancellor Konrad Adenauer to tackle the most fundamental issue: questions of economic sovereignty within capitalism.

With economic elites including managers, bankers, and small businessmen generally tainted by National Socialism, employees were the only realistic counterbalance. So in the end, pre-war work councils were resuscitated and strengthened to democratize German industry and society.

But that was only a fillip. Smith has written that economic sovereignty should rest with consumers, not producers, in his market capitalism. So, in a moment of Smithian inspiration in 1947, officials in the British zone of occupation mandated codetermination to dilute control exercised by the disgraced industrialists. Economist Walter Eucken and others, along with visionary economist Ludwig Erhard, the first postwar economic minister and later Chancellor, refined this approach to thoroughly reform and energize Germany's postwar market capitalism.

The strategy endorsed by the conservative Christian Democrats and British and US officials featured employee representatives sitting at the pinnacle of corporate governance as full members of boards of directors, which are called *Aufsichtsrats*. The ensuing competition among stakeholders in these boardrooms, rather than intrusive government regulations, is what revolutionized northern European corporate governance and fuels the world's most competitive capitalist economies.

Short-termism was not an issue in the later 1940s. So it's unlikely that even the brilliant Erhard or Eucken realized how effectively codetermination would lengthen the time horizon of enterprises, insulating management from short-term pressures and empowering an obsessive focus on maximizing productivity and stakeholder prosperity.

Codeterminism proved a success in the larger coal and steel firms where it was initially installed. The German industrial machine has never looked back as the practice spread to the entire economy by the 1970s and then to much of the rest of northern Europe. German employee representatives hold one-third of *Aufsichtsrat* seats at public corporations with 500-2,000 employees and one-half of all board seats in larger firms such as Daimler.[63]

These employee-employer *Aufsichtsrats* run German firms, setting all policy; they appoint all senior management and are analogous to American boards of directors. Only on tie votes do shareholder representatives hold an extra vote, ensuring the ownership rights important to capitalism are respected and preserved. While codetermination does not reorder ownership or control, it alters the dynamics of management. It gives lift to the talents and voice of employees and other stakeholders while providing them with major authority and responsibility in enterprise management; enabling them, for example, to demand that management adopt a long-time horizon. Here is how the American author Thomas Geoghegan describes the system:

> "They are responsible for other people. They are responsible for running the firm. They make up a powerful leadership class that represents the kind of people—low income, low education—who don't have much of a voice in the affairs of other industrialized countries."[64]

Based entirely on its proven potency, German law has steadily expanded codetermination, applying it to foreign-owned affiliates like GM's Opel. Codetermination has also withstood constitutional challenges.* Make no mistake: Germans are not fools. Had codetermination proved to be inefficient, harmed profits, slowed growth, corrupted share ownership, or weakened investment and productivity, the German and European business and government elite would long ago have dumped it in the dustbin of history.

In reality, codetermination and work councils have proven to convey such a competitive advantage that they enjoy wide support in German executive suites. One survey conducted anonymously of the largest German firms (DAX 100 stock market members) in 1997 by the auditing firm C&L Deutsche Revisions (Coopers & Lybrand) found that 71 percent opposed eliminating codetermination.[65]

The competitive advantage the two concepts bestow is also why they enjoy broad support increasingly in Eastern Europe, expanding to the Czech Republic, Finland, Hungary, Poland, Slovakia, and Slovenia. The applicability of these concepts varies between countries. But in most, as in Germany, they apply comprehensively to all larger enterprises, including corporate stock firms and privately held family firms such as the Bosch appliance and auto parts giant,[66] 92 percent owned by a foundation established by the late Robert Bosch.†

---

*Codetermination was upheld by the Federal Constitutional Court in 1979, which concluded that shareholder rights are protected because their nominee, the supervisory board chairman, casts tiebreaker votes. The court noted that codetermination served the public welfare by promoting industrial peace and improved economic performance.

†The only exceptions in Germany, for example, are tiny enterprises formed as sole proprietorships and the like, impractical for larger firms because of their unlimited personal liability.

The duality of codetermination and work councils enables northern European enterprise to do a better job than American competitors of maximizing productivity. For example, an extensive analysis by economist Steffen Mueller at the University of Erlangen-Nuremberg found that productivity was 10.5 percent greater at firms with work councils.[67] And, Trier University economist Uwe Jirjahn was quoted by *Handelsblatt* in January 2013, concluding that ". . . recent research suggests that codetermination has not only a positive effect on productivity, but also can have a positive impact on profitability and capital market valuation."[68] And, they accomplish it within a legal framework similar to America's. Both the American and German constitutions, for example, carefully protect property rights and codetermination does not impinge on those rights. Indeed, American law would readily accommodate codeterminism; it does not even give preference to shareholder over stakeholder capitalism, as noted by Cornell professor Stout:

> "It shows how the ideology of shareholder value maximization lacks any solid foundation in corporate law, corporate economics, or the empirical evidence. Contrary to what many believe, US corporate law does not impose any enforceable legal duty on corporate directors or executives of public corporations to maximize profits or share price."[69]

Codetermination Maximizes Human Capital and Productivity Growth

An important outcome of the governance and wage structures in the family capitalism countries is that it tends to enhance employee loyalty and intra-firm communication.* Employees embody human capital involving knowledge and skills about corporate operations and goals that even the best-informed corporate hierarchy can't adequately know. And too much of it does unfortunately remain unknown in the American transactional model characterized by *de facto* short-term contracts,where jobs are renewed every few weeks at each pay period.

*This aspect of the northern European economies is drawn from the Nordic model as elaborated in a book written by six Finnish scholars in 2007 (Torben M. Andersen, Bengt Holmström, Seppo Honkapohja, Sixten Korkman, Hans Tson Söderström, and Juhana Vartiainen), *The Nordic Model* (Helsinki: Research Institute of the Finnish Economy, Taloustieto Oy, 2007) and ably described in a 2008 book by that title by Mary Hilson at University College London. It embodies the concept of "Flexicurity," combined with an appreciation of the competitive advantage offered by the Nordic Model's tight employer-employee links.

Employees in such an environment have rationally responded by focusing on skills and knowledge that are not firm-specific, but rather more suited for locating the next job in a highly mobile labor market where pay is too disconnected from employees' marginal value to the employer.

Loyalty, upskilling, and worksite effort in America are further dimmed by hierarchical management schemes, along with outsized and typically unwarranted executive compensation. Very much unlike the family capitalism countries, most in the US business community reject the timeless Chinese proverb that investing in people is the way to build for 100 years of prosperity.[70] The major exceptions are higher tech firms and American multinationals forced to compete with firms armed with codeterminism.

The disparate attitudes in the United States and northern Europe toward human capital, and the responsibilities and expectations of employees, are reflected in data on employee loyalty and tenure. In France and Germany, average job tenure exceeds eleven years, compared to 4.5 years in the United States.[71] Both employers and employees in northern Europe covet long-term relationships that promote upskilling and yield robust productivity results. Here is how the value of human capital is explained by four economists from Queensland University of Technology in Brisbane, the European School of Management in Berlin, and led by Susanne Royer with the International Institute of Management at the University of Flensburg:

> "The longer an employee is with a company, the higher is his or her amount of firm-specific knowledge and this knowledge contributes to the added value of a firm . . . A shortsighted shareholder value orientation is ill advised and may impede performance. To secure success in the long run, these organizations have to bind the human resources to the firm and motivate employees to invest in firm-specific human capital. . . . A core element of successful companies in many environments is firm-specific human capital. Firms may build on this strength by committing to their employees in the long run. This approach traditionally formed one of the backbones of many European economies such as the German one."[72]

The work of American researchers like McInnes and George Akerlof provide a theoretical foundation for the relational work model in the family capitalism countries featuring close collaboration. As early as 1982, Akerlof had concluded that exceptional worksite performance hinges on a complicated matrix of one's own wages and those of colleagues, plus willingness of employers to treat employees as insiders. In their 2010 book, *Identity Economics,* exploring this new field, Akerlof and coauthor Rachel Kranton wrote that

> ". . . a firm operates well when employees identify with it and when their norms advance its goals. Because firms and other organizations are the backbone of all economies, this new description transforms our understanding of what makes economies work or fail."[73]

Codetermination pays off with strong productivity performance. Statistics gathered by the OECD document that labor productivity in French firms, for example, has overtaken American firms. Economists have concluded that one reason is two-way communication and the tight integration of employees in the operation and control of French firms. Here are the conclusions of an analysis conducted in May 2010 by David Fairris of the University of California, Riverside, and Philippe Askenazy of the Paris School of Economics:

> "Perhaps the most interesting findings from our analysis are that worker voice and information-sharing human resource practices are widely utilized in French firms, that this is true independent of work councils' status, and that these features are positive, statistically significant, and quantitatively important determinants of firm productivity."[74]

Other analyses document that the European or Nordic model enhances the productivity performance of German firms, including research published in 2001 by University of South Carolina economist John T. Addison and colleagues in the *Oxford Economic Papers.* And the effect appears to be large: Drawing on research published in the *Schmollers Jahrbuch* by German economists, Addison notes, "Plants with work councils have 25-30 percent higher productivity than their counterparts without work councils."[75]

Another expansive analysis undertaken for the Bonn-based Institute for the Study of Labor by British economists, Sarah Brown, Jolian McHardy, Karl Taylor, and Robert McNabb, also concluded that the Nordic model's enhanced employee identification and attachment increases productivity. The researchers developed a remarkably large database, drawing on a 2004 survey of employees and management in 1,432 major British firms. Firms where employees were the most committed and loyal, based on an independent survey, exhibited the highest productivity performance.[76] Perhaps of far greater importance for future competitiveness, they found that successful two-way communication has its most potent impact at the technology frontier, "... in firms where the principal occupation group is professional or associate professional, which are arguably occupations associated with a greater degree of autonomy and discretion over tasks performed."

American counterparts would be Silicon Valley software and biotechnology enterprises and American multinationals in harshly competitive environments such as northern Europe, where maximizing human capital is vital to success. The paradigm presented by these British economists draws from the original theoretical work of Akerlof, and documents that collaboration or reciprocal behavior, rather than an adversarial US model, produces superior productivity outcomes at the firm level.

These studies provide the weight of evidence that an emphasis on human capital is one reason the family capitalism countries have higher productivity growth. And that helps answer the question how northern European enterprises remain globally competitive, even while incurring significantly higher labor costs than American firms: they can pay high wages because their employees are highly productive. Millions of Americans are familiar with German Bosch products, but few realize how the late namesake founder embodied the ethos of Henry Ford discussed earlier. "I am not paying high wages because I have a lot of money," explained Bosch at one point, "but I have a lot of money because I pay high wages."[77]

Codetermination Maximizes Shareholder Return: The Fauver and Fuerst Analysis

Shareholder capitalism is presumed to maximize shareholder return, although we are learning that it rewards management at the expense of shareholders. In fact, codeterminism and stakeholder capitalism provide greater returns to shareholders than shareholder capitalism.

A growing number of American economists have concluded that shareholder capitalism fails to deliver shareholder value, fatally flawed by its short-termism. This includes Justin Fox and Jay W. Lorsch and also Harvard business professor Rosabeth Moss Kanter.[78] Fox and Lorsch concluded:

> "The argument here isn't that managers and boards always know best. It's simply that widely dispersed short-term shareholders are unlikely to know better—and a governance system that relies on them to keep corporations on the straight and narrow is doomed to fail."[79]

A number of analyses have sought to quantify the benefits of codetermination to shareholders, and I direct interested readers to the thorough literature survey of March 2011 by John T. Addison and Claus Schnabel.[80] The most comprehensive and methodologically advanced study applying rigorous analytical techniques to codetermination has been performed by American finance professors Larry Fauver at the University of Tennessee and Michael Fuerst at the University of Miami.[81] In December 2006, Fauver and Fuerst published a statistical analysis of performance differentials between those German firms with and without an employee presence on boards of directors. German firms with fewer than five hundred employees are not required to have employee representatives on their boards and served as their control.

Drawn from Bloomberg and Thomson Financial's *Worldscope* statistics from 2003, their database was the largest possible, comprising *all* 786 publicly traded German firms at the time. They concluded:

- Shareholder returns (profits per sale and dividend yield) were highest in firms with employee representatives on supervisory boards—more than double that of firms without codetermination; the employee representatives created relatively more value for shareholders.

- Employee board representation enhanced share values by acting as two-way conduits for the flow of new information, providing valuable firsthand operational knowledge to corporate boards.

- Employee board representation provides a powerful means of monitoring and reducing agency costs within the firm. Codetermination limits the abuse of smaller shareholders by management or by owners of large blocks of stock seeking to maximize individual remuneration.

- Employee representatives on enterprise supervisory boards provide unique insight into project feasibility and insist on a longer-term perspective in corporate decision making. The quality of investment decisions is higher and incidence of short-termism reduced.

- The greater degree of transparency achieved through direct board representation reduces labor-management antagonism, engenders a team approach to problem solving, and allows natural synergies to emerge that ultimately benefit shareholder value.

The most powerful finding by Fauver and Fuerst is that codetermination increases the share value assigned to such firms by the marketplace by about 10 percent, a notable bonus for shareholders. As noted in

Chart 7.4, they documented that German firms with employee representation had a "significantly higher" (1.126) median Tobin Q value than those lacking representation (1.038).

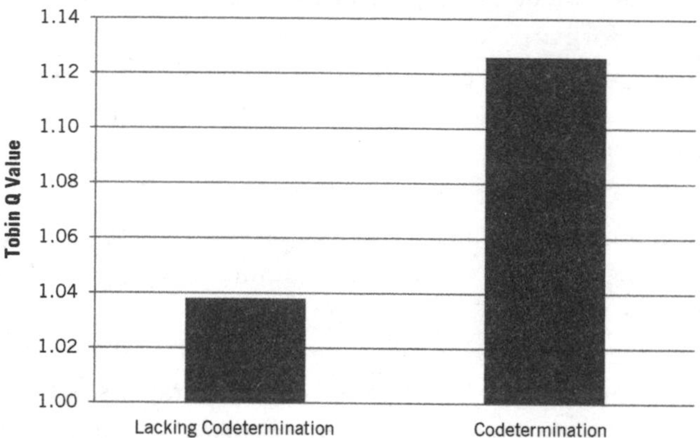

Chart 7.4.

Source: Larry Fauver and Michael E. Fuerst, "Does Good Corporate Governance Include Employee Representation? Evidence from German Corporate Boards," Journal of Financial Economics, volume 82, December 2006.

What does that mean? Devised by iconic American Nobel Laureate economist James Tobin, Q values measure the market value of any company compared to the value of its book assets. Tobin's Q answers the pivotal question of how well management utilizes a firm's resources. When Tobin's Q exceeds that of its competitors, the capital marketplace of analysts and investors views a firm as enjoying higher inherent worth due to unusual assets such as intellectual capital, higher-order management expertise, or other intangibles not valued by accountants. The fact that Fauver and Fuerst relied on the largest possible data set—every traded German firm—powerfully supports their conclusion that shares of codetermination firms are more highly valued by the market, presumably because of superior management. Fauver and Fuerst concluded that employees on supervisory boards serve as:

> ". . . highly informed monitoring agents. In such a whistle-blowing capacity, employees can provide information about the economic feasibility of projects and curb investment in managerial perquisites, or expropriation by large insiders seeking private benefits of control and cronyism."*

* These findings are reinforced by another analysis performed by Fauver and Fuerst. In the past, studies of German corporate governance have produced inconsistent findings because of small samples and other issues. For example, back in 2004,

Highly valuing employee expertise and information is scarcely the prevailing attitude of too many American executive suites that behave as though employees are something akin to cannon fodder in the stock-option wars. Worse, most American employees and voters docilely appear to accept this organizational construct. Voters in the family capitalism countries are considerably less indulgent.

Codetermination Maximizes Performance at the Technology Frontier

The second most powerful finding by Fauver and Fuerst emphasized by Addison and Schnabel is the comparative advantage that codetermination provides firms operating at the technology frontier. The competing interests and complexity of board-CEO interaction in firms across northern Europe result in longer-term perspectives and perhaps also a higher-order skill set than may be typical in American executive suites. It is an environment of intense managerial accountability for the longer term coupled with elaborate and demanding board oversight of executive decisions—the antithesis of American firm governance today. It means corporate decisions about wages and job security go hand in hand with the urgency of upskilling, investing in R&D, turning a profit, and remaining competitive over the longer term in the most hostile and unforgiving economic marketplace in the world.

Economists have explored the effect of codetermination on enterprise research investments. For example, Kornelius Kraft and Jörg Stank published research in 2004 in which they concluded that R&D activity measured by patents is modestly higher with codetermination. Their subsequent 2009 analysis in conjunction with Ralf Dewenter found activity would at worst be unaffected.[82]

Returning to the point drawn from the Bowles' Castle lectures at Yale during the winter of 2009–2010, the future winners in capitalism will be firms that best operate on the frontiers of science and technology. These are firms in environments requiring abnormally high

---

economists Gary Gorton and Frank Schmid examined the impact of employee representatives on German firms, but used only the 250 largest German firms as a data set and misclassified the status of employee representatives on boards. As Addison and Schnabel explain in their literature survey, Fauver and Fuerst tripled the data set, used actual employee data rather than a union proxy, and, importantly, included results that might flow from "the interaction of complex and high coordination industries and employee board representation neglected by Gorton and Schmid." See Gary Gorton and Frank Schmid: "Capital, Labor and the Firm: A Study of German Codetermination," *Journal of the European Economic Association*, vol. 2, 2004, 89–114.

coordination of labor and management, an integration of activities such as production and research, and, above all, maximization of specialized employee skill sets.

Managing a hundred software engineers and biotechnologists in a Palo Alto start-up demands a structure that can accommodate complexities and a high order of coordination featuring expansive human capital development and two-way communication. These research environments characterized by process complexities are the most challenging in science or commerce, yet are the seeds for giant enterprises of the future. The genius of the late Steve Jobs at Apple and Bill Gates at Microsoft was their ability to manage these complexities.

Fauver and Fuerst concluded that value added by the employee board representation model is pronounced precisely in such complex environments, in those sectors where special coordination, employee skills, or knowledge within individual firms is required for competitive success. Those are characteristics of quintessential, knowledge-driver enterprises in Silicon Valley; of research-intensive industries, such as pharmaceuticals or IT; and of autos and any manufacturing, such as electronics, with complex production or supply-train features. Those knowledge industries are precisely the type that benefit inordinately from human capital investment, placing a premium on employee motivation and skills. These complex environments are where employee motivation is a vital determinant of shareholder success and where employee representation yielded the strongest beneficial outcomes of all.

Now you understand why German firms are the global pacesetters in a host of complex engineering and industrial goods.

Fauver's and Fuerst's findings about the type of environment where codeterminism excels mirrored the conclusions of the four British economists Sarah Brown, Jolian McHardy, Karl Taylor, and Robert McNabb, and the economists from Australia and Germany led by Susanne Royer. This research represents the weight of evidence that codetermination provides practitioners with a strategic and structural comparative advantage over American and other global competitors, producing higher value for shareholders by maximizing human capital, the most valuable resource in such firms. Here is how Royer's researchers explained that advantage:

> "Strategic management literature suggests that firm-specific human capital is a central resource for the realization of competitive advantage. . . . Competitive advantages are firm-specific advantages that either cannot be imitated by other firms, or, if replicated, such replication can only be achieved at an extremely

> high price. . . . Systems that do not allow for the utilization of particular types of employee voice mechanisms . . . may harm both the firm and its employees. . . . Employees as a stakeholder group should be considered from an economic perspective as a strategic competitive advantage."[83]

Productivity is most readily born, and the wealth of tomorrow created, at the technology and knowledge frontiers. In a world where technology and capital are commodities, human capital is the single most important resource capable of conferring a strategic competitive advantage. The duality of work councils and codetermination is why Germany and its neighbors are the most competitive economies on earth.

This insight actually isn't new to American audiences. More than twenty-five years ago, American experts first began examining the weakening US economic performance, linking it to the debilitating features of what we now call Reaganomics. Here are economists Diane Werneke and Sar A. Levitan writing in 1984: "An organization may be resistant or unresponsive to management goals. Jobs may be incompatibly designed, given the existing skills of employees, or they may be inappropriately meshed." Looking abroad, they suggested that "the decision-making patterns of foreign business firms hold the key to improving US productivity performance. In particular, the industrial practices found in West Germany. . . ."[84] Researchers such as Werneke and Levitan lacked the rigorous hard evidence we have just reviewed about high-performing northern European firms, but their observations have proven prescient.

Of course, it isn't just high-technology firms that benefit from codetermination. Here is David Haines, the British CEO of Grohe, headquartered in Germany, Europe's largest bathroom fixtures firm:

> "It is working very well for us. The workers have supported all our decisions. Yes, the discussions were very hard and yes, they didn't always share our views, but they were enormously helpful."[85]

The Global Credit Crisis Affirmed the Superiority of Codetermination

The American and European economies have been burdened by the aftermath of the global credit crisis, an event that provided confirmation, however, of Fauver's and Fuerst's conclusions. That turmoil provided economists with a real-world opportunity to examine Reaganomics under stress. How did shareholder capitalism fare?

Reaganomics presumes that the best-governed US firms are those with shareholder-friendly boards: the greater the degree of shareholder control, the more efficiently such firms are assumed to be run. The validity of that notion would have become evident during the credit crunch, with superior performances scored by those financial intermediaries with boards ranked the most shareholder-friendly on corporate governance, according to MSCI's Risk Metrics. That hypothesis was tested by economists Andrea Beltratti and René M. Stulz in a March 2010 analysis. "To the extent that governance played a role, we would expect banks with better governance to have performed better," they suggested. Yet, their extensive study, involving over 500 of the world's largest financial institutions, led them to exactly the opposite conclusion:

> "However, banks with a shareholder-friendly board performed worse during the crisis. Such a result is consistent with the view that banks that were pushed by their boards to maximize shareholder wealth before the crisis took risks that were understood to create wealth but turned out poorly."[86]

Stulz and Rüdiger Fahlenbrach at the Ecole Polytechnique Fédérale de Lausanne, Switzerland, using a different data set comprised solely of US firms, reached the same conclusion: shareholder capitalism failed to perform under stress when superior management is most needed.[87]

These analyses document that Milton Friedman's shareholder-maximization model underperformed in the largest possible real-world experiment, yielding uncompetitively weak outcomes for shareholders precisely when superior management was needed. They add weight to the findings in Sonnenfeld's 2002 paper cited earlier, where he concluded that corporate success hinges on boards that are: ". . . strong, high-functioning work groups whose members trust and challenge one another and engage directly with senior managers on critical issues facing corporations."[88]

Codetermination in America: Family Firms

How would codetermination fare in America? The evidence suggests it would produce prosperous companies, based on experience with family firms managed by founders or (in later generations) by hired professionals. These are firms whose boards typically have long time horizons like those under codetermination. Indeed, an Ernst & Young 2013 analysis of family businesses primarily in the United States and northern Europe concluded that the first key to their success was that they managed for the long term. Philippe Vailhen, a French partner at the consulting firm, explained, "There is no dictatorship of the short term," enabling such firms to focus more on innovation "rather than the need to meet quarterly expectations of shareholders."[89]

Research by Ronald Anderson and David Reeb agreed; American family enterprises tend to be more focused on the long term than are non-family firms. They compared the performance of family and nonfamily firms listed on the S&P 500 stock market from 1992 to 1999, and concluded that:

> "Founding families view their firms as an asset to pass on to their descendants rather than wealth to be consumed during their lifetimes. Firm survival is thus an important concern for families, suggesting they are potentially long-term value maximization advocates."[90]

Family firms in their analysis had a higher return on assets (6.07 percent) compared to nonfamily firms (4.70 percent), "with family firms enjoying about a 10.0 percent greater Tobin's Q, relative to nonfamily firms." That superior outcome for shareholders nearly precisely mirrors the conclusions of Fauver and Fuerst based on German data. This bonus appears linked to superior prospects for survival, because such firms enjoy a lower cost of capital. Earlier research by Anderson, Reeb, and finance professor Sattar A. Mansi at Texas Tech University discovered that US family firms with professional management overseen by family had a 35.5 basis-point lower cost of capital than nonfamily firms.[91] Economists will tell you that spread is about the yield differential historically between A- and BBB-rated debt, a rather handsome bonus for shareholders in codetermination and in US family firms.

CHAPTER 8

SMALL GOVERNMENT HYPOCRISY

"America has let its infrastructure crumble, its foreign markets decline, its productivity dwindle, its savings evaporate, and its budget and borrowing burgeon."[1]

PETER G. PETERSON,
US Secretary of Commerce, Nixon administration, October 1987

"Reagan's tax cuts, whatever their merits as short-term fiscal policy, left large and growing budget deficits when combined with increased spending, and added to the national debt."[2]

RICHARD GAMBLE,
***American Conservative* magazine, May 2009**

Ronald Reagan refused to pay his bills.

Some view him as a transformational economic figure, but historians are likely to view him, and his Bush successors, as just three among many national leaders of his era—Mexico (1994), Indonesia and Thailand (1997), Russia (1998), Argentina (2000), and Greece (2009)—whose record deficits caused national debt crises.[3] Even so, conservatives persist in portraying President Reagan as a small-government *aficionado*. For example, the director of the American Enterprise Institute's National Research Initiative, Henry Olson, wrote in the *Wall Street Journal* in 2008 of "the limited government principles governing the GOP in the Reagan and post-Reagan era."[4]

Other less partisan conservatives with eyes wide open acknowledge the truth, expressing dismay at the iconic president's budget record. In eight years, Reagan nearly tripled the national debt, the single worst record by far among all American presidents, except for Franklin Roosevelt and Abraham Lincoln during wartime. As Austrian school economist Murray N. Rothbard wrote to his fellow conservatives at the Ludwig von Mises Institute in 2004:

> "So we have the curious, and surely not healthy, situation where a mass of politically interested people are totally misinterpreting, and

even misrepresenting, the Reagan record; focusing, like Reagan himself, on his rhetoric instead of on the reality."[5]

What was the reality that has left America's conservative intellectual aristocracy such as Pete Peterson so dismayed? Here is Rothbard again:

> "How well did Reagan succeed in cutting government spending, surely a critical ingredient in any plan to reduce the role of government in everyone's life? In 1980 . . . the federal government spent $591 billion. In 1986 . . . the federal government spent $990 billion—an increase of 68 percent. Whatever this is, it is emphatically *not* reducing government expenditures."

President Clinton campaigned to balance government budgets and met that promise. Presidents Ronald Reagan, George H.W. Bush, and George W. Bush campaigned even more aggressively on the promise of fiscal rectitude, with dire warnings of the dangers posed by big government and national debt. They demonized the threat posed by Washington—the government that won World War II, enacted Social Security and Medicare, the minimum wage, fought against discrimination, created the biggest middle class in history, went to the moon and won the Cold War. One is hard-pressed to identify a more effective government anywhere in history. Worse, once in office, these presidents proved to be big government guys, using their election mandates to engineer a grand episode of regulatory capture and the biggest-ever expansion of private debt and of government spending, debt, and credit.

Demonizing Beast Government

Fear of government has been a constant in political thought for centuries, ranging from European philosophers to the Founding Fathers, and for good reason because examples of tyrannical governments persist even today. Yet the reality is that governments in the postwar rich democracies have been benevolent, busily expanding the voting franchise, reducing ethnic inequality, expanding opportunity at home, and expanding democracy abroad.

Common history, social circumstances, and aspirations marked the golden age, when risks and obligations were shared between families and Washington. Government was an ally in realizing family aspirations, with laws and regulations promoting education, a respect for work, and steadily rising wages. As depicted in Chart 8.1 immediately prior to Nixon's election in 1968, barely one in three Americans viewed Washington as a threat despite the ongoing Vietnam War.

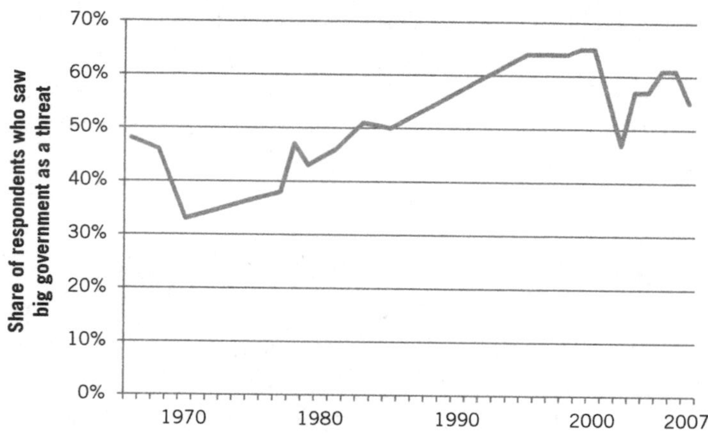

Chart 8.1. Gallup polling, various years. The question posed was, "In your opinion, which of the following will be the biggest threat to the country in the future—big business, big labor, or big government?"

Source: Joseph Carroll, "Public: Big Government Greater Threat Than Big Labor, Big Business," Gallup organization, January 5, 2007, and Charlotte Rampell, "Battle of the Bigs and Bads; Government vs. Business," New York Times, April 20, 2009.

The stagflation and gasoline lines of the 1970s reversed that sentiment. Those were eventful days. Antitax and antigovernment sentiment flourished, exemplified by enactment of California's Proposition 13 in June 1978, funded by commercial interests to freeze their own property taxes. That success was followed by Republican Congressional victories on a small-government platform that November, as political rhetoric began to darken attitudes toward government and question its oversight role of the business community. That period also saw the relaunch of the small-government agenda drawn from the earlier candidacy of US Senator Barry Goldwater of Arizona, with some 23 states in 1978 calling for a Constitutional amendment to balance the federal budget.[6]

Conservative politicians highlighted foolish regulations, demeaned the skill and temperament of civil servants, and ridiculed the motives of government with lines such as, "If it moves, tax it. If it keeps moving, regulate it. And if it stops moving, subsidize it."[7]

An important element was the demonization of Congress, which began in earnest with the ascendency of Newt Gingrich as leader of the minority Congressional Republicans in 1989. He embarked on a multiyear strategy of partisan attacks on the ethics and record of Congress then dominated by the Democratic Party. Criticism of taxes and big government emerged as the Republican Party *mantra*. And the partisan polarization succeeded; the changed tone contributed to the national sense of disaffection from government that occurred during the Reagan era. The magnitude of that shift is indicated by the health care reform debate in recent years, as explained by *Washington Post* columnist Steven Pearlstein:

> "It should tell you how far the country has moved to the right that the various proposals put forward by a Democratic president and Congress bear an eerie resemblance to the deal cooked up between Kennedy and Nixon, while Nixon's political heirs vilify it as nothing less than a socialist plot."[8]

By the end of the twentieth century, two out of three Americans surveyed in Gallup polls had grown to distrust government, a notable shift in opinion. That opprobrium also applied to civil servants. In an October 2010 survey by the *Washington Post*, some 49 percent of respondents denigrated federal employee work habits compared to private employees, and 36 percent felt they were less qualified than private employees.[9] A key element of the Reagan-era, antigovernment theme was sowing distrust about how well government utilizes tax revenue, as elaborated by researcher Marc Hetherington in his book *Why Trust Matters*:

> "When government programs require people to make sacrifices, they need to trust that the results will be a better future for everyone. Absent that trust, people will deem such sacrifices as unfair, even punitive, and, thus will not support the programs that require them."[10]

This transformation in public attitude repositioned government as a barrier, rather than as a broker, of prosperity and innovation, and a hindrance to the American Dream. Efficient and successful programs important to rising prosperity, including minimum wages, Medicaid, a progressive tax structure, upskilling, and even public education have come to be scorned by a sizable minority of Americans. The shift paid political dividends. Stanley B. Greenberg, chief of the polling firm Greenberg Quinlan Rosner, explains that this growing distrust of government:

> ". . . doesn't hurt Republicans. If government is seen as useless, what is the point of electing Democrats who aim to use government to advance some public end?. . . Today, a dispiriting economy combined with a well-developed critique of government leaves government not just distrusted but illegitimate."[11]

With government increasingly sitting on the philosophical sidelines and distrusted as a partner, individual economic distress has become internalized. Many Americans likely view wage stagnation and rising income disparities as a personal problem, rather than a consequence of Reagan era policies.

As we will now see, demonizing government was pursued disingenuously. It proved to be a mere stunt. Despite claiming allegiance to the ideals of small-government Jeffersonians, the Republican presidents proved to be big government men through and through.

Reaganomics: Big Government Spending

The budget deficits and government spending during the Reagan, G.H.W. Bush and G.W. Bush administrations dwarf the more recent deficits of the Obama administration, as we will see in a moment. Moreover, the source of the Obama deficits is different. They are recession-driven by greater safety-net spending and falling tax revenues from recession. In contrast, the relatively far larger deficits from 1981 to 2008 were an explicit consequence of a desire to greatly expand government spending, coupled with a premeditated political calculus to rebrand Republicans as the party of tax cuts. That toxic combination caused record budget deficits, while abandoning that party's history of fiscal probity.

It is certainly true that Republican politicians continue to fret about deficits. Yet, they attach a higher priority to tax cuts. Reaganomics marked a momentous transition point, where the *modus vivendi* of the two great American political parties switched fiscal roles: the Republican Party became a Hamiltonian party of big spending and big debt, while the Democratic Party became budget balancers. The switch in roles after 1980 is evidenced by Chart 8.2. Reproduced from US Department of Commerce statistics, *each* of the three Republican Reagan-era presidents increased the inflation-adjusted share of GDP devoted to government spending by an average of 1 percentage point—while President Clinton reduced it by more than 1 percentage point.

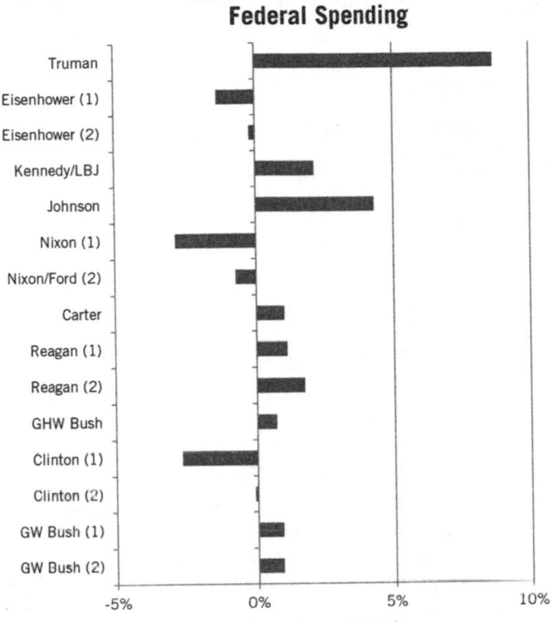

Chart 8.2. Change in inflation-adjusted share of GDP from direct government spending, compounded annual average for each presidential term.

Source: Floyd Norris, "Big Government Republicans," New York Times, May 6, 2009.

Including the Obama years in this chart, drawn from calculations in 2009 by economic reporter Floyd Norris at the New York Times, does not change this conclusion. Indeed, Presidents Obama and Clinton have been the most fiscally responsible leaders since 1980; spending during the first Obama term—with some credit certainly due to Tea Party Congressional Republicans—actually declined at a 1.4 percent annual pace in inflation-adjusted dollars.[12]

Examining government outlays in nominal terms does not change this picture either. For example, a Dow Jones & Company analysis in 2012 calculated the annualized growth in federal spending from 1980–2013. The conclusions reached by this Wall Street firm are reproduced as Chart 8.3. The largest increase since 1980 in Federal spending occurred during President Reagan's first term (8.7 percent annually), followed by George W. Bush's second term (8.1 percent) and his first term (7.3 percent). The slowest rise in spending since 1980 was by President Obama (1.4 percent), followed by President Clinton's first (3.2 percent) and second terms (3.9 percent).

Obama was dealt the worst economic hand of any President since Franklin Roosevelt. Yet despite sharply reducing the pace of government spending (which also slowed GDP), he successfully avoided a deeper recession.

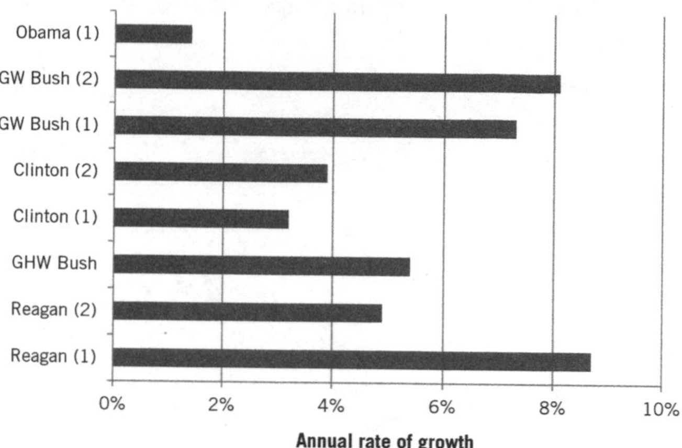

Chart 8.3. Annual growth in nominal federal spending, fiscal years 1982–2013, with a portion of spending during G.W. Bush fiscal year 2009 reassigned to Obama.

Source: Rex Nutting, "Obama Spending Binge Never Happened," MarketWatch, May 22, 2012, Dow Jones & Co., http://www.marketwatch.com/story/obama-spending-binge-never-happened-2012-05-22.

Despite a robust economic recovery during the latter part of his first term, Ronald Reagan had the worst spending record of any peacetime president. And his betrayal of campaign promises to restore Jeffersonian small government was lamented by a number of conservatives, including the Republican debt scold Pete Peterson:

> "In 1980, American voters decisively endorsed a smaller and leaner federal government, with special exceptions for defense spending and for poverty-related 'safety-net' benefits. Result: we ended up with a significantly higher level of federal spending in 1986 (23.8 percent of GDP) than we had in 1979 (20.5 percent of GDP)."[13]

Democrats were also dissatisfied with President Reagan's deficits. As early as 1982, as recounted by Republican David Frum, for example, Congressional Democrats urged that President Reagan balance the federal budget. Instead, "Ronald Reagan disregarded this advice. He held firm to his tax cuts."[14]

The late William A. Niskanen, a disappointed member of President Reagan's Council of Economic Advisors, concluded, "In the end, there was no Reagan revolution."[15] Niskanen was wrong: There *was* a revolution—just not one in which that administration and conservative economists can take pride.

Wasteful Outsourcing of Government Functions

The dramatic expansion of government spending during the Reagan era featured waste, and perhaps the most egregious example was stepped-up outsourcing of traditional government functions. The two Bush presidents were especially keen on conducting new military operations with contractors rather than expanding the military. Historic data are instructive on this point. During the Revolutionary War, there was one private-sector contractor for every six soldiers, according to research by Pentagon procurement officials, and that ratio held through the Vietnam War. The ratio rose sharply, however, during the Iraq War, where an undersized American military was supported by a growing legion of civilian contractors whose life-cycle cost was twice that of civil servants. There were so many that the ratio of contractors to troops fell to 1:1. Worse, the ratio has doubled in Afghanistan, with two very expensive contractors for each soldier.[16]

Certainly, contractors can produce value for taxpayers, but privatizing has proven not to be a default setting for the cost-effective delivery of public services. Quite the opposite: data show that outsourcing traditional governmental functions is usually a fiscal mistake, just another consequence of regulatory capture. In too many instances, it's simply a subsidy to the politically connected, such as Halliburton. The George W. Bush administration conducted an extensive set of competitions intending to prove the worth of privatizing, matching civil servants performing a variety of tasks with private enterprise. The elaborate analyses concluded that private firms couldn't match civil servants in efficiency.[17]

Moreover, privatizing proved to be considerably more expensive on a full cost basis in other comparisons as well. In 2008, Congressional investigators discovered that each private contract employee cost taxpayers an average $250,000 annually, well above the comprehensive cost, including health, retirement, and other benefits, of federal civilian or military employees doing the identical work.[18]

Similar results were found by the Washington-based nonprofit Project on Government Oversight, which concluded that contractors are paid about double the full cost of government employees performing the same work. Released in September 2011, their analysis determined that contractors were paid $268,653 for computer engineers, compared to a comprehensive cost of $136,456 for the same work by civil servants. Contractors were paid $228,488 for human resource managers, compared to $111,711 for civil servants doing identical work. Overall, costs were higher for the same work in 33 of the 35 occupations they examined.[19]

The most egregious example was the Pentagon during the Iraq War, where hundreds of thousands of expensive contractors were employed by taxpayers. The Pentagon's subsequent evaluation concluded that each defense contractor it replaced with a full-time federal official would have saved taxpayers $44,000 annually—a comprehensive cost savings which included all fringe and other direct and indirect costs.[20]

These wasteful contractor costs have been compounded by lax oversight. The number of US Department of Defense contracting auditors was *cut* by 2,850, or 30 percent, between 1987 and 2009, even as the number of Pentagon contracts increased by a factor of ten—from fewer than 45,000 to 500,000.[21] That is not a recipe for fiscal prudence. Firms with White House ties such as Blackwater were granted billions of dollars in contracts, with scant Pentagon review or later oversight and frequently on a noncompetitive, no-bid basis. These types of contracts, which more than doubled to $188 billion in the last year of the Bush administration, comprised one-third of all outsourcing: an invitation to malfeasance.[22] Some contractors also proved to be tax cheats, with Government Accountability Office investigators concluding that they dodged $3 billion in back taxes.[23]

Then-US Senator Harry Truman attained nationwide fame chairing a committee examining contractor practices during World War II. A similar bipartisan committee, the Commission on Wartime Contracting in Iraq and Afghanistan, was co-chaired by Michael Thibault and former Republican Congressman Christopher Shays. They are not likely to attain Truman's prominence, but their work was equally informative. The Commission documented in 2011 that some contractors delivered poor value; the nonpartisan Commission aimed it punches directly at the Bush administration's contracting shortcomings:

> "At least one in every six dollars of US spending for contracts and grants in Iraq and Afghanistan over the past decade, or more than $30 billion, have been wasted . . . through poor planning, vague and shifting requirements, inadequate competition, substandard contract management and oversight, lax accountability, weak interagency coordination, and subpar performance or outright misconduct."[24]

Outsourcing produces the same inefficiencies at the state level. An analysis found that prison outsourcing costs Arizonans as much as $1,600 more per inmate than traditional state prison management.[25] And that is a low-ball conclusion, because private prison contractors refuse to house sick or elderly inmates, leaving these most expensive inmates to reside in state prisons.

CHAPTER 9

TAX CUT CULTISTS

"The Republican Party has been infected by a faction that is more of a psychological protest than a practical, governing alternative. The members of this movement do not accept the logic of compromise . . . do not accept the legitimacy of scholars and intellectual authorities . . . have no sense of moral decency . . . have no economic theory worthy of the name. . . . To members of this movement, tax levels are everything . . . a sacred fixation."[1]

DAVID BROOKS,
***New York Times*, July 5, 2011**

"It's true that tax rates for higher-income brackets were cut; but for the average person, taxes rose, rather than declined."[2]

MURRAY N. ROTHBARD
***Mises Daily*, June 9, 2004**

"How Reagan ruined conservatism. . . . Under Reagan, they simply became the party of tax cuts, without any commitment to fiscal responsibility. . . . This drift in Republican thinking was actually profoundly anti-conservative—because it elevated ideology (cut taxes at any cost) over a pragmatic commitment to good governance."[3]

GIDEON RACHMAN,
***Financial Times*, March 1, 2010**

Remember your first love? That's the exciting way all presidents feel about lower taxes. They glory in cutting taxes. The voters love it, after all. The Reagan era rebranded the Republican Party in a number of ways, perhaps most significantly to economists as a fiscally feckless party of easy money and credit bubbles. Voters perceive a different rebranding, however. For many, it became a party that prioritized tax cuts and small government.

It was not a genuine small-government movement, as we have learned, but Reagan-era Republicans certainly met campaign promises to trim taxes. During the golden age, the top marginal federal income tax rate paid by the most affluent ranged from above 90 percent under President Eisenhower in the 1950s to 70 percent during the 1960s and

1970s. Repeated tax cuts during the Reagan era brought that rate below 40 percent in the last several decades. And the tax rate on capital gains income like stock speculation during the Reagan era was cut by more than one-half.

The outcome is that America's 400 wealthiest families paid 51.2 percent of their income in federal taxes in 1955, but only 18 percent in 2008.[4] Moreover, the Washington-based Tax Foundation calculated that the average income tax rate paid by the top 1 percent of earners declined from 34.47 percent in 1980 to 22.45 percent by 2007.[5]

There are two important points about these tax cuts:

First, as we see in detail in the following chapter, these tax cuts were financed with borrowed money; they are a major reason President Reagan nearly tripled the national debt in just eight years.

Second, they were skewed to favor the affluent political donor class identified by political scientists such as Larry Bartels, causing a historic redistribution of the American tax burden from the affluent onto the middle class. Some taxes were increased during the Reagan era, but almost uniformly, they were payroll taxes on wages and other regressive taxes disproportionately paid by the middle class. The outcome is that Reagan-era politicians abandoned the oldest and most timeless principle of taxation: vertical equity, or ability-to-pay, what economists call progressive taxation.

An example is the tax restructuring under President George W. Bush, examined in an October 2007 analysis by the Washington-based nonprofit Citizens for Tax Justice. The study drew on tax data from the US Department of the Treasury for the period 2000–2005, and concluded that the Bush administration cuts increased after-tax incomes a bare $464 on average for the bottom one-half of all taxpayers. Yet, those same tax cuts increased incomes for the top 1 percent by a stunning $46,868 apiece—100 times more per taxpayer.[6]

Thus, when George W. Bush left office, 200,000, or two-thirds of all earners with taxable incomes exceeding $1 million, paid a lower tax rate than the typical taxpayer making less than $100,000.[7] For example, the 14.1 percent federal tax rate paid in 2011 by multimillionaire presidential candidate Mitt Romney was less than the 15.3 percent payroll rate just for Social Security and Medicare paid by most employees in America.

How is that possible? What accounts for this upside-down federal tax structure? The explanation is that the tax rate on capital gains income is considerably below federal tax rates on wage income. Capital gains income is concentrated among the wealthiest Americans who fuel US politics, with one-half going to the 0.1 percent at the peak of the income pyramid.[8] Some 60 percent of the income received by the 400 highest earners in 2008 was capital gains, for example, while only 8 percent was wages. In contrast, 5 percent of the income received by everyone else was capital gains, while 72 percent was wages.

It is certainly true that America's leaders displayed sympathy on occasion to the tax equity concerns of families during this era. In a 1985 speech to students at Atlanta's Northside high school, for example, President Reagan invoked populist rhetoric to argue millionaires should pay more taxes than bus drivers. Loopholes "made it possible for millionaires to pay nothing, while a bus driver was paying 10 percent of his salary, and that's crazy," he exclaimed.[9] Yet Ronald Reagan's behavior shows that presidents need to be judged by deeds not rhetoric. And his deeds were remarkably broad, but scarcely lived up to this Atlanta speech regarding taxes as we now see.

Abandoning Progressive Tax Rates

A progressive tax system is one where those with lower incomes pay lower tax rates. Aristotle is an early hero to political scientists and philosophers because he spent a lifetime pondering the concepts of taxation, civilization, liberty, the popular will, and the intricacies and elements necessary for a democracy governed by equals to outperform tyranny. His concern with plumbing the elements necessary for the greatest economic and political good for the greatest number was fired by his distaste for the injustice that typically occurs when a nation's economic life is dominated by what he termed Oligarchs.

In his *Nicomachean Ethics*, Aristotle provided the philosophical grounding for what became modern tax theory; a tax system based on ability-to-pay. Attaining tax justice, he wrote, is found in this enduring concept of equality: "Equals are to be treated equally and unequals unequally."[10] That timeless teaching is the most fundamental principle of tax theory. Here is how David Cay Johnston, the tax specialist formerly with the *New York Times*, described the historical context of progressive taxation stretching back 2,300 years:

> "The Athenians jettisoned their flat tax, and with it tyranny in favor of a tax system based on ability to pay. From Aristotle to the Father of Capitalism, Adam Smith, the idea that taxes should be based on ability to pay has been at the core of the rise of Western civilization. John Stuart Mill, his father John Mill, David Ricardo, and every other leading worldly philosopher embraced this concept, which today is embodied in the progressive income tax, in which the higher your income, the greater portion of each additional dollar of income is paid in taxes."[11]

The admiration of America's Founding Fathers for economic justice and for the insights of Aristotle account for their vigorous support of the progressive tax principle. Thomas Jefferson, for example, explicitly expected taxes to be borne solely by income elites, not by the middle or working classes:

> "The farmer will see his government supported, his children educated, and the face of his country made a paradise by the contributions of the rich alone, without his being called on to spend a cent from his earnings."[12]

This seminal principle of the Founding Fathers was rejected by President Reagan. He inherited a modestly progressive tax system from President Carter and rapidly began replacing it with a flat one. A flat tax is where you, me, and the billionaires David Koch and Bill Gates all pay the same proportion of income as taxes. Aristotelian logic forcefully rejects flat taxes, because unequals are treated equally. Like Aristotle, Adam Smith wrote about the wisdom of avoiding such tax inequity. Smith had four maxims of taxation, and his first was progressivity based on ability-to-pay:

> "The subjects of every state ought to contribute toward the support of the government, as nearly as possible, in proportion to their respective abilities."[13]

Like citizens in all rich democracies, Americans pay a variety of taxes. Ensuring that progressivity prevails requires evaluating their cumulative impact, as explained in a 2007 tax policy concept paper by the American Institute of Certified Public Accountants: "Equity should be evaluated within the context of the entire tax system, not just the income tax."[14] Ability-to-pay has historically been achieved in America through a greater reliance on progressive income taxes than on sales, payroll, and other fixed-rate (and thus regressive) taxes, which extract a disproportionate share of earnings from the middle class.

It was that tradition which Ronald Reagan and his Bush successors abandoned. Their income tax rate cuts for the affluent, coupled with higher payroll, gasoline, and other regressive taxes, launched *de facto* tax-class warfare some 30 years ago. A nonpartisan Congressional Budget Office report in October 2011 examined the outcome, highlighting the impact between 1979 and 2007 of the Reagan era's tax structure shift this way:

> "The equalizing effect of federal taxes was smaller [in 2007] . . . the composition of federal revenues shifted away from progressive income taxes to the less-progressive payroll taxes."[15]

As recently as 2011, President Reagan's acolyte, Martin Feldstein, continued to lobby for this regressive tax shifting, urging the Congressional Joint Select Committee on Deficit Reduction to further cut taxes on the affluent and raise them on the middle class.[16] Feldstein was President Reagan's Chairman of the Council of Economic Advisors. Here is how David Cay Johnston explained the goal of this tax-shifting strategy conducted over the last three decades:

> "Since at least 1983 it has been the explicit, but unstated, policy in Washington to let the richest Americans pay a smaller portion of their incomes in taxes and to defer more of their taxes, which amounts to a stealth tax cut, while collecting more in taxes from those in the middle class."[17]

Because federal taxes are the major source of progressivity in America, Reagan's income tax cuts at the top sharply reduced overall progressivity. The outcome is depicted in Chart 9.1, reproducing statistics from the Tax Foundation. By 2004, the top 20 percent (quintile) of households were paying a lower share of total income in combined federal, state, and local taxes than families in the next highest quintile. In fact, the skewed Reagan and Bush cuts on elite earners caused their tax burden to fall so much that it now closely tracks the national average and is scarcely higher than middle-class tax burdens. At the other end, rising payroll and other regressive taxes have caused the tax burden of the poorest American households to rise; it is about 75 percent of the national average now.

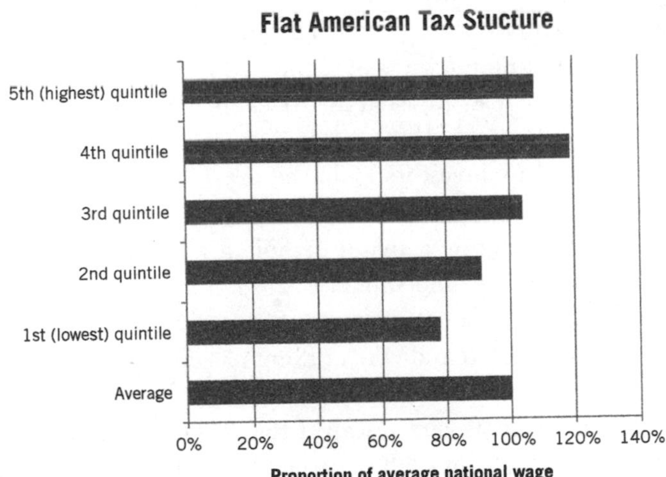

Chart 9.1. Household tax burden compared to average burden (100%).
Sources: Congressional Budget Office, "Data on the Distribution of Federal Taxes and Household Income," April 2009. Also: Andrew Chamberlain and Gerald Prante, "Who Pays Taxes and Who Receives Government Spending?" Tax Foundation Working Paper No 1, March 2007.

We know that Reagan-era presidents cut tax rates on higher incomes. How (and why) did they raise taxes on families in the middle, as Murray Rothbard explained in an epigraph to this chapter?

Raising Taxes on the Middle Class: The Alternative Minimum Tax

Reagan was borrowing $1 of every $3 he was spending by 1983 because of his large tax cuts. Budget deficits were up sharply, the government till empty.[18] Unwilling to cut much spending and adamantly against reversing his tax cuts on higher incomes, President Reagan anxiously sought new revenue. He contrived to raise two taxes on middle-class families, the Alternative Minimum Tax (AMT) and the payroll tax. Here is what happened.

The AMT was originally established in 1970 as a tax-reform device to ensure that millionaires paid at least some taxes. President Reagan made two changes in 1982 that spread its reach to also include the middle class. First, he required taxpayers to include some deductions heavily utilized by the middle class in calculating the tax base used for AMT, such as medical expenses and even the standard deduction. That greatly reduced the amount of these deductions. Lower deductions meant higher taxes.

Second, he eliminated the inflation indexation of the AMT. That raised the tax bill for millions of upper-middle-income taxpayers as inflation has since relentlessly pushed their income above the eligibility threshold for the AMT. Back in 1987, for example, only 140,000 mostly millionaire households paid the AMT tax; due to inflation; in 2009, however, some 4.5 million filers paid the AMT tax.

President Reagan also adjusted the AMT in 1986 to reduce its impact on high-income households by removing capital gains income and dividends received by investors from the tax. That completely nullified the original intent of the AMT, and saves investors about $90 billion annually.[19] This change is a major reason for the low tax burden of high-income households and thus, for the flat American tax structure. Economics reporter James B. Stewart of the *New York Times* explains how it happened in 1986 and why nothing has changed since:

> "The fact that capital gains escaped the AMT is testament to the power of the capital gains lobby, crucial Republican legislators, and their allies, who believe that low capital gains rates promote investment, hiring, and economic growth."[20]

Raising Taxes on the Middle Class: The Payroll Tax

The other major tax shifting onto the middle class by President Reagan was an increase in the payroll tax, which funds Social Security and Medicare. This is a sharply regressive tax, falling most heavily on middle- and working-class Americans; along with the AMT, it's an important reason their tax burden today exceeds that of many millionaires.

The regressivity of the payroll tax occurs, in part, because the payroll tax is not imposed on incomes above a certain level. Self-employed financial wizards or craftsmen such as carpenters, for example, paid a Social Security payroll tax of 12.4 percent on the first $110,100 of net income in 2012, but no tax on the balance of any income above that. Thus Warren Buffett—with an income 600 times larger than the successful carpenter with an income of $110,100 in 2012—paid the same Social Security tax amount.

Ronald Reagan had long harbored ideological objections to the Social Security and Medicare programs established during the New Deal era. At one point, he even advocated the *de facto* abolition of Social Security, a political embarrassment most of Reagan's admirers would just as soon forget. He proposed that participation in Social Security be made voluntary, knowing that higher-income folks with assets would immediately depart the program. Biographer Lou Cannon explained Reagan's mischievous proposal this way:

> "This idea would have undermined the system by depriving Social Security of the contributions of millions of the nation's highest-paid workers. In 1976, he said that Social Security 'could have made a provision for those who could do better on their own,' and suggested that such recipients be allowed to leave the program. . . . This declaration sent shudders through the ranks of Reagan's political advisers, who knew his true feelings about Social Security."[21]

Eager to find revenue to offset his tax cuts for top earners, Reagan's dislike of Social Security made it a fat target in his mind's eye. But raising middle-class taxes is tricky politically. His strategy was to obfuscate that goal by artfully creating a bogus Social Security "funding" crisis. The mythmaking worked this way: by the mid-1980s, dedicated payroll tax revenue for Social Security was projected to cover slightly less than 100 percent of Social Security benefit outlays. The remedy was simple: modest adjustments to tax rates and benefits to close the gap in perpetuity and place Social Security on a strict pay-as-you-go basis. In fact, modest future payroll tax hikes were already in law for that very reason.

Those adjustments already in law would preclude any funding crisis, but not Reagan's need for a geyser of new tax revenue. He solved his dilemma by ignoring the facts, arguing that Social Security was in jeopardy. The next step was to address the sudden new funding crisis by creating a Washington committee to frame the Social Security funding issue on his terms, this one headed by his trusted ally, Alan Greenspan. Here is how David Cay Johnston described events:

> "A commission, chaired by Alan Greenspan . . .said disaster was looming. If nothing was done, Greenspan said, Social Security would start running in the red, forcing the government to borrow money to pay benefits."[22]

The solution this stacked commission proposed was immediately higher payroll taxes to generate considerably more tax revenue than needed to fund Social Security. That was also when the Social Security earnings ceiling ($110,100 in 2012) was capped, ensuring the needed revenue geyser would flow mostly from middle- and working-class employees.

Three decades later, the success of this tax-shifting strategy remains evident in the fact that most Americans now pay *more* in payroll taxes than as actual income taxes.

And what a geyser it turned out to be, producing in the intervening years 20 percent *more* revenue than needed to close the Social Security gap, a surfeit of $1.7 trillion in tax receipts since 1983. The alternative solution of modestly tweaking payroll taxes and benefits to keep Social Security on a pay-as-you-go basis would have left that $1.7 trillion in family pockets. The amount translates to an average of more than $10,000 that would have been retained by each family. Here is how David Cay Johnston summarized the outcome:

> "Social Security taxes were used to pay the ordinary bills of the government, making up for the taxes that were no longer being paid by the rich, because of the 1981 income tax cuts. . . . What the government actually did with the excess Social Security taxes was use them to allow the rich to enjoy big tax cuts. It used the excess Social Security taxes to make up for part of the taxes from which the rich were excused in 1981."[23]

Shifting Taxes from Unearned Income onto Wages

The Reagan era also accentuated the difference in the taxation of work versus the taxation of income from capital. The changes were at odds with the principle embodied in the sixteenth amendment to the Constitution establishing the federal income tax. Enacted in 1913, the earliest income taxes applied solely to high incomes, including wealth transfers and wealthy estates, as David Cay Johnston explained:

> "Back then, income from capital was taxed more heavily than income from wages in the belief that it was morally offensive to take more money earned by the sweat of one's brow than from money obtained by clipping coupons."[24]

Even the most extreme robber barons of the day agreed, including the Gilded Age mogul, Andrew W. Mellon, who deigned later to serve Presidents Warren G. Harding, Calvin Coolidge, and Herbert Hoover as US Secretary of the Treasury. Mellon was far richer even than Croesus, King of Lydia, the first presumably to mint gold coins; Malcolm Gladwell ranks Mellon sixth among history's richest, behind Czar Nicholas II of Russia, but ahead of Basil II of Byzantium and the richest Pharaoh of all, Amenophis II.[25]

Richer than Pharaoh, billionaire Mellon was no socialist.* He was a genuine *laissez-faire* capitalist, believing that the Great Depression occurring on his watch served a useful purpose by wringing excesses from the system, eliminating what he termed "less competent people," in favor of "enterprising people." Ayn Rand must have loved this guy. President Herbert Hoover later wrote that this arrogant and grim robber baron urged him to, "Liquidate labor, liquidate stocks, liquidate the farmer, liquidate real estate. It will purge the rottenness out of the system."[26] Mellon was quite careful not to include his Gulf Oil among those who should be bankrupted, however.

Tough medicine for the tens of millions of struggling farmers, small businesses, and families of his day! Yet even one of the most ruthless, richest, insensitive, exploitative, and devoutly capitalist figures in world history drew the line at taxing work equal to or more than unearned income such as interest and dividends. Here is what Mellon wrote about the wisdom of taxing income from work at a lower rate than investments in his 1924 book, *Taxation: The People's Business*:

> "In the first case, the income is uncertain and limited in duration; sickness or death destroys it and old age diminishes it; in the other, the

*To the contrary, Mellon had a billionaire's sense of entitlement: he was a tax cheat. Even while overseeing the tax system as US Secretary of the Treasury, Mellon illegally used "fictitious gifts as a tax-dodging device," reports economic historian Liaquat Ahamed, *Lords of Finance* (New York: Penguin Group, 2009), 440.

> source of income continues; the income may be disposed of during a man's life and it descends to his heirs. . . . Surely we can afford to make a distinction between the people whose only capital is their mental and physical energy and the people whose income is derived from investments. Such a distinction would mean much to millions of American workers and would be an added inspiration to the man who must provide a competence during his few productive years to care for himself and his family when his earnings capacity is at an end."[27]

While President Reagan reoriented the Republican Party away from Mellon, some Democrats, including President Clinton, went along, too. Even so, Democratic politicians have been generally far more loyal to Mellon's principle, insisting in 1988, for example, that the tax on capital gains be raised from 20 percent to equal the top marginal tax rate on wages at 28 percent, an equivalence that was a watershed event in tax history. But that epic movement toward fulfilling Mellon's philosophy was only momentary. A gap in rates between wages and capital gains was opened anew by President H.W. Bush after only two years, the inspiring moment lost. And some time later in 1997, President Clinton assented to the demand of Congressional Republicans to cut the tax rate on capital gains back down to 20 percent.

This chapter has highlighted how the American tax burden was redistributed onto the middle class during the Reagan era. Another element of Reaganomics is reliance on debt to fund tax cuts, debt that will now be serviced and repaid in the future disproportionately by the middle class. Moreover, borrowing a billion dollars a day or more from thrifty German, Chinese, French, and Japanese families to give an average $46,000 tax cut to millionaires is scarcely a policy crafted to meet the economic challenges confronting most American families.

CHAPTER 10

"DEFICITS DON'T MATTER"

"The greatest credit bubble in history."[1]

JOHN PLENDER,
***Financial Times*, September 19, 2008**

"Reagan proved deficits don't matter."[2]

Vice President DICK CHENEY,
As quoted by US Secretary of the Treasury Paul O'Neill
November 2002

"Avoid the impulse to live only for today, plundering for our own ease and convenience, the precious resources of tomorrow."[3]

President DWIGHT DAVID EISENHOWER,
Farewell Address

"Admittedly the most embarrassing failure of Reaganomic goals is the deficit."[4]

MURRAY N. ROTHBARD,
***Mises Daily*, June 9, 2004**

The only office of the Jackson County Bank sat out where wildcats roamed, several days' ride west of the tiny trapper village of Detroit. Even so, promissory notes issued by Jackson circulated across Michigan during 1838; tradesmen accepted them as currency, although probably at a discount. It was far easier to use the discounted notes at the local sawmill or general store than make the hard horseback ride through dense woods for days to redeem them in full value for the promised gold or silver. Passing them along—and quickly—was also the smart move, because it turned out that Jackson dollars were worthless, the trip to redeem them certain to be futile.

The species, or money in coin, backing Jackson promissory notes was kept in nine strongboxes beneath the rustic bank counter in the distant wood. Here is the report of Michigan bank commissioners, who finally got around to examining Jackson County in 1839.

> "Beneath the counter of the bank, nine boxes were pointed out by the teller, as containing one thousand dollars each. The teller selected one of the boxes and opened it; this was examined and appeared to be a full box of silver American half dollars. One of the commissioners then selected a box, which he opened, and found the same to contain a superficies only of silver, while the remaining portion consisted of lead and ten-penny nails. The commissioner then proceeded to open the remaining seven boxes; they presented the same contents precisely, with a single exception in which the substratum was window glass broken into small pieces."[5]

Credit was created from thin air during this era of wildcat banking, so much that people in some victimized states such as Michigan suffered cash losses of 30–60 percent during regular bank panics. Banking historian Bray Hammond even argues that people in states without any banks in this era "were better off than the people of Michigan, Wisconsin, Indiana, and Illinois," which allowed wildcats.[6] Reforms were tried, including an Illinois law adopted in 1857, requiring banks be located in villages of at least 200 souls.[7] But this era of credit binging only ended with enactment of the National Bank Act in 1863, which created a uniform currency and effective regulation, a system heavily policed later by the gold standard. That is why it was nearly 120 years later in the Reagan era before the next great American credit binge occurred.

It seems intuitive to portray the Reagan era as a replay of the Roaring Twenties debt binge, where undisciplined stock speculation ended in the Great Depression. In reality, the (quite imperfect) gold standard in place during the latter nineteenth century until 1971 limited wholesale credit expansion. Thus, the more apt historical analogy to the Reagan era is the wildcat banking era from 1837 to 1863 prior to the gold standard.

The discipline over government credit creation imposed by the gold standard disappeared when President Nixon took America off gold in 1971. Other nations quickly followed suit. With that constraint absent when President Reagan took office, he and the successor Bush presidents acted like wildcat bankers. They deregulated banking oversight while engineering an unprecedented credit binge based on, well, iron washers, broken glass, and the same promise to repay that supported Jackson County dollars 140 years earlier. Credit expanded dramatically in the private sector, but also in the public sector, because they rejected government fiscal discipline: taxes were cut, spending jumped, and budget deficits burgeoned.

The Greatest Credit Bubble in History: The National Debt Increased Tenfold During the Reagan era

The combined budget deficits of the three Reagan and Bush presidents increased America's national debt more than tenfold, a startling statistic. That increase was vastly greater than the Obama deficits.

Moreover, their deregulation ethos denigrated prudent bank lending and credit standards, empowering financial engineers to spawn repeated asset bubbles inflated by insider S&L loans, technology stock speculation, loose credit standards, and new financial products like no-document mortgage loans. Easy credit practices swept up households as well, with loans made to aspiring homeowners and speculators alike, regardless of credit or work history. The outcome was that total American debt of all types more than *doubled* as a share of GDP during the Reagan era, too much of it opaque risky junk quality and worse, inadequately backed by bank reserves. The aftermath in 2007/2008 of these three decades of irresponsible fiscal leadership retaught the age-old lesson from the days of the swindler John Law: deregulation of commerce, and especially of finance, always ends badly in instability, joblessness, and wealth destruction.

Here are the facts: the Reagan era saw a jump to $53 trillion in overall American debt, from $5 trillion when that president took office. As the sober-minded *Financial Times* columnist John Plender concluded, this was "the greatest credit bubble in history." It exceeded even the Spanish splurge based on Potosi silver or the final decades of the Roman Empire in the third and fourth centuries AD, when fifty tons of silver coinage was minted each year.[8] Toward the tail end of this credit binge (during the administration of George W. Bush), America was borrowing a scarcely imaginable 70 percent of the world's surplus savings.[9]

How did the world's worst credit binge happen on the watch of small-government presidents? Let's begin with the federal budget. You are going to learn why economists, especially conservative economists, are harshly critical of President Reagan, the most fiscally irresponsible president in American history.

Borrow and Spend Reaganomics

The charismatic Ronald Reagan borrowed 19 cents of every dollar he spent as president, nearly tripling the national debt—the worst record of any peacetime US president.[10]

Think of his behavior this way. Since colonial times, American presidents had only resorted to sizable government budget deficits temporarily to address national crises such as the Civil War, Great Depression, or World War II. President Reagan converted that rare emergency practice into routine everyday policy, as explained by an obviously exasperated and disgusted Rothbard:

> "[Reagan deficits] seems to be permanent, despite desperate attempts to cook the figures in one-shot reductions . . . federal deficits now seem to be a recent, but still permanent, part of the American heritage."[11]

Worse, the iconic conservative Rothbard found President Reagan hypocritical because "the proposer of the biggest deficits in American history has been calling vehemently for a Constitutional amendment to require a balanced budget . . . trying to make Congress the fall guy for our deficit economy."[12]

Before Ronald Reagan, presidents managed the United States like governments manage Australia or Vermont, careful with their dimes and dollars. But the gullible President Reagan's evident belief that deficits don't matter sanctified a historic Washington shift to fiscal profligacy. He transformed what had been the rare transitory emergency practice of sizable budget deficits into a planned policy of enduring annual structural deficits.

In doing so, President Reagan turned his back on the fiscal prudence of presidents including Calvin Coolidge, Dwight David Eisenhower, John F. Kennedy, Jimmy Carter, and even Lyndon Johnson. They believed that a dollar spent should be paid with taxes. Not President Reagan; his philosophy of pursuing deficits of choice created enormous heartburn for the fiscally prudent of all political persuasions, especially among economists.

One of the greatest economic rivalries of the twentieth century, for example, pitted the Englishman John Maynard Keynes against Friedrich Hayek of the Austrian school. Hayek not only authored *The Road to Serfdom*, cautioning against overbearing and irresponsible government, he gained fame for predicting the great crash of 1929.[13] Like Smith, Keynes believed that markets serving careless mankind require oversight by careful and prudent regulators. Hayek distrusted central regulation of any sort, preferring a government bound by strict rules.[14] The Keynes viewpoint was explained this way by *Washington Post* columnist David Ignatius:

> "It wasn't that he liked government spending, but that he recognized that markets sometimes overreact—amplifying the fears and preferences of individual behavior that makes everyone worse off."[15]

For that and other insights, Keynes became the greatest economist of the twentieth century, even acknowledged by conservatives like N. Gregory Mankiw, who served as George W. Bush's Chairman of the Council of Economic Advisors:

> "If you were going to turn to only one economist to understand the problems facing the economy, there is little doubt that the economist would be John Maynard Keynes. Although Keynes died more than a half-century ago, his diagnosis of recessions and depressions remains the foundation of modern macroeconomics."[16]

Their philosophical differences aside, Keynes and Hayek admired one another, Hayek terming him "the one really great man I ever knew, and for whom I had unbounded admiration."[17] Both men would have been dismayed by the behavior of Ronald Reagan overtly crafting routine, large structural deficits merely to lower taxes on the wealthy. During eight years of peace in office, that president never once managed a balanced budget, precisely the sort of deplorable behavior that Hayek had come to expect of feckless American politicians.[18] Each would have seen the outcome in 2007/2008 as the inevitable consequence of Reagan's abuse of debt; with his remarkable track record, Hayek probably would have predicted the onset of the banking crisis to the month.

The biting criticism of President Reagan's budget policies by conservatives is justified because as the Reagan era matured, the only fiscally responsible Republicans were in graveyards. His presidency caused a stark transition that resulted in this proud party engineering the greatest peacetime deficits and greatest credit bubble in history. Back in 1963, President John F. Kennedy wanted to cut taxes. Democratic officials agreed, but the Republican Party resisted. Here is how tax authority and former colleague Bruce Bartlett explained events:

> "Kennedy's tax plan was exactly what Republicans today recommend, but they opposed it strenuously at the time. The Republican members of the [tax writing] Ways and Means Committee unanimously opposed it, saying, 'It is morally and fiscally wrong, and will do irreparable damage to the Republic.' When the tax cut came up for a vote in the House of Representatives on Sept. 25, 1963, only 48 Republicans supported it; 126 voted against it."[19]

The transition to spendthrifts went swiftly after 1980. By 1988, Pete Peterson was nearly a lone Republican voice, his disappointment and harsh evaluation of the fiscally irresponsible and self-indulgent President Reagan evident:

> "Reaganomics was founded on a bold new vision for America, yet today—another irony—we hear every politician who is warming up for the 1988 campaign, Republican and Democrat alike, complaining about the lack of vision in America. The reason we feel adrift is that we are waking up to the fact that blind and self-indulgent *gusto* is not vision at all."[20]

Writing nearly a generation later in 2010, here is a trenchant look back by President Reagan's budget director David Stockman:

> "Republicans used to believe that prosperity depended upon the regular balancing of accounts. . . . But the new catechism, as practiced by Republican policymakers for decades now, has amounted to little more than money printing and deficit finance. . . . This approach has not simply made a mockery of traditional party ideals. It has also led to the serial financial bubbles and Wall Street depredations that have crippled our economy. . . . This debt explosion has resulted not from big spending by the Democrats, but instead the Republican Party's embrace, about three decades ago, of the insidious doctrine that 'deficits don't matter' if they result from tax cuts."[21]

Reagan tripled the size of annual federal budget deficits to average 5 percent of GDP per year during his eight years in office (they averaged 1.7 percent during the 1970s). Worse, by politically credentialing sizable deficits, he freed successors George H.W. Bush and George W. Bush to engineer similar deficits.

"Starve the Beast"

Recall that President Reagan was unfamiliar with economics. Thus, the endorsement of these deficits of choice by advisors including Friedman, Feldstein, and former Federal Reserve Chairman Alan Greenspan was vital. As Stockman argues, Milton Friedman was his chief enabler, convincing Republican presidents since Richard Nixon that deficits don't matter, and to rely solely on washers and broken glass.

Ignoring history is especially parlous when it comes to credit. These seasoned economists surely knew the dismal history of nations broken by excessive debt. Starving economies of credit is a sure path to societal calamity and an observation that made Keynes and later Milton

Friedman justly famous. But the Austrian School, backed by history, also taught that excessive credit expansion is just as dangerous, which is why they support the gold standard. Like the bears' porridge, a Goldilocks economy cannot have either too much or too little credit. America struck that balance in the decades after World War II, which featured tough commitments to control government deficits, and regulations that limited consumer credit and credit leveraging by financial intermediaries. That economic balance enabled America's national debt, accumulated mostly in World War II, to decline by three-quarters measured as a share of GDP until President Reagan's inauguration.

The experts around Reagan surely knew this history, but it seems they feared missing an opportunity to cut taxes more than soaring national debt. For ideological (and in Greenspan's case, political) reasons, they hoped this time would be different. They should have been cautious about the dangers of unbridled tax cuts; the dangers were unmistakable and would grow enormous. Spending jumped during the Reagan era, but starving the government of revenue is the biggest reason why the national debt rose more than tenfold during the Reagan era: three decades of tax cuts reduced the federal tax base from 19 percent of GDP, when Ronald Reagan was elected, to 14.9 percent in 2010—a level not seen since Harry Truman was president.

Why didn't economists like Friedman or Greenspan move to halt the tax cuts causing the soaring national debt? A major reason is that, like Ayn Rand or wealthy donors to the Tea Party, they loathe government more than they like fiscal prudence. In one of the oddest episodes in American economic history, brilliant conservative economists like Friedman formed an ideological Greek Chorus, arguing that Reagan's unprecedented deficits of choice served a vital national objective. The deficits they caused must surely cap the size of government. Taking a page from Reagan who blamed Congress for his spending, Friedman wrote that deficits are "the only effective restraint on congressional spending," in the *Wall Street Journal* in 1988.[22]

I am not kidding. Despite soaring federal debt, Friedman remained delusional until the end about the mythical power of deficits to tame the beast government. When the large tax cuts of President George W. Bush produced sizable deficits, for example, Friedman went all-in again:

> "If anything, at the moment, the large deficit has a positive effect of holding down further spending. . . . In that sense, it is a good thing. But it is not a good thing if produced by more spending."[23]

Termed "starve the beast," this made-up notion lacks any basis in economic theory or history: tax cuts obviously do not shrink government;

they just balloon government debt. The Republican Party canard that cutting taxes is good policy in any and all conditions, never mind the inevitable deficits, perhaps originated with a *Wall Street Journal* editorial writer named Jude Wanniski in 1976.[24] Candidate Reagan and other *faux* small government politicians ever since have adopted that notion, providing ideological glue for a political party that otherwise is hopelessly schizophrenic about government spending. Its officials campaign promising small government while attacking opponents as in 2012 for cutting entitlements like Medicare. To this day, the Republican Party continues to find much of its political allure and comfort in the mistaken belief that tax cuts remediate any and all economic concerns. Even amid trillion-dollar deficits in 2012, a 20 percent across-the-board tax cut was a major plank of presidential candidate Mitt Romney. President Reagan's budget director, David Stockman, in mid-2012 explained the outcome:

> "Thirty years of Republican apostasy—a once-grand party's embrace of the welfare state, and the Wall Street-coddling bailout state—have crippled the engines of capitalism and buried us in debt."[25]

Amazingly, this apostasy has left the Democratic Party as the only force for fiscal rectitude in America, as lamented by *Financial Times* columnist Martin Wolf in mid-2010:

> "This is extraordinarily dangerous. The danger does not arise from the fiscal deficits of today, but the attitudes to fiscal policy, over the long run, of one of the two main parties. Those radical conservatives (a small minority, I hope) who want to destroy the credit of the US federal government may succeed. If so, that would be the end of the US era of global dominance. The destruction of fiscal credibility could be the outcome of the policies of the party that considers itself the most patriotic."[26]

One of the most remarkable aspects of this transformation of the Republican Party to enablers of enormous structural budget deficits has been how few members challenged Friedman and Greenspan. Until the Tea Party election of 2010, almost all Congressional Republicans went along, as Rothbard noted:

> "conservative Republicans . . . found themselves adjusting rather easily to the new era of huge permanent deficits."[27]

Republican Party Budget Deficits

Ronald Reagan's attributes, especially his joviality, his ability to inspire, and his fear of nuclear weapons, demand admiration. But balancing a checkbook was obviously not one of his talents. Ronald Reagan proved no more resistant to the siren call of deficit spending and easy credit than the most spendthrift Pharaoh, Roman emperor, or Oriental potentate shaving silver coins to debase their monetary base. In the Dark Ages, as trade dwindled and copper mines closed, coins became so shaven that some claimed they could float, like Jackson dollars 600 years later.[28]

In aping that behavior, Ronald Reagan was just another in a long line of irresponsible spendthrifts. His deliberate decision to pursue deficits of choice repudiated the foundation of the golden age, replacing it with the notion that America could somehow routinely prosper beyond its means by borrowing from its children. It is difficult to believe he was so gullible and untutored in history, but the proof is there, reproduced in Chart 10.1.

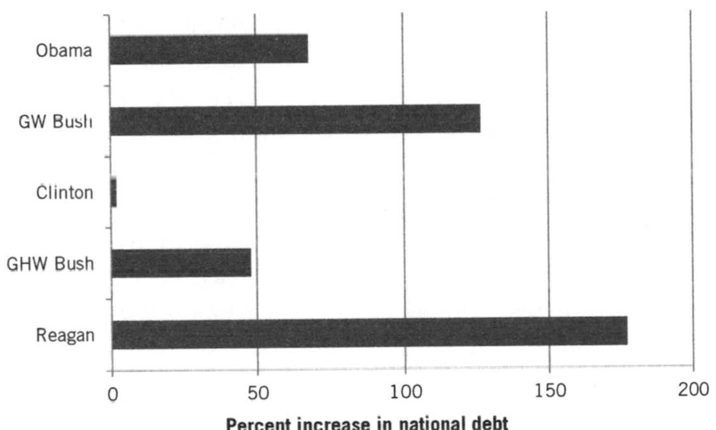

Chart 10.1. Increase in publicly held debt, Fiscal Years 1982–89 (Reagan), FY'90–93 (GHW Bush), FY'94–01 (Clinton), FY'02–09 (GW Bush) and FY'10–13(Obama I).
Source: US Department of the Treasury and Office of Management and Budget.

Here is how historian Paul Kennedy, in his book, *The Rise and Fall of the Great Powers*, describes the dangerous consequences of the Reagan budget deficits that converted America into an international financial supplicant:

"The only way the United States can pay its way in the world is by importing ever-larger sums of capital, which has transformed it from being the world's largest creditor to the world's largest debtor nation

> *in the space of a few years* [Kennedy's italics]. Compounding this problem—in the eyes of many critics, *causing* this problem—have been the budgetary policies of the US government itself. . . . The decisions taken by the Reagan administration in the early 1980s—i.e., large-scale increases in defense expenditures, plus considerable decreases in taxation, but without significant reductions in federal spending elsewhere—have produced extraordinary rises in the deficit, and consequently in the national debt."[29]

President Reagan's fiscal extravagance, and that of his successor George H.W. Bush, is why the Texan Ross Perot ran for president in 1992. Perot's quixotic campaign for fiscal rectitude succeeded, in the sense that his presence on the ballot enabled the election of President Clinton, who did in fact balance the national accounts. In contrast to President Reagan, Clinton proved to be a fiscal tightwad, raising taxes and limiting spending as we have learned, to the extent that half of his budgets actually ended in surplus. Thanks in part to outside factors like robust GDP growth, President Clinton added virtually nothing to the debt.

In fact, Clinton's budgetary record is remarkable, with credit due to his Treasury Secretaries Lloyd M. Bentsen, Robert Rubin, and Lawrence H. Summers. It was a proud time to be a Treasury official. Despite the bloated national debt that he inherited, Clinton controlled spending and raised taxes sufficiently to set the nation on a course to entirely eliminate the national debt. We know that because the Congressional Budget Office (CBO) in January 2001 predicted Clinton's policies would entirely pay off the national debt by 2008. Key was a tax increase in 1993, which every Republican in Congress opposed, arguing it would slow growth. Events proved them wrong, confirming that tax rates have little to do with economic performance. The weak performance of the economy in the years following the George W. Bush tax cuts further confirmed that truth.

Then George W. Bush arrived. Bush's father became the president who ended the Cold War by, well . . . doing nothing but allowing trends established under Reagan and Premier Gorbachev to play out. To become the towering president who eliminated America's national debt, all George W. Bush needed to do was, well . . . nothing. The heavy lifting had already been done by Bill Clinton. But like his father and President Reagan before him, George W. Bush believed that deficits don't matter and so reversed Clinton's successful policies. And just as he was earlier in the Reagan era, Alan Greenspan was pivotal in that decision.

It was a breathtaking moment in American fiscal history with budget surpluses projected to entirely eliminate the national debt in just seven years. But in one of the oddest and most memorable incidents in American fiscal history, the chairman of the Federal Reserve was aghast at the prospect. Days after George Bush took office, Greenspan appeared before the Senate Budget Committee on January 25, 2001, eagerly endorsing big tax cuts. His logic was bizarre, breathtaking nonsense: Clinton's budget surpluses were so large and certain that they would pay off the national debt in 2008, requiring the US Treasury to then invest further surpluses in private sector assets and cut taxes. Avoiding that prospect "required" immediate tax cuts to eliminate the budget surpluses.[30] And the Republican dominated Congress and George W. Bush quickly agreed.

The following year, Greenspan and President Bush also abandoned the 1990 pay-as-you-go budget rules (Paygo) instrumental in creating the Clinton surpluses. Paygo required that spending increases or tax cuts be revenue neutral. A precious and most remarkable opportunity to put America in the tiny category of fiscal prudes like Australia was lost.

War and other spending in the years that followed saw government outlays rise from 18.2 percent of GDP in 2001 to 20.7 percent in 2008, while the sizable Bush tax cuts reduced revenues. The deficit and national debt soared once again, as it had under Reagan; two weeks before President Obama took office, the CBO projected deficits for the last Bush fiscal year (containing no Obama initiatives) of a startling $1.3 trillion. Here is how the appalled editors at the *Financial Times* described what had happened under Alan Greenspan and George W. Bush:

> "It is hard to remember that the US was on a promising fiscal path in the 1990s. But the boom of the 2000s was frittered away in tax cuts, wars, and spending commitments that left the public purse in a parlous state. . . ."[31]

When President Bush departed in 2009, the national debt of $11.9 trillion was over tenfold larger than the $900 billion debt inherited by Ronald Reagan in 1981 from President Carter. Except for the Great Depression and World War II, America had been generally self-sufficient in capital during the twentieth century. But during this Reagan era, America became a debtor nation as Paul Kennedy had noted, an importer of unprecedented amounts of capital with consumption outrunning production as net imports surged. America has spent "the equivalent of 106 percent of what we produce each year" for the past two decades, explained *Washington Post* columnist Steven Pearlstein in 2009.[32]

Taking office amid the most severe economic crisis in eighty years, the Obama administration playbook drew from the lesson of World War II, where traditional Keynesian pump priming with government deficits sparked a recovery. The Wall Street bailout and stimulus legislation of George W. Bush, and the subsequent stimulus legislation of Barack Obama, succeeded in preventing another depression. Republican officials in the years since have routinely lamented the resulting budget deficits as too large. Yet most economists of all persuasions, from Paul Krugman to Bruce Bartlett, believed them too feeble to restore robust economic growth and events have proven them correct.

Critics of the Obama budget deficits fail to note they are dwarfed by the enormous deficits of his three Republican predecessors. For example, here is Haley Barbour, a former Mississippi governor and chair of the Republican National Committee in mid-2012:

> "We've been a country for 236 years; it took us 233 years to run up $10 trillion worth of debt, and another $5 trillion in just three years. This is mind-boggling to Americans."[33]

What's mind boggling is how this and other partisan politicians obfuscated the fact that virtually all of that $10 trillion debt was accumulated by President Reagan and the Bush presidents.[34] In fact, as budget statistics reproduced in the previous chart indicate, President Reagan alone increased the national debt by three times more than President Obama, and President George W. Bush twice as much. Taken together, the three Republican presidents increased the national debt by more than ten times or over 1,000 percent compared to the 60 percent increase under President Obama.

Deficits Do Matter: The Reagan era Created the American Debt Crisis

Vice President Richard Cheney was wrong—deficits *do* matter. Deficits matter a lot, because history teaches that excessive debt is a slippery slope threatening national bankruptcy—a reality visited recently on Iceland, Ireland, and across southern Europe. Nations can become bankrupt, and plenty of them do, just like Lehman Brothers, General Motors, and the Austrian bank CreditAnstalt in 1931, whose collapse helped trigger the Great Depression.

The difference is that nations enjoy some headroom, during which national debt can grow as a consequence of deficit spending for emergencies. But that headroom is not infinitely large. Researchers at Stanford call this headroom "fiscal space."[35] The most commonly discussed measure of fiscal space before national bankruptcy looms is the ratio of national (or sovereign) debt to GDP. That ratio is zero when a nation has no government debt and rises as deficits accumulate. A number of economists have examined sovereign debt statistics and the evidence indicates that no specific threshold for a danger zone exists. While that suggests the recent austerity policies in America and Europe have been misplaced, history clearly teaches that the use of budget deficits demands prudence clearly lacking during the Reagan era.

The implications of the deficits of choice accumulated during the Reagan era through 2008 may now be evident to you. They vaporized most of America's fiscal space. Here is the evidence: America's debt/GDP ratio peaked above 100 in the wake of World War II. It dwindled steadily thereafter, due to rapid economic growth and inflation, dropping to 25.8 in the final year of the Carter Presidency, FY'81.[36]

Ronald Reagan's deficits of choice reversed that trend. In combination with the deficits of George H.W. Bush, the ratio almost doubled, rising sharply to 49.3 by FY'93. The fiscal probity of President Clinton caused the ratio to decline once again to 32.5 by FY'01 as he left office. But the deficits of President George W. Bush raised that ratio even above President Reagan, to 54.1 in his final budget, FY'09. And due mostly to the various G.W. Bush tax cuts, spending on wars and recession, that ratio continued rising under the Obama administration.

My point is, in pushing the US debt to GDP ratio from 25.8 in 1981 to 54.1 in 2009 for no good reason, the Reagan, G.H.W. Bush, and G.W. Bush deficits eliminated much of America's emergency fiscal space available to address economic crises or war needs.

The golden age proved that the best remedy for recession and for excessive sovereign debt is economic growth, but history also teaches that recovering higher economic growth requires fiscal stimulus. Now you see the problem: by squandering much of America's fiscal space, Reagan-era Republicans left President Obama with limited room to engineer another traditional, robust American Keynesian rebound.

In hindsight, we know the Reagan-era leaders and economic advisors had it entirely wrong. The Reagan-era deficits mattered, and they mattered a great deal. They have placed at jeopardy your prosperity, and your children's prosperity, in a way you likely never imagined, because the fiscal space denied the Obama administration portends years of slow growth ahead.

Credentialing Debt by Other Nations

Leaders are role models, and that is especially true of American presidents who serve as leaders of the free world. That caused the fiscal indulgence of President Reagan to reverberate quickly among other politicians, removing a restraint on a profession already predisposed to wildcat banking.

The reputation of profligate politicians is richly deserved, evidenced by the plague of bankruptcies in the past. At one time the richest nation on earth, Spain, subsequently went bankrupt seven times in the nineteenth century alone. And France was bankrupt eight times between 1500 and 1800, including the momentous debt crisis that precipitated the French Revolution: in 1788, a bankrupt and economically despairing Louis XVI foolishly convened the quarrelsome and disrespectful Estates General. This body of ambitious local leaders hadn't been convened by monarchs since 1614 for good reason. The outcome was revolution, a civil war, tumbrels, the guillotine, economic turmoil, and eventually, a military dictatorship and continent-wide war.[37] Little wonder that Adam Smith, gazing on these events across the North Sea from Scotland, was a debt scold who would have been disgusted by the behavior of Reagan-era America.

The discipline of the gold standard and prudence of American presidents produced some global fiscal stability in the post–World War II era. Between 1960 and the early 1980s, for example, severe sovereign credit crises involving default or restructuring afflicted fewer than 15 percent of countries. That was easily the lowest share since 1827. But, as economists Carmen Reinhart and Kenneth Rogoff document in their book, *This Time is Different,* the number of profligate nations that became severely indebted leaped in the Reagan era. By the end of Ronald Reagan's Presidency, nearly 40 percent of nations across the globe had succumbed to his siren song of wildcat banking and were dealing with severe debt crises.[38]

America hopefully will not face a debt crisis in the years ahead. But, as we see in the next chapter, the serial budget deficits of the Reagan era are just one element of a much more wide-ranging collapse of prudent American credit management that occurred during this period.

CHAPTER 11

ILLUSORY PROSPERITY

"Republicans have been oblivious to the grave danger of flooding financial markets with freely printed money and at the same time, removing traditional restrictions on leverage and speculation. As a result, the combined assets of conventional banks and the so-called shadow banking system, (including investment banks and finance companies) grew from a mere $500 billion in 1970 to $30 trillion by September 2008."[1]

DAVID STOCKMAN,
Reagan Administration Budget Director

"The US has lived on borrowed money for too long."[2]

WOLFGANG SCHÄUBLE,
German Finance Minister
November 2010

The economic consequences of the transformation in debt and credit along with the other elements of Reaganomics launched in 1981 have been dark for almost all Americans. A nation once paying the world's highest wages became deindustralized, and is now routinely out-exported by a host of other rich democracies whose more competitive enterprises pay employees $10-per-hour higher wages. Acolytes rightly laud President Reagan as a transformational figure—but the transformational economic era he and his successors engineered was to a meaner nation that stripped economic sovereignty from families, redistributed income upward and tax burdens downward, and diminished economic opportunity.

Much of the prosperity of the Reagan era was based on the nearly tenfold ($48 trillion) rise in new credit created from four sources: federal deficits; rising leverage in the financial sector; deregulation of finance; and expanding money and credit aggregates from aggressive central bank credit policies. The four elements boosted US consumption at the expense of savings and investment for the most mundane of political reasons: to resuscitate economic growth hobbled by Reaganomics. Here is how Joseph Stiglitz explained the slowdown in growth:

> "Redistribution from the bottom to the top of the kind that has been going on in the United States lowers total demand. And the weakness of the US economy arises out of deficient aggregate demand. The tax cuts passed under President George W. Bush . . . put the burden of attaining full employment on the Fed, which filled the gap by creating a bubble, through lax regulations and loose monetary policy. And the bubble induced the bottom 80 percent of Americans to consume beyond their means."[3]

Transforming a Nation of Savers and Investors into Debtors and Consumers

The American economy thrives on consumer spending, but the Reagan era featured wage and tax policies that hampered household spending. The solution that produced new, convenient sources of credit for households was deregulation of the financial sector. A consumption surge resulted; and like Washington, households came to rely on credit to live beyond their means, drawing in goods from across the world. Pete Peterson spelled it out this way:

> "Deficit spending, of course, has been the primary engine behind this consumption *bacchanalia*—a superhot and super-Keynesian demand-side tilt. . . . In every previous decade, we consumed slightly less than 90 percent of our increase in production; since the beginning of the 1980s, we have consumed 325 percent of it—the extra 235 percent being reflected in an unprecedented increase in per-worker debt abroad and a decline in per-worker investment at home. That is how we managed to create a make-believe 1980s—a decade of 'feeling good' and 'having it all.'"[4]

The credit-based prosperity of the Reagan era is most evident in the household sector.

Household Savings and Borrowing

Household consumption during the Reagan era was sustained by reduced savings and rising debt. The household savings rate as a share of disposable income trended down steadily in those decades, falling by half from 10 percent in the early 1980s to 5 percent in recent years.

In addition, household consumption was sustained by a significant rise in family borrowing. Households began borrowing heavily beginning in the mid-1990s, causing household debt in real terms to nearly triple, rising from $24,000 per family in 1989 to peak at $68,000 per family by 2007 (in inflation-adjusted 2007 dollars), before declining with the recession.[5]

This entire epoch was merely a repeat of the decade preceding the Great Depression. Nearly a century ago during the Roaring Twenties, households similarly exploited copious credit and weak financial regulation to raise consumption, while also using bucket shops and the like to speculate in stocks. Household debt as a share of GDP nearly doubled between the end of World War I and 1929, which is why the Twenties roared. Similarly, household debt as a share of income doubled from 60 percent in 1981 to 119 percent at the 2007 peak.[6] For families, borrowing as a basis for prosperity sharply contrasted with the foundation of prosperity for families during the golden age, when rising consumption was built on real wage gains, not credit card debt and home equity loans.

This increase in household debt, in combination with the rise in business sector debt and the national debt, caused total American debt to more than double since 1980, approaching 400 percent of GDP in recent years.[7] That surge even surpassed the historic high of 287 percent in 1933, as noted in Chart 11.1.

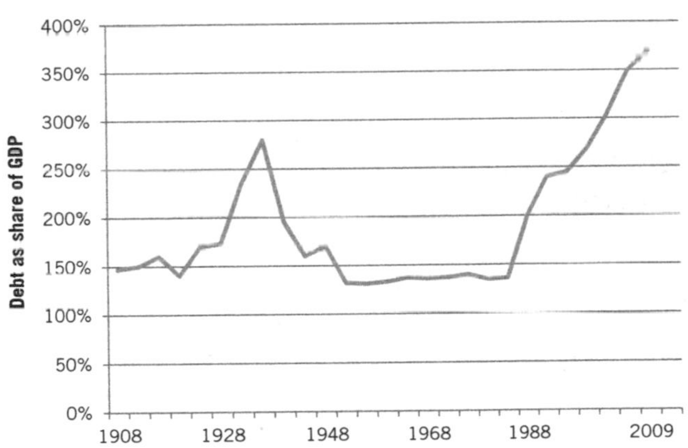

Chart 11.1. Total credit market public and private debt as a share of GDP.
Source: John Mauldin and Jonathan Tepper, Endgame, figure 1.1, St. Louis Federal Reserve and Census Bureau.

In dollar terms, as noted earlier, that debt rose from $5 trillion to $53 trillion in 2010, the rise acting as a growth accelerant. It enabled both President Reagan and the Bush presidents to increase economic growth with traditional Keynesian policies of tax cuts and higher spending.

The easy credit era also fed a generation-long surge in asset values for land and other physical assets, highlighted by bubbles in technology stocks and housing. These bubbles inevitably burst, as Keynes had explained seventy-five years ago: the Prisoner's Dilemma comes eventually to dictate behavior in a bubble environment, where cooperation among market participants proves unattainable. Some decide to cash out and run with their profits—eventually creating a speculative top—followed by a rush for the stairs and a price collapse with too many sellers suddenly chasing too few buyers. Here is how Keynes described this last stage of bubbles, as investors rush to offload abruptly unsalable assets:

> "It is, so to speak, a game of Snap, of Old Maid, of Musical Chairs—a pastime in which he is victor who says 'Snap!' neither too soon nor too late, who passes the Old Maid to his neighbor before the game is over, who secures a chair for himself when the music stops."[8]

The music stopped in 2007/2008 with almost all Americans holding an Old Maid card and the price has been steep: millions of jobs lost and several trillion dollars of household wealth vaporized, followed by years of anemic recovery as households deleverage to rebuild balance sheets. Instead of acting as temporary custodians of the economy and building prosperity for our children like Eisenhower, Kennedy, and Johnson, the politicians of the Reagan era acted like, well, profligate politicians intent on spiking growth to win reelection.

Debt-Averse Households in Family Capitalism Economies

The attitude toward debt in the family capitalism countries is more to the liking of Pete Peterson. The harsh lessons learned over its baleful past of wars, financial crises, and revolutions have encouraged a culture of caution in northern Europe. That attitude was reinforced by repeated real estate bubbles bursting on their doorsteps: the financial collapse of Norway (1987) and Finland (1991) and the 1992 bankruptcy of Sweden, where the bubble created by deregulation destroyed thousands of jobs. Their history has created extremely high public expectations that financial engineering and risk-taking by banks will be precluded by regulation and central bank credit controls, driven by a fear of inflation. "I haven't forgotten history . . . if you depend on paper money, you can lose everything," said Gert Heinz of Munich, quoted by *The New York Times* reporter Katrin Bennhold in October 2008.[9]

This wary culture means northern European households are debt averse. While 76 percent of US families were indebted in 2004, only 40 percent of Germans even owned a credit card, with academic research suggesting consumers there favor cash in order to more easily moderate spending. Australians are also far more comfortable paying for goods in cash than with credit.[10] Public policy reinforces prudence as noted by Sheldon Garon of the *New York Times* in 2011: "Supported by public opinion, policy makers in European countries have also restrained the expansion of consumer and housing credit, lest citizens become 'over-indebted.'"[11] Oh, and regulations preclude subprime mortgages.

The family capitalism countries display the Protestant ethic of thrift more so than Americans. Australians and northern Europeans are world-class savers, pinching pennies for years and salting away €3,000 year-end bonuses. As Americans used to do in the golden age, Australians saved 10 percent of their 2010 incomes, Germans 11 percent, and French households 15.3 percent.[12] To finance home purchases, the local *petit despote* bank loan officer in France will demand 20 percent down in cash, just like American bankers used to do. European families save for their first house the same way your parents or grandparents did, by living for years with relatives or in rentals. And they avoid the casino called stock markets. Despite high incomes and savings, few own stock outright; only 5.4 percent of Germans own stocks.[13]

Household savings is encouraged by public policies, including savings programs in schools for youths and postal savings programs accepting small deposits. They include the popular French Livret A accounts, tax-free and paying above market rates, and the ubiquitous government *Sparkassens* savings banks seemingly on every German corner.[14]

This mindset also carries over to the public square, where expectations are high for governments to promptly and efficiently ameliorate crises. For example, governments have programs to minimize enterprise layoffs during slow periods, and to ensure that credit continues to be available to employers. That includes the *Deutschlandfonds*, a €100 billion fund to support small- and medium-sized German firms.[15] In contrast, more than a few American banks utilized the Bush administration's bank bailout money for bonuses and mergers. M&T Bank, for example, received $600 million from the US Treasury and promptly used it to purchase Provident Bank.

Business sector practices also contributed to the American credit binge of recent decades, as we now see.

Higher Investment Bank Leverage and Deregulation of Derivatives

The American financial sector began life unregulated in the colonial era, and thus periodic banking crises burdened the real economy. The first was the panic of 1792, sparked by the collapse of a stock bubble involving Alexander Hamilton.[16] Regulation remained weak, causing crises to recur with regularity, most notably in 1873 and then the Great Depression. Beginning in the 1930s, however, comprehensive financial regulations were imposed broadly for the first time in American history. Banks were restricted in activities and the industry became boring as leverage declined and loan standards rose.

That stability diminished in the Reagan era, as the New Deal web of prudent and precautionary reforms began to be disassembled. Elimination of the firewall between banks and investment activities was an important milestone that occurred with abolition of the Glass-Steagall Act during the Clinton administration. That enabled banks whose deposits were insured by taxpayers to speculate on stocks, derivatives, and virtually anything else.

Another important milestone was Greenspan's abandonment of the Net Capitalization Rule in 2004. This so-called "Bear Stearns exemption" abolished the 1977 12:1 leverage cap requiring the five biggest investment banks to maintain $1 of reserves for every $12 invested.[17] With the cap lifted, leverage at these giant financial firms jumped as high as 33:1, meaning a scant 3 percent rise in investment return doubles profits. Risks went up as well, of course, because that leverage also means a 3 percent decline in asset value entirely wiped out equity and reserves.

A few efforts to reregulate, such as the Sarbanes-Oxley Act, occurred during the Reagan era. But they were overwhelmed by dozens of deregulatory mistakes with more impact, plus pervasive regulatory paralysis engineered by Alan Greenspan. At least one official at the bank lobby group called the International Swaps and Derivatives Association joked they didn't need a public relations firm, "because we have Alan Greenspan doing our PR for us."[18]

Deregulation was also endorsed by the Clinton administration, including the Commodity Futures Modernization Act of 2000, which minimized regulation of credit derivatives, removing them from bucket shop prohibitions. Underwriters such as AIG were not required to back derivative issues with a reasonable amount of reserves, causing the derivative market to grow enormously. AIG, with Lehman Brothers and Bear Stearns not far behind, issued $3 trillion of credit derivatives with little reserve backing.[19] Regulatory indulgence also included permitting Wall Street institutions to create vast, unregulated shadowy entities off their balance sheets, where new credit creation and leverage was extreme—and extremely opaque. The Reagan era also included weakened antitrust laws, permitting the most avaricious banks via mergers to become the Red Queens we discussed earlier, with the risks of imprudent speculation shifted from shareholders to taxpayers. Big banking became a one-way bet.

These changes enabled the debt of the American private financial sector to quadruple, growing from an amount comparable to 26 percent of GDP in 1985 to 108 percent in 2009.[20] We know how that ended, echoing the conclusion of Andrew Hilton, director of the London-based Centre for the Study of Financial Innovation: "You can make the case that banking is the only industry where there is too much innovation, not too little."[21]

Rising household, business sector, and government debt were three elements of the Reagan era credit binge. The fourth element was monetary policy, managed during much of this period directly by Alan Greenspan in his role as chairman of the Fed.

Manipulating Monetary Policy for Political Gain

Greenspan manipulated monetary policy, including the deregulation of the financial sector, to sustain growth and aid the political fortunes of his political party. That behavior followed in the tradition of some previous Fed chairmen, and validated the worst fears of nineteenth-century Jeffersonian populists such as President Andrew Jackson. Economists Daron Acemoglu and Simon Johnson have concluded that the conduct of monetary policy by the Federal Reserve has more often than not reflected regulatory capture by the business community. That is not surprising: bankers dominate the various Fed boards, and Friedrich Hayek correctly noted that Fed policy in the 1920s created unsound credit conditions that bolstered bank profits.[22] Similarly, Fed monetary policy conducted by Greenspan served to nurture profits at larger commercial banks during the Reagan era.

Central banks attract criticism for two main reasons:

First, they create credit, which always raises the risk of credit bubbles, deep recessions and inflation; that's why conservatives with the Austrian School endorse the discipline of the gold standard. Milton Friedman disagreed with them, placing his faith in robotic monetary growth targets administered by the Fed, rejecting fears of the Austrian School's Henry Hazlitt. President Nixon ignored the Austrians (and also the advice of Nobel Laureate Paul Samuelson) in favor of Friedman when he abandoned gold in mid-August 1971. Unlike the Austrians, President Nixon and his successors like President Reagan and Alan Greenspan perhaps never read the most famous fable of the German literary giant, Johann Wolfgang Goethe. It's right there in *Faust*: the creation of paper money is mere alchemy.[23]

History has proven Hazlitt, Samuelson, and Goethe right and Friedman wrong.[24]

Second, as mentioned, conservatives like Hayek believe that central banks are too easily captured by the business community, with monetary policies adopted for political ends. As Acemoglu and Johnson explained, ". . . clever politicians can use central banks to manipulate the business cycle, boosting output growth, and cutting unemployment ahead of elections."[25] Such manipulation has become common since Nixon departed the gold standard, and has favored Republican politicians, leaving Democrats to fume. For example, a 2007 study by a former colleague of mine, James K. Galbraith, along with Olivier Giovannoni and Ann J. Russo, documented that between 1969 and 2006, monetary policy was systematically engineered in the year preceding elections to produce lower interest rates on behalf of Republican incumbents:

> "The pattern is reasonably plain: periods of sustained, abnormally low interest rates all begin during Republican administrations. All end following an election involving a Republican incumbent or his immediate successor. . . . We find that in the year before presidential elections, the term structure of interest rates deviates sharply from otherwise-normal values. When a Republican administration is in office, the term structure in the pre-election year tends to be steeper, by values estimated at up to 150 basis points, and monetary policy is accordingly more permissive. . . . These findings are robust across model specifications and across time. . . . Taken together, they suggest the presence of a serious partisan bias at the heart of the Federal Reserve's policymaking process."[26]

This partisan strategy is fruitful because voters tend to respond to good economic news in the months before an election. Larry Bartels has determined that a one percentage point gain in real incomes during the second quarter of election years translates into a five percentage point jump in the incumbent party's popular vote margin, a whopping political payoff for temporarily spiking GDP.[27]

There is ample supporting documentation for Galbraith's conclusion of monetary policy manipulation for partisan gain. For example, Fed chairman Greenspan engineered a cut in the Fed's key interest rate to 3 percent in September 1992; that was the lowest rate in nearly *thirty years* and was timed to bolster the pre-election hopes of George H.W. Bush.[28] Later, Greenspan engineered another decline in interest rates to spark a quicker recover from the dotcom recession during the George W. Bush administration. Over the space of nine months in 2001, the Federal Reserve discount rate was cut drastically from 6 percent to 1.25 percent. A politicized Greenspan then kept rates low through the 2004 election cycle despite mounting evidence of a housing bubble.

At the same time, Greenspan collaborated with President Bush on the deepest tax cuts since World War II totaling $1.35 trillion, followed by another round of cuts totaling $350 billion in 2003. These cuts eviscerated President Clinton's steps that would have eliminated the US national debt by 2008. The 2003 tax cut was motivated entirely by politics, as reported by Paul O'Neill, President George W. Bush's first Treasury Secretary. Indeed, O'Neill resigned in protest because his interest in fiscal prudence was trumped by White House policies spiking growth in mid-2004 on the eve of the election: "I believed we needed the money to facilitate fundamental tax reform and begin working on unfunded liabilities for Social Security and Medicare. They wanted to make sure economic conditions were great going into the president's reelection," revealed Secretary O'Neill.[29]

Monetary manipulation also played a role in the redistribution of income upward during these years. It inflates asset values, disproportionately benefiting the wealthy. An econometric analysis by economists Olivier Coibion, Yuriy Gorodnichenko, Lorenz Kueng, and John Silvia reached the conclusion in mid-2012 that:

> "Monetary policy therefore may well have played a more significant role in driving recent historical inequality patterns in the United States than one might have expected."[30]

Alan Greenspan's Housing Bubble

The most prominent example of money policy manipulation for partisan advantage during the Reagan era was the housing bubble, engineered by Alan Greenspan as a prelude to the 2004 election. And there is a smoking gun.

In 1968, President Lyndon Johnson's administration authorized subprime mortgages, bank loans to homebuyers with poor credit. The program went into effect in 1970 under President Nixon and the results were a precursor to events thirty years later under Greenspan: fraud and scams, with speculators flipping houses so rampantly that President Nixon shut down the entire program after just one year.[31] This episode, involving the perils of deregulation and toxic subprime mortgages, was a lesson well-learned, or so economists believed.

But no one had counted on Alan Greenspan. In light of this widely known 1970 episode surely known to him, his deregulation of the housing finance sector during the 2000s was an error of commission—not omission. As the 2004 election loomed, Greenspan became a housing industry cheerleader, pressing it into known dangerous waters.

He was a full-throated advocate for degrading mortgage-lending standards and for easy credit instruments including interest-only mortgages, zero-down payments, adjustable rate loans, and so-called liar-loans made to borrowers lacking verification of income, assets, or even employment.

In February 2004, for example, Greenspan urged bankers to market adjustable rate mortgages to borrowers unqualified for fixed-rate loans: "American consumers might benefit if lenders provided greater mortgage product alternatives to the traditional fixed-rate mortgage," he said.[32] The financial sector seized the moment. Interest-only loans rose from only 1 percent of new mortgages in 2001 to 29 percent by 2005. And one-half of all new mortgages in 2006 were liar-loans requiring little or no documentation. The average down payment for first-time buyers fell from 10 percent in 1989 to a bare 2 percent by 2007.[33]

Deregulation added to the blaze. A majority of these unconventional loans came to be made by unregulated mortgage firms or S&Ls "not subject to routine supervision," according to Barry Ritholtz, CEO of the quantitative research firm Fusion IQ.[34]

Stolid firms refusing to join this race to the bottom in credit standards were penalized with shrinking market share and falling share prices.

Alan Greenspan's fingerprints were everywhere as the housing bubble expanded before the 2004 election, including successfully urging Wall Street to expand home equity loans. Such loans to households totaled $1.79 trillion during 2003–2005, adding spending comparable to an astounding 6 percent of GDP annually, a nice fillip for the reelection campaign of President George W. Bush.[35] Amazingly, the $719 billion equity withdrawn and converted to household spending in 2005 alone was about as large as the entire multiyear Obama administration's 2009 stimulus bill. Alan Greenspan was no better than President Reagan at balancing a checkbook, but he certainly knew how to spike GDP.

And there is a smoking gun, provided by Federal Reserve transcripts opened to the public in 2009. In a March 2004 Federal Reserve Board of Governors meeting, seven months before the election, then-Fed Governor Donald Kohn candidly acknowledged the efficacy of Greenspan's policy to boost housing. He was nervous about rising prices in the overstimulated housing sector:

> "Policy accommodation—and the expectation that it will persist—is distorting asset prices. Most of the distortion is deliberate and a desirable effect of the stance of policy. We have attempted to lower interest rates below long-run equilibrium rates and to boost asset prices. . . . It is hard to escape the suspicion that at least around the

margin some prices and price relationships have gone beyond an economically justified response to easy policy. House prices fall into this category. . . ."[36]

Greenspan and his board rejected caution, however, eager to continue the housing boom. Even Kohn opposed steps to "second-guess asset price levels," by tightening policy. "I'd be a little cautious about using monetary policy to try to damp asset price movements," he explained. Greenspan readily concurred, "I certainly agree with that." He misjudged events, insisting in 2005 that a bubble in housing prices "does not appear likely." And even should this mythical bubble burst, Greenspan argued that a collapse in housing prices would "not have substantial macroeconomic implications." Well, the bubble was real, and it caused the worst downturn in nearly 80 years. Acemoglu and Johnson evaluated his tenure at the Fed this way:

> "In recent decades the Fed has given way completely, at the highest level and with disastrous consequences, when the bankers bring their influence to bear—for example, over deregulating finance, keeping interest rates low in the middle of a boom after 2003, providing unconditional bailouts in 2007–08 and subsequently resisting attempts to raise capital requirements by enough to make a difference."[37]

And here is how George Soros explained his tenure as Fed chairman:

> "Since markets are bubble-prone, financial authorities must accept responsibility for preventing bubbles from growing too big. Alan Greenspan and others refused to accept that. . . . Second, to control asset bubbles it is not enough to control the money supply; you must also control credit."[38]

CHAPTER 12

ECONOMIC MYTHMAKING

"Workers' leverage is gone. Companies are not creating jobs. Unions that negotiated big wage increases in the 1970s are shadows of their former selves. Cost-of-living adjustments, once commonplace, have disappeared. And the movement of jobs offshore, or the threat of it, has conditioned workers to not even ask for a raise, fearing they will join the millions already laid off."[1]

LOUIS UCHITELLE,
***New York Times,* August 1, 2008**

"The conservative response to this trend verges somewhere between the obsolete and the irrelevant. Conservatives need to stop denying reality. The stagnation of the incomes of middle-class Americans is a fact."[2]

DAVID FRUM,
speechwriter,
President GEORGE W. BUSH
August 2008

"Insofar as Americans have any understanding of the alternative policies pursued by other affluent democracies, they mostly seem to reject those alternatives as inconsistent with America's core cultural values of economic opportunity and self-reliance. European welfare states, they tell themselves, are bloated, ossified and hidebound."[3]

LARRY BARTELS,
Vanderbilt University

"No one ever said that you could work hard—harder even than you ever thought possible—and still find yourself sinking ever deeper into poverty."

Author BARBARA EHRENREICH,
Nickel and Dimed,
***On (Not) Getting By In America* 2001**

For most Americans, a profound symbol of the Reagan era is bankers enjoying unwarranted millions of dollars, but at a personal level, the most pervasive symbolism has been income stagnation. Voters attribute this plight mostly to globalization, with remarkably few looking to Washington for remediation. Unaware of the prosperous family capitalism countries, most American families seemingly accept their fate as preordained by inexorable market forces beyond even the power of America.

These low expectations are reinforced by Democratic Party officials, who offer underwhelming tax, trade, and spending prescriptions. Republican Party officials are worse, weakening wages and defending the *status quo* desired by donors with government gridlock while appealing to voters with combustible social topics. Despite the shambles made of American family economics by Reaganomics, voters see little difference between the parties. Responsibility for this austere—if not to say, discouraging—landscape rests ultimately with pay-to-play politics. But vitally important in nurturing this dismaying environment has been a handful of myths about Reaganomics.

In past centuries, implied or actual military strength maintained a particular arrangement of economic sovereignty benefiting the Roman equestrian class, Chinese dynasties (and their equivalent today), medieval lords, or Renaissance courts.[4] The rise of the voting franchise in the nineteenth century altered that dynamic, requiring special pleaders to become imaginative in attracting voters. Thus, robber barons supported creation of the Interstate Commerce Commission to satisfy the farming community's clamor for lower railroad tariffs, for example, certain in their own ability to exploit pecuniary American politics to achieve regulatory capture; the same pattern has been repeated since. Similarly, economic myth made globalization a *bête noire* that facilitated the stripping of economic sovereignty from families during the Reagan era. And the canard that deficits don't matter eased the path to tax cuts. Another myth belied by American economic history is that taxes hamper growth, an important element of the supply-side canard.

The Canard of Supply-Side Economics

Tax cuts for millionaires or the business community are not political positions most voters support. Yet eager to do precisely that, President Reagan relied on message recalibration by Washington. President Reagan's reputation as a political genius is well earned, especially in reigniting American enthusiasm and confidence. But it was a political *tour de force* when he and his advisors conjured the canard called supply-side economics. This is the wistful notion that tax cuts pay for themselves by sparking an economic renaissance sufficiently robust to yield new, offsetting tax revenue. No economist believes it occurs, nor does President Nixon's harshly dismissive Secretary of Commerce, Pete Peterson.

> "Federal dollars spent should be paid for out of revenue [but] . . . the taxing rule was eliminated in the early 1980's by the *jihad* prayers of supply-side economists."[5]

The notion that tax cuts work this way has been discredited time and again by US economic history; only a John Law would argue that cutting tax rates from, say, 30 percent to 15 percent will spark a sufficient boom to replace the lost tax revenue. Early acolytes brought a religious fervor, making George Gilder's 1981 *Wealth and Poverty* a best-seller; media evangelist Pat Robertson argued that supply-side economics "was the first truly divine theory of money creation."[6] President Reagan himself was indifferent about whether this canard was accurate because, as former Republican US Senator Bob Packwood of Oregon explained, Reagan "wanted lower rates and didn't care how we got there."[7]

The lower taxes he and the Bush presidents implemented have not produced an economic renaissance, however, only deep national debt and a nation that consumes too much and invests too little. Even so, Reagan's intellectual heirs even today still sprinkle supply-side pixie dust to credential tax cuts as the prescription for any and all macroeconomic ailments. And the American business community has been little better, fecklessly urging tax holidays and cuts while exploiting tax havens, which worsen the national debt.

The Myth That Taxes Affect Economic Growth

That pixie dust has been magic for some. Comprehensive US tax rates are the lowest of any rich democracy, ranging between 8 and 15 percentage points of GDP lower than Australia, Germany, and France. Indeed, since American taxes don't provide comprehensive college or health care benefits, it would be surprising if the US did not have the lowest tax burden. (American corporations also pay about the least as a share of GDP of any rich democracy.)

This low tax burden has come about in part because of tax cuts during the Reagan era, featuring a redistribution of the tax burden onto the middle class, as discussed earlier. Top rates have been lowered and payroll taxes have increased. This redistribution has been sold to voters using the hoary myth that economic growth hinges on the risk-taking and entrepreneurial activities of higher-income households—you know, the job creators. Alan Greenspan argued before Congress in 1997 that the effect of capital gains taxation, "as best I can judge, is to impede entrepreneurial activity and capital formation. The appropriate capital gains tax rate is zero."[8]

History teaches that Greenspan was wrong. His assertion is directly contradicted by the postwar American experience. America's golden age featuring strong growth and job creation occurred when marginal tax rates on higher incomes were about double what they are today. Moreover, the economy performed quite well during the decade 1987–1996, when capital gains rates were nearly twice as high as they are now. Some Republican tax experts, including Bruce Bartlett, acknowledge that tax increases early in the Clinton administration didn't hinder the robust growth in the years that followed.[9] And a Congressional Research Service analysis by economist Thomas Hungerford found that GDP and productivity growth throughout the entire postwar period were unaffected by cuts in income tax rates.[10]

Taxes may matter a bit to some enterprises, but sales prospects, the economics of relocating abroad, interest rates, and macroeconomic conditions matter far more. That truth is magnified by the ready convenience of tax havens that enable the wealthy and multinationals to avoid taxes regardless of where actual production is located. Turning to individual entrepreneurs, when I'm evaluating whether to pursue a new real estate project, tax rates don't enter into my calculation at all, and they don't for most other entrepreneurs either. Not once during the real estate boom years did I accept or reject an investment opportunity because of tax rates. While I'm scarcely in his class, entrepreneurs like Warren Buffett have concluded the same thing:

> "It's not the *panacea* for economic growth that advocates make it out to be. I have worked with investors for 60 years, and I have yet to see anyone—not even when capital gains rates were 39.6 in 1976–77—shy away from a sensible investment because of the tax rate."[11]

A more consequential myth to almost every American family is that wage stagnation is inevitable, a result of global integration and thus beyond the ability of Washington to remediate.

The Myth That Washington Cannot Rectify the Impact of Globalization

Free trade is a wondrous wealth machine, enhancing the allocation of resources and providing higher-quality and cheaper imports, while improving wages abroad and for some employees at home. As consumers and investors, Americans welcomed globalization. But its severe impact on wages has caused many employees to loathe it.

Their ire is misdirected.

The impact of globalization has been extensively studied, as we see in detail in a later chapter. Perhaps the most comprehensive analysis is a 2011 OECD study, which concluded unequivocally that "In contrast, globalization had little impact on the gap between rich and poor."[12]

Unlike the United States, experience elsewhere in rich democracies is that globalization didn't have a significant impact on income disparities. That outcome reflects what has been accomplished by successful public policies in the family capitalism countries to exploit globalization rather than be victimized by it. The dismal effect of globalization in the United States is an exception to those widespread accomplishments. Let me explain.

Global integration has been allowed to become an important wage depressant by Washington officials who acquiesced in its effects redistributing income upward away from families. That is why the impact of globalization on wages, especially high-wage jobs held by non-college folks, has been as severe as the impact on buffalos of soaring global demand for industrial tanned hides in the nineteenth century; they were virtually extinguished in America. And that indulgence is why virtually all men earn less than their fathers or grandfathers before 1980.

Washington officials in thrall to Reaganomics stood aside and permitted wages to erode due to a soaring international labor supply. Here is a truly astounding statistic from a 2007 study by the International Monetary Fund (IMF):

> "There has been a dramatic increase in the size of the effective global labor force over the past two decades, with one measure suggesting it has risen fourfold. This expansion is expected to continue in the coming years."[13]

An update based on World Bank data published by *Handesblatt* in October 2012 concluded than 600 million new workers would be added between 2005 and 2020.[14] That will increase the global labor force today of 3 billion by about 20 percent, including perhaps 1.8 billion men and women with dubious or no jobs. Jim Clifton, the chairman of the polling firm Gallup, writes that only 1.2 billion regular jobs now exist.[15]

The entire American labor force totals 160 million or so men and women. Yet, just since 1990, more new workers than that (187 million) have appeared in China and India.[16] And these new entrants work cheaply; in 2008, for example, *China Daily* reported that Chinese factory workers averaged $3,544 in annual income, or about 11 percent of average US wages.[17] That labor overhang opened vast opportunities for executive suites at companies such as Apple to cut labor costs by conducting international wage arbitrage—shifting high-wage US jobs offshore to exploit low wages and docile workforces abroad.

In 2001, economists Lawrence Mishel, Jared Bernstein, and John Schmitt found that some American wages rose during this period, but they documented two factors creating powerful downdrafts linked to globalization:[18]

First, higher-wage jobs, especially unionized ones, were aggressively offshored, while deindustrialization ensured that virtually all new jobs being created were in low-wage services and at nonunion, lower-wage factories. Economist Michael Spence and Sandile Hlatshwayo concluded that nearly all of the 27 million or so American jobs added since 1990 were in nontradeable service sectors, such as health, where productivity growth is weak.[19] And, economist Robert E. Scott at the Washington-based Economic Policy Institute (EPI) has documented that service-sector wages in 2005 averaged 22 percent lower than wages for manufacturing jobs being offshored.[20] Worse, even the new jobs being created in the unionized manufacturing sector feature low wages, exemplified by the two-tier wage agreements in autos.[21] Some new jobs in tradeable goods sectors at firms like Boeing or on Wall Street and in Silicon Valley pay well, but they are few in number.

Second, the American business community effectively utilized the mere threat of globalization as an intimidator in wage talks. One quarter of almost 500 corporate executives who responded to a 1992 *Wall Street Journal* survey, for example, confessed to exploiting the threat of relocating abroad under the North American Free Trade Agreement (NAFTA) as a bargaining tool in wage talks.[22] And, Scott's report for EPI concluded that more than 50 percent of union organizing campaigns in the mid-1990s featured corporate spokesmen threatening to close some or all of the target plants.[23]

The use of such intimidation tactics doubled in elections monitored by the National Labor Relations Board (NLRB) after NAFTA was enacted in 1993.[24] Cornell economist Kate Bronfenbrenner examined the impact of NAFTA on union-organizing elections in 1998 and 1999. Threats of offshoring notably reduced the organizers' election success to 38 percent compared to 51 percent in elections where such threats were absent.[25]

The Reagan era has delivered precisely what many voted *against* in 1980. No one told American families that they were casting votes to terminate the golden age of stakeholder capitalism. Voters were unhappy with the 1970s stagflation, and likely knew that Ronald Reagan intended to weaken the government safety net; he certainly made no secret of his disdain for it. Americans rejected greater economic security, expecting the trade-off would be a more vibrant and dynamic economy that created a surfeit of good jobs. Grit, education, and effort would pay off, they believed, just as it had in the nineteenth century and the golden age.

American families gambled that Reaganomics would recapture the postwar good times. Instead, Washington abandoned them, admonishing them to respect globalization and the ensuing allocation of income and wealth dictated by the deregulated market. Or at least the market as interpreted by the business community and their Washington men.

Blaming Globalization for the Sins of Reaganomics

Here is conservative author Ross Douthat writing in February 2012, shifting responsibility for the outcome of Reaganomics onto globalization:

> "It was globalization, not Republicans, that killed the private-sector union and reduced the returns to blue-collar work."[26]

Too many economists were taken in by this canard delivered with certitude by folks like a writer for the *Economist* in June 2006:

> "The integration of China's low-skilled millions and the increased offshoring of services to India and other countries has expanded the global supply of workers. This has reduced the relative price of labour and raised the returns to capital. That reinforces the income concentration at the top, since most stocks and shares are held by richer people. More importantly, globalisation may further fracture the traditional link between skills and wages."[27]

And it was delivered with *gravitas* by folks such as the economist Michael Jensen of Harvard whom we met earlier. Here it is boiled down by Jensen and Perry Fagan in the *Wall Street Journal* in March 1996:

> "The political dynamics behind this third industrial revolution is the spread of capitalism in response to the worldwide failure of communism. . . . This move to market-oriented, open economic systems is putting 1.2 billion Third World workers into world product and labor markets over the next generation. Over a billion of these workers currently earn less than $3 a day. . . . The upshot of all this for Western workers is that their real wages are likely to continue

their sluggish growth and some will fall dramatically over the coming two or three decades, perhaps as much as 50 percent in some sectors. Wages will, however, reach a trough and recover as the cycle works its way through the system."[28]

With Chinese textile workers earning 86 cents an hour and Cambodians 22 cents, this chilling prospect, credentialed by Harvard professors, the *Wall Street Journal*, and the *Economist* was enough to make one seriously question the utility of an economic system that so severely penalizes Americans. After all, the United States had won the Cold War and all the rest, yet most citizens were seemingly destined to be treated like its losers while others grew rich. That made Jensen and other experts important apologists who could credential Reaganomics—busily explaining away how capitalism isn't broken, despite this grim prospect. We know that because of the title of Jensen's editorial:

"Capitalism Isn't Broken"

Jensen was wrong, at least, about the variant pursued in America during the Reagan era. American capitalism transformed into Reaganomics *is* broken. But that's only the beginning of the story.

The studied indifference by officials in Reagan-era Washington to offshoring and, more generally, to the wage impact of global integration, stands in sharp contrast to the results achieved by alternative policies in the family capitalism countries. In those countries, real wages continued rising, evidence that the economic loss and diminished living standards rationalized by Jensen and others were not preordained. Deindustrialization, the loss of good jobs to offshoring, and wage compression are not ineluctable. Americans didn't have to become the losers that Europeans such as *Handelsblatt* chief editor Gabor Steingart acknowledge, or those described in that newspaper by Norbert Häring, coauthor of the 2009 book *Economics 2.0*:

> "Many millions of Americans lack adequate health insurance and cannot afford medical care. The average life expectancy is significantly lower than in most other industrialized countries. In a comparative study by UNICEF of the quality of life of children in 21 industrialized counties, the US safety and health of children landed in last place, far behind much poorer countries like Greece, Hungary, and the Czech Republic. . . . A larger proportion of the population lives in absolute poverty than in many European countries and Canada."[29]

That grim rendition is not the consequence of capitalism, but of Reaganomics—and of American officials, economists, and voters who believed the myth that rich democracies are helpless before globalization.

Another myth is that policies to fend off the impact of globalization inevitably reduce economic efficiency.

The Myth That Promoting Income Equality Reduces Economic Efficiency

Iconic Yale economist Arthur Okun penned a book in 1975 entitled *Equality and Efficiency: The Big Trade-off*. The implication is that economic growth inevitably produces income disparities, and policies to ameliorate this side effect imperil economic growth. And a majority of Americans have come to accept that even the widening income disparity of today is an inevitable, if lamentable, price to pay for economic growth. In December 2011, for example, 52 percent of respondents to a Gallup poll viewed income disparities "an acceptable part" of attaining growth.[30]

They're wrong.

While true at times, the Reagan era has proven that trade-off to be mythical. Preventing income disparities doesn't inevitably impose an economic efficiency penalty. The family capitalism countries broadcast rising incomes widely across society even while nearly all attained better productivity performance than Reagan era America, and much stronger real wage growth as well. These decades of evidence from a host of rich nations reveal that any efficiency/equality penalty can be neutralized in the real world.

Indeed, economists Andrew Berg and Jonathan Ostry with the IMF have concluded that nations with less income disparity experience faster growth. Analyzing data from 1950 to 2006, they discovered that income equality is as important to growth as is openness to free trade. Nations with high-income equality experienced higher average rates of economic growth by avoiding disruptions such as credit crises that are precipitated when economic elites achieve financial deregulation.[31]

In family capitalism countries, gains from trade and economic growth are widely distributed. They met the challenges of globalization and technology change by opening borders to garner the enormous wealth from the improvement in resource allocations and efficiency. At the same time, they upskilled workforces and adopted institutions to ensure the gains would be broadcasted widely, not monopolized as in the United States. Income gains from globalization nurtured most families, rather than just tiny business elites along Berlin's elegant *Kurfurstendamm*, in the stylish sixteenth *arrondissement* of Paris, or in Sydney's beautiful Point Piper suburb. Their success reaffirms faith in capitalism and provides hope and a powerful model for America.

Another myth sustaining Reaganomics is that income stagnation for Americans can be avoided with education and upskilling.

The Myth That Education and Upskilling Can Solve Wage Stagnation

Many economists and commentators blame faltering American education as partly if not largely responsible for widening income disparities. The columnist David Brooks, for example, suggests that wage stagnation can be resolved by returning to America's education roots: "What's needed is not a populist revolt, which would make everything worse, but a second generation of human capital policies, designed for people as they actually are, to help them get the intangible skills the economy rewards."[32]

Brooks is precisely incorrect on the solution, but his point has merit. It is certainly accurate that global integration accelerates the usual creative destruction process of innovation and entrepreneurism described by Josef Schumpeter that rewards the educated. Their rising wages are price signals for employees to upskill and raise educational attainment. Bolstering the skill set of Americans with improved education and upskilling is a constructive, though not sufficient, resolution to wage stagnation. Educational attainment pays off at the individual level, as every parent knows. Among economists, this line of argument is driven by Nobel Laureate Gary Becker and others, who have convincingly shown that education yields benefits at the individual level; the more you learn, the more you earn. And episodes of joblessness are shorter, too.

America led the world a century ago in providing broadly based public education that became one foundation of the golden age. As Harvard economists Claudia Goldin and Lawrence Katz have noted in a careful, data-rich book, those receiving educations in the European nations at the turn of the twentieth century tended to be those who could personally afford schooling.[33] America rejected this elitism and greatly expanded its education base. The ensuing rise in human capital stock powered productivity growth, enabling America to become the richest nation in the world. Later, in the decades after World War II, rising productivity and wages linked to rising education attainment created the great American middle class.

Those verities still apply. Yet the notion of education as a panacea is deficient, because it ignores the structural problems reflected in the delinking of productivity and wages by Reaganomics. It would be a delight to learn that education was the solution to the middle-class ills of today, a much easier target politically to tackle than the national epiphany required in voting booths and in composition of the Supreme Court.

The structural nature of wage stagnation and why more education and upskilling in the Reagan era has *not* translated to better wages have been examined by a host of economists.[34] Here is how economists Ian Dew-Becker and Robert J. Gordon explained it in 2005:

> "Most of the shift in the income distribution has been from the bottom 90 percent to the top 5 percent. This is much too narrow a group to be consistent with a widespread benefit from SBTC [skill-biased technical change]. . . ."[35]

Educational attainment now in the family capitalism countries is not much different than in America, but wages are higher and continue rising. What *is* different are wage and labor market policies and national expectations about the behavior of corporate boards of directors.

If education paid off, surely those Americans with college educations would be at least out-earning college graduates forty years ago. Yet they are not. Economists have determined that college graduates have been among that 90 percent of Americans whose wages failed to even keep pace with inflation over the last 35 years: Heidi Shierholz at EPI has documented that inflation-adjusted starting wages for graduates in 2010 for both males ($21.77 per hour) and females ($18.43) were about 5 percent lower than in 2000 ($22.75 and $19.38).[36] It's the same story over a longer period for all male college graduates as documented by Adam Looney and Michael Greenstone of the Hamilton Project. Annual median earnings for male employees with college degrees in 2009 were 7 percent lower than in 1969 during the peak wage years.[37]

The only clear beneficiaries of rising wages among the college educated have been those relatively few with advanced or professional degrees, but even their gains have been mediocre. Indeed, wage stagnation is commonplace even in those professions most tightly linked to the information technology (IT) revolution. The 2005 study by Dew-Becker and Gordon included a detailed examination of the period 1989–1997, an era marked by the IT revolution and heightened demand for math and computer skills. They found that despite strong demand for computational-skill labor, real wages "in occupations related to math and computer science increased only 4.8 percent and engineers decreased 1.4 percent." Yet, ". . . total real compensation to CEOs increased 100 percent."[38] It is extremely difficult to see how a surge in American education attainment will reverse a pattern where CEO salaries double, while the wages of skilled computer engineers barely outpace inflation.

Some conservatives acknowledge this inconsistency, including N. Gregory Mankiw. He has noted that while education is "not irrelevant," one's educational attainment doesn't explain how a relative handful of Americans have prospered while the wages of all others stagnated since the 1970s: "It is less obvious whether it can explain the incomes of the super-rich. Simply going to college and graduate school is hardly enough to join the top echelons."[39]

Education as the cause or answer to wage stagnation is a myth of Reaganomics. Three smoking guns document its status as a canard: First, the share of Americans with college educations has risen from 19.7 percent in 1979 to 34.4 percent now, yet real average and median wages have stagnated or fallen.[40] Second, a significantly greater proportion of Americans than Germans (34.4 percent versus < 25 percent) have college degrees, yet wages are significantly higher there.[41] Third, compensation for most Americans does not rise with productivity, which is the best measure of their skill and education (and value to employers), as judged by labor markets.

With globalization and faltering education ruled out as sources of wage stagnation, what are the factors responsible?

Why Wages Stagnate

The elements of Reaganomics are major factors in wage stagnation, including its Randian corporate culture, offshoring, short-termism, and quarterly shareholder or managerial capitalism. Another factor has been the failure of Washington officials to mimic the tactics of the family capitalism countries in ameliorating the impact of globalization. Economists cite three other significant factors: employer collusion to limit wage increases, the sagging minimum wage, and the weakening of employee collective bargaining power.[42]

Employer Collusion to Minimize Wages

Even blue-chip enterprises cross the line in colluding to suppress wages. For example, the Obama administration's Department of Justice settled two antitrust lawsuits in 2010, in which several leading high-tech firms agreed to pay penalties for conspiring against their own highly skilled artisans. Lucasfilm and rival Pixar were found to have illegally colluded to avoid wage-bidding wars for prized digital animators. Adobe Systems, Apple, Google, Intel, and Intuit were similarly caught for colluding to dampen the wages paid to top technical talent.[43]

Kneecapping the Minimum Wage

As a student in 1968, I earned the minimum wage stocking grocery shelves, which was comparable to $10.11 measured in 2008 dollars. And it was still high, around $9/hour in today's currency, when amiable President Reagan was elected. That substantial level for the minimum wage provided a solid economic floor beneath American incomes during the golden age. It also proved to be a muscular antipoverty mechanism, setting a living wage floor sufficient to prevent abject family poverty.

The logic of the minimum wage is straightforward: without a robust market for labor or a wage floor beneath them, history since the industrial revolution teaches that market forces produce a race to the bottom for wages. The American experience during my first years of work demonstrated how successful minimum wages can be. During its peak years in the late 1960s and early 1970s, America enjoyed the lowest poverty rates ever in its history (11.1 percent in 1973) and higher real wages than today. And the lowest recorded rate of childhood impoverishment ever in America was in 1969, at 13.8 percent.[44] Most persuasive is that year after year in this period, America recorded among the lowest unemployment levels in postwar history despite the high minimum wage.

But that was before the Reagan era. A prominent target of the business community, the minimum wage became a quick victim after 1980, despite its centrality to the prosperity of America's lower-income employees. As depicted in Chart 12.1, it began a steady slide eroded by inflation, falling a third over the following decades, before being raised modestly during the Clinton administration and again in 2007 at the insistence of Congressional Democrats. This erosion has had a generalized impact because minimum wages serve as an escalator, pushing up wages for workers further up the income scale. The US experience sharply contrasts with policies in the family capitalism countries, where minimums are considerably higher, as we will learn in a later chapter. The minimum wage, for example, in France during 2012 was €9.22 per hour; in purchase-power parity terms that is over $11 per hour, or 60 percent above the federal minimum in America. The minimum wage in Australia is higher still.

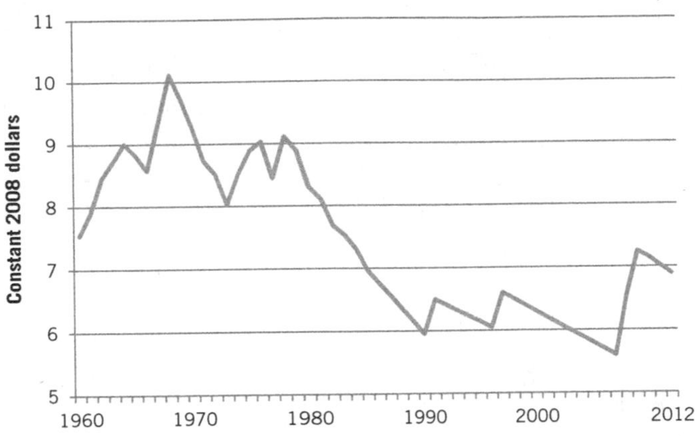

Chart 12.1.

Source: Wage and Hour Division, "History of Changes to the Minimum Wage Law," Department of Labor, Washington, DC. Also: Phyllis Korkki "Keeping an Eye on the Low, Point of the Pay Scale," New York Times, August 31, 2008, and Ralph E. Smith and Bruce Vavrichek, "The Minimum Wage: Its Relation to Incomes and Poverty," Monthly Labor Review, June 1987.

Another important explanation for the wage stagnation of recent decades was regulatory capture, particularly of federal labor market regulators who turned hostile to unions promoting higher wages.

Diminishing the Golden Age Role of Unions

You may recall that the organization Human Rights Watch criticized European firms in September 2010 for exploiting weak American labor rights. HRW concluded the firms were, "adopting practices common in America but banned in Europe," by seeking ". . . to create a culture of fear about organizing in America."[45]

The business community has targeted trade unions in its pursuit of the gains from growth because they raise wages and because they support opponents of Reaganomics. Research by economists Bruce Western and Jake Rosenfeld determined, for example, that union membership confers a lifelong wage premium on blue-collar employees comparable to that of a college education. "The decline of the US labor movement has added as much to men's wage inequality as has the relative increase in pay for college graduates," they concluded.[46] Moreover, the existence of trade unions is a precursor to a high-wage economy as in Australia or Germany, because they elevate the wages of nonmembers as well. Economist Henry Farber, for example, has concluded that wages of nonunion employees are 7.5 percent higher if at least 25 percent of a particular industry's jobs are unionized.[47] Their presence strengthens family economic sovereignty.

Their importance to family prosperity also accounts for the centrality of unions in historic Catholic social teachings for well over a century. Leaders including Pope Leo XIII taught that a strong trade union movement is "greatly to be desired." In his 1891 encyclical *Rerum Novarum*, Pope Leo explained that unions "have always been encouraged and supported by the Church." And that support has remained steadfast in the modern era, as indicated by this 1986 pastoral letter from the United States Conference of Catholic Bishops:

> "No one may deny the right to organize without attacking human dignity itself."[48]

The success of wage compression tactics targeting unions in the Reagan era is indicated not only by wage stagnation, but also by the union share of the private sector workforce, which has dwindled to below 7 percent from 35 percent in the 1950s; including the public sector, that share has dropped to about 11 percent. A major reason has been the barriers erected during the Reagan era to union organizing.

A comparison with Canadian law and practice is instructive. While the share of employees interested in joining unions is similar to the US, membership is nearly three times higher in Canada because labor organizers face fewer roadblocks. Indeed, the Canadian membership rate is close to the US rate during the golden age, when organizing rights were better enforced.[49] As Kris Warner with the Washington-based Center for Economic and Policy Research noted, a Canadian union is generally recognized once a majority of employees indicate intent to join over employer objections. Unlike US employers, Canadian employers do not have a second opportunity (involving an election and lengthy delays) to derail organizers using American-style tactics.[50]

Labor rights set forth in the National Labor Relations (Wagner) Act were weakly policed during the Reagan era. The National Labor Relations Board (NLRB), traditionally composed of prominent scholars, attorneys, and career civil servants, became toothless, increasingly filled with lobbyists and other ideologues.

Cornell professor Kate Bronfenbrenner examined more than 1,000 union election campaigns over a recent five-year span. Most featured employers conducting Madison Avenue-style campaigns targeting employees, with 57 percent threatening to export jobs, and even entire plants, if unionization occurred. And 34 percent of the campaigns included the illegal firing of union advocates.[51] Here is the outcome, as described by labor attorney Thomas Geoghegan.

> "Employers found out they could just ignore the Wagner Act and fire pro-union workers right before so-called 'secret-ballot' elections; they found out there was no real limit on what they could use as a threat."[52]

These public relations campaigns were conducted in conjunction with niche law firms specializing in union busting. Lawyers taught executive suites where enforcement was weak, how to bend the rules, and how to greatly muddy the simplicity of union-organizing elections. *New York Times* journalist David Leonhardt explained: "Companies pay minimal penalties for illegally trying to bar unions and have become expert at doing so, legally and otherwise."[53] The ultimate goal was to slow-walk the union election process, in order to buy time for executive suites to ferret out and fire union sympathizers.

Fired union advocates frequently complained, but pleas fell on deaf ears at a US Department of Labor behaving like the Interstate Commerce Commission in the nineteenth century. It was more interested in protecting employers from employees than achieving the balance prescribed by the Wagner Act. Even when legal steps by aggrieved employees forced NLRB action, official foot-dragging was common, with Labor Department administrative-law judges taking an average of eighteen months to rule on a complaint of unfair labor practices.[54] Here is how the *Washington Post* in an editorial summarized these tactics:

> "From the point of hiring, employers have unfettered access to workers to make the case against forming a union. When unions launch organizing campaigns, employers can require workers to attend repeated antiunion presentations, while unions have no comparable access to workers and are left to try to contact them off company premises. Although it is illegal for employers to fire or threaten workers for joining a union, enforcement is inadequate, with penalties too late and too small to deter violations."[55]

The NLRB during the G.W. Bush administration permitted employers to place new hurdles in the path of unions, even those managing to win organizing elections. Researchers John-Paul Ferguson and Thomas Kochan of the MIT Sloan School of Management examined the outcome of organizing campaigns from 1999 to 2004. In cases where employees prevailed—winning a majority vote to organize—they were subsequently able to negotiate a contract only 56 percent of the time.[56] Why? There were at least three reasons:

First, many employers who lost organizing elections simply refused to negotiate a union contract. If they stonewalled election outcomes for one year, Bush administration regulators generally allowed them a second bite at the apple: employers could request that the union victory a year earlier be decertified, forcing the entire time-consuming and expensive electoral process to be repeated.[57] Victories thus delayed became victories denied.

Second, as exemplified by the tactics of Walmart, executive suites routinely flouted the intent of laws by simply shuttering facilities, such as a meat department where the majority of employees had voted to organize. Punishment for such illegalities, consisting of employee reinstatement and back pay, was *de minimus,* too small to deter large corporations.

Third, nearly forty years ago, employers discovered that Chapter 11 of the bankruptcy code was a useful tool in avoiding or breaking labor contracts. Business units that voted to unionize were suddenly discovered to be money-losers, declared bankrupt by employers and temporarily closed—only to reopen later with a newly hired, chastened workforce. Worse, *faux* Chapter 11 bankruptcy became a tactic to break existing labor agreements, particularly those that required high wages or benefits be paid for many years in the future. Here is how labor attorney Geoghegan explained this scam:

> "Right around the time Reagan took office, companies began to figure out that they could go in and out of Chapter 11 in order to dump their obligations, not just to workers but also to retirees. Often the companies weren't 'bankrupt.' The parent firm was simply shutting down the subsidiary. . . . With a competent lawyer, any employer can cancel any promises to any worker."[58]

The Chapter 11 ploy was utilized to obviate or sharply pare back retiree pensions or health-care obligations to only pennies on the dollar. In bankruptcy, employees "managed to hang on to five cents on the dollar, maybe ten" cents of prior obligations promised by employers, concluded Geoghegan.

Taking the totality of these various union-busting strategies into account, Bronfenbrenner concluded that the balance between labor and management that had empowered the golden age has been knocked askew since.

> [Employers take] ". . . full advantage of current labor law to try to keep workers from exercising their full rights to organize and collectively bargain under the National Labor Relations Act. Far from an aberration, such behavior by US companies during union-organizing campaigns has become routine, and our nations' labor laws neither protect workers' rights nor provide disincentives for employers to stop disregarding those rights."[59]

The final myth examined in this chapter is that stakeholder capitalism underperforms.

The Myth That European Economies Are Sclerotic

The most authentic European version of Milton Friedman was the late German economist Herbert Giersch. He emulated Friedman in fierce antigovernment rhetoric and writings, and also in conducting a public relations effort to discredit stakeholder capitalism under the auspices of the Kiel-based Institute for World Economics. During the 1980s, for example, Giersch coined the catchy term "Euro-sclerosis."[60] It has been mimicked since by some American conservatives to denigrate European economies as ossified, with stultified labor markets and firms cowering behind protectionist tariff walls.

Henry Olson of the American Enterprise Institute, writing in the *Wall Street Journal* during 2008, miscast Europe this way: "Germany, Italy, Belgium, and the Netherlands are poorer than the United States, with substantially higher unemployment rates and slower economic growth."[61] France is regularly demonized, including a 2007 editorial in the *Washington Post* arguing it needs "weaning . . . from a mind-set that disdains and devalues work."[62] And here is reporter Simon Heffer of London's *Daily Telegraph*, cheerleader for the conservative Tory party and critic of continental Europe: "While much of the rest of the World moves on through the application of free-market disciplines, France is demoralized, impoverished, overtaxed, and in despair."[63]

A similar verdict was issued in 2001 by law professors Henry Hansmann and Reinier Kraakman, who described stakeholder capitalism and codetermination as "a failed social model."[64] Disciples of Milton Friedman and Ayn Rand, their article was entitled "The End of History for Corporate Law." Their writing was reminiscent of political scientist Francis Fukuyama's inaccurate commentary on the end of the Cold War or Oswald Spengler's much earlier prediction amid the carnage of World War I, in his chilling *The Decline of the West*, that Western civilization had begun an inevitable downturn.

Even the *Economist* magazine promotes the canard of a sickly Europe, as it did in June 2006 with unfortunate timing, not long before the US housing bubble burst. Editors fretted that income and wage stagnation in America may embolden European resistance to the spread of Reaganomics, thereby "setting back the course of European reform even further." Later, amid the 2007/2008 credit crises, editors there persisted in praising Reaganomics:

> "This is a black week. Those of us who have supported financial capitalism are open to the charge that the system we championed has merely enabled a few spivs [petty thieves] to get rich. But it helped produce healthy economic growth and low inflation for a generation."[65]

Well, the part about spivs is spot on, but the balance of the editorial is mendacious. One is hard-pressed to term what has happened to American families and their household wealth as "healthy economic growth." And the economic outcomes were even more sickly in the United Kingdom, Ireland, and Spain, which had foolishly mimicked Reaganomics.

Even so, the expansive Reagan era demonization of European stakeholder capitalism was successful in forming public opinion, as noted by Princeton political scientist Andrew Moravcsik. He was quoted in the *New York Times* in October 2008, saying that "Americans, especially conservatives, have a particular view of Europe as over-regulated, therefore suffering from weak growth and Euro-sclerosis."[66] Political scientist Bartels wrote similarly in an epigraph to this chapter, and here is Mark Leonard at the Center for European Reform:

> "Many Americans see the European economy as the business equivalent of a hippy commune—mired in the 1970s, unable to reform because of the cacophony of voices that erupt every time a decision needs to be made, and more interested in soft-headed ideas of quality of life than economic performance. They argue that it will not succeed until it emulates the United States with lower taxes, less social protection, a smaller state, and a narrow focus on shareholder value."[67]

As we are learning, reality is much different.

Northern Europe Is an Economic Powerhouse

 A number of European firms such as Ikea and Siemens are among the most profitable multinationals in the world. Some European internet startups such as Angry Birds have become part of America's social fabric. BMW, Daimler, and VW-Porsche-Audi perennially compete to claim the title of the world's best-managed auto firm in what has become an intramural German competition. The widespread prowess of firms across northern Europe results from their deep integration with globalization and codetermination. Europe is not an easy market for US firms, because its openness to trade also has made it the richest and the most fiercely competitive market in the world. And it is the world's largest market, easily exceeding American share of global output. In the 2000s, some 61 of the world's 140 largest firms on the Global Fortune 500 were European, compared to only 50 from the United States and 29 from Asia.[68]

Some might think that its high wages exist only because of trade barriers or inflexible labor market rules shielding uncompetitive firms. Reality is starkly different: superior corporate governance, high investment, and robust productivity growth enable northern European firms to pay high wages while out-investing and out-exporting America's finest. Globalization means Schumpeter's creative destruction process occurs at a faster pace than in America. Since 2000, for example, some 5 million Germans in 340,000 firms have lost their jobs from bankruptcy, reports Neuss-based Economic Reform Credit.[69] And wages can and do decline, even in France. Employees at the Bosch facility in Beauvais agreed to wage and benefit cuts in 2004, as did employees at Hewlett-Packard in 2005, at Continental Clairoix in 2007, at Peugeot Motorcycles in 2008, and at GM's Strasbourg gearbox plant in 2010. Sometimes lower labor costs preserve jobs, but sometimes not: the Bosch and Clairoix plants subsequently closed.[70]

Americans have fretted about the rising economic prowess of China since their exports surpassed US exports in 2007. Few realize that stealthy northern Europe is the real global export colossus. Despite the American advantages in commodity exports such as food and coal, exports from Belgium, France, Germany, and the Netherlands grew faster from 1999 to 2009.[71] No democracy except Australia has benefited more from globalization. Here is the European specialist economist Barry Eichengreen:

> "European exporters continue to dominate international markets in precision manufactures ranging from luxury sedans to dialysis machines. It is the United States, not Europe, whose auto companies and airlines are on the ropes owing to low productivity and poor product quality and which have massive trade and current account deficits. . . . [And] . . . the stronger hand of government in setting product standards has given European firms producing high-tech

products a leg up on their American competitors. After all, for much of the 1990s, it was not some US high-tech giant but Nokia, from tiny Finland, that dominated the global cell phone market. The point is general: European firms continue to compete successfully in a wide range of high-tech products, from pharmaceuticals to high-speed trains."[72]

And Germany is the greatest beneficiary of all; codetermination. makes that country easily the globe's most competitive economy measured by exports per capita, where the long term is measured in years rather than in months. For even the canniest American CEO to step into the executive suite or boardroom of a German firm such as VW would be like stepping onto the bridge of the starship *Enterprise*. Expectations of competence, vision, and expertise would be higher. Every decision would be ruthlessly parsed by expert colleagues wielding a great deal of detail and their own competing robust visions for the firm. And he or she would be paid a great deal less as CEO in the bargain. American CEOs would hate it.

Led by France and Germany, northern Europe is reformulating the EU, with a final amalgam still to be determined as the region's sovereign debt crisis plays out. The current challenges should not obscure the fundamental strength found in the superior corporate governance and resulting superior economic performance of these family capitalism economies. And the key is their openness to globalization, making them investment magnets. Nearly one-half of the funds invested in the French stock market (the CAC 40) come from abroad.[73] And, between 2000 and 2005, the EU received nearly one-half of global foreign direct investment, far more than China and the United States combined.[74] Yet, northern Europe's cutthroat competitive environment is not for every American corporation, as we will see in a moment.

Competition is fierce. We learn that from the behavior there of the iconic American firm McDonald's. Its outlets in northern Europe deploy more upscale décor and menus than in America. Tough competition has left it little choice but to grant local management almost *carte blanche* to innovate. Instead of competing by hiring Washington men to harp about taxes and regulation, the company reinvented its railway station café image with innovations first introduced there: table service, automated order kiosks, and café settings with upholstered or Danish-style egg chairs that compete directly with local coffee shops.[75]

McDonald's is not an isolated example. Most Americans pay little attention to northern Europe. But that isn't true for a key cohort of influential, wealthy, and important Americans who run the largest and most competitive US multinationals. These keen observers have led a wholesale flight of American firms to northern Europe in recent decades. Thousands of America's most competitive and vibrant enterprises have invested there, including 3,000 in France alone,[76] creating more than 500,000 jobs, with more than $1 billion a week in commerce flowing between that country and the United States.[77] In Germany, the 4,000-strong US Chamber of Commerce claims that US firms account "for approximately 800,000 direct jobs and over $100 billion in investment."[78] Pete Sweeney with *European Voice* acknowledges that European affiliates of American companies in total employ millions of Europeans,[79] including more than 100,000 Ford and GM auto workers alone.[80] Even amid the current debt crisis and slowdown, firms like Amazon continued adding thousands of jobs across Europe during 2012 and 2013.[81]

And, not a single one is a crummy US-style job.

Their investments evidence the normal greed motivating capitalism. But they also highlight the disingenuous attitude of American executives toward stakeholder capitalism. Back home, US multinationals lobby *against* higher wages, preventing their American employees from living as well as their European employees.

The word you're searching for is duplicity.

American Business Keeps You in the Dark While Creating Jobs and Paying Higher Wages in Europe

I first noticed the phenomenon in 2004. Rental cars in Europe began to baffle me, with power-window rocker switches you had to pull up instead of down. Really odd, because new cars back home still came with the old switches. The explanation was a new EU regulation—one which American firms successfully fought at home. It turns out that toddlers can accidentally push down window rocker switches with tiny toes, and some were strangling as a result, including seven American youngsters in just three months in 2004. Worried about profits, Detroit killed remedial regulation—the safer pull switch—but Europe puts families ahead of profits. It wasn't until 2006 that the death toll grew sufficiently large to convince the Bush administration to do what parents and safety advocates had been demanding for years.[82]

Rules have consequences, and rules like this embodying family capitalism in Australia and northern Europe annoy American firms. What CEO likes being told what to do, especially by employees and moms? Yet, as business professor Rakesh Khurana argues, "If there's an ideology of management, it is pragmatism."[83]

American firms abroad comply with local customs wherever on the globe they do business. That sometimes produces behavior their American shareholders and employees would find startling—none more surprising than their behavior in northern Europe. There, they pay close attention to the concerns of all stakeholders, including employees, customers, and debt holders, and follow the rules of family capitalism, because they have to.

That means all US firms operating in northern Europe negotiate openly and in good faith with trade unions and government agencies about annual wage increases. They agree to split productivity gains with their employees each year, pay wages above what they pay in America for the identical work, grant year-end bonuses and the conventional four to six weeks of vacation. And, they interact routinely with employee work councils. Moreover, firms like Ford eagerly use European government programs to limit layoffs and retain skilled workforces, a decidedly un-American practice.[84] And they pay many billions of Euros into government health care, pension, worker training, and other programs supporting family capitalism.

Multinationals do it for the profit with eyes wide open. Their attitude is exemplified by TIAA-CREF, the American global pension and investment manager. Like most other American multinationals these days, it can be found in every nook and cranny of Europe. They know firsthand that family capitalism works and acknowledge that Reagan-era America "is not necessarily the best model for everyone. I think there is a great awareness that other models make sense. There is no one-size-fits-all for companies," according to John Wilcox, former head of corporate governance in 2010.[85]

The reality is that American firms readily comply with the customs in stakeholder capitalism of work councils, codetermination, splitting annual productivity gains with employees, and union bargaining agreements.

They will do the same thing in America when voters change the rules to prioritize family, rather than firm, prosperity.

America's Low-Wage Model Fails in Europe: Walmart

Institutionalizing stakeholder capitalism rules in the United States would require firms to adopt the model used by American multinationals in Europe. It may not be a happy experience for some. Consumers in family capitalism countries have high expectations that firms will support, rather than exploit, customers and employees. That makes them poor fits for enterprises reliant on the disposable labor model.

Forced to pay double their accustomed American wages, US firms in northern Europe must draw deeply from innate management expertise to adapt. Many like Amazon, McDonald's, and Starbucks have displayed the superior management skills needed to survive, paying high European wages while providing quality service and products. There are similar success stories in Australia. Domino's Pizza, for example, has prospered in Australia and New Zealand despite what CEO Don Meij describes as their "Scandinavian labor costs. The labour cost of a US delivery driver is one-third the price in Australia."[86] Despite paying high wages, Domino's exploited the internet to raise profits by 15 percent in 2011 in Oceania. But other US firms with weaker management have foundered badly under stakeholder capitalism.

The most instructive example is Walmart; the company's experience offers multiple lessons. The adventure began when Walmart purchased the Wertkauf retail chain in 1997 and the 74-store Spar Handels chain in 1998. The result was 85 German Walmart stores, with 11,000 employees and excellent economies of scale. But it was downhill from there.

Walmart is among the world's largest firms, but management was overmatched when confronted *mano a mano* with rules and expectations about corporate behavior in Germany, and with seasoned German retailing giant Metro. Self-inflicted damage by Walmart executives seeking to apply its American business model rapidly doomed the expansion. One challenge was that the lush German retail sector places a premium on customer relations, while Walmart's strong suit is low prices based on low employee wages and inexpensive Asian imports. Moreover, what could charitably be termed its quirky corporate culture alienated far too many potential customers. For example, it quickly garnered unhelpful publicity for poor employee relations, treating German workers like its American workforce: as problems rather than partners. Management-labor relations supporting high wages are vital to family prosperity, which means that European shoppers are generally unwilling to support "bad citizens" who chisel employees by legalistically manipulating rules to find loopholes. Forced to adhere to demanding consumer expectations about firm behavior—and eventually forced to pay nearly double its American wage structure—Walmart had difficulty viewing its expensive employees as assets useful in improving its corporate image and interpreting local consumer inclinations.

From the start, poor labor relations were a problem, as controversy with its employees erupted into public squabbling. Walmart stalled wage negotiations and demonized its employees' unions. It also slow-walked implementing traditional northern Europe nonwage workplace practices that management found inconsistent with the hierarchical American mode. Work councils, for example, are useful early warning tripwires for European firms eager to draw on experienced employees.

Indeed, veteran local hires were potentially of great value to a neophyte like Walmart. But Walmart instead simply wanted trade unions, work councils, and high wages to disappear—as in America.

Walmart's management adopted practices that repeatedly resulted in public ridicule. One consequence of failing to consult with employees was the unfortunate instigation of an anonymous informer hotline, apparently common in its American stores. German employees were encouraged to secretly inform on one another, in an astounding display of insensitivity in light of Germany's recent history. This episode was in a class by itself for amateurish management and proved far too redolent of Germany's Communist and Nazi past for customers. Even so, Walmart ended the policy only when a German court declared it illegal. The informer hotline episode was then magnified by widespread publicity in Germany surrounding Walmart's decision at around the same time to close its Jonquière store in Quebec, Canada; the firm eliminated hundreds of Canadian jobs rather than accept a collective bargaining agreement.

As curious Germans digested these events, they voted with their feet, staying away by the millions.* Burdened with a tarnished image, Walmart confronted a choice after just a few years: adapt or abandon Europe. Other firms in similar straits—the grocery convenience retailer Lidl, for example, which had a similarly unsavory reputation for spying on employees—had succeeded in adapting to community expectations.[87]

But reform seemingly is not Walmart's strong suit. And so it bolted, abandoning its European operations in 2006 in favor of expansion in Asia, Latin America, and India, where local rules are more accommodating to its low-wage and disposable labor practices. Walmart sold its operations to competitor Metro after losing nearly $5 billion, according to the leading German retail industry weekly magazine *Lebensmittelzeitung*. Hans-Joachim Körber, CEO of competitor Metro, was reported to have said he "cannot hide his satisfaction . . . that the US retail giant lost out and paid dearly for it."†

---

*The most comprehensive source of detailed public information on Walmart's failed attempt to enter the Continental market are the "Walmart pages," a series that appeared periodically on the United Food and Commercial Workers' website. The series included: "Ridicule and Anger Instead of Results and Profits," April 12, 2005; "Critical Walmart Documentary is Well Received at Berlin Film Festival," Feb. 13, 2006; "Walmart Throws in the Towel in Germany as Social Dumping Did Not Work," July 28, 2006; "Social Dumping Does not Pay: Walmart Lost 4.5 Billion Dollars on Its German Fiasco,"Aug. 7, 2006; and "Walmart Says No to Personnel Representatives Training in Germany, May Have to Answer in Court," Sept. 4, 2006.

†Other American firms have found high-wage family capitalism a hindrance to profitability and also bolted, even closing up shop in the middle of the night, unpaid bills

McDonald's in Europe

Walmart's flight stands in contrast to the experience of other American firms in northern Europe, even those such as McDonald's that rely on the same low-wage model. McDonald's established its first store in Europe over thirty years ago, and continues to expand today, carving out markets across Europe and into Russia. It has over 1,350 outlets and 60,000 employees in Germany alone, and Europe has emerged as a vital contributor to McDonald's bottom line.

McDonald's success is built in part on avoiding some of the miscues of Walmart. As noted earlier, management has been willing to adapt its business model, drawing on local expertise, relying on local ingredients, and preserving local architecture. Moreover, it exhibited flexibility, modifying its low-wage model, paying about double its US wages in Scandinavia, for example.[88] Even so, old habits die hard; the firm has persistently endeavored to exploit loopholes to avoid paying more than the absolutely lowest wage.[89]

Europe tends to regulate by goals. Officials provide plenty of written guidance, but rely on firms to meet the spirit of those guidelines in a collaborative fashion. The presumption is that the business community will not seek to thwart public intent by legalistically exploiting regulatory leeway. American executives are schooled in the adversarial *über* legalistic US model, however, where lawyerly evasion is the *modus operandi*, and every comma, adverb, and adjective relentlessly parsed for wiggle room.

For example, McDonald's established its own captive trade union and work councils, comprising mostly compliant store managers.*

---

fluttering in the taillights of the moving vans. For example, the US auto parts firm Molex had a factory with nearly 300 employees in the French town of Villemur-sur-Tarn, Haute-Garonne, supplying the auto giants Renault and PSA. Molex closed the plant in October 2009 and skipped town, owing perhaps €4 million ($5 million) to employees. The move seems to have helped profitability; a year later, the firm reported record earnings per share, and announced a 14 percent dividend to shareholders. Laws in northern Europe support employees more strongly than in America, however, and government officials can be persistent in chasing wage chiselers, including firms like Molex that use legalities to obfuscate ownership and thwart debt collection. Officials initiated legal action against Molex. The French Minister of Industry at the time, Christiani Estrosi, also "asked PSA and Renault—two important clients of Molex—to cease all trade with the US company," reported *Le Figaro*. See Agence France-Presse, "Molex Displays Record Results," Le Figaro, Oct. 27, 2010, and "The Government Calls for a Boycott of PSA and Renault Molex," *Le Figaro*, Oct. 27, 2010.

*Professor Tony Royle at the National University of Ireland in Galway is the leading European expert on McDonald's and author of *Working for McDonald's in Europe*. His analyses have also appeared in a variety of professional journals, including:

Other tactics include discriminatorily firing trade union supporters and slow-walking wage negotiations.[90] In a frustrated France, the repeated use of these tactics caused courts to order the arrest of some McDonald's managers.[91]

Other American firms like Amazon have adopted some of McDonald's tactics. Amazon is a resounding commercial success in northern Europe. Sales have tripled since 2006 in Germany alone, with distribution centers at Bad Hersefeld, Rheinberg, Leipzig, and Werne employing as many as 9,000 temporary hires during busy periods. But management is apparently unhappy paying wages of €9.65 ($12) per hour, well above American wages.

To compress wages, both Amazon and McDonald's aggressively game the government subsidized apprentice programs in northern Europe. Amazon exploits a German Federal Employment Agency subsidy, for example, where taxpayers fund the entire wage for the first two weeks for new employees; the German program is designed to avail firms a window to costlessly evaluate the suitability of new hires. Rules to prevent repetitive reemployment of the same men and women (at taxpayer expense) were thought unnecessary because such practices clearly violate the law's intent. Amazon viewed that presumption as a loophole: as many as one-half of its workers are repetitive rehires, an abusive exploitation of the program that was termed "scandalous" by the North Rhine-Westphalia labor minister Guntram Schneider in 2010. The tactic saved Amazon €1 million in wages just in that one German state alone that year.[92]

"Just Vote No! Union-Busting in the European Fast-Food Industry: The Case of McDonald's," *Industrial Relations Journal*, vol 33, 262–276, 2002, http://ssm.com/abstract=320668; Tony Royle, "Worker Representation Under Threat? The McDonald's Corporation and Effectiveness of Statutory Works Councils in Seven European Union Countries," *Comparative Labor Law & Policy Journal*, vol. 22, no. 2/3, 2003.

Section 3

THE RESULTS

CHAPTER 13

WAGES RISE IN FAMILY CAPITALISM

"If we are able to grow, as our German friends, the productivity of our economy, then of course we must increase wages."[1]

CHRISTINE LAGARDE,
Former Economic Minister, France
Managing Director, International Monetary Fund

"The share of every dollar of value added to the US economy going to American workers has also fallen to a record low of 57.1 cents in the US dollar, down from more than 62 cents before the subprime mortgage crisis, and well below an average of 63.9 cents in the previous century."[2]

MALCOLM MAIDEN,
Sydney Morning Herald
December 14, 2011

"Europe is often held up as a cautionary tale, a demonstration that if you try to make the economy less brutal, to take better care of your fellow citizens when they're down on their luck, you end up killing economic progress. But what the European experience actually demonstrates is the opposite: social justice and progress can go hand in hand."[3]

PAUL KRUGMAN,
Nobel Laureate, Princeton University

Mervyn Le Roy's film *I am a Fugitive from a Chain Gang* exquisitely captured 1932, the darkest and most despairing year in American economic history. Paul Muni is rendered bankrupt, jobless, and disgruntled by a malevolent government and callous society. The film contains perhaps the most evocative scene in American cinematic history, when Muni is unable to hock his Army medals because the pawnshop already had purchased too many.

Two years later, *It Happened One Night* became the only film ever to win all the major Academy Awards, even though it was far from Frank Capra's best. He rejected the pessimism of *I Am a Fugitive* crafted early in the New Deal to present a message of optimism in *One Night*.

Capra's antagonist was a plutocrat who selfishly resists reforms initially, but its message was uplifting in the end, when Claudette Colbert's wealthy father abandons his narcissism.

As the Great Depression persisted with despair deepening, Capra revised his narrative again in his best work, the nuanced *Mr. Smith Goes to Washington* (1939).[4] The plutocrat businessman Edward Arnold remains corrupt to the end, bending government to his bidding and forcing the hero James Stewart and moviegoers alike to confront the enormous challenge and complexities in bestowing economic sovereignty on families. Capra taught that Aristotelian democracy is possible in America only if voters are willing to struggle mightily to attain it. Even today, audiences react to its powerful emotive message: only a visionary sense of community can overcome a society dominated by a greedy and cynical extractive elite.

Both American and northern European families have been on a journey since those dark days, but their destinations have proven quite different. The American journey, which began so brightly with the postwar flush of prosperity, has ended badly. Why? Blessed with abundance and a sense of exceptionalism that lured too many to believe that *One Night* portrayed reality, it was much easier for Americans to be misled by politicians. In contrast, jaundiced voters in northern Europe were not so foolish to believe that family prosperity was a default setting for capitalism. Scarred by pitched street battles with communists, Weimar inflation, the Depression, and devastating war, voters there knew firsthand the ghastly terror, anger, and frustration of Paul Muni's character. They knew far too well the shortcomings of democracy to believe that innate goodness resides in its DNA, as Capra argued in *One Night*. Unlike Americans, they had learned what economists Daron Acemoglu of MIT and James Robinson of Harvard concluded in *Why Nations Fail*, that episodes of broadly based opportunity for innovation, entrepreneurship, and prosperity are so rare in economic history over thousands of years that they can be counted on the fingers of one hand. They are absolutely not default settings for capitalism or any other economic system in America or anywhere else.

Europeans knew the manipulative Edward Arnold—and far worse—was reality, which is why, after World War II, they voted to craft a new and clever capitalism that granted economic sovereignty to families, not firms. Moreover, beginning in the 1950s, they adopted Jean Monnet's vision of a common market in hopes of escaping the continent's baleful history of war and bloodshed.

His goal was to dilute nationalism by coalescing economic and trade interests within Europe to render war less likely.[5] Monnet realized that relying on economics to defuse nationalism had failed, nowhere more harshly and recently than in Europe. In 1909, the *Daily Mail's* Norman Angell had published *Europe's Optical Illusion*, arguing that with intertwined economic and credit ties among the Great Powers, even the winner of war would be worse off.[6] Austrian Stefan Zweig's sobering and poignant 1942 autobiography, *The World of Yesterday,* rejected the *faux* security described by Angell and others. The great nineteenth-century wave of European globalization and wealth creation had failed to prevent the bloodiest thirty years in history. Zweig wrote of the optimistic era prior to the Archduke Ferdinand's assassination in 1914, which sparked World War I. In *Belle Époque* Vienna,

> "There was as little belief in the possibility of wars between the peoples of Europe as there was in witches and ghosts. . . . Our fathers honestly believed that the divergences and boundaries between nations and sects would gradually melt away into a common humanity. . . . Now that the great storm has long since smashed it, we finally know that the world of security was naught but a castle of dreams; my parents lived in it as if it had been a house of stone."[7]

Converting Zweig's ephemeral castle to stone in post–World War II Europe required economic unification to create stability. With fears of the expansionist Soviet Union providing a wind at his back, Monnet evolved unification bit by bit, beginning with Europe's coal and steel industries. He built his castle on the philosophy of Adam Smith, relying on the invisible hand of the market to allocate resources most efficiently. As Mark Leonard, director of foreign policy at the Centre for European Reform, explained in 2005:

> "Monnet's genius was to develop a 'European invisible hand' that allows an orderly European society to emerge from each country's national interest. . . . He did not try to abolish the nation-state or nationalism—simply to change its nature by pooling sovereignty."[8]

The Emergence of Family Capitalism

The genius of Adam Smith was not in his depiction of the age-old market process for allocating resources, but the much more nuanced melding of human nature and careful government regulation to sketch how markets can best be corralled and exploited to nourish mankind. Australia and the northern Europe economies have implemented Smith's vision: mankind doesn't serve markets in the fashion of the Reagan era, but rather is served by markets. The dictates of the marketplace and age-old greed are yoked to the higher priority of nurturing society and families.

Family prosperity is the postwar national covenant of the family capitalist countries, because citizens have been given clear choices at the polls and they've logically chosen self interest. Selfish voters have implemented Adam Smith's dream of markets serving mankind by voting for public institutions and policies to institutionalize family economic sovereignty as national covenants. They strive at every election to implement the lesson Capra taught in *Mr. Smith*.

In contrast, Americans have voted since 1980 to shift economic sovereignty to the business community. Like families in *fin de siècle* Vienna, American voters by 1980 had come to believe—erroneously—that their golden age was built of stone rather than sand. Your parents or grandparents mistakenly believed that family prosperity was America's default position, seemingly destined to persist regardless of choices at the poll. In reality, history teaches that the Aristotelian elites described by Acemoglu and Robinson virtually always extract all the gains from growth. The default setting for families since the beginning of time is to be victimized just as Americans have been under Reaganomics by those Adam Smith called "merchants and master manufacturers."

Half a world away in Australia, voters also have avoided the American illusion that broadly based prosperity is the default setting for capitalism. Instead, like northern Europe, both conservative and liberal governments have labored to institutionalize stakeholder capitalism, featuring a nationwide wage determination system along with collaborative worksite environments. And also like northern Europe, but unlike America, the consequence has been real wages that have risen apace with productivity.

Wages and Productivity

Throughout history, wages have been what landowners, entrepreneurs, or owners of capital said they were. Rising real wages were rare, except for specialists, medieval guilds, or when plagues or other catastrophes caused labor shortages. Wages were highest at the economic height of Rome in the first century AD, late medieval England, and perhaps also in eleventh-century Kaifeng, capital of the Song dynasty, when early manufacturing specialization raised labor demand.*

* Rising industrial specialization caused wages in first century AD Rome to be higher in real terms than at anytime over the following sixteen centuries in Europe. See Robert Allen, "How Prosperous Were the Romans? The Evidence of Diocletian's Price Edict, 301 AD," Oxford University Department of Economics working paper no. 363 (2007).

The trump card wielded by employers systematically began to weaken only as productivity and labor demand rose for workers in the pottery, textiles, and other industries at Stoke-on-Trent, where the miraculous eighteenth-century Industrial Revolution began. Adam Smith was mesmerized by the productivity at a pin factory, for example, and concluded that wages had begun to be influenced by skill and education, rather than brute employer market power alone. Historian Ian Morris explains:

> "By about 1830, these investments were making the mechanically augmented labor of each dirty, malnourished, ill-educated 'hand' so profitable that bosses often preferred cutting deals with strikers to firing them and competing with other bosses to find new ones."[9]

Rising wages in the two centuries since lulled many into believing that wages naturally reflected value added by employees. Had the law of supply and demand been negated, as they thought? Would employees instead be paid according to their productivity level? This issue has dogged economics since the early industrial revolution, when data first began to appear regarding wages and productivity and inspired a series of famous (among economists) debates during the 1880s: Alfred Marshall faced down enthusiasts of Henry George and John Stuart Mill, who believed that competition among workers always had the potential to cause stagnating or declining real wages regardless of rising productivity. Marshall demurred.[10] Armed with decades of statistics from the era of labor shortages created by the industrial revolution then driving up real wages, Marshall argued that private property and competition were succeeding in raising wages where socialism could not.

The outcome was that a wage-productivity link became standard theory among economists. This presumed linkage between wages and productivity was also credentialed by the iconic American automaker Henry Ford, whose legacy remains embodied in the Australian wage mechanism of the rich democracies today. Here is how *New York Times* Washington bureau chief David Leonhardt described that legacy in 2006:

> "Henry Ford was 50 years old, and not all that different from a lot of other successful businessmen, when he summoned the Detroit press corps to his company's offices on January 5, 1914. What he did that day made him a household name. . . . Mr. Ford announced that he was *doubling* the pay of thousands of his employees, to at least $5 a day. With his company selling Model T's as fast as it could make them, his workers deserved to share in the profits, he said. His rivals were horrified. The *Wall Street Journal* accused him of

injecting 'Biblical or spiritual principles into a field where they do not belong.' The *New York Times* correspondent who traveled to Detroit to interview him that week asked him if he was a socialist."[11]

Ford could pay higher than market-clearing wages, because the productivity of his workers was relatively high; a Model T was produced every twenty-four seconds, compared to 12 hours previously.[12] Better productivity performance also enabled Ford to grow fabulously rich, despite paying better wages than his competitors. Malcolm Gladwell has concluded that Ford is the most successful auto man ever and the seventh richest person in history, resting between Andrew Mellon and the Roman Senator Marcus Crassus.[13] He was no fool, producing 15.5 million model Ts and revolutionizing the global auto industry; Ford certainly didn't become wealthy overpaying for anything. This quintessential capitalist recognized that wages, based on value-added rather than market forces, were affordable—and even vital—in ensuring the prosperity of both his empire and of America:

> "Our own sales depend in a measure upon the wages we pay. If we can distribute high wages, then that money is going to be spent, and it will serve to make storekeepers and distributors and manufacturers and workers in other lines more prosperous, and their prosperity will be reflected in our sales. . . . Countrywide high wages spell countrywide prosperity."[14]

Henry Ford was a ferocious capitalist, but realized more was at stake than his own bank account. Higher wages meant greater economic prosperity. And his logic has prevailed in family capitalism nations such as Australia, as explained in this June 2010 editorial in the *Sydney Morning Herald*:

> ". . . businesses in a market economy depend on consumer confidence and spending. Nothing hurts more than workers who can't make ends meet. Every cent that goes to low-paid workers will be spent, whereas freezing wages can only cause consumer spending to contract."[15]

Rising productivity results from the efforts of both employees and employers. Employers such as Henry Ford or General Motors provide most tools, equipment, and machinery in the workplace, which is an important determinant of productivity. Tim Slaughter's information technology boss in Detroit certainly provided him computers and software. Likewise, the education, job skills, work ethic, talent, suggestions for improvement, and skill upgrading that employees such as Augustine, Tim, and you and I bring to the workplace are also important contributors to productivity. Making productivity rise is a shared project between employees and employers pulling together and jointly improving efficiency.

During most of the industrial era, some sizable portion of such efficiency improvements have been shared between employers and employees, just as Adam Smith and Alfred Marshall presumed. But the whole story is more nuanced and less encouraging—a lot less encouraging. It turns out that productivity growth is a necessary, but not sufficient, determinant of wages. Rising productivity spreading from the eighteenth-century Midlands across the globe didn't repeal the law of supply and demand after all. Certainly during the golden age, and during the previous two centuries when labor markets were tight, Alfred Marshall's marginal value theory was a reasonably accurate depiction of labor market realities, with wages rising more or less apace with productivity. In America, for example, Augustine reaped high wages in Detroit as his productivity increased—just like the theory predicted.

That ceased beginning in the 1970s. During the Reagan era, Washington stood by passively as offshoring, "us vs. them," international wage arbitrage, and weaker trade unions tilted the balance of power in worksite negotiations in favor of employers. American men and women have continued to do their part, finishing high school or college, becoming better educated and adept at information technology, working harder and more productively. Yet wages became delinked from productivity, as depicted in Chart 13.1.

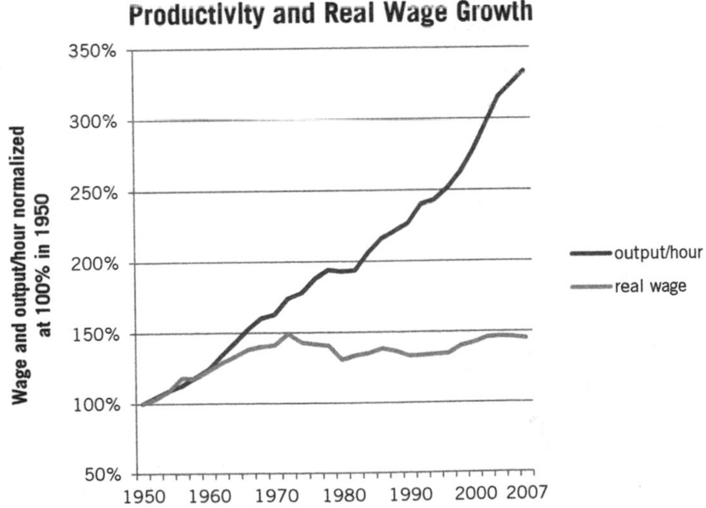

Chart 13.1. Real wage is average weekly earnings from 1950–1979 and wage component of Employment Cost Index 1979–2007. Output/hour is private nonfarm sector productivity growth. *Source: "National Employment Survey and Employment Cost Survey," Bureau of Labor Statistics.*

Adam Smith would have found that odd, because the American workforce is better educated and more productive today than ever in its history, yet wage earners for three decades have received little of the added bounty created. It would also stun Alfred Marshall, Smith's successor as the greatest British economist, because it defied the generalized nineteenth- and twentieth-century experience and the shared presumption of economists across the political spectrum ever since. Even the most conservative economists endorse the wage-productivity linkage. Henry Hazlitt of the Austrian school of economic persuasions argued that "wages are basically determined by labor productivity."[16]

Yet Smith and Marshall hadn't confronted Reaganomics, which severed the productivity-wage link. Alfred Marshall would embarrassingly lose his debates today, which has sparked an extensive reexamination of the link by a host of economists, including Robert H. Frank and Phillip Cook, Edward Wolff, Robert Kuttner, Ian Dew-Becker, and Robert J. Gordon.[17]

The Reagan era Delinked Wages from Productivity

Not only did President Reagan and his heirs apparently not read Greek—no crime there—they didn't appreciate the most iconic of all American capitalists, an embarrassing lapse for any US leader. Real wages rose during the remarkable American golden age economic renaissance after World War II to become the highest in the world because of Henry Ford's perspective. And wages rise in the family capitalism countries today for the same reason, because their national covenant is to spread the bounty from rising productivity to all, beginning with employees. Here is how Berthold Huber, head of the large German IG Metall trade union, explained the centrality of linking wages to productivity growth: "A big part of our wage-setting formula is always productivity. It's not the same in other nations."[18]

It is certainly not the same in America.

A brief economics lesson: The income generated by an economy from one year to the next will rise for only two reasons. Population growth is the first. The other is productivity growth, which enables more to be produced with the same amount of effort. Both factors spurred the postwar American golden age, until 1973. Population growth averaged better than 1 percent annually. But much more important was the rapid and persistent growth in labor output per hour—productivity—which averaged 2.8 percent annually. That hefty rise in productivity was key to raising living standards. More could be produced with the same work effort, making productivity growth the standard for assessing genuine economic performance.

It was President John Adams who famously said, "Facts are stubborn things; and whatever may be our wishes, our inclinations or the dictates of our passion, they cannot alter the state of facts and evidence."[19] Let's begin with facts about wages in the generations since World War II. US agencies such as the Bureau of Labor Statistics conduct a handful of wage and labor cost surveys and they all depict the same story: inflation-adjusted wages rose handsomely until 1973, which turns out to be the peak year for wages in American history. During the rest of the 1970s, wages continued rising briskly, but inflation took away all of the gains, which caused real wages to sag.

Real wage stagnation continued after the Reagan era dawned in 1981, but the reasons why became different. Rather than stagnating because of inflation, real wages went flat because wages on offer from employers began growing far more slowly. Wages went flat as American employers chose to stop rewarding rising labor productivity. For most Americans, the outcome was wage increases that trailed slightly behind inflation. The only exception was about 5 percent of the labor force, especially those with graduate school and professional degrees, valuable skills, senior business executives, or bankers. Their earnings outpaced inflation. These results are summarized in Table 1.

Annual Real Wage Change

	1950–1973	1979–2011
Average wage changes:		
Earnings of all employees[1]	n/a	+ 0.1
Earnings of middle/working class employees[2]	1.8	– 0.1
Median weekly earning[3]	n/a	+ 0.1
Index: Productivity growth/year	2.8	1.9

Table 1.

[1] Wage and salary component of Employment Cost Index; survey began in 1979.

[2] Current Employment Survey of real weekly average wages covers the lower paid 80 percent of all private sector employees (those in nonsupervisory and production occupations).

[3] Fulltime workers; series began in 1979.

Source: Employment Cost Index, Current Employment Survey and Private Nonfarm Business Sector Productivity Series, http://data.bls.gov/cgi-bin/print.pl/lpc/prodybar.htm, Bureau of Labor Statistics.

Wage data for middle- and working-class employees (nonsupervisory and production employees) is the most comprehensive private-sector time series across the entire postwar period. It excludes compensation paid to the top 20 percent of the American workforce, such as CEOs and other white collar and supervisory employees. Because this series includes the wages and salaries earned by the bottom 80 percent of all Americans, college and noncollege, male and female alike, it provides the most accurate snapshot of how most Americans working in the private sector have fared.

Real wages increased an average of 1.8 percent each year (nearly 50 percent overall) during the postwar decades through 1973, before hitting a stone wall. Total real labor compensation, which includes benefits as well as wages, performed better than wages alone, at least until 2004.[20] But total compensation has gone flat since then as well, because employers have succeeded in capping benefit outlays after years of shifting pension and health insurance costs to employees. In combination with stagnant paychecks, this shifting has caused important out-of-pocket costs for health (co-pays, premiums, and deductibles), housing, child care, and education to now consume 75 percent of middle-class household incomes compared to only one-half of incomes back in the 1980s.[21] This budget squeeze is why families in recent decades resorted to debt and the widespread breaching of retirement accounts like 401(k)s to meet household expenses.[22] In recent years, about 28 percent of participants have borrowed against retirement, and 42 percent completely cash out pension funds when changing jobs.[23]

This epoch of wage stagnation is acknowledged by economists across the ideological spectrum. Details show that the Reagan-era erosion in earnings has been most severe among men, whose wages are down nearly 20 percent in real terms since 1980. About one-half of that drop is the result of pay lagging inflation, and the other half the result of an (unwelcomed) decline in annual work hours. Work has become less secure and more erratic, with millions of men cycling in and out of the labor force over the course of a year, unable to find full-time work because job growth has lagged workforce growth. For example, 94 percent of men between the prime ages of 25–64 worked in 1970, but only 81 percent worked in the recovery year 2010, the "new normal" of a weak economy that bedevils American families today. The hourly earnings of women performed better during the Reagan era but remain below male earnings.[24]

Productivity growth rates are also noted in Table 1. By comparing real wage growth and productivity growth, an approximation of how the gains from economic growth have been distributed can be determined. During the golden age, productivity growth averaged 2.8 percent annually and real employee wages rose about 1.8 percent, meaning employees received about 60 percent of that growth. That is how the greatest middle class in history was created. It explains how your parents or grandparents, along with Augustine, were able to leave farms and become solid members of the middle class, buy a home and a new car, take vacations, and step onto a career path. That outcome was responsible for driving poverty in America down to record low levels not seen since, enabling tens of millions of farm boys like Augustine and my father to live the American Dream.

The relentless rise in wages earned by these men and women across America made them equal beneficiaries with bankers and business executives of the wondrous American postwar boom. It breathed life into the American Dream. And this postwar model of stakeholder capitalism was studied intently and mimicked by Japan, Australia, and northern European nations eager to create their own flourishing middle classes after World War II.

America was heroic. It had managed to turn the genius of John Locke and Adam Smith into broadly rising prosperity for most, regardless of the meanness of their birth. And the broad rise in living standards from American stakeholder capitalism tossed socialism and communism into the dustbin of history.

Voters ended it all in 1980.

Wage Compression

This postwar span of America's wage history has been studied by a host of economists including Thomas Piketty and Emmanuel Saez.[25] Their analyses tell the same story of robustly rising wages through the golden age, followed in the decades since by stagnation. For example, Isabel Sawhill, senior fellow at the Brookings Institution, and John Morton, director of the Economic Mobility Project at the Pew Charitable Trusts, examined the earnings of fathers and sons using data from the US Census Bureau. As a baseline, Sawhill and Morton looked at men who were in their thirties in 2004 and compared their incomes to their fathers' at the same age in 1974. It is very likely that the males in your family were part of their giant database. They found that real median incomes of men in their thirties in 2004 was 12 percent ($5,200) lower than in 1974, vividly documenting how the Reagan era delinked productivity and hard work from wages.[26]

This pattern holds across all education levels. For example, the Economic Policy Institute concluded that the entry-level wage for men with secondary school diplomas was $11.68 per hour in 2010, down from $15.64 per hour in constant dollars in 1979. Moreover, as noted earlier, men and women with college degrees also earn less now, adjusted for inflation, than during the golden age. Among broad categories, only earnings of graduate school degree-holders are higher.[27]

The outcome since 1980 has been wage compression, the consequence of elements such as offshoring and short-termism, with mediocre jobs replacing good ones. It is exemplified by the anecdotal behavior we reviewed earlier of auto companies and firms such as Snapple Dr. Pepper. And it's statistically documented extensively as well. The analysis noted earlier found that some 79 percent of the 6 million jobs lost in 2008–2009 paid more than $13.84 an hour, yet only 42 percent of the jobs created in 2010-2012 paid as well.[28] Moreover, in January 2011, the National Employment Law Project found that 40 percent of jobs lost during the recent recession were high-wage ones, but only 14 percent of the new jobs in the recovery paid the same high wage. In contrast, only 23 percent of jobs lost were lower-wage ones paying less than $15 per hour, but they comprised 49 percent of all new jobs.[29]

This degrading of America's job mix confirms that little of the gains from growth during the Reagan era accrued to employees, with wages delinked from productivity. As we will soon learn in detail, such decoupling has not occurred since World War II in the other rich democracies. In the United States, the most recent previous episode was the Roaring Twenties when productivity grew 63 percent between 1920 and 1929, but real wages fell 9 percent.[30] But that disconnect nearly a century ago was too brief to convince economists that the productivity-wage link portrayed by Adam Smith and Alfred Marshall had been severed.

By contrast, the current disconnect has persisted for three decades and counting, through recession and recovery—virtually the entire span of the Baby Boomer work experience. And unfortunately, it seems this delinking will persist until either policies are changed in Washington or a billion new high-value jobs are created globally, enough to create US labor shortages.

Wages and the Gains from Growth in the Family Capitalism Countries

As we learned earlier, real wages have continued rising in the family capitalism countries, with paychecks closely mirroring the statistics on the cover (covering wages, benefits, and employer taxes for manufacturing blue-collar workers) as well as the French experience (just wages) depicted in Chart 13.2.[31] The statistics on the cover depict a considerably larger rise than this figure because the full cost of French workers such as fringe benefits and government fees for health care and the like has outpaced the rise in wages alone.

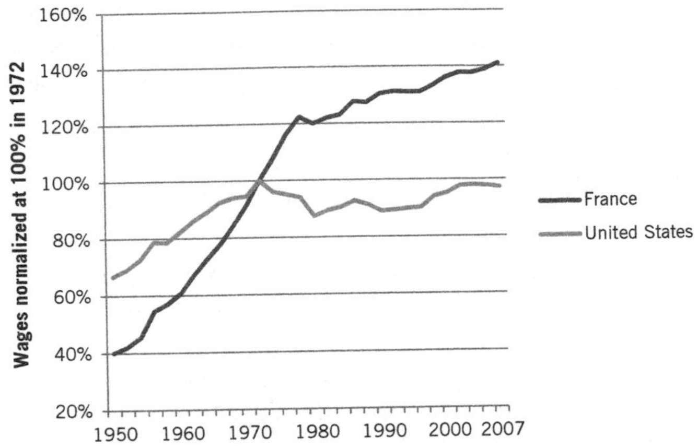

Chart 13.2. The US series is average real weekly earnings (1950–1979) and the wage and salary component of the Employment Cost Index (1979–2007) for the private nonfarm sector. French wages are average wage index series net of government taxes for the private and semi-public sectors, and includes apprentices and trainees, but excluding government employees.

Sources: National Employment Survey and Employment Cost Survey, Bureau of Labor Statistics; "Revenus-Salalres-Evolution du Salaire Moyen et du Salaire Minimum," Insee, Paris, 2008.

The French data indicate that the growth rate of real wages slowed a bit after the 1970s, but has risen about one-half a percentage point annually since. You may recall the economists Piketty and Saez determined that wages of only 5 percent of American workers have outpaced inflation since then. In contrast, the average French employee over the entire span of the Reagan era has earned wage gains exceeding those received by 95 percent of Americans.

Other scattered wage data indicate that this French pattern of modest, but persistently rising real wages occurred in the other family capitalism countries as well. And it has continued in more recent years, according to the International Labor Organization (ILO). From 2001–2007, for example, inflation-adjusted, real average wages grew 4.2 percent in France (0.6 percent annually); 3.5 percent in Germany (0.5 percent annually); and nearly 10 percent in booming Australia (1.41 percent annually). In contrast, real median wages in the United States grew a minuscule total of only 0.21 percent (0.03 percent annually) during this same period.[32]

A moment ago we learned how the gains from growth were distributed in America during the golden age. Productivity and wage data can similarly be used to determine who reaped the gains from growth in the family capitalism countries during the Reagan era. The most comprehensive statistics over the long span of the Reagan era are from Australia, the United States, and France. In Australia, labor productivity rose about 1.6 percent annually between 1979–2007, according to the

OECD, and real wages rose about half as fast; thus, about half of the gains from growth accrued to employees as higher wages. As depicted in Chart 13.3, about one-third of the rise in labor productivity was reflected in the paychecks of French workers over this span, while virtually none (< 2 percent) of the gains from growth was reflected in American wages during the Reagan era.

Compatible statistics for all the family capitalism countries are available for recent years from the ILO and are also reproduced in this figure. These data show that the robust share of employee gains from growth across these nations has continued to far outpace the American experience.

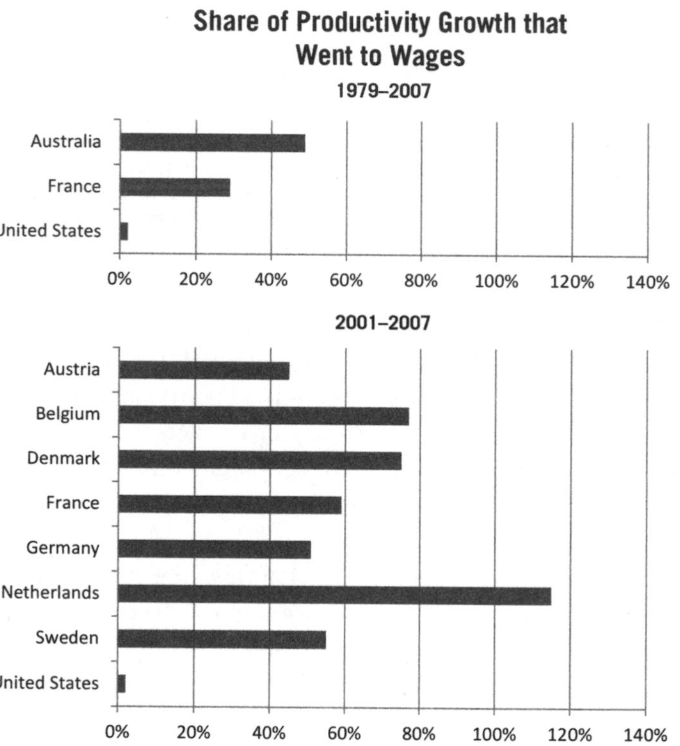

Chart 13.3. Average annual real wage growth as share of average annual productivity growth. US data is median weekly earnings for fulltime employees, in all industries, from 1979 to 2007, http://data.bls.gov/pdq/SurveyOutputServlet); average weekly earnings 1979–2006 for Australia; and median real wages 2001–2007 for the United States.

Sources: "Global Wage Report 2008/9," statistical appendix, table A1, International Labor Organization, Geneva; "Employee Earnings, Benefits and Trade Union Membership 63100TS0002," Australian Bureau of Statistics, Canberra; "Du Salaire Minimum et du Salaire Moyen (Net) Annuels Depuis 1951 (en Euros Constants), Salaries du Secteur Privé et Semi-Privée, y Compris les Apprentis," Insee. Paris; US Bureau of Labor Statistics; and "Economic Outlook," OECD, no. 82, December 2008.

There are relatively few share-of-growth analyses such as this one; the most comprehensive was published in October 2011 by economists Jess Bailey, Joe Coward, and Matthew Whittaker under the auspices of the British Resolution Foundation. They reached similar conclusions. Looking at full-time employees, they concluded that the portion of real GDP per capita growth reflected in US median wages has lagged far behind the Australian, French, or German share since 1980. Their commentary regarding the robust French experience, in particular for lower-wage groups, may strike most Americans as simply unfathomable in light of their own wage experience during the Reagan era:

> "France may offer the best example of a country in which ordinary workers continue to prosper. That is, although wages at the median have fallen some way behind economic growth, this has [occurred] . . . because of a disproportionate increase in the wages of those at the bottom."[33]

Since 2001, lower-paid French workers have received annual wage gains averaging 0.9 percent in real terms, which is 50 percent larger than French average national gains.[34] Indeed, wage statistics suggest that Australia and France best embody the principle spelled out eloquently by John Rawls in 1971, likely America's most prominent twentieth-century philosopher. The late Harvard professor argued that a society is most meaningfully judged by its treatment of the least advantaged.[35] The best spots on earth to be born poor are Australia or France, the nations that come closest to fulfilling Adam Smith's dream of prosperity for all mankind.

In 2012, the International Labor Organization statistics showed that labor income in Germany has stagnated in recent decades even as wages continued rising. This trend was a consequence of steadily rising real wages coupled with a sharp decline in hours actually being worked as employees there and elsewhere across northern Europe and increasingly affluent Australia substituted leisure for work.[36]

Leisure Instead of Work

Thorstein Veblen argued in his 1899 classic, *The Theory of the Leisure Class,* that employees will work long and hard to enable status-related conspicuous consumption. The northern Europe experience is evidence that supports this theory, if we view leisure time as a variant of conspicuous consumption. A more contemporary descriptor of attitudes in other rich democracies toward work and leisure is provided by the political scientist Andrew Moravcsik. He posits that Europeans have been more willing than Americans to substitute additional leisure for work as European wages rose; data confirm his hypothesis.[37]

In northern Europe, wages have risen steadily for decades, enabling folks to reduce their work effort at a measured pace without unduly forgoing income. The consistent quality of real-wage gains year after year in northern Europe is responsible for the trend toward more leisure and less work there. Wages roughly equal American wages, but the history of steady wage gains in the postwar era gave northern Europeans the confidence to reduce work effort in expectation that gains will persist in the decades ahead. No such expectation has existed in America since the 1980s, however. Here is how Barry Eichengreen contrasted the impact of these divergent trends on work effort in the United States and in Europe:

> "Although hours [worked] had been falling since the mid-1960s, they had moved in tandem in the two economies, reflecting the common desire of workers to take some of their increased income in the form of leisure. After 1975, however, hours worked per employee stabilized in the United States, but in Europe they continued falling."[38]

Back in 1970, as we see in Chart 13.4, northern Europeans worked about the same as or longer than Americans; French men and women, for example, worked over 2,000 hours annually or 7 percent longer than Americans, who were a third richer at the time. Since then, Europeans have reduced their work effort about 20 percent across the board as real wages continued rising, substituting more leisure. In contrast, yoked to their offices and factories by wage compression and job insecurity, Americans have been willing to pare back work hours a trivial 5 percent. For many, that reduction has been involuntary.

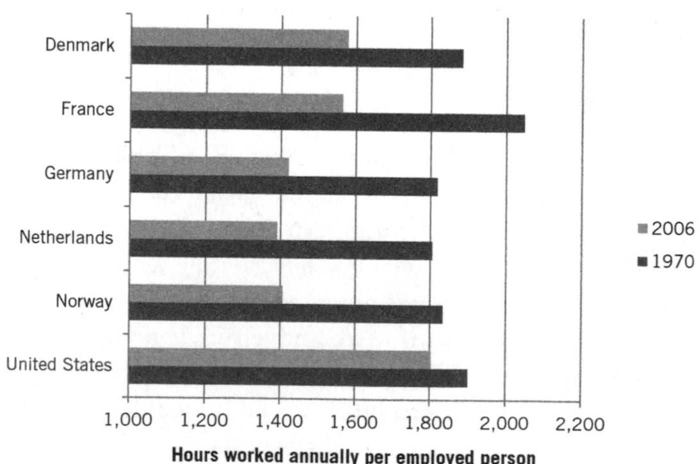

Chart 13.4. German data is for West Germany and for 1976.
Source: OECD Employment Outlook, 2007 Statistical Annex, Table F, OECD.StatExtracts.

Long Vacations

Australians and northern Europeans have more leisure than Americans, especially long vacations, as noted in Table 2. Fringe benefits are also higher in the family capitalism countries, where many employees routinely receive large year-end bonuses and more paid vacation days. In contrast, 23 percent of Americans receive no vacation or holiday time, and tens of millions are only paid for Christmas, New Year's, or Easter if they work those holidays.[39]

Hours Worked and Benefits Paid to Employees

	Bonuses[1]	Annual Paid Holiday Leave	Hours Worked/ Year
Australia	n/a	20 days	1,714
Austria	14.7%	24.7 days	1,655
Belgium	11.1%	19.5 days	1,571
Denmark	2.2%	24.9 days	1,577
France	12.3%	30.9 days	1,564
Germany	8.9%	28.8 days	1,436
Netherlands	9.5%	21.9 days	1,391
Sweden	1.4%	n/a	1,583
United States	2.1%	8 days	1,804[2]

Table 2. Hours worked data from 2006, paid leave and bonus data 2002.
[1] Nonproduction-related bonus; amount paid as share of annual gross wage.
[2] US national average, including public sector; private-sector average was 1,758 hours.
Sources: Hans-Joachim Mittage, "Statistics in Focus," Eurostat 12 (2005); "Employee Benefits in Private Industry," Employment Cost Index series, and "National Compensation Survey," Bureau of Labor Statistics, March 2006; Australian Bureau of Statistics; and "Economic Outlook 2007," OECD, table F.

Wages in Northern Europe Likely Exceed American Wages

Earlier we learned that comprehensive labor costs paid by employers are $10 per hour higher in northern Europe. But these figures include social insurance taxes and fees, which are considerably higher in the family capitalism countries. How does pay in the United States compare if such taxes and also fees for health, pensions, and other benefits are stripped out? Americans certainly receive less health and pension coverage than Australians and northern European employees, but do they at least earn more than these folks abroad in wages and the cash value of paid leave and other direct benefits?

We can only speculate about wages across the board in all sectors internationally because of data limitations. However, the Bureau of Labor Statistics in Washington, DC gathers internationally comparable data on wages in manufacturing sectors. And we learned earlier that wage patterns in manufacturing are broadly representative of overall wages. So what does the BLS data show?

In 2010, the average value of wages, paid leave, and cash benefits for Americans in the manufacturing sector was $26.27 per hour. That was lower than the comparable figure for employees in every family capitalism country. The closest was manufacturing sector pay in France ($27.61 per hour). Comparable figures for Australia ($32.40) and the other nations in northern Europe, including Belgium ($34.30), Denmark ($42.40), Germany ($34.23), and Netherlands ($32.23) were notably higher.[40]

That means Reagan-era wage stagnation has been sufficiently severe so that manufacturing-sector employees in every family capitalism country—and probably employees in all sectors—now make more money than their US counterparts. Employees abroad also receive better (i.e., cheaper and more comprehensive) health care, enjoy secure pensions, and benefit from sending their youngsters to college tuition-free.

CHAPTER 14

THE GAINS FROM GROWTH

"The rich are getting fabulously richer, the vast majority are somewhat worse off, and the bottom half—for all practical purposes, the poor—are being savaged by our current economic policies."[1]

DAVID CAY JOHNSTON,
Free Lunch, 2007

"The most important contributor to higher profit margins over the past five years has been a decline in labor's share of national income."[2]

Goldman Sachs,
Profits Report, 2006

"The baby boomers, you can basically treat them terribly and they don't quit."[3]

IRA T. KAY,
CEO Pay Consultant, 2007

"Our merchants and master manufacturers complain much of the bad effects of high wages in raising the price and thereby lessening the sale of their goods. . . . They can say nothing concerning the bad effects of high profits. They are silent with regard to the pernicious effects of their own gains. They complain only of those of other people."[4]

ADAM SMITH,
The Wealth of Nations

The Roman Empire of Caesar Augustus was an extractive behemoth built on trade, specialized labor in factories and farms, well-developed markets, and, most importantly, slavery. This post-Republic era of Rome featured oligarchs just like those of Aristotle's era, as Washington University historian Timothy H. Parsons explains:

"Aristocrats in Rome and the central provinces were the ultimate beneficiaries of this comparatively efficient extractive system. These were the senatorial and equestrian classes, which constituted less than 1 percent of the total imperial population . . . the empire's most prominent financiers and businessmen."[5]

There are few surface similarities between the first-century AD and America at the turn of the twenty-first century. But one area where Reagan-era America resembles ancient Rome is how the gains from growth are distributed. The American economy has grown handsomely during the decades since 1980, producing trillions of dollars in additional wealth. Yet wages have stagnated or declined, while gains disproportionately flowed to the 1 percent Smith called merchants and master manufacturers—the same way gains from growth were distributed in the Roman Empire.

Since then, there have been episodes of great wealth being redistributed, including the coerced transfers from religious sects in the Roman era. More recent examples include the confiscation of wealth by the Soviet Union a century ago and the contemporary transfer from consumers to oil-exporting nations (OPEC) that manipulate production and price, and whose net export earnings were about $1 trillion in 2012.[6] What Virginia Commonwealth University economists Robert Trumble and Angela DeLowell earlier termed "the largest peacetime transfer of wealth in history" since 1980 in America is another contemporary example.[7] During the Reagan era, wage compression has caused the share of GDP comprising wages and salaries to drop about 5 percentage points while the share of GDP representing profits has risen about as much. With each point of GDP worth on the order of $150 billion in 2011, the redistribution from wage earners upward, mostly to Smith's merchants and master manufacturers, totaled roughly $750 billion in that one year alone. That represents the greatest extractive windfall in history, a redistribution from American families each year comparable to three-quarters of the annual net global export earnings of OPEC. Little wonder the *New York Post* headlined in August 2010, "So Long, Middle Class."[8]

The families of wage earners were the losers, but what is the evidence about winners?

The winners whose income grew dramatically in the Reagan era are executive suites, shareholders, finance sector employees, and others with connections to the business community. And it's a remarkably small slice of America—tiny, really. A number of economists, such as Dew-Becker and Gordon, have documented that the gains disproportionately flowed to the top 1 percent and top one-tenth of 1 percent (0.1 percent) of the US income distribution.[9] As Warren Buffett explained, "There's been class warfare going on for the last 20 years and my class has won."[10]

Michael Cembalest of JP Morgan Chase concluded in July 2011 that compressed wages and fringe benefits account for about 75 percent of the rise in profit margins.[11] It's a war where the middle class has been firing blanks, while the tiny deregulated business community came locked and loaded. If you think it's not a war, check your wallet and 401(k), or read David Cay Johnston's detailed book published in 2012, *The Fine Print*. The *Economist* magazine put it this way:

> "The fruits of productivity gains have been skewed toward the highest earners, and toward companies, whose profits have reached record levels as a share of GDP."[12]

Higher Profits

The 1980s marked the beginning of a wondrous era for American enterprise. The information technology revolution and burgeoning global trade improved the efficiency of US firms, just as their executives began acting out Ayn Rand, seizing most of the gains from rising productivity by compressing wages and reducing investment. Firms profited inordinately by historical standards from reductions in labor compensation rather than from the traditional sources of profits, including entrepreneurship, improved efficiency, lower capital costs, and the like. The outcome was a rising share of corporate cash flow being realized as profit. Profit margins fluctuate with the business cycle, but each new macroeconomic rebound since 1980 has seen profit margins reach new highs. The business community frets endlessly about labor costs, taxes, and regulatory compliance costs. Those complaints have proven vacuous, because profits as a share of US national income have become the highest ever recorded. After-tax profits more than doubled, from below 5 percent in 1980 to 10 percent of GDP in 2011, higher even than during the peak Gilded Age year of 1929.

Some of this profit surge was paid out as executive compensation and dividends, but about $2 trillion filtered down to sit on accounting statement bottom lines as record cash balances; and for the subset of US firms that are multinationals, much of that cash sits in tax havens abroad. Amazingly—if spread evenly among all firms—this cash hoard would entirely eliminate American corporate debt. In fact, academic researchers have determined that the American business community *in toto* has been debt free since 2004, when the corporate debt ratio fell below zero.[13] Some undercapitalized banks, small businesses, and struggling manufacturing enterprises are hard pressed and indebted, but they're the exception in an American business community flush with profits and cash three decades into the Reagan era.

Economists talk about two types of extraordinary profits, named to honor economists David Ricardo and Joseph Schumpeter. Ricardian rents accrue to owners of fixed (nonreproduceable) resources, such as quite fertile land, oil, or gold deposits, while Schumpeterian rents flow to individuals or firms because of entrepreneurial insights in a risky or complicated environment—think of the early days of Bill Gates or Steve Jobs. But the Reagan era created a third category I term Reagan rents, which accrue to enterprise leaders who command neither scarce resources nor unusual skill; they have the good fortune simply to hold senior corporate positions during the Reagan era of regulatory capture and shareholder capitalism, commanding only their supine boards of directors. And their Reagan rents have been extraordinary. For example, an analysis by economists Lucian Bebchuk and Jesse Fried concluded that the top five executives at US firms received about 10 percent of firm profits in recent years—that's double their share in the 1990s.[14]

Economists have determined with some precision where these profits and compensation, as well as other income flows during the Reagan era, went: most ended up in a relatively few pockets.

Income Flowing to the Peak of the Income Pyramid

After adjusting for population growth and inflation, the American economic pie available to be sliced on a per-person basis rose 66 percent between President Reagan's election and 2005 before the recession. Such hefty income gains didn't go to servicemen and women in uniform, or to factory, store, or office workers, computer scientists, schoolteachers, physicians, or policemen. So who's left? Some went to innovators, IT entrepreneurs, media commentators, real estate developers, Hollywood actors, and athletic stars. But they're a tiny few in a nation of 315 million. So, where did that 66 percent rise in incomes go?

We turn to economists Piketty and Saez for the answer. In analyses for the National Bureau of Economic Research noted earlier, they determined that it all went to the top 5 percent since 1970, the only slice of America whose incomes actually outpaced inflation.[15] The actual redistribution was far more lopsided, however, with the top 1 percent receiving fully one-half of the gains from growth.[16] In 1980, the so-called Brandeis Ratio showed that average income of the top 1 percent was 12.5 times larger than median household income; by 2006, it had *tripled* to be 36 times larger.[17] The average income of this modern-day equestrian class has added so much to their household wealth that they own as much collectively as the entire bottom 90 percent of all Americans.[18] And that trend has become even more exaggerated in recent years, as indicated by the statistics from Piketty and Saez presented earlier: the share of income growth accruing to the top 1 percent during the Clinton boom (1993–2000) was 45 percent. Yet that share has risen steadily, to 93 percent of all income during the recovery years 2009 and 2010.[19] The lastest statistics developed by the income expert Emmanuel Saez show that trend continuing with the 1 percent actually receiving *all* gains from growth during 2009–2011. In fact, they claimed more than 100 percent because incomes declined 0.4 percent on average for everyone else.[20]

Other statistics make the same point: the top 1 percent's share of all national income averaged about 8 percent during the administrations of Presidents Kennedy, Johnson, Nixon, Ford, and Carter. It was 8.03 percent when Ronald Reagan took office in 1981—but their share more than doubled thereafter to peak above 18 percent in 2007.[21]

Pinnacle of the Pyramid: 13,400 American Families

David Cay Johnston in his book *Perfectly Legal* examined the 13,400 richest American men, women, and children. They include managers of hedge funds and entrepreneurs with familiar names, including Warren Buffett, Bill Gates, David Koch, and George Soros. Collectively, this fortunate fistful of families saw their annual incomes rise more than six-fold since 1970 to now average about $27 million. For every *dollar* of additional income earned by the bottom 99 percent of Americans since 1970, each member of these dynastic families received $7,500 additional, as I noted earlier. Collectively, this cohort—small enough to fit inside a couple of high school basketball gyms—received as much income in 2000 as the poorest 96 million Americans, an amazing statistic that likely resembles first-century Rome.[22] And from 2002 to 2006 during the Bush boomlet, these few families received one-quarter of all household income growth, a startling statistic.[23]

And at the very top? Each of the highest-earning 400 families in 2007 received $345 million.

The decline in taxes has been important to these households, too: they paid only 16.6 percent of their income in taxes in 2007, down from 29.4 percent as recently as 1993.[24]

Relaxed Enforcement of Tax Laws on the Richest Americans

Affluent Americans benefited both from lower tax rates and from lax enforcement during the Reagan era. Audits of returns from the wealthy plunged during these years. By 1999, those making less than $25,000 had a higher audit rate than those earning more than $100,000, a stunningly inefficient use of scarce tax agency resources. Other procedures changed as well. For example, the IRS for many decades had routinely examined returns of folks who appeared to be living well above their income; that's how Al Capone was fingered. Indicative of this new forbearance toward affluent filers, however, a 1997 law signed by President Clinton ended that policy. This strategy of forbearance for the affluent was reversed by the Obama Administration.[25]

Lower Taxes on Corporations

As we learned, the tax burden was shifted during the Reagan era from the affluent to middle- and working-class families. An even more significant redistribution in tax burdens occurred from corporations to individual taxpayers. Measured as a share of GDP, corporate taxes were 6 percent during the golden age, for example, but had declined to 1.3 percent by 2010, according to IRS data developed by the Washington-based Center for Tax Justice.[26] Statutory rates fell, but enforcement also weakened. In 1993, under President Clinton, some 2,400 tax penalties were imposed on firms for negligence. Such penalties fell during the administration of George W. Bush by 99 percent, with only 22 negligence penalties imposed in 2002.[27] Another significant contributor to lower corporate taxes has been the use of tax havens by multinationals, which we will discuss in a moment.

This combination of lower rates and weak enforcement caused the effective corporate tax rate during 2011 to be only one-half the effective rate when Reagan took office.[28] (It was 21 percent rather than the nominal rate of 35 percent, with multinationals, in particular, paying far less than the nominal rate.)[29] These changes have enabled American firms in recent years to have the lowest tax burden as a share of GDP of any rich democracy, comparable to that of the corporate sector in Turkey. American business contributes less than one-third the share of taxes by Australian firms, for example.[30]

Piratical Tax Havens: Stealing Tax Revenue from Neighbors

There are plenty of American firms with tax rates approaching the nominal rate of 35 percent, but the average effective rate is 21 percent because thousands of others pay far less. And most are multinationals exploiting tax havens abroad, small rogue nations, such as Switzerland or the Cayman Islands, which parasitically pirate their neighbors' taxes. Tax havens are state-sponsored thieves that have created an enormous industry serving drug and arms dealers, despots, American multinationals, blood diamond warlords, and African elephant killers (tusk smugglers)—along with your ordinary wealthy tax dodger.

Experts such as the economist Martin Sullivan, formerly with the US Treasury Department and now at Washington-based Tax Analysts, have found that havens enable many profitable American multinationals to pay little or no tax. Over the last five years, for example, Prudential paid taxes of only 7.6 percent of profits; Yahoo, 7 percent; Boeing, 4.5 percent; and the Carnival cruise firm exploited an obscure loophole enabling it to incorporate in tax haven Panama and pay taxes of only 1.1 percent on $11 billion in profits.[31]

These tax rates are far lower than those paid by international competitors that jostle for customers with US firms in global markets. For example, the head of GE's tax department, John Samuels, told a tax forum in February 2011 that his firm's effective tax rate for earnings purposes was 7 percent. Its major German competitor, Siemens, pays an average tax rate of 31 percent; its major Japanese competitor, Mitsubishi, pays 40 percent; and its major Dutch competitor, Phillips, pays 26 percent.[32]

Because the biggest loopholes involve foreign operations, the American firms that are most effective at sheltering taxes are multinationals. It is big business for them: the Government Accountability Office (GAO) in 2009 concluded that such US firms avoided about $100 billion each year in taxes.[33] How does it occur? The answer is found in statistics provided by GE, suggesting that it earned only 18 percent of its taxable profits in the United States in 2008–2010, despite receiving 46 percent of its revenues there.[34] It would be delightful to learn that GE is subsidizing you and me by settling for low prices and profits in the United States, but that's unlikely.

Here's what's going on: Domestic American firms cannot easily utilize tax shelters. But GE and other multinationals can; they aggressively juggle revenue and expense accounting in order to launder profits through tax shelters. They exploit outdated US tax laws unreflective of the contemporary global business environment inordinately driven by intellectual property issues and the internet. Their foreign income has become enormous in the last fifteen years. Treasury Department economist Harry Grubert in 2012 examined tax returns from 754 US multinationals and found that the share of their pretax income coming from overseas had increased to 51.1 percent in 2004 from 37.1 percent in 1996.[35] This jump reflects a strategy whereby firms record most profits abroad in low-tax jurisdictions rather than in higher-tax jurisdictions such as America. Is this strategy effective? You bet it is, making multinationals one of the least-taxed industries. Grubert concluded that virtually none of the sharply rising income reported from overseas by the hundreds of firms in his database was being taxed because it is sequestered in tax shelters. "This increase in the foreign share of total income was almost completely in the form of income that is not repatriated from abroad, which rose from 17.4 percent of worldwide income in 1996 to 31.4 percent in 2004."

Weak laws and even weaker international cooperation are the problems, exacerbated by an under-resourced Internal Revenue Service. Despite a complex tax code and sizeable national deficits, the IRS budget for fiscal year 2012 was cut $300 million from the prior year by Congressional Republicans, leaving an estimated $385 billion, or 16 percent, of corporate taxes uncollected, according to IRS estimates.[36] Perhaps the most aggressive tax dodgers are the subset of multinationals involved in high technology, rich in patents and selling intangibles such as digitized products that enable them to readily select favorable locations where intellectual property ownership is claimed. In 2010 and 2011, technology firms in the *Standard & Poor's 500* stock index reported an average global tax rate one-third less than the rest of the S&P according to a *New York Times* study.[37] Apple had a tax rate of only 9.8 percent in 2011, saving some $2.4 billion in taxes, according to estimates by Martin Sullivan; it sloshed profits around the globe using tactics with names like the Double Irish with a Dutch Sandwich.[38]

A favorite haven is Luxembourg, where servicing tax dodgers accounts for up to one-half its national income.[39] The profit on your Apple music or app downloads, for example, is recorded at a mail drop called iTunes S.àr.l. in Luxembourg. Oh, and that Apple product you bought in Berlin? You likely purchased it through a reluctant German *commissionaire*, a cutout for a firm in low-tax Singapore, where the profits of the German transaction are actually recorded.[40] The example of Google is also instructive. That firm asserts that ownership rights and patents to technologies developed by its US engineers in fact are held by a subsidiary at a tiny law firm in tax-free Bermuda. Google funneled $5.4 billion in royalties during 2009 through that tax haven, a practice that cut its US tax bill by $3.1 billion during 2007–2009.[41]

Another tax-sheltering tactic involves juggling the price of production inputs to cut taxes. This practice of intentionally mispricing intermediate goods is so widespread that it has its own category; "transfer pricing" enabled Chevron and Texaco to save $3.25 billion in taxes between 1970 and 2000 by overpricing oil bought from a subsidiary in low-tax Indonesia for sale in the United States. Inflated prices on inputs from abroad result in low taxable profits on US sales, with profits recorded in low-tax nations.

By shifting profits on American sales to tax havens abroad, blue-chip firms such as Apple, Chevron, Cisco Systems, GE, Google, Microsoft, Oracle, and Pfizer perforce end up with sizeable portions of their corporate cash resting in havens like the Cayman Islands or Luxembourg. For example, Cisco holds 80 percent of its $40 billion cash balance abroad[42] and Apple holds two-thirds of its even larger hoard abroad.[43] In May 2011, American multinationals held over $1 trillion abroad in such accounts, according to JP Morgan Chase.

As these figures suggest, tax sheltering is highly profitable and firms reasonably devote considerable internal resources to it. Shell and BP have created nearly 1,000 paper entities in tax parasites to filter profits, including more than 100 in the Caribbean.[44] Nearly 19,000 US firms, including hedge funds and large banks such as JP Morgan Chase, maintain tax addresses at a single Cayman Island law firm, Maples and Calder.[45] In 2009, Congressional GAO investigators determined that 83 of the largest 100 American firms exploit tax havens.[46] Such behavior isn't punished; in fact, 63 of those firms including Boeing, Caterpillar, Kraft Foods, and Merck receive large federal contracts. Tax-haven *habitués* also include 14 banks that were saved from bankruptcy by the 2008 taxpayer bailout.

The family capitalism countries confront the same problem, although two of their number (Belgium and Netherlands) are also significant tax havens. For example, McDonald's and Starbucks count Europe as important markets, but pay virtually no tax on sales there. Since opening its first store in 2002, the Starbucks chain of over 200 stores in France and Germany has never reported a taxable profit. In 2011, Starbucks reported a loss of €5.3 million on sales of €117 million. Those outlets are profitable, but manipulate cash flows to report no profit to tax authorities there. The coffee chain paid no tax because its European corporate headquarters in Netherlands imposes a hefty franchising fee, 6 percent of sales in the case of Starbucks, roughly comparable to profits. Moreover, in a transfer-pricing stratagem, Starbucks adds an extravagant 20 percent cost margin on all coffee sold in bulk to its European stores, imposed internally by offices in the tax haven of Switzerland.[47] Thus, European profits end up being recorded in Switzerland and Dutch tax havens in the Caribbean.[48]

Google dodges taxes on its European sales in a similar fashion, shuttling billions in profits between subsidiaries in Ireland and Netherlands that end up in tax-free Bermuda. *Le Monde* reported that Google paid a bare €5 million in taxes on 2011 sales in France of at least €1.25 billion. This occurs because its European operation like that of Starbucks pays a hefty licensing fee to a mailbox in Amsterdam (Google Netherlands

Holdings B.V.), and then to Bermuda.[49] Sheltering profits is common for sales across the world. India is demanding over $10 million in back taxes for domestic Google transactions that the company channeled through low-tax Ireland. [50] Revenues from Google sales in Australia are recorded in Singapore and then Bermuda, enabling it to pay a scant A$74,176 in taxes in 2011 on sales there of as much as A$2 billion.[51] When applied globally, these tactics are spectacularly successful, with the *Brisbane Times* reporting that Google paid only 3.2 percent in taxes during 2011, while sweeping $9.8 billion in international revenues, mostly from high-tax Australia and Europe, into its Bermuda mail drop.[52] Apple sales in Australia are recorded in Cork, Ireland, with profits recorded eventually in the tax haven of the British Virgin Islands.[53]

Amazon utilizes the Luxembourg tax haven, recording its European book sales in that tiny nation, which enabled the company in 2011 to pay taxes of about €8 million on sales of €9.1 billion. That charade is one reason the French government is demanding $252 million in back taxes from Amazon as of this writing.[54]

CHAPTER 15

INCOME DISPARITY

"The Walton family of Walmart fame is wealthier than the bottom third of the US population."[1]

BEN FUNNELL,
***Financial Times*, June 30, 2009**

"Conservatives need to recognize that the most pernicious sort of redistribution isn't from the successful to the poor. It's from savers to speculators, from outsiders to insiders, and from the industrious middle class to the reckless, unproductive rich."[2]

ROSS DOUTHAT,
***New York Times*, July 11, 2010**

". . . none of the changes seem transitory. The middle of America's labour market are likely to become ever more squeezed."[3]

***Economist*,**
June 17, 2006

"US labor compensation is now at a 50-year low relative to both company sales and US GDP."[4]

MICHAEL CEMBALEST,
Chief Investment Officer, JP Morgan Chase
***Eye on the Market*, July 11, 2011**

The skewed allocation of the gains from growth in recent decades in America has reasserted the traditional extractive pattern common prior to the Industrial Revolution as outlined by economists Doran Acemoglu and James Robinson. It caused American income disparities to widen noticeably. Some of the most extensive contemporary research on US income inequality is by Larry Bartels of Vanderbilt University. Chart 15.1 is reproduced from his 2008 book, *Unequal Democracy*. During the golden age, income inequality remained relatively stable, with incomes at the 80th percentile of the income spectrum about three times greater than at the 20th percentile.

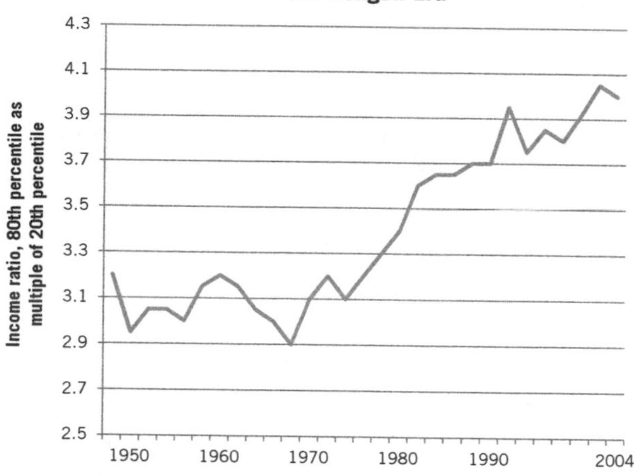

Chart 15.1.
Source: Larry M. Bartels, Unequal Democracy, fig. 2.2.

This stable pattern began to deteriorate in the late-1970s due to inflation, a cyclical event. But once the Reagan era began, that change was dramatically exaggerated because of structural factors such as wage compression. The outcome is an American income distribution resembling that of a developing nation.

American Income Disparity Is the Worst Among Rich Democracies

One of the first scholars to detect the impact of Reaganomics on income disparities was economic historian Paul Kennedy; as early as the mid-1980s, he wrote, "The 'earnings gap' between rich and poor in the United States is significantly larger than in any other advanced industrial society."[5] Another was economic historian Kevin Phillips, who concluded in 2002, "Among the major Western industrial nations, it was the United States—its revolution 225 years distant—that now has the highest level of inequality."[6] Kennedy and Phillips have proven prescient: income disparities have widened by about 25 percent since 1980.[7]

There's great irony in that change. America was settled by Europeans fleeing the limited-income opportunity exemplified by the early industrial revolution's Dickensian income pattern, where legacy capital owners, landowners, and emergent entrepreneurial tycoons dominated income flows and wealth. Those early immigrants to America would be dismayed to learn our generation has voted repeatedly to allow a reincarnation of that system two centuries on.

How much of an international outlier is the US income distribution? The answer is presented in Chart 15.2, reproduced from statistics compiled by the OECD. For each dollar of income received by the poorest 10 percent of Americans in 2005, the richest 10 percent received $16 dollars. That disparity is comparable to the income distribution in Turkey and nations (not shown) such as Bulgaria, Cameroon, Ivory Coast, Jamaica, Uganda, and perhaps Rome after the fall of the Republic in 49 BCE—economies dominated by thin layers of the traditional historic extractive elite. The American multiple is twice as severe as any other rich democracy. As the *Economist* magazine noted in June 2006, the exaggerated American income distribution is nearly halfway to the range typical of nations such as Brazil, "notorious for the concentration of income and wealth."[8] And, the Gini Coefficient measure of inequality shows that the American income distribution is even more skewed than a number of other middle-income nations like Egypt and India.[9]

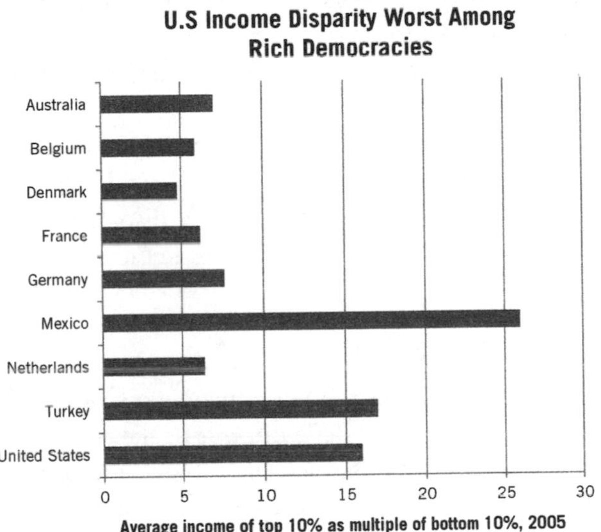

Chart 15.2
Source: "Are We Growing Unequal?" OECD, table 1, October 2008.

Income disparities in some other rich democracies such as Germany have grown slightly more exaggerated in this period, but the extreme scale and the pace of the American income disparity in recent decades sets the United States apart. Even those Anglo-Saxon nations most resembling the United States in culture and ethnic background, such as Australia or Canada, have income distributions resembling Austria, Germany, or France rather than Turkey or the United States. There are millions of wealthy individuals in the family capitalism countries, but their advantage over their countrymen is markedly less than in the

United States. In the mid-2000s, for example, the share of pretax national income received by the top 1 percent of earners was 5.6 percent in the Netherlands, 6.3 percent in Denmark and Sweden, 9.8 percent in Australia (2007)—but 17.4 percent in America.[10]

This American exceptionalism is a consequence of wage stagnation, in contrast to widely broadcast prosperity up and down the population distribution in these other nations. The average income of the bottom 90 percent of Australian households rose 30 percent in real terms from 1980–2007, for example, while it rose a bare 2 percent for the bottom 90 percent of American families.[11] That is, the bottom 90 percent of Australian households received as much income gain every two years as that identical cohort of Americans received over the entire 27 years of the Reagan era. The statistics from Canada are similar. In 1970, the distribution of family incomes in Canada was only slightly more even than in the United States. But by 2000, historian James W. Loewen, professor *emeritus* at the University of Vermont, noted that American income inequality had deteriorated sharply, and "was much greater than Canada's; the United States was becoming more like Mexico, a very stratified society."[12]

There is nothing innate about the American economic structure, geography, globalization, its peoples or other physical, ethnic, or cultural attributes that account for widening income disparities in recent decades. It is solely the consequence of Reaganomics.

The Gilded Age Reincarnated

To find analogous periods of such wide income disparity in the United States, we must search the early *Belle Époque* or the ensuing Gilded Age. Then, as now, America was characterized by regulatory capture and economic sovereignty resting with firms. Here is how historian James MacGregor Burns described the Roaring Twenties:

> "Collaboration among capitalists, politicians, and justices was a defining feature of the Gilded Age. . . . A president's use of his appointing power on behalf of powerful economic interests . . . [was] not an exception in the Gilded Age but the rule."[13]

Members of Congress who pandered to elite earners were as common in those earlier periods as in today's Reagan era. Supreme Court justices enthralled with economic power were commonplace in both periods as well. In language describing the dollar-friendly Fuller and Waite Courts of the latter nineteenth century, Burns could just as well have been writing about the economic Darwinism perspective of most court appointees by Ronald Reagan and the two Bush presidents:

> "Americans might have mused that corporation heads packed the court as much as presidents. Exerting their overpowering influence on the White House and Congress, an astonishing number of railroads and other industries put their people on the Supreme Court. All of Grant's appointees . . . were railroad attorneys."[14]

Middle-Class Societies

The rising American income disparity of recent decades has made Australia and Northern Europe much more middle-class societies than the United States. When a nation's productivity and economic growth are enjoyed broadly as in those nations, the middle class expands and the economy itself performs more efficiently, as Joseph Stiglitz has argued.[15] That's what happened in America and other rich democracies after World War II, and it has continued to occur in the family capitalism countries since 1980, even as the United States took another path.

The OECD defines the middle class as those earning between .5 and 1.5 times a nation's median income. While slightly more than one-half of the US workforce earned an income in 2007 within that range, about two-thirds of working-age men and women elsewhere received incomes in that range. That is even true in Germany, where employees in the former GDR enjoy rising, but still relatively low wages.

Moreover, the relatively small middle class in America is shrinking. US Census Bureau statistics showed the share of national income in 2011 received by the three middle quintiles (60 percent) of households declined to 46.4 percent, from nearly 55 percent in 1980. That may explain why one-third of Americans now describe themselves as lower or lower-middle class, compared to 25 percent who did so as recently as 2008.[16] As *Washington Post* columnist Harold Meyerson explains, "What emerges is a picture of a nation in decline. The first nation in human history to create a middle-class majority looks increasingly to be losing it."[17]

The Income Share of Top Earners

The share of income received by elite earners is much lower in other rich democracies than in the United States. In 1960, the share of national income going to the top one-tenth of 1 percent of earners was 2 percent in France and America; that share remained the same 2 percent during the ensuing twenty years of the golden age in both nations. But the share began rising in the United States after 1980, and by 2001, the share of national income accruing to that top slice of Americans had nearly quadrupled, to almost 8 percent. In contrast, that share has remained at 2 percent in France.[18]

The picture is the same in Germany. Back in 1970, the top 1 percent of German households garnered 11 percent of all income; that was *higher* than the 9 percent received by the top 1 percent of Americans at the time. Through 2010, that figure remained stable at 11 percent in Germany, while the share of income received by the top 1 percent of Americans more than doubled to 22 percent by 2005.[19]

Beyond issues of fairness, does the deteriorating US income disparity matter? Not all economists agree, but some economists, including Joseph Stiglitz and Thomas I. Palley, argue persuasively that it slows economic growth. Additionally, economist Robert H. Frank and others have argued that standards beyond just income should be used to measure the plight of American families during the Reagan era. I've adopted one such alternative standard in this book, using families in other rich democracies as a control group.

Frank suggests educational access as another standard. Since the 1980s, for example, concerns about school quality have grown as families seek solutions to stagnant incomes through better education. For their children, families covet quality school districts, yet prices in those neighborhoods have remained stubbornly high even in recent years, while sagging wages have made homes there less affordable, dimming that element of the American Dream for many. Frank's statistics are compelling. Near the peak of wages in 1970, for example, he determined it took 41.5 hours of work a month for an employee earning the median wage to afford housing in the top half of school districts. But by 2000, the required work effort to live in such districts had increased sharply to 67.4 hours; wage compression requires that Americans work 60 percent more than before Reaganomics to afford housing in desirable school districts.[20]

This darkening of the American Dream has become generalized across the nation, with economic mobility dwindling during the Reagan era. As we will see in detail in the next chapter, that era has had an even more corrosive impact on opportunity, reversing what had been an American strength in the golden age.

CHAPTER 16

THE OPPORTUNITY SOCIETIES OF STAKEHOLDER CAPITALISM

"Free market capitalism is . . . the engine of social mobility, the highway to the American Dream."[1]

GEORGE W. BUSH,
President, November 2008

"The economics literature, based on correlation or regression coefficients, suggests that the United States may, indeed, be exceptional, but not in having *more* mobility, but in having *less*, a finding our results support."[2]

MRAKUS JÄNTTI, et al,
University of Oslo, 2005

[College in America] "Rich, stupid children are more likely to graduate than poor, clever ones."[3]

Economist,
April 17, 2010

[The dominant role of parental wealth] ". . . very manifestly displays the anti-meritocracy in America—the reproduction of social class without the inheritance of any innate ability."[4]

DALTON CONLEY,
Director, Center for Advanced
Social Science Research, New York University, December 2007

America is the only rich democracy in the twenty-first century where birth remains destiny—and I think it's because Ronald Reagan never understood John Ford.

I can understand him not appreciating Jean-Jacques Rosseau, maybe John Locke, or even Frank Capra. But John Ford?

It's all there in the greatest Western of all, *My Darling Clementine*. President Reagan loved his cowboys, especially stories about individual heroes like Wyatt Earp. He watched *Clementine* but didn't see it, and proved clueless when it came to Ford's evocative message. After all, it was the community that hired Earp and sparked the gunfight at the OK Corral, banding together in joint action to improve their lives by creating new opportunity, their eyes set on the future. In contrast, the politician Ronald Reagan chose to demonize the communitarian spirit and the notion that the business community has broad responsibilities to society. Like Ayn Rand, he glorified individualism—precisely the dark societal trade-off rejected by the greatest director of Westerns—over an individual's responsibility to strengthen community. President Reagan empowered the narcissists among us, instead of the good citizens of Tombstone rightly deified by Ford.

In stripping economic sovereignty from families, Ronald Reagan mocked the concept of opportunity symbolized by the visionary families of Tombstone. By targeting minimum wages, promoting an Us vs. Them culture disinterested in productivity, upskilling, wages, or jobs, and shirking public commitments to education, poverty alleviation, sober monetary and fiscal policies, or trade unions, he undercut the precise policies that made golden age America the land of opportunity. Reagan savaged the only proven tools in the entire sweep of human history to expand opportunity. And in the process, his cultural shift abandoned the Republican Party's historic focus on improving broad opportunity and reducing poverty.

The Myth of American Economic Mobility

Americans face sour economic prospects, but many retain a mythical sense of US prowess and mobility from the experience of their parents or grandparents. How could economic mobility not be high in America, they ask? After all, it was founded by settlers fleeing the rigid, class-rooted, economic, religious, and social elitism of England and continental Europe, societies where since time immemorial those born poor died poor, and those born rich died rich. This unfounded belief is perpetuated by politicians, such as former vice-presidential candidate and Congressman Paul Ryan:

> "We are in an upwardly mobile society with a lot of movement between income groups. [In Europe] . . . top-heavy welfare states have replaced the traditional aristocracies, and masses of the long-term unemployed are locked into the new lower class."[5]

Congressman Ryan is a leading Republican Party spokesman on budget issues and is known to substitute fiction for truth as when he said this at the Heritage Foundation. Politicians can do that, pandering to donors. The facts are that America has devolved into an inopportune society, its Reagan-era policies reducing opportunity by a quite large 40 percent.

The family capitalism countries have become the new land of opportunity. They pay the world's highest wages. They consistently spread the gains from growth broadly, rewarding hard work with real wage gains. And they inordinately raise the incomes of lower-paid employees, thereby improving economic mobility. In spreading prosperity to the least advantaged, they meet the key test posed by philosopher John Rawls.

America flunks the Rawls test. France and Australia do the best of any nation in world history of meeting the Rawls standard. During the last two decades, rising real wages for low-income French employees have reduced their wage gap with the middle class.[6] France even makes it cheap to hire minimum-wage workers; their employers pay a Social Security tax of only 2 percent. Economists at the UK Resolution Foundation in October 2011 concluded that France showed:

> ". . . a substantial improvement in outcomes for the lowest paid, rather than a concentration of the proceeds of growth in the hands of the highest earners. . . . For example, in the decade to 2005, the proportion of employees below the low-pay threshold in France fell, with just 11 percent in this position at the end of the period, compared with 22 percent in the UK and 25 percent in the US. Similarly, while the real value of the US federal minimum wage declined significantly between 1970 and 2005, the French minimum wage doubled in real terms."[7]

There are profound differences between Reagan-era America and the family capitalism countries, but perhaps the most significant is how they succeed where America fails in creating economic opportunity for the least advantaged at birth. The development of institutions to accomplish this surely ranks among the noblest accomplishments in human history. The judgment of Rawls renders them superior societies, as would the judgment of most economists, including Nobel laureate Amartya Sen of Harvard, who argues that families view the degree of economic mobility and opportunity as more important than actual income.[8]

One might think that the hyperflexible American markets for capital, venture capital, and labor, coupled with world-class innovation, years of robust profits, and superb university educations, would at least enable anyone with energy and diligence to prosper. It's certainly a bedrock article of faith among many that your odds of beating the game, escaping even dodgy roots, and landing in Beverly Hills are better in America than in stodgy Europe. So many Americans believe this notion of exceptionalism that it entered national folklore. Moreover, too many seem willing to tolerate striking inequality, believing that opportunity remains available for anyone to succeed. Some 76 percent of respondents to a 2004 survey by Syracuse University's Maxwell School of Citizenship and Public Affairs, for example, agreed that most or all Americans have "an opportunity to succeed."[9] And *The Economist* carried a story in 2006 saying this about Americans:

> "Eight out of ten, more than anywhere else, believe that though you may start out poor if you work hard, you can make pots of money. It is a central part of the American Dream."[10]

That impression is based on history reaching back nearly to America's earliest days. The colonization of America was a miraculous time when opportunity so rare in human history was available. Of course, this opportunity came at the expense of many millions of Native Americans murderously cast aside. Impoverished and youthful adventurers from Europe such as Abraham Smith arrived in seventeenth-century Virginia with only the clothes on their backs, owing six or seven years of labor to others who paid for their dangerous passage.[11] But the promise was utterly breathtaking—and real: adventurers arriving penniless could become landowners (and voters, if male) in less than a decade simply by the sweat of their brow, privileges denied all but well-born males back home or at any other period in world history.

For many in the old countries, the impossibly rare character of the colonial economy defined opportunity. Dominating elites were less present than at almost any point in economic history, allowing grit, innovation, and entrepreneurship to flourish. Even those of the meanest birth could fulfill great ambition. Aspiring to success through self-improvement was a common outcome and became a defining feature of the American experience. Most of our parents did it. Scotsman Samuel Smiles wrote *Self Help* in 1859, encouraging the theme of personal improvement through hard work and grit.[12] The famous American optimist Horatio Alger penned formulaic novels such as *Strive and Succeed*, popularizing the concept of success through individual effort, although always with a vital dollop or two of good luck along the way. Real-life examples are common in American history: Benjamin Franklin, Andrew Carnegie, John Henry Heinz, Phineas Barnum, and Henry Ford all rose from poor roots; Heinz and Ford even overcame bankruptcy to attain great success.

The belief in America as an opportunity society was realistic prior to the Reagan era, and supported by institutions and politicians across the voting spectrum. Ironically, while Reagan's legacy is one of dwindling opportunity, Milton Friedman in 1955 worried that rising college costs would limit opportunity and "perpetuate inequalities in wealth and status."[13] He was prescient in fretting about excessive college costs, yet his ideological crusade of demonizing government and shifting economic sovereignty from families to firms has been vastly more damaging to opportunity than rising college costs.

Belief in this elemental aspect of American uniqueness is responsible for the expectation that, like Augustine in Detroit, everyone can live the American middle-class dream through hard work. And the mechanism of such rising opportunity is hard work rewarded through rising wages, which make all things possible: a spouse, a home, and a stable family life with children who can hope for a still better future. Though dimmed by a few years of stagflation, that American dream still glimmered brightly when Ronald Reagan took office in 1981, elected by voters who erroneously believed both prosperity and opportunity were their default positions as Americans. Ronald Reagan believed it, too, because his uplifting life story embodied the notion of the United States as a meritocracy where hard work, ability, and education inevitably produce rising wages and opportunity—even as his policies were making it mythical.

Think of the transformation in American opportunity during the Reagan era this way: The essence of American exceptionalism is not whether self-made success is possible, but whether that opportunity is open to most citizens rather than just a few of the plucky and lucky like Horatio Alger's heroes. Has the Reagan era sustained the historic American promise of opportunity for all bequeathed it? The answer is a unanimous *no* from scholars.

To succeed today, American children need to pick their parents very, very carefully.

Poor American Economic Mobility

Americans have tumbled onto that truth after three decades of Reaganomics. In a nationwide poll for the Pew Economic Mobility Survey in 2009, some 55 percent of respondents acknowledged that "in the US, a child's chances of achieving financial success is tied to the income of his or her parent." And more than half believed that it will be "harder for [their children] to move up the income ladder."[14]

In the past forty years, American wages have never regained their 1972 high. Alarmed by the implications for economic mobility, a host of economists have examined how well Americans in the intervening decades have been able to move between income groups during their careers.[15] These expansive studies examined different time periods and looked at different population cohorts, but all reached the same conclusion: economic mobility in America is poor.

For example, government economists at the US Treasury Department in 2007 used income tax data to divide nearly 100,000 filers into quintiles: five equal-sized groups. They found that 42 percent of those men and women in the lowest quintile in 1996 were still there ten years later, highly indicative of poor mobility[16]; in a perfectly mobile society, only 20 percent would still be there. An analysis for the Pew Mobility Project by economist Julia B. Isaacs of the Brookings Institution reached the same conclusion. Isaacs compared income data for parents from the late 1960s with that of their children in the late 1990s and early 2000s.[17] She also discovered that 42 percent of children from poor households ended up in the lowest-earning quintile a generation later as adults. A subsequent update by the Pew Mobility project released in mid-2012 found that trend continuing. Drawing on statistics from 2,200 families from 1968 to 2009 (admittedly a small sample), 43 percent of youngsters born poor remained in the lowest-earning quintile as adults.[18]

The odds may be high of youngsters born poor remaining poor as adults, but what are the odds of moving up? Treasury economists also examined the prospect of achieving the "rags to riches" story of American lore. They found that the odds of a poor person in America striking it rich and rising from the bottom quintile all the way to the top earning quintile ten years later was a scant 5.3 percent. The Pew Economic Mobility Project examined the same question and found that the share who accomplished that between 1994 and 2004 was 6 percent, and the 2012 update lowered that figure to a bare 4 percent. Only a handful of musicians, athletes, Nascar drivers, or a coterie of scholarship students in the Ivy League or Ohio State achieve the American rags to riches story today. Isaacs concluded:

> "Contrary to American beliefs about equality of opportunity, a child's economic position is heavily influenced by that of his or her parents. Forty-two percent of children born to parents in the bottom fifth of the income distribution remain in the bottom. . . .The 'rags to riches' story is much more common in Hollywood than on Main Street. Only 6 percent of children born to parents with family income at the very bottom moved to the very top."[19]

In Reagan-era America, if you are poor, you have a 43 percent chance of still being poor a decade or generation hence, and you have only a 1-in-17 chance of becoming rich. That's not quite the very long odds of winning a lottery, catching on in the NBA or Hollywood, but they are quite weak odds nonetheless. In contrast, Isaacs found that 39 percent of children born to rich parents were themselves rich some forty years later; the figure was updated to 40 percent in 2012. In other words, the odds of an American child ending up rich are nearly seven times greater if he or she does a superior job picking parents. Mobility is a bit better for those children from the middle class. But opportunity is so poor for the bottom quintiles that Reagan-era America fails the Rawls test.

American Economic Mobility Has Deteriorated

Is Reaganomics to blame? Mobility may be poor, but has it at least remained stable or even improved during the three decades of the Reagan era? Again, the answer is no. To the contrary, Reaganomics has proven toxic to opportunity.

During the golden age, economic mobility improved. Economists Emily Beller and Michael Hout utilized data going back to the 1940s to compare the economic status of sons with their fathers. Economists frequently focus on fathers and sons, because female economics is heavily biased by marriage outcomes. Their work began when youths like Augustine first began to leave farms for assembly-line jobs in the industrial heartland as the golden age emerged. Beller and Hout concluded that parental income became *less* important to the economic success of men between 1940 and 1980, meaning economic mobility had improved.[20]

The arrival of Reaganomics changed all that. Since 1980, the economic status of a son's parents has become more determinant and predictive of a child's ultimate economic status. Plucky poor was out. Lucky rich was in. A sharp decline in mobility since 1980 has been documented extensively by economists. In 2002, for example, Kathleen Bradbury and Jane Katz looked at the impact of Reaganomics decade by decade since the 1970s and found that mobility had declined steadily.[21] Perhaps the most extensive analysis of mobility trends in the twentieth century was performed in 2008 by Federal Reserve Bank economists Daniel Aaronson and Bhashkar Mazumder. Using six million data points from decennial censuses, they used the Beller-Hout formulation to evaluate the economic status of middle-age sons and their fathers at the same age. Their discouraging findings are reproduced in Chart 16.1.

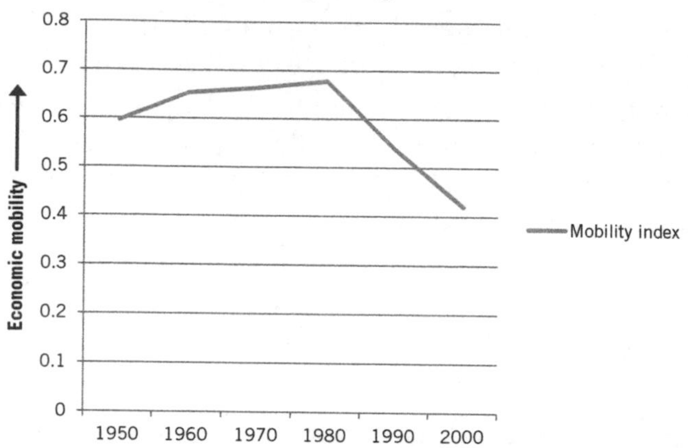

Chart 16.1. Mobility is (1 minus the estimated intergenerational earnings elasticity coefficient implied for 40- to-44-year-olds. A mobility index of zero indicates a boy's position in the income spectrum as an adult will be identical to his father's forty years earlier; a value of 1 indicates a completely mobile society, where a son's eventual status bears no relationship to his father's income, and his odds are the same of becoming rich, poor, or anywhere in between.

Source: Daniel Aaronson and Bhashkar Mazumder, "Intergenerational Economic Mobility in the United States, 1940 to 2000," The Journal of Human Resources 43: 1, table I (2008).

Aaronson and Mazumder concluded:

> "We find that mobility increased from 1950 to 1980 but has declined sharply since 1980. . . . [It's lower] now than at any other time in the post World War II period."[22]

These studies provide the weight of scholarly evidence that the opportunity of Americans to bootstrap themselves like Horatio Alger's heroes through education and hard work has deteriorated sharply during the Reagan era to the lowest level in more than 60 years. If not born rich, boys and girls have had to resort to the thin reed of diminishing opportunity to improve their lot, relying on weakening schools, indifferent if not hostile employers, rising college costs, and limited upskilling opportunity.

Since 1980, America has been transformed into a society that works in reverse: the poor are less likely to become rich, and the rich less likely to become poor. And that trend is cemented by rising income inequality, which limits the ability of lower-income parents to nurture childhood achievement. With schools in working-class neighborhoods underresourced, college costs rising, and good jobs shrinking, working-class youths have grown cynical and pessimistic, increasingly sidelined by the Reagan era's diminishing opportunity. Innate ability, height, education, grit, sex, ethnic origin—nothing comes close to parental wealth in determining the economic opportunity for youth today. As Michael Kinsley concluded in June 2005,

> "The problem in short may not be that reality is receding from the national myth. The problem may be the myth."[23]

Even before the recession and the 2012 election, a sense of diminished prosperity and a darkening future was palpable among voters, with Kinsley explaining it was becoming easier every day to slip out of the middle class from just bad luck, like an accident. Too few blame Reaganomics, even though only a bare handful of its acolytes and supporters have matched their opportunity society rhetoric with deeds. Most prominent is the late Congressman Jack Kemp, nominated for vice president at the Republican Party's 1996 convention. He spoke glowingly of expanding opportunity, pointing to education and better housing as key measures of economic justice. As noted by Michael Gerson, a speechwriter for George W. Bush, Kemp argued that opportunity "is the most important measure of economic justice; capitalism is perfected by the broadest possible distribution of capital."[24] Kemp seems to have read his Aristotle, Adam Smith, and perhaps even Rousseau. But he was nearly a lone voice in the Republican Party.

It may surprise you, but evidence of reduced opportunity has become so persuasive that even conservatives get butterflies about the impact of Reaganomics on mobility. Here is how Stuart Butler, vice president for economic studies at the business lobby Heritage Foundation, put it:

> "It does seem in America now that for people at the very bottom it's more difficult to move up than we might have thought or might have been true in the past."[25]

What really may be causing them to blush is that evidence of dwindling American opportunity in the Reagan era has gone viral globally; the United States is now routinely fingered as a cautionary tale when compared to the higher mobility in other rich democracies. Here is how economists Jo Bladen of the London School of Economics, Paul Greeg of University College, London, and Stephen Machin of the University of Bristol put it in 2005: "The idea of the US as 'the land of opportunity' persists; and clearly seems misplaced."[26] Experts at the OECD writing in the 2012 survey of the United States put it this way:

> ". . . socioeconomic background has a much greater impact on student outcomes in the United States than it does in most other countries, resulting in much wasted talent."[27]

Greater Economic Mobility in the Family Capitalism Countries

Responding to a wave of international analyses in recent years, economists have concluded that Kinsley and other researchers are correct: the notion of exceptional American opportunity not only has become mythical, experience since 1980 has turned that presumption upside down. Not only has mobility declined quite significantly, that decline has made American opportunity the lowest and weakest of any rich democracy, a national humiliation. "It's becoming conventional wisdom that the US does not have as much mobility as most other advanced countries. I don't think you'll find too many people who will argue with that," concluded Isabel Sawhill in January 2012.[28] Studies informing that consensus include a number conducted in recent decades and evaluated in 2006 by economist Anna-Cristina d'Addio for the OECD.[29] The d'Addio conclusions are reproduced as Chart 16.2, drawing heavily on researchers led by Mrakus Jäntti at the University of Oslo and Professor Miles Corak at the University of Ottawa.[30]

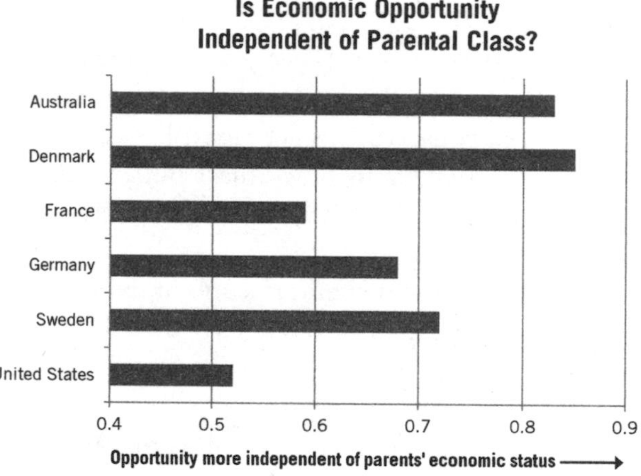

Chart 16.2. 2006. Mobility measure ranges from 0 to 1.0 and the variable is (1-estimated intergenerational earnings elasticity coefficient). High values denote greater economic mobility, with adult status more independent of parental status a generation earlier.

Source: Anna-Cristina d'Addio, "Intergenerational Transmission of Disadvantage: Mobility or Immobility across Generations? A Review of Evidence for OECD Countries," OECD, 2006.

This chart depicts the extent to which earnings of adults differ from parental earnings a generation earlier. The family capitalism countries, along with nations such as Canada, Norway, and Finland, have high economic mobility and notable churning of individuals among income categories from one generation to the next; earnings of children display a wide variation compared to their parents. These are genuine opportunity societies, where pluck and skill determine outcomes and one's success bears little relationship to the economic status of one's parents. Indeed, economic mobility or opportunity in nations such as Australia and Denmark is nearly 50 percent greater than in the United States. These enormous differences, documented in the d'Addio compendium, were highlighted by the *Economist*:

> "Several new studies show parental income to be a better predictor of whether someone will be rich or poor in America than in Canada or much of Europe. In America, about half of the income disparities in one generation are reflected in the next. In Canada and the Nordic countries, that proportion is about a fifth."[31]

D'Addio also assessed mobility by determining the prospects of poor sons remaining poor as adults. Recall the US Treasury Department economists and Brookings Institution's Julia Isaacs, who concluded that about 42 percent of adult sons from poor parents in America also were poor. As depicted in Chart 16.3, these US odds are considerably worse than in any other rich democracy, almost double that of Denmark. This chart displays the probability that the son of a father in the lowest quintile will land in that quintile as an adult. Even in the class-ridden United Kingdom, cluttered with moneyed blue bloods of title and wealthy global expatriates, the odds of remaining poor are 30 percent. In fact, sons born into low-earning households in any of the other rich democracies examined have quite significantly better opportunities to escape an impoverished birth than do American boys.

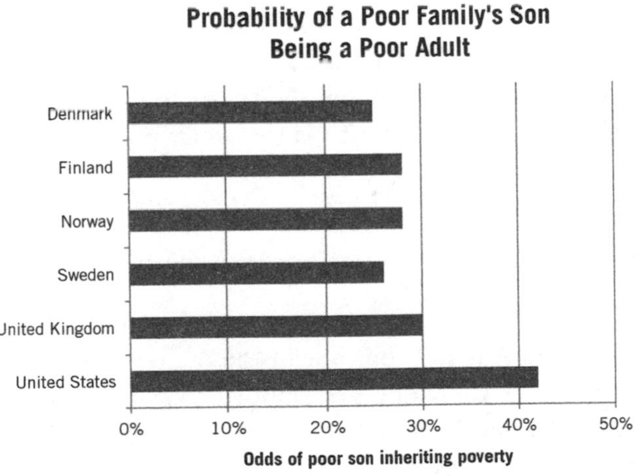

Chart 16.3.
Source: Anna-Cristina d'Addio, "Intergenerational Transmission of Disadvantage: Mobility or Immobility Across Generations? A Review of Evidence for OECD Countries," Paris, OECD, table 1, 2006. This data based on Jäntti, et al. University of Oslo, 2006.

You can see why Isabel Sawhill has concluded that "a number of advanced countries provide more opportunity to their citizens than does the United States."[32]

The low and declining American intergenerational mobility is most pronounced where it is most meaningful, pinning far too many children from lower-income households in what has become a multigenerational cycle of poverty. Here is how the University of Oslo economists describe that consequence of Reaganomics, including their quote in the epigraph to this chapter:

> "Comparative studies of socioeconomic mobility have long challenged the notion of 'American exceptionalism,' a term that was invoked by Tocqueville and Marx to describe what was then thought of as exceptionally high rates of social mobility in the United States . . . the United States has more low-income persistence and less upward mobility than the other countries we studied. . . . The probability that the son of a lowest-quintile father makes it into the top quintile group—'rags to riches' mobility—is lower in the US than in all other countries. . . . These two findings—higher low-income persistence and a lower likelihood of rags-to-riches mobility—seems to us quite powerful evidence against the traditional notion of American exceptionalism consisting of a greater rate of upward social mobility than in other countries. In light of this evidence, the US appears to be exceptional in having less rather than more upward mobility."[33]

After thirty years of the Reagan era, the only American odds higher than a rich man's son becoming rich himself as an adult are the odds of a poor man's son staying poor. And the worst odds of all? The likelihood that opportunity will enable a poor man's son to become rich. Of all the world's rich democracies, America is the worst poor son's country, and the best rich son's country.[34]

The American Education Auction: Widening Class-Based Disparities

Birth is destiny in America, but not in the family capitalism countries, which are the true contemporary opportunity societies. Their public policies have been instrumental in this success, especially institutional arrangements such as codetermination that generates good jobs and upskilling to ensure employees have the skills to qualify for such jobs. For families, high wages have resulted from Australian-style national wage policies, supported by quality education, free college, and public upskilling programs; those programs enable most families to invest more effectively in their children's future than resource-deprived American families.

Almost from birth, a web of mutually reinforcing policies, including preschool, childcare programs, and nationwide student spending standards, are utilized to create and enhance human capital while minimizing poverty. Remarkably, 89 percent of German three-year-olds attend preschool (two-thirds are private), as do 96 percent of four-year-olds.[35] In contrast, only 69 percent of American four-year-olds are enrolled in early education, ranking the United States in twenty-sixth place in the world. Participation is greater in Austria (89 percent); Belgium (99 percent); Denmark (98 percent); France (100 percent); the Netherlands (100 percent); and Sweden (94 percent), according to the OECD.[36] And the same pattern persists for five-year-olds. In Germany, every youngster is guaranteed a kindergarten spot, and OECD statistics show 97 percent are in public or private facilities in contrast to 80 percent in America. Comparable figures for Australia, Belgium, and the Netherlands are 99 percent.[37]

Economists including Tarjei Havnes at the University of Oslo and Magne Mogstad with *Statistics Norway* have determined that such preschool investments yield big payoffs for society. Writing in the 2011 *American Economic Journal: Economic Policy*, they concluded:

> ". . . subsidized child care had strong effects on children's educational attainment and labor market participation and also reduced welfare dependency. Subsample analyses indicate that girls and children with low-educated mothers benefit the most from childcare."[38]

Similar evidence is provided by for a National Institutes of Health analysis; preschool interventions with low-income children in America were determined to generate anywhere from $4 to $11 in benefits per dollar invested.[39] Even so, the more limited US availability of preschool support is symptomatic of a generalized American problem of uneven and limited access to internationally competitive education. Ironically, education has served in the past as an opportunity escalator for Americans, but quality education has become a luxury item in the Reagan era, with college and the price of neighborhoods featuring good public schools well outpacing wages. Recall economist Robert H. Frank had concluded that families must devote 60 percent more work hours now than they did in 1970 to afford neighborhoods with above-average school systems. Moreover, school districts exacerbate the resource disparity by assigning the most capable veteran teachers and principals to higher-income neighborhoods, according to a November 2011 report by the US Department of Education.[40]

Education attainment improved dramatically during the nineteenth century and through the 1970s, but the auctioning of education opportunity during the Reagan era has reversed this trend. There is considerable evidence that a class-based education gap has been exacerbated rather than eased by Reaganomics. Current research by education statisticians like Sean F. Reardon document that the achievement gap between students from impoverished *versus* higher-income families has widened in recent decades; the standardized testing score gap between rich and poor children is 40 percent larger now than in 1970, for example.[41] And, National Assessment of Education Progress studies have concluded that 40 percent of reading score variations and 46 percent of math score variations among the states today are associated with childhood poverty. Indeed, poverty now easily trumps race as the more potent indicator of low achievement; the poverty/achievement gap is 50 percent wider than the gap between black and white youngsters.[42] And here is how Isabel Sawhill describes the conclusion of her recent research into this area:

> "An examination of preschool, K-12, and undergraduate and graduate education in the United States reveals that the average effect of education at all levels is to reinforce rather than compensate for the differences associated with family background and the many home-based advantages and disadvantages that children and adolescents bring with them into the classroom. There is no reason to expect change in the disappointing effect of education on economic mobility unless reforms are aggressively pursued at all levels."[43]

Class-Based College Opportunity

Rising college costs have contributed to this class-based deterioration in education opportunity. The Economic Mobility Project of the Brookings/Pew analysis examined the impact of a college degree on mobility. Recall our earlier evidence that the odds of a poor son jumping to the top-earning quintile as an adult are 6 percent or less? If they finish college, those odds triple to 19 percent.[44] The troubling news is the increasingly class-ridden nature of American society means children from resource-deprived schools, neighborhoods, and homes have only modest opportunity to attend college or to succeed once there. The brightest youngsters from poor backgrounds have opportunity, but few of their siblings or classmates do.

While college completion rates for all youngsters increased during the Reagan era, virtually all the rise was among students from higher-income households, with the gap between rich and poor widening quite significantly. The statistics responsible for this conclusion are disheartening, especially for a nation priding itself on educational opportunity. Only 5 percent of youngsters born in 1961–1964 to families in the lowest-quartile (25 percent) income group completed college, compared to 36 percent of youngsters born those years into the highest quartile. Yet the completion rate for the lowest-income youngsters growing up in the Reagan era (born at its cusp in 1979–1982) is only 4 percentage points higher, or 9 percent total. But the completion rate for those born into the highest-income quartile soared 18 percentage points at the same time, to 54 percent total. Thus, during the Reagan era, the *increase* in college completions by richer youngsters was four and one-half times greater than for poor youngsters, as depicted in Chart 16.4. Thus, students from more affluent households completed college at a rate six times greater than students from the lowest-income quartile. And they do it faster, too. Students from highest-income households are eight times more likely than those from the lowest-income families to earn a bachelor's degree by age 24.[45] And these results parallel those reached by other researchers such as Ron Haskins, Harry Holzer, and Robert Lerman.[46]

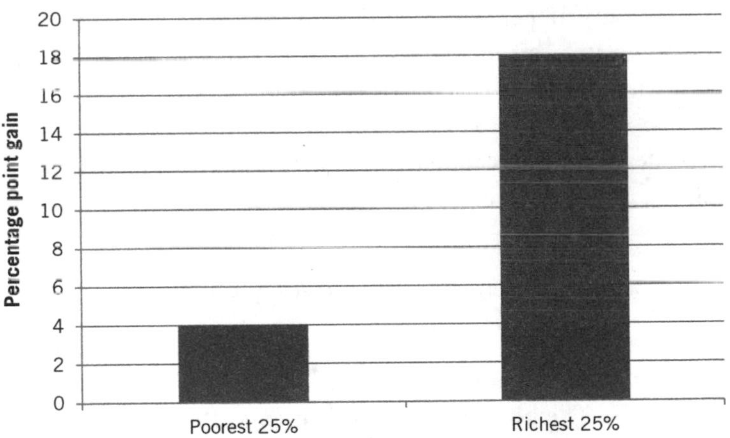

Chart 16.4.

Source: Martha J. Bailey and Susan M. Dynarski, "Gains and Gaps: Changing Inequality in US College Entry and Completion," NBER working paper no. 17633 (December 2011); "College Completion by Income and Year of Birth," Inequality in America, The Stanford Center for Poverty and Inequality, September 2012.

The actual situation is worse. A Century Foundation Report in 2010 concluded that 44 percent of low-income students with high standardized test scores enroll in four-year colleges, while 50 percent of those from high-income households but with only average test scores enroll.[47]

And the world knows it. The US college education system was captured editorially by the *Economist* magazine in April 2010, as indicated by its epigraph to this chapter:

> "Rich, stupid children are more likely to graduate than poor, clever ones."[48]

The outcome is that American college attainment in relative terms is deteriorating. The share of Americans from 25 to 34 years old with college degrees ranks only 14th among the richest nations, lagging behind nations such as Australia, Canada, France, Korea, and Norway.[49] The US attainment rate used to be second, behind only Canada.[50] And some believe the outcomes and performance in higher education today have ceased improving in absolute terms. David Brooks concluded in 2008 that "the US needs a more skilled workforce, but for the first time in our history, it is getting a generation no better educated than its parents."[51]

Public policy has failed to slow the class-based consequences of the US education auction. Lacking family resources of the more affluent, capable poor and middle-class college students are penalized by inadequate public education support. Pell Grants for low-income students covered 72 percent of costs at a public university in 1976, for example, compared to only 38 percent in 2003; and that trend has worsened since with the downturn.[52] Students have compensated by going heavily into debt with student loans.

American competitors abroad are not so foolish as to squander the talents of deprived but capable youths by diverting resources to give $46,000 tax cuts to millionaires.

The American Multigenerational Poverty Cycle

Stagnant wages, a weak minimum wage, and the disposable labor syndrome at worksites feature prominently in the disjointed life of lower-income families. The blight of impoverishment afflicting the chronically underemployed in many, if not most, instances reflects a life bereft of quality employment opportunities, a reality ensnaring more of the middle class each year. The genesis in many instances is not dysfunctional homes or inappropriate work habits, but insufficient jobs and especially insufficient jobs paying livable wages, which create or dramatically exacerbate family pathologies.

Evidence comes from three sources:

First, America is a low-wage country lacking sufficient quality jobs. ILO statistics reveal that nearly one-fourth of US jobs paid less than two-thirds the median hourly wage in 2010; this US rate is *four times* the incidence of low-wage jobs in Sweden, double the rate in New Zealand, and 50 percent higher than Australia's. Worse, this comparison was just among full-time workers, which minimizes the actual incidence of crummy American jobs, many of which are temporary or part time.[53] America really is a low-wage country and socioeconomic outcomes merely reflect that.

Second, the absence of quality jobs creates pathologies. For example, an important element creating the multigenerational poverty cycle is teenage pregnancies. Demographers have found that the incidence of teen births is linked to unemployment. Cynthia Cohen, Arline Geronimus, and Maureen Phipps, for example, concluded in a study in the journal *Social Science and Medicine* that declining jobless rates in the 1990s explained 85 percent of the drop in rates of first births to 18- and 19-year-old African Americans. That cohort is among those most prone to teen pregnancies. "Young Black women, especially older teens, may have adjusted their reproductive behavior to take advantage of expanded labor market opportunities," was their conclusion.[54]

Third, impoverished Americans work very hard. Research conducted by economist Timothy Smeeding, while director of the Center for Policy Research at Syracuse University, produced the smoking gun. The poverty expert discovered that poor American families with children work *more* annual hours than families in any other rich democracy, yet they earn less, and too little to escape poverty:

> "The United States also has the highest proportion of workers in poorly paid jobs, and the highest number of annual hours worked by poor families with children. . . ."[55]

If hard work was the key to success in Reagan-era America, the poor would be atop the income pyramid. They are poor because they are paid low wages in insecure jobs, despite working hard. Their impoverishment is the consequence of too few good jobs, not deficient work efforts or inappropriate family cultures.

Already losers in the education auction, education attainment by students in lower-wage households is further weakened by frequent relocations. Scholars have found that it is common for lower-income families to relocate many times in a single school year, disrupting family environments for childhood learning as youngsters repeatedly adjust to new teachers, new curriculums, and new friends. Little appreciated by economists, the US-disrupted education syndrome is described this way by David Kerbow, a University of Chicago education researcher:

> "Such house-hopping and school disruption is common in low-income urban areas across the country, with annual turnover of students typically ranging from 30 percent to 50 percent."[56]

Thirty to fifty percent means little education is occurring. Turnover at one school in hard-pressed Flint, Michigan, reached an astounding 75 percent, noted Kerbow. *New York Times* reporter Erik Eckholm explains:

> "Children switch from school to school, even returning repeatedly to the same one, as their parents become overextended on rent in one place, try another rental, flee an unsafe block, or move in with a relative or a new partner."[57]

With the poorest intergenerational mobility and weakest opportunity of any rich democracy, America is plagued by inherited poverty: American youngsters with poor schooling are destined to become disposable workers, like their parents, a squandered resource, their genius lost. And their plight is exacerbated by a weakened economic safety net. President Clinton's Temporary Assistance for Needy Families reform, which appeared remarkably innovative in good economic times, has been revealed as senselessly cruel and draconian when times toughened. In 1996 before the changes, 68 of every 100 impoverished families with children received welfare support; by 2010, the share had plunged to only 27 of every 100 families, despite unemployment doubling.[58] Intended to incentivize job searches, the reforms fail when the need is greatest: in the real world, employment opportunities collapse when the need is greatest, with five or ten applicants for every opening. The Clinton reform is like a car whose headlights cease functioning at dusk.

New Research Debunks Traditional Beliefs: Nurture Trumps Nature

Why are Americans indifferent to the multigenerational poverty cycle, leaving 20 percent of the United States chronically mired in or near poverty, and 20 million living in extreme poverty? Certainly, stagnation of real incomes amid rising costs for health, education, and other necessities makes families disinclined to support taxes. But responsibility for this indifference among voters also rests in some measure on their belief that the disadvantaged are a natural and ineluctably ordained phenomenon. The success of family capitalism countries in building genuine opportunity societies from top to bottom proves those beliefs erroneous. Poverty is permitted, not ordained.

Education expert Paul Tough argues in his book *How Children Succeed* that culture, family environment, and preschool support are instrumental in shaping youths to become valued members of society. And important studies by Americans such as psychologists Eric Turkheimer and Richard Nisbett have produced new insights from studies of twins. These analysts searched for separated twins so that they could assess the influence of different learning environments. Turkheimer concluded that the economic status of households in which youngsters are raised can trump the impact of genetics. "The IQ of the poorest twins appeared to be almost exclusively determined by their socioeconomic status." He concluded that the cognitive abilities of even the least advantaged children are extremely malleable.[59]

Nisbett reached a similar conclusion: "It is now clear that intelligence is highly modifiable by the environment." Psychologist Ulman Lindenberger at Berlin's Max Planck Institute for Education Research came to the same conclusion: "The proportion of genetic factors in intelligence differences depends on whether a person's environment enables him to fulfill his genetic potential."[60]

In an important conclusion, Nisbett determined "50 percent to be the maximum contribution of genetics," with the importance of environment to cognitive ability typically more pronounced, especially among the least advantaged. The issue of nurture versus nature is a complex field. Yet such research provides evidence that the successful approach of family capitalism countries to poverty alleviation is based on sound science and could be duplicated by the United States.

The family capitalism countries behave as though childhood impoverishment is only a temporary birth defect to be remediated by support, jobs, and education. Communities amid an abundance of jobs paying livable wages are communities where hope and opportunity flourish, where cultural norms are strong, and where employed parents and neighbors provide stable role models. They are communities where families accumulate social capital and where the predicates of a good education and personal responsibility become self-evident to youths who perceive opportunity. Conservatives attribute American poverty to the many low-wage workers entering world labor markets or fault cultural norms among the poor and a breakdown of US family structures. The factors making for American poverty are varied and complex, but its origin is not too many Chinese or missing fathers, but too few American jobs paying livable wages.

The success of the family capitalism countries powerfully affirms that poverty alleviation cannot succeed in the absence of good jobs. Preschool, inexpensive child care, good quality schools, and inexpensive college are resources that families can reasonably expect from the public sector. But the single certain necessary and sufficient condition to ameliorate the pathologies, inopportunity, disrupted communities, and despair that beset impoverished Americans is a sufficient number of good jobs.

CHAPTER 17

AUSTRALIAN-STYLE WAGE DETERMINATION IN FAMILY CAPITALISM

"There is also a system of generalized regular arbitration that served for a long time as the pillar of industrial relations in New Zealand and Australia. This system originated in legislation of 1894 and 1904. . . ."[1]

SABINE BLASCHKE, BERNARD KITTEL, and FRANZ TRAXLER,
***National Labour Relations in International Markets*, February 2001**

"The real point is that humans are meant to be the object of the economic exercise. When you seek to raise productivity and material living standards by making peoples' working lives a misery of uncertainty and insecurity, damaging people's family lives and even their health, you confuse means with ends."[2]

ROSS GITTINS,
Economics Editor, *Sydney Morning Herald*, July 2011

"Over the past few decades, several European nations, like Germany and the Netherlands, have played by the rules and practiced good governance. They have lived within their means, undertaken painful reforms, enhanced their competitiveness, and reinforced good values."[3]

DAVID BROOKS,
***New York Times*, December 2, 2011**

"The Netherlands has achieved what others only dream of: collective agreements without strikes, coupled with a healthy economic growth and a reduction in unemployment."[4]

RUTH REICHSTEIN,
***Handelsblatt*, October 2010**

Australian-style national wage determination is the heart of family capitalism's ability to widely broadcast the gains from growth and attain broadly enjoyed prosperity amid globalization. The pivotal concept first emerged 120 years ago in Australia and New Zealand, and features collaboration by employees and employers to raise real wages annually. How did that happen?

The nineteenth-century roots of Australian-style wage determination were explained this way by University of Vienna sociologists Sabine Blaschke, Bernhard Kittel, and Franz Traxler in 2001:

> "There is also a system of generalized regular arbitration that served for a long time as the pillar of industrial relations in New Zealand and Australia. This system originated in legislation of 1894 and 1904 that enabled the unions to make all employers party to the arbitration procedures, resulting in a binding decision on the terms of employment (i.e. the award) by special tribunals. . . ."[5]

These researchers are part of a global community of scholars examining how wages are reached in the rich democracies, a community including Americans like sociologist and political scientist Lane Kenworthy at the University of Arizona.[6] Reaching back well before the Hallmark 1907 Harvester decision, New Zealand and Australia established the legal foundation for laws and practices embodying a livable wage that evolved to the nationwide wage agreements common in rich democracies. This important element of family capitalism emerged perhaps independently early in the twentieth century in Denmark, later during the 1930s in France and Switzerland, and during the war years in Sweden. It was adopted as a key component of the hyper-competitive German codeterminism model introduced in the aftermath of World War II. German reformers such as Konrad Adenauer, Ludwig Erhard, and Walter Eucken were vital. But absolutely critical to its emergence was the exigency of the Cold War that justified a dramatic experiment by the Allies. The experiment included drawing on the successful experience of neighbors with Australian-style wage setting mechanisms ensuring that productivity gains are shared by both employees and employers. Employers reach wage agreements with families who are represented in negotiations by surrogates from unions in a process closely monitored by government officials.

Australian-style wage policies and northern European codeterminism, where employees and employers closely collaborate to enhance family and firm success, must appear strange indeed to Americans after a generation of Reaganomics. Yet ironically, codeterminism and the Australian wage system are drawn directly from American business practice and economic research, their roots and intellectual provenance resting firmly in American economic history. Indeed, the success of the family capitalism countries rests as much with a number of American and British visionaries and scholars as it does with their own economists and politicians, as we see now.

The Ford Model Prioritizing Productivity, with Wages Based on Value-Added

One American visionary was a wealthy Utah businessman named Marriner Eccles, Franklin Roosevelt's chairman of the Federal Reserve System. A stout defender of legacy capital, Eccles was no socialist. He provided both the muscle and the vision during the New Deal era that gave lift to Adam Smith's centuries-old hope for capitalism to improve the lot of all mankind:

> "Mass production must be accompanied by mass consumption, and this in turn implies a distribution of wealth—not of existing wealth, but wealth produced during the same period—as it provides men purchasing power equivalent to the quantity of goods and services offered by the country's productive apparatus."[7]

The Smith/Eccles/Roosevelt recipe of family capitalism is straightforward: the moral sentiments of society should be harnessed in support of widely broadcasting the gains from productivity growth. Attaining that goal hinges on two elements from Henry Ford adopted by these countries: prioritizing productivity growth in order to maximize economic growth, and linking wages to labor productivity growth.

Prioritizing productivity reaches back to the British economist Alfred Marshall and the Austrian Joseph Schumpeter who first preached the seminal importance of raising productivity as the precursor to prosperity.[8] This lesson was emphasized anew in the postwar era by a number of nations, including the family capitalism countries and Japan. Indeed, the first great challenge to America's postwar economic preeminence was Japanese firms such as Toyota in the 1970s and 1980s. Initially mocked, the quality, consumer appeal, and pace of productivity improvements embodied in postwar Japanese products in the space of a decade or two revolutionized global manufacturing. We have learned that American management's attention to productivity concerns waned with the introduction of Reaganomics as executive suites turned inward, pursuing the windfalls abruptly on offer. But the family capitalism countries were not sidetracked. They remained attentive to the urgency of productivity growth in order to compete with the American postwar juggernaut and the first tendrils of global integration represented by Japanese exporters.

Innovations like just-in-time inventory control were important, but the genuine Japanese revolution was a ferocious focus on quality (*kaizen*). In turn, that placed a premium on what has become a northern European strength in the decades since, thanks to work councils and codetermination: active intrafirm communications up and down the hierarchy chain leading a relentless search for improved productivity. Their evolved approach has emerged as the *sine qua non* for enterprise success in modern capitalism. And the management structure most attuned to its implementation in the postwar era has proven to be codetermination, yielding the competitive superiority the northern Europe nations enjoy today on the technology frontier.

The second tenet of family capitalism drawn from Henry Ford is to link wages to productivity growth. We learned earlier that productivity growth in the US became decoupled from wages during the Roaring Twenties and again during the Reagan era. In contrast, practices in the family capitalism countries reflect the teachings of Ford that wages should reflect something approximating employees' marginal value to employers. Even more significant, the design of the Australian-style wage determination system practiced in these nations is a direct mimicry of the human resource policy of every American enterprise.

Family Capitalism Applies American Corporate Wage Practices

Australia and northern Europe translate rising productivity into rising wages using various permutations of a collaborative public and private mechanism, with most wages nationwide increasing by an amount each year tied to the rate of inflation plus some sizable portion of the rise in productivity. That's the outcome of the Australian-style wage mechanism even though countries use different arrangements. That system resembles what occurred in America during the golden age where wage settlements at blue chip firms like GM became national templates for wage setting in all sorts of other enterprises.

The family capitalism system draws explicitly from American business practices at another conceptual level as well. How do these nations justify what tend to be somewhat uniform wage hikes across their economies in light of the fact that productivity growth is far from uniform between sectors like retailing or manufacturing?

It turned out to be simple. They just looked at what American firms were doing in the golden age.

In designing their wage mechanisms, officials in family capitalism countries examined how the best performing enterprises in the world at the time determined wage increases among their own employees. The officials merely mimic the behavior common to every single American office, plant, and corporation. Senior American human resource officials today from Fox News to GE and Koch Industries would instantly recognize the mechanism as their own. In American firms as we know, wage gains on average have struggled even to keep pace with inflation. Even so, whatever nominal wage increases that do occur are allocated with the most productive employees receiving rather less than their marginal product while the least productive receive rather more. Drawing on analyses by researchers like Stanford business professor Jeffrey Pfeffer, Alison Davis-Blake who is Dean of the University of Michigan business school, and Alison Konrad at the University of Western Ontario,[9] Cornell economist Robert H. Frank explained in *The Darwin Economy* just how pervasive this distributive pattern mimicked by the family capitalism countries is within American enterprises:

> "The pattern is widespread. In every occupation for which data facilitate the relevant comparisons, the most productive workers in any unit are paid substantially less than the value they contribute, while the least productive workers are paid substantially more. . . . That's precisely the pattern we'd predict if people assign considerable value to high-ranked positions within work groups. . . . In effect, each employer administers an implicit income distribution scheme that taxes the most productive workers in each group and transfers additional pay to the least productive."[10]

He specifically referred to the pay pattern in the US private business sector:

> "In short, the startling fact is that private business typically transfers large amounts of income from the most productive to the least productive workers. Because labor contracts are voluntary under United States law, it would be bizarre to object that these transfers violate anyone's rights."

The Australian-style national wage systems of the family capitalism countries allocate the gains from growth among workers the same way that the private labor market does at Apple, Ford, Google, Microsoft, and the *Wall Street Journal*. They mimic the precise pattern in firms that libertarians and market fundamentalists laud as exemplars of innovation and high-performing work places. In Germany during 2012, this system produced wage gains averaging about half a point above the consumer price index, ranging from a nominal 3.3 percent in the highly productive capital goods industry to only 2 percent in the banking and insurance sectors.

Wage Determination Features Compromise—Not Conflict

The wage-setting mechanisms that have evolved in the family capitalism countries are rooted in American corporate practices, but the job site orientation is entirely different. Rather than wage compression featuring commoditized and disposable employees, these high-performing economies place a premium on job site productivity and rewarding John Calvin's work ethic. The enterprise cultures abroad are profoundly different, with employees viewed as assets, not liabilities.

That seminal difference can best be grasped by examining the potential wage crisis confronting Germany in 2011. Workers from lower-wage Eastern Europe would be permitted unfettered access to the booming jobs market in Germany after May 1, 2011 under EU rules. Predictions were dire, with up to 800,000 moderately skilled Poles, Czechs, and others expected to flood Germany, overwhelming job markets and suppressing wages. But forecasters hadn't counted on the character of northern European job sites after decades of globalization, where highly productive, seasoned, and skilled employees are more vital to firm success than cheap wages.

Fear quickly turned to puzzlement when the flood turned out to be a dribble; only 26,000 migrants arrived in the first three months after May 1, not markedly more than the 10,000 migrants in the preceding three months before May. And the German trade union federation DGB determined that only 67,000 came in the first six months.[11] What happened? There were simply few jobs on offer for the newcomers. Explanations such as language barriers were given, but the Institute for Labour Market and Employment Research (IAB) in Nuremberg figured it out. They fingered the German labor model, which prioritizes worksite performance over wage compression: only the highly skilled need apply.[12] Herbert Brucker of the IAB explained the outcome was the consequence of the explicit German rejection (because it hobbles productivity growth) of the American-style "hire-and-fire" labor model.

How are nationwide wage increases set by the family capitalist countries? Recall that we reviewed the process in Australia in Chapter 3, including this explanation from that government's Bureau of Statistics: "In Australia, the 1983 Wage Accord established a centralized wage fixing system that took into account economic policies and the Consumer Price Index. By 1987, the replacement was a two-tier system that distributed a flat increase to all workers and made further increase provisional on improvement in efficiencies."[13]

This Australian-style approach with its roots reaching back to 1894 is common in the other family capitalism countries, where economy-wide parameters for wage gains are devised and applied to the vast majority of jobs. Regional and nationwide wage and benefits agreements are negotiated by employer groups with trade union organizations, who act as agents for families, and then reviewed by governments.[14] The system resembles the Nordic model mentioned earlier, with scholars Åge Johnsen at Olso University College and Jarmo Vakkuri at the University of Tampere writing that it features a high degree of consensus building, with decisions being evidenced-based rather than ideology based.[15]

As applied specifically in the Netherlands, Ruth Reichstein's epigraph summarized the outcome of its Australian system this way: "The Netherlands has achieved what others only dream of: collective agreements without strikes, coupled with a healthy economic growth and a reduction in unemployment." Emphasizing collaboration and compromise rather than conflict, and revised continually to enhance labor market flexibility, this consensus system is the heart of family capitalism.

The Australian mechanism has been modified locally in each nation. In some, wages are set locally or regionally between employees and employers with little public sector oversight, while in others—Norway and France, for instance—government input is more direct.[16] Negotiators are careful to avoid settlements that significantly differ in magnitude from those in neighboring countries. As in Australia, labor federations are at the center, as representatives for all employees and their families. Government can step in should negotiations falter, a prospect that incentivizes negotiators to reach agreement on their own. Failure of employers and employees to collaborate is punished, not rewarded.

These negotiations focus on key economic variables, including profits, inflation, taxes, fees for social programs, and especially productivity. And it is common for wage settlements in one sector or region to establish benchmarks for salary settlements to a greater or lesser degree in most sectors and throughout each country. Some major industries conduct their own individual wage negotiations, but collective agreements or nationwide benchmarking covers anywhere from 62 percent of employees in Germany to 90 percent or more in neighboring nations, according to the ILO and the *Berliner Zeitung*.[17] Chart 17.1, using statistics from the German Economic and Social Research Institute, indicates that broad wage settlements are most comprehensive in Austria and least comprehensive in America.

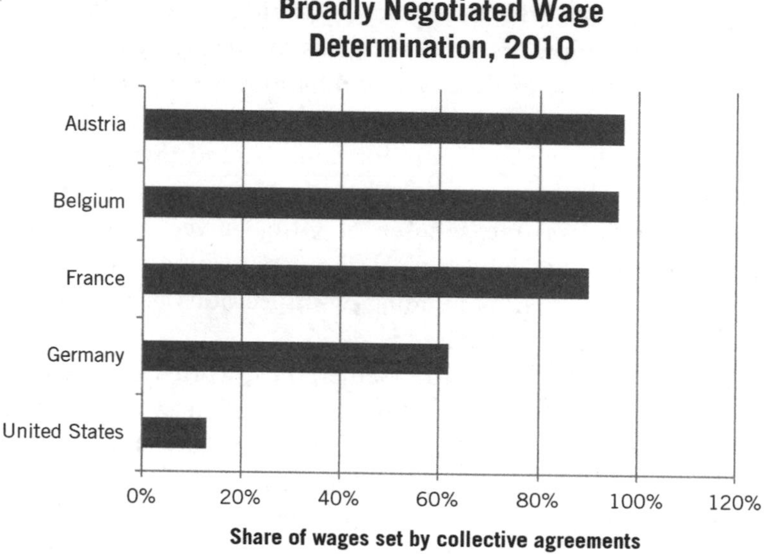

Chart 17.1.

Source: Economic and Social Research Institute, Berlin, October 24, 2012, and Stefan Sauer, "Collective Bargaining Coverage in Germany: Wages No Lower Limit," Berliner Zeitung, Oct. 15, 2012, http://www.berliner-zeitung.de/wirtschaft/tarifbindung-in-deutschland-loehne-ohne-untergrenze,10808230,20706404.html.

Here is how the wage-setting mechanism in hyper-competitive Germany functions. Only larger firms such as VW-Audi-Porsche engage in direct talks with employee unions. Instead, most wages are negotiated at the state level, as in the Saarland, Hess, or Rhineland-Palatinate, between employer groups and trade federations, with the outcome setting national templates.[18] In July 2011, for example, a *de facto* national guideline emerged from the collective agreement reached in the state of Baden-Württemberg. It provided for about 1 percent real wage gains, with retail employees receiving a 3 percent nominal wage hike (and 36 paid vacation days for some), with inflation at about 2 percent. Here is how the German Federal Statistical Office explains its regionally based process for reaching national wage determination: "The impact of collective agreements goes far beyond that. Many businesses and employers who are not bound by them nevertheless use the agreements negotiated for the relevant branches for orientation purposes."[19]

As a result, most employees in each of the family capitalism countries typically receive annual wage increases comprising two components.[20]

The first component hews to a broad standard intended to offset the erosion of inflation on employee earnings, while the second component is intended to ensure that employees receive a portion of the gains from growth, with total wage settlements typically exceeding inflation. This second element is where the gains from growth are sliced, and negotiations are vigorous and detailed. Individual company product lines and prospects can be exhaustively examined and debated.

Employees have a stake in striving for wage increases, of course, but not at the expense of firm survival because they have long-term attachments to employers; they covet enterprise success and that moderates wage demands. For their part, keenly sensitive to the urgency of productivity growth, employers have a stake in maintaining an energetic workforce while avoiding strikes. Yet employers also prioritize flexibility to hire and fire workers, to control labor costs while meeting sudden market changes, to optimize low labor turnover, and to be profitable for their shareholders and thereby able to invest in new technology to meet competition.[21] Wages do not rise beyond a cost-of-living adjustment if productivity growth is poor: "Salaries in France should be increased only if there is an increase in productivity," is how Reuters quoted former Economic Minister and now IMF chief Christine Lagarde in March 2011.[22]

Here is how this system worked in France in 2006. Productivity in 2005 rose 1.8 percent—better than the United States, but only one half that of Sweden, for example. Inflation at the retail level was about 1.6 percent. As it unfolded, average monthly gross salaries at French companies were negotiated upward by about 2.6 percent in nominal terms, yielding an increase of 1 percent in real terms.[23] That means a bit more than one-half of the gains from growth from rising productivity in the previous year flowed to employees in 2006, with the rest to employers to cover investment, R&D, and other expenses, and corporate profits.

At both domestic firms and American transplants in the family capitalism countries, trade federations play a pivotal role in coalescing public opinion, modulating or accelerating wage demands, and representing employees and families in this process, even though actually union membership is low. In Australia, France, and Netherlands, for example, only a minority of employers are directly covered by trade union agreements; union membership in the Netherlands was only 21 percent in 2010, down from 28 percent in 1995. Even so, voters expect trade union negotiators to exercise broad responsibility in the annual wage talks for nonunionized citizens and families, because the outcome establishes *de facto* national wage raises covering almost all employees.[24]

Avoiding Inflationary Wage Drift

Negotiators are especially vigilant against the dangers of inflationary wage settlements. Indeed, a major purpose of a significant 1983 Australian wage accord was to end inflationary "wage drift" there that had caused firms to become internationally uncompetitive. Various European countries and Australia struggled with what economists call wage drift in the decades after World War II, when wage hikes well above productivity growth generated inflation. Inflation disincentivizes investment and sends interest rates skyward, slowing growth, reducing employment, and perhaps precipitating instability resulting in currency devaluation. Indeed, controlling wage drift was a critical element in the launch of the EU over a decade ago. The fact that national currencies such as the German mark and the French franc were being replaced with a continent-wide euro meant that wage and price decisions (and government budget decisions, as we have learned) anywhere affected employers and employees everywhere. The safety valve of currency devaluations was no longer available for individual nations.

After decades of experimentation, the northern Europe wage mechanism adopted by the EU attacks wage drift in four ways:

First, automatic indexing of wages such as the Italian *Scala Mobile* was sharply scaled back or abolished, replaced with more flexible annual negotiations.

Second, the process has evolved so that a portion of wages is paid as variable and flexible thirteenth-month bonuses tied to profits. Sizable bonuses are nearly universal in northern Europe and are a major component of incomes; they typically represent 10 percent or more of annual earnings for many workers. Relying heavily on variable bonuses linked to firm profitability maximizes employee wage increases while also maximizing employer flexibility to control labor costs in the future, because it moderates base wage increases. Bonuses are adjusted each year during wage talks to reflect enterprise success. The logic of this practice in northern Europe is precisely analogous to the practice on Wall Street, where financial sector bonuses fluctuate with firm success.

Third, the public sector stands ready to assist firms in moderating inflation. Occasionally, government officials will intervene directly in wage negotiations, using the lure of public benefits in order to avoid inflationary wage increases. In the past, for example, wage negotiations in the Netherlands have sometimes included government-proffered tax cuts, enabling negotiators to hold down wage hikes and thus moderate labor costs and prices.[25]

Fourth, perhaps the most important element in avoiding inflationary wage drift is the responsibility forced on participants by the concept of unified wage negotiations. In the early postwar period characterized by labor shortages, wage drift occurred in part because of competitive forces among employers eager for workers and also by trade unions in competition to boost wages. By imposing a higher degree of responsibility, the Australian wage mechanism changed those dynamics, greatly easing wage-push pressures. With employees assured of reasonable wage gains in the future, pressure to score excessive wage gains today is eased. The added responsibility the current system imposes on trade union and employer negotiators has had similar salutary effects on inflation in Australia.[26]

CHAPTER 18

GLOBALIZATION CAN BE A BOON OR A BANE

"The positive conclusions of the cross-country study of inequality were that widening income gaps were not inevitable and technology forces driving incomes apart could be successfully countered with active government policies. . . . Globalisation had little impact on the gap between rich and poor."[1]

Editorial,
***Financial Times*, December 2011**

"Germany has been the winner in the globalization process."[2]

KENNETH ROGOFF,
***Der Spiegel*, February 20, 2012**

"67 percent of French employees believe globalization is 'good for employment in France.'"[3]

ANNE RODIER,
***Le Monde*, June 26, 2011**

Globalization holds a potent lesson for America. But as we are learning, it isn't the one you might anticipate: families in almost all other rich democracies benefited from the acceleration of international trade in recent decades. For that reason, future scholars are likely to view globalization as the nail in the coffin of Reaganomics.

Globalization Hit Europe Harder

Americans despise globalization. By a margin of better than 2:1, a July 2007 *Financial Times*/Harris poll found that Americans believe globalization has harmed, rather than helped, the US.[4]

But northern Europeans and Australians don't seem to get it. A remarkable 94 percent of French employees, for example, in May 2011 considered globalization "good for the development of the company," and 67 percent believed it's "good for employment in France." Americans have complex feelings toward foreigners, but few believe the French to be utterly delusional. *Good for employment*? Didn't they receive

Jensen's memo about their plight, dictated by the impersonal forces of the marketplace and international wage arbitrage?

Buckle up. We're going to learn that the story of globalization is not what happened in America, a discouraging and atypical experience which is the just the opposite of experiences in other rich democracies. The real story of globalization is what happened in Australia and northern Europe.

In America, global integration is a convicted wage killer. But we know that not all Americans suffered. Its dynamic forces improved resource allocation, greatly expanded world trade, and became a wealth machine for a thin slice of America. That meant greater rewards to owners of capital, innovators, and the most skilled, whose shares of national income rose. But for others, a race to the bottom in wages ensued, with workers in Milwaukee, Brooklyn, and Dallas competing one-on-one with workers in Sri Lanka, New Delhi, and Shanghai. And the biggest losers have been less skilled workers and high-wage union shops targeted by the offshoring and wage compression features of Reaganomics.

European economies are much more integrated and influenced by world trade than is America's. Logically, losses and labor market churning from global integration should have been even more severe in Europe. Three-quarter of the sales of the thirty German firms listed on the blue-chip DAX stock exchange in Berlin were overseas in 2010, for example, up from 66 percent in 2006; that includes Adidas, where 95 percent, and Merck, where 86 percent, of sales were abroad.[5] Even two thirds of all sales by the giant Metro supermarket chain occur abroad, including subsidiaries Media Market and Saturn. In many European countries, the sum of exports and imports in any single year has a value not far short of total GDP. The equivalent GDP trade component for the United States is far less—around 20 percent of GDP.

Because they're more integrated in world trade, the family capitalism countries faced a stiffer adjustment to the forces of globalization than did the United States. Indeed, the potential wage depressant and labor market effects of globalization were more than twice as harsh in France and nearly three times greater in Germany than in America. Unlike America, the economies of these nations prosper or wither by international trade. And make no mistake, many skilled jobs are lost in northern Europe due to globalization.[6]

The Impact of Globalization on Labor Markets

The following two tables present the detailed impact of globalization on labor markets in the United States and Europe. They're reproduced from a 2007 econometric study, *The Globalization of Labor*, by IMF economists Florence Jaumotte and Irina Tytell.[7] The study focused mostly on the United States and northern Europe, and the results are most applicable there, although statistics from Italy and Portugal were included. The IMF analyzed data from 1980, just as global integration accelerated, until 2003 well before the recession; it parsed the impact of globalization and technology progress on subsets of workers, divided by overall skill levels.

The analysis concluded that globalization and technology change put a premium on job skills, just as economic theory would predict. Table 3, for example, shows a rising share of labor's overall income going to employees in occupations classified as skilled by the OECD in both America (from 39 percent to 43 percent) and in Europe amid globalization. Job prospects improved as well for such workers in the upper echelons of the labor hierarchy: employment in skilled sectors in America grew 25 percent (the index number rose to 125 from 100), while skilled-sector employment grew an even larger 57 percent in Europe.

Skilled Labor Benefits from Technology Progress and Globalization

	1980	2003
The share of labor income received by skilled-sector labor[1]		
United States	39%	43%
Europe[2]	38%	41%
Index of skilled labor employment		
United States	100%	125%
Europe	100%	157%

Table 3.

[1] Measured as share of economy-wide value added.

[2] Includes: Austria, Belgium, Denmark, Finland, France, Germany, Italy, Norway, Portugal, and Sweden.

Source: World Economic Outlook, fig. 5.7 and 5.9, IMF, 2007.

The much greater magnitude of growth in the skilled labor category in Europe is a first surprise, the tip of the iceberg: the IMF economists determined that skilled-sector employment in Europe grew much more strongly than in America amid globalization. We will return to this evidence of European economic prowess in a moment.

Unsurprisingly, as we see in Table 4, American and European workers in relatively unskilled, labor-intensive sectors fared less well. That's consistent with the famous conclusion reached in 1941 by Wolfgang F. Stolper and Paul Samuelson, which is the source of the received wisdom among economists that freer trade permanently harms some employees in rich democracies.[8] The IMF analysts concluded that the unskilled worker share of total wages fell somewhat sharply in both America and Europe.

The Impact of Technology Progress and Globalization on Unskilled Labor

	1980	2003
Labor's income share in unskilled sectors[1]		
United States	25%	18%
Europe[2]	34%	24%
Index of unskilled employment		
United States	100%	121%
Europe	100%	86%

Table 4.
[1] Measured as share of economy-wide value added.
[2] Includes: Austria, Belgium, Denmark, Finland, France, Germany, Italy, Norway, Portugal, and Sweden.
Source: IMF, World Economic Outlook, fig. 5.7 and 5.9, 2007, IMF.

For a second surprise, look at the data on the last lines of this table. While unskilled jobs rose 21 percent in America, the absolute number of unskilled employees in Europe actually declined over these decades of rapid global integration and technology change. Think of the implications of that sentence. Unlike America, the European process of adapting to globalization resulted in the elimination of unskilled, low-wage jobs, replacing them with ones in higher-skilled economic sectors. The IMF analysis reveals that European employers upskilled the domestic job mix, with good jobs supplanting unskilled ones. In contrast, American employers during the Reagan era sat on their hands, doing little to change the economy's skill mix, with the number of skilled and unskilled jobs rising about the same.

Europe Managed Globalization by Upskilling Employees

The IMF labor force data is a big surprise. While the forces of globalization hit Europe much harder than America, the IMF found that Europe adapted by eliminating jobs in lower-skill sectors, replacing them with jobs in higher-skill ones. Jaumotte and Tytell described their significant finding this way: "In Europe . . . employment in unskilled sectors lost ground to employment in skilled sectors (and actually contracted by a cumulative 15 percent)."[9] Did Europe really pull that rabbit out of its hat in the Reagan era? A conclusion this significant can be double-checked using data from another international agency, from OECD statistics on the job skill mix in the United States and Europe.

The OCED studied the skill distribution of labor forces in its 2008 edition of *Education at a Glance*, with statistics from the most intense period of globalization, 1998 to 2006. Their results are replicated in Chart 18.1, and confirm in detail the IMF results. The OECD found that nearly every nation in northern Europe and Scandinavia increased the proportion of its population employed in categories classified as skilled, such as managers, professionals, technicians, and associated professionals. The only exception to this upskilling was the Netherlands, where the share fell 1 percentage point; that occurred because the Dutch already had an astoundingly skilled workforce by 1998. A whopping 54 percent of its entire workforce was classified as skilled that year, the highest in the world. It's as though Silicon Valley in its entirety was transformed into a nation called Holland and plunked down on the cold North Sea beaches between Belgium and Germany.

Australia isn't far behind; it has the second most skilled workforce in the world and the smallest share (not shown) of unskilled employees (6 percent) aside from Norway (4 percent). The story is much different in the United States, as we see in the chart, where the proportion of Americans working in skilled jobs moved little in the Reagan era. That confirms the trend over the longer period of 1980–2003 uncovered by the IMF economists Jaumotte and Tytell.

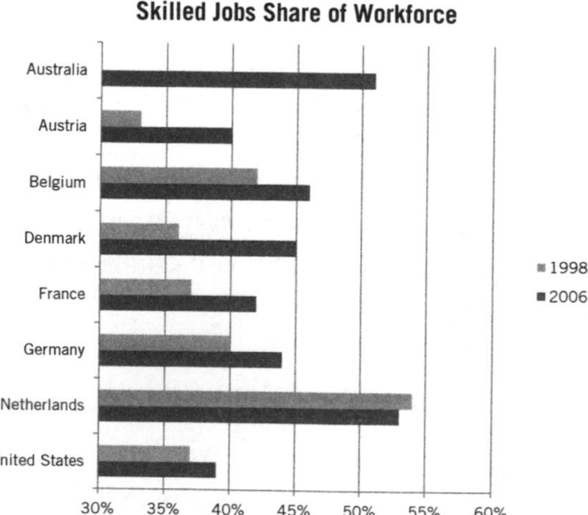

Chart 18.1. Ages 25-64. Australian data not available for 1998 or earlier periods.
Source: Education at a Glance, table A1.6, OECD, 2008, Paris.

The OECD data also show that upskilling by Austrian and Danish employers was so dramatic that the share of skilled employees in each of their workforces leapfrogged America. And the share in France went from parity with the United States in 1998 to well above (42 percent) by 2006. Consequently, by 2006, the share of American jobs classified as skilled on the OECD global standard was lower than every nation in northern Europe, and far below Australia as well.

You have just read what should be the obituary for Reaganomics. In a world where family prosperity hinges on adapting to globalization and on upskilling to boost productivity and grow wages, it proved to be absurdly inadequate. It certainly redistributes income from families to those Adam Smith called merchants and master manufacturers. But it weakens productivity growth, and has proved to be the variant of capitalism you want your stoutest competitor to adopt.

A third major matrix of workforce skill levels during the era of globalization is the share of students with STEM (science, technology, engineering, and math) backgrounds. These are folks with technical training beyond the secondary school level and their numbers indicate workforce capability and prowess vital to international competitiveness. In 2012, the OECD examined the share of STEM graduates in the labor forces of the rich democracies and determined that the share in Germany is 20 percent larger and the share in France and Australia is 50 percent larger than in the United States.[10]

This profile is reflected in the relative erosion of engineering students in recent decades. The United States ranked 27th out of 29 rich countries in the share of college students studying science or engineering, according to an October 2010 report from the National Academy of Sciences in Washington.[11] That portends competitive problems in the years ahead for the American economy as explained this way by the OECD:

> "STEM graduates are a key input to innovation. However, they represent a relatively low share of persons aged 25–34 years in employment in the United States. Moreover, below the PhD level, the share of STEM in total graduates has not increased over the past decade despite wage data pointing to persistent, and at lower qualifications levels, worsening shortages of STEM workers."

Moreover, it seems that the quality of American technical teaching has stagnated as well, while competitors edged past: the World Economic Forum at Davos ranked the United States 48th out of 133 nations in 2010 in the quality of science and math instruction.[12]

What these impartial IMF, National Academies, and OECD analyses reveal is that, in an era where superior job skills are the key to future prosperity, Australia and every northern European nation has surpassed the United States to acquire a more skilled and competitive labor force. That transformation helps explain higher productivity growth rates abroad and higher wages there, too. Even more significant, Europe's ability to supplant unskilled with skilled jobs amid globalization can't be an accident. These data are strongly suggestive that family capitalism countries have evolved a panoply of practices to ensure that globalization enhances, rather than harms, family prosperity. The major one is codeterminism, which results in employers raising domestic skill levels and competitiveness routinely year after year. Codeterminism and other policies, such as work councils and Australian-style national wage policies, succeed in ensuring that better jobs replace those being lost to global integration, with those new jobs justifying rising real wages.

Take a breath. This is a lot of unconventional information to absorb. But the bottom line is this: America's competitors in the rich democracies have adopted policies exploiting globalization to steadily improve family prosperity.

This rather profound outcome holds two obvious lessons for America:

First, policies such as codeterminism, an Australian wage system, work councils, and upskilling have proven effective in converting the dangers of globalization into broadly based prosperity and steadily rising wages. As the epigraph to this chapter from the *Financial Times* asserts, the harmful potential of global integration can be entirely ameliorated by public policies. And you have just read what those policies are.

Second, the evidence in this chapter exposes as mendacious the assertion of American market fundamentalists that US wages are being inexorably compressed by globalization. Indeed, economists at the OECD have studied the performance of the northern European countries and the US, and determined that globalization is not responsible for weak US wages or rising income disparities. "Neither rising trade nor financial openness had a significant impact on either wage inequality or employment trends," concluded the OECD experts.[13] And as just noted, journalists at the *Financial Times* know it, too. Recall the newspaper editorially concluded in 2011 that

> ". . . forces driving incomes apart could be successfully countered by active government policies."[14]

That conclusion is one of the most significant findings in this book. Globalization is a canard, a straw man to deflect attention and blame from the redistributive nature of Reaganomics. America's failure to mimic the stakeholder capitalism policies of Australia, Germany, and other rich democracies accounts for wage stagnation, the plight of American families, and eroding US competitiveness. The vaporous American Dream originates in US voting booths, not the low-wage factories surrounding Shanghai, Taipei, or Mumbai.

CHAPTER 19

HOW FAMILY CAPITALISM PROSPERED FROM GLOBALIZATION

"As you know, the Prime Minister has articulated clearly that boosting productivity is at the very heart of this government's agenda. Productivity growth will be the prism through which the government will weigh and consider industrial relations."[1]

CHRIS EVANS,
Australian Minister for Tertiary Education, Skills, Jobs, and Workplace Relations, November 2010

"Minimum wages do not result in employment losses in countries in which minimum wages are set by some type of national collective bargaining process. . . . A higher minimum wage may encourage low-skilled individuals to acquire more skills in order to raise their marginal product above the minimum wage floor."[2]

DAVID NEUMARK and WILLIAM WASCHER,
***Minimum Wage*, 2008**

"We are currently in the middle of a shallow national debate around productivity, in which business groups and the right-wing media are attempting to convince us the only way to increase productivity is to cut wages and conditions. This ignores the fact the main long-term drivers of productivity are investment in industry, infrastructure, and in the skills of workers."[3]

BRIAN HOWE,
Former Australian Deputy Prime Minister, May 2012

Economists know that international trade enhances productivity by shrinking employment in industries subject to import competition and expanding it in more efficient industries, especially exports.[4] This process features job churning and the creative destruction process,

which places a premium on the upskilling tactic common to family capitalism countries required to seize the gains from globalization.

Driven by codeterminism and supported by work councils and Australian-style national wage policies that reward the work ethic, upskilling has been a central element in converting globalization to widespread prosperity.

But there is a problem—a huge problem—because globalization is so dynamic, exposing even the most skilled to instability, abrupt changes in fortune, and job insecurity, precisely the circumstances and events any rational person despises. Voters have managed to resolve some of this challenge with codeterminism, avoiding the Apple Problem of runaway offshoring by tightly focusing the business community on domestic prosperity. But huge adjustment challenges remain. How have the family capitalism countries managed to accommodate the same powerful forces of globalization that Americans loathe?

The Logic of Social Welfare States

The social welfare character of northern Europe has nothing to do with a desire for big government and everything to do with seizing the gains from global trade. The conundrum of capturing the gains from globalization while securing stable and prosperous family economics was resolved by creating the social welfare state. Voters have demanded education and upskilling along with income, unemployment, and retirement safety nets to avoid becoming collateral damage in the creative destruction process.

Economists have determined that the social welfare model in northern Europe is a direct consequence of this bargain crafted to accommodate globalization by protecting families. Yale political scientist David R. Cameron and Harvard economist Dani Rodrik, in separate analyses, have concluded that openness to world trade is a major factor in the relatively large government safety nets across northern Europe.[5] Their conclusions have been reinforced by other economists, including research from the National Bureau of Economic Research by Anna Maria Mayda of Georgetown University, Kevin H. O'Rourke of Trinity College, Dublin, and Richard Sinnott of University College Dublin.[6] The more volatile and unpredictable the market because of unusually high international trade exposure, as in nations like Germany, the greater is the inclination of voters to insist on insurance. Here is Rodrik in 2011 explaining his research results:

> "The evidence seemed to point strongly toward the social insurance motive. People demand compensation against risk where their economies are more exposed to international economic forces; and

governments respond by erecting broader safety nets. . . . It is also because they are needed to preserve the legitimacy of markets by protecting people from the risks and insecurities markets bring with them."[7]

Rodrik's last sentence is a restatement of Adam Smith, and is important. He explains the underlying logic this way:

"Markets are most developed and most effective in generating wealth when they are backed by solid governmental institutions. Markets and states are complementary, not substitutes."[8]

That same logic was on display in the nineteenth century amid the blooming of globalization, featuring worker rights embodied in the British Factory Acts of 1844 and introduced later by Europeans, notably Germany's Chancellor Bismarck.[9] And it was on display again nearly a century later as Keynes, George Orwell, and Franklin Roosevelt introduced social insurance elements such as unemployment aid and enhanced employee worksite rights to nurture the survival of capitalism against collectivism during the Great Depression. Today, northern Europeans vote for big government not out of infatuation with taxes or bureaucrats; their jaundiced perspective toward them differs little from your own. Instead, they accept them out of a desire to protect families from the greater risks inherent in maximizing wealth creation through international trade.

What are the elements of their system that support the creation of widespread wealth in the age of globalization?

Traditional Education

American university education is quite expensive, but university-level research institutions are the world's best. Yet the foundation below is sagging. Between 1875 and 1975, the duration of schooling increased by an average of seven years, making America the best-educated nation. Public education was a vital pillar in the foundation of the golden age.

Since then, however, education success in primary and secondary schools has become uneven, bedeviled by the skewed allocation of education resources favoring more affluent neighborhoods. School performance in the United States now ranks near the bottom among rich democracies—marginally worse than some former Soviet bloc nations such as Hungary, Poland, and Slovakia. For example, the typical 15-year-old Canadian is now more than one year ahead of Americans in educational achievement.[10] Most humiliating for a society that prided itself in equality of opportunity, American education fails rather spectacularly to rectify socioeconomic disadvantages at birth, as we have learned. The discouraging multigenerational poverty cycle is the consequence.

Even worse, America's international achievement gap grows wider as education careers advance, with students falling further behind those abroad as they rise through grades. That phenomenon is the strongest possible evidence that American education has failed the competitive test during the Reagan era. And that dirty secret is out. As *Financial Times* columnist Clive Crook noted in May 2009, "Far from leaning against economic inequality, US schools make it worse."[11]

America spends more on education than competitors, but it matters a great deal how the funding is spent, such as enhancing teacher quality. As concluded by economists Raj Chetty and John N. Friedman of Harvard, and Jonah E. Rockoff of Columbia University, teachers can change lives. Their analysis drew on an enormous data base of 2.5 million students over 20 years. And they concluded that being exposed to a superior teacher for even one year who can genuinely raise standardized test scores has an enduring impact on students by increasing college matriculation rates, lowering teenage-pregnancy rates, and raising lifetime earnings.[12]

Another goal is smaller classes that can increase the amount of attention each student receives. Student-teacher ratios in American secondary schools are 15.5:1, well above the 12:1 ratio in Australia and France or in Belgium, 10:1.[13] These data are from 2005, and layoffs during the recession as local budgets dwindled have likely widened this disparity.

Secondary school graduates in America desirous of higher education confront greater barriers than in the family capitalism countries. College is free in northern Europe. In 2011, France budgeted €11,630 ($14,000) for each of its 2.3 million college students, about the cost of tuition at a US public college.[14] College is not free in Australia, but tuition rates are linked (as in the United Kingdom) to subsequent earnings and are much more affordable than American colleges. These efforts have been effective in raising educational attainment. Some 50 percent of the French workforce in 2009 held a degree beyond high school compared to only 24 percent in 1984.[15]

College grants for the most able are available in the United States, but most students must rely on loans that can total $100,000 upon graduation. Government income-based repayment and loan forgiveness programs exist. But a report in October 2012 by the New America Foundation found those programs favored students pursuing high-income careers: "If left unchanged, the program is set to provide huge financial windfalls to people who, far from being in need, are among the most financially well-off graduates in today's job market."[16] Finally, while I'm optimistic, it is far from certain as of this writing whether the potential of the massive Open Online Courses movement to lower college costs will be realized.

Education/Work Transition and Career-Long Upskilling

In the middle of 2010, some 171,000 Danes were unemployed. Of that number, 58,000, or one-third, were actively being retrained, upskilled in preparation for new and more lucrative employment in the near future.[17] Next door in Germany, over 500,000 youths were in formal training at firms as apprentices, and firms were aggressively recruiting to fill another 75,000 empty slots. By the 2012–2013 academic year, the vacancies in apprenticeship slots had swelled to 100,000.[18] In France, the government in 2011 announced policies to raise the number of apprentice slots from 600,000 to 1 million by 2015.[19]

These snippets surely appear decidedly strange to Americans: One-third of the unemployed being formally upskilled? Employers recruiting to fill 100,000 empty apprentice slots and government adding more training capacity?

Traditional education in the family capitalism countries is supplemented by extensive school-to-work transition programs. Secondary schooling can extend to 19 or 20 years of age, integrated with strong transitional vocational education programs. That's why education participation rates for young males from 15–19 years old across northern Europe in countries such as France (84 percent) and Germany (93 percent) exceed American rates. These are nonuniversity youngsters remaining in the education system, gaining skills promising productive futures.[20]

The northern Europe business community such as Siemens strongly supports these transitional vocational programs, which can extend two or three years and feature on-the-job and classroom time. The number of youths enrolled in German vocational apprenticeships in 2011, for example, exceeded the number of university students.[21] And as careers advance, employers routinely provide on-the-job retraining because it pays off. In 2007, for example, an OECD analysis concluded that a 10 percent increase in skills arising from worksite training boosts what economists call multifactor productivity by more than 1.4 percentage points.[22] While tricky to measure, multifactor productivity is a proxy for worksite innovation. In other words, this study concluded that upskilling has an effect on enterprise productivity and long-term success similar to that of investment in R&D. The rationale for this career-long upskilling culture is described by OECD economists Andrea Bassanini and Wooseok Ok this way:

> [In the future] "... the bulk of the labor force will still be represented by individuals who are currently in the labour market. The education and training they receive after having started their working life is therefore crucial for output growth as well as individual career prospects."[23]

This awareness has created an upskilling culture in northern Europe, along with high employee and employer expectations that lifetime training is an integral part of the work experience. Here is how economist Barry Eichengreen described it:

> "The continent's system of vocational education and apprenticeship training produced workers with the specialized knowledge to identify the technological challenges facing their employers and the skills needed to devise solutions. Firms that might have been reluctant to invest in on-the-job training for fear of losing workers to their competitors were reassured by the existence of cohesive employer associations that discouraged poaching."[24]

Family capitalism countries utilize their education-to-job transition to enhance social stability, minimizing the threat to social cohesion posed by high youth unemployment. The outcome is that youth unemployment in nations such as the Netherlands, Austria, and Germany is less than one-half the rate in America, although the rate in France is as high as the United States. The goal is to ensure that youths have the skills suitable for employment, to avoid them behaving like amoral American bankers. Reporter Karl Fluck with Vienna-based *Der Standard* explains:

> "If, despite a hard-won education, one sees precious few opportunities for oneself and one's dreams, eventually Facebook ceases to be an adequate safety valve. Then—as in England—a truly tragic but ultimately mundane reason is enough to unleash all people's pent-up frustration under cover of the mob. . . . On a small scale, such chaos merely reflects the example handed down from above: grab what you can and make off with it. In spirit, these are the bankers of the street."[25]

Support and Upskilling for the Jobless

An important aspect of the upskilling culture is muscular public-sector programs like that in Denmark that utilize periods of joblessness to upgrade workforces. OECD statistics on program size are depicted in Chart 19.1.

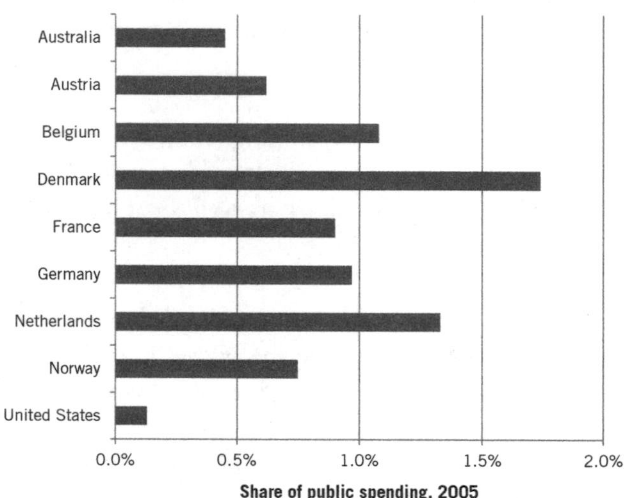

Chart 19.1. Includes: upskilling support, training, temporary employment to facilitate upskilling, and incentives to employers for hiring.
Source: "Employment Outlook, Statistical Annex, 2007," OECD, table J.

In the United States, however, support for the unemployed is relatively low, raising the odds that the jobless are more likely to experience skill-degradation instead of skill-upgrading. Moreover, unemployment benefit payouts equal only 14 percent of prior incomes in America, well below the average income replacement rate of 38 percent across Europe,[26] reducing the capacity for the unemployed to retrain. And such support declined during the Reagan era. Howard F. Rosen of the Peterson Institute testified before Congress in 2007 that tighter rules imposed since 1980 reduced the share of jobless Americans eligible for unemployment compensation by nearly a quarter.[27] Eligibility was sharply reduced, for example, to include only former full-time employees with at least one year of employment. That excluded the rapidly growing legions of independent contractors and part-timers being utilized today to implement just-in-time staffing needs in the vast service sector and elsewhere.

The Obama administration and Congressional Democrats reversed this trend in February 2009, nearly doubling eligibility to about 70 percent. They also extended coverage to 99 weeks during the recession.[28] Even so, the duration of support in nations such as Belgium, Denmark, and Australia is at least double this temporary American maximum of 99 weeks, according to OECD data.[29]

Unemployment benefits are supplemented in America mostly with food stamps and smaller assistance programs administered locally or by states. But recall that the share of eligible very-poor families who actually receive such public benefits has declined to 40 percent, from 80 percent in the early 1980s. This is a contrast with northern Europe's safety net that is designed to upskill and quickly reintegrates job losers.

The priority assigned to upskilling in the family capitalism countries is intended to facilitate and accommodate the creative destruction aspect of globalization. It reflects a serious national commitment to reap the gains of globalization absent in America. About 5 percent of northern Europe's workforce is interacting with public support and reintegration programs at any point in time, running much higher in some nations including 10 percent in Germany; the comparable American participation rate in such programs is one-third of 1 percent of the labor force.[30] That is a lot of upskilling for the jobless. But it's justified by economic research, including a study by the OECD, "Employment Outlook for 2007," by economists seeking to answer whether unemployment compensation encourages retraining that measurably raises productivity. The researchers concluded:

> "These results suggest that any negative impact of unemployment benefits on employment is fully offset by a net positive impact of unemployment benefits on average measured productivity . . . overall, the net impact of unemployment benefits on average measured productivity appears to be positive."[31]

This determination is explained by the authors in part by suggesting that job matches seem to be of a superior quality in northern Europe. That's a consequence of the ability of the jobless to be a bit choosy in taking new employment, while taking advantage of upskilling opportunities in the interim to expand the universe of jobs for which they qualify.

Unemployment support and upskilling programs in America are both modest by comparison and at least some suffer from poor conceptualization. In a 2009 study, for example, the US Department of Labor found that the biggest federal job training program during the George W. Bush administration produced "small or nonexistent" improvements in earnings or job opportunity.[32] One group that received training at Macomb Community College outside Detroit, for example, was examined in depth by *New York Times* investigative reporters; within a year of completing training, over 60 percent were unemployed or working in jobs unrelated to their training.[33] No wonder German experts, such as Felix Rauner, professor of vocational education at the University of Bremen, dismiss the American vocational education system. "In fact, the studies in terms of academic standards [are] completely inadequate. They fall far short of the qualifications of skilled workers."[34]

Utilizing Minimum Wages to Drive Productivity

Minimum wages spread from New Zealand and Australia to Britain and Europe over a century ago. They arrived in America decades later, when President Franklin Roosevelt introduced a nationwide minimum wage of 25 cents per hour in 1938. It was set at a low rate, about half what Henry Ford paid twenty years earlier. Even so, it was a pivotal moment in American history, marking a moral turning point in which leaders endorsed the concept of a minimum living standard, at least for those working. In adopting a minimum wage, Roosevelt understood its powerful symbolism as a commitment to a middle-class society, as noted in 2008 by Adam Cohen of the *New York Times*: "The minimum wage can play a vital role in lifting hardworking families above the poverty line. But, as Roosevelt understood, it is also about something larger: what kind of country America wants to be."[35]

Statutory minimum wages in the rich democracies hover in the range of $10–$12 per hour, considerably above the American rate of $7.25 per hour. Statutory rates are important, but minimum wages measured as a share of average take-home pay is a more important indicator of national commitment to poverty alleviation. That statistic measures relative purchasing power and therefore the relative benefit to employees. Calculated by OECD economists and reproduced in Table 5, effective minimum wages measured in this fashion are set above 40 percent of post-tax average wages in the family capitalism countries.

That robust rate (and broad coverage of the minimum wage) is the reason so few working in those nations are impoverished, as we learn later. By contrast, the American minimum wage is lower than the effective rate in Romania or Turkey, and about two-thirds the rate in the family capitalism countries. It is set so low that 10.5 million *working* Americans lived below the official US poverty line in 2010, according to data from the Bureau of Labor Statistics.[36]

Minimum Wage Rates

	Relative to average wage
Australia	45%
Belgium	43%
France	48%
Mexico	19%
Netherlands	42%
New Zealand	51%
Romania	31%
Turkey	35%
United States	28%

Table 5. Value of minimum wage for fulltime workers as share of average wage, 2010. *Source: "Real Hourly Minimum Wage and Minimum Wage Relative to Average Wages of Fulltime Workers," Statistical Extracts, OECD, Paris, http://stats.oecd.org/Index.aspx?QueryId=7219, and http://stats.oecd.org/Index.aspx?DatasetCode=MIN2AVE.*

A signal of the important role assigned to the minimum wage by family capitalism countries is that it is adjusted frequently and independent from politics to at least keep pace with inflation. The independent Fair Work Australia commission, for example, adjusts minimums every July, resulting in a 4.8 percent rise in mid-2010 and 3.4 percent in mid-2011.[37] By design, increases such as these since 2006 have outpaced inflation by about one percentage point annually in order to bolster incomes of the least-advantaged employees. The French *Salaire Minimum Interprofessionnel de Croissance* (SMIC) is also adjusted annually based on recommendations from the independent National Commission on Collective Bargaining. That commission also has the authority to further increase the SMIC during the year should inflation exceed 2 percent. In 2012, the SMIC was raised 2.3 percent, while inflation was 1.3 percent, meaning wages for the 2.6 million men and women at the bottom rung of the French workforce that year received a 1 percent wage hike in real terms.[38]

Germany has minimum wages in selected industries and is debating setting a comprehensive nationwide wage because it has the highest proportion of low-wage workers in northern Europe, 20.6 percent in 2010.[39] It has also seen a rise in part-time employment and a tripling of temporary work assignments to nearly one million since labor markets were deregulated in 2003.[40]

A second signal of their importance in family capitalism is that violators of minimum wage laws are aggressively prosecuted, as we learned earlier. Over 6,000 provincial detectives in Germany monitor minimum wage laws.[41] The policy goal is straightforward: voters expect enterprises to pay a livable wage sufficient to avoid taxpayers *de facto* having to subsidize firms paying so little that employees are eligible for welfare benefits. That expectation contrasts with voters in America, who support corporate welfare policies by assenting to minimum wages so low that employees qualify for taxpayer-funded food stamps and Medicaid. Indeed, economists have long recognized that the modest American minimum wage constitutes a clandestine taxpayer subsidy to low-wage employers such as Walmart. I mention that firm, because some years ago, the company actively encouraged its working-poor employees in California to make use of taxpayer supported programs, such as Medicaid.[42]

Taxpayer subsidies to the business community are less common in Australia and northern Europe because voter expectations are considerably higher regarding reasonable behavior by enterprises. Moreover, the media is alert to corporations that fall short of these expectations and are quick to mobilize public opinion as we learned earlier, a critical element in sustaining stakeholder capitalism.

Higher Minimum Wages Incentivize Productivity Growth

Returning to the question of productivity, employers in the family capitalism countries adjusted to globalization by dumping endangered jobs in unskilled sectors and recycling workers into jobs requiring higher skills. A relatively high minimum wage aids this process. Unemployed, unskilled workers who lose their jobs cannot be hired in growing sectors at lower wages as occurs in America. Instead, employers ensure that the skill level of new hires justifies their higher wages, if necessary by upskilling them or collaborating with public officials in upskilling programs. Economic justification for this approach comes from the OECD analysis we noted earlier by economists Bassanini and Ok. Their research highlighted the fact that less-educated workers receive more training when their wages are relatively close to the average wage, which occurs when minimum wages are high.[43]

These various aspects move economies in the direction of faster productivity growth. Conceptually, think of the family capitalism countries' tactic this way: their relatively high minimum wages have an impact on the *composition* of employment. These countries craft minimum-wage structures to forcibly shift employment preferences toward higher-productivity jobs that justify higher wages. Support for this tactic comes from another OECD analysis by Andrea Bassanini and Danielle Venn, in which they found that higher minimum wages lead to a statistically significant improvement in average productivity. Based on data from rich democracies, the researchers concluded that boosting minimum wages by 10 percent increased worker productivity by nearly 2 percentage points over time. And that gain occurred without evidence of higher unemployment.[44]

These analyses are significant indicators that minimum wages are intentionally set relatively high to reinforce the productivity focus of Australia and northern Europe. Reaping productivity growth is serious business in the family capitalism countries; it is a war, and no stone is left unturned in finding ways to win it, including a high minimum wage. That emphasis is in contrast to American firms where the rare discussion of productivity seemingly only appears as a foil in *Wall Street Journal* editorials urging business community tax cuts.

Minimum Wages Are an Effective Antipoverty Mechanism

Another important policy objective of minimum wages is to ameliorate poverty. That appears to be the rationale for President Obama's proposal in February 2013 to raise the US minimum wage to $9.00 per hour, while also indexing it for inflation. In 2008, he had proposed $9.50 per hour. What is the evidence that his proposal will accomplish that goal?

First, a large number of employees cluster at the minimum wage in the family capitalism nations, indicating that they pull up wages at the low end of the earnings spectrum. This is most evident in the two rich democracies that attach the most emphasis to improving the lot of the working poor. Between 10.6 and 15.1 percent of the workforce in France has earned the SMIC in recent years, for example, and 12 percent of the labor force in Australia in 2011 earned the minimum.[45] In contrast, the minimum wage is set well below prevailing wages in the United States; only 2.3 percent of hourly workers clustered there in 2007.[46]

Second, historic data from the United States suggest how powerful high minimums can be in alleviating poverty. The American poverty rate for children and adults has never been as low as it was in the 1969–1973 period, when the US minimum peaked at $10 per hour in current dollars. Moreover, *New York Times* reporter Steven Greenhouse cites studies indicating that an increase to $9.80 per hour, from $7.25 today, would raise more than 28 million Americans above the poverty threshold.[47] That expectation has caused nineteen states and a few prosperous local governments to mandate higher minimums to fight poverty, with Washington state and Oregon maintaining the highest domestic rates in 2013, of about $9 per hour. And, despite the refusal of America to index the minimum wage, nine states, including Florida, Ohio, and Montana index their higher individual minimum wage rates.[48]

Further evidence comes from research by economists David Card at the University of California, Berkeley, and Princeton professor Alan Krueger, chairman of President Obama's Council of Economic Advisors. Their analysis concluded that over "35 percent of the earnings gain generated by the 1990 and 1991 minimum wage hikes were concentrated among families in the bottom 10 percent of the family earnings distribution."[49] Research by economist David S. Lee in 1999 affirmed that conclusion.[50] These studies document that raising the US minimum wage is one important element in reducing poverty and moving to family capitalism, where the gains from growth would be more broadly enjoyed.

Raising the minimum wage is also preferable to expanding the Earned Income Tax Credit (EITC), an income-based welfare benefit program targeted at the working poor. Funded from general revenues administered through the federal tax system, the EITC can be carefully targeted, making it a cost-effective favorite among economists. However, unlike the minimum wage, it does not incentivize employers to upskill. In addition, it has limited coverage, because the working poor must file tax returns to obtain benefits. Moreover, it's bureaucratic and expensive to operate. Its complexity further reduces its effectiveness: there are 50 pages of instructions for single mothers and others to follow when filing for the tax benefit.[51] Finally, like food stamps and other support received by the working poor, the EITC is an opaque taxpayer subsidy to low-wage employers whose balance sheets in many instances are far stronger than those of taxpayers.

Do Minimum Wages Cost Jobs?

Minimum wages redistribute income from employers and customers to lower-wage workers. The business community contends the minimum wage causes unemployment. They are correct that an economic tradeoff exists, but misidentify it: a high minimum wage reduces poverty—not employment—a myth we now examine.

Economists assume that employers react to high minimum wages by hiring fewer workers. It just makes intuitive sense. That logic led the United Kingdom, under Prime Ministers Margaret Thatcher and John Major, to honor executive suite pleas and abolish minimum wages in the early 1990s during that nation's flirtation with Reaganomics. In so doing, they rejected Adam Smith, as well as Winston Churchill, who had shepherded the first UK minimum-wage provision into law in 1910.[52] Thatcher and Major may not have read Aristotle, but it seems odd that they were also unfamiliar with Adam Smith's *Wealth of Nations*, not only the greatest economics book, but the greatest British economics book. In his book, Smith ridiculed the precise complaints of employers about wages that Thatcher and Major chose to honor:

> "Our merchants and master-manufacturers complain much of the bad effects of high wages in raising the price and thereby lessening the sale of their goods. They can say nothing concerning the bad effects of high profits. They are silent with regard to the pernicious effects of their own gains. They complain only of those to other people."[53]

A subsequent British government relented and reestablished a comprehensive and high minimum wage in 1999; employment in the aftermath was seemingly unaffected. For example, an OECD analysis of the impact of restoring the minimum wage entitled "The Use of Wage Floors As Policy Tools," concluded: "The Confederation of British Industry has declared that the moderate minimum wage has had little noticeable impact on employment according to their members."[54] Even ten years later, no unemployment effects had become evident; in 2008, the UK Low Pay Commission declared itself:

> ". . . [at the] forefront of the search for evidence of any damage caused by the minimum wage to the economy or to jobs. So far, we have not found any significant negative effects, either in the work we have done ourselves or in the work we have commissioned from others."[55]

The restoration of high minimum wages in the United Kingdom provided a perfect lab experiment and academics were quick to seize the opportunity. Peter Dolton, Rosazza-Bondibene Chiara, and Jonathan Wadsworth from the University of London, for example, divided the United Kingdom into hundreds of geographic subunits. Beginning before restoration of the minimum wage in 1999, their 10-year study determined that "the minimum wage over the entire period of time has a neutral effect on employment."[56]

No evidence of an unemployment effect exists in northern Europe either. Indeed, economists there have come to learn that high and rising minimum wages coexist with job creation and falling unemployment. For example, the French unemployment rate fell to a 25-year low in

June 2008 before the Wall Street recession despite minimum wages hovering around $10 per hour.

With Germany considering establishing a nationwide minimum wage, some six research institutes were commissioned by the Federal Ministry of Labor in recent years to examine the potential impact on employment of that step. Industries like construction and painting where minimum wages already existed became a control group for comparison to other sectors lacking them. Their 2011 analyses concluded that any unemployment impact of minimum wages "could not be detected quantitatively."[57]

American Minimum Wages and Employment

Economists have had difficulty identifying any employment effects of American minimum wages as well. One of the most comprehensive analyses was performed in 2010 by economists Arindrajit Dube, T. William Lester, and Michael Reich at the Institute for Research on Labor and Employment at the University of California, Berkeley. They utilized lower-wage employment data from a number of adjacent US counties separated by state lines where state minimum wage laws differed. The economists determined that raising minimum wages had no employment effect, but did succeed, as intended, in boosting incomes in lower-wage service occupations such as food service, retailing, and the like: "We find strong earnings effects and no employment effects of minimum wage increases."[58] The higher wages also diminished turnover, which lowered employer training costs.

A second analysis focused on the impact of minimum wage increases by US cities, and reached the same conclusions. John Schmitt and David Rosnick at the Washington-based Center for Economic and Policy Research examined the impact of an increase to $8.50 per hour in San Francisco's minimum wage in 2004; the prevailing state minimum was $6.75. They concluded that the hike boosted employee incomes without eroding the employment base.[59]

A third data-rich analysis was conducted by economists Card and Krueger in 1995 and updated in 2000. They examined the effects of an 80 cent per hour increase in the New Jersey state minimum wage in 1992. Data from nearly 400 fast food restaurants there and in adjacent lower-wage Pennsylvania showed that employment *increased* in the New Jersey sample despite the higher wages, while falling in Pennsylvania.[60]

These analyses are supported by anecdotal evidence. For example, Florida established a minimum wage $1 per hour above the federal minimum shortly after 71 percent of voters demanded it in a 2004 referendum. In the year following enactment, Florida added 248,000 new jobs, and unemployment fell to a 30-year low.[61]

More broadly, an absence of linkage between minimum wages and employment is buttressed by experience with the US minimum wage since the 1960s. As depicted in Chart 19.2, the American minimum wage in inflation-adjusted dollars (left axis) rose steadily during the golden age to peak in 1968 even as the US unemployment rate fell by nearly half. Over the next 40 years, however, the minimum wage trended downward, eroded by inflation, which presumably incentivized employers to step up hiring. Instead, unemployment rose, peaking close to 11 percent in the early 1980s. That same dissociative pattern has persisted in the years since.

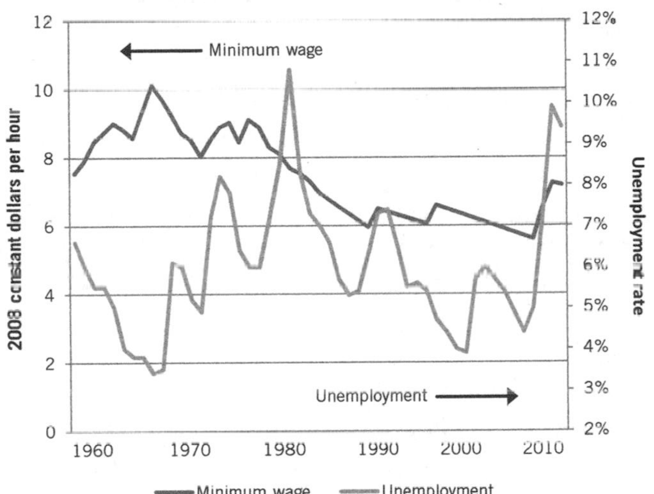

Chart 19.2.

Sources: Bureau of Labor Statistics, US Department of Labor, Washington, DC. Ralph E. Smith and Bruce Vavrichek "The Minimum Wage: Its Relation to Incomes and Poverty," Monthly Labor Review, June 1987. Phyllis Korkki, "Keeping An Eye on the Low Point of the Pay Scale," New York Times, Aug. 31, 2008.

Economists have devoted considerable effort to understanding why the intuitive link between minimum wages and employment is so difficult to detect in the real world. One explanation came from Nobel laureate George J. Stigler as far back as 1946, who contended that labor markets are imperfect, characterized by poor information.[62] Another explanation harkens back to the earliest days of the Industrial Revolution, when employers dominated labor markets. Either because of employer collusion or isolated locations, the wages on offer from employers were frequently set below the employees' actual value to the enterprise. That is why Winston Churchill supported minimum wages a century ago to counter what he termed "employee exploitation."[63] Higher minimum wages are not likely to produce unemployment in such circumstances.

In contrast, if minimum wages are set above workers' value, as perceived by employers, they will certainly reduce employment. David Neumark and William Wascher, for example, concluded that the minimum wage hike to $7.25 per hour in July 2009 cost 300,000 jobs. Yet, the overall impact of any minimum wage increase even in these circumstances is small for two reasons. First, as economist John Schmidt has noted, employers offset higher wage bills with savings from reduced labor turnover and improved productivity, plus small price hikes.[64] The second factor is that economists have come to learn that other factors dwarf the influence of minimum wages in determining whether low-wage jobs are being created or lost. Here's how economists Neumark and Wascher explain it:

> "The influence of modest changes in the minimum wage on the national economy is undoubtedly small relative to business cycle fluctuations and other macroeconomic shocks. . . . Even the largest estimates of disemployment effects pale in comparison with movements in unemployment over the business cycle or with the monthly gross rates of job flow in the US economy."[65]

Even so, fretful about potential unemployment, particularly among youth, officials in northern Europe have tinkered with minimum wage offsets for many years. (These lower minimum wages intended for trainees have provided opportunities for manipulative firms like McDonald's and Amazon to shave labor costs as we learned earlier.) In Belgium, France, and the Netherlands, officials in the past have cut taxes an average of 20 percent for employers hiring lower-wage workers, with encouraging results.[66] One study by Bruno Crepon and Rozenn Desplatz, for example, found that reduced government fees and charges on lower-wage workers created or saved 460,000 jobs in France between 1994 and 1997.[67] American economists have been impressed: Despite its relatively high minimum wages, Newmark and Wascher concluded in 2008 that "France may have a combination of labor market institutions that makes it less likely that minimum wages will have detectable disemployment effects on young workers."[68]

Another question is whether minimum wages are inflationary. Neumark and Wascher have concluded that they are not:

"Even if minimum wages boost prices in low-wage industries, the inflationary impact of modest minimum wage increases in the aggregate economy is unlikely to be important in industrialized countries. . . . The effect of a minimum wage increase on the overall price level is likely to be small . . . small enough that they are far outweighed by fluctuations in prices for products such as gasoline and apparel."[69]

CHAPTER 20

OFFSHORING AND THE APPLE PROBLEM

"Manufacturing in America is in serious decline, with 40,000 factory closures and more than 4 million jobs lost over the last decade."[1]

Manufacturing: A Better Future for America,
Alliance for American Manufacturing, 2009

"We stood by as big American companies became global companies with no more loyalty or connection to the United States than a GPS device."[2]

ROBERT REICH,
Aftershock

"The problem with that strategy is that for the past two decades we have allowed our industrial and technological base to deteriorate as talent and capital were grossly misallocated toward other sectors of the economy. . . ."[3]

STEVEN PEARLSTEIN,
***Washington Post*, September 2010**

"American companies often save on costs by finding lower wages abroad, not by enhancing the abilities of American workers."[4]

TYLER COWEN,
George Mason University, August 2011

"These are the jobs that have created the Midwestern middle class for generations. Manufacturing jobs paid for college educations, including mine. They have been cut in half over the past two decades."[5]

JEFFREY IMMELT,
CEO, General Electric, December 2009

Lord Uxbridge was Wellington's deputy commander as the combined forces arrayed against Napoleon fought desperately in Belgium against the fearsome French *cuirassiers* and cannoneers who had conquered Europe. At a crucial stage of the battle, Uxbridge stationed himself with the cavalry. The British historian Max Hastings described what occurred next:

"Placing himself at the head of the Dutch–Belgium cavalry at Waterloo, Uxbridge ordered a charge and galloped a hundred yards toward the French line, before his aide-de-camp felt obliged to point out that no other horseman was following his dash for glory."[6]

A few American firms, such as GE, are experiencing Uxbridge moments, charging ahead to open new factories at home while their fellow US multinationals look away. Offshoring occurs in all rich democracies, but its scope and the rationale for it is much different in the family capitalism countries than in the United States. American offshoring reflects the pursuit of lower wages, using cheap and docile foreign workers to replace US workers, which directly diminishes the prosperity of American families. In contrast, firms in the family capitalism countries routinely offshore production and jobs for the exact *opposite* reason—as a tactic to sustain their domestic economic position.

American workers take offshoring very personally. Some 77 percent of respondents to a 2006 Pew Research Center survey viewed the practice as harming, rather than helping, employees.[7] And, 86 percent of respondents in an NBC News/*Wall Street Journal* poll in 2010 agreed that offshoring to low-wage nations was a leading cause of America's economic problems.[8] Ironically, some of these same employees likely voted for Presidents Reagan or Clinton, who supported wholesale offshoring. All four Reagan-era Presidents supported trade agreements that facilitated offshoring, assenting to vital details demanded by multinationals eager to profit by reducing the number of high value jobs in America.

There are two recent examples. In October 2000, President Clinton signed legislation establishing permanent normal trade relations (PNTR) with China. That ended decades of uncertainty about prospective American taxes on imports from China for American firms eager to offshore high-wage jobs there. The impact of PNTR on offshoring was dramatic. Indeed, one study in December 2012 by Justin R. Pierce of the Federal Reserve System and Yale management professor Peter K. Schott attribute the loss of as many as 4 million US manufacturing jobs between 2000 and 2007 to the new certainty provided by PNTR. Utilizing census data, they concluded:

> "Absent the shift in US policy, US manufacturing employment would have risen nearly 10 percent between 2001 and 2007, versus an actual decline of more than 15 percent."[9]

The second example is the North American Free Trade Agreement (NAFTA), enacted earlier in the Clinton administration (1993). A key provision forced Mexico to guarantee that foreign investors for the first time could actually own a majority controlling interest in domestic factories. In its eagerness for the new jobs promised by NAFTA, the Mexican government overturned centuries of xenophobia. Enacted by the Clinton Administration in collaboration with Congressional Republicans, NAFTA also contained a second important caveat: any dispute with Mexican officials would automatically bring the full weight of Washington into the settlement process, overwhelming complaining local officials. A proposed third policy was a union initiative to protect the right of Mexican workers to organize independent unions, with the goal of raising local wages. The business community's Washington men torpedoed that provision, ensuring that exporting US jobs to low-wage Mexico would remain quite profitable.

Here is how economist Robert E. Scott of the Washington-based Economic Policy Institute explained the consequences: ". . . NAFTA tilted the economic playing field in favor of investors, and against workers and the environment, resulting in a hemispheric 'race to the bottom' in wages. . . ."[10] Scott's observation points out the most severe impact of offshoring by American firms which is wage compression. That is the first of three elements of American offshoring that we now review:

- Wage compression
- Offshoring domestic jobs
- The Apple Problem: production abroad for export to the United States

Wage Compression

The actual export of jobs as well as the potential for offshoring compresses wages. As Princeton economist Alan Blinder explains, the mere threat of offshoring creates an environment that depresses wages.[11] It has proven to be an effective tool to coerce concessions from employees or to fend off unionization, with extortion commonly practiced even by the largest and most illustrious US firms. For example, some 40 percent of Microsoft's employees already work abroad, yet chief executive Steve Ballmer has threatened to export even more jobs if Democratic politicians close foreign tax havens. "We're better off taking lots of people and moving them out" of the United States, citizen of the world Ballmer asserted.[12]

Any obligation of industry leaders to nurture the American economy and its workers by even the most profitable and bluest of blue-chip US multinationals has been vitiated by Reaganomics. Foreign enterprises in the US practice the same wage compression behavior as Microsoft, commoditizing American employees with offshoring threats. Here is how Nissan-Renault CEO Carlos Ghosn tamped enthusiasm for higher wages among employees at the Smyrna, Tennessee plant: "We'll be making decisions on where future growth will occur in the United States and in Mexico based on the efficiency of operations. Bringing a union into Smyrna could result in making Smyrna not competitive."[13]

Offshoring Domestic Jobs

The second element of offshoring is the actual export of existing US jobs, which is the subject of much economic research. Prior to the 1980s, American firms tended to supply foreign markets from high-wage, efficient US plants. That changed after 1980 as management at multinationals pursued Reagan rents by offshoring millions of high-value manufacturing jobs to low-wage platforms, beginning in Mexico. Starting from an admittedly low base, direct foreign investment abroad by US firms soared in the early Reagan era, as explained by *Handelsblatt* editor Gabor Steingart in 2006:

> "Capitalists left their home turf and went looking for suitable locations to invest. Direct investment abroad . . . rose dramatically. Global production increased a solid 100 percent between 1985 and 1995. But direct investment abroad increased by 400 percent during the same time period."[14]

The pace of foreign investment and job exports accelerated after 2000. In their analysis for the US–China Economic and Security Review Commission, for example, economists Kate Bronfenbrenner and Stephanie Luce determined that the number of production operations being offshored to Mexico, China, and India in 2004 was nearly triple the number just three years earlier, in 2001. Many of these transplants fabricate goods merely being sold directly back to the United States, displacing the identical goods previously produced domestically.[15] Not all studies agree.[16] But the weight of evidence provided by scholarly analyses is that net US job exports have been significant and are a notable cause of the sustained deindustrialization of the US economy during the Reagan era. The evidence is powerful, because factories being closed during this period—and reopened abroad—utilized about the same number of employees. Let's look at several of the most comprehensive studies.

One analysis by reporter David Wessel of the *Wall Street Journal* in

April 2011 concluded that American multinationals cut US employment by a net 2.9 million between 2000 and 2009, while expanding jobs abroad by a net 2.4 million.[17] This conclusion was reaffirmed by other analyses, including one by Martin Sullivan, the former US Treasury Department economist with Washington-based *Tax Analysts*.[18] He parsed BLS data and concluded that US multinationals eliminated 1.9 million domestic jobs between 1999 and 2008, while creating 2.35 million jobs abroad; in other words, they eliminated five American jobs for every six they created overseas, as noted in Chart 20.1.

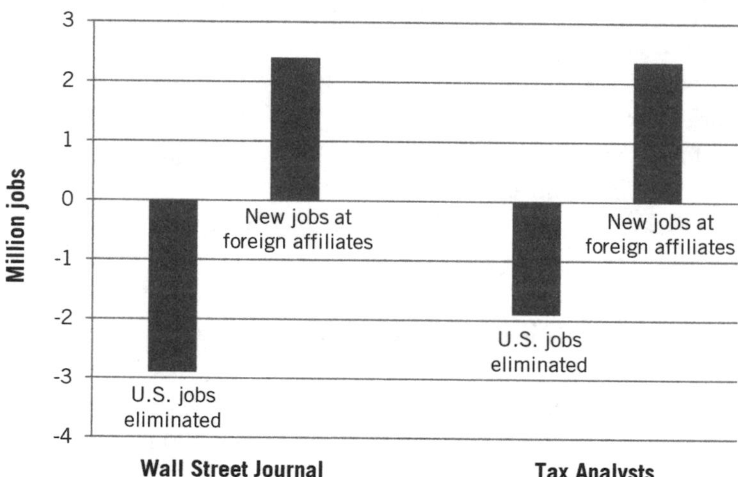

Chart 20.1. *Wall Street Journal* study period 2000–2009, Tax Analysts study period 1999–2008. *Sources: Catherine Rampell, "Is a Multinational CEO the Best Jobs Czar?" New York Times, Jan. 27, 2011. David Wessel, "Big US Firms Shift Hiring Abroad," Wall Street Journal, April 29, 2011.*

Offshoring has proven to be a particular plague on the industrial Midwest. The Bronfenbrenner and Luce analysis concluded that nearly 40 percent of jobs being lost were exported from the Midwest, especially Illinois and Michigan. Offshoring has cut deeply into the industrial heart of the American workforce, with an impact broader than suggested by the bare figures from Wessel and Sullivan. It depresses wages, as Blinder noted. Many of the jobs being exported are from the unionized manufacturing sector; their high wages make them especially attractive targets for offshoring.[19] Moreover, each lost job has a ripple impact on jobs at associated enterprises and suppliers. As we will see later, five or six jobs in the fabrication/supply chain are linked to each manufacturing job; those jobs are also lost when a single manufacturing job is offshored.

There is a similar multiplier impact when higher-wage jobs are exported from the technology and services sectors. Utilizing a database of 1,600 service sector firms beginning in 2004, researchers at Duke University and the Conference Board documented widespread offshoring in these sectors, too. This study also assessed the motivation for exporting jobs by these service-sector enterprises, with the authors concluding that few of the respondents pursued the strategy to enhance domestic employment.[20] As in the manufacturing sector, the profits on offer from exporting high wage US jobs to low-wage platforms is the lure.

"The Apple Problem"

The third element of offshoring involves the creation of jobs at production facilities abroad intended to supply the US market with new products never fabricated domestically. This was a notable pattern detected by the Bronfenbrenner and Luce analysis. Some of the new jobs abroad support foreign sales. But millions of such foreign jobs involve fabricating for the US economy. Apple alone has nearly 700,000 employees at subcontractor Foxconn scattered across Asia, 40 percent of whom are producing goods for the American market. The consequence of such behavior by Apple and others is to hollow out the domestic industrial base. When the multiplier effects are included, the opportunity cost is far larger than measured just by the jobs figure.

The American technology jewel Apple is a poster child for this category of offshoring. Despite its products being envisaged, conceived, researched, financed, developed, and managed from America, Apple fabricates most of its products—iPhones, for example—in low-wage countries, such as China, for export to the United States. The late visionary Steve Jobs was an innovative genius, but despite agreeing under pressure in December 2012 to resume some domestic US production, his successor, Timothy D. Cook, has proven to be far from an economic patriot.

Unlike their predecessor CEOs during the golden age, Cook, Ballmer, and other citizens of the world feel little compunction to support American families. Son of an immigrant, Steve Jobs' genius was nurtured by the schooling, opportunity, resources, and venture capital available to him in America's Silicon Valley, a phenomenon nearly as unique in the history of mankind as the eighteenth-century Midlands. But the Americans now running his firm scarcely return the favor. About 43,000 of Apple's 63,000 or so direct employees reside in the United States, but almost none of the 700,000 contract employees work in America.[21]

Multinationals like Apple should strive to locally source wherever they operate, of course. But their unwillingness to match US sales with production hollows out the American industrial and R&D base. It means less opportunity in the future for other start-ups to benefit from the same education, venture capital opportunities, and entrepreneurial outlets that were instrumental in nurturing their infancy and growth. It means fewer new Apples in the future. Leaders at most multinationals from the family capitalism countries appreciate that dynamic, as we see in the next chapter. But CEOs at Apple and Microsoft, among other companies, divert their eyes, the Reagan rents on offer trumping economic patriotism. Indeed, taking a page from the Walmart playbook, Apple treats many of its American employees poorly as well. Most of its domestic employees are in sales, and its low-wage business model induces rapid staff turnover. Some three-quarters of its retailing employees earn about $25,000 annually and work at Apple an average of only two-and-a-half years before moving on.[22] While Apple has the highest profits and sales per square foot ($6,050) of any large firm in America, its hardworking employees don't share in that bounty.[23]

Its low-wage strategy elicits few complaints in the United States, but has proven controversial in the family capitalism countries. Employees in Paris, for example, publicly complained in September 2012 of "remuneration considered too low, opacity in wage scales, working hours too fragmented by part-time, and a lack of perspective developments in the company," according to *Le Figaro*.[24] In Munich and Frankfurt, employees at Apple stores bristled at the unfamiliar imperious Apple management style and established work councils during 2012 to strengthen their hand in negotiations on issues such as work hours and vacations.[25]

If Apple and other American firms hire more expensive Americans, they might not even incur a profit penalty because Americans are considerably more productive. In any case, it is likely to be small, comparable to background noise for such firms. Certainly, dealing with more productive and assertive American employees requires a higher order of management skill, but that should not be a problem for firms such as Apple or Google. If the global powerhouses Siemens or VW can manage such tradeoffs, Apple can, too.

Onshoring, or bringing jobs from abroad to US soil, by firms like Apple, would be inexpensive, because labor is a small element of manufacturing costs. In the case of iPhones, for example, paying American rather than Chinese wages would add $65 or so to each unit's cost, reported Charles Duhigg and Keith Bradsher of the *New York Times*.[26] Put that in perspective: Apple fetched an average $427 per iPhone in 2007, but jumped its price to average $620 during the first half of 2012 as reported by Elsa Bembaron in *Le Figaro*, a price hike three times larger than the US employment cost differential.[27] That presumably added in the neighborhood of $200 per unit to profits.

What would be the absolutely worst-case outcome if Apple hired Americans to produce for its US customers? Think of the answer this way: Apple reported profits of $41.7 billion in its fiscal year 2012. The use of tax havens (remember its Luxembourg mail drop?) kept its 2012 taxes modest, enabling the firm to increase its foreign cash hoard in the Caribbean and elsewhere to $82.6 billion at fiscal year-end. Had it used Americans to produce the 40 percent of its output sold in the United States, Apple's foreign cash holdings under the worst-case scenario would have been $80 billion instead.[28]

A bit embarrassed by foreign production of goods for American customers, mendacity has come to color the business community's justification, exemplified by this comment from one Apple executive in the winter of 2011–2012:

> "We shouldn't be criticized for using Chinese workers. The US has stopped producing people with the skills we need."[29]

That would be news to Silicon Valley community colleges, nearby Stanford University, the Universities of California at San Francisco and Berkeley, San Jose State University, or the broader scientific community. If that were actually a valid explanation, all Apple need do to create hundreds of thousands of American jobs is adopt the upskilling culture of its competitors in family capitalism countries. That's seems unlikely, however. *New York Times* reporters Duhigg and Bradsher seem convinced that Apple management is pivotally reliant on a docile and eminently disposable workforce always on call, living in dormitories with twelve-hour, six-day schedules.

With products now routinely shifted for fabrication abroad that were envisioned and developed in the United States, firms like Apple exacerbate—rather than ameliorate—the US trade balance. Offshoring of Apple's iPhone, for example, contributes $1.8 billion to the bilateral American trade deficit with China.

Offshoring carries a human toll as well. Women have become as important as men in the American labor force. Yet traditionalists still view the key workforce cohort in any economy as males aged 25 to 54 years old. Back in 1954, 96 percent of them worked according to the Department of Labor. Only 80 percent were working in 2011, a difference representing over thirteen million prime-age men without jobs. Some of that erosion is cyclical, but most is not, with millions of them victimized by offshoring. Even a few conservatives fret about the problem and one or two acknowledge that government should play a role in reversing this tide. Here is David Brooks in May 2011:

> "There are probably more idle men now than at any time since the Great Depression, and this time the problem is mostly structural, not cyclical. . . . Many will pick up habits that have a corrosive cultural influence on those around them. The country will not benefit from their potential abilities. . . . It can't be solved by simply reducing the size of government. . . ."[30]

Offshoring Weakens Productivity

Beyond its impact on jobs and wages, offshoring haunts America's longer-term prospects by hobbling future productivity growth in two ways:

First, it shrinks employment in the highest productivity manufacturing sector, because those jobs are disproportionately higher-wage (frequently unionized) ones and thus prime targets for offshoring. In addition, their high wages also make them unlikely targets to be onshored.

Second, economists such as MIT's Jerry A. Hausman have argued that the weak US productivity record also reflects offshoring of associated R&D and innovation investments that accompany the export of manufacturing jobs.[31] Some of this offshoring is also a consequence of explicit, coercive industrial policy strategies abroad in some low-wage platforms. A portion of American offshoring, for example, occurs to accommodate the basest of mercantilist policies pursued by nations like China. Such nations blackmail firms eager for access to their burgeoning markets, extorting technology secrets under duress from US innovators. For example, GM was required in 2011 to reveal several innovations in its Volt plug-in hybrid in exchange for receiving the same $19,300 subsidy received by its Chinese domestic hybrid competitors like BYD's e6 model.[32] Such commercial blackmail violates rules of the World Trade Organization, to which China belongs.

Offshoring and Collapse of the Great American Jobs Machine Since 2000

Private-sector job creation has been paltry since the turn of the twenty-first century in America. The bare statistics are that fewer than 59 percent of American adults were working in 2011, compared to 64 percent in 2000.[33] Offshoring broadly defined to include the Apple problem is the major reason. Indeed, virtually no private-sector jobs on a net basis were created during the halcyon days of offshoring from 1999–2007 prior to the credit crisis and ensuing recession. Economists such as Nancy Folbre have determined that offshoring weakens the link between economic growth and domestic job creation. Using capacity at foreign affiliates, US firms can meet rising American demand with imports, without adding proportionately to domestic employment during recoveries.[34] Imports have risen, not employment.

The data are informative. Prior to 2000, US companies opening or expanding domestic operations added nearly eight employees for every 100 already on the payroll. That dropped to a rate of seven during the 2001 recession. Surprisingly, it remained there during the boom period which followed before declining yet again, to a rate of six during the 2008 recession.[35] And Robert Shapiro, former undersecretary of commerce for economic affairs in the Clinton administration, noted in February 2013 that private-sector job growth has averaged only 1.25 percent annually since the recovery began in 2009. That is just a fraction of the rate during the comparable recovery periods following the 1981 recession (3.7 percent) and 1990 recession (2.3 percent).[36] This new dynamic obviating Okun's Law has added greatly to the woes of attaining enduring American prosperity through the creation of high-value jobs domestically. And the solution rests largely with resolving the Apple problem.

CHAPTER 21

DOMESTIC CONTENT AND THE APPLE PROBLEM

"We can't compete as a low-wage, low-skill nation. We have to compete as a high-wage, high-skill nation."[1]

CHRIS EVANS,
Australian Minister for Tertiary Education,
Skills, Jobs, and Workplace Relations, November 2010

"A new consensus has emerged in influential policy circles that the American labor market and educational system are unable to equip workers with sufficient skills . . . too much job turnover and too little training on the job."[2]

ROBERT J. GITTER and MARKUS SCHEUER,
Rheinisch-Westfällsches Institut für Wirtschaftsforschung (Essen)
***Monthly Labor Review*, March 1997**

"[German] Company managers set long-term policies while market pressures for short-term profits are held in check. The focus on long-term performance over short-term gain is reinforced by Germany's stakeholder, rather than shareholder, model of capitalism. . . ."[3]

HAROLD MEYERSON,
***Washington Post*, March 2009**

President Obama cast the 2012 election in populist terms and became only the third President elected with that theme. His opponent, former Governor Mitt Romney, cast the election choice quite differently: as a decision between intrusive big government and benign small government. Voters naturally distrust big government, but key voter cohorts made clear that they also favor a government that is interested and involved in improving their lives. The 2012 election was not a referendum won by "takers" who view government largess as a birthright. It had little to do with redistribution by government and everything to do with the broader role that voters believe government should play in building a better future.

The evidence is buried deep in exit-polling data. Asian-Americans are among the most, if not the most, aspirational ethnic groups in the United States, and richer and better educated than their neighbors. They are over-represented as small business proprietors, as entrepreneurs and in every meritocracy competition, ranging from the nation's most selective public high schools to elite universities or as STEM graduates. They are one of the population cohorts with a vital role to play if America is to reverse what I term the Reagan decline and innovate its way to parity—or better—with muscular global competition. Republicans call them the "Party of Work."[4]

They voted three to one for President Obama.

While the President's populism had broad appeal, something else worked strongly in his favor. And we find the answer by looking at why both Asian-Americans and young voters favored his reelection. Here is how the veteran political reporter of the *New York Times* Sheryl Gay Stolberg explained it:

> "On a central philosophical question of the day—the size and scope of the federal government—a clear majority of young people embraces President Obama's notion that it can be a constructive force. . . ."[5]

Like the fictional citizens of Tombstone, a majority of key aspirational Americans have concluded that the US government should be an ally in recapturing the frontier era combination of individualism leavened with collaborative and collective action. They hope and expect the public sector to become their ally in reversing tough family economics and dismal opportunity. It starts with good schools and expands from there to a public sector able to ensure competitive markets and that eschews favors for elite earners and corporate subsidies. They want Washington to adopt a different version of capitalism, one which rewards hard work and grit, one capable of offering a future for their children. They want America to recreate a new golden age.

Here is the way I think of it: given the choice at the polls in November 2012, Americans voted like the Danes and the Germans. They voted for a government that worries about the prosperity of families and prioritizes good jobs at home, even if that requires new policies. That means a government that thwarts deleterious market outcomes such as Red Queens, widening income disparities, or bank accounts in the Cayman Islands. And that means a government that focuses on creating good jobs despite the wishes of American multinationals. It means a government that embraces the goals of family capitalism.

Nurturing High-Value Jobs

In October 2012, the German government vetoed a merger of the French-German defense contractor EADS with the British firm BAE. The story of that veto actually began back in 1998, when the German pharmaceutical firm Hoechst merged with the French firm Rhône-Poulenc to form Aventis. Like EADS-BAE, Aventis was intended to be a merger of equals. But as events transpired, the brunt of job losses fell on Hoechst employees in Germany, especially when Aventis subsequently merged with Sanofi, another French drug firm. Fearing another sacrifice of high-value jobs to France or the United Kingdom, the 2012 defense merger was killed in Berlin.[6]

It is certainly true that German collaboration with France to restructure the jeopardized EU is proving productive, starting with budget constraints and a banking union. And it is also true that French, and especially German, economic success is built on strong commitments to free trade and investment, with care generally taken to avoid sheltering inefficient domestic firms. At the same time, they also take care to nurture a sturdy and secure domestic economic base. Indeed, that balancing act is common to all the family capitalism countries. For example, in the wake of the GM/Peugeot merger talks announced in early 2012, Xavier Bertrand, then French labor minister, wasted no time publicly reminding PSA Peugeot-Citroen to preserve its French employment levels.[7]

This domestic orientation by governments is matched by a similar commitment from corporate boards across northern Europe due to codeterminism, an institution absolutely vital to the long-term success of stakeholder capitalism. That commitment explains why offshoring in the family capitalism countries enhances—rather than erodes—family prosperity as we see momentarily. These countries have the most skilled workforces in the world and pay the world's highest wages, because entrepreneurs, enterprises, factories, and offices in Bremen, Vienna, Cherbourg, and Amsterdam provide good jobs paying good wages. They have active industrial bases and a host of industries operating at the technology frontier, where their embrace of codeterminism, work councils, and upskilling provide a competitive edge.

And not one of them has an Apple Problem.

Codeterminism is the reason. It's the fulcrum sustaining a domestic content perspective in enterprise board rooms. Northern Europe avoids the Apple Problem because codeterminism encourages firms to behave as economic patriots. This creates a soft *de facto* domestic content imperative that envelops many if not all board deliberations. That perspective means more jobs at home, with firms such as VW-Audi-Porsche passing up offshoring opportunities to keep Wolfsburg bustling and rich. And, codeterminism prevents short-termism and management rent-seeking.

Voter and consumer expectations are important in sustaining this domestic orientation by enterprise management. Families and public policies tend to nurture stakeholder capitalism by prioritizing domestic products over those from low-wage competitors or firms practicing wage compression. The collapse of Walmart in Germany is instructive in that regard, as is the current Franco-German focus on crafting meaningful standards and enforcing strictures against products inappropriately claiming EU origin. This latter theme was echoed recently by the industrialist Lakshmi Mittal, CEO and board chairman of the Luxembourg-based steel giant ArcelorMittal, who urged a "buy European" program when interviewed by the *Financial Times* in May 2012:

> "We need measures to encourage more purchases of European goods both to boost demand and to ensure any benefits are felt by European industry rather than leading to more imports."[8]

Consumers are sensitive to the broader values promoted by domestically produced goods, as indicated by data from France, where nine of the top sell ten cars in 2010 were French brands.[9] Price points are important, but *Le Figaro* journalist Isabelle de Foucaud notes survey data showing that 49 percent of French consumers are willing to pay more for local products.[10] A separate poll in October 2012 found that 50.5 percent of respondents were willing to pay 10 percent or more for Christmas gifts made in France, and a few were willing to pay as much as a 40 percent premium.[11] Websites helping identify domestic products have proliferated. And some 90 percent of respondents to a poll by the French National Association of Food Industries in April 2012 favored creation of "made-in-France" product labeling.[12] Reporter Charlotte Haunhorst of *Der Spiegel* explained that firms naturally react to consumer attitudes reflected in such polls:

> "Of course, industry representatives know that a label that says 'made with ingredients from China' isn't exactly good for sales."[13]

The Theoretical Foundation for Domestic Sourcing

There's a belief rooted in the nineteenth-century work of David Ricardo that expanding international trade benefits all, eventually even those initially suffering wage and job loss. Yet recall from an earlier discussion that economists have known that to be false since at least 1941, when

Wolfgang F. Stolper and Paul Samuelson's famous research appeared in the *Review of Economic Studies*. They didn't just acknowledge that some will lose from international trade; they concluded that some losses will be substantial and persevere for the long term. Worse, *ex post* attempts to redistribute income from winners to losers are problematic; there is no happy ending for all, one of the disheartening, enduring truths of capitalism.[14] Economist Rodrik explained the Stolper-Samuelson redistributive conundrum this way:

> "Advocates who claim that trade has huge benefits, but only modest distributional impacts either do not understand how trade really works, or have to jump through all kinds of hoops to make their argument halfway coherent. . . . It is not just that some win and others lose when tariffs are removed. It is also that the size of the redistribution swamps the 'net' gain. This is a generic consequence of trade policy under realistic circumstances."[15]

This 1941 explanation of the downside to free trade had little relevance at first in the postwar golden age of an America whose currency and multinationals dominated global trade. That was the era where paternalistic business leaders led families to conclude erroneously that broad prosperity was America's default setting. In those wondrous decades, a rising tide of trade and incomes did in fact lift most boats.

That outcome eroded quickly in the 1980s, however, as we have learned, when Washington endorsed offshoring and the other elements of Reaganomics. Washington paid little heed as US wages stagnated and fell, but economists and leaders in the family capitalism countries had been wrestling with the Stolpher-Samuelson conundrum for decades by then, anxious to continue domestic wage growth and job creation tied to world trade. In the end, they rejected trade controls and restraints, and instead relied primarily on codeterminism and its soft domestic content element to ensure that domestic economic health is a priority concern of all employers.

Importantly, codeterminism enabled the family capitalism countries to become ferocious advocates of free trade, and firm adherents to international trade rules. Those rules provide considerable flexibility and maneuvering room for nations to custom-design variants of capitalism. Rodrik explains:

> "Democracies have the right to protect their social arrangements, and when this right clashes with the requirements of the global economy, it is the latter that should give way."[16]

Those requirements give way in two meaningful ways in northern Europe:

First, private internal corporate deliberations in a codeterminism setting favoring domestic employment and production are beyond the reach of international trade law.

Second, voters expect public sectors in France, Germany, and elsewhere in northern Europe to be inhospitable to foreign investment involving the leveraged buyouts of larger domestic employers. Officials are well aware of the LBO business model and history in which jobs and assets of target firms are too often stripped in order for buyers to seize short-term productivity and profits before the enterprise is resold. Some LBO targets subsequently prosper, but the business model is centered on short-termism that frequently yields outcomes antithetical to the long-term prosperity goals of stakeholder capitalism.

The Family Capitalism Countries Oppose Barriers to International Trade

Regarding government trade restrictions on imports, the family capitalism countries are the globe's leading traders. That gives them an obvious incentive to nurture free trade and to police foreign mercantilist practices. In 2012, for example, countries threatened reciprocal retaliation if equal access for EU exporters to public procurement by the Chinese, American, and Japanese governments continued to be thwarted.[17]

This and occasional similar controversies have given rise to the incendiary notion of a protectionist Europe, an absurd libel against nations whose foreign trade sectors are two, three, or even four times larger as a share of GDP than the United States. Indeed, they're stout advocates of globalization, free trade, the World Trade Organization, and multilateralism. And they should be, because they are big winners from globalization. Here is German Chancellor Merkel in June 2008: "We are witnessing an exponential increase in the penetration of globalisation. There is a protectionist temptation. This is not the right way to address the challenge of globalisation."[18] Northern Europe has displayed great tolerance in the face of invidious mercantilist practices of nations such as China. In fact, they have been too tolerant. After all, laws in the family capitalism countries delineate workplace practices, including safety, wages, and hours of work. Yet international trade features imported goods sometimes produced in exploitative conditions by Chinese and other firms such as Apple that violate such standards. Indeed, foreign firms can seize a competitive advantage over firms in the rich democracies, not from more efficiency, advanced technology, superior products, or R&D, but merely by exploiting their own nation's lack of worksite conditions or livable wages.

Why should any rich democracy tolerate foreign firms reliant on prohibited practices seizing a competitive advantage and entering their markets through a back door? During the Reagan era, a handful of American economists argued the merits of penalizing such tactics, imposing compensatory taxes on foreign enterprises that seized advantage in this fashion. They included Jeff Faux at the Economic Policy Institute; Robert Kuttner, co-editor of *Prospect Magazine*; Clyde Prestowitz at the Economic Strategy Institute; and Joseph Stiglitz. But most economists, like Alan Blinder and Paul Krugman at Princeton, or Harvard President *emeritus* and former Treasury Secretary Lawrence Summers, were free-trade advocates.

Yet these prominent US free traders did what good economists do when confronted with convincing new data: they changed their minds in the face of surging Chinese goods, mercantilist policies such as the persistent undervaluation of the Chinese currency, the *yuan*, expansive offshoring, and wage erosion. It wasn't just the impact of trade, which directly accounts for maybe 15 percent of American wage declines, or the magnitude of offshoring. Instead, it was the combined impact of offshoring, deindustrialization, Us versus Them and all the rest, plus technology change, which intensified the impact of trade on wages and deindustrialization.

Alan Blinder, for example, concluded that even good jobs in "safe" domestic service sectors (health care, education, and finance) are jeopardized by global integration and the threat of offshoring. He determined that the number of sectors at risk is two to three times larger than the number of manufacturing jobs subject to offshoring—and that the danger is growing.[19]

Krugman's conversion occurred in 2007; global integration was exacerbating income disparities and "fears that low-wage competition is driving down US wages have a real basis in both theory and fact," he concluded.[20] And Summers grew concerned with multinationals behaving like "stateless elites whose allegiance is to global economic success and their own prosperity rather than the interest of the nation where they are headquartered. . . . Such firms are disinterested in the quality of the workforce and infrastructure in their home country."[21] He urged international labor standards to stem a race to the bottom in labor market regulations.

This sea change in mainstream economic thinking brought perceptive, hardnosed American realists into compatibility with conclusions reached years earlier by the bow wave of prescient colleagues such as

Stiglitz, and by officials in the family capitalism countries. Like them, American economists support international trade; none wants to reverse globalization. The riches are undeniable. Their goal rather is to corral and render globalization compatible with broadly enjoyed prosperity.

American economists critical of Reaganomics or offshoring, however, have little influence in the pecuniary US political arena. And so trade policy remains *ad hockery* writ large, relying too much on temporary solutions forged at the behest of influential political donors rather than consistent, long-term planning.

Offshoring in Family Capitalism Strengthens Domestic Employment

Firms in Germany and in other family capitalism countries routinely offshore, but their motivation for such foreign investment is different than American multinationals, as captured in these comments by Horst Mundt, head of the International Department at the German trade union IG Metall. Speaking in October 2009 regarding a new plant being offshored by BMW to low-wage South Carolina, Mundt explained:

> "The success of German carmakers depends on the ability to sell cars abroad. We cannot expect all the cars to be made in Germany. . . . The affected plant got other models to work on and other jobs—so no one was losing."[22]

Motivated by an eagerness to strengthen the domestic employment base, enterprises in northern Europe do not offshore with the same vigor as American firms. Journalists at the *Economist* examined offshoring in some detail in January 2013, concluding that "European firms had been off-shoring less in the first place," than American firms in recent decades:

> "Cultural factors are partly responsible; Germany's *mittelstand* or mid-sized family firms, for instance, sell their products globally but are more inclined to make things in their own backyards."[23]

Perhaps the most thorough studies of offshoring in the family capitalism countries and Reagan-era America have been done by Bronfenbrenner and Luce. Drawing on their data, Jacob Funk Kirkegaard with the Washington-based Institute for International Economics determined that offshoring is considerably less prevalent among European firms than American ones. His results are reproduced in Chart 21.1. Kirkegaard concluded that firms from the EU 25 offshored only about one-third the jobs as a share of domestic private employment as the share exported by American firms during the same first quarter of 2004.* An even more exaggerated difference was found in statistics and projections gathered by the consulting firm Forrester Research beginning in 2002.[24]

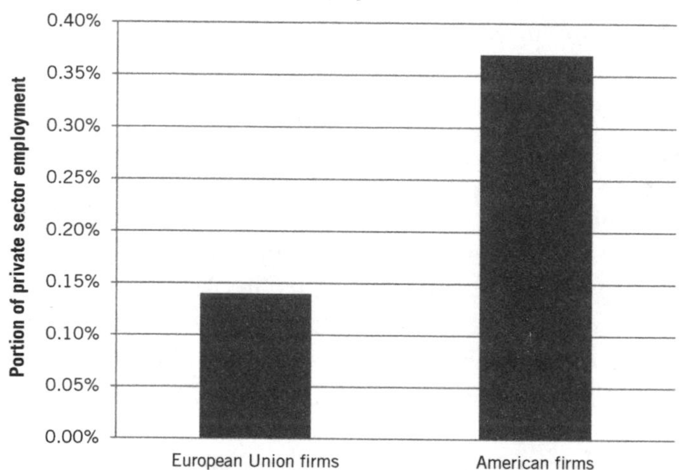

Chart 21.1. Announced or reported job exports. EU 25 includes Norway and Switzerland. *Sources: Jacob Funk Kirkegaard, "Outsourcing and Offshoring: Pushing the European Model Over the Hill, Rather than Off the Cliff," Washington, DC, Institute for International Economics, March 2005. Kate Bronfenbrenner and Stephanie Luce, "The Changing Nature of Corporate Global Restructuring: The Impact of Production Shifts on Jobs in the US, China and Around the Globe," U.S.–China Economic and Security Review Commission, Oct. 14, 2004.*

Unlike America, offshoring in northern Europe is accompanied by domestic job growth by the same multinationals. Presumably their offshoring reduces the enterprise-wide cost profile, helping sustain investments in new employment, factories, and R&D back home. In France, during the boom period 2002–2005, for example, data from the French statistical agency Insee show that 12 percent of French firms with more than 20 employees offshored some production, averaging 36,000 jobs created abroad yearly during the study period. That isn't surprising. French firms vie with German ones as the world's

*Moreover, offshoring may have diminished in recent years, at least by German firms, according to the Fraunhofer Institute for Systems and Innovation Research. It appears to have dwindled to the lowest levels in fifteen years in part because European multinationals are troubled by persistent foreign production-line quality issues and logistical challenges, plus rising Chinese wages. See Jakob Schlandt, "Goodbye China–Company Returns to Germany," *Berliner Zeitung*, March 16, 2012.

second largest international investor abroad after the United States. But the motivation for this French offshoring is revealed by the fact that the firms involved expanded domestic operations simultaneously, creating 41,000 new jobs yearly at home over the same period.[25] That is a dramatic contrast with the conclusions of the American offshoring studies reviewed earlier.

The *Economist* magazine suggests that this pattern is not universal, with the very largest French firms belonging to the CAC-40 Paris exchange exporting jobs on a net basis during the financial crisis years of 2008–2010.[26] Even so, research by economists Lionel Fontagné and Farid Toubal concluded that, as a group, all French multinationals are net domestic job creators. Moreover, the French multinationals investing abroad simultaneously created more new jobs at home than did other French firms that didn't offshore at all; three years after their study began, French firms investing abroad were employing an average of 25 percent more French staff at home than firms that stayed put.[27] The only exception was those French firms that invested in poor countries such as Vietnam. Even French firms investing in the middle-income countries of Brazil, India, or China netted new jobs back home.

German firms also utilize offshoring to support domestic operations. Powerful evidence is the fact that some 42 percent of all jobs at firms on the Berlin DAX 30 stock exchange are in Germany, even though only 25 percent of sales come from Germany.[28] The German business model is the precise opposite of Apple. Scholarly analyses support this conclusion. Martin Falk with the Centre for European Economic Research in Mannheim and Bertrand Koebel at the Otto von Guericke University in Magdeburg determined in 2002 that offshoring did not supplant domestic employment in the key German manufacturing sector.[29]

In a data-rich 2004 study, economist Dalia Marin at the University of Munich found that efficiencies realized by offshoring, especially lower labor costs abroad, led to an increase in domestic employment by both Austrian and German firms. Marin's extensive analysis examined 1,200 projects representing 80 percent of all German offshoring in Central and Eastern Europe (CEE) and 100 percent of such CEE investments by Austrian firms from 1998 to 2000. This study included investments in former Soviet republics, such as the Ukraine, where wages were only 5 percent of German wages at the time, and investments in higher-wage nations including the Baltic States, Poland, and Slovenia. Marin concluded that such offshoring specifically produced net job growth in Germany:

> "Lower costs of Eastern European affiliates help firms to lower overall production costs and to stay competitive. . . . The estimated

> employment demand functions show that a 10 percent decline in affiliate wages in CEE countries leads to a 1.6 percent increase, rather than decline, in the parent company's employment demand in both Austria and Germany. These estimates suggest that the outsourcing activity of German and Austrian firms to the accession countries has actually helped to create jobs in Austria and Germany."[30]

These data and analyses provide the weight of evidence supporting the conclusion that the priority of Austrian and German corporate boards is to sustain domestic prosperity. Another indicator may be the issue identified earlier, when the final opening of the European labor market in 2012 caused little employment or wage dislocation in Germany. The extraordinarily high-skill level of the northern European workforce causes employers there to prioritize applicant job skills over low wages. Indeed, the US consulting firm Ernst & Young examined the behavior over five years of 360 small- and medium-sized German firms (SMEs) during the 2000s. It determined that offshoring had dwindled since 2005 because of the sharp drop-off in labor skills available abroad. Analyst Peter Englisch noted that firms had found it

> ". . . difficult to find the skilled labor, particularly in Eastern Europe, which—with China—has become the prime production area of German industrialists. The best candidates have been recruited by the firms that settled earlier. Instead of venturing outside the borders, SMEs prefer to consolidate their positions in Germany."[31]

Several threads in this narrative are brought together in the next chapter assessing in more detail the economic prowess of the family capitalism countries, starting with their robust productivity performance.

CHAPTER 22

PRODUCTIVITY AND INVESTMENT

"Fire the research and development group. The cost cutting will goose my stock options so I can cash out before the death spiral."[1]

SCOTT ADAMS,
Dogbert the CEO, "Dilbert"

"The competitiveness problem of the 1980s and early 1990s didn't really go away. It was just hidden during the bubble years behind a mirage of prosperity, and all the while the country's industrial base continued to erode."[2]

GARY PISANO and WILLY SHINE,
***Harvard Business Review*, July 2009**

"Trillions of dollars vanished, along with American competitiveness."[3]

JEFFREY IMMELT,
CEO, General Electric, July 2009

"In the three years to September 2007, companies in the S&P 500 used more money to buy back stock than to invest in production."[4]

LAWRENCE MITCHELL,
George Washington University, July 2009

Europe began as a tragic love story. The tale is that the beauty of Europa, daughter of a Phoenician king, captivated Zeus after he was struck by an Eros arrow. Alas, the princess proved mortal as the years passed, and the anguished Zeus named the continent to memorialize her for all time. The Eurozone may still prove mortal like the mythical Europa as it struggles with poor conceptualization, undisciplined fiscal policies, and excessive sovereign debt. But as we have learned, countries in northern Europe have gained a measure of at least economic immortality in sustaining faster productivity and wage growth than the United States during the most severe decades of globalization. No American economist in 1980 would have bet on that outcome.

Not all European nations are the same, of course. The sober north does not much resemble the Mediterranean members of the EU or Iceland, the United Kingdom, and Ireland, which adopted major behaviors of Reaganomics. These practices caused the same economic turmoil as they did in America. André Sapir at the Brussels-based consultancy Bruegel explained:

> "Everything we feared about the Mediterranean model has proven right—only it was worse. In Holland, Germany, and the Nordic countries there was more of a longer-term view of the challenges that societies were facing."[5]

Reporters Ralph Atkins and Matt Steinglass of the *Financial Times* elaborated in August 2011:

> "Germany, the Netherlands, and a few other northern European counties tell another story, however. Their success is the flip side of the Eurozone debt crisis. While the economic models of some in the 12-year-old monetary union have been blown apart—in Greece unemployment has hit 15 percent—others have turned out to be surprisingly efficient."[6]

Productivity Growth in Northern Europe Outpaced America

It was just another in the long line of reports about auto firms establishing new assembly plants abroad to supply the American market, and always in places like Mexico. But it was a Japanese firm moving production from Japan itself, which is unusual, and the firm was world-class Toyota, so I read on. Moving from Japan made sense, since it involved the Yaris, a mid-mini model where the labor component of costs loomed relatively large.

But where on earth was Onnaing?

It turns out to be a small town outside Valenciennes—in Europe. In France, actually.

"This export to the United States demonstrates our commitment to European manufacturing . . ." is how Didier Leroy, director of Toyota Europe, explained the decision in mid-2012.[7] The transfer to France of auto production for the North American market by a leading Japanese exporter is surprising, and this chapter explains how high-wage northern Europe has emerged to be one of the world's most competitive industrial export platforms. And it occurred despite labor costs of $10–$20 per hour more than crummy American wages.

We start with a conundrum. American management holds all the cards needed to raise productivity. They can behave exactly like Apple. They have access to the world's best technology, its lowest-cost capital, the world's best universities and labs, a cheaper workforce than competitors in other rich democracies like Germany or France, complete freedom to outsource and offshore, to innovate and reduce costs, and to open and close plants. Moreover, they have a unique flexibility among rich democracies to commoditize domestic employees: treat them as inanimate production inputs, such as coal, staplers, or computers, with virtual total control over pay and schedules; put them on erratic night or weekend shifts; export their jobs to China; cut wages; adjust weekly hours of work; relocate them across state and national boundaries; demand work on Easter or Christmas; or to abruptly fire them—after first requiring that they train cheaper replacements.

Yet these remarkable advantages have been squandered decade after decade since the 1980s by American executives. Short-termism, offshoring, the American hierarchical management style, and other aspects of Reaganomics are the reasons. This subpar performance has been a disappointment to Republican Party leaders, such as Peter Peterson, who hoped that the Reagan era would be an improvement over the sluggish 1970s:

> "From a decade of feeble productivity growth (0.6 percent yearly in the 1970s) and early signs of rising poverty rates, we entered the 1980s flush with expectations of 'supply side' prosperity. Result: We have ended up with still feebler productivity growth (0.4 percent yearly from 1979–1986) and, despite a debt-financed rise in personal income, with an upward leap in every measure of overall poverty."[8]

We learned earlier that an economy can grow by the sum of the percentage rate rise in productivity and in population. While northern Europe's population growth is sluggish, productivity has risen at a brisk rate over the entire postwar period. There are a variety of sources of productivity growth, including upskilling employees, R&D, adopting more efficient technologies, and adding additional capital to the workplace with new machinery or computers. Playing catch-up from the devastation of World War II, Europeans utilized all these elements to stimulate productivity growth in the early postwar period until the 1960s, benefiting in good measure from technology transferred from the United States. Productivity experts such as Barry Eichengreen term this sort of period (similar to the economies of Brazil, Russia, India, and China today) one of "extensive" productivity growth, in which existing technologies were imported and combined with new investment.[9] In addition, productivity benefited from former agricultural workers in Europe moving into more productive manufacturing jobs. This catch-up period ended about 1970, with labor productivity still lower than America.

For the last nearly forty years, the nature of productivity growth in the European economies has been different, increasingly generated mostly from internal innovation, R&D, upskilling, and investment. Like Japan, growth morphed to an "intensive" process no longer unduly reliant on foreign technology transfers or breakthroughs, with employees working harder and smarter and sharing ideas for innovation with employers. In his book, *The European Economy Since 1945*, Eichengreen described the transformation this way in 2007, harking back to Henry Ford:

> "The Fordist model of using assembly-line methods to divide, conquer, and scale up the labor process gave way to flexible production and decentralized work organization. . . . Today, Europe has converged to the technology frontier, and its growth derives from internally generated innovation."[10]

We see the consequence of these trends in the United States and in the family capitalism countries depicted in Chart 22.1. During the postwar golden age, when stakeholder capitalism characterized America, labor productivity growth averaged 2.8 percent annually. Then Reaganomics arrived and in the long span from 1979 through 2006 immediately preceding the credit crisis, American labor productivity grew only 1.6 percent annually based on internationally standardized data from the OECD.* And, while comparable to the rate in Australia, productivity in the big family capitalism countries of France and Germany has grown a third faster than the United States over the entire span of the Reagan decline. That's why historians like Paul Kennedy, writing even as early as 1986, observed that Germany's "long-term productivity growth has been extremely impressive."[11] This is the sort of superior relative performance suggested earlier by OECD and IMF statistics on labor-force skill levels: it seems that European managers spent the last three decades upskilling and investing, while American executives assiduously did not.

*Note this figure is lower than the BLS figure of 1.9 percent for this period, which is not comparable to OECD internationally-standardized statistics.

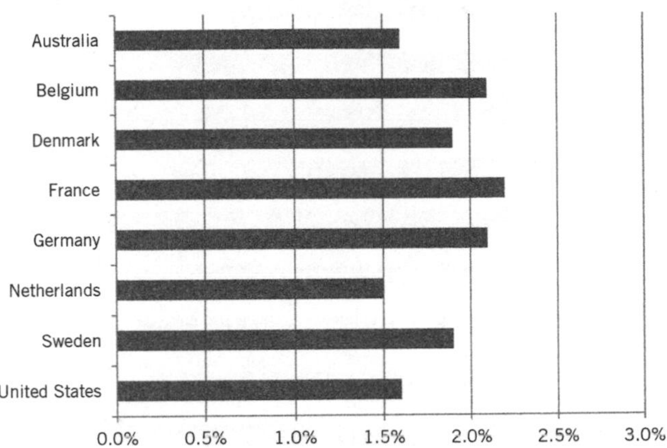

Chart 22.1. Output/hour worked, average annual growth rate.
Source: OECD statistical base, OECD, Paris. For the United States, 1947–1973: "Productivity Change in the Nonfarm Business Section," Bureau of Labor Statistics, Washington, DC, http://data.bls.gov/cgi-bin/print.pl/lpc/prodybar.htm.

This long Reagan-era erosion rings ominously familiar to economic historians, as explained by Peter Peterson:

> "The 1980s and 1990s may be remembered, with bitterness, as a turning point in America's fortunes—a period of transition when we took the British route to second-class economic status. Britain's decline took seventy-five years of productivity-growth rates that were half a percentage point lower than those of its industrial competitors. Because America's corresponding gap is more than three times as large, its relative decline is proceeding far more swiftly."[12]

The weak Reagan-era performance has completely wiped out the American productivity edge that emerged from the catastrophe of World War II and powered the golden age. It is gone, entirely lost. Productivity in northern Europe has overtaken America, with the levels at the shop floor now quite close, as evidenced from OECD statistics reproduced in Chart 22.2. These numbers have varied a bit in the past few years of recession and recovery, but on the cusp of the credit crisis, Belgium's workers had become the most productive in the world, with the US, Dutch, French, and German workforces bunched quite closely behind, followed by employees in the other family capitalism countries.

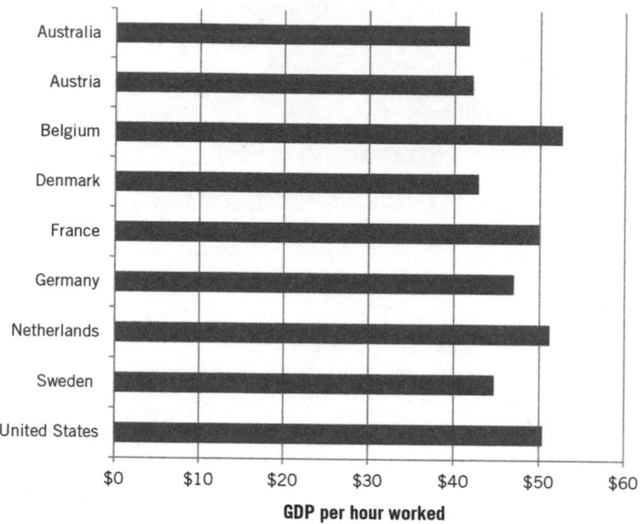

Chart 22.2. Converted at purchase power parities.
Source: "Productivity," OECD.stat, Paris. http://stats.oecd.org/WBOS/Index.aspx?DatasetCode=LEVEL.

Even more concerning for America, experts have concluded that this snap-shot presents an overly optimistic picture of US performance. Compared to nations like Germany, the United States has relatively large agricultural, banking, and energy sectors where returns per employee are spectacular, skewing productivity figures based on GDP statistics. Moreover, Department of Commerce data neither independently captures nor adjusts for the US productivity drain from offshoring and the overseas supply chains at firms such as Apple. Instead, they inaccurately attribute productivity gains actually achieved abroad in Chinese and other factories to US importers. Here is how Michael Mandel, former chief economist at *Business Week* (now with the Washington-based Progressive Policy Institute), and Susan Houseman, senior economist with the W.E. Upjohn Institute for Employment Research, explained these phantom US productivity gains:

> "In 2000, imports of computer and electronic products from China and Mexico accounted for about 10 percent of the net supply to the US market. . . . By 2010, that percentage had risen to 37 percent. . . . These shifts in sourcing from high-cost to low-cost suppliers can show up as productivity growth in the United States."[13]

The one-third faster productivity growth in France and Germany during the Reagan decline means the economic pie there has grown faster. Only a few American conservatives argue otherwise. Ross Douthat, for example, simply made up the claim in 2010 that Reaganomics had "kicked off a long era of impressive economic growth. . . . Even now, there isn't a major power in the world that wouldn't happily change places with the United States."[14] With American wages stagnant for a generation, productivity growth poor, and investment weak, this sort of economic jingoism is dismissed by economists, such as these at the OECD:

> "It has been claimed by some that only countries which emphasize market-oriented policies (limited welfare benefits, light regulation) may enjoy both successful employment performance and strong labour productivity growth simultaneously. . . . This claim is not supported by the evidence in this chapter, however. Indeed the chapter finds that other successful employment performers (which combine strong work incentives with generous welfare protection and well-designed regulation) had, on average over the past decade, similar GDP per capita growth to that recorded in more market-reliant counties."[15]

Moreover, most voters in Australia or northern Europe would find risible the notion of switching places with the 95 percent of Americans whose wages have stagnated for a generation. Why would they prefer an economy that redistributes each year from families to American firms an amount equal to three-quarters the value of net export earnings of OPEC? After all, their own real wages have risen faster, they earn about the same wages as Americans now even while taking longer vacations, and college tuition for their children is free. Oh, and their societies do not suffer from the American dynamic of sharply declining economic mobility or tens of millions trapped in a multigenerational poverty cycle.

European self-doubters need only look closely at neighbors in the United Kingdom, Ireland, or Spain, which actually did mimic Reaganomics. Launched in 1979 by Prime Minister Margaret Thatcher, for example, the UK outcome featured a credit bubble just like America: the volume of new housing mortgages rose from £6 billion to £63 billion and non-housing loans rose from £4 billion to £28 billion during the 1980s.[16] And just like America, the UK bubble burst, destroying wealth and jobs. Here is how British historian Max Hastings in December 2009 described the current sentiment there toward Prime Minister Thatcher's misadventure:

> "Historians are likely to look back on 2009 as the year in which Britain was confronted by truths of lasting significance. For two

> decades, we have supposed ourselves a successful society. It has been an article of faith that the revolution wrought by Margaret Thatcher transformed a sclerotic, declining nation into a dynamic and robustly prosperous one. We decided that we manage our affairs better than our European partners do theirs. The events of the past 18 months suggest otherwise. Britain is emerging from the crisis weaker than other developed economies, and notably more vulnerable than Germany and France. It seems hard to overstate the pain in store when the next government embarks on the steps necessary to restore the public finances."[17]

Productivity in France and Germany has drawn close to America because of those structures discussed earlier, such as codeterminism, work councils, and supportive labor policies that have been quite effective incentivizing workplace diligence and upskilling. Northern European labor markets are less flexible than in the United States, but reforms have made them obviously sufficiently flexible to accommodate a rate of productivity growth one-third higher for decades. And this superior performance occurred amid the tumult of rapid globalization.

Short-termism has been a major determinant of weak US performance, but extreme executive remuneration may also be demoralizing workforces in America. Why be gratuitously innovative or unusually energetic at your work station when the only reward is higher executive compensation? This reality at worksites in the United States featuring extreme executive compensation was editorially summarized in 2010 by the *Financial Times*:

> "There is no evidence that such packages promote exceptional performance—and much to suggest they destroy the social fabric of companies as the gap between chief executives and workers soar."[18]

US productivity performance has not been uniformly weak. There have been several periods in recent decades when it improved, but the details of those episodes dramatize just how gravely and pervasive the Reagan decline has undermined American productivity. The first episode was a spike between 1995 and 2006 when it temporarily matched or even exceeded rates in France and Germany. Productivity expert Robert J. Gordon of Northwestern University attributes this blip to the fruits of the dot-com boom.[19]

The second episode was another spike that coincided with the 2008 credit crisis and ensuing recession. It is quite discouraging to ponder the factor responsible for this latter spike, because it was a byproduct of sizable job cuts by American managers shedding employees to shield profit margins amid the downturn.[20] Recall that this new CEO behavior has obviated Okun's Law. Here is how mutual fund guru John P. Hussman described events:

> "It is a good time to be a corporate insider, particularly at major financial companies. First you report productivity gains and 'operating profits'—not by making smart investments in productive assets, but instead . . . at industrial firms, by cutting the number of workers per unit of capital."[21]

American Management Reacting to Reagan-Era Policies Are Responsible for the Weak US Productivity Record

American productivity growth swooned because a variety of incentives created by Reaganomics induce management behavior that is anti-growth. Reagan-era deficits raised the inflation-adjusted cost of capital. Entrepreneurs are indifferent to tax rates as long as they aren't confiscatory, but the cost of capital is vitally important. Moreover, these deficits also raised the value of the dollar, harming exports. As economic historian Kennedy explained, "The increasing federal deficits . . . sent the dollar's price to artificially high levels and turned the country from a net lender to a net borrower."[22]

Perhaps most importantly, as I have emphasized, the reaction of American executives to the policies embedded in Reaganomics cause short-termism, which disincentivizes domestic R&D and investment. Informed observers without a political agenda, such as the worldwide consulting firm McKinsey and Company, have reached the same conclusion. Economists at the McKinsey Global Institute (MGI) note that responsibility for weak productivity rests squarely with disincentivized American executives, not US government policies such as high or low taxes or with regulation. Far too many narcissistic American executives for decades have squandered the opportunity to implement the Japanese model of continually reforming the production process called *kaizen,* to incrementally and continually upskill employees, or to invest aggressively to match northern Europe's productivity performances. As recently as 2011, MGI analysts concluded that American business leaders simply ignore readily adoptable practices able to boost efficiency:

> "There is a large untapped potential to increase productivity and growth in the United States, MGI finds. Businesses can achieve three-quarters of the necessary productivity growth acceleration in the current regulatory and business environment. Companies can achieve one-quarter of the acceleration by more wisely adopting

> best practices. Even in such sectors as retail . . . by taking lean practices from the stockroom to the storefront. Aerospace companies . . . have yet to adopt lean practices in the systematic way seen among best in-class automotive players. . . . Health-care players have just begun to adopt lean [practices]. . . . Implementing emerging business and technology innovations can achieve a further half of the necessary acceleration. Opportunities lie in enhanced supply chain integration, greater responsiveness to evolving customer preferences and behavior, and innovating in what, and how, goods and services are provided to customers."[23]

Similar forces may account for the weak productivity performance in Australia. While its nationwide wage determination mechanism is as effective as those in other family capitalism countries, corporate governance there exhibits the debilities of Reagan-era America: its adversarial rather than collaborative workplaces act as an anchor on productivity growth. Just like the MGI economists, Australian researchers have concluded that enterprise failure to pursue best practices by Australian executive suites has slowed productivity growth. Too many CEOs there perhaps obsess about scoring American-style Reagan rents rather than obsessing like the Germans or Swedes about positioning firms for the next decade. Here is how Australian productivity consultant Tom Bevington and University of Melbourne management professor Danny Samson explained the outcome of their analyses in mid-2012:

> "One of the things that has happened in the last 30 years is that business processes have become more complex and this trend is accelerating as a result of outsourcing, off-shoring, service bundling, production extensions. . . . The research behind our book identifies how organizations can, by managing their ever more complex interfaces, lift productivity by about 20 percent quickly and at little or no capital cost and efficiently engage their staff in the delivery."[24]

Weak American Nonfinancial Sector Profits and Investment

Despite the surge in American corporate profits during the Reagan decline as labor and other costs compressed, much of that increase benefited financial firms rather than nonfinancial firms in manufacturing vital to productivity growth. Indeed, as reproduced in Chart 22.3 from Eurostat data, profit margins in the American nonfinancial sector during the boom years after 2000 fell short of margins at nonfinancial firms in northern Europe.

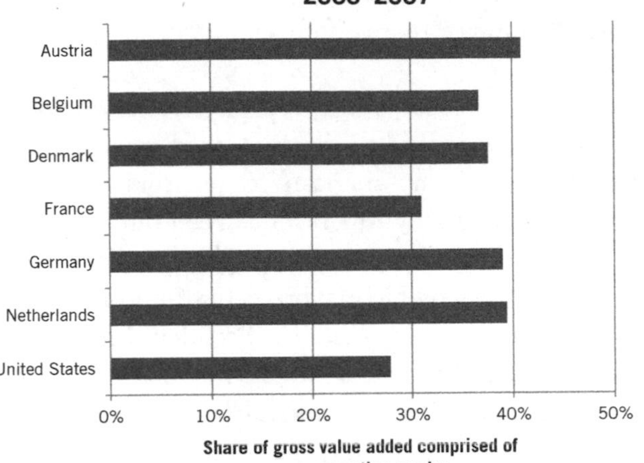

Chart 22.3.

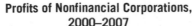

Source: Denis Leythienne and Tatjana Smokova, "Business Profit Share and Investment Rate Higher in the EU Than in the USA," Eurostat 28, table 1, 2009. Bureau of Economic Analysis, US Department of Commerce.

This result to some degree reflects the benefit of codeterminism. Recall that the 2006 analysis by Larry Fauver and Michael Fuerst, reviewed earlier, concluded that returns to shareholders were higher in German firms featuring codeterminism. Their research findings were summarized this way in 2011 by Edith Ginglinger and Timothée Waxin of the Université Paris-Dauphine and William Megginson, a finance professor at the University of Oklahoma: "Fauver and Fuerst show that firms with employee representation are consistently more profitable and are significantly more likely to pay out cash as a dividend than are firms without worker representation. They also find that Tobin's Q is significantly higher for firms with greater employee representation in industries that demand high levels of coordination—principally industries with complex supply chains."[25]

In the same article published in 2011 by the *Journal of Corporate Finance*, Ginglinger, Waxin, and Megginson reached similar results in their study of the impact of codeterminism on French firms, published in 2011 by *The Journal of Corporate Finance*. Their data base was drawn between 1998 and 2008 from a sample of the largest 120 French firms, those comprising the SBF 120 share index.

> "We find that directors elected by employee shareholders increase firm valuation and profitability. . . . This effect is economically significant . . . the marginal impact is comprised between 0.0116 and 0.0172 (an increase of 1.16 percent to 1.72 percent of the ROA), or a 10 percent increase in ROA [return on assets]."[26]

That is quite a significant bonus to shareholders, and is acknowledged and coveted by executive suites. That is why over one-third of German firms had *more* employee representatives on corporate boards than legally required.

Higher corporate and shareholder returns certainly made it easier for northern European enterprises to invest in productivity-enhancing projects at a heavier pace than American competitors during this period. But other factors explain why America has been out-invested during the Reagan decline. One reason is the record budget deficits of President Reagan and his successors which favored consumption over investment. In 1986, for example, Peterson noted that President Reagan's budget deficits drained 90 percent of private-sector savings away from investment.[27] Adding the impact of short-termism featuring strategies like stock buybacks and unwise mergers at the expense of R&D, and the stage was set for a perfect storm, for the decades of chronically poor investment by American firms which followed. Harvard economist Benjamin Friedman explains:

> "The 1980s has been by far the worst period for business investment in physical assets like plant and equipment since World War II. Instead of borrowing to build new facilities or even to build liquidity, the corporate business sector as a whole has mostly used the proceeds of its extraordinary volume of borrowing since 1980 to pay down equity through mergers and acquisitions, leveraged buy-outs, and stock repurchases."[28]

Here is how the frustrated Peterson described the disappointing collapse of investment under his friend Ronald Reagan:

> "After a decade of worry about our low level of net private domestic investment (6.9 percent of GNP from 1970–1979) . . . we wanted the 1980s to be a farsighted decade of thrift, healthy balance sheets, and accelerating capital formation. Result: we ended up with by far the weakest net investment effort in our postwar history (averaging 4.7 percent of GNP from 1980–1986) and have acquiesced in the crumbling of our infrastructure. . . . This is, quite simply, the dirty little secret of Reaganomics: Behind the pleasurable observation that real US consumption per worker has risen by $3,100 over the current decade lies the unpleasant reality that only $950 of this extra annual consumption has been paid for by growth in what each of us produces; the other $2,150 has been funded by cuts in domestic investment and by a widening river of foreign debt."[29]

Except for the sober Clinton Presidency, that same trend persisted throughout the Reagan decline. Not only has American investment been subpar, too much was malinvestment as in the Roaring Twenties, investment capital frittered away bidding up the price of assets like technology stocks or housing that merely inflated bubbles in the dot-com and real estate sectors. As Hussman explained in mid-2010:

> "There is little question that we have, for more than a decade, squandered our productive resources in the pursuit of bubbles. Almost unbelievably, real private gross domestic investment is lower today than it was 12 years ago, and much of the gross domestic investment that we have made in the interim has been destroyed in mispriced speculative activity, such as residential construction and commercial real estate development."[30]

The most telling evidence documenting the erosion of US investment is portrayed in Chart 22.4. It reproduces a time series developed by the *Economist* magazine displaying American private-sector gross fixed capital formation during the entire span of the Reagan decline. Hovering at above 13 percent of GDP as the Reagan administration arrived, American private business investment has never recovered from the forces set in motion by voters in that that election. Since then, the US share of capital investment has trended to below 10 percent of GDP, with the peak of each boomlet lower than the previous one. Worse, the two episodic boomlets during the dot-com and housing bubbles were composed mostly of malinvestments, as Hussman notes, and were no more productive than the capital poured into the Roaring Twenties stock market or the Facebook IPO in 2012.

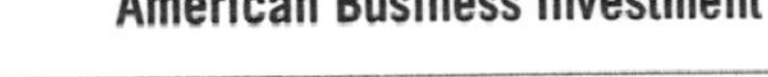

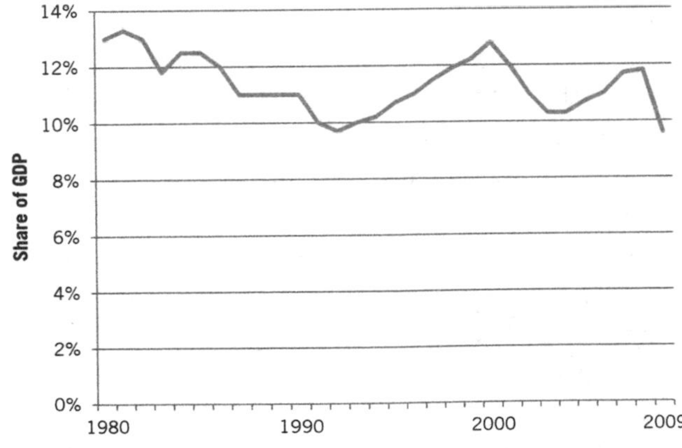

Chart 22.4. Private-sector gross fixed capital formation.
Source: "Show Us the Money," The Economist, July 3, 2010, Bureau of Economic Analysis, US Commerce Department.

Stakeholder Capitalism Out-Invests Reaganomics

A focus on the long term, upskilling, codetermination, robust profits, and vertical two-way intrafirm communication involving work councils are elements of the superior productivity performance of northern Europe. Another element is their superior investment performance. Eurostat and US Bureau of Economic Analysis data from the American boom period beginning in 2000 are reproduced in Chart 22.5 and document that non-financial firms in northern Europe have out-invested American firms.

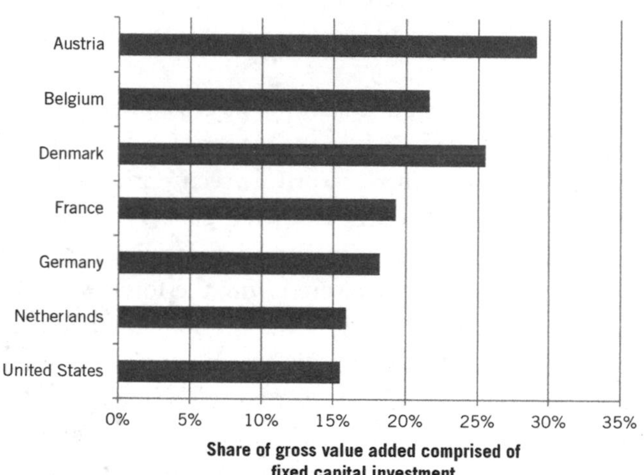

Chart 22.5.

Source: Denis Leythienne and Tatjana Smokova, "Business Profit Share and Investment Rate Higher in the EU Than in the USA," Eurostat 28, table 2, 2009. Bureau of Economic Analysis, US Department of Commerce.

There are other international statistics on gross fixed capital formation that display this same story of an underperforming America compared to northern Europe. One of these statistical series focuses on the *growth rate* of gross fixed capital formation, with OECD statistics reproduced as Chart 22.6. Between 2001 and 2008, annual growth in American gross fixed capital formation averaged less than one percent (.87 percent), while growth rates were multiples of that at firms across northern Europe. The only exception was the export powerhouse Germany, whose industrial base was already in far better shape than the United States in 2001. Because of its resource boom, investment rates in Australia (not shown) were actually a huge ten times American rates over this period. Recall that these data are drawn from an American boom period, when the private sector was flush with cash, flush with high consumer demand, and the excitement of deregulation and unfettered free trade.

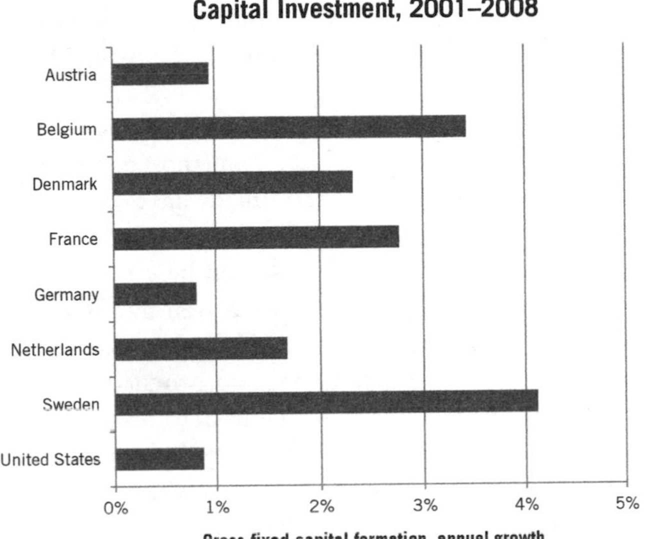

Chart 22.6.
Source: "National Accounts at a Glance," OECD, 2009 edition.

These data also confirm the argument, presented earlier, that taxes have little or no impact on growth or investment. This weak American investment record has occurred despite tax rates on investment capital at historic lows in the United States, and low compared to rates in other nations as well. For some years, US rates have been only 15 percent on assets held longer than one year, while the comparable capital gains tax rate on investment property in Australia, for example, is 50 percent higher (23.25 percent on long-term and 46.5 percent on short-term gains). Yet that nation handily out-invests America. That portrayal is general: the family capitalism countries collect higher taxes from their firms and citizens. Yet they routinely out-invest, pay higher wages, and enjoy higher productivity growth than the United States. Taxes are irrelevant; it is customers that matter.

That reality applies even more forcefully to corporate tax rates. Pleas for lower taxes on profits are a perennial favorite in the business community and their acolytes at the *Wall Street Journal* and among Republican politicians in Washington. The notion is that lower taxes on profits equal more jobs and investment. That claimed nexus has long baffled economists, because taxes on profits make no difference to the costs of conducting business. As Stiglitz notes, profit taxes are applied to profits, the surplus above production costs:

> "If it were profitable to hire a worker or buy a new machine before the tax, it would still be profitable to do so after the tax . . . what is so striking about claims to the contrary is that they fly in the face of elementary economics: no investment, no job that was profitable before the tax increase, will be unprofitable afterward."[31]

The disconnect between investment, jobs, and corporate tax rates is most evident when it comes to the largest and most competitive US firms, which tend to be multinationals. They already have complete freedom to juggle revenues and costs to land profits in tax havens.

Do not mistake the arguments presented here for codetermination, work councils, and the like as primarily driven by notions of fairness. The stakes for Americans are much graver than considerations of equity. As we see next, the dismal investment and productivity performances that are hallmarks of the Reagan decline have also caused a notable deindustrialization of the American economy. It is simply impossible to conjure a bright economic future for America when the number of high-value jobs is not rising and firms are being out-invested by the margins just noted by international competitors.

CHAPTER 23

DEINDUSTRIALIZING AMERICA MARKS THE REAGAN DECLINE

"The progression of an economy such as America's from agriculture to manufacturing to services is a natural change."[1]

RONALD REAGAN

"A strong manufacturing sector is not a requisite for a prosperous economy."[2]

New York Stock Exchange, 1984

"The US de-emphasized technology. Our economy tilted instead toward the quicker profits of financial services. . . . The United States ranks last among major manufacturers in export intensity. . . ."[3]

JEFFREY R. IMMELT,
CEO, General Electric

"When you're manufacturing anything, even if the work is done by robots and machines, there's an incredible value chain involved. Manufacturing is simply this huge engine of job creation."[4]

SUSAN HOCKFIELD,
President, MIT

"A key difference between the US and Germany is the power of the financial sector is much more limited. The circulation of funds for investment is much more driven by the strategies of business than the profit-making interest of financiers."[5]

GARY HERRIGEL,
University of Chicago

American manufacturing hegemony lasted 110 years, little more than a century.[6] Its dominance in high-value services, such as engineering and computer design, was even shorter.

This chapter begins with a cautionary tale from history. Two grand economic empires have collapsed since the sixteenth century and America is exhibiting some of their characteristics. In its erosion of manufacturing, the Reagan decline certainly resembles the British Edwardian decline a century ago. But the most accurate analogy is the European Habsburgs. The first truly global economic empire was the Habsburgs, whose economic dominance ran throughout Europe and stretched from Latin America past Goa to the Philippines beginning in the sixteenth century, including expansive trade with South Asia and China. Its windfall of precious metals from modern-day Bolivia powered the empire and collateralized enormous credit creation. Until the Reagan-era credit bubble increased American public and private debt tenfold, Habsburg silver and borrowings had produced by far the greatest cash bonanza in world history, fueling the most lavish court ever, acquisitive wars in Europe, and imports of luxuries from across the globe. Indeed, so robust was the global Habsburg trade that about one-half of all the silver mined in South America eventually made its way to the cashboxes of Chinese merchants.[7]

That wealth and credit distorted the Spanish economy, inflation eroding real incomes. And innovation suffered as the clever and ambitious were deflected from improving the domestic investment base, decamping to seek windfall colonial fortunes. As the historian Timothy H. Parsons noted,

> "Although they dominated Europe from the mid-sixteenth century to mid-seventeenth centuries, they could not translate the wealth of the Americas into sustainable power in Europe. It may seem nonsense that the enormous wealth of the overseas empire would be of so little benefit to Spain, but hindsight clearly shows that plunder and extraction had toxic consequences in the imperial metropole."[8]

This history is being replayed by America, although the debt binge of the Reagan decline is optimistically not going to end in serial bankruptcies as it did for Philip II (in 1557, 1560, 1575, and again in 1596). Even so, the Reagan decline has seen the greatest credit bubble in history, diminishing manufacturing and inducing widespread windfall-seeking by America's clever and ambitious. It has even featured extraction of a sort, with the deregulated banking industry mining customers, families, and even taxpayers, using the tools made available by credit creation and deregulation to conduct opaque financial engineering. Like Hapsburg Spain, record wealth has been redistributed during the Reagan decline to enrich relatively few, while weakening the American metropole, especially the high-value technical services sector and industrial foundation that made the twentieth century the American century.

The Financialization of America

That portion of the American economy composed of financial engineering by Alan Greenspan's pollinators was 8.3 percent of GDP in 2011, surpassing health care to be the second largest sector. Only the share of value added by manufacturing at 12.2 percent is larger. The trend lines are moving in the wrong direction. Since 1980, the value added by finance and insurance has increased by 3.5 percentage points as a share of GDP while the manufacturing share has declined 7.8 percentage points. Finance and insurance has already become the largest when measured by profits. Its share of US corporate profits has risen from around 16 percent at the election of President Reagan to over 40 percent in some recent years. In contrast, the profit share from manufacturing has slumped to a *de minimus* 10 or 12 percent.

Easy credit and especially deregulation hastened growth in the financial sector, featuring rising bank leverage, opaque off-balance-sheet entities, and abuse of borrowers. The Harvard banking expert Kenneth Rogoff argues that this growth occurred because deregulation created vast new—if risky—opportunities for the financial sector to speculate: "How could financial services be a third of the economy? And the answer was that it was taking much bigger risks that it should have."[9] Peter Boone of the London School of Economics and Simon Johnson also finger deregulation:

> "Before 1935 and after 1980, however, the Fed's financial regulation was and has been weak. At the heart of this weakness are the large profits that can be earned by taking advantage of lax regulation in the financial sector."[10]

Johnson of MIT argues that this invidious deregulation during the Reagan decline was rooted in the divinity of market fundamentalism:

> "In a society that celebrates the idea of making money, it was easy to infer that the interests of the financial sector were the same as the interest of the country—and that the financial sector knew better what was good for America than did the career civil servants in Washington. Faith in free financial markets grew into conventional wisdom—trumpeted on the editorial pages of the *Wall Street Journal* and the floor of Congress."[11]

Rising remuneration and profits in finance lured intellectual and financial assets from manufacturing. Some 58 percent of Harvard male graduates and 43 percent of female graduates from the class of 2007 took jobs in finance or consulting, uninterested in manufacturing or start-ups in Silicon Valley.[12] And the lure of Wall Street, rather than manufacturing, is such that the United States now ranks only twenty-seventh among the twenty-nine richest democracies in the share of college students studying engineering or science, as determined you may recall by the National Academies of Sciences.[13] *Washington Post* columnist Steven Pearlstein explains:

> "No longer is it the entrepreneurial capitalism of Google or Amazon and Nucor Steel that animates the American imagination—it is the financial capitalism of Enron and Drexel Burnham Lambert, of Goldman Sachs and the Blackstone Group, of publicly traded real estate investment trusts and multibillion-dollar hedge funds."[14]

Benjamin Friedman of Harvard adds that:

> "For years, much of the best young talent in the Western world has gone to private financial firms. While some part of what they do helps to allocate our investment capital more effectively, much of their activity adds no economic value. The largest individual returns seem to flow to those whose job is to ensure that microscopically small deviations . . . persist for only one millisecond instead of three. . . . At the level of the aggregate economy, we are wasting one of our most precious resources. While some part of what they do helps to allocate our investment capital more effectively, much of their activity adds little to economic value."[15]

An Enlarged Financial Sector Slows Growth

Economists since Bagehot and Schumpeter have realized that a sound and robust financial system is vital for economic growth, but needlessly large financial sectors are another situation entirely. Analyses performed by economists in recent years have concluded that a financial sector can become so large as to destabilize and slow—rather than nurture—economic growth. Research by John Joseph Wallis of the University of Maryland found that countries that grow the best over time are precisely those, such as Australia or Germany, that avoid Reaganesque financial gyrations.[16]

His conclusions were confirmed by economists Jean Louis Arcand of the Graduate Institute in Geneva, Enrico Berkes of the IMF, and Ego Panizza of the United Nations, drawing on a trove of global data beginning in 1976. They determined that overly large financial sectors due to weak regulation can drive economies into a volatile red zone characterized by speculative credit bubbles swelling and bursting:

> "Marginal effects of financial development on output growth become negative when credit to the private sector surpasses 110 percent of GDP."[17]

Iceland, the United States, Ireland, Portugal, Spain, and the United Kingdom were adoptees of financial deregulation—and each has struggled to attain solid growth in the years since unharnessing the financial sector. Their conclusion that growth suffers from bloated financial sectors is also consistent with research by Subal C. Kumbhakar and George Mavrotas under auspices of the World Institute for Development Economics Research in Helsinki. Their 2005 global analysis highlighted the benefits of a mature financial sector to developing economies, but also comfirmed that a bloated finance sector poses harm for developed economies such as the United States. Specifically, they determined that a ten-percentage point increase in their financial-sector development index was predictive of a decline in GDP growth by 0.5 percent.[18] Finally, I hark back to the earlier noted research by Moritz Schularick and Alan M. Taylor, along with the studies of Reinhart and Rogoff, which determined that the aftermath of a banking crisis can slow growth for up to a decade. Now you see why Benjamin Friedman of Harvard has concluded, "Overmighty finance levies a tithe on growth."[19]

Finance Deregulation Reduced Productivity

These analyses form the weight of evidence that financial deregulation, when coupled with the other features of Reaganomics such as short-termism, account for the drop in American productivity growth rates. It would be strange indeed to think otherwise, to seriously entertain the notion that productivity is enhanced by a business sector prospering due to risky speculation, credit booms and busts, betting against customers, insider trading, Ponzi schemes, computerized arbitrage, and illegally front running clients (by placing bets immediately before placing their customer bets). Its prosperity has come at the expense of American society, draining resources from sectors characterized by innovation and real engineering. Sustained and robust productivity growth year after year is scarcely likely from a sector where output is highly volatile, risky behavior is routine, time horizons are measured in months, and income is highly skewed and gyrates wildly.

In 2009, former Fed chairman Paul Volcker famously dismissed financial engineering, asserting that ATMs were the most useful financial innovation of the past 30 years. "I wish that somebody would give me some shred of neutral evidence about the relationship between financial innovation recently and the growth of the economy."[20] *Financial Times* columnist Wolfgang Münchau in December 2009 agreed with his theme:

> "We know that financial innovation, in combination with macroeconomic imbalances, produces bubbles. But there is not a shred of evidence, theoretical or empirical, that the financial instruments invented in the past 10 years produce sustainable growth."[21]

Alan Greenspan couldn't do it, acknowledging the absence of such evidence justifying his policies in a *Financial Times* column of his own in March 2011. Deciding belatedly to seek a factual basis for his deregulation covenant, Greenspan admitted the need "to address the as-yet unproved tie between the degree of financial complexity and higher standards of living."[22]

Greenspan is wrong. There *is* a tie, but it's a negative one, as scholars like Wallis documented. And US statistics document the harm from deregulation on productivity. Phyllis Otto, supervisory economist at the Bureau of Labor Statistics, explained in August 2005 that productivity in the financial services sector has traditionally grown at about the same rate as the entire business sector. That means the (smaller Wall Street) of yesteryear was neither a contributor nor liability to American productivity growth. That traditional pattern was altered by Greenspan, and the financial sector swelled to become a drag on productivity, and thus on GDP growth. From 1997 to 2008, productivity growth in the nonfinancial business sector averaged nearly one percentage point higher (.95 of 1 percent) than when the financial sector is also included in the statistics.[23]

Reaganomics Incentivizes Deindustrialization

Like nineteenth-century economic Darwinians such as Andrew Carnegie, today's banking sector and the business community generally argue that their narcissism is divinely ordained by the marketplace. But the outcomes we are reviewing make their claims as specious as that of medieval British monarchs who claimed a divine right to govern ("Dieu et mon droit"). The Glorious Revolution of 1688 that overthrew King James II, the American and French Revolutions, and philosophers such as the great John Locke changed this age-old iron law, arguing the startling presumption that economic and political sovereignty rests with you and me, not elites wearing business suits or royal purple.

Allowing economic sovereignty to rest with the business sector has proven lethal to the US industrial base, evidenced by the loss to China and Germany of the historic American prowess and advantage in manufacturing output and exports. Manufacturing in each of those competitors comprises one-quarter of their GDPs, double the US share. And despite having a GDP barely 40 percent as large, China's factories outproduce American ones. Germany is close behind.

Washington stood aside as manufacturing and high-value services such as engineering design became *passé,* President Reagan believing it to be some sort of natural evolution. Along with other US firms, Hewlett-Packard, Apple, and Dell became domestic marketing and design shells, offshoring manufacturing and R&D. Alan Greenspan best expressed the equanimity of Ayn Rand's acolytes in the face of deindustrialization, demeaning manufacturing as "something we were terrific at fifty years ago . . . essentially a nineteenth- and twentieth-century technology."[24] Business professor Brad Jensen of Georgetown University's McDonough School later added, "We need to be clear-eyed: manufacturing is not really where the US comparative advantage lies."[25]

That would be news to Germans. Their superior corporate governance, product quality, and innovation fuel a more competitive economy, despite paying $10 an hour higher wages. They likely think Reaganomics is a grand system—for their manufacturing competitors to adopt. That nation has surpassed America as an exporter of industrial goods even though its unit labor costs rose 41 percent between 2002 and 2010, while they fell 11 percent in America.[26] Superior management, human capital investments, the small labor component of industrial costs, and rising productivity more than offset rising wages. Contrary to sentiments of America's merchants and master manufacturers, the quality of executives and the incentive structure they confront are more determinant of enterprise prospects than labor costs.

The problem for American families is this: what Reaganomics portrays as the antiquated practice of manufacturing computers or engineering design is at the heart of growing productivity. Greenspan and his colleagues are mistaken. Deindustrialization is certainly not an inevitable evolution, in light of the experience of Germany or Japan that had only modest manufacturing sectors two generations ago. As recently as 1998, Germany had a trade deficit of $5.9 billion. Yet, by 2011, its surplus was $170 billion, with manufacturing responsible for the metamorphosis. That elicits only a shrug from American executives, eyes firm set on next quarter's earnings per share. As *Washington Post* columnist Harold Meyerson notes:

> "The decline of American manufacturing has saddled us not only with a seemingly permanent negative balance of trade, but with a business community less and less concerned with America's productive capacities."[27]

Sagging Trade Balances and Job Loss

A signal indicator of economic prowess is trade balances in manufacturing. The US balance began to deteriorate in the 1980s. In 1980, for example, the United States had a trade surplus in manufactured goods of $17 billion. Just seven years later, that had deteriorated to a deficit of $137 billion, including an unprecedented deficit in high-technology goods. In the years since, Americans have not quite turned to taking in each others' wash, although relying on an economy where finance is expanding and manufacturing weakening to create broadly based wealth has the same outcome.

Turning to high-technology goods specifically, the United States enjoyed a trade surplus from World War II through 2000; by 2007, it had flipped to a deficit of $53.6 billion. A second example is the deterioration in manufactured machine tools, which used to be another American strength. Despite a home field advantage, too many US machine tool fabricators underperformed in the last several decades. The result? Foreign producers accounted for more than 90 percent of metal-forming machine tool and plastics-forming machinery sales in the United States in 2007. A third example is electrical equipment. America is the home of GE, yet importers now supply about two-thirds of the US market for turbines, generators, a host of electric components, and computer storage equipment. The picture is the same in higher-valued services, where technology is devised and refined, translating innovation into goods and services yielding productivity gains.[28]

The erosion is also reflected in manufacturing employment, which peaked at 19,426,000 in 1979 on the eve of President Reagan's election. There was a 41 percent decline in manufacturing jobs thereafter, to fewer than 11,500,000 by early 2010, before turning up a bit with the recovery. Manufacturing employment was actually lower in 2009 than in 1941 prior to Pearl Harbor, or in any year in between.

The thinning out of manufacturing employment was intense. Writing about the middle years (1984–1986) of the Reagan administration, Peter Peterson noted:

> "Over the past three years America's import deluge has resulted in pink slips for one to two million domestic manufacturing workers each year. More than a third of them remain indefinitely out of work; more than half of the rest have taken pay cuts of 30 to 50 percent in new jobs that cannot make use of their experience."[29]

In that same year, Paul Kennedy prophetically wrote:

> "In terms of commercial expertise, levels of training and education, efficiency of production, standards of income . . . the 'number-one' power of 1900 seemed to be losing its position, with dire implications for the country's long-term strategic position."[30]

Employment in manufacturing is cyclical, but each upturn in the macroeconomy during the Reagan decline has featured disproportionate job loss in the manufacturing sector. During the recent recession, manufacturing employment fell nearly 29 percent through October 2009, over *five-fold faster* than the pace of job loss across all sectors.[31] Once such jobs are gone, as economist Nancy Folbre explained earlier, firms have mostly proven loathe to recreate high-value manufacturing jobs at home, and thus the losses become permanent. Any new jobs are low-wage ones in today's two-tier manufacturing pay structure. Higher wages in China are encouraging some reshoring now, with Boston Consulting touting a survey a year or so ago that larger multinationals are reexamining domestic US manufacturing. And, the *Economist* examined this encouraging trend in a special report in January 2013. As an aside, it importantly noted that the trend of "Reshoring is largely an American phenomenon," because relatively little offshoring is undertaken by European firms.[32] Intriguingly, Google's Nexus Q product is being manufactured in Silicon Valley as in the days of yore (the 1970s), and even Apple may return some jobs to the United States.[33] Ideally, these dribs and drabs will become a torrent. Even then, a huge problem would remain: there is no evidence that reshoring boosts wages in the manufacturing sector.

Lost Multiplier Impacts

Manufacturing jobs are coveted as the heart of a robust economy because they are more productive and better paying than most other jobs. But they are also particularly valuable because they have a direct multiplier impact on job creation, sustaining a number of jobs in affiliated industries. In analyses documenting such effects, like the OECD's *Economic Surveys: United States 2012*, economists refer to this phenomenon as "agglomeration and knowledge spillover benefits from manufacturing activity."[34] The effect is pronounced. As reproduced in Table 6, every new steel industry job in America, for example, has traditionally created nearly 12 additional jobs in management, marketing, shipping, parts, fuel production, and so forth. About five new ancillary jobs are created by every single new auto plant or innovation industry job.

Ancillary Jobs Created by New Manufacturing, Design, and Innovation Jobs

For each new job in this sector ...	these new ancillary jobs are created
Computer system design services	1.12
Hospital	0.67
Innovation industry[1]	5.00
Motor vehicle manufacturing	4.71
Retailing	0.24
Steel manufacturing	11.89

Table 6.

[1] Innovation industry includes: information technology, medical R&D, engineering, and digital design.

Source: Charles Duhigg and Keith Bradsher, "How US Lost Out on iPhone Work," New York Times, Jan. 22, 2012. Eduardo Porter, "The Promise of Today's Factory Jobs," New York Times, April 4, 2012.

In recent decades, harm from the sharp deterioration in the American manufacturing trade balance has been modulated by the expansion of good jobs in services. A number of these jobs pay better than factory work and are in what economists like Enrico Moretti at the University of California, Berkeley refer to as the innovation industry. These are service firms designing or managing software, medical R&D, telecom applications, and the like. New jobs in vibrant firms such as Facebook have a muscular multiplier profile similar to manufacturing. Moretti has concluded, for example, that each innovation industry job creates five others, including two that are highly paid professional slots.[35] It also presumably means that firms such as Apple that shift jobs back to America would generate hundreds of thousands of highly valued jobs in addition to those directly onshored.

The benefits of reindustrializing America seem evident, but the erosion is far advanced. Here is how Rolf Langhammer, vice president of the Kiel Institute for the World Economy, described the US plight in 2010:

> "In many cases, companies that are based in the US can't survive on the global market because they don't have the innovative products or the qualified workforce required to develop them. . . . The crucial thing is that a country must be well positioned with the range of goods that it wants to export. The US is still lagging well behind in that aspect."[36]

Here is the assessment *Handelsblatt* editor Gabor Steingart penned when American manufacturing was still 17 percent of GDP (it's below 13 percent now):

> "Undoubtedly superior United States doesn't exist anymore. As a center of power, it is still more powerful than others, but for some years now that energy has been flowing in the opposite direction. . . . The world's greatest exporter became its greatest importer. The most important creditor became the most important debtor. Today, foreigners dispose of assets in the United States with a net value of $2.5 trillion, or 21 percent of gross domestic product. . . . Neither laziness nor the obvious American penchant for consumerism can be blamed for this changed reality in America. US industry—or at least what little is left of it—is responsible. In the span of only a few decades, US industry has shrunken to half what it once was. It makes up only 17 percent of the country's GDP, compared to 26 percent in Europe. Every important national economy in the world now exports to the United States without purchasing an equivalent amount of US goods in return."[37]

Observers like these know what economic historian Kevin Phillips glumly noted in 2008 about America's hopes for a substantial manufacturing revival:

> "Financialization has a long record of being an unhealthy late stage in the trajectory of previous leading world economy powers. . . . No previous leading world economic power has enjoyed a full-fledged manufacturing renaissance after becoming unduly enamored of finance."[38]

Recall the analogies drawn earlier between the Reagan decline and the sunsetting of Spanish and English economic empires? In manufacturing, America looks to keen observers as merely a grander version of the nineteenth-century Edwardian decline of England. In both the United Kingdom and America, the sunset was not in absolute measures but rather in relative position to global competitors, and notably marked by swooning productivity growth. In contrast, northern Europe is more attune to manufacturing, exemplified by Germany. The production of cars, machine tools, rapid rail systems, computers, and the like has swelled to become major drivers of GDP growth there. Many of her exports are manufactured goods with best-in-class reputations. The explanation is codetermination and the absence of Reaganomics enabling enterprises to out-invest US firms while paying higher wages and sustaining a domestic economy replete with high-value jobs. Here is the *Washington Post* columnist Harold Meyerson:

> "In Germany, manufacturing still dominates finance, which is why Germany has been the world's leader in exports. German capitalism didn't succumb to the financialization that swept the United States. . . . Company managers set long-term policies while market pressures for short-term profits are held in check. The focus on long-term performance over short-term gain is reinforced by Germany's stakeholder, rather than shareholder, model of capitalism. . . . German companies are among the world's most competitive in their financial viability and the quality of their products."[39]

Deindustrialization is one tell of America's Reagan decline, and another is slowing innovation.

Reaganomics Has Weakened Innovation

It was a goose-bump moment, one that exemplified the most unique attribute of Americans, a relentless drive to innovative and willingness to take risks. History will likely never record another transformational epoch of innovative genius such as the eighteenth-century Midlands, but Silicon Valley runs a close second. Yet innovation isn't cheap and—far, far worse—it isn't linear. That means government support is vital.

Parsing protein folding is an exemplary public good, a vital key to plumbing diseases. And for years, medical researchers have desperately sought solutions to puzzles like the three-dimensional protein structure of the retroviral protease contributing to AIDs. But it proved too complex for Silicon Valley to unravel despite aggressive support from the national treasure called the Defense Advanced Research Projects Agency (DARPA). The puzzle went unsolved for fifteen frustrating years, until DARPA figured out a solution. No, not the answer, just the solution.

They configured the challenge into an online puzzle video game called Fold.it and crowdsourced it to let global gamers figure it out (ask your teenage son or daughter). Nearly an infinite universe of tiny interactions: a perfect puzzle. A perfect game.

MSNBC reports it took the gamers ten days in September 2011 to solve it.[40]

Innovation is the lifeblood of economic growth and future prosperity. Here is how Thomas Mason, director of the Oak Ridge National Laboratory, and Persis Drell, director of the SLAC National Accelerator laboratory atop Sand Hill Road overlooking Stanford, explained its importance:

> "Fully half of US economic growth since 1945 can be attributed to investments in science and technology. . . . Innovation—not trade policy or labor costs—is the most important factor in global economic competitiveness and continued American prosperity."[41]

This statement clarifies why the narcissistic American business community that prioritizes mergers, stock buybacks, and quarterly earnings over R&D is America's Achilles heel, deemphasizing innovation, which, ". . . is the most important factor in global economic competitiveness and continued American prosperity."

Public support for science R&D through entities such as DARPA has historically been a critical accelerant to innovation. American policy since the 1930s has been to supplement private-sector R&D, because such private spending exhibits an important market failure: the yawning gap between the smaller return to an individual enterprise from R&D and the larger return to society from that same research.

This gap was extensively evaluated by technologists at the Washington-based Center for Strategic and International Studies in 1996. Indeed, various researchers have concluded that social returns from private-sector R&D are from two to seven times greater than the returns to the business sector alone. Public supplements for private-sector R&D is the most efficient way to bridge this gap and reap those higher returns, thereby more rapidly expanding the technology frontier.[42] Indeed, the National Science Foundation has estimated that from 20 to 50 percent of American GDP is linked to innovative technologies such as the computer, advances most efficiently, and perhaps only brought to fruition with public-private collaboration.[43] No firm could justify investing in the Internet decades ago, for example, which is why government support to divine, devise, and especially to commercialize Arpanet proved vital.*

Because innovation isn't linear, the entire frontier of technology needs to be continually plumbed for breakouts like the internet. Yet, Reaganomics has imposed two significant hurdles in the path of American innovation: deindustrialization, which has empowered offshoring of R&D, and short-termism, which has harmed US private-sector R&D itself and incentivized its export.

The Offshoring of Innovation

Financialization of the United States along with offshoring has shrunk the expanse of the technology frontier being explored domestically. Firms such as Apple, selling tens of millions of iPhones and iPads to Americans, have moved too much of their technology R&D and production base abroad. Considerable innovation occurs in the manufacturing process, which is why research centers typically are located in proximity to production. That vital synergism is lost to America when firms offshore or they mimic the Apple business model. Indeed, economists Yuqing Xing and Neal Detert at the Asian Development Bank in 2010 documented that America's high-tech firms routinely offshore production of even the most advanced products, along with associated R&D and high-value jobs, to low-wage platforms such as China.[44] That pattern adds another troubling dimension to the Apple problem as noted earlier.

In some instances, this offshoring involves technologies recently supported by the US government, spending that should instead benefit American employees and taxpayers who funded the research. For example, the synergistic combination of resources from academia, industry, and the federal government created the semiconductor industry and its later spinoffs, including renewable-energy technology, the World Wide Web, and LED-lighting industries in the United States. But much of the related production and services, in these and other fields in the years since, has been offshored to Asia, despite the large investments made by American taxpayers.

The offshoring of R&D by American firms is well advanced. GE's biggest health-care research center in the world is in Bangalore. Nearby, Cisco has spent $1 billion on its alternative global headquarters. The biggest Microsoft R&D center outside of Redmond, WA, is in Beijing.

*The Pentagon funded the Arpanet network, whose technology then-Senator Al Gore legislatively insisted (in 1991) be revealed to the public, overruling the Department of Defense. It is uncertain if the Internet would exist without government seed money and Gore's action to open the new technology.

In 2009, Applied Materials opened its largest research center in Xian. Moreover, contractors to firms such as Apple in these low-wage platforms, dissatisfied with mere fabrication, are engineering new products, funding start-ups, and seizing more control over the critical design stage. Judy Estrin, chief technology officer at Cisco, for example, notes that basic technologies for the iPad or the Facebook social network are increasingly being developed abroad, shrinking the stock of innovation in the domestic pipeline now.[45]

These trends have helped propel Chinese scientists to author the second highest number of peer-reviewed papers in international journals, and to trail only innovators in America, Japan, and Germany in filings with the Munich-based European Patent office in 2011.[46] Here is how the *Economist* described this new world:

> "The world's creative energy is shifting to the developing countries, which are becoming innovators in their own right rather than just talented imitators. . . . Emerging economies are not merely challenging that lead in innovation. They are unleashing a wave of low-cost, disruptive innovations that will, as they spread to the rich world, shake many industries to their foundations."[47]

Technology transfer from the United States in combination with indigenous R&D explains how China has been able to export more high-technology goods than the United States since 2004. In a 2009 *Harvard Business Review* article, Gary Pisano and Willy Shin reviewed that process. "When one industry moves, there can be other industries in the future that follow it that you couldn't even anticipate." They concluded that offshoring of R&D and the ensuing technology development abroad tied to it has darkened US growth prospects.[48] Moreover, the deindustrialization characteristic of the Reagan decline is especially debilitating to research because manufacturing firms innovate much more than do service firms. Manufacturing employs a disproportionate share of US scientists and engineers, for example, and some 68 percent of R&D spending by the business community comes from manufacturers.[49]

Reaganomics: American Innovation Prospects Reduced to 43rd Among Global Leaders

Quarterly capitalism is a cudgel, punishing firms that divert cash flow to long-term investments, and making R&D and innovation a luxury too few choose to afford. Moreover, the short-termism of Reaganomics has settled into domestic research labs, truncating research time horizons.

Silicon Valley experts agree. Judy Estrin traced the transition toward short-term, rather than long-term, investments there in her 2008 book, *Closing the Innovation Gap*. She explains that America's cutting edge in innovation—venture capitalists, innovators, and technology wizards—have been supplanted by bankers who focus on starting new companies only in order to flip them; they seek quick profit rather than nurturing them and the underlying technologies for success in the longer term. "Starting in 1998," she wrote, "there was such a shift in Silicon Valley toward chasing money and short-term returns."[50]

Eroding domestic innovation from deindustrialization, offshoring, and short-termism is well documented. Once the leaders, miserly US firms now devote less (measured as a share of GDP) to civilian scientific R&D than competitors including France, Japan, Korea, Denmark, or Finland. The share of university R&D financed by German industry, for example, is double the 6 percent share funded by US industry.[51] And between 1999 and 2006, US firms increased R&D spending by 3 percent while South Korean firms increased spending by 58 percent, Finnish firms by 28 percent and German firms by 11 percent.[52]

Moreover, government civilian R&D has become collateral damage of the starve-the-beast syndrome, with Republican politicians concentrating their small-government efforts on discretionary nondefense spending. With other rich democracies keenly aware of the value of R&D, the consequences were easily predictable: in 2009, for the first time, more foreign entrepreneurs and scientists were awarded US patents than Americans.[53]

As an aside, government infrastructure investment is also being starved. American railroads and highways are ranked twentieth in quality behind Taiwan, Malaysia, and France; its ports rank twenty-third, behind Estonia and Namibia; and its airports rank thirty-first, behind Singapore and the Czech Republic.[54] And the future promises worse. The American tax burden is easily the lowest among rich democracies. Yet resource deprivation has darkened the future of US innovation, especially the key sectors of high-value services and manufacturing, as observers such as Edward Luce of the *Financial Times* have explained.[55] The evidence comes from the international Information Technology and Innovation Foundation. In 2009, it ranked America only sixth in the world in innovation competitiveness, based on sixteen encompassing indicators. And that snap-shot is the good news; the Foundation also projected future performance by examining factors that determine prospective innovation, including the pace and trendlines of human capital investment and R&D. Burdened by starve-the-beast policies harming government R&D

and elements of Reaganomics, such as short-termism harming corporate R&D, the Foundation in July 2011 ranked the United States *next to last* of the forty-four nations and regions examined as a competitive innovator in the future.[56]

That respected global analysis is a stark tell of the Reagan decline, robbing you today and your children tomorrow. A darkening national economic future will be the most lasting legacy of this era. And some of the most visionary minds in Silicon Valley agree, including Paul Otellini, former Intel CEO:

> "Unfortunately, long-term investments in education, research, digital technology, and human capital have been steadily declining in the US. So too has the commitment to policies that made us such an entrepreneurial powerhouse for more than a century. This is the bitter truth and we don't hear enough about it."[57]

The rather startling Foundation ranking is a harbinger. Panglossian supporters of Reaganomics seem to believe that American wage stagnation and deindustrialization can be redeemed with heavier doses of deregulation and tax cuts. The Apple business model proves that to be a mirage. International innovation experts at the Foundation and elsewhere know it.

The Foundation warning marks an appropriate spot to summarize where we are. It is disheartening. Households are beset by stagnant wages and employment insecurity, reduced economic mobility, the national embarrassment of a multigenerational poverty cycle, and darkening futures. Corporations are beset with managers who have survived the Darwinian competition to be the fittest at maximizing quarterly earnings. And the public sector is beset by resource deprivation. The seminal features of the Reagan decline at a macroeconomic level are just as discouraging:

- relatively weak investment, R&D, and innovation
- the commoditization of employees and squandering of human capital at the worksite
- offshoring of high-value jobs rather than upskilling to counter globalization
- the Apple Problem in which high-value jobs supplying the US market are established in low-wage platforms

- erosion in relative industrial performance
- trade policies that encourage offshoring rather than incentivize onshoring

It doesn't require a degree in economics to figure out the unsettling implications of the Reagan decline on America's macroeconomic capabilities.

Weak Investment Has Lowered America's Growth Potential

A nation's potential growth rate is reduced when the business community prioritizes short-term windfalls and discounts the future, investing less than its competitors. Business investment has dwindled to a 40-year low and continuation of this unsettling decline seems guaranteed in the decades ahead. Investment will surely respond a bit when the recovery accelerates. But the expectation of a weak trend line ahead in investment reflects the structural nature of short-termism and other antigrowth features of Reaganomics responsible for weak investment since 1980. Here is how *Washington Post* columnist Steven Pearlstein described the US investment situation during the recovery in July 2010:

> "Right now they are sitting on more cash than they know what to do with, thanks to strong profits, depreciation that exceeds new investment, and meager spending on researching, developing, and marketing new products. . . . We know that financial markets have become particularly risk-averse, ready to punish any company that makes investments in long-term growth that might negatively impact short-term profits. We know that, during the bubble years, companies misallocated capital—buying up their own stock, making overpriced acquisitions, overpaying executives, and bidding up financial assets. That money could have been used to develop new products and new markets."[58]

No economist envisages a resurgent American economy improving its international competitiveness and the quality of its jobs, while investing and innovating less than its competitors. Nor is a brighter future to follow from the Reagan-era strategy of engineering prosperity with credit bubbles, productivity only an afterthought. The weakening of American capital investment has had quite serious long-term effects on productivity growth. Accordingly, experts have adjusted their projections.

Here is the current situation: The uptick noted earlier in American productivity from the IT revolution has dissipated, and productivity growth has sagged back to its long term trend line in recent years. Even the business community is uneasy about this return to the weak productivity performance characteristic of the Reagan era. Here is how one study funded by the Business Roundtable put it in 2009:

> "US productivity growth in the nonfarm business sector has decelerated since 2002—to annual rates in 2005–2007 of just 1.7, 1.0, and 1.4 percent, respectively. There is now greater uncertainty about the underlying structural rate of US productivity growth, with commensurate greater concern of slipping back to slow rates of the pre-1995 generation."[59]

The American dean of productivity, Robert J. Gordon, had initially decided that long-term US productivity growth would simply return to its low Reagan-era trajectory, just as the Business Roundtable speculated. In a March 2010 analysis for the National Bureau of Economic Research, Gordon concluded that US productivity growth between now and 2027 will settle at a long-term average of just 1.7 percent a year.[60]

Within two years, however, that projection proved outdated and optimistic. Annual labor productivity growth averaged only 1.3 percent annually from 2004–2012, and Gordon concluded it was not likely to improve. In August 2011, he published a more sobering update for NBER that projected even lower per capita growth rates in the future, likely just one percent for virtually all Americans. Gordon identified six causal factors responsible for weakening productivity and innovation, including rising college costs, sagging education performance, and the national debt overhang.[61]

This news is especially troubling, because Gordon's research is emerging as a consensus. There are some more pessimistic forecasts, including one by economist Jeremy Grantham in November 2012.[62] The Congressional Budget Office (CBO) is slightly more optimistic, but is convinced, like Gordon, that the weak Reagan-era outcome will persist. Their nonpartisan experts expect the future maximum potential productivity growth rate to range around the 1.4–1.5 percent level, a rate barely one-half the level during the golden age.[63]

When combined with slowing population growth, the consequence of this mediocre productivity outlook is to significantly lower the ceiling on potential growth in US GDP. During the golden age, robust investment led to robust productivity growth, with America's potential GDP growth ceiling averaging 3.9 percent from 1950–1973, as reproduced in Chart 23.1 from CBO statistics. But as investment and innovation dwindled in the Reagan decline, productivity growth descended to a lower plane, reducing the ceiling on potential GDP growth to an average of 2.3 percent from 2002–2011. Through at least 2017, the CBO is projecting a continued decline in the GDP growth ceiling to only 2 percent due to weakening productivity.

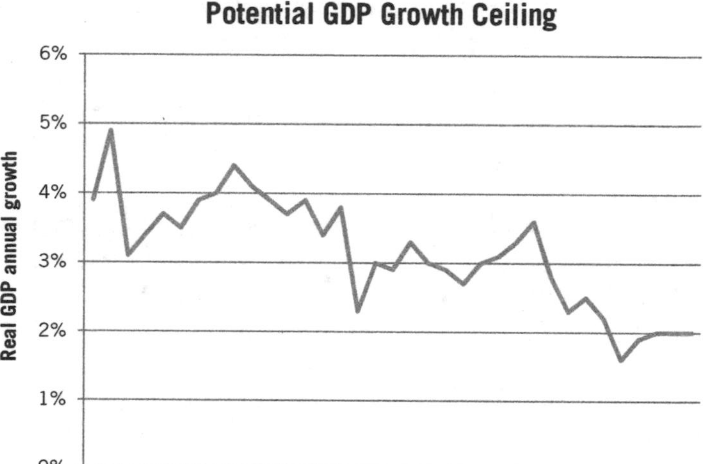

Chart 23.1.

Source: "What Accounts for the Slow Growth of the Economy After the Recession," Congressional Budget Office, fig. 2, November 2012, http://www.cbo.gov/sites/default/files/cbofiles/attachments/43707-SlowRecovery.pdf. "An Update to the Budget and Economic Outlook: Fiscal years 2012–2022," Congressional Budget Office, table 2.3, August 2012, http://www.cbo.gov/sites/default/files/cbofiles/attachments/08-22-2012-Update_to_Outlook.pdf.

After three decades of Reaganomics, the potential national economic pie from growth each year has diminished to be only one-half as large as during the preceding era. This grim outcome reflects the thousands of decisions made each day by the business community under Reaganomics that are unhelpful to growth. Instead, the business community should invest domestically rather than abroad and should bend toward domestic investment rather than stock buybacks, higher dividends, inopportune mergers, and other characteristics of short-termism.

Admittedly, this lower US growth ceiling may be of little concern to households, because they receive little of the gains from growth anyway, although it means weaker job prospects for them as well.

CHAPTER 24

POVERTY

"American children, the poorest in the developed world."[1]

Le Figaro,
November 3, 2009

"The United States also has the highest proportion of workers in poorly paid jobs, and the highest number of annual hours worked by poor families with children. . . . Our poverty rates are higher for two reasons: because our jobs pay low wages and because, even with high levels of low-wage work, US antipoverty policy does less to compensate low-wage workers than do other nations."[2]

TIMOTHY SMEEDING,
University of Wisconsin-Madison, 2008

In a Presidential election campaign that touched on so many aspects of American life, the modest discussion about poverty in 2012 reflected diminished concern for the least advantaged Americans. That is a stark contrast with voters in the family capitalism countries, who have proven willing to support programs that limit poverty, provide livable wages for the working poor, and secure a decent retirement for all. These disparate attitudes toward the least advantaged reflect better opportunity under stakeholder capitalism and expectation by voters of real wage gains continuing in perpetuity. Those expectations engender a spirit of community and optimism, undercut in America during the Reagan decline.

Recall that the late philosopher John Rawls believed the measure of a society is how well it deals with the less able. His gold standard for evaluating the variants of capitalism is how well families prospered while also enabling meaningful economic participation by the disadvantaged including the working poor, single parents, and high school dropouts. How do the family capitalism countries compare with Reagan-era America in meeting the Rawls standard?

Attenuating Poverty

With 20 percent of American adults considered to be working poor in near-poverty-income jobs or worse, according to MIT's Osterman, the closest thing to a magic bullet to attenuate US poverty is higher wages, especially higher minimum wages. Other steps include access to a quality public education for all families and more expansive upskilling by the public and private sectors. Yet Reagan-era policies have pursued the opposite course in each instance. Unsurprisingly, poverty has worsened.* Here is how the Brookings Institution's Ron Haskins and Isabel Sawhill describe events in 2009:

> "The lack of progress in combating poverty is especially surprising. . . . Economic growth should have automatically reduced the portion of people falling below (poverty) thresholds. The primary reasons for this lack of progress are the stagnation of wages at the bottom of the skill ladder and changes in family composition. . . . Men in their thirties have lower wages than their fathers' generation did at the same age."[3]

American poverty is measured utilizing a system devised in the 1960s by an innovative and justly famous Social Security Administration economist, the late Molly Orshansky. It relies on costs of various baskets of goods and services considered to be necessities for lower-income households. Much has changed in the past half-century. Her approach has been criticized from both the left and right, and by Orshansky herself. The Census Bureau now publishes a variety of alternative measures, yet that concept remains the fundamental matrix of American poverty. Nearly one in six Americans, or more than 45 million adults and children, are meeting the Orshansky official threshold for impoverishment in 2013.

Even so, poverty is understated. Critics at the National Academy of Sciences, among others, have determined that the Orshansky concept undercounts poverty by as much as 20 percent in high-cost areas such as New York City.[4] Moreover, because it excludes common expenses such

*During the Reagan-era decline, Washington has been more interested in trimming poverty programs than expanding them. A report by Elaine Maag in 2005 found that only 58.1 percent of low-income parents even knew about the major American antipoverty program, the EITC. Moreover, the EITC is only available to those who file tax returns, not a priority for the impoverished. See Elaine Maag, "Disparities in Knowledge of the EITC," Tax Policy Center, Urban Institute and Brookings Institution, March 14, 2005.

as health care and some sources of income, Orshansky is not utilized by any other nation. The EU countries, for example, rely on continent-wide standards established in 2001 at Laeken, in the Netherlands. We can compare the extent of poverty in the United States and northern Europe using both measures, thanks to a 2007 analysis by researchers at Maastricht University in collaboration with Harvard and the University of Michigan. The results are reproduced as Table 7.

Poverty Rates in America and Northern Europe

Population Share Below Poverty Standards, 2000

	Measured by European Laeken Standard	Measured by U.S. Orshansky Standard
Poverty Rate:		
Austria	11.9%	4.8%
Belgium	13.3%	3.6%
Denmark	10.8%	3.4%
France	15.4%	6.5%
Germany	11.1%	5.1%
Netherlands	11.3%	6.6%
Sweden	10.4%	5.7%
United States	23.5%	8.7%

Table 7.

Source: Geranda Notten and Chris de Neubourg, "Poverty in Europe and the USA: Exchanging Official Measurement Methods," Table 2, Graduate School of Commerce, Maastricht University, August 2007.

The northern European amalgam of widely broadcasted wage gains, higher minimum wages, numerous high-value jobs, and expansive safety nets translates to considerable less poverty than in America when measured with uniform statistics. The northern European Laeken standard is the more demanding one, requiring a higher income to avoid official penury. For example, the American poverty rate of 8.7 percent in 2000 would have measured 23.5 percent on the Laeken standard; nearly one in four Americans that year, or about 70 million, lived in poverty by European standards. In contrast, poverty in northern Europe would be nearly defined away by the less-demanding Orshansky standard.

Measured by either standard, the incidence of poverty in America is about twice as severe as in northern Europe. And if differences in the out-of-pocket cost of health care, pensions, and education required for membership in the middle class were included in these measures, the difference in poverty rates would be even greater. Here is how the authors Notten and de Neubourg put it:

> "Generally speaking, the out-of-pocket costs of post-secondary education for a family with children are considerably lower in continental Europe than in the United States. To provide children similar education opportunities, US families thus need a higher income than continental European families. Ideally, such differences should be taken into account."[5]

Chronic Poverty Is Twice as High in America as Northern Europe

Is *chronic* poverty more widespread in the United States? We learned earlier that the decline in American opportunity since 1980 is especially evident for lower-income Americans, too many trapped in a multigenerational poverty cycle. This cycle is an especially telling matrix for the performance of Reagan-era America. Lacking good incomes or social capital, families suffering chronic impoverishment have difficulty effectively empowering their children for a life of achievement, mobility, and accomplishment. Their children have a diminishingly small opportunity to break free of their economic class, perpetuating the poverty cycle.

Notten and de Neubourg captured these families in their analysis by defining long-term or chronic poverty as those who had lived impoverished during two of the previous three years. Like overall poverty, the Maastricht study revealed that the incidence of chronic poverty in northern Europe was generally less than half that in America; uniformly applying the Laeken standard, chronic poverty ranged down from 8.7 percent in France to 6.1 percent in Germany to 5.2 percent in Denmark, compared to 13.8 percent in the United States during their study year 2000.

American Childhood Poverty Is Double the Rate in Northern Europe

The Reagan decline has been destructive to American families and in particular children. Low opportunity has weakened households, stagnant or falling wages raising havoc with its structure and impoverishing a greater share of US children than in northern Europe.

How severe is childhood poverty in America?

There are two comprehensive analyses that have recently answered that question:

First, a 2010 analysis of childhood poverty among the global 24 richest OECD nations by UNICEF ranked the United States twenty-third, stuck at the bottom between Hungary and Slovakia.[6]

Second, Notten and de Neubourg of Maastricht University examined the incidence of childhood poverty, using both the Laeken and Orshansky standards. Their results are reproduced as Chart 24.1. A stunning one in every three American children lived in poverty in 2000, when measured by the Laeken standard. That rate was twice the childhood poverty rate of any nation in northern Europe. Moreover, because of income churning by lower-income households, the actual reach of childhood poverty in the United States is underestimated by Notten and de Neubourg. A remarkable one-half of all American youths during childhood are destined to experience bouts of poverty, reliant at some period on food stamps, a startling statistic.

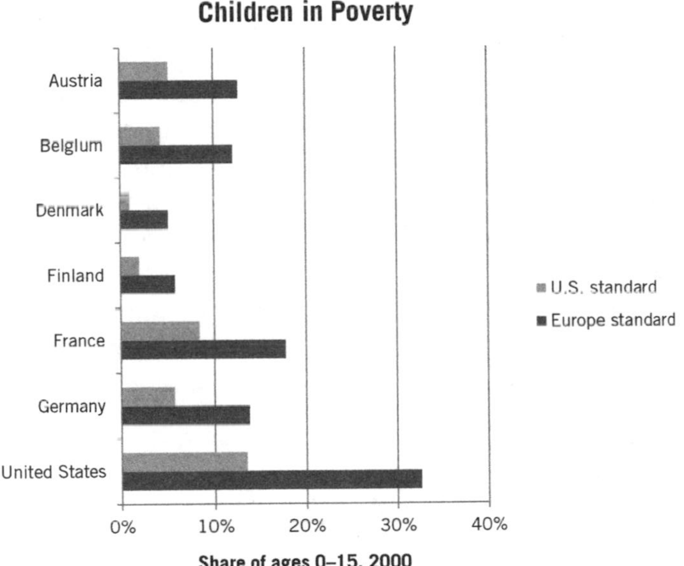

Chart 24.1.
Source: Geranda Notten and Chris de Neubourg, "Poverty in Europe and the USA: Exchanging Official Measurement Methods," table 7, Graduate School of Commerce, Maastricht University, August 2007.

High and rising wages helping to preserve the traditional family structure is a major reason the family capitalism countries are more successful in ameliorating childhood poverty. In contrast, inopportunity and the absence of high-value jobs create unhelpful pathologies and a corrosive dynamic destabilizing families and family formation in America. That outcome is documented by an American rate of single-parent households that is 50 percent greater than in France and Germany.[7] And researchers including Isabel Sawhill and Robert Lerman have determined that the rise in single-parent households accounts for most of the increase in childhood poverty since the 1970s.[8] When combined with low minimum wages and weak public antipoverty support, the outcome is that American children are the poorest of all among rich nations. And Europeans know it, with headlines like this one in the epigraph appearing in *Le Figaro*:

> "American children: the poorest in the developed world."[9]

The Notten and de Neubourg study and similar analyses are strongly suggestive that the documented Reagan decline in high-wage jobs short-changed the economic prospects, opportunity, and mobility of American families and their children. It leaves one-third of youngsters languishing in or near poverty when calibrated by the standard used by most other rich democracies, too many struggling in single-parent households, doomed to squandered lives of lost opportunity and frustration. No economic system should permit the loss of up to one-third of its human resource, particularly since a superb model for maximizing human capital has evolved in other rich capitalist democracies.

Research and statistics on childhood poverty document that America during the Reagan decline failed to meet the Rawls test. Has it performed any better in addressing the two other groups historically most disadvantaged by market economies—the working poor and school dropouts?

The Working Poor

Families unable to escape poverty despite working fulltime blight any economic system. Unlike most other rich democracies, America chooses not to provide those who work with a wage sufficient to avoid impoverishment. Indeed, its wage structure causes taxpayers to subsidize low-wage employers. Even working full-time, the American minimum wage does not lift a single parent and child above even the *de minimus* Orshansky threshold. In 2010, for example, a minimum wage paycheck for working the US average of 1,800 hours would have earned $2,000 less than the poverty level for a two-person family.

How many working poor are there? BLS determined some 10.5

million working Americans lived below the official US poverty line in 2010.[10] And, including the near poor, recall that MIT economist Osterman determined in August 2011 that nearly one in five working adults was mired in poverty-level jobs paying the minimum wage or little better. International measures based on more demanding standards place the figure higher still. For example, statistics from the International Labor Organization show that one in four working Americans in 2010, some or many of them full-time workers, were considered to be working poor by international standards. They earned less than two-thirds the median wage threshold standard adopted by the United Nations for impoverishment.[11]

What is the lifestyle of this bottom 20 percent or more of our neighbors? Working full-time at the minimum wage in America in 2013 means earning a bit less than $1,100 a month. That income must cover comprehensive expenses for housing, food, transportation, health care, and everything else. It means a hand-to-mouth existence reliant on public transportation, shared housing, food stamp allotments, free school meals, little if any savings, scant health coverage, high-credit costs from usurious payday lenders, little or no worksite upskilling, prey to unscrupulous employers, and the continual stress of a grinding paycheck-to-paycheck life frequently featuring two jobs and inattention to children. It means the harrowing life evocatively described by Barbara Ehrenreich in her 2001 bestseller, *Nickel and Dimed: On (Not) Getting By in America.*

Dropouts

The other sizable component of the most disadvantaged is school dropouts. Sizable dropout cohorts are a problem in every rich democracy. The Scandinavian countries do a better job than Australia, France, Germany, or the United States of retaining youths in school and minimizing their number. Yet, because of their higher-wage structures, earnings by dropouts approach middle-class wages in the family capitalism countries. That is less true in America, as indicated by statistics in Chart 24.2, reproducing OECD data from 2006 (see next page). Indeed, dropouts in America bear the most severe earnings penalty of any rich democracy, receiving less than two-thirds (63 percent) the average wages for high school and university graduates in 2006. In contrast, German male dropouts earned 93 percent of what graduates earned, nearly a 50 percent larger share than in America. And in a global first, female drop-outs in Denmark and Sweden out-earn male dropouts.

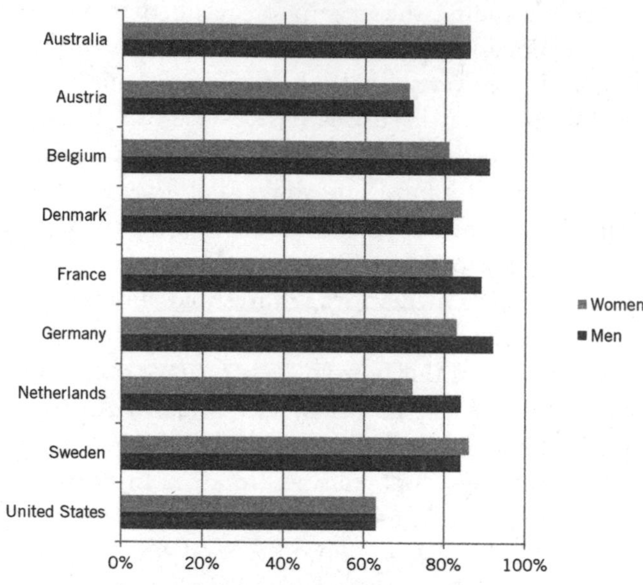

Chart 24.2.

Source: "Education at a Glance," Table A9.1a, OECD, Paris, 2008.

CHAPTER 25

DELAYED AMERICAN RETIREMENT

"The number of those working past 65 is at a record high."[1]

FLOYD NORRIS
***New York Times*, May 2012**

"I'll probably be working for the rest of my life. Some golden years."[2]

American JEAN CELINE, 64,
Starting a new job, September 2008

"Regardless of how much you throw 401(k) advertising, pension cuts, financial education, and tax breaks at Americans, the retirement system simply defies human behavior. Basing a system on people's voluntarily saving for 40 years and evaluating the relevant information for sound investment choices is like asking the family pet to dance on two legs."[3]

TERESA GHILARDUCCI,
New School of Social Research, July 2012

Teresa Ghilarducci, a prominent American researcher on retiree economics, was blunt in this February 2013 assessment:

"This is the first time that Americans are going to be relatively worse off than their parents or grandparents in old age."[4]

The prospect of a lengthy and a comfortable retirement is an important quality of life issue. Like other elements of the American Dream, that promise has become ephemeral for most. The Reagan decline has diminished the prospects of realizing the presumptive American birthright of retiring at age 65 or 67. The reasons are weak wage growth, low savings, a weak private pension system, family wealth stagnation, and Social Security benefits set near the poverty level. Three-quarters of men and women close to retirement have less than $30,000 in their retirement accounts, and 28 percent of actual retirees have no savings of any kind.[5]

A major factor is that the private pension system prioritizes financial sector profits and reduced employer costs rather than retirement security for employees; it is mostly a commercially sponsored, voluntary, and self-directed system, each characteristic posing high danger for families. In too many instances, it forces families to go *mano a mano* with front-running investment firms, as explained by economist Ghilarducci at the New School for Social Research in New York:

> "It is now more than 30 years since the 401(k) Individual Retirement Account model appeared on the scene. . . . It has failed because it expects individuals without investment expertise to reap the same results as professional investors and money managers. What results would you expect if you were asked to pull your own teeth or do your own electrical wiring?"[6]

The profit-motivated private system is skewed against those most in need. While 76 percent of white-collar employees enjoy private pension plans at work, over half of employees earning $27,000 or less lack access to any pension plan at work, their golden years destined to be spent working under the golden arches of McDonald's or living in penury.[7] These employees are more likely to work part time or have a broken work history, with absences that prevent steady participation in whatever pension programs might have existed at their various jobs. Moreover, they are the workers most prone to be among the 42 percent of all employees who cash out retirement funds when changing jobs, a grim augury for their retirement.

The retirement prospects of most Americans have been sharply reduced by the seminal shift of employers during the Reagan decline away from sponsoring defined benefit plans for their employees to defined contribution plans. The latter plans are far cheaper for the business community, enabling them to dodge the financial risk of providing a steady income stream to retired employees. Instead, that financial risk has been shifted to employees left to fend for themselves to find a reasonable return on retirement savings over a span of decades in competition with Wall Street professionals. Many have turned to those same professionals to manage (401)k and IRA accounts, providing plentiful profit opportunities for the financial sector.

Far worse from a national perspective, as elaborated by Michael Clowes in *The Money Flood*, the abandonment of defined benefit plans is a major factor promoting short-termism among money managers, pension funds, and stock market investors that exacerbates the Randian short-termism of executives.

The Reagan decline has been a perfect storm for older Americans. Led by Alicia Munnell, the Center for Retirement Research at Boston

College projects post-retirement incomes in assessing how many senior are likely to fall well short of pre-retirement living standards. Since 1983, the share of retirement households likely to fall at least ten percent shy of previous living standards has jumped by two-thirds. In 2010 for the first time, more than half (53 percent) of all such American households face significantly reduced livings standards as pensioners.[8] Their reaction has been to delay retirement.

There are a number of charts in this narrative, but the next one perhaps most eloquently summarizes the consequences for most Americans of the Reagan decline. As depicted in Chart 25.1, labor force participation rates for both men and women age 65 to 69 ceased dropping early in the Reagan era, and reversed course thereafter. Now nearly one in every three seniors works, competing for jobs with their grandchildren. This rise in delayed retirements is quite a contrast to the experience of our parents or grandparents during the golden age, particularly men. Rising real wages back then enabled them to substitute leisure for labor like northern Europeans now, a happy phenomenon which caused the annual work effort of Americans to decline to about 1,800 hours, where it has been stuck ever since.

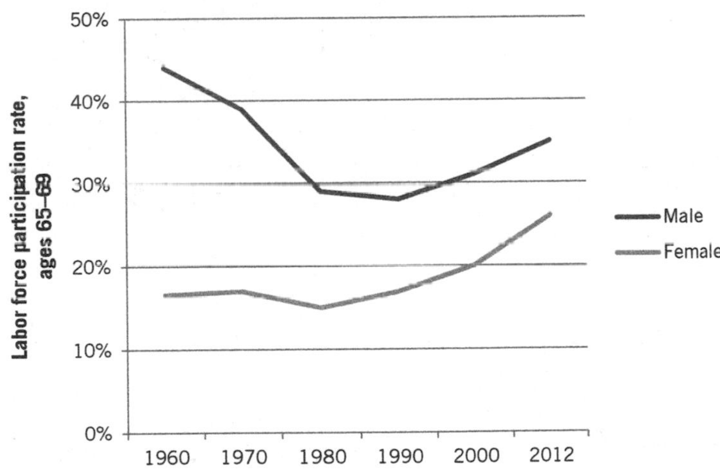

Chart 25.1.
Sources: Floyd Norris, "The Number of Those Working Past 65 Is at a Record High," New York Times, May 12, 2012. "Labor Force Participation Rates of Persons 50 years and Over by Age, Sex, and Race, 1950-1990," table 4-2, US Bureau of Census, Washington.

Although from a very low base, the number of seniors working increased *eleven* times faster than overall employment from 1999 to 2008. And the actual number of working seniors over age 65 has doubled since 1999, their share of the workforce rising disproportionately.[9] These are not just part-time jobs being taken to top-off pensions. In 2007, 56 percent of working men age 65 and older were doing so full time, up from 46 percent in 1999.[10] And it not just the young seniors; some 11 percent of American men over age 75 were working in April 2012.[11]

Eager for work, responsible, experienced, and gaudily flashing their Medicare cards, seniors work cheaply and outcompete others for jobs. That is why, since 2009, the number of senior males working has remarkably exceeded the number of teenage workers.[12] For millions of senior citizens, that outcome is captured in the epigraph to this chapter by disgruntled former retiree Jean Celine as the recession unfolded in 2008. In dismay, Celine, then 64, was forced to reenter the workforce and hope that good health would enable her to continue participating for many years. "Some golden years," she summarized, her secure retirement perhaps undermined repeatedly by her own votes since the 1980s.[13]

Early Retirement in Northern Europe

The situation is more optimistic in family capitalism countries where retirement ages have fallen steadily in recent decades, quite a change since the early postwar years. In France, for example, 70 percent of men between the ages of 60 and 64 worked in 1970, but only 19 percent do now.[14] Moreover, while the sluggish European economy and government policies to discourage early retirement have reversed these trends to some degree in recent years, both men and women in northern Europe still retire years sooner than Americans. This pattern reflects solid public pension systems, along with decades of steadily rising real wages and the robust personal savings they fund. For example, families in Australia and northern Europe saved 12 to 15 percent or so of their incomes for decades to supplant pensions, well above paltry American savings rates.[15]

Only a small minority of men, and especially women, worked past age 60 there in 2006 as depicted in Table 8, even though they are denied full pension or Social Security benefits until age 65 or 67, as in the United States. Indeed, the share of American men continuing to work beyond age 60 (59 percent) was nearly three times higher than in France that year. In addition, five out of six French women retired early, by age 60, while little better than one-half of American women chose (or could afford) to stop working before age 65. These trends are starker for older cohorts. Between ages 65–69, the share of American men working in these traditional retirement years was over eight times greater than Frenchmen, and nearly four times greater than in Germany.

Early Retirement in Northern Europe and U.S.

Labor Force Participation Rates, 2006

	Men			Women		
Ages	**25–54**	**60–64**	**65–69**	**25–54**	**60–64**	**65–69**
Austria	93%	22%	10%	81%	10%	5%
Belgium	92%	21%	7%	77%	11%	2%
France	94%	19%	4%	81%	17%	2%
Germany	94%	43%	9%	80%	25%	5%
Netherlands	92%	34%	14%	78%	20%	5%
United States	91%	59%	34%	76%	47%	24%

Table 8.

Source: "Labor Force Statistics by Sex and Age," Employment Outlook 2007, Statistical Annex table C, OECD, Paris.

Unfortunately for American women, Reaganomics has proven to be an equal opportunity blight: nearly one in four American women between the ages of 65 and 69 continued to work. Unlike Ms. Celine, only a few European women toil past age 65.

Northern European governments are moving aggressively to ensure a secure public retirement system. German reforms, for example, succeeded in reversing the trend toward unduly early retirement. Though still low, the share of German women and men aged 60–64 working in 2009 was nearly double their share a decade earlier.[16] And France, like the United States and Germany, has increased the threshold age for full retirement benefits for most to age 67 from age 65, and the early retirement threshold to age 62 from 60. The Hollande government last year allowed a few quite limited exceptions to those tougher standards (for those who began working careers as teenagers and the like). These reforms have worked. In combination with earlier pension reforms (1993, 2003), the net impact is projected by the French statistical agency Insee to increase the workforce there by two million employees by 2030.[17]

CHAPTER 26

INCENTIVIZING AND REWARDING WORK

"France's labour force . . . has never had an international reputation as being work-shy."[1]

CHRISTOPHER CALDWELL
***Weekly Standard*, November 2008**

Critics of stakeholder capitalism might argue the superior work incentives of Reaganomics. As we will now learn, the facts do not support that notion. Employees in the family capitalism countries now retire before Americans and work less over the course of a year, as well. By those measures, they do work less. But when on the job, most work hard, as shown by these nations overtaking US productivity levels.

Christopher Caldwell notes in the epigraph to this chapter that the French are not averse to hard work. Indeed, international experts, including business elites at the annual mid-winter conclaves in Davos, Switzerland, have concluded that they have a sturdier work ethic than Americans. Here is how editors at the *Economist* summarized the conclusion of surveys at Davos conducted at the behest of the World Economic Forum: "The French rank and file has a much stronger work ethic than American, British, or Dutch employees."[2] The same can be said of Australian employees and those in the balance of northern Europe, as we now see.

More Work in the Family Capitalism Countries Than in America

The family capitalism countries did not evolve to become the most competitive rich democracies in the world with indolent work habits. Employees work under the same arduous conditions as Americans, contending with odd hours, deadlines, and demanding customers, employers, and production standards. Their broad middle-class societies have not overtaken America economically by sitting in cafés drinking Pilsner *lager*, Foster's VB, or sipping *espresso* while smoking *Gauloises*. We know that because a greater share of their population than America's works. Even though 2005 was a boom year in America, the labor-force participation rate was higher in *every* family capitalism country than in America. These statistics are reproduced from OECD data in Table 9. Note that the gap is actually larger than these statistics suggest, because they include Europeans aged 60–64, many of whom are happily retired.

Labor Force Participation Rate

Ages 25–64 Men and Women, 2005

	High school graduates	College graduates
Australia	82.6%	86.6%
Austria	77.3%	86.8%
Belgium	79.5%	87.4%
France	80.9%	86.8%
Germany	79.3%	87.7%
Netherlands	81.3%	88.1%
United States	76.7%	84.7%

Table 9.
Source: Employment Outlook, 2007, table D, OECD, Paris.

Another way to gauge work effort is to compare statistics for the key cohort between ages 25 and 54. Table 8 in the previous chapter noted the participation rate was 94 percent for such males in France and Germany in 2006, compared to 91 percent in America. And the rates for women in France (81 percent) and Germany (80 percent) were higher than in the United States (76 percent) as well.

Codeterminism and the soft domestic content corporate culture it dictates is vital to ensuring a growing stock of high-wage jobs and avoiding the Apple problem. But a handful of public policies also importantly enable the higher rate of workforce participation in family capitalism countries, while promoting stable family environments. These policies include family support, flexible labor markets continually being refined to incentivize work, and employment support during recessions like the "short-work" programs discussed in a moment.

Supportive Family Policies

The paucity of good jobs in America, a feature of the Reagan decline, is responsible for emergence of a culture of welfare dependency, described by *Washington Post* columnist Petula Dvorak in 2010:

> "There is the familiar narrative of low-income parents who figure out that it pays more to leave the crummy minimum wage job and collect welfare at home than to get child care. And often, when they do work, they deal with substandard child care, erratic work schedules, no sick days, no health care, and a host of other horrors."[3]

Officials in northern Europe are anxious to incentivize job growth to avoid Reagan-era welfare dependency and the unstable family situations and pathologies that follow. Northern Europe has splurged on youth-nurturing infrastructures in recent decades, implementing a web of mutually reinforcing policies almost from birth that include quality, standardized, and inclusive education, preschool, childcare, expansive school-work transitions, high minimum wages, and Australian-style national wage-setting mechanisms that reward workforce participation and encourage stable lifestyles. The goals are to socialize youth, while enhancing their human capital to warrant high wage, career-long employment. Family program spending is as high as 3.8 percent of GDP in France, for example. And we learned earlier about the near-universal availability of preschool, daycare, and kindergarten spots across northern Europe.[4] Recall research by economists including Tarjei Havnes at the University of Oslo and Magne Mogstad with *Statistics Norway* found that such investments yield big payoffs.[5]

These programs in part are intended also to enable new moms to rejoin the workforce speedily. Their success is marked by female labor force participation rates and wages in northern Europe that are the highest in the world.

"Flexicurity" to Ensure Northern Europe Labor Market Flexibility

The family capitalism countries recognize the vital role played by flexible labor markets in enhancing productivity growth. They are keenly aware that the Schumpeterian creative destruction process means job churning is an inevitable byproduct of highly beneficial entrepreneurial activity and of economies integrated with international trade. And they have taken to heart economist Eichengreen's admonition. "Trying to prevent this creative destruction from happening is a recipe for less economic growth and less productivity."[6] As economists at the OECD have explained, there is awareness now in countries such as the Netherlands that "strict employment protections reduce labor market fluidity and prolong unemployment."[7] That appreciation has inculcated a culture of labor market experimentation and continual reform in recent decades in northern Europe with names like "flexicurity." First coined in Scandinavia, flexicurity describes steps to enhance labor market flexibility by pairing an enhanced employer ability to hire and fire with greater unemployment support and incentives for jobless workers to upskill and recycle rapidly back into the labor force.[8]

Examples include German reforms that made it easier to hire and fire employees beginning in 1998. How deeply are the objectives of flexicurity ingrained in the culture of northern Europe now? Here is how Steffen Kampeter, parliamentary state secretary in the German Ministry of Finance, described the intensity of that culture: "We have learned that reform is not only a 10-year program but an everlasting challenge."[9] That commitment to flexible labor markets explains why the European Central Bank demanded reduced labor market protections in Greece, Portugal, and Spain as a condition for support during the sovereign debt crisis.

New York Times reporter Liz Alderman described the consequence of flexicurity in Denmark this way: "Each year, a remarkable 30 percent of Danes change jobs, knowing the system will allow them to pay rent and buy food so they can focus on landing a new position." At the same time, the government provides retraining, adult education, and up to 80 percent of prior wages in jobless benefits for a time to ease the transition to new employment.[10] Robert Kuttner described the outcome of the Danish reforms this way:

> "Thanks to these reforms, Denmark enjoys a new economic dynamism and a lower unemployment rate than the United States, and has not sacrificed broad social benefits or income inequality."[11]

The results of this approach have been on display during the recent decades of global integration. When coupled with private and public resources for upskilling, these labor market reforms facilitated the job shifting we discovered in favor of more skilled employment amid the intense labor market churn of globalization. A virtuous cycle has been created across northern Europe in which rising skill levels support still further innovation and higher wages, accommodating an outward-moving technology frontier. Flexcurity and similar reforms have demonstrated that while the family capitalism countries fret about job security, that goal is not allowed to slow workplace flexibility needed to drive productivity and accommodate dynamic global trade.

A distinct, but equally effective, set of labor reforms were undertaken over the past several decades in Australia. Ric Battellino, former Deputy Governor of the Reserve Bank of Australia, explained the changes in August 2010:

> "... labour market reforms, some extending back to the late 1980s, gave the labour market increased flexibility to respond to changing economic conditions without producing large swings in unemployment or unsustainable pressure on wages."[12]

The boost in efficiency also meant improved tax receipts, enabling that country to maintain an enviable budgetary picture, with government surpluses recorded in ten of the last nineteen years. And its tight banking regulations has made Australia a global winner among the rich democracies over that period, piecing together over two decades of broadly rising wages and debt-free growth without an American-style credit bubble.

Despite their broader social safety nets, voters in the family capitalism countries are no more tolerant of malingering than Americans; they insist that unemployment support programs accomplish a rapid return to work. The Danes, for example, demand that the unemployed accept retraining and placement in reasonable new jobs when offered or risk benefit cuts.[13] And similar no-malingering provisions are common in the other family capitalism countries, as explained by economist Jan van Ours at Holland's Tilburg University:

> "Unemployment benefits have been reduced and qualifying for them has become harder. While our Social Security system still pays a fair amount, especially compared to other countries, you can only draw on it for a limited time. The unemployed are also required to actively seek new jobs. If they don't apply for jobs, or refuse work they are offered, they are penalized."[14]

Employee Protections Enhance Productivity Growth

Flexicurity reforms are designed to promote productivity, and family capitalism countries also utilize worksite standards to encourage productivity growth. In an era where human capital is pivotal to firm competitiveness, well-crafted worksite rules can enhance the contribution of human capital to productivity, as we now see.

Firms in the family capitalism countries typically must comply with standardized and transparent labor market procedures when hiring or firing. These standards include advance notice, negotiations with the affected employees regarding terms of employment and dismissal, and severance pay.

These standards and procedures contrast rather sharply with the disposable employee pattern of American labor markets. Aside from some jobs covered by trade union agreements, few standards exist for US private employers regarding advance notice or transparency when conducting layoffs, for example. Indeed, US employers even stoutly resist posting a worksite notice as simple as explaining the right of employees under American law to form unions and bargain collectively.[15] Somewhere, Ayn Rand is beaming.

According to OECD data reproduced as Chart 26.1, America is an international outlier with the weakest labor protection policies and practices among both the rich democracies and middle-income countries like Mexico and Turkey. Indeed, the OECD utilizes the low American standard on workplace protection to establish the null or zero point for its spectrum of policy intensity. Each of the forty-four richest nations surveyed by the OECD maintains greater protections against capricious or arbitrary dismissals by employers without cause than the United States.

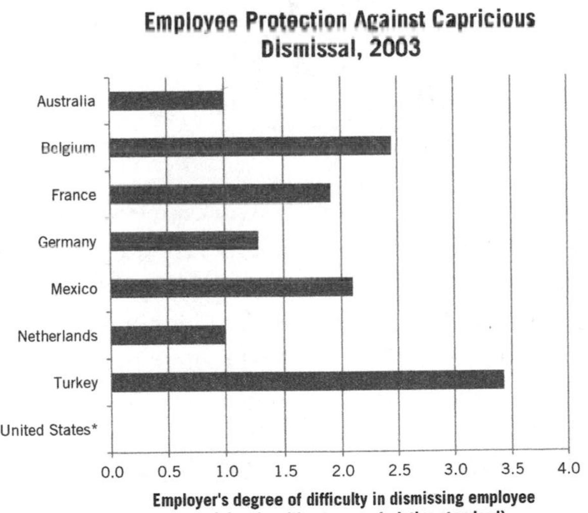

Chart 26.1. Relative measure of protection against dismissal by employers without cause based on a uniform OECD standard.
* Protection measures zero in the United States.
Source: "Dataset: Strictness of EPL, Regular Employment," OECD, Paris, OECD.StatExtracts.

Additional evidence of *de minimus* American labor standards is provided by academic analyses. With support from the Ford Foundation, the Harvard-McGill University Project on Global Working Families published a report in 2007 examining workplace standards in one hundred and seventy-seven countries. They found America to be an international outlier. For example, one hundred and thirty-seven countries mandated that employers must provide something as common as paid annual leave to their workers, but not America. Some one hundred and thirty-four countries cap the maximum length of a workweek, but not America; nor is overtime work capped in the United States. And some fifty countries mandate that employers pay wage premiums for evening and night work, but America is not among them.[16] These statistics validate the disposable labor sobriquet associated with the commoditization of American employees during the Reagan decline.

The investment and productivity performance of the family capitalism countries indicate that worksite standards don't inhibit superior global competitiveness and productivity growth. Indeed, evidence indicates that worksite standards are analogous to high minimum wages in encouraging employers to value employees rather than commoditize them, which incentivizes upskilling and thus productivity growth by firms. Australian Brian Howe, deputy prime minister in the Paul Keating government during the 1990s, chaired a 2012 investigation of jobsite practices in that country. He explained the connection between labor standards and productivity this way:

> "[The] greatest cost of insecure work is the impact it is having on productivity and skills when the world is moving into a globalised, information-based economy."[17]

Look at the importance of competitive worksite labor standards this way: Firms seek competitive advantage in any fashion possible. For employers, worksite standards that encourage a sense of job security is among a set of policies that includes high minimum wages, codeterminism, and work councils explicitly crafted to maximize human capital and enterprise collaboration with employees. From the employee side of this equation, higher-order worksite standards encourage them to more fully buy into behaviors aiding the longer-run success of their employers.

Moderating Unemployment During Recessions

Unemployment is a major challenge as the EU struggles to establish banking standards and prudent government budget behavior while recovering from the sovereign debt crisis of some members. Growth has slowed and unemployment has increased in recent years to extremely high levels. This temporary distress should not obscure the important lesson to be drawn from the disparate ways that labor markets react to downturns in northern Europe and America. We learned earlier that one element of Reaganomics is a quick trigger by executives, cutting jobs inordinately during slowdowns, invalidating Okun's Law. This pattern was discussed earlier, and a number of economists in addition to Nancy Folbre, such as Deepankar Basu and Duncan K. Foley, have documented its emergence. Basu and Foley concluded in a February 2011 analysis:

> "In 2009, the official unemployment rate in the US rose about twice what would have been predicted by conventional models of output-employment dynamics."[18]

This pattern of disproportionate, exaggerated job loss during recessions is at odds with the behavior of executive suites under codetermination. Driven by fears that extended unemployment will erode job skills and self-esteem—the process economists term *hysteresis*—northern European executives collaborate with public officials to minimize layoffs even amid the current macroeconomic difficulties. The different outcomes there and in the United States have been on display since the credit crisis recession unfolded and are noted in Chart 26.2, reproduced from OECD statistics. Despite equally large declines in GDP (except for stolid Australia) during the 2007/2008 recession, the unemployment rate grew less in family capitalism countries than in America.

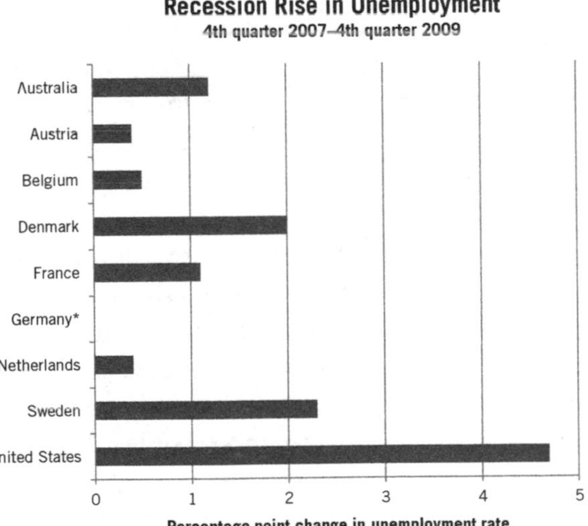

Chart 26.2.
*Rate declined by 0.9 percent in Germany.
Sources: "Unemployment Rates," OECD.StatExtracts, OECD, Paris, 2010. Floyd Norris, "In Great Recession, Other Nations Have Suffered More," New York Times, Sept. 18, 2010.

The different reactions by employers in the United States and abroad caused the American unemployment rate at the economic trough (10 percent) to rise well above Australia (5.6 percent) and northern Europe, including Germany (7.5 percent), Austria (5.5 percent), and the Netherlands (4 percent). Only the rate in France was as high as the US rate and it remained high in 2013. In fact, unemployment actually declined in Germany despite the European recession. That surprised some experts, including Jörg Krämer, chief economist for Commerzbank in Frankfurt, who declared the German outcome, "something of an economic miracle."[19] And it has continued, with German unemployment in 2012 reaching a 20-year low; many factories there resemble the evocative scenes of busy industrial might in the 1927 Fritz Lang film, *Metropolis*. Export growth has been important, but an unusual collaboration between the public and private sectors in Germany has played a role, as well.

Kurzarbeit: Cost-Effective Job Preservation

The major tactic to minimize layoffs during recessions in northern Europe is so-called "short-work" programs. These are public/private partnerships, where employers reduce work hours across a large proportion of their entire workforce rather than conducting targeted layoffs of some employees. First established in the potash industry in 1910 and expanded in 1924, the German *Kurzarbeit* program is the most comprehensive in Europe. It grew out of experience in past recessions, when layoffs hampered the subsequent recovery as firms scrambled to hire and train new workers. Short-work programs like *Kurzarbeit* are intended to enable enterprises to bridge episodic downturns, while keeping workforce skills intact. The programs spread the cost of unemployment among employers, employees, and taxpayers, rather than the costs falling mostly on the jobless and their families, as they do in the United States.

The most expansive deployment occurred during the recession of 2008–2009 where some 22 nations initiated short-work programs. Employers cut work hours across the board, but with much of the lost wages offset by temporary top-ups from public funds and also from employee benefits stockpiled earlier.[20] Only 39,000 German employees were participating in the *Kurzarbeit* program in September 2008; by May 2009, 1.5 million at nearly 60,000 firms were involved.[21] *Le Monde* carried a French Associated Press report that some 258,000 imperiled French employees were participating in the short-work program in the peak second quarter of 2009 at more than 1,000 firms.[22]

The moderating impact on unemployment rates was significant.

Among Germany's midsize firms, for example, sales fell 4.9 percent in 2009, but employment barely declined (0.27 percent), according to the employer group, the German Confederation of Skilled Crafts.[23] The recession reduced labor required by 24 percent in the sizable metal and electrical industries, jeopardizing 870,000 jobs, but *Berliner Zeitung* journalist Matthias Loke reported that employers in those industries laid off only 105,000, while preserving another 765,000 jobs using *Kurzarbeit.*[24] The Nuremburg-based Institute of Labor Research released a report in February 2010 documenting that Kurzarbeit in total saved 1.2 million work years of German jobs in 2009 alone.[25] Overall, OECD labor market economists have concluded that short-work programs preserved jobs representing about 1 percent of workforces, although the benefits in heavier users such as Germany, Belgium, and France were greater. Nearly 6 percent of the Belgian workforce, for example, was involved at one point.[26] *Le Figaro* economics reporter Marc Landré in his blog concluded that the French program shaved two percentage points off the unemployment rate there in 2010.[27]

Employees are naturally supportive, but so are employers. American multinationals in Europe and domestic firms in northern Europe participate because a short-work strategy saves them money. Analyses document that the expense of training new employees when a recovery arrives exceeds the employer expense of participating in *Kurzarbeit.* Professor Gerhard Bosch at the University of Duisburg Essen, for example, estimated that redundancy/training costs for 500,000 German layoffs would be €22 billion, while estimated firm costs for participating in the short-work program totaled a much smaller €5 billion.[28]

Here is how David Haines of the German bathroom fixtures firm Grohe put it. "It is a great tool. It is fantastic because it keeps our costs down but allows us to keep our trained workers."[29] Even major American transplants—Ford, for example—are quick to use Kurzarbeit. For example, Ford collaborated with the Federal Employment Agency to shield 4,000 employees from layoffs at its Cologne plant in 2012.[30]

Beyond these immediate advantages to direct participants and families, short work reinforces the northern European business model by not squandering expensive training and human capital during episodic business cycle downturns. Franz Fehrenback, CEO of Bosch, the auto supplier, explained why the firm had few layoffs in 2009: "We are trying to retain our core workforce. . . . We are taking advantage of the short-time working program or reducing working hours."[31] Barbara Kux of Seimens explained the logic of such employee hoarding this way: "It gives you a chance to keep experienced people, to keep their knowledge in-house and develop a high level of loyalty and trust so they feel like part of a family rather than just doing a job."[32] Dutch economist Erik de Gier of Nijmegen University wrote how employers in that country remembered the tight labor markets earlier in the 2000s:

> "Unemployment was at a historic low and businesses were having a very hard time finding new staff. Now that times are hard, they are hesitant to fire the staff that they have worked so hard to find in the first place. Particularly because they will need these people even more when the baby boomers start to retire en masse."[33]

Manfred Wittenstein, president of the German engineering firm Wittenstein AG in Igersheim, explained the broader logic framing the German *Kurzarbeit* program:

> "You cannot consume in the good times and let the employees pay for it in the bad times. We as an employer are stronger than our employees, so it is for us to take on the financial risk of lower working hours, instead of loading it on their shoulders."[34]

Milton Friedman would grimace to hear that and American CEOs would shake their heads. But Wittenstein would have made Adam Smith proud of the remarkable stakeholder capitalism he first envisioned more than two centuries ago that has blossomed in the family capitalism countries.

Section 4

RECOVERY

CHAPTER 27

REBUILDING THE AMERICAN DREAM

"One of the lessons of the global economic transformation of the past 20 years is that when incentives change, cultures can change, too."[1]

CHRYSTIA FREELAND,
***Financial Times*, January 29, 2010**

"What is required is nothing less than a shift in the culture of . . . capitalism."[2]

RICHARD LAMBERT,
Chancellor, University of Warwick

Is Apple the future?

I begin this chapter with a cry from the heart by the generations coming up. Written by Alexandra Petri in February 2013, it is their future envisaged by Apple and guaranteed by Reaganomics and pay-to-play:

> "Millennials are grotesquely underemployed. We waded bravely into the workforce waving extremely expensive sheets of paper that turned out to be almost meaningless. Nearly half of college graduates have jobs that don't require four-year degrees. And those are the ones who are working."[3]

Apple is touted as perhaps America's finest firm, an innovative giant, highly productive and profitable. Its business model involves transferring the fruits of R&D, venture capital, and innovation nurtured in American labs abroad where Asian production utilizes a cheap, flexible, docile, and disposable workforce. Offshoring virtually everything in the value chain from R&D to production with barely 6 percent of its workforce in America, it is also an unusually disloyal American multinational. Moreover, like most multinationals, much of its profit is channeled through overseas cutouts to be hidden in tax havens, its tax burden shifted onto families and purely domestic US enterprises.

That is the business model of the firm synonymous with the very best of American capitalism in the Reagan decline. Apple behaves like some sort of global citizen, refusing to nurture broadly based American family prosperity. Permitted by voters to commoditize employees, its officials cynically blame America for the firm's decision to abandon the nation that nurtured its creation and creator and enabled its success.

Along with other firms, Apple exploits the nearly unique assets of the American economy, but displays little concern for the impact of its business model on US society. Apple's behavior—multiplied thousands of times—is a major reason why American wages are stagnating, opportunity shrinking, and income disparities widening in contrast to the family capitalism countries. The plight of millenials and their parents is not a temporary condition. Looking ahead, the Apple business model promises more stagnation and more family economic distress. The US business community is offshoring too many high-productivity jobs, exporting the source of traditional US growth. That compounds the drain on productivity from short-termism. And that's why economists such as Robert Gordon, Jeremy Grantham, and experts at the Congressional Budget Office in 2012 downgraded your future.[4] Recall that Gordon concluded that American productivity growth in the future will average a bare 1 percent:

> "Future growth in real GDP per capita will be slower than in any extended period since the late nineteenth century, and growth in real consumption per capita for the bottom 99 percent of the income distribution will be even slower than that."[5]

The antigrowth aspects of Reaganomics have caused an enduring downshift in the potential growth rate of America. With growth slowing and the gains from growth certain to continue being redistributed upward, most families and their children will be hard-pressed to avoid further economic deterioration. Of course, forecasts can be wrong; in the era of the floppy disc, Bill Gates argued that "640 kilobytes ought to be enough for anyone."[6]

Not this time. Most Americans hope for the best, but reality keeps pressing in. And that reality is the global labor overhang and a Washington that chooses not to ameliorate the impact of globalization. Wages in China and elsewhere are rising, but they will remain small fractions of US wages because of glutted global labor markets. Recall how the chairman of Gallup, Jim Clifton, explained the reality of the overhang, featuring some 3 billion jobseekers worldwide:

"There are currently only 1.2 billion full-time, formal jobs in the world. This is a potentially devastating global shortfall of about 1.8 billion good jobs. . . ."[7]

In America, that reality is Apple and firms such as Dr. Pepper Snapple. As a result, men and women today find new employment mostly in the service sector, dominated by lower-wage enterprises such as Walmart, Apple, or McDonalds. Those are good jobs only in comparison to being unemployed: weak hourly pay, limited career potential, unpleasant and tiring working conditions, and too many are part-time. And it isn't much better in more upscale service jobs, as journalist Ben Austen explained in *Harper's* magazine a few years ago:

> "Even in service-sector jobs at businesses on Fortune's '100 Best Companies to Work For' list, such as nonunion Whole Foods or Starbucks, employees are paid just above minimum wage and benefits are repeatedly downgraded, all in the service of a business model that relies on young workers quitting in a short time."[8]

It is certainly true that improving minimum wages, more education, and stronger unions can raise individual wages. But these conventional remedies flounder on the sharp reefs of extreme offshoring and that labor compensation for most Americans has become structurally decoupled from productivity. Increasing reliance on robots threatens to further decouple wages from rising productivity. There is no path to reverse the Reagan decline without drawing on the lesson offered by Australia and the other family capitalism countries in structurally modulating offshoring while linking wages broadly to national productivity performance.

Reversing the decline requires fundamental reforms in the way firms are governed, the way gains from growth are received, the way management interacts with employees, and the way domestic content is nurtured. Are these reforms likely under Reaganomics?

Adam Smith wouldn't think so. Recall his warning about governments comprised of merchants? To frame the answer, I first return to Joseph Stiglitz. Reprising Aristotle and also Acemoglu and Robinson, here is how Stiglitz in his book, *The Price of Inequality,* explains what I believe is the most accurate perspective on the origin of the Reagan decline:

> "When one interest group holds too much power, it succeeds in getting policies that benefit itself, rather than policies that would benefit society as a whole."[9]

Only a relative handful of Americans have benefitted from the credit bubbles, deregulation, and other Reaganomic policies and outcomes since 1980, garnering most of the gains from growth. Side effects of those policies wiped out an entire generation of toil and savings for virtually all American families. And those policies promise a future that is equally bleak.

Do not be deluded that the Stiglitz description of America today is rare or an anomaly soon to be reversed. As economists Daron Acemoglu and James Robinson make clear in their book, *Why Nations Fail*, the Reagan decline featuring an upward income redistribution is *the* template throughout economic history. For many thousands of years, mankind has continually labored under an extractive economic model that narrowly benefits the few.

Family Capitalism Is the Anomaly

With a rare few exceptions, economic elites such as Aristotle's oligarchs, Roman equestrians, medieval kings, Ottoman Sultans, and southern plantation owners, have always dominated the less fortunate, extracting through slavery, feudalism, or tenant farming whatever surplus those souls managed to produce. Economies stagnated because such elites are Luddites, stymieing the creative destruction process because change threatens their positions. The first exception was the era of the Roman Republic from around 510 BCE until the time of Julius Caesar in 49 BCE; slavery was widespread, but property rights somewhat broadly evolved and at least plebeian "Roman political institutions had pluralistic elements," concluded Acemoglu and Robinson. Importantly, this weak grip by elites allowed economic opportunity to flourish, enabling New Men to challenge vested interest, opening the door to innovation and entrepreneurship that evolved to be the vast Roman Empire.

The second exception flared momentarily in the thirteenth century in Venice, until it was extinguished beginning in 1286 when "Political and economic institutions became more extractive," ending broad-based prosperity.[10] The third exception was the medieval textile regions of northern Italy, Germany, Holland, and Lancaster, as explained by historians Charles Foster and Eric Jones in *The Fabric of Society and How it Creates Wealth*. Entrepreneurship broadly flourished, but the gains came to be concentrated in a few families, their Luddite instincts ending the saga. The fourth exception is the historically quite recent prosperity and economic equality that evolved from the industrial and political revolutions of the seventeenth and eighteenth centuries. The Glorious

Revolution, the defeat of the Spanish Armada, and other historically unique conditions enabled strivers in England and later Europe and America to serendipitously thwart the luddite instincts of elites. Inclusive, pluralistic economic and political institutions evolved that facilitated rising and broadly spreading prosperity.*

But as Acemoglu and Robinson make clear, these tiny few examples of a serendipitous happenstance are not destiny. The examples of Republican Rome, thirteenth-century Venice, Europe's medieval textile centers, and Britain's industrial and political revolution are no guarantee of future prosperity: "Moves toward inclusive institutions, as our account of Venice shows, can be reversed. . . . It is neither automatic nor easy."[11] Within the framework of this long sweep of history, the Reagan decline is readily categorized as merely another iteration of this traditional pattern. The annual redistribution of gains from growth upward over the span of this decline differs from the usual pattern throughout economic history only in detail and of course, in its gargantuan magnitude.

It differs in another far more important fashion, however, which is why this book was written. The decline was created in American voting booths and can be reversed in those same voting booths.

Does the 2012 Election Portend Reforms?

For only the third time in American history in 2012, a winning President melded the politics of hope and change with economic resentment. It's tempting to conclude that Americans are therefore receptive to returning economic sovereignty to families. The millenials are certainly supportive. And polling data suggest public dismay at widening income disparities. A Pew Research Center survey in January 2012 found a 40

*Emerging property rights in Britain gave the New Men challenging the established order the ability to innovate and enrich themselves and society, upending the political and economic order centered on the aristocracy and landed gentry. A prospering America emerged in a quite different fashion bucking even longer odds. Indeed, the English settling Virginia in the seventeenth century intended to emulate the wildly profitable extractive economic model in Spanish and Portuguese America, just as they did in fact duplicate that model in British colonies in the Caribbean, Bengal and Africa. Only the absence of precious metals, a readily apparent plantation crop or numerous exploitable local natives forced them (luckily) to abandon that traditional colonial strategy. They cut their losses by introducing settler farming from which eventually emerged inclusive political and economic institutions outside the slave-holding American south. Only a few other outliers in similar circumstances like Australia, Canada and New Zealand had the same rare luck. See Daron Acemoglu and James Robinson, *Why Nations Fail* (New York: Crown Business, 2012) 105, 332, 433, 458.

percent jump since 2009 in respondents who believe that a conflict now exists between rich and poor Americans. Two-thirds of respondents believed that. Indeed, more respondents believed that income differences are a source of conflict (66 percent) than believe the nation is divided instead by immigrants *versus* native born (62 percent) or on questions of race (38 percent).[12]

These polling results, coupled with financial crises and weak economic recovery, have led some to conclude that reform is inevitable. Here is *Financial Times* journalist Francesco Guerrera writing during the depths of the stock market decline in March 2009 about corporate governance reforms:

> "Long-held tenets of corporate faith—the pursuit of shareholder value, the use of stock options to motivate employees, and a light regulator touch allied with board oversight of management—are being blamed for the turmoil and look likely to be overhauled. . . . As a result, the composition of boards is likely to change dramatically."[13]

Mutual fund manager John P. Hussman is similarly optimistic:

> "Economies that generate high profits, weak wage gains, and low capital accumulation are like old-style monopolies that . . . fail to produce long-term prosperity or growth. No economy in the history of the world has tolerated that sort of situation for long. . . ."[14]

Not so fast.

Reform is unlikely, thwarted by nineteenth-century economic Darwinians comprising a majority of the Roberts Supreme Court. They endorse a Washington firmly in legislative gridlock resulting from judicially indulged gerrymandering and pay-to-play. Washington will continue treating American families like deer in the headlights of globalization.

Recent world history offers clear lessons about how families fare when elites capture government. America has now come to resemble those nations, according to Simon Johnson, former chief economist at the International Monetary Fund (IMF), and nowhere more evident than in finance. Despite the regulatory collapse of recent decades, even reform of Wall Street is proving to be a bridge too far, an alarming tell for the future. "A whole generation of policy makers has been mesmerized by Wall Street," explained Johnson, unwilling to regulate with prudence because of pecuniary politics. Drawing on his experience, Johnson identifies disturbing similarities between lagging developing nations and gridlocked Washington:

"The finance industry has effectively captured our government—a state of affairs that more typically describes emerging markets, and is at the center of many emerging-market crises. . . . But there is a deeper and more disturbing similarity: elite business interests—financiers, in the case of the US—played a central role in creating the crisis . . . [and] are now using their influence to prevent precisely the sorts of reforms that are needed. . . . The financial industry has not always enjoyed such favored treatment. But for the past 25 years or so, finance has boomed, becoming ever more powerful. The boom began with the Reagan years, and it only gained strength with the self-regulation policies of the Clinton and George W. Bush administrations."[15]

The similarities between mismanaged nations and America in 2013 are unsettling: weak productivity growth, stagnant wages, Red Queens, deteriorating economic mobility, and widening income disparity. Johnson's analogy is extended by statistics suggesting the United States also has come to resemble a mismanaged nation on social indices, as described by Australian journalist Leon Gettler, drawing on research by epidemiologists Kate Pickett and Richard Wilkinson, authors of *The Spirit Level*:

"The US has the worst health and social problems in such areas as numeracy and literacy, infant mortality, homicides, imprisonment, teenage pregnancies, lack of trust, obesity, mental illness including drug and alcohol addiction, and social mobility."[16]

Voters can end gridlock by reasserting their economic self-interest at the polls, weighing carefully the consequences of policies expected from the leaders they elect. But history has not been kind to such hopes. Certainly, the Reagan decline provides evidence for behavioral economists such as Dan Ariely, who argue that millions don't vote in their economic interest.[17] It may be that too many have poor information. For one thing, Americans have a fundamental misimpression of how wealth is distributed today as a consequence of Reaganomics. Surveys by Michael Norton and Ariely found that respondents believe the top 20 percent own less than 60 percent of American wealth, when their actual share is close to 90 percent.[18]

Reform hinges on new rules from Washington. Yet, despite the 2012 election outcome, many voters remain distrustful of government, the lingering effects of decades of demonization. This attitude is reinforced by the rather pervasive cognitive dissonance of Americans regarding the sizable role played by government in their lives, documented in research by economist Suzanne Mettler of Cornell University. She found that 44 percent of Social Security recipients, 43 percent of those receiving unemployment benefits, and 40 percent of both Medicare and GI Bill beneficiaries say they "have not used a government program."[19]

Even so, American voters are not fools and realize they are economically downtrodden. So why have a majority of Americans voted repeatedly for political leaders who reject Adam Smith's concept practiced in the family capitalism countries, where the ultimate purpose of an economy is the prosperity of families and not firms?

There are at least two complementary explanations: betrayal by economic elites and small ball policy options offered voters.

Betrayal by Economic Elites

Reestablishment since 1980 of the traditional historic extractive economic system described by Acemoglu and Robinson had an important political element. Political scientists such as Larry Bartels writing in *Unequal Democracy* have concluded that electoral choices and economic consequences are rendered opaque for many voters buffeted by extravagant half-truths.[20] And "half-truths" is a kind interpretation of the unprecedented intensity of outright fabrications by the wealthy conservative fringe, such as swift-boaters in 2004 or birthers in 2012, tarring Presidential candidates. Democrats agree, of course, arguing that pecuniary politics enables plutocrats to obfuscate economic options, large donations empowering their hired politicians to exploit social and value issues to bamboozle voters. You may disagree, but some conservatives do agree, including David Brooks, who wrote of this charade and Machiavellian manipulation in January 2012:

> "The Republican Party is the party of the white working class. They overwhelmingly favor Republicans. . . . The Republicans harvest their votes but have done a poor job responding to their needs. The leading lights of the party . . . have a more individualistic and even Randian worldview than most members of the working class."[21]

Moreover, voter myopia and inattention appears to enable Republican Party officials to tend subsequently to the concerns of donors rather than constituents. Economist Nancy Folbre cites Tea Party supporters as an example. While polling results confirmed that 53 percent of members supported higher taxes and spending cuts to shrink deficits during the 2011 budget battles, Tea Party Republicans in Congress ignored them. Folbre explains:

"Their views . . . are not primarily shaped by the views of their constituents. . . . Its elected representatives quickly began relying on Political Action Committees and major contributions from Wall Street firms. . . . Many Tea Party members may be unaware of the extent to which wealthy political conservatives like the Koch brothers have controlled their efforts and shaped legislative priorities."[22]

Such donors have taken the measure of Republicans, insisting the Party's careerists fiercely support the present distribution of gains from growth by gridlocking Washington. And that Party has naturally responded by subordinating every other legislative issue to that donor imperative.

Economists explain the success of this relatively small donor class through the lenses provided by Mancur Olson's 1982 classic, *The Rise and Decline of Nations*. Olson explained that the popular will in the United States is routinely thwarted by the focused efforts of a concentrated minority with more at stake.[23] Groups like the pharmaceutical industry, hedge fund managers, the extremely wealthy, or sugar farmers that have an intense stake in public policy tend to prevail even when massively outnumbered by opponents, each of whom has a far less intense stake in the outcome. Billionaire businessman David Koch or the Red Queens have much more to lose than you have to gain from environmental or banking regulations, and their donations reflect that calculus. That is the essence of regulatory capture empowered by pay-to-play.

Another explanation why folks don't vote in their self-interest is that they're offered limited choices at the polls.

Limited Policy Choices Hamstring Voters

Scholars argue persuasively that Democratic Party officials knowingly play small ball. Drawing on research prior to 2012, law professor Joan C. Williams at the University of California, Berkeley has suggested, for example, that the Democratic Party only reluctantly raises middle-class concerns. That is because opponents have succeeded in portraying its efforts on health-care expansion and improving public education as invidious redistribution aiding only impoverished households and teacher unions. Williams argues that "Republicans have made working-class resentment a powerful weapon for achieving the policy goals of the business elite." The consequence has been quite odd electoral battles featuring the "have-a-littles fighting the have-nots."[24] That changed in 2012.

The 2012 campaign by President Obama featured a full-throated defense of the New Deal legacy of government activism, but the prescriptions were underwhelming. Probably from limited familiarity, proven options drawn from family capitalism countries were ignored.

Leadership to Restore the American Dream

The small-ball reality of Democratic Party options and loyalty of Republican Party politicians to its donor class eager for gridlock have left American firms free to pursue international wage arbitrage and offshore valuable jobs. Reversing these trends with the only proven means of remediation—Australian-style wage policies, German codeterminism, work councils, and *de facto* domestic content—will be a herculean task for voters. Americans are ambivalent about enterprises, rightly distrustful of their priorities and morality in the wake of the financial sector crisis and their offshoring of jobs. Yet the business community is connected to families by golden handcuffs, because enterprises are the device contrived in capitalism to create wealth. Even so, as we have learned, the terms of that complex relationship are not preordained, and history teaches they can be shaped by rules cast by voters.

Renewal requires leadership. America's greatest President, Abraham Lincoln, understood the unique opportunity offered by leadership; the potential to mobilize public opinion by appealing to the better angels in each of us. Later, Franklin D. Roosevelt seized the opportunity to lead, channeling American frustration with economic outcomes to begin assembling family capitalism. And a number of courageous leaders abroad subsequently challenged entrenched economic interests as well, in order to broaden prosperity. Japan, South Korea, and Taiwan instituted dramatic and contentious economic reforms in the 1950s to allow independent action by elected leaders in the face of oligarchs and landed aristocracies interested in maintaining the *status quo*.[25]

The barriers hindering reform today are no less formidable than in 1933, and remediation must be at least as fundamental in scope as the grand bargain crafted between families and the business community then. The concepts of a minimum wage, Social Security, and bank deposit insurance that Roosevelt championed were as unfamiliar to the Americans of his day as codeterminism and the Australian wage mechanism are today.

Three years ago, the economist Ross Garnaut, Vice Chancellor's Fellow at Melbourne University, explained the vital role that leadership plays in mobilizing public opinion to support family economic sovereignty. And his perspective is equally applicable to Americans pondering reforms to duplicate Australia's success:

> "The vested interests have large advantages, but they don't hold all the cards. The big card in the hand of the public interest is the community's capacity and tendency to respond to leadership. . . . The independent centre cannot exist unless there are academic and other centres of policy analysis, media, and mass communications that are funded independently of interest groups. Public institutions can play a role in expanding the independent centre. . . . On the latter, the Australian Productivity Commission and its role in the analysis of the effects of protection is an outstanding example. . . . The outcome of the struggle between the national interest and special interests determines the prosperity, and in the end the security and longevity of the national community. The prospects for policies in the national interest and for stable outcomes once adopted are shaped by the quality and strength of leadership. Good outcomes are unlikely without effective, strong, and clear-headed leadership, drawing support from an informed electorate."[26]

Lessons from the Family Capitalism Countries

The family capitalism countries have demonstrated that steps to reassert family economic sovereignty are not on the path to serfdom. On the contrary, they put America on a path that began with the Glorious Revolution and the American Revolution, one lit by John Locke and Adam Smith, and trod by Thomas Jefferson, James Madison, and FDR.

Aside from the need for leadership and the adoption of a reform agenda built around the urgency to recouple wages with productivity, there are four specific lessons the family capitalism countries offer for those Americans pondering the journey.

First, the arguments marshaled in this book evidence that rising middle-class prosperity is incompatible with shareholder or managerial capitalism; their goals are simply different. Reaganomics has slowed growth and rendered the American family something of a free-fire zone, as David Brooks acknowledges, even as he offers no remedies:

> "The social fabric is fraying. Human capital is being squandered. Society is segmenting. The labor markets are ill. Wages are lagging. Inequality is increasing. The nation is over-consuming and under-innovating. . . . Not all of these challenges can be addressed by the spontaneous healing powers of the market."[27]

Second, in reasserting family economic sovereignty, the United States doesn't face a trade-off between income equality and economic efficiency.

The weight of evidence we have reviewed proves false the notion that policies rebalancing the gains from growth will reduce efficiency or economic growth. Indeed, the reverse even seems to be the case. Northern Europe has benefited from the superior efficiencies of stakeholder capitalism and codeterminism, while avoiding the growth penalties imposed by short-termism and other elements of Reaganomics. It also has proven false the notion that widening income disparities are an ineluctable consequence of maximizing economic efficiency.

Third, the economic viability of American enterprise is not jeopardized by paying high wages, adopting a long time horizon, or cutting CEO compensation. As noted earlier, wages are only a small component of overall enterprise costs, between 10 and 20 percent in manufacturing, for example, a figure swamped by gyrations in the macroeconomy or other costs, such as debt service or energy. Moreover, American firms have long operated around the world under a wide variety of capitalist models based on disparate rules, including those insisting on high wages. These foreign rules vary a great deal, but American corporations adjust and prosper under each; that's what corporations are designed to do, after all. Indeed, the best American firms, such as Ford, invest hundreds of millions of Euros and employ many thousands of Europeans at $10, $20, or even $30 more per hour than they pay Americans at home. They will do the same thing at home, promoting middle-class prosperity, when voters demand it.

Fourth, stakeholder capitalism is sustainable for the long term. The prowess of the family capitalism countries in recent decades amidst globalization is the most compelling evidence conceivable of the model's potency. Its sustainability rests on stakeholder capitalism's superiority in driving productivity, the magic elixir powering a virtuous circle of greater investment and rising wages.

Australian Reforms

Productivity growth in both the United States and Australia has been lackluster compared to northern Europe, and both nations should seize the competitive advantages from codeterminism. Unlike America, Australia does have a national wage mechanism. But upgrading that Australian foundation to include codeterminism will be hindered by many of the same barriers confronting American reformers. While Australia balances its budgets, tightly regulates banks, and avoids recession, it has begun exhibiting unprecedented signs of American-style government gridlock fueled by its own version of pay-to-play politics. Reminiscent of collaborative governance in golden age Washington, Australia enjoyed a bipartisan bloom of government in the 1980s and early 1990s.

While opposing Medicare, opposition leaders collaborated on many other initiatives with the Labor Party government. Today the nation enjoys a sturdy foundation of alert voters and unions, public institutions, watchful media and scholars, and a vigilant public sector. Yet that foundation is threatened by Rupert Murdock's success in morphing domestic conservatives into US-style uncompromising politicians. That has created dangerous new dynamics challenging Australian voters because, as Garnaut explains, "Special interests have powerful incentives to obscure the real effects of various interventions. . . . The special interests are favored by ignorance and the fog of politics."[28]

The ability of mining interests, in particular, to derail inspired efforts to mimic Norway's sovereign wealth fund highlights the need to end pay-to-play in Australia. Here is a frank assessment of that nation's contemporary political environment by *Sydney Morning Herald* reporter Tim Colbatch, writing in mid-2012:

> "Conservative leader Tony Abbott's war against everything has made good government in Australia almost impossible. . . . Whatever it [the Labor party] proposes, he opposes."[29]

CHAPTER 28

AMERICAN FAMILY CAPITALISM

"Control of rent-seeking requires decentralization of economic power."[1]

JOHN KAY,
***Financial Times*, Nov. 10, 2009**

"Many of the factors that have long driven American innovation have dried up. Droves of investors, disappointed by their returns, have abandoned the venture capital firms of Silicon Valley. At pharmaceutical companies, computer-driven research is making fewer discoveries than intuitive chemists once did. We cannot simply assume that, when the recession ends, American dynamism will snap back in place."[2]

EDMUND S. PHELPS,
Columbia University, 2010

"What is to be done? That demands a huge agenda. It must cover employment, education, corporate governance and financial reform. . . . It will be unavoidable divisive."[3]

MARTIN WOLF,
***Financial Times*, Dec. 22, 2011**

American voters launched the Reagan era in hopes of recapturing the American Dream. For almost all, those hopes have been dashed, leaving sharp divisions exemplified by recent national elections. On one side are elite earners naturally eager to perpetuate what has seemingly become their entitlement to most of the gains from growth. Politically, they rely on gridlock engineered by the bought men of Upton Sinclair that contemporary scholars such as Thomas Mann and Norman Ornstein have fingered. On the other side is everyone else, 300 million strong, each with his or her own opinion, the choices blurred by pay-to-play politics and limited options in the voting booths.

This chapter discusses explicit steps to return economic sovereignty to American families. But they cannot occur in isolation from politics, and so we begin the renewal agenda with goals for reforming American politics.

Reform the Political Process

The first step to political reform is to mobilize private institutions and academia in support of family economic sovereignty. Credible information is pivotal. Washington should craft a research entity mimicking in quality and purpose the independent Australian Productivity Commission to provide sound economic research and information. Credible data on the extent of wage stagnation, the disconnect between wages and productivity, and the annual taxpayer subsidy to low-wage employers such as Walmart could be developed, for example. A second step is the enormous task of extracting money from politics, a step awaiting reduction in the economic Darwinians comprising a majority of the Roberts Supreme Court.

Third, electoral politics should become regularized, reforms that also require reconfiguration of the Roberts Court. Gerrymanderd voting districts is an example. President Obama won the 2012 popular vote in Ohio and Virginia, but fewer than 30 percent of Congressional elections there went his way. Mann and Ornstein, along with many other economists and political scientists (e.g., Lawrence Lessig, Jeff Faux, and Larry Bartels), have advanced meritorious reform agendas. These involve voting and redistricting procedures, public financing of campaigns, legislative procedures, and the like, and warrant attention.[4]

Lastly, confidence in government can be rebuilt by banning conflicts of interest involving public officials. An analogous institution to stem regulatory capture, such as the French Committee on Standards in Public, should be created, and peopled by nonpartisan judges, to close the revolving door for senior government officials and regulators.[5] Lengthier cooling-off periods than the one-year US standard would help. The family capitalism countries have revolving door issues, too, and Berlin-based political scientist Timo Lange of the public interest group Lobby Control has proposed a cooling-off period of three years before departing officials can engage in lobbying activity.[6]

Turning to the judiciary, that profession does a poor job of avoiding conflicts of interest, particularly in state-level judicial elections; judgeships are too often sold blatantly to the highest donor with business before the court. All judges should be appointed, rather than elected. In the interim, mandatory recusal from issues involving larger donors, family interests, or spousal employers seems sensible. For the longer term, an independent American judiciary career path should be created, replete with graduate education to wring politics from the judicial system. And the assets of all judges should be placed in blind trusts.

Preventing such conflicts in the legislative branch is more difficult, with elected members frequently involved in local economies as attorneys or in business. Yet Congress does a poor job of policing conflicts or precluding members lobbying colleagues and voting on matters involving their direct personal financial interests. Moreover, some Members of Congress exploit inside information, routinely juggling portfolios within a day or two of confidential White House briefings on imminent market-changing policies.[7]

Lobbying by relatives of Congressional members is widespread as well. Despite restrictions imposed by Congress in 2007, a *Washington Post* investigation in December 2012 found that

> "[thirty-six] congressional relatives—including spouses, children, siblings, parents, and in-laws—have been paid to influence 250 bills passing through their family members' congressional committees or sponsored by the members."[8]

Blind trusts, full and prompt disclosure, and recusal of members (and Supreme Court Justices) from issues in which they or relatives have an economic stake are the obvious solutions.

Turning to an American economic reform agenda, Nobel Laureate Edmund Phelps has described the contentious task ahead for Americans where "Regaining a well-functioning capitalism will require re-education and deep reform."[9] What are components of the deep economic reforms comprising my agenda?

Codeterminism: Superior Corporate Governance and Greater Shareholder Returns

Time magazine calls Germany, "The most competitive industrial sector of any advanced economy."[10] That superiority is a consequence of codeterminism creating a long horizon, high-productivity economy where the gains from growth created by enterprises are enjoyed broadly and the domestic employment base is nurtured.

Matching German prowess is improbable unless American (and Australian) firms seize the competitive advantage provided by codeterminism. The incentives created by Reaganomics have made corporate governance America's Achilles' Heel. Managerial or shareholder capitalism exalts executive compensation and the short-term over returns to shareholders, investment, R&D, or firm prosperity and survivability. Corporate leaders have mastered the art of self-aggrandizement and become millionaires. But in terms of delivering value for others, they have proven to be lemons. Those Adam Smith called merchants and master manufacturers must be reoriented to eliminate short-termism, here lamented editorially by the *Financial Times* in March 2009:

> "Good business results often require long-term relationships based on trust between managers, employees, customers, and suppliers. But long-term trust between two parties is impossible unless their respect for each others' interests is anchored in something deeper than the effect on the next quarterly profit numbers."[11]

The golden age tradition of long time horizons in corporate boardrooms was abandoned by Reagan era folks such as GE CEO Jack Welch. Welch has since had second thoughts. Nearly 30 years later, he recanted his advocacy of shareholder capitalism. In March 2009, Welch wrote:

> ". . . shareholder capitalism is the dumbest idea in the world. Shareholder value is a result, not a strategy. Your main constituencies are your employees, your customers, and your products."[12]

Eliminating managerial capitalism starts at the top with corporate boards of directors, as noted by governance experts Gillespie and Zweig: "Corporate boards remain the weakest link in our free enterprise system."[13] "Reform must begin in the boardroom," instructed Paul Myners, a former UK Minister of the Exchequer and hedge fund manager. "It is vital to the economy that corporations generate long-term value. To achieve it, we need a new enlightenment in governance."[14]

Some thoughtful alternatives have been proposed to deal with short-termism, such as proportionately weighting the votes of long-term shareholders in board elections.[15] But a fundamental solution is needed to eliminate the bias against investment, R&D, and productivity in American enterprises and labs. More rules to be endlessly lawyered and loopholed are not the solution. The reform with the strongest track record is for the boards of all larger US firms to gain the superior perspective and efficiency provided by codeterminism and its corollary work councils. That should include privately owned firms which also prosper under codeterminism, as indicated by the giant German family firm Bosch. As the most comprehensive research on codeterminism by Fauver and Fuerst concluded,

> "Codetermination provides for the credible exchange of information between the firm's board and workers . . . and lead[s] to a team approach to management. Indeed, because codetermination provides workers with operational expertise a forum for sharing operational

insights with the highest levels of management, this increased flow of information should result in efficiency gains."[16]

Codeterminism and work councils would boost the mediocre performance of Australian as well as American executives and boards, helping give more focus to the real challenge of raising productivity.

Beyond the arguments and studies already cited, my endorsement of codeterminism is also based on academic research that won the 2009 Nobel Prize. Research by Nobel prize winners Oliver Williamson and the late Elinor Ostrom concluded that imposition of rules from outside an entity appears to be a less effective scheme generally than refocusing management from within.[17] While this exact point was not discussed by them, their work suggests the superiority of boards featuring codeterminism over government rules or pressure from beyond the boardroom from employees, trade unions, voters, or the media. And internal *diktats* are honored more regularly when enforced by insiders as well, including engaged and responsible mid-management, and boards half-filled with employees refocusing corporate attention on the longer term.

Germany has the best-managed firms in the world, upskilling and investing for the long term, and it is the nation where codeterminism is the most mature and widespread. The seminal source of this economic prowess is not northern European culture or work ethic, large public sectors, or safety nets, but intense vertical communication and sharp competition between competing visions within supervisory boards. As American researchers such as Lucian Bebchuk and Jesse Fried have explained, independent and powerful directors bolster board independence, driving more critical decision making by management, resulting in better performance.

Are shareholders disadvantaged by codeterminism? As we learned, research has documented the opposite case: German CEOs do not mimic American CEOs. They do not shortchange R&D, conduct value-eroding mergers, or offshore high-value domestic jobs to compress wages in order to spike quarterly returns. Their tactics better utilize corporate resources than their US competitors. And shareholders benefit, with financial markets rewarding codetermination firms with higher Tobin Qs. That is the most powerful possible endorsement of codeterminism by capital markets and investors. If you believe that markets ferret out superiority, their evaluation of codeterminism is a compelling and determinant accolade. Moreover, those attributes are most important to firms on the technology frontier relied on for future economic prosperity.

Are enterprise ownership rights disturbed? German courts have affirmed that full shareholder rights are maintained by double-counting

CEOs votes in board deliberations. Since it maximizes shareholder returns, codeterminism would pass legal muster in American courts as well. In fact, American law provides leeway for willing executives to go well beyond any perceived parameters of codetermination. They have the specific legal flexibility to pursue an agenda of broad social enhancements, as noted by Harvard professors Forest L. Reinhardt, Robert N. Stavins, and Richard H.K. Vietor in 2008:

> "The judicial record, although supportive of a duty to maximize profits for shareholders, also leaves room for the possibility that firms may sacrifice profits in the public interest. . . . The business judgment rule prevents many public-minded managerial actions from being legally challenged. . . . In addition, twenty-nine states have statues that allow managers to consider the interests of non-shareholders such as employees, customers, suppliers, creditors, and society at large."[18]

A reoriented business school curriculum would complement codeterminism with professors becoming corporate whisperers, addressing governance shortcomings to help the American business community re-adopt stakeholder capitalism. A new wave of business school leaders such as Harvard dean Nitin Nohria could perhaps play that role. Nohria and colleague Rakesh Khurana argued in 2008 for "turning managers into agents of society's interest in thriving economic enterprises."[19] And business professor Michael Porter has suggested that firms strengthen the commons by focusing outward and blending community goals with the bottom line.[20]

It won't be easy to reform business education. Observers including Mary Gentile and *Financial Times* associate editor Michael Skapinker, for example, acknowledge that the current crop of MBA students generally identifies with shareholders rather than stakeholders. That may be because business students self-select for those who "want to make money," as Skapinker suggests, incurring sizable debt to do so.[21] A better profile for admissions committees would be students who believe it is wrong for prospering firms to fire employees and cut R&D merely to reward executives and transitory shareholders. GE CEO Jeffrey Immelt could guest lecture on occasion to channel a predecessor, Owen D. Young, in suggesting, "Ethically, leaders do share a common responsibility to narrow the gap between the weak and the strong."[22]

Short-termism is the consequence of behavior by both management and investors. To focus investors on the long term, the American pension system must also be reformed to mandate defined benefit plans as the private pension system; critically, that would encourage longer horizons by managers of the trillions of dollars invested in pensions. Only 20 percent of employees have access to such plans now compared to 80 percent in 1980 before Reagan.*

Raise Real Wages: Australian-Style Wage Determination

The only proven approach to raising real wages and broadcasting the gains from growth widely is an Australian-style wage determination mechanism based on national productivity performance. When productivity rises, all American employees should receive a portion of the new bounty, just like families in other rich democracies and as Alfred Marshall presumed more than a century ago. Moreover, the Australia system has proven effective in fighting inflation because productivity is the determinant metric; that accounts for northern Europe's pronounced bias *against* inflationary wage increases.

Will the Australian system saddle American enterprises with uncompetitive labor costs? Many decades of real-world evidence, the best kind there is, belie that concern. Is it your impression that Daimler or VW/Audi/Porsche is uncompetitive? Indeed, when combined with codetermination, the weight of evidence accumulated over decades is that productivity and corporate governance effects offset any labor cost impact. Analyses of decades of European data have concluded that firms become more competitive to the benefit of shareholders from the Australian and German wage and corporate governance reforms proposed here.

A national wage-setting mechanism patterned on Australia would mean establishing an analogous platform to Fair Work Australia where neutral experts oversee negotiated national annual wage increases hinged to productivity. A Fair Work America and an American Productivity Commission would devise annual wage-gain parameters as guidance for all worksites. The standard outcome should be higher wages everywhere that outpace inflation by perhaps one-half the rise in national productivity growth, giving American families the same wind at their backs enjoyed by their grandparents. Fair Work America should also enjoy the same mandatory arbitration authority provided Fair Work Australia, with short deadlines to settle wage disputes.

Other wage-related reforms should enhance employee organizing and bargaining rights and rigorously police the employer tactic of

---

*The Netherlands has a pension system that uses all three pillars of the World Bank pension system model. See http://www.pensioenfederatie.nl/Document/Publicaties/English%20publications/Nederlandse_pensioensysteem_Engelstalige_versie.pdf.

misclassifying employees as independent contractors. Importantly, work councils should be mandated to ease the drag on productivity from the hierarchical structure of American firms. After all, American firms in northern Europe routinely operate with work councils, and their shareholders would benefit from the same system back home.

Turning to minimum wages, the higher levels proposed repeatedly by President Obama are important ancillary steps to boosting productivity and wages. Where should the American minimum wage be set? The family capitalism countries establish the after-tax value of minimum wages at about 45 percent of the average wage for full-time workers, meaning the US minimum should approach ten dollars an hour in 2013. Raising the minimum wage would resonate with voters as well; a 2004 ballot initiative in Florida to boost that state's minimum wage, for example, was supported by 71 percent of voters, winning in every county and fetching 1 million more votes than President George W. Bush and 2 million more than Senator John Kerry.[23] Additionally, nine states already adjust their individual minimum wages for inflation and inflation indexation as proposed by Obama should also be adopted as national policy.[24]

Improve Economic Mobility with Education and Apprenticeship Programs

Improving mobility means rewarding hard work with good pay. That requires an abundance of good jobs and steps to ensure that all Americans can maximize their capabilities. The challenge is enormous but the family capitalism countries prove it can be met with the right policies. These include improving infant and child health and expanding preschool, incentivizing secondary school completion, identifying and rewarding extraordinary teachers, and making college more affordable.

Early intervention is vital to improving mobility, as pointed out more than thirty years ago by a prescient business group called the Committee for Economic Development, which concluded that ". . . an early and sustained intervention in the lives of disadvantaged children both in school and out is our only hope of breaking the cycle of disaffection and despair."[25] As noted earlier, researchers such as Nobel laureate James Heckman have concluded that the most vital years in youth development are the first years. America must make a commitment to act on the likelihood that nurture matters as much as nature, and that childhood education and sound parenting are vital foundations for a life rich with opportunity.

The benefits of Head Start programs can be lost by weak K-12 education. The prescriptions are more effective public support for parents and turning around struggling public schools. As in the family capitalism countries, a quality education should be the birthright of every American child.

With college a certain pathway out of poverty, America should mimic Australia and the United Kingdom in lowering college costs by expanding its new (2012) program linking education loans repayment amounts to subsequent earnings. College educations are national investments in human capital that the family capitalism countries make and the returns warrant an expanded American effort to ease college costs as well.[26]

A major effort to improve the school-to-work transition is also warranted for those Americans not headed to college. Scholars including Heckman, Robert Lerman, Rebecca Roselius, and Jeffrey Smith have documented that the disorderly transition harms productivity and squanders human potential.[27] America has apprentice programs, but fewer than one-half as many slots *per capita* as international competitors such as Germany, as noted earlier. Those programs should be expanded in close collaboration with enterprises to facilitate a more productive and rewarding transition. Some guidance is offered by the methods of German auto firms in the American South, which collaborate with local schools to train needed workers.[28]

Reversing mobility, wage, and poverty trends, while creating more apprentice opportunities, cannot succeed without reindustrialization and an abundance of high-value domestic jobs it can create.

Returning High-Productivity Jobs to America

Reagan era officials viewed deindustrialization as inevitable, akin to aging. Many others believed it, too, including a *Washington Post* editorial board in 2012, which pooh-poohed hopes of matching the German success in rebuilding an industrial base: "It's unrealistic to imagine a return to the relatively high levels of manufacturing employment and wages that the United States enjoyed in the 1950s."[29]

US families cannot rekindle the American Dream by taking in each other's wash. Moreover, the inevitability of deindustrialization is belied by history and rejected by a number of economists and US business leaders, such as retired Intel CEO Paul Otellini and Andrew Liveris of Dow.[30] They have not only Japanese and German history on their side but American history as well, one replete with the successful deployment of policies that have stimulated domestic enterprises and facilitated the creative destruction process. Incentivizing manufacturing has been woven into the fabric of America since the tea tariff raised colonists' ire and Prime Minister William Pitt declared in 1770 that the colonists not be allowed to fabricate so much as a horseshoe nail.[31] An agrarian future held such dire implications for the fledgling nation that one of the first Congressional acts in 1791 was Hamiltonian tariffs to shield infant industries, probably including horseshoe nails. Alexander Hamilton even undertook industrial espionage to lure skilled artisans from the British Midlands to open colonial factories.

Along with a host of other factors, these Hamiltonian trade policies, featuring tariffs as high as 50 percent well into the late nineteenth century, were instrumental in propelling the United States to become the world's richest economy. These policies succeeded in some measure because Britain, the world's greatest trader of the day, looked the other way, allowing its industrial base to deteriorate in relative terms, marking the Edwardian decline.[32] The late economic historian Charles Feinstein described it this way:

> "In the first half of the century Britain's exports had expanded at an exceptionally rapid rate, and the country flourished on the back of export-led growth. In the second half of the century that process came to an end, and was replaced by what might be called export-retarded growth."[33]

America's analogous Reagan decline a century later has different roots, but is replicating the outcome of the Edwardian era. Liveris argues that policy reforms are needed to end the decline:

> "At a time when US companies—run by patriotic people—are moving offshore at the fastest rate in history, we should, at a minimum, recognize that the model we are relying on isn't working."[34]

The erosion of American dynamism in manufacturing and in high-value services like computer design means new jobs are being concentrated in less-remunerative services where productivity growth tends to be weaker. These trends lend support to Robert Gordon and the Congressional Budget Office's unsettling prognoses of slow growth in the years ahead. To create more high-productivity jobs, America needs new jobs in high-value services, in the innovation industry including Hollywood and especially in manufacturing where productivity growth is most promising and multiplier effects large. Despite slipping behind northern Europe in productivity performance, the United States remains the most innovative nation on earth. It has valuable precursors to innovation-driven reindustrialization, including an unmatched entrepreneurial culture, superb R&D institutions, an enormous consumer base, trained workers, efficient capital markets, and a superior venture capital culture.

And that brings me to the Apple Problem. Apple and other innovative US firms both offshore existing jobs and build new facilities abroad to fabricate new products. This pattern, characteristic of the Reagan decline, creates an exaggerated mismatch between US sales and US production. In 2011, for example, 39 percent of Apple sales but only around 10 percent of its global labor force were in the United States. The rest of the jobs are offshored to Brazil and Asian countries.

To reindustrialize, America could rummage around in its historic economic tool kit of Hamiltonian trade policies, and demand that US firms like Apple build here if they want to sell here. The goal would be the return of high-value jobs and the associated R&D and service industry feedback opportunities.

An alternative path is offered by northern European codeterminism in which executives avoid extreme offshoring and nurture the domestic enterprise base. The model embodies a bias toward domestic content that is *sine qua non* for reindustrializing America, with reconstituted, invigorated, and commanding corporate boards prioritizing domestic investment and production. In March 2013, VW granted a $8,600 bonus to each of 100,000 employees. If firms like VW or Siemens can manage to support millions of high-wage jobs at home and pay handsome bonuses as well, well-managed and profitable American enterprises like Apple with reconstituted boards can do the same.

Neutralizing Beggar-Thy-Neighbor Mercantilism

Codeterminism should address the Apple Problem. But reindustrialization also hinges on neutralizing the drain of high-value jobs caused by mercantilist policies in nations such as China. Its firms and officials have crafted an array of opaque tactics to aid domestic producers that would dazzle Hamilton, starting with the most potent and important of all: low wages and weak labor, safety, health, and environmental standards that keep production costs well beneath Europe or America. These tactics and practices saw China increase its renewable energy product market share worldwide to 54 percent from 6 percent in less than a decade. The same policies are mostly responsible for the US share dwindling from 40 percent to barely 5 percent.[35]

Chinese firms also routinely engage in intellectual property (IP) theft from US and European competitors.* Even VW has fallen prey. VW

*European enterprises are victimized as much as US firms by IP theft. For example, a Chinese firm was caught red-handed conducting industrial espionage at a Lorraine-based GE affiliate in France called Converteam (Jean Chichizola, "New Chinese Espionage in France," *Le Figaro*, Oct. 12, 2011). And only a random customs

agreed to establish a joint venture with the Chinese government some years ago in exchange for market access. Its price of entry was proprietary engine and gearbox technology exposed to its Chinese partner in the venture called FAW. By 2010, suspicious VW officials had concluded that FAW was engaging in systematic IP theft, reproducing secret VW engine technology for a separate line of Chinese vehicles being marketed in Russia, for example. The competing cars were patterned on vehicles from VW and its subsidiary Skoda. That technology was also illegally transferred to another entity producing vehicles directly for the domestic Chinese market. Despite being perhaps the best-managed large firm in the world, VW is stymied in seeking redress, because it has a market of over 2 million vehicles annually in China to protect.[36] If it can happen to VW, every private enterprise in the world is vulnerable.

"The world is awash in trade-distorting subsidies," is how a 2012 document from the Washington-based libertarian Cato Institute described the global trade environment.[37] Yet as Alan Beattie of the *Financial Times* has noted, the new tactics are not easily eliminated, having outpaced laws at the World Trade Organization (WTO) intended to police free trade: "Disputes over state subsidies are spreading, the trade law to constrain them is not easy to use. . . ." Criticized for its mercantilist practices, the Chinese government response to WTO investigations has been the typical American one of lawyering up, throwing legal sand in WTO gears.[38] Beattie concludes, "it would be optimistic to imagine that WTO litigation or the widespread use of CVDs [countervailing duties] will bring the subsidy wars to a near and rapid end. Applying WTO rules is neither simple nor straightforward."

Indulging its mercantilism might be justified for some period if China were progressing toward democracy apace with prosperity, but skeptics such as Martin Jacques of the *Guardian* abound.[39] Moreover, the reality is that mercantilist trade practices abroad are incompatible with American hopes to reestablish family prosperity. And its practitioners should appreciate that the rich democracies are justified in reacting, as explained by Harvard economist Dani Rodrik:

> "If China and other developing nations want their policy space, they will have to allow rich nations to have theirs as well. China has every right to maintain its distinctive institutions; but it cannot expect other nations to alter their own economic and social models under threat

---

inspection of luggage at O'Hare airport prevented the telecom giant Huawei from stealing technology that Motorola spent $600 million developing. See Jamil Anderlini, Peter Marsh, John Reed, Joseph Menn, Peggy Hollinger, and Daniel Schäfer, "Industrial Espionage: Data Out the Door," *Financial Times*, Feb. 1, 2011.

from Chinese competition. Furthermore, China's nondemocratic political regime requires that its trade receive much greater scrutiny than the trade of other countries like Brazil, Turkey, or India."[40]

Presidents as far apart politically as Ronald Reagan and Jimmy Carter have selectively adopted Hamiltonian policies in the past to neutralize foreign mercantilist trade practices. President Carter, for example, insisted on US domestic content by high-performing Japanese auto firms in the late 1970s. His demands quickly became bipartisan, drawing in support from Republican governors such as (now Senator) Lamar Alexander. And it resulted in a wave of auto firms establishing manufacturing in Tennessee and elsewhere, supplanting vehicles being exported from Japan. American University professor emeritus Stephen D. Cohen explained what happened: "The pressure put on the Japanese was absolutely critical for them to agree to export restraints."[41]

Leaders of the family capitalism countries and President Obama need to apply this history today. They certainly have a target-rich environment. For example, Chinese currency undervaluation has become a chronic irritant, equivalent to a tax on GE or Daimler imports being sold there as well as a hidden subsidy to Chinese exports, such as giant wind generators. The Obama administration hopes to include prohibitions on currency manipulation in trade agreements, beginning with the Trans-Pacific talks in spring 2013. And aggressive steps are needed to neutralize other illegal trade practices, a difficult challenge as Beattie notes. A poster child for the ineffectiveness of policies to neutralize such illegal trade practices is the predicament dramatized by Maurice Taylor, CEO of the US tire firm Titan International. Titan had limited success in enlisting Washington to help preserve US jobs in the face of Chinese export subsidies. The experience helped convince Taylor to become a citizen of the world like Microsoft's Ballmer or Apple's Cook. "Titan is going to buy a Chinese tyre company or an Indian one, pay less than one euro per hour wage and ship all the tyres France needs," explained the former American Republican Party politician in February 2013.[42]

More difficult still is the urgency of formulating a response to exporters in mercantilist countries exploiting cheap domestic wages and weak labor standards. They gain a competitive advantage not related to superior efficiency or innovation, but due to poor standards at home that are illegal in the rich democracies. They gain market share in the United States and European Union through the backdoor. The rich democracies do have mechanisms to tax foreign suppliers whose cheap imports exploit the weak standards loophole; the EU imposed such penalties on imported oranges in February 2013, for example, because of lax food safety requirements in China.[43] But the process is creaky, with relief occurring belatedly and episodically; the policies are ineffective in stemming the destruction of valuable jobs by producers in mercantilist countries or firms like Titan pursuing the Apple business model. Reform of this process to close the backdoor should be the highest priority for the rich democracies.

Stabilize Precarious Employment

A gridlocked Washington enshrines the disposable labor model, leaving most Americans to find job stability and rising real wages only in grandparents' scrapbooks. The commoditization of employees during the Reagan decline has featured the rise of precarious employment, with new jobs increasingly being insecure ones. As sociologist Erin Hatton at the State University of New York in Buffalo notes, "Over the last three years, the temp industry added more jobs in the United States than any other. . . ."[44] Part-time employment has also increased dramatically. In the retail and hospitality sectors, for example, part timers are two and one-half times more numerous than in 2006. And overall in the retail and wholesale service sectors, about 30 percent of employees are part-time, according to BLS data, with the share considerably higher among industry leaders such as the big box giant Walmart.[45]

This trend reflects two phenomena. First, it's more profitable for employers; BLS statistics show that part-time employees in the service sector received an average $10.92 an hour in June 2012, including benefits, while full-time employees received $17.18 per hour, or 57 percent more. Second, the gush of computing capacity provided by the IT revolution has facilitated matching store needs with employee hours even down to the quarter hour, enabling employers to elaborately apply the just-in-time inventory concept to human beings. Many part-timers are required to call in each morning before reporting.[46]

These new characteristics add to the unsatisfying nature of work in today's economy for tens of millions of commoditized Americans, their wages and working hours shorn, too many reliant on food stamps and Medicaid, with little prospect of ever living the American Dream. Moreover, taxpayers are footing the bill: the public benefits these workers receive constitute opaque taxpayer subsidies to low-wage employers. It seems odd for American families to be subsidizing profitable firms such as Walmart.

In recent years, these features of the American disposable labor model have cropped up in some family capitalism countries, thwarting traditional protections and compressing some wages. Foreign economists such as Guy Standing at Bath University have provided valuable analysis of this trend abroad, which has also been informed by analyses prepared for the 2013 debate over establishing the nationwide German minimum wage.[47] Some employees—students, for example—may enjoy the flexibility provided by these nontraditional employment arrangements, but most men and women in rich democracies seek job stability and the higher wages provided by ordinary employment. Employers argue that job insecurity is necessary to accommodate fluctuations in the need for labor. And labor market flexibility has improved across northern Europe in the past decade, thanks to flexicurity and other reforms. But the low wages that are also common for such jobs dramatize the importance even in the EU of rules mandating livable wages. German sociologist Hajo Holst contends that these loopholes are profit-driven rather than reaction to inflexible labor markets.[48]

Among the family capitalism countries, precariats are perhaps most common in Australia. Indeed, Australians were likely stunned by data showing a sharp rise during 2012 in those holding precarious employment.[49] At a few Australian multinationals such as the giant miner BHP Billiton, systematic management strategies have seen regular employees dwindle to be a minority.[50] Precariats also include victimized Australians working for employers adopting the American-style independent contractor scam, common at US firms such as FedEx or SuperShuttle.[51]

While comprising a smaller share of the German workforce, the number of precariats has risen there as well since the 2003 labor market reforms. Trade unions have responded by negotiating worksite agreements in some sectors, which require that precariats receive the same pay as regular employees.[52] The rise in precariats was an important factor in the German minimum wage debate.

Expanding codeterminism to Australia and America may neutralize the precarious employment business model to some degree. Yet the German trend is sobering and emphasizes the need for strengthening family-friendly labor market rules everywhere. In particular, precariats should receive competitive pay and fringe benefits after a limited training period as suggested by the German Bertelsmann Foundation.[53]

Tax Reform, Including Closing Tax Havens

A first priority is improving tax equity. Revenue lost from corporate tax cuts have been replaced by regressive payroll taxes. Lifting the earnings cap on payroll taxes will improve equity; the poorest Americans pay a combined 14.6 percent FICA rate while the effective rate on the top one percent is just 1.8 percent. Another source of inequity is the disparity in taxes on various forms of income. The oligarch Andrew W. Mellon is scarcely an historical figure one might associate with family prosperity. Yet Mellon believed that taxes on income from capital should not be favored and rates should be set at least as high as taxes on wages.

Will higher rates on capital gains harm investment, hiring, and economic growth? President Reagan didn't think so when raising the rate by nearly half to 28 percent in 1986. Nor do former Treasury Secretaries Robert Rubin or Lawrence Summers. Low taxes on capital benefits owners of legacy capital, but entrepreneurs have other priorities; they are interested in creating new wealth not shielding old wealth. Tax rates have no detectable impact on GDP or productivity, and the historical record bears this out: US growth and hiring have been the weakest when capital gains rates have been the lowest, a pattern that has persisted throughout the entire Reagan decline. GDP has grown more than twice as fast in periods of high tax rates on capital gains (1982–2002) as in periods of low rates (2003–2011).[54] Such causality is not proof, but rigorous scholarly analyses examining the evidence provide that proof. One recent example is a 2012 Congressional Research Service study by economist Thomas L. Hungerford. He concluded: "Analysis of such data suggests the reduction in top tax rates have had little association with savings, investment, or productivity growth."[55] Other factors influence these macroeconomic variables, but tax rates on capital do not.

Equally important to the question of tax fairness is elimination of tax havens used by wealthy citizens and multinational enterprises to shift their taxes onto others. Tax havens launder money. They are pirates, surfing the global economy, indulged by politicians in Berlin, London, Paris, Tokyo, and Washington. The OECD has identified forty-two tax havens, such as the Cayman Islands and Switzerland, where hiding foreign money is an economic mainstay. Local economies there prosper from banking laws promising low taxes and secrecy to wealthy foreigners, drug dealers, smugglers, multinationals, arms merchants, and tyrants with bloody hands.

The United States is a big loser from the piratical tax haven business model.[56] In combination with weakly drawn American laws and under-resourced tax officials, havens have converted the payment of taxes by wealthy Americans and US multinationals such as Apple, Caterpillar, and GE to a voluntary exercise. "Taxes are only paid by the naïve," is how the OECD described this tax environment in February 2013.[57] Tax fairness and large American budget deficits argue for closing havens, which could generate as much as $100 billion annually in tax revenue alone just for the United States, according to government estimates reported by Gretchen Morgenson of the *New York Times*.[58]

Turning first to personal taxes, Swiss banks accommodate American and other foreign tax cheats utilizing a contrived distinction between tax fraud and tax evasion, the latter defined as legal in Swiss law. A prominent Swiss strategy involves selling tax indulgences to wealthy foreign tax dodgers, the purchaser becoming a Swiss citizen of convenience for a year at a time—for the price of a hotel stay. It works this way: At the end of 2010, 5,445 foreigners, including the wealthiest German, Baron von Finck, and French singer Johnny Hallyday, purchased Swiss citizenship for a *forfait* fee tied to a small multiple of the cost of renting accommodations for a year. Thus, for an average cost reportedly of about $130,000 annually, foreigners can significantly reduce or avoid income taxes elsewhere in the world. The Swiss like the scheme because these tax fugitives spend an average of $250,000 each, supporting an estimated 23,000 jobs.[59]

The rich democracies have grown impatient with such chicanery, and several years ago called for havens to terminate their business models or be blacklisted and face economic sanctions; officials at the April 2009 G-20 meeting in London authorized such sanctions. The Obama Administration has been supportive and began aggressively pursuing Americans with hidden wealth abroad, using scofflaw laws enacted early in its first term over the strenuous objection of Congressional Republicans. Since then, the Justice Department has prosecuted eleven Swiss banks for aiding tax dodgers.[60] And international agreements have been reached requiring Swiss and other foreign banks to identify US accounts exceeding $50,000, opening the door to audits from which the IRS expects to reap $8 billion in tax receipts. Uncooperative foreign banks face sizable penalties on their US-based income, causing many now to shy away from US customers.[61]

In Europe, some tax dodgers, such as former tennis great Boris Becker, are snared for misclaiming residence in tax havens like Monaco; Becker actually lived in Munich. The crackdown there has also inspired entrepreneurial instincts among some European bankers in these tax havens; they have begun whistle-blowing, selling electronic files listing the names of wealthy tax dodgers to officials in the United States, Germany, and elsewhere. It can be quite profitable. The IRS paid a record $104 million in 2012 to a former UBS banker who shared records on 5,000 American tax cheats, for example. Those records resulted in UBS paying a fine of $780 million and audits that produced $5 billion in taxes and penalties.[62]

Whistle-blower bounties have proven to be good investments for Germany and Australia as well. In recent years, finance ministers in the German states of North Rhine-Westphalia and Lower Saxony, along with national tax officials, have paid millions of Euros to purchase purloined account information fingering thousands of tax dodgers.[63] For bounty payments of €4.6 million, for example, the Merkel government has recouped nearly €200 million from German tax cheats laundering income through the Liechtenstein bank LGT. One tax cheat was the then-CEO of Deutsche Post, Klaus Zumwinkel, who was fined €1 million in January 2009.[64] And another €200 million was recouped from German tax evaders hiding funds in Swiss banks, according to a 2010 report in *Handelsblatt*.[65] Germany also shared a compact disc listing account holders at the LGT bank with Australia, whose tax investigators and courts have gone after more than twenty of those listed. At least one tax dodger there (and now fugitive) was hiding sufficient wealth to trigger a $36 million tax bill.[66]

Swiss officials are certainly aware that they are conspiring with drug smugglers, African warlords, and arms merchants. Swiss president Eveline Widmer-Schlumpf acknowledged in a *Der Spiegel* interview in December 2012 that her nation's refusal to expose names enables foreign bank account holders to evade prosecution until statutes of limitation abroad expire.[67] Yet bankers and politicians there appear unembarrassed by the piratical business model. The powerful banking industry has even prevailed upon Widmer-Schlumpf to accuse German tax authorities purchasing compact discs of "organized crime." I doubt the irony was lost on Ms. Widmer-Schlumpf.[68] Swiss officials have also reacted by criminalizing whistle blowing. And, provincial German tax officials paying bounties for compact discs have been indicted, with arrest warrants issued by Swiss prosecutors across the border.[69] The controversy has sparked a bit of reform in Bern, although the Swiss idea of tax reform was for the legislature in mid-2012 to raise the *forfait* to a slightly higher multiple of the cost of an annual stay.[70]

Turning now to corporate taxes, US Treasury department economist Harry Grubert indicates that an era of competitive tax cuts internationally for corporations began with the arrival of the Reagan era in the United States and United Kingdom.[71] Multinationals began to conduct tax arbitrage, promising new jobs to eager nations like Ireland, causing a race to the bottom in global corporate taxes.

There are effective remedies if voters choose to demand them. Reform must begin with accurate data. Domestically that means Congress should require that corporations report how much tax they paid. Internationally, that means adopting something resembling a global tax information system patterned on the Common Consolidated Corporate Tax Base concept, credentialed editorially by the *Financial Times*.[72] In 2012, the European Parliament also endorsed that concept which would resolve uncertainty around complex issues such as digitized sales and transfer pricing exploited by firms such as Apple.[73] The EU's first step was to require country-by-country reporting of income and taxes in 2014. This applies just to banks, however, and uniformity in tax rates will be facilitated by widespread adoption of a comprehensive international database of corporate sales and expenses from all economic sectors, greatly aiding those officials hoping to stem the race to the bottom in corporate tax rates.*

Fairness and ending tax dodging are important, but there are also important economic reasons for the United States to support international tax conformity. The Congressional Budget Office in a January 2013 report concluded that the current tax regime hurts American employment, reduces economic efficiency, and penalizes taxpayers and shareholders:

> "The current tax system provides incentives for US firms to locate their production facilities in countries with low taxes as a way to reduce their tax liability at home. Those responses to the tax system reduce economic efficiency—the extent to which resources are allocated so as to maximize their value—because the firms are not allocating resources to their most productive use. Those responses also reduce the income of shareholders and employees in the United States, and they lead to a loss of federal tax revenue."[74]

The February 2013 OECD report cited earlier also stressed the harm posed by the current tax regime to domestic competitors of multinationals and to economic efficiency:

> ". . . [multinationals] have unintended competitive advantages compared with enterprises that operate mostly at the domestic level. In addition to issues of fairness, this may lead to an inefficient allocation of resources by distorting investment decisions toward activities that have lower pre-tax rates of return, but higher after-tax rates of return."[75]

A final step is enforcement of existing laws, an area where Australia offers a useful lesson. The Australian Tax Office (ATO) has imposed a A$738 million ($760 million) tax bill on the American private-equity firm Texas Pacific Group from its sale of the Myer department store

---

*Not all European governments appear sincere about tax reform. The Tory government of Prime Minister Cameron, for example, laments the low tax burden of multinationals like Starbucks and Google. Yet it has cut British tax rates on corporate profits and importantly introduced a patent tax loophole shielding high value intangibles from taxes. See John Gapper, "Corporate Tax Posturing Should Stop," *Financial Times*, Jan. 30, 2013.

chain there a few years ago. Texas Pacific obfuscated the accounting trail, immediately secreting the proceeds by rushing them from Australia to a Dutch shell company called NB Swanston BV, then to another in Luxembourg—NB Queen SARL—and finally to TPG Newbridge Myer in the Cayman Islands. The ATO is demanding that the Luxembourg and Cayman Island shell companies pay taxes, interest, and penalties due Australia.[76] The lesson for the United States is this: The ATO's Texas Pacific tax bill presumes logically that the proceeds of the Myer transaction be taxed as ordinary income, rather than as capital gains, as lobbied by Texas Pacific. In December 2010, the ATO determined that since buying and selling firms is the main activity of enterprises such as Texas Pacific, proceeds on such transactions are taxable as ordinary business income, not as capital gains.[77] This is the same logic involved in the carried-interest debate in the US Congress, where reform is presently gridlocked by Congressional Republicans.

Restore Financial Market Discipline by Eliminating Red Queens

The American economy needs to be protected from the baker's dozen Red Queens that have emerged in recent decades of willful neglect of antitrust laws. The goal of that protection was spelled out by Walter Bagehot a century and a half ago:

> "The business of banking ought to be simple. If it is hard it is wrong. The only securities which a banker, using money that he may be asked at short notice to repay, ought to touch, are those which are easily saleable and easily intelligible."[78]

Joseph Stiglitz verified Bagehot's principle using contemporary evidence in December 2011. It turns out that the most severe economic crises in recent history all share a common root, even though nominally attributed to a variety of different factors such as excessive national borrowing (Latin America, 1980s) or weak national governance (Asia, 1990s). Stiglitz determined that the common denominator was a deregulated financial sector.[79] Thus, the absolutely nonnegotiable condition necessary to minimize the recurrence of financial crises such as 2007–2008 is a well-regulated financial sector. Other conditions, such as prudent government finance and sound money policies, are also important, but the major lesson taught by history is that unless the banking sector is corralled, turmoil is inevitable.

Tighter regulation does not substitute for eradicating Red Queens, banks too big to fail. The regulatory collapse marking the Reagan decline demonstrates that even tight rules are inevitably suborned by the financial sector over time. There are current examples of solid bank regulation, with the banking crisis bypassing nations such as Australia and Canada. Yet history teaches that tight regulation does not survive the test of time measured in decades or centuries. It is simply an uneven struggle as memories fade, with affluent banks always pressing for weaker rules, as Martin Wolf of the *Financial Times* explained in mid-2012:

> "My interpretation of the Libor [interest rate fixing] scandal is the obvious one: banks, as presently constituted and managed, cannot be trusted to perform any publicly important function, against the perceived interests of their staff. Today's banks represent the incarnation of profit-seeking behavior taken to its logical limits, in which the only question asked by senior staff is not what is their duty or their responsibility, but what can they get away with."[80]

Washington should move in a deliberate, transparent, and investor-friendly manner to eliminate the thirteen Red Queens, as proposed by bipartisan experts including former Federal Reserve System chairman Paul Volcker, Richard W. Fisher, president of the Dallas Fed, Thomas Hoenig, former president of the Kansas City Fed and current Fed governor Dan Tarullo. Even former private bankers—Sandy Weill and John Reed of Citigroup and Phil Purcell of Morgan Stanley, for example—acknowledge the wisdom of eliminating Red Queens.[81] According to Fisher, ". . . the social costs associated with those big financial institutions are much greater than any benefits they may provide. We need to find some international convention to limit their size."[82] He later described the calamitous Greenspan-Mankiw-Hubbard regulatory collapse of the Reagan decline as one "that coddles survival of the fattest rather than promoting survival of the fittest."[83]

Shrinking commercial behemoths is not uncommon in US history. America broke up Standard Oil in 1911, AT&T later, and bank downsizing is commonplace in the United States and abroad today during financial crises, with a proven record of success. Indeed, breakups abroad are even frequently conducted in troubled nations at the *insistence* of US officials. European regulators do the same thing, recently ordering the giant bankrupt Dutch conglomerate ING broken up, and its insurance and online American banking subsidiaries sold.

A variety of options for eliminating Red Queens have been discussed; the *Financial Times* and Volcker have proposed that their depository (retail) activities be entirely sold off from investment activities, for example.[84] Another option is to limit bank size as proposed by Tarullo, Ohio Senator Sharrod Brown and MIT's Simon Johnson to a set proportion of US GDP, say 1 or 2 percent.[85] The resulting size would still be larger than the optimal suggested by Andrew Haldane and colleagues at the Bank of England. They concluded that economies of scale for banks disappear when assets exceed $100 billion, which should be an internationally adopted size ceiling.[86] In the interim before such reforms, New York University professor Nassim Nicholas Taleb of "black swan" fame has proposed eliminating all bonuses at Red Queens to reduce risk and the odds of further taxpayer bailouts.[87]

Deflate Executive Compensation

While the most dramatic examples of market failure in pay-for-performance occurred on Wall Street, it has been broadly characteristic of the American business community during the Reagan decline. It also occurs in other nations that adopted Reaganomics: The British High Pay Commission in 2011 found little correlation between pay and performance there either. So the Commission recommended restricting executive pay to a reasonable multiple of median pay within the firm, a position editorially endorsed on a global basis by the *Financial Times*.[88] Fortunately, there is a model pay standard, based on research by the US management expert Peter Drucker. Compared to median enterprise pay, he determined that "a 20-to-1 salary ratio is the limit beyond which [management] cannot go if they don't want resentment and falling morale to hit their companies."[89] The exception? CEOs in very good years at large firms should be capped to $10 million as discussed in Germany.

A first step toward implementing Drucker's ratio is the introduction of codeterminism, with employees joining compensation committees in the boardroom. A second step is to make US executive pay packages simple and transparent, as proposed by the High Pay Commission. Opaque compensation presentations are a widespread abuse in the United States as well as Australia. Public ire has forced Australian firms to release more executive pay information. Yet the giant mining firm BHP Billiton responded with a 25-page remuneration report in September 2012, difficult to navigate and even more difficult to understand. The challenge is general, with firms too often responding with opaque reports filled with intricate and obfuscating calculations and details. An extreme example is another Australian mining firm called Aquila Resources whose CEO, Tony Poli, was paid A$169 million ($180 million) in 2011 but whose compensation listed in the annual report was A$572,000.[90]

A third step is to strengthen the role of shareholders in approving executive remuneration. The Dodd-Frank reforms mandate "say-on-pay" votes by shareholders, but the vote is nonbinding, an approach already proven ineffective when tried in the United Kingdom.[91] That is changing under a proposal adopted in 2012 by the British conservative government to mandate binding shareholder approval of executive compensation. Listed UK firms must also provide a single—and presumably transparent—figure for each executive's total pay as well.[92] In March 2013, Swiss voters also approved a "say-on-pay" law requiring shareholder approval of executive pay. And the *Financial Times* endorsed that process:

> "Approval votes [on remuneration] should be made binding. . . . The strongest case for empowering shareholders is that the nature of their protest still seems to pass many executives by. This is not a problem of 'poor communication,' as some companies seem to think, but one of substance. Shareholders want executives to perform for their pay. Is that so much to ask?"[93]

Empowering shareholders with binding say-on-pay voting has dampened remuneration, and is an important step to incentivize pay-for-performance. In the Netherlands, for example, shareholders have held binding votes on pay since 2004, resulting in reduced or modified remuneration schedules even at world-class giants such as Phillips, DSM, Royal Dutch Shell, and Heineken.[94]

An effective say-on-pay tactic was enactment of the Australian Two Strikes law in 2011. It has forced boards to improve accountability on pay, as reported in November 2012 by journalist Michael West:

> "And so it is that executive bonuses are down to their lowest levels since 2003, and in nominal dollars to boot. The 'two strikes' regime is working. It has personalized the issue of pay. Boards don't like the embarrassment of having their remuneration report rejected."[95]

Boards at firms suffering first strike votes in 2011, such as Crown Ltd or Sirtex, have become much more engaged with shareholders, paring back pay packages, foregoing bonuses not reflective of performance, and adopting more demanding standards for any extra pay.[96] In total, eight of the ten largest firms subject to first strike votes in 2011 cut executive remuneration significantly.[97] Another measure of its success is that few firms in the second year of the law suffered a first or second strike vote. Moreover, it is significant that many of the discussions preceding strike votes at general shareholder meetings in 2012 focused on reasons for firm underperformance as well as compensation levels. The global bionic hearing aid firm Cochlear, for example, suffered a first strike vote in 2012 mostly because of poor management performance, not remuneration.[98] This trend reflects a desirable heightened degree of shareholder engagement in overall enterprise operation.

Deincentivize Risky Management: Limit Variable Pay Incentives

As important as they are in their own right, correcting extreme remuneration and reestablishing pay-for-performance are less urgent than the need to terminate business community compensation practices that incentivize short-termism. Variable pay options linked to share prices should be largely banned in order to eliminate quarterly capitalism. Moreover, stock options thwart pay-for-performance goals because payouts are determined in too many instances by obsequious boards or gyrating share markets unreflective of executive performance. Options don't punish incompetence either, as Michael Jensen and Kevin Murphy observed many years ago; indeed, the broken market for executive compensation is symbolized by boards renegotiating strike prices or even backdating option terms, enabling American executives to bizarrely profit from failure as well as success. These behaviors reveal that the goal of variable pay schemes is to maximize executive compensation, not pay-for-performance.

Banning options would likely reduce mergers as well, a good thing for shareholders as determined by the National Bureau of Economic Research analysis of Malmendier, Moretti, and Peters. Recall they concluded that shareholders in acquiring firms consistently fared poorly from [Mark] Hurd-like merger activity.[99]

Deferring option payouts for some years is no solution, and proved a failure during the 2000s, as evidenced by firms such as Lehman Brothers and Bear Stearns. While driving their firms bankrupt with risky behavior, Bear Stearns CEO James E. Cayne, Lehman CEO Fuld, and their top four lieutenants cashed out over $2.4 billion from 2000–2008, according to the Program on Corporate Governance at Harvard Law School.[100] Much was deferred for a few years, reports Louise Story of the *New York Times*, but this failed to prevent bankruptcy.[101] Moreover, internal reform of the options system is unlikely because boards are in denial: 83 percent of US boards believe that options improve executive performance, according to a 2010 PricewaterhouseCoopers survey. And they dislike being second-guessed with reforms such as Two Strikes: three-quarters of them oppose granting shareholders any vote on compensation packages.[102]

Subject to abuse and manipulation, stock options should be permissible only for start-ups as a tool to encourage entrepreneurship. Americans benefit from the entrepreneurial spirit inspiring firms such as Apple, Facebook, Google, and Microsoft, and options are a useful compensation adjunct for cash-strapped firms at a nascent stage of product development. That scarcely describes these high-tech enterprises, Red Queens or the vast majority of US firms today that use options, however.

Despite the harmful incentive effects of variable pay linked to share prices, there is certainly a role for performance *bonuses;* some firms in Europe are adopting them in lieu of options, in the belief that they can be more carefully calibrated to induce pay-for-performance. The French global giant GDF Suez, for example, went some distance in that direction in 2010, abandoning options and instead linking prospective executive bonus incentive payments to demanding performance standards measured two years hence.[103] And L'Oreal abandoned options in 2012, replaced by a transparent variable bonus tied to four-year performance measures.[104]

The ideal variable or performance pay structure would be to mimic the historic but discarded investment bank partnership risk-reward calculus linking management remuneration to prudent asset stewardship. Recreating that calculus today would consist of four elements. First, bonuses should be linked to long-term performance measures, not share performance, with options banned. Second, bonuses should be payable primarily in unsecured firm debt, ranked the lowest within the hierarchy of debt commitments on its balance sheet with weakest claims on assets. That reform was proposed in the Liikanen report in October 2012 to the EU banking commission, and was adopted in 2013 by the troubled Swiss bank UBS for its most valuable 6,500 employees. Bonuses fully vest there only after five years, and are paid in UBS bonds that can be wiped out if legal capital requirements are breached by investment losses.[105] I suspect bankers at least at that firm now watch the behavior of their colleagues carefully.

Third, bonuses should be limited to a ratio of 1:1 with salary as required by the European parliament in March 2013 (although just for banks). Fourth, it seems sensible to include clawbacks as a standard element of any variable pay scheme; the Dutch financial conglomerate ING, for example, asked its best-paid 1,200 employees in March 2009 to return bonuses after a difficult 2008.[106] Clawbacks are uncommon in the United States, although JP Morgan Chase recently cancelled millions of dollars in bonuses to employees involved in a $5.8 billion investment loss. They are more common in Europe and even in the United Kingdom since the Financial Services Authority in London imposed clawback rules in 2009, targeted at bad apples. That is perhaps why Lloyds Banking Group reclaimed bonuses paid to senior executives who engineered a consumer scam.[107] And it seems likely that the LIBOR scandal will eventually involve clawbacks at firms such as Barclays.

The general framework just outlined, with modest bonuses featuring delayed vesting and dependent on long-term performance metrics, has been endorsed by academics, notably the Squam Lake Group of economists including Kenneth French of Dartmouth and Robert Shiller of Yale.[108] And its principles are reflected in Germany's VorstAG law enacted in July 2009, explicitly intended to lengthen executive time horizons, with incentive pay vesting only after four years.[109] Moreover, risky decision-making is discouraged by its legal provisions precluding management profiting from extraordinary developments such as takeovers or other realization of hidden assets.

The March 2013 cap imposed by the EU on bank bonus payments satisfies most of these criteria. Indeed, the reforms were a remarkable achievement as noted by the usually understated *Financial Times* journalist Alex Barker:

> "Politicians the world over have huffed and puffed about excessive pay at banks since 2008. While remuneration curbs were put in place, nothing fundamentally challenged bank operations, or their ultimate flexibility to reward staff. The European Parliament has bucked that trend with the mother of all bonus clampdowns."[110]

Bonuses paid in the future to bankers anywhere in the EU cannot exceed fixed pay. That absolute cap can be temporarily raised to twice fixed pay if a super majority of 66 percent of voting shareholders approve; in that case, some of the bonus must be linked to longer-term performance, and be subject to clawback. The cap may also be extended beyond bankers to apply to asset managers, large hedge funds, and private equity funds. The adoption of similar caps by the United States would modulate the risky behavior of Wall Street.

A Larger American Government?

Family capitalism featuring Australian-style wage determination and codeterminism is compatible with either small or large public sectors, because the size of government has nothing to do with whether families or firms enjoy economic sovereignty. With that in mind, the steps proposed above to return economic sovereignty to families are consistent with the Jeffersonian tradition featuring "limited but energetic governments that used aggressive federal power to promote growth and social mobility," as described by David Brooks, a small-government conservative. He noted in September 2010 that the founding fathers,

> ". . . didn't build their political philosophy on whether government was big or not. Government is a means, not an end. They built their philosophy on making America virtuous, dynamic and great. They supported government action when it furthered those ends and opposed it when it didn't."[111]

Time for Political Courage

Hope.

Hope is among the most powerful of human emotions, and the themes in this book provide hope by introducing a pathway for restoring family prosperity as the American economic covenant. The Eurozone is dealing with a flawed design, excessive sovereign debt, and slow economic growth. Yet beneath that macroeconomic uncertainty, public institutions in sober northern Europe as in Australia continue functioning smoothly in delivering the American Dream.

In America, it's far too late for baby boomers or Tea Partiers to recover the generation of toil lost during the Reagan decline. The question is whether their children will fare any better. Yet families have the means as voters to rekindle another golden age of stakeholder capitalism, where their children's hard work will mean a good paycheck and wages that rise apace with productivity. Transformation through the ballot box also requires political courage from leaders willing to challenge established routines in order to return economic sovereignty to families. They can take some courage from polling data indicating that at least independents and Democratic Party–leaning Americans are as supportive of additional regulation of the business community as respondents in Australia, France, and Germany.[112]

Can the political base for reform be expanded further? It is certainly true that the donor class favors legislative gridlock to perpetuate the present allocation of the gains from growth. But that gridlock is sustained by Republican-Party leaning voters, typically conservative, who actually receive few of those gains. Their conviction that government cannot deliver value is compounded by the reality in their daily lives of economic stagnation. Harvard economist Benjamin Friedman draws from history to argue that periods of economic malaise like today can induce deep social fragmentation that reduces the inclination of voters to compromise. Politics becomes in the eyes of many voters a zero-sum game:

> "The unwillingness to entertain compromise with one's political opponents on the central issues of the day is a phenomenon all too familiar in times when participants in a democratic society lose the sense that society is delivering any material improvement in their lives."[113]

Australian-style wage determination and codeterminism carry the promise of side-stepping the Friedman conundrum because evidence is persuasive that they can enable virtually all to gain. That could translate into support from across the political spectrum.

One thing is certain. The reforms proposed provide the only viable pathway for restoring the promise of Adam Smith. He gazed across lands where income disparities were stark and envisioned a better world, one where economic sovereignty resided with families. Americans face that same environment today and the challenges are equally formidable because the necessary reforms bear on the most fundamental step any democracy can peacefully undertake: transferring economic sovereignty.

History is encouraging. Eighteenth-century Europe pivoted away from the age-old historic model of wide income disparities. The United States did the same thing in the Great Depression by creating conditions for the greatest middle class in history to emerge and live the American Dream. Moreover, those seeking to reestablish family economic sovereignty come armed with the certitude that these reforms will restore the American Dream just as they are sustaining that Dream now in the family capitalism countries. America prides itself as the embodiment of the universal principles of democracy, freedom, free enterprise, and the rule of law. It is time once again to also become the embodiment of the American Dream.

A new golden age awaits only the courage of leaders to sharpen the policy choices facing voters, and for American families to bootstrap themselves at the ballot box.

ACKNOWLEDGMENTS

This book exists because of Hellen Gelband, who asked me to coauthor the concept paper for what became the Geneva-based medical research nonprofit organization, Drugs for Neglected Diseases initiative. Hellen is now Associate Director for Policy at the Center for Disease Dynamics, Economics & Policy in Washington and New Delhi.

Three economists and friends offered support and sage advice that have been invaluable in forming my ideas and in critiquing these pages as they took shape. All were members of a remarkable group of colleagues with me at the Congressional Joint Economic Committee. Daniel Bond moved on to establish the country risk analysis protocols at the Export Import Bank of the United States in Washington and later performed in similar capacities at Duff & Phelps Credit Rating Company and Ambac Assurance Corporation in New York. Dan now serves as a consultant to several public and private groups. James Klumpner went on to serve as chief economist for both the House and Senate Budget Committees and more recently has been a Visiting Lecturer at Princeton University, George Washington University, and at Georgetown University. David Podoff became Senator Daniel Patrick Moynihan's Chief of Staff for the Senate Finance Committee and is now an Adjunct Professor of Public Policy at Georgetown University and at the University of North Carolina–Chapel Hill.

Many others—some of whom will recognize their ideas in the text—were critical to the evolution of my thoughts. I particularly want to thank Stephen Pursey and Kristen Sobeck with the International Labor Organization in Geneva and Roland Schneider with the Organization for Economic Cooperation and Development's Trade Union Advisory Committee in Paris for their valuable advice and direction. I also want to thank the research professionals at the Fair Work Commission library in Melbourne and at the Australian Productivity Commission, whose guidance and support has been vital.

I am grateful to Erin Kelley, Leigh Camp, and Sarah Dombrowsky at BenBella Press for their expertise and careful review of the manuscript and especially to Glenn Yeffeth for his enthusiasm for this project. Finally, I want to acknowledge the vital role of my agent, Howard Yoon at the Ross Yoon Literary Agency in Washington, for his early and persistent encouragement.

ENDNOTES

SECTION ONE

CHAPTER 1

[1] James Goldsmith, *The Trap* (London: Carroll & Graf, 1994), 50.

[2] Thomas Schulz, "On the Way Down: The Erosion of America's Middle Class," *Der Spiegel*, August 19, 2010, http://www.spiegel.de/international/world/on-the-way-down-the-erosion-of-america-s-middle-class-a-712496.html.

[3] Paul Mason, "The graduate without a future," *The Guardian*, July 1, 2012.

[4] Thomas Piketty and Emmanuel Saez, "Income Inequality in the United States, 1913 to 1998," *Quarterly Journal of Economics* 118, no. 1 (2003): 1-39.

[5] Emmanuel Saez, "Striking it Richer: The Evolution of Top Incomes in the United States," *Pathways*, Stanford Center on Poverty and Inequality (Winter 2008), 6–7.

[6] Alexander Keyssar, "The real grand bargain, coming undone," *Washington Post*, August 21, 2011.

[7] "Australia near top ranking in economic freedom," *Sydney Morning Herald*, January 13, 2012.

[8] An October 2012 Credit Suisse survey identified Australia as having the world's highest median wealth per capita ($193,653) of 216 nations. "Australians are the world's wealthiest," *Brisbane Times*, October 11, 2012, http://www.brisbanetimes.com.au/business/world-business/Australians-are-the-worlds-wealthiest-20121011-27enm.html.

[9] Our proposal featured what was an unprecedented collaboration of nonprofits with the pharmaceutical industry to conduct research on medicines for neglected diseases in tropical nations, such as malaria and African Sleeping Sickness. It was advanced in collaboration with Dr. Yves Champey, former research director at Sanofi Aventis, and a working group chaired by the remarkable Dr. James Orbinski, then International President of Doctors Without Borders. Dr. Orbinski was the aid organization's Head of Mission in Kigali during the Rwandan genocide of 1994 and Head of Mission in Goma, Zaire, from 1996–1997 during the refugee crisis. In 1999 he accepted

the Nobel Peace Prize awarded to Doctors Without Borders. Headquartered in Geneva, the CEO of DNDi is Dr. Bernard Pecoul.

[10] Steven Greenhouse, "A Company in Good Health Seeks Cuts; Strife Follows," *New York Times*, August 18, 2010.

[11] Louis Uchitelle, "An Argument Against a Two-Tier Pay System," Economix (blog), *New York Times*, November 25, 2010.

[12] Charles Duhigg and Keith Bradsher, "How the U.S. Lost Out on iPhone Work," *New York Times*, January 21, 2012.

[13] Adam Smith, *An Inquiry into the Nature and Causes of the Wealth of Nations* (London: Oxford University Press, 1993), 94.

CHAPTER 2

[1] Peter Whoriskey, "A bargain for BMW means jobs for 1,000 in S. Carolina," *Washington Post*, October 27, 2010.

[2] James Goldsmith, "The Case Against GATT: An interview with James Goldsmith," *Multinational Monitor*, 1994, http://www.multinationalmonitor.org/hyper/issues/1994/10/mm1094_06.html.

[3] Dani Rodrik, *The Globalization Paradox: Democracy and the Future of the World Economy* (New York: W.W. Norton and Company, 2011), 237.

[4] Jonathan Mahler, "Slipping Away," *New York Times Magazine*, June 28, 2009.

[5] Ben Austen, "End of the Road," *Harper's Magazine*, August 2009.

[6] Timothy Noah, *The Great Divergence: America's Growing Inequality Crisis and What We Can Do About It* (New York: Bloomsbury Press, 2012).

[7] Bill Vlasic and Nick Bunkley, "U.A.W. Urges Automakers to Raise Entry-Level Pay in New Labor Deal," *New York Times*, August 30, 2011.

[8] Michael A. Fletcher, "In Rust Belt, manufacturers add jobs, but factory pay isn't what it used to be," *Washington Post*, May 17, 2011. For minimum wages, see http://www.dol.gov/elaws/faq/esa/flsa/001.html.

[9] Austen, "End of the Road."

[10] Bernie Woodall, Ben Klayman, and Jan Schwartz, "U.A.W. takes aim at foreign automakers," *Reuters on AutosonMSNBC.com*, December 29, 2011.

[11] Patrik Jonsson, "America's 'other' auto industry," *Christian Science Monitor*, December 5, 2008.

[12] Michael Luo, "$13 an Hour? 500 Sign Up, 1 Wins a Job," *New York Times*, October 21, 2009.

[13] Associated Press, "Union drive at IKEA plant in US takes aim at Swedish furniture giant's worker-friendly rep," *Washington Post*, July 23, 2011.

[14] Bernard Simon and Matt Kennard, "Two-tier system divides US carmaker workers," *Financial Times*, December 14, 2011.

[15] Vickie Elmer, "Show them the money," *Washington Post*, October 24, 2007.

[16] "2007 Job Satisfaction: A survey report by the Society for Human Resource Management," *Society for Human Resource Management,* June 2007, http://www.workplacesolutionspros.com/resources/Job%20Satisfaction%20Survey%20Report.pdf.

[17] Emma Schwartz, "How a good job hit a dead end," *Washington Post*, April 22, 2012.

[18] Woodall, Klayman, and Schwartz, "U.A.W. takes aim at foreign automakers."

[19] Vlasic and Bunkley, "U.A.W. Urges Automakers to Raise Entry-Level Pay in New Labor Deal."

[20] Paul Osterman, "Yes, We Need Jobs. But What Kind?," *New York Times*, August 6, 2011.

[21] Catherine Rampell, "Majority of New Jobs Pay Low Wages, Study Finds," *New York Times*, August 30, 2012. The data was developed by the National Employment Law Project.

[22] "The American-Western European Values Gap, American Exceptionalism Subsides," *Pew Global Attitudes Project*, November 17, 2011, http://www.pewglobal.org/2011/11/17/the-american-western-european-values-gap/?src=prc-headline.

[23] Ibid.

[24] Harold Meyerson, "Unhappy Labor Day," *Washington Post*, September 7, 2009.

[25] Robert R. Trumble and Angela N. DeLowell, "Connecting CEO performance to corporate performance: Examining intangible metrics of shareholder value," *Journal of Compensation and Benefits*, November/December 2001.

[26] Alan Auerbach, "BEA Advisory Committee Meeting," *Bureau of Economic Analysis*, May 1, 2009.

[27] Steven Greenhouse and David Leonhardt, "Real Wages Fail to Match a Rise in Productivity," *New York Times*, August 28, 2006.

[28] See Robert Frank, "The 1% Captures Most Growth From Recovery," The Wealth Report (blog), *Wall Street Journal*, March 6, 2012, http://blogs.wsj.com/wealth/2012/03/06/the-1-captures-most-growth-from-recovery/.

[29] David Cay Johnston, *Free Lunch: How the Wealthiest Americans Enrich Themselves at Government Expense (and Stick You with the Bill)* (New York: Portfolio Trade, 2008), 277. See also: David Cay Johnston, "Richest Are Leaving Even the Rich Far Behind," *New York Times*, June 5, 2005.

[30] David Cay Johnston, *Perfectly Legal: The Covert Campaign to Rig Our Tax System to Benefit the Super Rich—and Cheat Everybody Else* (New York: Portfolio Trade, 2005), 41.

[31] By 1988, for example, the iconic conservative Murray M. Rothbard had concluded that "the monetarists, devoted to a money rule of a fixed per centage increase of money growth engineered by the Federal Reserve, have come a cropper. . . . The monetarists self-destructed by making a string of self-confident but disastrous predictions in the last several years." Murray M. Rothbard, "The Myths of Reaganomics," *Mises Daily*, June 9, 2004. John C. Williams, President of the Federal Reserve Bank of San Francisco, explained: "Viewing them as definitive in today's world is like thinking that rock and roll stopped with Elvis Presley." John C. Williams, "Economic Instruction and the Brave New World of Monetary Policy," *FRBSF*, June 6, 2011.

[32] See Ian Morris, *Why the West Rules—for Now: The Patterns of History, and What They Reveal About the Future* (New York: Picador, 2011), 259–60.

[33] Thomas J. Lewis, "Acquisition and Anxiety: Aristotle's Case against the Market," *The Canadian Journal of Economics* 11, no. 1 (1978): 69–90.

[34] Aristotle, *The Politics*, translated by T.A. Sinclair (Harmondsworth: Penguin Classics, 1962), 117.

[35] Larry M. Bartels, *Unequal Democracy: The Political Economy of the New Gilded Age* (Princeton, NJ: Princeton University Press, 2008): 283–4.

[36] Smith, *Wealth of Nations*, 129.

[37] Ibid., 376.

[38] The successful value investor George Soros has figured this all out and prospered by rejecting the illusionary virtual world of Friedman. Soros views markets as inherently irrational, afflicted by chronic ignorance. The only certainty in his world and in the real world is uncertainty. It is no accident that Soros' Quantum fund is named in honor of physicist Werner Heisenberg.

[39] John Kay, "How economics lost sight of the real world," *Financial Times*, April 21, 2009.

[40] Joseph Stiglitz, "Bleakonomics," *New York Times*, September 30, 2007.

[41] John Plender, "Capitalism in convulsion: Toxic assets head toward the public balance sheet," *Financial Times*, September 19, 2008.

[42] Nouriel Roubini, "Anglo-Saxon model has failed," *Financial Times*, February 9, 2009.

[43] Richard Thaler, "Markets can be wrong and the price is not always right," *Financial Times*, August 4, 2009.

[44] Ken Silverstein, "Labor's Last Stand," *Harper's Magazine*, July 2009.

[45] Naomi Klein, *The Shock Doctrine: The Rise of Disaster Capitalism* (New York: Picador, 2007), 68.

[46] David E. Hoffman, *The Dead Hand: The Untold Story of the Cold War Arms Race and Its Dangerous Legacy* (New York: Knopf Doubleday, 2009), 41.

[47] See David Frum, *Comeback: Conservatism That Can Win Again* (New York: Broadway Books, 2008).

[48] See Simon Johnson, "The Quiet Coup," *The Atlantic*, May 2009.

[49] Christine Mattauch, "The Secret Lobbyists," *Handelsblatt*, February 28, 2011. In reaction to a letter crafted by University of Massachusetts economist Gerald A. Epstein and signed by 300 of his colleagues including Nobel Laureate George Akerlof, the American Economic Association is considering a code of conduct, mostly to ensure transparency of outside connections for publicly opining economists.

[50] Jin-Hyuk Kim, "Corporate Lobbying Revisited," *Business and Politics* 10, no. 2 (2008).

[51] My former professor Gordon Tullock wondered why the business community didn't contribute more. Of course, that was decades ago, long before the Roberts Court empowered unlimited and, more importantly, anonymous firm donations. See Eduardo Porter, "Unleashing Corporate Contributions," *New York Times*, August 29, 2012.

[52] Steven Brill, "On Sale: Your Government. Why Lobbying Is Washington's Best Bargain," *Time Magazine*, July 12, 2012.

[53] Raquel Alexander, Steven Mazza, and Susan Scholz, "Measuring Rates of Return for Lobbying Expenditures: An Empirical Case Study of Tax Breaks for Multinational Corporations," *Journal of Law and Politics 25*, no. 401 (2009). doi:10.2139/ssrn.1375082. See also Dan Eggen, "Investments Can Yield More on K Street, Study Indicates," *Washington Post*, April 12, 2009.

[54] Kim Phillips-Fein, "One Notion: Individual—The Two Lives of Ayn Rand," *Harper's Magazine*, December 2009.

[55] See Tony Jackson, "Changing top pay is a long haul," *Financial Times*, January 8, 2012.

[56] Steven Pearlstein, "Toward a New International Capitalism," *Washington Post*, November 11, 2008.

[57] Greg Smith, "Why I am Leaving Goldman Sachs," *New York Times*, March 14, 2012.

[58] See Kyle Crichton, "Return of the theorist of capitalism's doom," *International Herald-Tribune*, February 16, 2009.

[59] Sylvia Nasar, *Grand Pursuit: The Story of Economic Genius* (New York: Simon & Schuster, 2011), 390.

[60] Simon Johnson, "No One Is Above the Law," Economix (blog), *New York Times*, December 23, 2011.

[61] Editorial, "Starting the Regulatory Work," *New York Times*, January 7, 2009.

[62] Martin Wolf, "Why the credit squeeze is a turning point for the world," *Financial Times*, December 12, 2007.

[63] David Pilling and Ralph Atkins, "A quest for other ways," *Financial Times*, March 15, 2009.

[64] Reena Aggarwal, Isil Erel, Rene Stulz, and Rohan Williamson, "Do U.S. Firms Have the Best Corporate Governance?: A Cross-Country Examination of the Relation Between Corporate Governance and Shareholder Wealth," *USC FBE Finance Seminar*, December 2006.

[65] See Ken Jacobson, "Whose Corporations? Our Corporations!" *AlterNet*, April 3, 2012, http://www.alternet.org/story/154789/whose_corporations_our_corporations.

[66] Ibid.

[67] Jacob S. Hacker and Paul Pierson, *Winner-Take-All Politics: How Washington Made the Rich Richer—and Turned Its Back on the Middle Class* (New York: Simon & Schuster, 2010).

[68] Peter G. Peterson, "The Morning After," *The Atlantic*, October 1987.

[69] Michael Pascoe, "US already half way into a lost quarter century," *Sydney Morning Herald*, October 20, 2011.

[70] Bartels, *Unequal Democracy*, figure 2.2.

[71] Robert B. Reich, *Supercapitalism: The Transformation of Business, Democracy, and Everyday Life* (New York: Knopf, 2007), 108.

[72] Schulz, "On the Way Down." See also Michael T. Snyder, "So long, middle class," *New York Post*, August 1, 2010.

[73] Thomas Schulz, "The Second Gilded Age: Has America Become an Oligarchy?," *Der Spiegel*, October 28, 2011.

[74] Sheryl Gay Stolberg and Robert Pear, "Bush Speaks in Defense of Markets," *New York Times*, November 14, 2008.

[75] Paul Osterman as quoted by Steven Greenhouse, "The Challenge of Creating Good Jobs," Economix (blog), *New York Times*, September 7, 2011.

[76] Anna Fifield, "Last decade worst for US middle class," *Financial Times*, August 22, 2012.

CHAPTER 3

[1] As quoted by Ralph Atkins and Matt Steinglass, "Employment: A fix that functions," *Financial Times*, August 3, 2011.

[2] Jess Bailey, Joe Coward, and Matthew Whittaker, "Painful Separation: An international study of the weakening relationship between economic

growth and the pay of ordinary workers," *Resolution Foundation, Commission on Living Standards*, October 2011, 19.

[3] Gideon Rachman, "The end of the Thatcher era," *Financial Times*, April 27, 2009.

[4] Lynn A. Stout, "The Shareholder Value Myth," *The Harvard Law School Forum on Corporate Governance and Financial Regulation* (blog), June 26, 2012, http://blogs.law.harvard.edu/corpgov/2012/06/26/the-shareholder -value-myth/.

[5] Jonsson, "America's 'other' auto industry." See also: "AP, "New contract with UAW only minimally increases GM fixed costs," *Washington Post*, September 19, 2011. Additional news reports on auto industry wages can be found at: Editorial, "Saving Germany's Auto Industry," *BusinessWeek International*, November 1, 2004; Jonathan Cohn, "Debunking the Myth of the $70-per-hour Autoworker," *New Republic*, November 21, 2008; and Daniel Schäfer, "Daimler pledges to preserve 37,000 jobs," *Financial Times*, December 10, 2009.

[6] Costs in Germany plants ranging from $55 to $60 per hour including benefits vary with exchange rates, but routinely exceed US wages by as much as $20 per hour. Keith Naughton and Jeff Green, "Ford Said to Reverse Plans to Make SUV in Kentucky for Export," *Bloomberg*, September 9, 2010.

[7] Jack Ewing, "Relying on Middle Class, Ford Is Tested in Europe," *New York Times*, April 27, 2012.

[8] For one thing, American firms restyled during model years 1995–2006 every fourth year while European, Korean, and Japanese producers restyled every three years. See: George Hoffer, Oleg Korenok, and Edward Millner, "Non-Price Determinants of Automotive Demand: Restyling Matters Most," *Journal of Business Research* 63, no. 12 (2010): 1282–1289. In German eyes, French management, at least in the weak auto sector, has been little better, lacking vision and too reliant on government support. See: Dietmar Hawranek and Isabell Hülsen, "Peugeot on the Brink: How Paris Is Killing French Industry," *Der Spiegel*, August 17, 2012, http://www.spiegel.de/international/europe/french-industrial-policies-are-aiding-rapid-decline-of-peugeot-a-850348.html.

[9] As quoted by David Gordon Smith, "A Costly Defeat for Deutsche Bank," *Der Spiegel*, March 23, 2011.

[10] "Legal costs put Centro in the red," Sydney Morning Herald, August 28, 2012, http://news.smh.com.au/breaking-news-business/legal-costs-put-centro-in -the-red-20120828-24xq3.html.

[11] Ian Verrender, "Now it's clear: the buck stops with the board," *Sydney Morning Herald*, June 28, 2011.

[12] Elisabeth Sexton, "Court case should remind directors of their duty," *Sydney Morning Herald*, June 28, 2011.

[13] Leonie Wood, "Reality check for Centro," *Sydney Morning Herald*, June 28, 2011.

[14] Phil Ross, "Directors must be financially literate," *Sydney Morning Herald*, June 30, 2011.

[15] Neil Hume, "Australia upholds tobacco branding ban," *Sydney Morning Herald*, August 15, 2012. See also AFP, "Australia/Tobacco: packages

uniform," *Le Figaro*, November 30, 2012, http://www.lefigaro.fr/flash-eco/2012/11/30/97002-20121130FILWWW00297-australietabac-les-paquets-uniformes.php.

[16] Leonie Lamont, "Hardie directors breached duties: High Court," *Sydney Morning Herald*, May 3, 2012.

[17] "The Millionaire Party: Germany's Free Democrats Accused of Serving the Rich," *Der Spiegel*, January 20, 2010.

[18] Gerrit Wiesmann, "Pirates' gains raise Merkel's hopes," *Financial Times*, April 6, 2012.

[19] "German labor costs remain low," *Handelsblatt*, December 12, 2011. An update in 2012 included these wage figures: Germany €30.10 per hour, Belgium €39.30, Sweden €39.10, Denmark €38.90, France €34.20, and the Netherlands €31.10. See "German companies have to pay higher wages," *Handelsblatt*, September 7, 2012.

[20] "Domino's defies 'Scandinavian labour costs,'" *Sydney Morning Herald*, August 10, 2011.

[21] Malcolm Maiden, "Decision time as Toll's US truckies wait for state-of-the-union redress," *Sydney Morning Herald*, April 12, 2012.

[22] "European Corporate Hypocrisy: Global Firms Violate International Labor Standards in America," *Human Rights Watch*, September 2, 2010, http://www.hrw.org/news/2010/09/01/us-european-corporate-hypocrisy. See also "Human Rights Watch denounced wasteful practices of some European companies in the US," *Le Monde*, September 2, 2010; and Jeremy Lerner, "Groups attacked on US labour practices," *Financial Times*, September 2, 2010.

[23] Daniel Schäfer, "Daimler pledges to preserve 37,000 jobs," Financial Times, December 10, 2009.

[24] Steven Rattner, "Let's Admit It: Globalization Has Losers," *New York Times*, October 16, 2011. See also Woodall, Klayman, and Schwartz, "U.A.W. takes aim at foreign automakers."

[25] Joe Nocera, "Factory Field Trip," *New York Times*, September 27, 2011.

[26] Gabor Steingart and Thomas Schulz, "America Must 'Reassert Stability and Leadership,'" *Der Spiegel*, December 12, 2009.

[27] Harold Meyerson, "Is China's bad news good for America?," *Washington Post*, May 11, 2011.

[28] David Leonhardt, "A Pay Gap in Autos Is Less Than It May Seem," *New York Times*, December 10, 2008.

[29] "Wages and labor costs, UAW bargaining 2007," *UAW*, 2007.

[30] Jon Gertner, "Make," *New York Times Magazine*, August 28, 2011.

[31] Gabor Steingart, "America's Middle Class Has Become Globalization's Loser," *Der Spiegel*, October 24, 2006.

[32] "Australia near top ranking in economic freedom," *Sydney Morning Herald*, January 13, 2012.

[33] Editorial, "Fair pay underpins our prosperity," *Sydney Morning Herald*, June 7, 2010, http://www.smh.com.au/opinion/editorial/fair-pay-underpins-our-prosperity-20100606-xn5c.html.

[34] "Harvester Judgment: Basic Wage," *Skwirk* (Red Apple Education Ltd.), 2010.

[35] "Harvester Judgment," *History of Wages in Australia*, Victoria Trade Hall Council, 2010.

[36] "IR reform no productivity 'magic bullet': Treasury chief," *Thomson Reuters Workforce News*, September 20, 2011.

[37] Chris Evans, "Fair Work: The Big Picture" (speech, 9th Annual Workforce Conference, Melbourne, Australia, November 22, 2010).

[38] Australian Bureau of Statistics, "Income Distribution: Trends in earnings distribution," 4102.0—Australian Social Trends, Annual, November 22, 2006, http://www.abs.gov.au/ausstats/abs@.nsf/2f762f95845417aeca25706c00834efa/A4C296ED2B41CF20CA2570EC0078703D?opendocument.

[39] Australian public support for this arrangement with the public sector monitoring wage settlements has strengthened in recent years. The Kevin Rudd Labour government reaffirmed the traditional centrality of collective bargaining rights and government monitoring of wage agreements in the 2009 Fair Work law. While prior reforms had established a commission to monitor wages and prices, it lacked teeth to bring recalcitrant employers or trade unions to agreement. The Rudd reforms assigned Fair Work Australia a mandate to sanction bad-faith negotiators and to impose outcomes when necessary; its conciliation powers regarding wage settlements have been elevated to the extent that "a single national system for around 96 percent of the private sector" now exists, according to minister Chris Evans. That mechanism enables the Australian Productivity Commission to anticipate and prevent inflationary wage drift while monitoring important worksite variables like profits, gender wage parity, upskilling and investment to maximize productivity growth. See Chris Evens, "Fair Work: The Big Picture," 9th Annual Workforce Conference, Melbourne, Australia, November 22, 2010; and Rae Cooper, Bradon Ellem, and Patricia Todd, "Workers' Rights and Labour Legislation: Reviving Collective Bargaining in Australia," *Wharton, UPenn Referred Papers*, July 2012, http://ilera2012.wharton.upenn.edu/RefereedPapers/EllemBradon%20RaeCooper%20PatriciaTodd.pdf.

[40] Jeremy Rifkin, *The European Dream: How Europe's Vision of the Future Is Quietly Eclipsing the American Dream* (New York: Tarcher/Penguin, 2004), 148.

[41] Nasar, *Grand Pursuit*, 9–10.

[42] Ibid.

[43] Norbert Häring, "Man As A Yardstick," *Handlesblatt*, August 19, 2010. Häring explains: "Francis Edgeworth, Alfred Marshall, Irving Fisher, Arthur C. Pigou, and John Bates Clark, the founding fathers of the currently dominant neoclassical mainstream, shared the then consensus among economists that reallocation was necessary from the rich to the poor to increase welfare. The idea was of diminishing marginal utility: the more of a good a person has, the less value he estimates for an additional unit."

[44] Timothy H. Parsons, *The Rule of Empires: Those Who Built Them, Those Who Endured Them, and Why They Always Fall* (New York: Oxford University Press, 2010), pp. 170, 194, 201, 202.

[45] Smith, *Wealth of Nations*, 325.

[46] Ibid., 348.

[47] Rifkin, *The European Dream*, 149.

[48] Economic historians like Jerry Z. Muller or Joyce Appleby argue that the default condition of mankind is dictatorship and corrupted markets. See

Joyce Appleby, *The Relentless Revolution: A History of Capitalism* (New York: W.W. Norton and Co, 2012); and Jerry Z. Muller, *The Mind and the Market: Capitalism in Western Thought* (New York: Anchor Books, 2003). See also Brad Ziesemer, "Is capitalism just a random question?," *Handeslblatt*, April 16, 2011.

[49] Liaquat Ahamed, *Lords of Finance: The Bankers Who Broke the World* (New York: Penguin, 2009), pp. 118, 121.

[50] Ret Marut, "Spartakism to National Bolshevism—the KPD 1918–1924—Solidarity," *libcom.org*, November 8, 2009. Niall Ferguson, *Civilization: The West and the Rest* (New York: Penguin, 2012), pp. 188, 228.

[51] Ferguson, Ibid.

[52] Francois Furstenberg, "Welfare state, or collapse?," *Washington Post*, July 3, 2011.

[53] Ahamed, *Lords of Finance*, 358.

[54] Ibid., 436.

[55] Nasar, *Grand Pursuit*, 383.

[56] Editorial, "State Capitalism," *Financial Times*, February 3, 2009.

[57] Robert Skidelsky, *John Maynard Keynes: Vol. 2, The Economist as Saviour, 1920–1937* (London: Macmillan, 1994), xv.

[58] Robert Shiller, "A failure to control the animal spirits," *Financial Times*, March 8, 2009.

[59] The orientation is quite at odds with the prosperity gospel with its Randian roots in tracts like Russell H. Conwell's "Acres of Diamonds," infusing Reagan-era America. See Benjamin Anastas, "Mammon from Heaven," *Harper's Magazine*, March 2010.

[60] Paul Rayment, "There is an alternative to market fundamentalism," letter to editor, *Financial Times*, February 9, 2009.

SECTION TWO

[1] Murray N. Rothbard, "The Myths of Reaganomics,"*Mises Daily*, June 9, 2004, http://mises.org/daily/1544.

CHAPTER 4

[2] Amit R. Paley, "Bailout Oversight Panel Calls for More Regulation," *Washington Post*, Jan. 29, 2009.

[3] As quoted by Jo Becker, Sheryl Gay Stolberg, and Stephen Labaton, "White House Philosophy Stoked Mortgage Bonfire," *New York Times*, Dec. 21, 2008.

[4] Dani Rodrik, *The Globalization Paradox* (New York: W.W. Norton, 2011), 237.

[5] Irwin Stelzer, "US Regulators Run to Catch Up with EU," *Financial Times*, May 27, 2009.

[6] Catherine Rampell, "Lax Oversight Caused Crisis, Bernanke Says," *New York Times*, Jan. 4, 2010.

[7] Greg Smith, "Why I Am Leaving Goldman Sachs," *New York Times*, March 14, 2012.

[8] Peter S. Goodman, as quoted in "A Fresh Look at the Apostle of Free Markets," *New York Times*, April 13, 2008.

[9] Catherine Rampell, "Same Old Hope: This Bubble Is Different," *New York Times*, Sept. 14, 2009.

[10] Mathias Döpfner, "On the Search for the Honor of the Merchant," *Handelsblatt*, Nov. 19, 2011.

[11] John Carswell, *The South Sea Bubble* (London: Cresset Press, 1960). Catherine Rampell, "Same Old Hope: This Bubble Is Different."

[12] Timothy H. Parsons, *The Rule of Empires* (New York: Oxford University Press, 2010), 170, 194, 201–202.

[13] John Gillespie and David Zweig, *Money for Nothing* (New York: Free Press, 2010), 20–24 and Jan Edwards, "Challenging Corporate Personhood," *Multinational Monitor,* November 2002.

[14] Amrit Dhillon, "Fresh Brew," *Sydney Morning Herald,* June 5, 2010.

[15] Ralph Nader, *The Nader Reader*, Feb. 21, 2000, speech.

[16] R. Jeffrey Smith, "DeLay Trial a Window Into Influence," *Washington Post,* Dec. 1, 2010.

[17] Justin Fox, "What the Founding Fathers Really Thought about Corporations," *HBR Blog Network, Harvard Business Review*, e-mail exchange between Justin Fox and Brian Murphy, April 1, 2010, http://blogs.hbr.org/fox/2010/04/what-the-founding-fathers-real.html

[18] John Kay, "Beware the Bailout Kings and Backbench Barons," *Financial Times,* May 20, 2009.

[19] Luke Mitchell, "Understanding Obamacare," *Harper's Magazine*, December 2009.

[20] Hedrick Smith, *Who Stole the American Dream* (New York: Random House, 2012).

[21] Charles Morris, "A Recession Can Clear the Air," *Washington Post,* Nov. 16, 2008.

[22] Northeast Public Power Association (NEPPA), "Deregulation Continues to Impact Retail Electric Prices in Region," NEPPA News Line, vol. 43, no. 12, December 2007. David Cay Johnston, "Unregulated Electricity Costs More, Studies Say," *NewYork Times*, Nov. 6, 2007. Marilyn Showalter, "Electricity Price Trends, Deregulated vs. Regulated States," Power in the Public Interest, Feb. 12, 2008.

[23] Christopher Weare, "The California Electricity Crisis: Causes and Policy Options," Public Policy Institute of California, 2003. Niall Ferguson, *Ascent of Money* (New York: Penguin, 2008*),* 173.

[24] As quoted by Kevin Phillips in *Bad Money* (New York: Penguin, 2008), 29.

[25] As quoted by Gretchen Morgenson, "Given a Shove, Americans Dig Deeper into Debt," *New York Times*, July 20, 2008.

[26] Simon Johnson, "No One Is Above the Law," *New York Times,* Dec. 23, 2011.

[27] Thomas Frank, *The Wrecking Crew* (New York: Metropolitan Books/Henry Holt, 2008), 42–43.

[28] Ross Douthat, "The Class War We Need," *New York Times,* July 11, 2010.

[29] David Brooks, "The Bloody Crossroads," *New York Times,* Sept. 8, 2009.

[30] George Packer, "Washington Man," *The New Yorker*, Oct. 29 and Nov. 5, 2012.

[31] David S. Hilzenrath, "CFTC Judge Says Colleague Issues Biased Rulings," *Washington Post,* Oct. 20, 2010.

[32] Joseph Stiglitz, "Of the 1%, by the 1%, for the 1%," *Vanity Fair,* May 2011.

[33] Robert Reich, *Aftershock: The Next Economy and America's Future* (New York: Vintage Books/Random House, 2010), 110.

[34] Thomas Frank, *The Wrecking Crew,* 153.

[35] James B. Stewart, "As a Watchdog Starves, Wall Street Is Tossed a Bone," *New York Times*, July 16, 2011.

[36] Frank Rich, "What Happened to Change We Can Believe In?," *New York Times,* Oct. 24, 2010. Secretary Rubin played a role in President Clinton signing into law the misnamed Commodity Futures Modernization Act, which deregulated derivatives. See also Robert Kuttner, *A Presidency in Peril* (White River Junction, VT: Chelsea Green Publishing, 2010), 103. See also Sheila C. Bair, *Bull by the Horns* (New York: Free Press, 2012).

[37] Murray N. Rothbard, *The Myths of Reaganomics.*

[38] Richard V. Allen, "Ronald Reagan, a Man with a Plan," *New York Times,* Jan. 31, 2010.

[39] Watt had been a lobbyist against land conservation protections in the West prior to his appointment. Thomas Frank, *The Wrecking Crew,* 159.

[40] Benjamin Hart, ed., *The Third Generation: Young Conservative Leaders Look to the Future* (Washington, D.C.: Regnery Gateway, 1987) and Thomas Frank, *The Wrecking Crew*, 128.

[41] Interview with Homer Ferguson, "Nation's Business." US Chamber of Commerce magazine, 1928. As cited in Thomas Frank, *The Wrecking Crew,* 131.

[42] Irene S. Rubin, *Shrinking the Federal Government: The Effect of Cutbacks on Five Federal Agencies* (New York: Longman, 1985) and Thomas Frank, *The Wrecking Crew*, 134–135.

[43] James K. Galbraith, *Predator State, How Conservatives Abandoned the Free Market and Why Liberals Should Too* (New York: Free Press, 2008), 182.

[44] Niall Ferguson, *The Ascent of Money*, 50.

[45] Leon Gettler, "It Will Happen Again," *Sydney Morning Herald*, July 20, 2010.

[46] Brooke Masters, Tom Braithwaite, and Helen Thomas, "Bankers Target 'Anti-US' Parts of BASEL III," *Financial Times,* Sept. 15, 2011.

[47] Paul Krugman, "Reagan Did It," *New York Times,* June 1, 2009.

[48] Gretchen Morgenson, "Into the Bailout Buzzsaw," *New York Times,* July 2012.

[49] Niall Ferguson, *The Ascent of Money,* 255.

[50] Kevin Phillips, *Bad Money,* 41.

[51] Paul Krugman, "Disaster and Denial," *New York Times,* Dec. 14, 2009, and Thomas Heath, "Making Money From the Collapse," *Washington Post*, Oct. 4, 2008.

[52] "Insiders Off Side," Editorial, *Financial Times,* Nov. 28, 2010.

[53] Paul Krugman, "Blindly into the Bubble," *New York Times,* Dec. 21, 2007.

[54] Alan Greenspan, "Corporate Governance," Speech to 2003 Conference on Bank Structure and Competition, Chicago, May 8, 2003. http://www.bis.org/review/r030509a.pdf. See also John Kay, "Look Back in Anger at the Spirit of the Age," *Financial Times,* Dec. 28, 2009.

[55] Andrew Sorkin, "Big, in Banks, Is in the Eye of the Beholder," *New York Times*, Jan. 19, 2010.

[56] "Securities and Exchange Commission," Government Accountability Office, March 2009, GAO-09-358, http://www.gao.gov/new.items/d09358.pdf.

[57] Zachary A. Goldfarb, "In Cox Years at the SEC, Policies Undercut Action," *Washington Post*, June 1, 2009.

[58] Amartya Sen, "Adam Smith's Market Never Stood Alone," *Financial Times*, March 10, 2009.

[59] Robert J. Shiller, "Challenging the Crowd in Whispers, Not Shouts," *New York Times,* Nov. 2, 2008.

[60] Arthur Levitt, Jr., "Don't Gut the SEC," *New York Times*, Aug. 8, 2011.

[61] Steven Pearlstein, "Stop the Pharmacy Consolidation Train," *Washington Post,* Dec. 11, 2011.

[62] Niall Ferguson, *Ascent of Money,* 351.

[63] Mario Monti, "Watchdogs of the World, Unite!," *Financial Times,* July 28, 2009.

[64] Mathilde Visseyrias, "Brussels Increasingly Tough on Cartels," *Le Figaro,* Jan. 6, 2011.

[65] Adam Davidson, "It's Not Technically an Oligopoly," *New York Times Magazine*, Dec. 11, 2011.

[66] Editorial, "Lagarde En Garde," *Financial Times*, Nov. 17, 2009.

[67] David Stockman, "Four Deformations of the Apocalypse," *New York Times,* Dec. 1, 2010.

[68] Douglas W. Diamond and Raghuram G. Rajan, "Illiquid Banks, Financial Stability, and Interest Rate Policy," University of Chicago, May 2012, http://faculty.chicagobooth.edu/douglas.diamond/research/Illiquidty%20JPE%20May%2010%20%202012%20with%20refs.pdf .

[69] Olaf Storbeck, "Too Big to Fail," *Handelsblatt*, Feb. 7, 2011.

[70] Elijah Brewer III and Julapa Jagtiani, "How Much Would Banks Be Willing to Pay to Become 'Too-Big-To-Fail' and to Capture Other Benefits?," Federal Reserve Bank of Kansas City, July 2007, research working paper, 07-05.

[71] Priyank Gandhi and Hanno Lustig, "Size Anomalies in US Bank Stock Returns: A Fiscal Explanation," National Bureau of Economic Research, working paper no. 16553, November 2010. See also Rob Cox and Lauren Silva Laughlin, "Another Advantage for Biggest Banks," Reuters Breaking News, *New York Times*, March 29, 2010.

[72] Interactivebrokers.com, "How We Handle Customer Assets," November 2010, http://www.interactivebrokers.com/en/?f=ibgStrength.

[73] Heidi N. Moore, "Beware of the FTC," Dealbook, *New York Times,* Nov. 4, 2010.

[74] "Another Thumb on the Scales," Editorial, *New York Times,* Nov. 1, 2008.

[75] Eric Lichtblau,"Antitrust Document Exposes Rift," *New York Times,* Sept. 9, 2008. Stephen Labaton, "Administration Plans to Strengthen Antitrust Rules," *New York Times*, May11, 2009. "The World Is In Turmoil," Editorial, *New York Times,* Nov. 1, 2008.

[76] Mario Monti, "Watchdogs of the World, Unite!"

[77] James Kanter, "New Snag for Oracle in Sun Deal," *New York Times,* Sept. 4, 2009.

[78] Mathilde Visseyrias, "Brussels Increasingly Tough on Cartels," *Le Figaro*, Jan. 6, 2011.

[79] Kanter, "New Snag for Oracle."

[80] Stephen Labaton, "Cracking Down, Antitrust Chief Hits Resistance," *New York Times,* July 26, 2009.

[81] "US Returns to Its Trust-Busting Roots," Editorial, *Financial Times,* May 12, 2009.

[82] Harold Meyerson, "The Occupiers and the Suites," *Washington Post,* Nov. 17, 2011.

[83] Peter Lattman, "Judge in Citigroup Mortgage Settlement Criticizes SEC's Enforcement," *New York Times,* Nov. 10, 2011. Edward Wyatt, "Promises Made, and Remade, by Firms in SEC Fraud Cases," *New York Times,* Nov. 8, 2011.

[84] James B. Stewart, "Bribes Without Jail Time," *New York Times,* April 28, 2012.

[85] Peter Lattman, "Judge in Citigroup Mortgage Settlement Criticizes SEC's Enforcement."

[86] John Cassidy, "After the Blowup," *New Yorker,* Jan. 11, 1010. See also Phillip Blond, "Let Us Put Markets to the Service of the Good Society," *Financial Times,* April 13, 2010.

[87] David Brooks, "The Day After Tomorrow," *New York Times,* Sept. 14, 2010.

[88] "Chris Christie Defers Truth at Congressional Hearings on Deferred Prosecution Agreements," Editorial, *The Star-Ledger,* June 28, 2009; and Neil Gordon, "John Ashcroft Lands Lucrative Corporate Monitor Gig Courtesy of Former Employee," *The Project On Government Oversight (POGO) Blog*, Dec. 11, 2007.

[89] Lynnley Browning, "US Curbs Deals as Prosecution Tactic," *International Herald Tribune,* Feb. 7, 2009.

[90] Eric Lichtblau and Kitty Bennett, "30 Ex-Government Officials Got Lucrative Posts as Corporate Monitors," *New York Times,* May 23, 2008.

[91] Jean-Michel Bezat, "The Ethics Commission Judges Alexander Juniac Cannot Run Areva," *Le Monde*, Dec. 16, 2010. Mary Visot, "Areva, the Candidate of Juniac 'Incompatible,'" *Le Figaro,* Dec. 15, 2010.

[92] "Bonus Windfall Tax," Editorial, *Financial* Times, Nov. 20, 2009.

[93] Adam Smith, *The Wealth of Nations* (New York: Oxford University Press Classics), 376.

[94] P.J. O'Rourke, "Adam Smith Gets the Last Laugh," *Financial Times*, Feb. 10, 2009.

[95] Ibid.

[96] Adam Smith, *The Wealth of Nations*, 129.

[97] Adam Smith, *The Wealth of Nations*, 188.

[98] Trevor Manuel, "Let Fairness Triumph over Corporate Profits," *Financial Times,* March 16, 2009.

[99] Nicholas Phillipson, *Adam Smith: An Enlightened Life* (Hartford, CT: Yale University Press, 2010).

[100] James K. Galbraith, *Predator State,* 162.

[101] "Bonus Points," Editorial, *Financial Times,* Dec. 7, 2009.

[102] David Brown, "Blood Levels of Trans Fats Plunge after Food-Labeling Decree," *Washington Post,* Feb. 9, 2012.

[103] Michael E. Porter, "Green Competitiveness," *New York Times,* April 5, 1991.

[104] Matthew Murphy, "Breathe Easy, Regulation's No Dirty Word," *Sydney Morning Herald,* Sept. 9, 2011.

[105] Lucrezia Reichlin, Michele Lenza, and Domenica Giannone, "Market Freedom and the Global Recession," Universite Libre de Bruxelles,

working papers ECARES 2010-020, 2010; Olaf Storbeck, "Less Government, More Crisis,"*Handelsblatt*, July 9, 2010.

[106] "Germany's Free Democrats Accused of Serving the Rich," *Der Spiegel*, Jan. 20, 2010.

[107] Ibid.

[108] Ibid.

[109] Ibid.

[110] DAPD News Agency, "Justice Minister Wants to Make Buying Tax CDs Under Penalty," *Handelsblatt*, Sept. 1, 2012.

[111] "CDU Politician Wants to End Subsidy," *Handelsblatt*, Aug. 15, 2011.

[112] Gerrit Wiesmann, "Pirates' Gains Raise Merkel's Hopes," *Financial Times*, April 6, 2012.

CHAPTER 5

[1] Joseph Stiglitz, "Bleakonomics," *New York Times*, Sept. 30, 2007.

[2] Jefferson Cowie, "That '70s Feeling," *New York Times,* Sept. 1, 2010.

[3] Susanne Royer, Jennifer Waterhouse, Kerry Brown, and Marion Festing, "Employee Voice and Strategic Competitive Advantage in International Modern Public Corporations—an Economic Perspective," *European Management Journal* vol. 26, no. 4, August 2008, 3, 5.

[4] Robert S. McElvaine, *The Great Depression* (New York: Three Rivers Press, 1984), xxxvii–xxxviii.

[5] Ibid, xi.

[6] Sean Wilentz, *The Age of Reagan* (New York: HarperCollins, 2008). Douglas Brinkley, editor, *The Reagan Diaries* (New York: HarperCollins, 2007).

[7] Jackie Calmes, "Both Sides of the Aisle See More Regulation, and Not Just of Banks," *New York Times,* Oct. 14, 2008.

[8] "Top Marginal Income Tax Rates. 1993–2003," Truthandpolitics.org.

[9] Timothy Noah, *The Great Divergence* (New York: Bloomsbury Press, 2012.)

[10] Carola Fryman and Raven E. Saks, "Executive Compensation: A New View from a Long-Term Perspective, 1936–2005," Figure 1, National Bureau of Economic Research, working paper no. 14145, June 2008.

[11] Hedrick Smith,"When Capitalists Cared," *New York Times*, Sept. 3, 2012.

[12] Leo Hindery, "Obama Must Act to Curb Executive Greed," *Financial Times*, June 24, 2009.

[13] Ken Jacobson, "Whose Corporations? Our Corporations!" AlterNet.org, April 3, 2012, http://www.alternet.org/story/154789/whose_corporations_our_corporations!

[14] Jacobson, Ibid.

[15] Robert S. McElvaine, *The Great Depression,* 210.

[16] Alfred Rappaport, *Creating Shareholder Value* (New York: Free Press/Simon and Schuster, 1986).

[17] Andrew Martin, "In Company Town, Cuts but No Layoffs," *New York Times*, Sept. 25, 2011.

[18] Jena McGregor, "In Praise of Jim Sinegal, Costco's No-Frills CEO," *Washington Post,* Sept. 11, 2011.

[19] Joseph A. McCartin, "The Strike That Busted Unions," *New York Times*, Aug. 2, 2011.

[20] Joseph A. McCartin, Ibid.

[21] Milton Friedman, "The Social Responsibility of Business Is to Increase Its Profits," *New York Times Magazine*, Sept. 13, 1970.

[22] Milton Friedman, Ibid.

[23] Michael C. Jensen and William H. Meckling, "Theory of the Firm: Managerial Behavior, Agency Costs, and Ownership Structure," *Journal of Financial Economics*, vol. 3, no. 4, 1976.

[24] John Plender, "Investing: Rules of Engagement," *Financial Times,* July 11, 2010.

[25] Justin Baer, Francesco Guerrera, and Richard Milne "A Need to Reconnect," *Financial Times*, March 13, 2009.

[26] Rakesh Khurana and Nitin Nohria, "Management Needs to Become a Profession," *Financial Times*, Oct. 20, 2008.

[27] Adam Smith, *The Wealth of Nations*, 368–69.

[28] Joe Nocera, "Nice Wasn't Part of the Deal," *New York Times*, Aug. 1, 2009.

[29] Adam Smith, *The Wealth of Nations.*

[30] Milton Friedman, "Rethinking the Social Responsibility of Business," *Reason*, October 2005.

[31] David Magee, *Jeff Immelt and the New GE Way* (New York: McGraw-Hill Professional, 2009).

[32] John P. Hussman, "Misallocating Funds," *Weekly Market Comment*, July 12, 2010, hussmanfunds.com, http://www.hussmanfunds.com/wmc/wmc100712.htm.

[33] Truman F. Bewley, *Why Wages Don't Fall During a Recession* (Cambridge, MA: Harvard University Press, 1999).

[34] Robert J. Gordon, "Okun's Law, Productivity Innovations, and Conundrums in Business Cycle Dating," American Economic Association meetings, Jan. 4, 2010, 22.

[35] Harold Meyerson, "The Unshared Recovery," *Washington Post*, Sept. 6, 2010.

[36] Catherine Rampell, "Majority of Jobs Added in the Recovery Pay Low Wages, Study Finds," *New York Times*, Aug 31, 2012. The data was developed by the National Employment Law Project.

[37] Robert J. Gordon, "Okun's Law, Productivity Innovations, and Conundrums in Business Cycle Dating," 22.

[38] Richard Sennett, *The Corrosion of Character* (New York: W.W. Norton, 1998).

[39] As quoted by Kevin Phillips, *Wealth and Democracy* (New York: Broadway Books, 2003), 148.

[40] David Brooks, "The Great Seduction," *New York Times*, June 10, 2008.

[41] Robert J. Samuelson, "Capitalism's Enemies Within," *Washington Post*, Jan. 23, 2008.

[42] Greg Farrell, "Lynched at Merrill," *Financial Times*, Jan. 25, 2009, and *Financial Times,* Editorial, "Thain Behaviour," Jan. 23, 2009.

[43] Steven Pearlstein, "So You Just Squandered Billions . . . Take Another Whack at It," *Washington Post*, Sept. 2, 2009.

[44] Steven Pearlstein, Ibid.

[45] Dana Milbank, "29 Dead, and a Coal CEO Blames the Government," *Washington Post*, July 26, 2010.

[46] "Unsettled Justice at Upper Big Branch," Editorial, *New York Times*, Dec. 8, 2011, and David M. Uhlmann, "For 29 Dead Miners, No Justice," *New York Times*, Dec. 10, 2011.

[47] Dana Milbank, "29 Dead, and a Coal CEO Blames the Government."

[48] Kerin Hope, "History of Statistics That Failed to Add Up," *Financial Times*, Sept. 30, 2011.

[49] Nelson D. Schwartz and Sewell Chan, "In Greece's Crisis, Fed Studies Wall St.'s Activities," *New York Times*, Feb. 26, 2010.

[50] Gerrit Wiesmann and Kerin Hope, "Merkel Hits Out at Banks Over Greek Deals," *Financial Times,* Feb. 17, 2010.

[51] Robert H. Frank, "Income Inequality: Too Big to Ignore," *New York Times*, Oct. 17, 2010. An excellent biography of Smith is Nicholas Phillipson's *Adam Smith: An Enlightened Life.*

[52] Adam Smith, *The Wealth of Nations.*

[53] Amartya Sen, "Adam Smith's Market Never Stood Alone."

[54] As quoted by Hedrick Smith, "When Capitalists Cared," *New York Times,* Sept. 3, 2012.

[55] John Martin and Herwig Immervoll, "The Minimum Wage: Making It Pay," *OECD Observer*, May 2007. See also: "Wages," Victorian Trades Hall Council, Melbourne, vthc.org, http://www.vthc.org.au/index.cfm?section=4&category=49.

[56] Lionel Barber, Bertrand Benoit, and Hugh Williamson, "March to the Middle: Merkel Celebrates Germany's Social Market Model," *Financial Times*, June 10, 2008.

[57] Lionel Barber, Bertrand Benoit, and Hugh Williamson, Ibid.

[58] Hugh Williamson, "Kohler Warning to Germany's Business 'Elite,'" *Financial Times*, Feb. 18, 2008.

[59] Chris Bryant, "German Unions Put Imprint on Stimulus Package," *Financial Times*, June 18, 2009.

[60] Ralph Atkins, "German Industry Warns on Tax Cuts," *Financial Times,* Nov. 1, 2009.

[61] Matthew Franklin, "Tony Abbott Eyes Working Families with Paid Potential Leave," *The Australian*, March 9, 2010.

[62] "FW Act Is Not a 'Business Tool' and Irrelevant for Productivity: Holden," Workplace, *Thomson Reuters*, April 14, 2011.

[63] Michael Pascoe, "In an Era of Self-Interest, the Upright Flier Declines to Recline," *Western Australia Today*, April 23, 2011.

[64] Leonie Lamont, "Absconder's Wife Fails in Freedom Appeal," *Sydney Morning Herald*, April 28, 2012.

[65] Steven Greenhouse, "Low-Wage Workers Are Often Cheated, Study Says," *New York Times*, June 2, 2009. "Workers in America Cheated," Editorial, *New York Times,* Sept. 3, 2009.

[66] Michael A. Fletcher, "Labor Dept. Accused of Straying from Enforcement," *Washington Post*, Dec. 1, 2008. Andrea Chang, "Walmart to Settle Lawsuits Over Wages," *Los Angeles Times*, Dec. 24, 2008. Steven Greenhouse and Stephanie Rosenbloom, "Walmart to Settle Suits Over Pay for $352 Millon," *New York Times*, Dec. 23, 2008.

[67] Chris L. Jenkins, "GAO Report Faults Labor Dept. on Wage Complaints," *Washington Post*, April 7, 2009.

[68] "HR Report," Thomson Reuters, Oct. 31, 2012, and "Fair Work Australia Step Change," *Workplace Insight*, Thomson Reuters, Nov. 11, 2012.

[69] Larissa Ham, "Store Fined $67K for Underpaying Worker," *Sydney Morning Herald*, Nov. 12, 2010.

[70] Ben Schneiders, "Student Paid 'Just $3.30 an Hour,'" *Sydney Morning Herald*, Sept. 5, 2011.

[71] Eva Roth, "Kik Announces Minimum Wage," *Berliner Zeitung*, Aug. 24, 2010.

[72] "Collective Agreement at Schlecker—No More Wage Dumping," *Berliner Zeitung*, Jan. 6, 2010.

[73] Jutta Maier, "Wages for All: Schlecker Pays Equal Wages in the Future XL Stores," *Berliner Zeitung*, June 2, 2010. Eva Roth, "The Schlecker Drama," *Berliner Zeitung*, June 1, 2010.

[74] "Sentence for Illegal Work in Slaughterhouses," *Berliner Zeitung*, Dec. 9, 2010.

[75] Elsbeth Stoker, "Employer Court Puts Stop to Move Trick Employers," *de Volkskrant*, Amsterdam, Oct. 22, 2010.

[76] AP, "Employees Compensated by Recylex," *Le Figaro*, Dec. 18, 2009.

[77] Agence France-Presse, "Time Workers—the New Slaves," *Berliner Zeitung*, April 2, 2012.

[78] "Cameron Quizzes EU Work Directive," *The Daily Telegraph*, Sept. 6, 2011.

[79] Lauren Cohen, Christopher Malloy, and Lukasz Pomorski, "Decoding Insider Information," National Bureau of Economic Research, working paper 16454, October 2010. Karl A. Muller, III, Monica Neamtaiu, and Edward J. Riedl, "Insider Trading Preceding Goodwill Impairments," Harvard Business School working paper, July 2009.

[80] David S. Hilzenrath, "SEC Says 'Dark Pool' Operator Traded Ahead of Its Customers," *Washington Post*, October 25, 2011.

[81] Mark Landler, "US Credit Crisis Adds to Gloom of Arctic Norway's Long Night," *New York Times*, Dec. 2, 2007. Julia Werdigier, "Subprime Woes Hit Norwegian Brokerage," *New York Times*, Nov. 29, 2007.

[82] John Gillespie and David Zweig, *Money for Nothing*, 63–64. Michael West, "Lawyers the Big Victors in Lehman Saga," *Sydney Morning Herald*, Sept. 24, 2012.

[83] Michael West, "Toxic Rembrandts—Rating Agency 'Sandbagged,'" *Sydney Morning Herald*, Oct. 4, 2011.

[84] Adele Ferguson, "Storm Ahead for Riders of the GFC [Global Financial Collapse] Apocalypse," *Sydney Morning Herald*, Nov. 6, 2012.

[85] Michael West, "Councils Win Fight Against S&P Over 'Rembrandt' Notes," *Sydney Morning Herald*, Nov. 5, 2012, http://www.smh.com.au/business/rembrandt-ruling-puts-heat-on-sp-20121105-28t4y.html.

[86] Editorial, "Holding the Rating Agencies to Account," *Financial Times*, Nov. 5, 2012.

CHAPTER 6

[1] Gretchen Morgenson, "Enriching a Few at the Expense of Many," *New York Times*, April 10, 2011.

[2] George A. Akerlof and Rachel E. Kranton, *Identity Economics* (Princeton, NJ: Princeton University Press, 2010), 41.

[3] Robert H. Frank, "A Remedy Worse Than the Disease," *Pathways*, Stanford Center for Poverty and Inequality, Summer 2010.

[4] Jesse Eisinger, "Challenging the Long-held Belief in 'Shareholder Value,'" *New York Times*, June 28, 2012.

[5] Justin Fox and Jay W. Lorsch, "What Good Are Shareholders?," *Harvard Business Review*, July–August 2012.

[6] Milton Friedman, *Essays in Positive Economics* (Chicago: University of Chicago Press, 1953), 22.

[7] Mark Armstrong and Steffen Huck, "Behavioral Economics As Applied to Firms: A Primer," January 2010, University Library of Munich, MPRA paper no 20356. See also Anja Müller, "The Myth of the Rational Enterprise," *Handelsblatt*, Oct. 14, 2010.

[8] R. Hall and C. Hitch, "Price Theory and Business Behavior," Oxford Economic Papers 2, 2–45, 1939. Nabil Al-Najjar, Sandeep Baliga, and David Besanko, "Market Forces Meet Behavioral Biases: Cost Misallocation and Irrational Pricing," *Rand Journal of Economics* 39, 214–237, 2008.

[9] Richard Roll, "The Hubris Hypothesis of Corporate Takeovers," *Journal of Business* 59, 197–216, 1986.

[10] Mark Armstrong and Steffen Huck, "Behavioral Economics As Applied to Firms: A Primer," January 2010.

[11] Robert Reich, *Supercapitalism* (New York: Vintage Books/Random House, 2008), 108.

[12] David Cay Johnston, *Perfectly Legal* (New York: Portfolio/Penguin Group, 2003), 240.

[13] Diane Coyle, *The Economics of Enough: How to Run the Economy As If the Future Matters* (Princeton, NJ: Princeton University Press, 2011).

[14] Paul K. Piff, Daniel M. Stancata, Stephane Cote, Rodolfo Mendoza-Denton, and Dacher Keltner, "Higher Social Class Predicts Increased Unethical Behavior," *Proceeds of the National Academy of Sciences*, February 27, 2012.

[15] For example, see: Randall Morck, Andrie Shleifer, and Robert Vishny, "Alternative Mechanisms for Corporate Control," *American Economic Review*, 1989, 79:842–852.

[16] Ian Austen, "Shake-Up at Canadian Pacific Railway As Activist Investor Takes Control," *New York Times*, May 18, 2012.

[17] Peter Whoriskey, "The Lake Wobegon Effect Lifts CEO's Pay," *Washington Post*, Oct. 4, 2011, and Ryan Chittum, "Cronyism and Executive Compensation," The Audit, *Columbia Journalism Review*, Oct. 4, 2011.

[18] Whoriskey, Ibid.

[19] Heather Landy, "Executives Took, But the Directors Gave," *New York Times*, April 5, 2009.

[20] David Cay Johnston, *Perfectly Legal*, 2003, 250.

[21] David Carr, "Why Not Occupy Newsrooms?," *New York Times*, Oct. 24, 2011.

[22] *Executive Viewpoints on Employee Benefits*, "Corporate Director Compensation Grew Modestly in 2008," Liberty Publishing vol. 52, no. 11, 2009.

[23] John Gillespie and David Zweig, *Money for Nothing*, 2.

[24] Steven M. Davidoff, Dealbook, "On Boards, Little Cause of Anxiety," *New York Times*, Aug. 3, 2011.

[25] John Gillespie and David Zweig, *Money for Nothing*, 82.

[26] Jeremy W. Peters, "For Murdock, a Board Meeting with Friendly Faces," *New York Times*, Aug. 10, 2011.

[27] Lucian A. Bebchuk and Jesse M. Fried, "Tackling the Managerial Power Problem," *Pathways*, Stanford Univeristy Center for Poverty and Inequality, Summer 2010.

[28] "Executive Pay," Editorial, *Financial Times*, Feb. 7, 2010.

[29] Michael C. Jensen and Kevin J. Murphy, "Beware the Self-Serving Critics," *New York Times*, May 20, 1984.

[30] John Gillespie and David Zweig, *Money for Nothing*, x and 97.

[31] Adam Liptak, "Justices to Weigh In on Corporate Culture and Its Paychecks," *New York Times*, Aug. 18, 2009.

[32] Steven Pearlstein, "How HP, Silicon Valley's Darling, Became a Soap Opera," *Washington Post*, Sept. 25, 2011.

[33] James B. Stewart, "Rewarding CEOs Who Fail," *New York Times*, Oct. 1, 2011.

[34] Ian Verrender, "Corporate Ranks Start to Divide on Bonuses," *Sydney Morning Herald*, Aug. 9, 2012.

[35] John Gillespie and David Zweig, *Money for Nothing*, 35.

[36] John Kay, "Powerful Interests Are Trying to Control the Market," *Financial Times*, Nov. 10, 2009.

[37] Richard Lambert, "Blueprint to Put Bosses' Pay in Order," *Financial Times*, Nov. 4, 2011.

[38] Ian Verrender, "Running to Save Their Executive Bacon—Alas, It May Be Too Late," *Sydney Morning Herald*, Oct. 15, 2011.

[39] Gretchen Morgenson, "Enriching a Few at the Expense of the Many."

[40] Kate Burgess, "More Calls for Reform of Executives' Pay," *Financial Times*, Nov. 27, 2011.

[41] Ian Verrender, "Running to Save Their Executive Bacon—Alas, It May Be Too Late."

[42] Ekkehard Wenger (University of Würzburg finance professor) and Leonhard Knoll, as quoted by James Wilson and Chris Hughes, "Pull Back from the US, Deutsche Urged," *Financial Times*, April 8, 2008, http://www.ft.com/intl/cms/s/0/effdda98-0592-11dd-a9c0-0000779fd2ac.html#axzz24CFwaGsQ.

[43] Robert Reich, *Supercapitalism*, 108.

[44] Martin Wolf, "Why Today's Hedge Fund Industry May Not Survive," *Financial Times*, March 18, 2008. http://www.ft.com/intl/cms/s/0/c8941ad4-f503-11dc-a21b-000077b07658.html#axzz24CFwaGsQ.

[45] "Shareholder Values," Editorial, *Financial Times*, April 19, 2011.

[46] Robert R.Trumble and Angela N. DeLowell, "Connecting CEO Performance to Corporate Performance: Examining Intangible Metrics of Shareholder Value," *Journal of Compensation and Benefits*, November/December 2001.

[47] Alex Edmans and Xavier Gabaix, "What's Right, What's Wrong and What's Fixable," *Pathways*, Stanford Center for Poverty and Inequality, Summer 2010.

[48] Jessica Silver-Greenberg and Alexis Leonsis, "How Much Is a CEO Worth?," *Bloomberg Businessweek*, April 26, 2010.

[49] Michael C. Jensen and Kevin J. Murphy, "Performance Pay and Top-Management Incentives," *Journal of Political Economy* vol. 98, no. 2, April 1990. "CEO Incentives: It's Not How Much You Pay, But How," *Harvard Business Review*, May-June 1990, no. 3, 138–153.

[50] Scott Thrum, "Oracle's Ellison: Pay King," *Wall Street Journal*, July 27, 2010. Georges Ugeux, "Demystifying Finance, The Mega Salaries of American Business Leaders: Oracle and Apple," *Le Figaro*, July 28, 2010.

[51] Rakesh Khurana, *Searching for a Corporate Savior* (Princeton, NJ: Princeton University Press, 2002). See also Steven Pearlstein, "CEO Pay: Why They're Winning," *Washington Post*, June 26, 2011.

[52] Thomas Philippon and Ariell Reshef, "Wages and Human Capital in the US Financial Industry, 1909–2006,"working paper 14644, National Bureau of Economic Research, January 2009, www.nber.org/papers/w14644.

[53] Alex Edmans and Xavier Gabaix, "What's Right, What's Wrong, and What's Fixable," Pathways, Stanford Center for Poverty and Inequality, Summer 2010.

[54] "Managing High Pay in Companies," Editorial, *Financial Times*, Nov. 21, 2011.

[55] As quoted by James B. Stewart, "Rewarding CEOs Who Fail," Oct. 2, 2011.

[56] See C. Frydman and R. Saks, "Executive Compensation: A New View From a Long-Term Perspective, 1936–2005," Federal Reserve Board, Washington, D.C. 2007-7-35, 2–3. Robert H. Frank, "A Remedy Worse Than the Disease," *Pathways*, Stanford Center for Poverty and Inequality, Summer 2010.

[57] Gretchen Morgenson, "What Iceberg? Just Glide to the Next Boardroom," *New York Times*, Dec. 27, 2009.

[58] Robert H. Frank and Philip Cook, *The Winner-Take-All Society* (New York: Penguin Books, 1996). See also: Robert H. Frank, "A Remedy Worse Than the Disease," *Pathways*, Stanford Center for Poverty and Inequality," Summer 2010.

[59] Robert H. Frank and Philip Cook, *The Winner-Take-All Society*. For a variation of this argument, see Kevin J. Murphy and Ján Zábojník, "CEO Pay and Appointments: A Market-Based Explanation for Recent Trends," *American Economic Review: Papers & Proceedings* May 2004.

[60] Scott Thrum, "Oracle's Ellison: Pay King."

[61] Adam Smith, *The Wealth of Nations*, book V, chapter I, part 3, article I.

[62] Liu Zheng and Xianming Zhou, "The Effects of Executive Stock Options on Firm Performance: Evidence From Retiring CEOs," University of Hong Kong, 2010, *Employee Benefits, Compensation & Pension Law Abstracts*, vol. 10, no. 37: Oct. 2, 2009. See also: L. Zheng and X. Zhou, "Stock Options May Negatively Affect Company Performance," *Executive Viewpoint on Employee Benefits*, Liberty Publishing vol. 52, no. 11, 2009.

[63] Eric Dash, "The Lucrative Fall from Grace," *New York Times*, Sept. 30, 2011.

[64] Eric Dash, "Stock-Hedging Lets Bankers Skirt Efforts to Overhaul Pay," *New York Times*, Feb. 6, 2011.

[65] Eric Dash, Ibid.

[66] Erik Lie, "On the Timing of CEO Stock Option Awards," *Management Science*, vol. 51, no. 5, May 2005. Erik Lie and Randall A. Heron, "Does Backdating Explain the Stock Price Pattern Around Executive Stock Option Grants?," *Journal of Financial Economics*, vol. 83 (2), February 2007. See also Lucian A. Bebchuk and Jesse M. Fried, "Tackling the Managerial Power Problem," *Pathways*, Stanford Center for Poverty and Inequality, Summer 2010.

[67] David Cay Johnston, *Free Lunch* (Portfolio/Penguin Books, 2008), 263.

[68] Peter Lattman, "Prosecutions in Backdating Scandal Bring Mixed Results," *New York Times*, Nov. 12, 2010. Backdating prosecutions are rarely pursued, although Jacob Alexander (the former CEO of Comverse Technology) and two colleagues were fined $46 million in 2010 for a swindle involving millions of dollars in backdated options hidden from shareholders.

[69] George Akerlof and Rachel E. Kranton, *Identity Economics*, 58–59.

[70] Louis Uchitelle, "Revising a Boardroom Legacy," *New York Times*, Sept. 28, 2007.

[71] W. G. Sanders and D. C. Hambrick, "Swinging for the Fences: The Effects of CEO Stock Options on Company Risk Taking and Performance," *Academy of Management Journal* vol. 50, no. 5, 1055–1076.

[72] Ulrike Malmendier, Enrico Moretti, and Florian S. Peters, "Winning by Losing: Evidence on the Long-Run Effects of Mergers," working paper 18024, National Bureau of Economic Research, April 2012, http://emlab.berkeley.edu/~moretti/mergers.pdf.

[73] Jeffrey S. Harrison and Derek K. Oler, "The Influence of Debt on Acquisition Performance," *Academy of Management Journal*, August 2008.

[74] Michael West, "When Fourth Out of Five Earns You a Squillion," *Sydney Morning Herald*, Oct. 25, 2011. "Pacific Brands Shareholders Get Chesty," *Sydney Morning Herald*, Oct. 25, 2011. Scott Rochfort, "Rockin', Shocking: The Market's Hits, Hype and Horrors," *Sydney Morning Herald*, Dec. 31, 2011.

[75] Ian Verrender, "Running to Save Their Executive Bacon—Alas, It May Be Too Late."

[76] Michale Pascoe, "Unions on the Way Back," *Sydney Morning Herald*, Oct. 31, 2011, www.smh.com.au/.../unions-on-the-way-back-20111031-1mrcl.html.

[77] David Bradbury, Opening Keynote Address to the Australasian Investor Relations Association Conference, 2010, Nov. 26, 2012. David Bradbury, "Australian Laws to Curb Executive Pay Due Soon," *The Age*, Nov. 26, 2012.

[78] Elizabeth Knight, "Shareholders Set for a Season to Remember," *Sydney Morning Herald*, Oct. 21, 2011. Scott Rochfort, "Fireworks on Cards at Kagara AGM," *Sydney Morning Herald*, Oct. 20, 2011.

[79] Colin Druger, "Investors Rebel Against Cabcharge Exec Pay," *Sydney Morning Herald*, Nov. 16, 2011 and Adele Ferguson, "Directors Sweating the Outcome of Pay Votes," *Sydney Morning Herald*, Sept. 24, 2012, http://www.smh.com.au/business/directors-sweating-the-outcome-of-pay-votes-20120924-26gcd.html.

[80] AAP, "Globe Shareholders Force Board Spill," *Sydney Morning Herald*, Nov. 14, 2012.

[81] Malcolm Maiden, "Pinning Boom Bulls and Policing Post-Bust Trust a Tall Order," *Sydney Morning Herald*, July 24, 2010.

CHAPTER 7

[1] Justin Fox and Jay Lorsch, "What Good Are Shareholders?"

[2] Richard Lambert, "Sir Ralph's Lessons on Short-Termism," *Financial Times*, May 22, 2011.

[3] Antoine Reverchon, "Employee Satisfaction and Shareholder Value Are Correlated," *Le Monde*, Sept. 26, 2011.

[4] Bill George, "What Minnesota Can Learn from Germany," *Star Tribune,* Jan. 7, 2012.

[5] John Kay, "Why the Rioters Should Be Reading Rousseau," *Financial Times*, Aug. 16, 2011.

[6] Thomas Hobbes, *Leviathan, or the Matter, Form, and Power of a Commonwealth, Ecclesiastical and Civil*, chapters xiii and xiv, Blackstone Audio, 2011.

[7] John Kay, "Why the Rioters Should Be Reading Rousseau."

[8] Edmund Phelps, "Uncertainty Bedevils the Best System," *Financial Times*, April 14, 2009.

[9] Jeffrey S. Harrison and Derek K. Oler, "The Influence of Debt on Acquisition Performance," *Academy of Management Journal*, August, 2008.

[10] Edmund S. Phelps, "The Economy Needs a Bit of Ingenuity," *New York Times*, Aug. 7, 2010.

[11] See Robert Lerman, "Training Tomorrow's Workforce," Center for American Progress, Dec. 9, 2009. *Handelsblatt*, "Labor Market, More and More Apprenticeship Spaces Remain," May 11, 2011. Jack Ewing, "Germany's Answer to Jobless Youth," *Der Spiegel*, Oct. 8, 2009.

[12] Robert J. Gordon, "The Demise of Okun's Law and of Procyclical Fluctuations in Conventional and Unconventional Measures of Productivity," Northwestern University and the National Bureau of Economic Research, 2010. Also see James Surowiecki, "Mind the Gap," The Financial Page, *The New Yorker*, July 9, 2012.

[13] Adam Smith, *The Wealth of Nations*, book IV, chapter vii, 372–73.

[14] Claire Gatinois, "The Bosses' Lament," *Le Monde*, May 28, 2012.

[15] Alfred Marshall, *Principles of Economics* (London: Macmillan, 1895), book 3, chapter 5.

[16] As recounted by Justin Baer, Francesco Guerrera, and Richard Milne, "A Need to Reconnect," *Financial Times,* March 13, 2009.

[17] James Surowiecki, "Sputnikonomics," The Financial Page, *The New Yorker*, Feb. 14–21, 2011.

[18] Edmund Phelps, "Uncertainty Bedevils the Best System," *Financial Times*, April 14, 2009.

[19] Sheila C. Bair, "Stop Selling the Long Term Short," *Washington Post*, July 10, 2011.

[20] Justin Fox and Jay Lorsch, "What Good Are Shareholders?"

[21] Andrew G. Haldane and Richard Davies, "The Short Long," *29th Société Universitaire Europèene de Recherches Financières Colloquium: New Paradigms in Money and Finance*, Bank of England, May 2011.

[22] Justin Fox and Jay Lorsch, "What Good Are Shareholders?"

[23] Jesse Eisinger, "Challenging the Long-Held Belief in 'Shareholder Value,'" *New York Times*, June 28, 2012.

[24] Michael Clowes, *The Money Flood: How Pension Funds Revolutionized Investing* (New York: Wiley, 2000).

[25] James M. Poterba and Lawrence H. Summers, "A CEO survey of US Companies' Time Horizons and Hurdle Rates," *Sloan Management Review*, Fall 1995.

[26] Thomas Schulz, "How the German Economy Became a Model," *Der Spiegel*, March 21, 2012.

[27] Ulrike Malmendier, Enrico Moretti, and Florian S. Peters, "Winning By Losing: Evidence on the Long-Run Effects of Mergers," working paper 18024, National Bureau of Economic Research, April 2012, http://emlab.berkeley.edu/~moretti/mergers.pdf.

[28] Joe Nocera, "The Real Reason HP's Board Ousted Its Chief," *New York Times*, Aug. 14, 2010.

[29] Robert Cryan and Rob Fox,"HP After Hurd Is a Risky Play," Reuters Breaking Views, *New York Times*, Aug. 10, 2010.

[30] Herb Greenberg, "Was HP Really That Good Under Hurd?," cnbc.com, Aug. 9, 2010, http://www.cnbc.com/id/38621499/.

[31] Quentin Hardy, "Meg Whitman's Toughest Campaign: Retooling HP," *New York Times*, Sept. 30, 2012.

[32] Quentin Hardy, "HP Shares Fall as Chief Sees Trouble," *New York Times*, Oct. 4, 2012.

[33] Steve Lohr and Damon Darlin, "Playing Catch-Up, Nokia and HP Try to Innovate," *New York Times*, Feb. 9, 2011.

[34] Quentin Hardy, "Hewlett-Packard's Plans Include 30,000 Job Cuts," *New York Times*, May 18, 2012.

[35] Yves Smith and Rob Parenteau, "Are Profits Hurting Capitalism?," *New York Times*, July 6, 2010.

[36] Marianne Bertrand and Antoinette Schoar, "Managing With Style: The Effect of Managers on Firm Policies," September 2002, MIT-Sloan, working paper no. 4280-02, http://ssrn.com/abstract=376880 or doi:10.2139/ssrn.376880.

[37] Nancy Folbre, "The Fat Cat Hypothesis," Economix, *New York Times*, May 17, 2010.

[38] John R. Graham, Campbell R. Harvey, and Shiva Rajgopal, "The Economic Implications of Corporate Financial Reporting," *Journal of Accounting and Economics* vol. 40, 1–3 Dec. 2005, 3–75.

[39] See Nelson D. Schwartz, "As Layoffs Rise, Stock Buybacks Consume Cash," *New York Times*, Nov. 22, 2011.

[40] As quoted by Jia Lynn Yang, "Companies Spend Their Stash of Cash to Buy Back Stock," *Washington Post*, Oct. 7, 2010.

[41] Andrew Jack, "Drugs: Supply Running Low," *Financial Times*, Feb. 9, 2011.

[42] Nelson D. Schwartz, "As Layoffs Rise, Stock Buybacks Consume Cash."

[43] Lawrence Mitchell, "Protect Industry from Predatory Speculators," *Financial Times,* July 8, 2009.

[44] Richard Waters, "Microsoft Begins $40 Billion Share Buyback," *Financial Times*, Sept. 22, 2008. Details reported also on CNN.com and MSNBC.com, Sept. 22, 2008.

[45] As quoted by Steven Greenhouse, "The Challenge of Creating Good Jobs," Economix, *New York Times*, Sept. 7, 2011.

[46] J. Morris McInnes, "Corporate Management of Productivity—An International Comparison," Alfred P. Sloan School of Management, Massachusetts Institute of Technology, working paper 1, 398–83, January 1983.

[47] Andrew B. Bernard, Jonathan Eaton, J. Bradford Jensen, and Samuel

Kortum, "Plants and Productivity in International Trade," *American Economic Review*, February 2003.

[48] J. Morris McInnes, "Corporate Management of Productivity."

[49] Nicholas Bloom, Benn Eifert, Aprajit Mahajan, David McKenzie, and John Roberts, "Does Management Matter? Evidence from India," National Bureau of Economic Research, working paper 16658, January 2011.

[50] Bradley R. Staats, Francesca Gino, and Gary P. Pisano, "Varied Experience, Team Familiarity, and Learning: The Mediating Role of Psychological Safety," *Harvard Business School working papers, 10-016,* Sept. 16, 2009.

[51] Heike Hennig-Schmidt, Bettina Rockenback, and Abdolkarin Sadrieh, "In Search of Workers' Real Effort Reciprocity—A Field and Laboratory Experiment," *Journal of the European Economic Association*, June 2010. Also, "Governance and the Efficiency of Economic Systems," discussion paper, Research Centre, University of Bonn, June 2008.

[52] Samuel Bowles, "Machiavelli's Mistake: Good Incentives Are No Substitute for Good Citizens," Castle Lecture Series, Yale University, Santa Fe Institute, January 2010.

[53] Robert J. Shiller, "Stuck in Neutral? Reset the Mood," *New York Times*, Jan. 31, 2010.

[54] Lynn A. Stout, "The Shareholder Value Myth."

[55] Edmund S. Phelps, "The Economy Needs a Bit of Ingenuity," *New York Times*, Aug. 7, 2010.

[56] William D. Cohen, "Want to Fix Wall Street? Work There," *Washington Post*, Sept. 18, 2011.

[57] "German Economy Has Excellent Reputation," *Berliner Zeitung*, Jan. 26, 2011.

[58] Gerrit Wiesmann and Chris Bryant, "Long View: Berthold Huber Has a Reputation for Keeping an Eye on the System as a Whole," *Financial Times*, July 22, 2012.

[59] Bill George, "What Minnesota Can Learn From Germany," *Star Tribune*, Jan. 7, 2012.

[60] John Gillespie and David Zweig, *Money for Nothing,* 239–40. Jeffrey A. Sonnenfeld, "What Makes Great Boards Great," *Harvard Business Review*, September 2002.

[61] As reported by Edward Luce, *Time to Start Thinking* (New York: Atlantic Monthly Press, 2012), 175.

[62] Timothy H. Parsons, *The Rule of Empires,* 364.

[63] Larry Fauver and Michael E. Fuerst, "Does Good Corporate Governance Include Employee Representation? Evidence from German Corporate Boards," *Journal of Financial Economics*, December 2006, 3.

[64] Thomas Geoghegan, "Consider the Germans' Codetermination and Works Councils," *Harper's Magazine*, March 2012.

[65] Thomas Paster, "Do German Employers Support Board-Level Codetermination? The Paradox of Individual Support and Collective Opposition," *Socio-Economic Review*, (2011) 1–25, Aug. 17, 2011.

[66] Roland Schneider, Trade Union Advisory Committee to the Organisation for Economic Co-Operation and Development, e-mail exchange with the author, Paris, April 27, 2012.

[67] Steffen Mueller, "The Productivity Effect of Non-Union Representation," 2004, http://centros.uv.es/web/departamentos/D132/data/tablones/tablon_general/PDF160.pdf.

[68] "Worker Participation in the Judgment of Economists," *Handelsblatt*, Jan. 25, 2013, http://www.handelsblatt.com/politik/oekonomie/nachrichten/arbeitnehmermitsprache-die-mitbestimmung-im-urteil-der-oekonomen-seite-all/7683538-all.html.

[69] Lynn A. Stout, "The Shareholder Value Myth," Harvard Law School, Forum on Corporate Governance and Financial Regulation, June 26, 2012, http://blogs.law.harvard.edu/corpgov/2012/06/26/the-shareholder-value-myth/.

[70] See David Ignatius, "Smart Power Amid the Social Whirl," *Washington Post*, Jan. 21, 2011.

[71] Susanne Royer et al., "Employee Voice and Strategic Competitive Advantage," in International Modern Public Corporations—An Economic Perspective," *European Management Journal* vol. 26, no. 4, August 2008, 4.

[72] Royer et al., "Employee Voice and Strategic Competitive Advantage," 10, 14, 15.

[73] George A. Akerlof and Rachel E. Kranton, *Identity Economics*, 15.

[74] David Fairris and Philippe Askenazy, "Works Councils and Firm Productivity in France," *Journal of Labor Research*, May 22, 2010.

[75] See J.T. Addison, C. Schnabel, and J. Wagner, "Work Councils in Germany: Their Effects on Establishment Performance," *Oxford Economic Papers* 53, 2001, 659–694. Paul J. Welfens and J.T. Addison, "The Performance Effects of Unions, Codetermination and Employee Involvement: Comparing the United States and Germany (with an addendum on the United Kingdom)," *Innovation, Employment and Growth Policies' Issues in the European Union and the United States* (Heidelberg, Germany: Springer Verlag Berline, 2009). B. Frick and I. Möller, "Mandated Work Councils and Firm Performance: Labor Productivity and Personnel Turnover in German Establishments," *Schmollers Jahrbuck* 123, 435–454, 2003.

[76] Sarah Brown, Jolian McHardy, Robert McNabb, and Karl Taylor, "Workplace Performance, Worker Commitment, and Loyalty," *Institute for the Study of Labor*, January 2011.

[77] As quoted in Daniel Schäfer, "Keeping the Lights On," *Financial Times*, Nov. 10, 2009.

[78] Rosabeth Moss Kanter, "How Great Companies Think Differently," *Harvard Business Review*, November 2011.

[79] Justin Fox and Jay W. Lorsch, "What Good Are Shareholders?"

[80] John T. Addison and Claus Schnabel, "Worker Directors: a Germany Product That Did Not Export," *Industrial Relations: A Journal of Economy and Society* 50:354–374, March 24, 2011.

[81] Larry Fauver and Michael E. Fuerst, "Does Good Corporate Governance Include Employee Representation? Evidence from German Corporate Boards," *Journal of Financial Economics*, December 2006.

[82] Kornelius Kraft, Jörg Stank, and Ralf Dewenter, "Codetermination and Innovation," *Cambridge Journal of Economics* vol. 35 (1), 2011.

[83] Royer et al., "Employee Voice and Strategic Competitive Advantage," 3, 4, 7–8, 10, 11.

[84] Diane Werneke and Sar A. Levitan, "Worker Participation and Productivity Change," *Monthly Labor Review* vol. 107, 1984.

[85] As quoted by Richard Milne, "A Meeting of the Minds," *Financial Times*, Feb. 28, 2010.

[86] Andrea Beltratti and René M. Stulz, "The Credit Crisis Around the Globe: Why Did Some Banks Perform Better?," Ohio State Fisher College of Business, working paper series, 2010–05, March 2010, http://areas.kenan-flagler.unc.edu/Accounting/Documents/Beltratti_and_Stulz_March_16_2010.pdf.

[87] Rüdiger Fahlenbrach and René M. Stulz, "Bank CEO Incentives and the Credit Crisis," National Bureau of Economics, August 2009 (updated March 2010), http://www4.gsb.columbia.edu/rt/null?&exclusive=filemgr.download&file_id=7214553&rtcontentdisposition=filename=Stultz_Bank%20CEO%20Incentives%20and%20the%20Credit%20Crisis%2020100508%20RMS.pdf.

[88] As quoted in John Gillespie and David Zweig, *Money for Nothing*, 239–40.

[89] See Hayat Gazzane, "Family Businesses Are More Resilient to The Crisis," *Le Figaro*, Jan. 21, 2013, http://www.lefigaro.fr/entrepreneur/2013/01/21/09007-20130121ARTFIG00700-les-entreprises-familiales-resistent-mieux-a-la-crise.php.

[90] Ronald C. Anderson and David M. Reeb, "Founding Family Ownership and Firm Performance: Evidence from the S&P 500," *Journal of Finance* vol. LVIII, no. 3, June 2003.

[91] Ronald C. Anderson, Sattar A. Mansi, and David M. Reeb, "Founding Family Ownership and the Agency Cost of Debt," working paper, Feb. 6, 2002, http://papers.ssrn.com/sol3/papers.cfm?abstract_id=303864.

CHAPTER 8

[1] Peter G. Peterson, "The Morning After."

[2] Richard Gamble, "How Right Was Reagan," *The American Conservative*, May 2009.

[3] Lliaquat Ahamed, *Lords of Finance*.

[4] Henry Olson, "The GOP's Time for Choosing," *Wall Street Journal*, Jan. 5, 2008.

[5] Murray N. Rothbard, "The Myths of Reaganomics."

[6] Kenneth S. Baer, "The Spirit of '78, Stayin' Alive," *Washington Post*, July 13, 2008. Proposition 13 had an even more momentous impact on governance, imposing a supermajority requirement on most elements of California's budget, allowing the small Republican Party minority in the state legislature to gridlock policy vastly out of proportion with its numbers. See Edward Luce, *Time to Start Thinking*, 207.

[7] Robert H. Frank, *The Darwin Economy*, 57.

[8] Steven Pearlstein, "Kennedy Saw Health-Care Reform Fail in the '70s; Today's Lawmakers Don't Have To," *Washington Post*, Aug. 28, 2009.

[9] Lisa Rein and Ed O'Keefe, "A Negative Poll for Federal Workers," *Washington Post*, Oct. 18, 2010.

[10] Marc J. Hetherington, *Why Trust Matters: Declining Political Trust and the Demise of American Liberalism* (Princeton, NJ: Princeton University Press, 2006).

[11] Stanley B. Greenberg, "Why Voters Tune Out Democrats," *New York Times*, Aug. 5, 2011.

[12] The explanation for this counterfactual Obama record is based on an unbiased evaluation of the fiscal year 2009 budget. The surge in federal spending related to the credit crisis and recession occurred in FY'09. Is that the responsibility of the departing President Bush or Obama? Well, that fiscal year began on October 1, 2008, amid the credit crunch, four months before President Obama took office. Outlays originated by George W. Bush were already one-third spent before Obama arrived, the magnitude of the budget on a trajectory determined by G.W. Bush, including the bank bailout he signed into law. After January 2009, the new President Obama added some new stimulus and child health spending; the Dow Jones & Company analysis reflects that division of responsibility in FY'09 for federal spending between Presidents George W. Bush and Obama.

[13] Peter G. Peterson, "The Morning After."

[14] David Frum, "Post-Tea-Party Nation," *New York Times Magazine*, Nov. 14, 2010.

[15] David Segal, "William A Niskanen, 78, a Blunt Libertarian Economist," *New York Times*, Oct. 29, 2011.

[16] Dana Hedgpeth, "The Man Behind the Army's Monetary Might," *Washington Post*, June 1, 2010.

[17] The Bush Administration's Office of Management and Budget concluded that civil servants outperformed private sector contractors in 83 percent of competitions between 2003 and 2006, producing quality outcomes cheaper. This occurred even though the watchdog Government Accountability Office subsequently found that the Administration had secretly jiggered results to favor the private firms. Professor Paul Light of New York University's Wagner Graduate School of Public Service evaluated the competitions this way: "The competitive sourcing initiative did little to improve management, produced a ton of worthless paper, demoralized thousands of workers, and cost a bundle, all to prove that federal employees are pretty good after all." See Christopher Lee, "Bush Plan to Contract Federal Jobs Falls Short," *Washington Post*, April 25, 2008.

[18] Walter Pincus, "Congress Gives Pentagon Funds to Replace Expensive Contractors," *Washington Post*, Dec. 24, 2009.

[19] Ron Nixon, "Government Pays More in Contracts, Study Finds," *New York Times*, Sept. 13, 2011.

[20] Walter Pincus, "Congress Gives Pentagon Funds to Replace Expensive Contractors."

[21] Dana Hedgpeth, "The Man Behind the Army's Monetary Might."

[22] Anna Fifield, "Obama Looks to Slash Contracting Costs," *Financial Times*, Dec. 21, 2009.

[23] Dana Hedgpeth, "Spending on Iraq Poorly Tracked," *Washington Post*, May 23, 2008.

[24] Christopher Shays and Michael Thibault, "Reducing Waste in War Contracts," *Washington Post*, Aug. 29, 2011.

[25] Richard A. Oppel, Jr., "Private Prisons Found to Offer Little in Savings," *New York Times*, May 19, 2011.

CHAPTER 9

[1] David Brooks, "The Mother of All No-Brainers," *New York Times*, July 5, 2011.

[2] Murray N. Rothbard, "The Myths of Reaganomics."

[3] Gideon Rachman, "How Reagan Ruined Conservatism," *Financial Times*, March 1, 2010.

[4] Harold Meyerson, "End Slacker-State Subsidies," *Washington Post*, May 18, 2011.

[5] "Summary of Latest Federal Individual Income Tax Data," Fiscal Fact no. 183, The Tax Foundation, July 30, 2009.

[6] David Cay Johnston, "Tax Cuts Increased Income, But Hardly Equally," *New York Times,* Oct. 12, 2007.

[7] "We Thought They Wanted to Be Like Buffett," Congressional Research Service, cited on the Editorial Page, *New York Times*, Oct. 16, 2011.

[8] Steven Mufson and Jia Lynn Yang, "Tax Policy Feeds Gap Between Rich, Poor," *Washington Post*, Sept.12, 2011.

[9] Al Kamen, "Ronald Reagan, the Original Class Warrior?," In the Loop, *Washington Post,* Oct. 7, 2011.

[10] H. Rackham, trans., *Aristotle, The Nicomachean Ethics* (Cambridge, MA: Harvard University Press, 1975).

[11] David Cay Johnston, *Perfectly Legal*, 3.

[12] Sean Wilentz, "Confounding Fathers," *The New Yorker,* Oct. 18, 2010.

[13] Adam Smith, *The Wealth of Nations*, 451, and "Tax Policy Concept Paper," American Institute of Certified Public Accountants, 2007, 1.

[14] "Tax Policy Concept Paper," American Institute of Certified Public Accountants, 2007, 3.

[15] Robert Pear, "It's Official: The Rich Get Richer," *New York Times*, Oct. 26, 2011.

[16] Martin Feldstein, "The Tax Reform Evidence from 1986," *Wall Street Journal*, Oct. 24, 2011.

[17] David Cay Johnston, *Perfectly Legal*, 20.

[18] David Cay Johnston, Ibid., 123.

[19] "An Incomplete Fix," *New York Times,* Jan. 14, 2013.

[20] James B. Stewart, "Troubling Favoritism in Tax Code," *New York Times*, April 21, 2012.

[21] Lou Cannon, *The Role of a Lifetime* (New York: Public Affairs, 2001), 243.

[22] David Cay Johnston, *Perfectly Legal*, 123–4.

[23] David Cay Johnston, Ibid., 125–26.

[24] David Cay Johnston, Ibid., 19.

[25] Malcolm Gladwell, *Outliers* (New York: Little, Brown and Co., 2008), 56.

[26] Peter L. Bernstein, "When Should the Fed Crash the Party," *New York Times,* May 11, 2008.

[27] Andrew W. Mellon, *Taxation: The People's Business* (New York: Macmillan, 1924), and Joseph J. Thorndike, "Was Andrew Mellon Really the Supply-Sider That Conservatives Like to Believe?," *Tax Analyst*, March 24, 2003.

CHAPTER 10

[1] John Plender, "Capitalism in Convulsion: Toxic Assets Head Towards the Public Balance Sheet," *Financial Times*, Sept. 19, 2008.

[2] John F. Dickerson, "Confessions of a White House Insider," *Time Magazine*, Jan. 10, 2004.
[3] David Brooks, "The Ike Phase," *New York Times*, March 15, 2011.
[4] Murray N. Rothbard, "The Myths of Reaganomics."
[5] Gerald P. Dwyer, Jr., "Wildcat Banking, Banking Panics, and Free Banking in the United States," Federal Reserve Bank of Atlanta, *Economic Review*, December 1996.
[6] Bray Hammond, *Banks and Politics in America, from the Revolution to the Civil War* (Princeton, NJ: Princeton University Press, 1957).
[7] Gerald P. Dwyer, Jr., "Wildcat Banking, Banking Panics, and Free Banking in the United States."
[8] Timothy H. Parsons, *The Rule of Empires*, 35.
[9] Martin Wolf, "Seeds of Its Own Destruction," *Financial Times*, March 8, 2009.
[10] "Budget, United States Historic Tables," Office of Management and Budget, FY 2011, table 1.1.
[11] Murray N. Rothbard, "The Myths of Reaganomics."
[12] Murray N. Rothbard, Ibid.
[13] See Simon Johnson, "No One Is Above the Law," *New York Times*, Dec. 23, 2011.
[14] Sylvia Nasar, *Grand Pursuit*, 263.
[15] David Ignatius, "A Political Crisis of Faith," *Washington Post*, Aug. 10, 2011.
[16] Dana Milbank, "Keynes, the GOP's New Whipping Boy," *Washington Post*, Sept. 12, 2010.
[17] Sylvia Nasar, Ibid, 402
[18] Sylvia Nasar, Ibid, 408.
[19] Bruce Bartlett, "When Tax Cuts Were a Tough Sell," *New York Times*, Jan. 22, 2013.
[20] Peter G. Peterson, "The Morning After."
[21] David Stockman, "Four Deformations of the Apocalypse," *New York Times*, Aug. 1, 2010.
[22] Thomas Frank, *The Wrecking Crew*, 264 and 360 (notes 9 and 10).
[23] Thomas Frank, Ibid.
[24] Catherine Rampell, "Tax Pledge May Scuttle a Deal on Deficits," *New York Times*, Nov. 19, 2011.
[25] David Stockman, "Paul Ryan's Fairy-Tale Budget Plan," *New York Times*, August 14, 2012.
[26] Martin Wolf, "The Political Genius of Supply-Side Economics," *Financial Times*, July 25, 2010.
[27] Murray N. Rothbard, "The Myths of Reaganomics."
[28] Ian Morris, *Why the West Rules for Now* (New York: Farrar, Straus and Giroux, 2010), 320.
[29] Paul M. Kennedy, *Rise and Fall of the Great Powers* (New York: Vintage, 1989), 527.
[30] James Klumpner (Chief Economist, Senate Budget Committee), e-mail to author, January 14, 2013,
[31] "A Warning Shot to Washington," Editorial, *Financial Times*, April 18, 2011.
[32] Steven Pearlstein, "Debt Doesn't Have to be a Burden," *Washington Post*, March 4, 2009.

[33] Richard McGregor, "The Republicans: Sloganeers to Supremos," *Financial Times*, April 25, 2012.

[34] Another example is *Washington Post* columnist Robert J. Samuelson, who argued in mid-2012 that President John Kennedy was responsible for setting American on a deficit course. The facts belie Samuelson. The ratio of US national debt held by the public to GDP stood at 45 in FY'61 when Kennedy took office, but dwindled to 40 by FY'64, and fell even lower after that to 25.8 in FY'81 on the eve of Ronald Reagan's election. See Robert J. Samuelson, "The Mistake We're Still Paying for," *Washington* Post, July 9, 2012.

[35] T.J. Augustine, Alexander Maasry, Damilola Sobo, and Di Wang, "Sovereign Fiscal Responsibility Index 2011," Stanford University and the Comeback America Initiative, March 23, 2011.

[36] Publicly held debt statistics are from "Fiscal Year 2013 Historical Tables," Office of Management and Budget, Table 7.1, 2013.

[37] Niall Ferguson, *Civilization* (New York: Penguin Group, 2011), 149–50.

[38] Carmen M. Reinhart and Kenneth S. Rogoff, *This Time Is Different*, fig 1. John Mauldin and Jonathan Tepper, *Endgame* (Hoboken, NJ: John Wiley & Sons, 2011), 27.

CHAPTER 11

[1] David Stockman, "Four Deformations of the Apocalypse."

[2] Michale Sauga and Peter Müller, "Interview with German Finance Minister Schäuble," *Der Spiegel*, Nov. 8, 2010.

[3] Joseph E. Stiglitz, "Breaking the Vicious Cycle of Inequality," *New York Times,* June 24, 2012.

[4] Peter G. Peterson, "The Morning After."

[5] "Rising Debt Burden," Inequality in the US," The Stanford Center on Poverty and Inequality, September 2012, http://www.stanford.edu/group/scspi/slides/Inequality_SlideDeck.pdf, download slides at www.inequality.com.

[6] "Inequality, Debt and the Financial Crisis," Editorial, *New York Times,* May 4, 2012.

[7] A majority of this was household and business community debt, which rose as a share of GDP from 123 percent in 1981 to 290 percent in late 2008. Martin Wolf, "Japanese Lessons for a World of Balance-Sheet Deflation," *Financial Times*, Feb.18, 2009.

[8] John Maynard Keynes, *The General Theory of Employment, Interest, and Money* (out of print; 1936). John Cassidy, "Rational Irrationality," *The New Yorker*, Oct. 5, 2009.

[9] Katrin Bennhold, "Hardships Past Haunt Europe's Search for Financial Safety," *New York Times*, Oct. 27, 2008.

[10] See Colin Brinsden, "Consumers Prefer Cash as Wages Grow," *Sydney Morning Herald*, Nov. 19, 2009. "Federal Bank Study: Why the Germans Prefer to Pay with Cash," *Handelsblatt*, Nov. 7, 2011.

[11] Sheldon Garon, "Why We Spend, Why They Save," *New York Times*, Nov. 25, 2011.

[12] Nicholas Kulish, "Smarting From Crises in the Past, Germans Approach Bailouts With Reluctance," *New York Times*, Oct. 5, 2008, and "Outside the CAC 40 Companies, An Executive of a Listed Company Receives an

Average Salary of 502,000 Euros, with Wide Variation Depending on the Size of the Company," *Le Figaro*, Nov. 25, 2009.

[13] Nicholas Kulish, "Smarting from Crises in the Past, Germans Approach Bailouts with Reluctance."

[14] Sheldon Garon, Ibid.

[15] Daniel Schäfer, "Keeping the Lights On," *Financial Times*, Nov. 10, 2009.

[16] John Gillespie and David Zweig, *Money for Nothing*, 23.

[17] A concise review of these deregulation events is provided by Barry Ritholtz, "Debt Ceiling: Ten Lessons Beyond That Crisis," *Washington Post*, July 29, 2011.

[18] As reported by Gillian Tett, "Insight: Big Steps Taken to Reform Wall Street," *Financial Times*, May 14, 2009.

[19] Barry Ritholtz, "Debt Ceiling: Ten Lessons Beyond That Crisis."

[20] Phillip Coggin, "Betting the Balance Sheet," *Economist*, June 26, 2010.

[21] As quoted by John Plender, "Originative Sin: The Future of Banking," *Financial Times*, Jan. 4, 2009.

[22] Martin Wolf, "Central Banks Must Target More Than Just Inflation," *Financial Times*, May 5, 2009.

[23] See Derek Scally, "Germany's Pact With the Devil," *Irish Times*, Dec. 14, 2012, http://www.presseurop.eu/en/content/article/3163701-germany-s-pact-devil.

[24] Here is how Joseph Stiglitz explained the failure of Friedman's theory: "Few would hold that now, as the velocity of circulation turned out to be less constant than the monetarists anticipated. Countries seduced by apparent certainties of monetarism found themselves in a highly uncertain world." Joseph Stiglitz, "It Is Folly to Place All Our Trust in the Fed," *Financial Times*, October 18, 2010. Research by economists in the United States and abroad, such as Harald Uhlig at the University of Chicago and Pedro Teles of the Portuguese Central Bank in 2010, rejects linkages of the sort envisioned by Friedman: "The connection is at best vague, or does not even exist." See Olaf Storbeck, "Quantity Theory of Money: Printing Does Not Always Lead to Inflation," *Handelsblatt*, October 25, 2010.

[25] Daron Acemoglu and Simon Johnson, "Who Captured the Fed?," Economix, *New York Times*, March 29, 2012, http://economix.blogs.nytimes.com/2012/03/29/who-captured-the-fed/.

[26] James K. Galbraith, Olivier Giovannoni, and Ann J. Russo, "The Fed's Real Reaction Function: Monetary Policy, Inflation, Unemployment, Inequality—and Presidential Politics," University of Texas Inequality Project Working Paper 42, July 17, 2007. See also James K. Galbraith, "With Economic Inequality for All," *The Nation*, Sept. 7–14, 1998.

[27] Larry Bartels, "Nearsighted Voters," *New York Times*, April 15, 2012.

[28] Binyamin Appelbaum, "Economic Stimulus As the Election Nears? It's Been Done Before," *New York Times*, Sept. 12, 2012.

[29] Lori Montgomery, "On the Way to a Surplus, a $12-Trillion US Detour," *Washington Post*, May 1, 2011.

[30] Olivier Coibion, Yuriy Gorodnichenko, Lorenz Kueng, and John Silvia, "Innocent Bystanders? Monetary Policy and Inequality in the US,"

University of California, Berkeley, May 30, 2011, http://emlab.berkeley.edu/~ygorodni/CGKS_inequality.pdf.

[31] Louis Hyman, "The House That George Romney Built," *New York Times*, Jan. 31, 2012.

[32] Michael J. Barry, "I Saw the Crisis Coming. Why Didn't the Fed?," *New York Times*, April 4, 2010.

[33] Dennis Cauchon, "Why Home Values May Take Decades to Recover," *USA Today*, Dec. 15, 2008.

[34] Barry Ritholtz, "Debt Ceiling: Ten Lessons Beyond That Crisis," *Washington Post*, July 29, 2011.

[35] John Mauldin and Jonathan Tepper, *Endgame* (Hoboken, NJ: John Wiley & Sons, 2011), 16.

[36] "Open Market Committee Minutes," Federal Reserve Board of Governors, January 27–28, 2004 and March 2004 meetings.

[37] Acemoglu and Johnson, "Who Captured the Fed?"

[38] George Soros, "Do Not Ignore the Need for Financial Reform," *Financial Times*, Oct. 25, 2009.

CHAPTER 12

[1] Louis Uchitelle, "Fed Fears Wage Spiral That Is Little in Evidence," *New York Times*, Aug. 1, 2008.

[2] David Frum, "The Vanishing Republican Voters," *New York Times*, Aug. 5, 2008.

[3] Larry M. Bartels, *Unequal Democracy* (Princeton, NJ: Princeton University Press, 2008), 296–97.

[4] See Timothy H. Parsons, *The Rule of Empires*, 36.

[5] Peter G. Peterson, "The Morning After."

[6] George Gilder, *Wealth and Poverty* (1981; out of print), and David Graeber, *Debt* (Brooklyn, NY: Melville House, 2011), 377–78.

[7] Albert Hunt, "Reagan Offers Lesson for Obama on Tax," *Sydney Morning Herald*, Jan. 10, 2011.

[8] Steven Mufson and Jia Lynn Yang, "Tax Policy Feeds Gap Between Rich, Poor," *Washington Post*, Sept. 12, 2011.

[9] Bruce Bartlett, "The Fiscal Legacy of George W. Bush," Economix, *New York Times*, June 12, 2012.

[10] Thomas L. Hungerford, "Taxes and the Economy: An Economic Analysis of the Top Tax Rates Since 1945," Congressional Research Service, Washington, Sept. 14, 2012, http://graphics8.nytimes.com/news/business/0915taxesandeconomy.pdf.

[11] James B. Stewart, "Questioning the Dogma of Tax Rates," *New York Times*, Aug. 20, 2011.

[12] Michael Förster, "An Overview of Growing Income Inequality in OECD Countries: Divided We Stand: Why Inequality Keeps Rising," OECD, December 2011, 29.

[13] "World Economic Outlook 2007," *International Monetary Fund*, 180.

[14] "World Bank Report: Economy Must Create 600 Million Jobs," *Handelsblatt*, Oct. 5, 2012.

[15] Jim Clifton, *The Coming Jobs War* (New York: Gallup Press, 2012), 2.

[16] “Labour Markets in Brazil, China, India, and Russia,” Organisation for Economic Co-Operation and Develoopment, Paris, 2007, table 1.A1.3.

[17] “Henry Ford Raising Wage May Give Tip on Worker Prosperity,” *China Daily*, Jan. 20, 2010.

[18] Lawrence Mishel, Jared Bernstein, and John Schmitt, *State of Working America, 2000–01* (Ithaca, New York: Cornell University Press, 2001). Studies suggest that trade may account for 10–15 percent of income disparities, with other factors more important. See Paul Krugman, “Growing World Trade: Causes and Consequences,” Brookings Papers on Economic Activity, 1995, vol. 26, issue 1, 327–377. Robert Z. Lawrence, “Blue-Collar Blues: Is Trade to Blame for Rising US Income Inequality?,” Peterson Institute for International Economics, January 2008. Josh Bivens, “Globalization, American Wages, and Inequality,” Economic Policy Institute, working paper 279, 2007. “Krugman’s Conundrum,” *Economist*, April 17, 2008.

[19] Sandile Hlatshwayo and Michael Spence, “Jobs and Structure in the Global Economy,” Project Syndicate, March 16, 2011. See also Edward Luce, “Can America Regain the Most Dynamic Labour Market Mantle?,” *Financial Times*, Dec. 11, 2011, and Steven Pearlstein, “Good for GDP = (Does Not Equal) Good for Workers,” *Washington Post*, March 13, 2011.

[20] Robert E. Scott, “The Burden of Outsourcing,” Economic Policy Institute, Oct. 2, 2008.

[21] See Louis Uchitelle, “An Argument Against a Two-Tier Pay System,” Economix, *New York Times*, Nov. 25, 2010.

[22] Robert E. Scott, “The High Price of ‘Free’ Trade,” November 2003, Economic Policy Institute, http://www.epi.org/publication/briefingpapers_bp147/.

[23] Robert E. Scott, Ibid, 9.

[24] Robert E. Scott, Ibid.

[25] Kate Bronfenbrenner, “Uneasy Terrain: The Impact of Capital Mobility on Workers, Wages, and Union Organizing,” report prepared for the United States Trade Deficit Review Commission, Washington, D.C., September 2000. See also Thomas I. Palley, “Trade, Employment, and Outsourcing: Some Observations on US-China Economic Relations,” *Offshoring and the Internationalization of Employment* (Paris: International Labour Organization, International Institute for Labour Studies, Symposium Proceeds, Annecy, 2005), 84.

[26] Ross Douthat, “Can the Working Class Be Saved?,” *New York Times*, Feb. 11, 2012.

[27] “The Rich, the Poor and the Growing Gap Between Them,” Special Report: Inequality in America, *Economist,* June 15, 2006.

[28] Perry Fagan and Michael C. Jensen, “Capitalism Isn’t Broken,” *Wall Street Journal,* March 29, 1996, A-10.

[29] Norbert Häring, “Man As a Yardstick,” *Handelsblatt*, Aug. 19, 2010.

[30] Charles Lane, “Obama’s Leaky Bucket,” *Washington Post*, Dec. 20, 2011.

[31] Andrew G. Berg and Jonathan D. Ostry, “Equality and Efficiency: Is There a Trade-off Between the Two or Do They Go Hand in Hand,” *Finance and Development*, International Monetary Fund, Washington, September 2011.

[32] David Brooks, “The Biggest Issue,” *New York Times*, July 29, 2008. See

also Tyler Cowen, *The Great Stagnation* (New York: A Penguin Group e-Special from Dutton, 2011).

[33] Claudia Goldin and Lawrence F. Katz, *The Race Between Education and Technology* (Cambridge, MA: Harvard University Press, 2008).

[34] This includes: Alan Blinder, Edward N. Wolff, Deborah Reed, Daniel Cohen, Gordon Lafer, Frank Levy, and Peter Temin. For a survey of their analyses, see Edward C. Kokkelenberg's book review in "Human Resources, Management, and Personnel," *Industrial & Labor Relations Review*, vol. 61, issue 4, 2008. Also see Richard B. Freeman, *American Works: Critical Thoughts on the Exceptional US Labor Market* (New York: Russell Sage Foundation, 2007). Robert B. Reich, *Supercapitalism: The Transformation of Business, Democracy, and Everyday Life* (New York: Borzoi/Alfred A. Knopf, 2007).

[35] Ian Dew-Becker and Robert J. Gordon, "Where Did the Productivity Growth Go? Inflation Dynamics and the Distribution of Income," Brookings Panel on Economic Activity, Washington, D.C., Sept. 8, 2005.

[36] Steven Greenhouse, "For Graduates, a Shrinking Payoff," Economix, *New York Times*, Aug. 31, 2011.

[37] Catherine Rampell, "Do College Grads Earn Less Now Than 40 Years Ago?," Economix, *New York Times*, Jan. 12, 2012.

[38] Dew-Becker and Gordon, "Where Did the Productivity Growth Go?"

[39] N. Gregory Mankiw, "The Wealth Trajectory: Rewards for the Few," *New York Times*, April 20, 2008.

[40] Harold Meyerson, "Labor's Power Gap," *Washington Post*, Sept. 3, 2012.

[41] Stefan Sauer, "Many Students, Some Apprentices," *Berliner Zeitung*, Aug. 30, 2012.

[42] These other economists include Robert J. Gordon, "The Demise of Okun's Law and of Procyclical Fluctuations in Conventional and Unconventional Measures of Productivity," National Bureau of Economic Research, Cambridge, MA, 2010. For a broad survey of the wage compression literature, see Frank Levy and Tom Kochan, "Addressing the Problem of Stagnant Wages," Employment Policy Research Network, March 2011. Also Jess Bailey, Joe Coward, and Matthew Whittaker, "Painful Separation," Resolution Foundation, October 2011.

[43] "What Century Are We In?," Editorial, *New York Times,* Jan. 3, 2011.

[44] Thomas Gabe, "Poverty in the United States," Congressional Research Service, Aug. 27, 2008.

[45] "Human Rights Watch Denounced Wasteful Practices of Some European Companies in the US," *Le Monde,* Sept. 2, 2010. Jeremy Lerner, "Groups Attacked on US Labour Practices," *Financial Times*, Sept. 2, 2010.

[46] Steven Greenhouse, "Labor's Decline and Wage Inequality," *New York Times*, Aug. 4, 2011.

[47] Harold Meyerson, "When Unions Disappeared," *Washington Post*, June 13, 2012.

[48] Mark Oppenheimer, "For Duquesne Professors, Union Fight That Transcends Religion," *New York Times*, June 23, 2012.

[49] Harold Meyerson, "Corporate America's Chokehold on Wages," *Washington Post*, July 20, 2011. For an analysis of the relationship between union membership and income disparities, see Stephen Machin of University College London and John van Reenen of the London School of Economics,

"Changes in Wage Inequality," Centre for Economic Performance, Special Paper 18, London School of Economics, 2007. See also Jacob Hacker, "Northern Exposure, Learning from Canada's Response to 'Winner-Take-All' Inequality" (Stanford University: *Pathways*, Spring 2009).

50 An attempt to introduce this Canadian-style system in American failed in Congress early in the Obama Administration. Kris Warner, "Protecting Fundamental Labor Rights: Lessons from Canada for the United States," Center for Economic and Policy Research, August 2012, http://www.cepr.net/documents/publications/canada-2012-08.pdf.

51 Kate Bronfenbrenner, "The NLRB Got It Right on Boeing," *Washington Post*, June 23, 2011.

52 Thomas Geoghegan, "Infinite Debt," *Harper's Magazine*, April 2009.

53 David Leonhardt, "In Wreckage of Lost Jobs, Lost Power," *New York Times*, Jan. 19, 2011.

54 Ken Silverstein, "Labor's Last Stand," *Harper's Magazine*, July 2009.

55 "The Imperfect Union Bill," Editorial, *Washington Post*, May 11, 2009.

56 Harold Meyerson, "Card Check and Gut Check," *Washington Post*, May 14, 2009.

57 Silverstein, "Labor's Last Stand."

58 Geoghegan, "Infinite Debt."

59 Ibid.

60 Norbert Häring, "The Economist Who Wanted to Make a Difference," *Handelsblatt*, July 27, 2010.

61 Henry Olson, "The GOP's Time for Choosing," *Wall Street Journal*, Jan. 5, 2008.

62 "The 'Omnipresident's' Crucible," Editorial, *Washington Post*, Nov. 23, 2007.

63 Quoted by Martin Newland, *The Observer*, May 6, 2007.

64 Henry Hansmann and Reinier Kraakman, "The End of History for Corporate Law," 89 *Georgetown Law Journal*, 439–468, 2001. Also see Irene Lynch Fannon, "The European Social Model of Corporate Governance: Prospects for Success in an Enlarged Europe," European Union Studies Association Conference, March 30, 2005.

65 "The Financial Crisis: What Next?," *Economist*, Sept.18, 2008.

66 Andrew Moravcsik, as quoted in "Suddenly, Europe Looks Pretty Smart," Dealbook, *New York Times*, Oct. 20, 2008.

67 Mark Leonard, *Why Europe Will Run the 21st Century* (New York: Public Affairs, 2005), 70.

68 Mark Leonard, Ibid., 74.

69 "Bankruptcies Eliminate Millions of Jobs," *Berliner Zeitung*, Dec. 28, 2009.

70 Mary Bartnik, "They Could Renounce Their RTT to Save Their Jobs," *Le Figaro*, July 19, 2010.

71 Floyd Norris, "A Shift in the Export Powerhouses," *New York Times*, Feb. 20, 2010.

72 Barry Eichengreen, *The European Economy Since 1945* (Princeton, NJ: Princeton University Press, 2008), 380.

73 "France Is Open for Business with Foreign Investors," Paris: Invest in France Agency, November 2007.

74 Steven Hill, "5 Myths about Sick Old Europe," *Washington Post*, Oct. 7, 2007.

[75] Julia Werdiger, "To Woo Europeans, McDonald's Goes Upscale," *New York Times*, Aug. 25, 2007.

[76] Daniel S. Hamilton and Joseph P. Quinlan, "France and Globalization," Washington, D.C.: Center for Transatlantic Relations, Paul H. Nitze School of Advanced International Studies, 2008.

[77] "France Is Open for Business with Foreign Investors," Paris: Invest in France Agency.

[78] Fred B. Irwin, "Networking for the Future," 100 years—American Chamber of Commerce in Germany.

[79] Pete Sweeney, "Europe Still Vies for US Investment," *EuropeanVoice.com*, Oct. 11, 2004, http://www.europeanvoice.com/article/imported/europe-still-vies-for-us-investment/51104.aspx.

[80] Nelson D. Schwartz, "Global Car Industry Fearful for Detroit," *New York Times,* Dec. 16, 2008.

[81] Guy Dutheil and Dominique Philippe Gallois, "EDF, McDonalds's, Airbus. . . . These Companies Create More Jobs in France," *Le Monde,* Jan. 1, 2013.

[82] Gibson Vance, "Lawsuits Are Making Our Cars Safer," *Washington Post,* April 16, 2011.

[83] As quoted by Steve Lohr, "How Crisis Shapes the Corporate Model," *New York Times*, March 29, 2009.

[84] "Ford Plans to Short-time Working in Cologne," Democratic Action Party, *Berliner Zeitung,* April 25, 2012.

[85] As quoted by Richard Milne, "Europe: A Meeting of Minds," *Financial Times,* Feb. 28, 2010.

[86] "Domino's Defies 'Scandinavian Labour Costs,'" Australian Associated Press/ *Sydney Morning Herald*, Aug. 10, 2011.

[87] Eva Roth, "Lidl Strikes Ten Euro against Minimum Wage," *Berliner Zeitung,* Dec. 21, 2010.

[88] Tony Royle, *Working for McDonald's in Europe: An Unequal Struggle?* (London: Routledge Studies in Employment Relations/Taylor & Francis, 2001), Table 7.3.

[89] Tony Royle, Ibid., 172. See also John Tagliabue, "A McDonald's Ally in Paris," *New York Times,* June 20, 2006.

[90] Tony Royle, *Working for McDonald's in Europe,*134.

[91] Ibid.,135.

[92] Janko Tietz, "Amazon Accused of Systematic Job Subsidy Abuse," *Der Spiegel,* Nov. 28, 2011.

SECTION 3

CHAPTER 13

[1] Christine Lagarde, as quoted in "Wages Increases Linked to Productivity," Reuters, *Le Figaro*, March 4, 2011.

[2] Malcolm Maiden, "US in a Bind as Traditional Drivers of Economic Recovery Are Broken," *Sydney Morning Herald*, Dec. 14, 2011.

[3] Paul Krugman, "Learning from Europe," *New York Times*, Jan. 11, 2010.

[4] Robert S. McElvaine, *The Great Depression* (New York: Three Rivers Press, 1984), 212–218.

[5] Mark Leonard, *Why Europe Will Run the 21st Century* (New York: Public Affairs, 2005), 9–19.

[6] Liaquat Ahamed, *Lords of Finance* (New York: Penguin Books, 2009), 20.

[7] Stefan Zweig, *The World of Yesterday* (Lincoln, NE: University of Nebraska Press, 1964).

[8] Mark Leonard, *Why Europe Will Run the 21st Century*, 13.

[9] Ian Morris, *Why the West Rules—for Now* (New York: Farrar, Straus & Giroux, 2010), 505.

[10] Nasar, *Grand Pursuit*, 86–90.

[11] David Leonhardt, "The Economics of Henry Ford May Be Passé," *New York Times*, April 5, 2006.

[12] Mary Bellis, "Henry Ford (1863–1947) I Will Build a Car for the Great Multitude," Money/Inventors, About.com, http://inventors.about.com/od/fstartinventors/a/HenryFord.htm.

[13] Malcolm Gladwell, *Outliers*, 56.

[14] Mary Bellis, "Henry Ford (1863–1947), I Will Build a Car for the Great Multitude."

[15] "Fair Pay Underpins Our Prosperity," Editorial, *Sydney Morning Herald*, June 7, 2010, http://www.smh.com.au/opinion/editorial/fair-pay-underpins-our-prosperity-20100606-xn5c.html#ixzz209mlVU4v.

[16] Henry Hazlitt, *Economics in One Lesson* (New York: Three Rivers Press, 1979), 149.

[17] Robert H. Frank and Phillip J. Cook, *The Winner-Take-All Society* (New York: Free Press, 1995). Edward N. Wolff, *Top Heavy* (New York: The New Press, 2002), 11, and "The Squeeze Before the Storm," *Pathways*, Stanford Center for the Study of Poverty and Inequality, Fall 2009. Robert Kuttner, *The Squandering of America* (New York: Vintage Books, 2007), 20. Robert Gordon and Ian Dew-Becker, "Where Did the Productivity Go? Inflation Dynamics and the Distribution of Income," National Bureau of Economic Research (NBER) working paper no. 11842 (December 2005).

[18] Gerrit Wiesmann and Chris Bryant, "Long View: Berthold Huber Has a Reputation for Keeping an Eye on the System as a Whole," *Financial Times*, July 22, 2012.

[19] Ron Haskins and Isabel Sawhill, *Creating an Opportunity Society* (Washington, DC, Brookings Institution Press, 2009), 32.

[20] For example, see the analysis reproduced by the International Labour Organization (ILO) in "Falling Labour Shares and Equitable Growth," section five of the "Global Wage Report 2012/2013, Wages and Equitable Growth," Geneva, ILO, December 2012, http://www.ilo.org/wcmsp5/groups/public/--dgreports/--dcomm/documents/publication/wcms_194843.pdf.

[21] Elizabeth Warren, "The Middle Class on the Precipice," *Harvard Magazine*, Jan.–Feb., 2006.

[22] Some economists, including Columbia University Business School Dean R. Glenn Hubbard, former chairman of George W. Bush's Council of Economic Advisors, suggest that rising benefit outlays belie frozen wages. It is certainly true that employer outlays for benefits (led by health insurance) increased in real terms between the 1980s and the early 2000s. Yet executive suites have been shifting health and other fringe benefit costs onto employees, as outlined by *Wall Street Journal* reporter Ellen E. Schultz in her book, *Retirement Heist* (New York: Portfolio/Penguin, 2011). This

shifting strategy succeeded. Employer outlays for fringe benefits ceased rising after 2003, with such costs capped in real terms at about 30 percent of stagnant paychecks. The success of this cost-shifting strategy by employers is reflected in the Milliman Medical Index: Employee out-of-pocket insurance and health costs for a family of four increased by $1,395 from 2002 to 2006, racing far ahead of any wage gains. Those costs have accelerated since, as firms continue shifting the cost of fringe benefits, with employee out-of-pocket health costs rising another $1,804 between 2006 and 2009.

[23] Michael A. Fletcher, "More Workers Raiding Retirement Accounts to Pay Bills," *New York Times*, Jan. 15, 2013.

[24] Michael Greenstone and Adam Looney, "The Uncomfortable Truth About American Wages," Economix, *New York Times*, Oct. 22, 2012.

[25] Thomas Piketty and Emmanuel Saez, "Income Inequality in the United States: 1913–1998," NBER working paper no. 8467, September 2001, published in the *Quarterly Journal of Economics* 118(1): 1–41 (2003), http://www.nber.org/papers/w8467, and updated Aug. 5, 2009, with 2007 estimates, http://elsa.berkeley.edu/~saez/saez-UStopincomes-2007.pdf. See also Bill Moyers, "The Rule of the Rich," *The Progressive*, February 2011.

[26] Isabel V. Sawhill and John E. Morton, "Economic Mobility: Is the American Dream Alive and Well?," the Economic Mobility Project, an initiative of the Pew Charitable Trusts and the Brookings Institution, May 2007, http://www.brookings.edu/research/papers/2007/05/useconomics-morton.

[27] Michael Cooper, "Lost in Recession, Toll on Underempoyed and Underpaid," *Washington Post*, June 19, 2012.

[28] Catherine Rampell, "Majority of Jobs Added in the Recovery Pay Low Wages, Study Finds," *New York Times*, Aug. 31, 2012. The data was developed by the National Employment Law Project.

[29] Harold Meyerson, "The Unshared Recovery," *Washington Post,* March 9, 2011.

[30] Scott Lilly, "Understanding Bushonomics," Center for American Progress, August 2008, 2, http://www.americanprogress.org/issuesopen-government/report/2008/08/04/4763/understanding-bushonomics/.

[31] The average labor cost time series by the Bureau of Labor Statistics depicted on the cover graph is the most comprehensive international data set covering the entire span of the Reagan era. It reflects the experience of blue-collar employees in manufacturing and is inclusive of all labor costs—including wages, all benefits, and employment taxes such as social insurance fees. In contrast, the statistics in this chapter are wages alone. However, they are more comprehensive, inclusive of all sectors and all workers, and are comparable, drawn from the database at the Geneva-based International Labour Organization. Unfortunately, such time series are available only for recent years. National statistical agencies such as the French Institut National de la Statistique et des Études Économiques (INSEE) or Australian Bureau of Statistics have excellent historical time series and have been relied upon for historical data when available. However, the reader is cautioned that these series are not particularly cross-comparable, due to varying definitions and methodologies.

[32] "Average Wages and the Wage Share, Global Wage Report 2008/9," statistical

appendix, table A1, Geneva, ILO. After rising robustly in the 1980s and 1990s, real German wages declined during some years of the 2000s, increasing international competitiveness. See Holger Görg and Dennis Görlich (at the Kiel Institute for the World Economy) and Christian-Albrechts (University of Kiel), "Trade and Labour Market Outcomes in Germany, Policy Priorities for International Trade and Jobs," OECD, September 2012, chap. 6, 220, http://www.oecd.org/site/tadicite/policy-prioritiesforinternationaltradeandjobs.htm.

[33] Jess Bailey, Joe Coward, and Matthew Whittaker, "Painful Separation, an International Study of the Weakening Relationship Between Economic Growth and the Pay of Ordinary Workers," Resolution Foundation, October 2011, http://www.resolutionfoundation.org/media/media/downloads/Painful_Separation.pdf.

[34] "Les Salaires en France, Édition 2008," *Fiches Thématiques* table 6, Paris, INSEE, 2009.

[35] Sylvia Nasar, *Grand Pursuit*, 457.

[36] "Wages and Equitable Growth, Global Wage Report 2012/2013," Geneva, ILO, December 2012, http://www.ilo.org/global/research/global-reports/global-wage-report/2012/WCMS_194843/lang--en/index.htm.

[37] Moravcsik is chair of Princeton University's European Union program. See *The Choice for Europe: Social Purpose and State Power from Messina to Maastricht* (Ithaca, NY: Cornell University Press, 1998). See also Rutger van der Hoeven, "Those Work-Shy Europeans," *De Groene Amsterdammer*, July 19, 2010.

[38] Barry Eichengreen, *The European Economy Since 1945* (Princeton, NJ: Princeton University Press, 2007), 381.

[39] "National Compensation Survey: Employee Benefits in Private Industry in the US," Washington, DC, Bureau of Labor Statistics, US Department of Labor, March 2006.

[40] "Components of Compensation, US Dollars," Washington, DC, Bureau of Labor Statistics, table 3, December 2011, http://www.bls.gov/news.release/ichcc.t03.htm.

CHAPTER 14

[1] David Cay Johnston, *Free Lunch* (New York: Portfolio, 2007).

[2] Steven Greenhouse and David Leonhardt, "Real Wages Fail to Match a Rise in Productivity," *New York Times*, Aug. 28, 2006.

[3] As quoted by David Cay Johnston, *Free Lunch*, 270.

[4] Adam Smith, *The Wealth of Nations*, book I, chap. IX, 94.

[5] Timothy H. Parsons, *The Rule of Empires* (New York: Oxford University Press, 2010), 36.

[6] Javier Blas, "OPEC cartel to reap record $1tn" *Financial Times*, Dec. 30, 2012.

[7] Robert R. Trumble and Angela N. DeLowell, "Connecting CEO performance to corporate performance: examining intangible metrics of shareholder value," *Journal of Compensation and Benefits*, Nov/Dec 2001.

[8] Michael T. Snyder, "So Long, Middle Class," *New York Post*, Aug. 1, 2010.

[9] Robert Gordon and Ian Dew-Becker, "Where Did the Productivity Go? Inflation Dynamics and the Distribution of Income," NBER working paper no. 11842 (December 2005), http://www.nber.org/papers/w11842.

[10] As quoted by Martin Wolf, "America's Inequality Need Not Determine the Future of Britain," *Financial Times*, Dec. 22, 2011.

[11] Harold Meyerson, "Corporate America's Chokehold on Wages," *Washington Post*, July 20, 2011.

[12] "The Rich, the Poor and the Growing Gap Between Them," *Economist*, June 17, 2006.

[13] Thomas W. Bates, Kathleen M. Kahle, and Rene M. Stulz, "Why Do US Firms Hold So Much More Cash than They Used To?," *The Journal of Finance, American Finance Association* vol. 64(5), 1985–2021 (October 2009).

[14] Steven Pearlstein, "Why They're Winning on CEO Pay," *Washington Post*, June 24, 2011.

[15] Thomas Piketty and Emmanuel Saez, "Income Inequality in the United States, 1913 to 1998." Their analysis has been updated repeatedly. For example, see Emmanuel Saez (based on previous joint work with Piketty), "Striking it Richer: The Evolution of Top Incomes in the United States," *Pathways* (Stanford Center for the Study of Poverty and Inequality, Winter 2008), (updated with 2008 estimates and published July 17, 2010), http://elsa.berkeley.edu/~saez/saez-UStopincomes-2008.pdf; and 2009–2010 updates (published March 2, 2012), http://elsa.berkeley.edu/~saez/saez-UStopincomes-2010.pdf.

[16] Emmanuel Saez, "Striking It Richer," July 17, 2010.

[17] Ian Ayres and Aaron S. Edlin, "Don't Tax the Rich, Tax Inequality Itself," *New York Times*, Dec. 19, 2011.

[18] David Cay Johnston, "Tax Cuts Increased Income, But Hardly Equally," *New York Times*, Oct. 12, 2007.

[19] Emmanuel Saez, "Striking it Richer," March 2, 2012. "A Long Way Down," Editorial, *New York Times*, Sept. 16, 2009.

[20] Bonnie Kavoussi, "Top One Percent Captured 121 Percent of all Income Gains During Recovery's First Years: Study," *Huffington Post*, Feb. 12, 2013.

[21] Facundo Alvaredo, Tony Atkinson, Thomas Piketty, and Emmanuel Saez, "The World Top Income Database," Paris School of Economics, 2012, http://g-mond.parisschoolofeconomics.eu/topincomes/. For similar see calculations, Ian Ayres and Aaron S. Edlin, "Don't Tax the Rich, Tax Inequality Itself."

[22] David Cay Johnston, *Perfectly Legal*, 41.

[23] Scott Lilly, "Understanding Bushonomics," Center for American Progress, August 2008, 2.

[24] Bloomberg News, "Top-Earning US Households Averaged $345 Million in '07," Economix, *New York Times*, Feb. 18, 2010.

[25] Lynnley Browning, "IRS Says Its Audits of Wealthy Are Rising," *New York Times*, March 13, 2010. David Cay Johnston, *Free Lunch*, 18, 83–84, 132, 136.

[26] David Kocieniewski, "280 Big Public Firms Paid Little US Tax, Study Says," *New York Times*, Nov. 3, 2011.

[27] David Cay Johnston, *Perfectly Legal*, 141.

[28] Floyd Norris, "For Business, Golden Days; For Workers, the Dross," *New York Times*, Nov. 26, 2011.

[29] Charles Duhigg and David Kocieniewski, "How Apple Sidesteps Billions in Taxes," *New York Times*, April 29, 2012.

[30] Bruce Bartlett, "Are Taxes in the US High or Low?," Economix, *New York Times*, May 31, 2011.

[31] David Leonhardt, "The Paradox of Corporate Taxes," *New York Times*, Feb. 2, 2011.

[32] Allan Sloan and Jeff Gerth, "The Truth About GE's Tax Bill," *CNN Money*, April 4, 2011.

[33] Tom Cardamone, "Is the Sun Setting on Tax Dodgers?," *Washington Post*, April 12, 2009.

[34] David Kocieniewski, "GE Turns the Tax Man Away Empty Handed," *New York Times*, March 25, 2011.

[35] Harry F. Grubert, "Foreign Taxes and the Growing Share of U.S. Multination Company Income Abroad: Profits, Not Sales, are Being Globalized," Office of Tax Analysis, Working Paper No. 103, February 2012. http://www.treasury.gov/resource-center/tax-policy/tax-analysis/Documents/OTA-W2012-103-Multinational-Income-Globalized-Feb-2012.pdf.

[36] Lisa Rein, "Budget Cuts Hurt IRS, Watchdog Says," *Washington Post*, Jan. 13, 2012.

[37] Charles Duhigg and David Kocieniewski, "Inquiry into tech giants' tax strategies nears end," *New York Times*, Jan. 1, 2013.

[38] Charles Duhigg and David Kocieniewski, "How Apple Sidesteps Billions in Taxes."

[39] Stanley Pignal, "Madoff Puts Luxembourg on Defensive," *Financial Times*, Jan. 29, 2009.

[40] Charles Duhigg and David Kocieniewski, "How Apple Sidesteps Billions in Taxes."

[41] Jesse Drucker, "Google 2.4% Rate Shows How $60 Billion Lost to Tax Loopholes," *Bloomberg*, Oct. 21, 2010. This strategy was facilitated by the "check the box" blunder, a $10-billion business loophole mistakenly created by the Clinton Administration that has since survived two efforts by Democratic Party politicians to close, including by the Obama Administration in 2009. A US Treasury Department rule intended to cut business red tape in 1996 inadvertently allowed US multinationals to legally misclassify taxable foreign subsidiaries as branches, opening the door to the rejiggering of profits and expenses between high- and low-tax jurisdictions. See Vanessa Houlder, Megan Murphy, and Jeff Gerth, "Tax Wars: The Accidental Billion-Dollar Break," *Financial Times*, Sept. 27, 2011.

[42] Tom Braithwaite, Helen Thomas, and Jeremy Lemer, "Companies in Appeal for US Tax Amnesty," *Financial Times*, Oct. 18, 2010.

[43] Charles Duhigg and Keith Bradsher, "How US Lost Out on iPhone Work," *New York Times*, Jan. 22, 2012.

[44] "The Netherlands, a Tax Haven for Many Multinationals," Amsterdam, *De Volkskrant*, Nov. 14, 2011. Tax sheltering bedevils other rich democracies such as the United Kingdom. Its 100 largest multinationals listed 8,492 mostly tax-inspired foreign subsidiaries in 2011, according to ActionAid.

[45] Robert Kuttner, *A Presidency in Peril* (White River Junction, VT: Chelsea Green, 2010), 82.

[46] Carol D. Leonnig, "Bailed-Out Firms Have Tax Havens, GAO Finds," *Washington Post*, Jan. 17, 2009.

[47] Stéphane Lauer, "For Amazon, Google or Starbucks, Tax Has No Borders (blog), *Le Monde*, Nov. 13, 2012, http://lauer.blog.lemonde.fr/2012/11/13/pour-amazon-google-ou-starbucks-limpot-na-pas-de-frontieres/.

[48] RTR, "How Starbucks Expects to Poor," *Berliner Zeitung*, Nov. 5, 2012.

[49] Sven Böll, Markus Dettmer, Frank Dohmen, Christoph Pauly, and Christian Reiermann, "Tango with the tax man: Multinationals find loopholes galore in Europe," *Der Spiegel*, Nov. 14, 2012, http://www.spiegel.de/international/business/effort-to-close-multinationaltax-loopholes-gaining-steam-a-866989.html.

[50] "Facebook Has Also Been Raided by the French Tax Authorities," *Le Monde*, Nov. 14, 2012. http://www.lemonde.fr/technologies/article/2012/11/14/facebook-a-aussi-ete-perquisitionne-par-le-fisc-francais_1790455_651865.html.

[51] Ben Butler and Georgia Wilkins, "Bringing Web Transactions Home for Their Just Deserts," *Sydney Morning Herald*, Nov. 17, 2012.

[52] Louise Armitstead, "Bermuda Shelter Helps Google Duck $2 Bn Tax Bill," *Brisbane Times*, Dec. 11, 2012, http://www.brisbanetimes.com.au/business/bermuda-shelter-helps-google-duck-2bn-tax-bill-20121211-2b6su.html.

[53] Ben Butler and Georgia Wilkins, "Bringing Web Transactions Home for Their Just Deserts."

[54] Eric Pfanner, "European Countries Seek More Taxes from US Multinational Companies," *New York Times*, Nov. 19, 2012, http://www.smh.com .au/business/bringing-web-transactions-home-for-their-just-deserts-20121116-29hmu.html. Cecile Crouzel and Marc Cherki, "IRS: Multinationals in the Crosshairs," *Le Figaro*, Nov. 14, 2012, http://www.lefigaro.fr/societes/2012/11/13/20005-20121113ARTFIG00587-fisc-les-multinationales-dans-le-collimateur.php.

CHAPTER 15

[1] Ben Funnell, "Debt Is Capitalism's Dirty Little Secret," *Financial Times*, June 20, 2009.

[2] Ross Douthat, "The Class War We Need," *New York Times*, July 11, 2010.

[3] Special Report, "Inequality in America: The Rich, the Poor, and the Growing Gap Between Them," *Economist*, June 15, 2006.

[4] Michael Cembalest, "Eye on the Market" (report to private banking clients), JP Morgan Chase, July 11, 2011.

[5] Paul Kennedy, *The Rise and Fall of the Great Powers* (New York: Vintage Books/Random House, 1969), 531.

[6] Kevin Phillips, *Wealth and Democracy* (New York: Broadway Books, 2002).

[7] Michael A. Fletcher, "Income Inequality on the Rise in Wealthy Nations, Report Finds," *Washington Post*, Dec. 5, 2011.

[8] "The Rich Are the Big Gainers in America's New Prosperity," *Economist*, June 17, 2006.

[9] "Out of the Bottle," *Economist*, Jan. 26, 2013, 42.

[10] Saul Eslake, "Why Some Incomes Are Just Gross," *Sydney Morning Herald*, Oct. 29, 2011. Martin Wolf, "America's Inequality Need Not Determine the Future of Britain," *Financial Times*, Dec. 22, 2011.

[11] Saul Eslake, "Why Some Incomes Are Just Gross." Martin Wolf, "America's Inequality Need Not Determine the Future of Britain."

[12] James W. Loewen, *Lies My Teacher Told Me* (New York: Simon & Schuster, 2007), 206.

[13] James MacGregor Burns, *Packing the Court* (New York: Penguin Press, 2009), 93, 96.

[14] Ibid.

[15] Joseph Stiglitz, *The Price of Inequality* (New York: Norton, 2012).

[16] Carol Morello, "Middle Class Caught in the Squeeze," *Washington Post*, Sept. 13, 2012.

[17] Harold Meyerson, "Unhappy Labor Day," *Washington Post*, Sept. 7, 2013.

[18] Thomas Piketty and Emmanuel Saez, "The Evolution of Top Incomes: A Historical and International Perspective," Cambridge, MA, NBER working paper no. 11955 (January 2006), http://www.nber.org/papers/w11955. "Employment Outlook, 2007," fig 3.9, OECD, http://dx.doi.org/10.1787/023654854812.

[19] David Leonhardt, "The German Example," *New York Times*, June 8, 2011.

[20] Robert H. Frank, "Gauging the Pain of the Middle Class," *New York Times*, April 2, 2011.

CHAPTER 16

[1] Sheryl Gay Stolberg and Robert Pear, "Bush Speaks in Defense of Markets," *New York Times*, Nov. 14, 2008.

[2] Mrakus Jäntti, Bernt Bratsberg, Knut Roed, Oddbjorn Raaum, Robin Naylor, Eva Osterbacka, Anders Bjorklund, and Tor Eriksson, "American Exceptionalism in a New Light: A Comparison of Intergenerational Earnings Mobility in the Nordic Countries, the United Kingdom, and the United States," Nordic Program on Welfare Research, memorandum no. 34 (2005), Department of Economics, University of Oslo. Also reproduced as discussion paper no. 1938, Bonn, Institute for the Study of Labor. Other studies are surveyed in an OECD analysis by Anna Cristina d'Addio, "Intergenerational Transmission of Disadvantage: Mobility or Immobility Across Generations? A Review of the Evidence for OECD Countries," OECD, Paris. See also Editorial, *New York Times*, "Land of Opportunity," July 13, 2007.

[3] "The Way Up," *Economist*, April 17, 2010, 30.

[4] Joshua Holland, "The American Dream is Alive and Well—in Finland!," AlterNet, Dec. 11, 2007, http://www.alternet.org/story/70103/the_american_dream_is_alive_and_well_..._in_finland! (Interview with Dalton Conley, director of New York University's Center for Advanced Social Science Research.)

[5] Congressman Paul Ryan, as quoted by Fareed Zakaria, "Broken Bootstraps," *Washington Post*, Nov. 10, 2011.

[6] Jess Bailey, Joe Coward, and Matthew Whittaker, "Painful Separation," October 2011, table 5, 19.

[7] Ibid.

[8] Sylvia Nasar, *Grand Pursuit*, 458.

[9] Larry Bartels, *Unequal Democracy*,150.

[10] "Inequality in America: The Rich, the Poor and the Growing Gap Between Them," *Economist*, June 15, 2006.

[11] Niall Ferguson, *Civilization*, 112.

[12] John Lloyd, "The Mobile Society Stalls at the Gates of Academe," *Financial Times*, July 24, 2009.

[13] "A Political Trauma, But a Policy Success," Editorial, *Financial Times*, Dec. 29, 2011.

[14] The Economic Mobility Project, an initiative of the Pew Charitable Trusts, Greenberg Quinlan Rosner Research, February 2009.

[15] A literature survey is presented in Rosemary Hyson, "Differences in Intergenerational Mobility Across the Earnings Distribution," Washington, DC, Bureau of Labor Statistics working paper no. 364 (January 2003). This study contains an excellent survey of the mobility literature, as does the d'Addio study. A thorough listing of resources can be found in Julia B. Isaacs, "International Comparisons of Economic Mobility," The Economic Mobility Project of the Pew Charitable Trusts.

[16] "Movin' On Up," *Wall Street Journal*, Nov. 13, 2007.

[17] Julia B. Isaacs, "Economic Mobility of Families Across Generations." The Economic Mobility Project, the Pew Charitable Trusts, November 2007, http://www.brookings.edu/research/papers/2007/11/generations-isaacs.

[18] Diane Elliott, "Pursuing the American Dream: Economic Mobility Across Generations," Economic Mobility Project, the Pew Charitable Trusts, July 9, 2012. Some conservatives lauded another aspect of this report, arguing it proved that economic mobility had actually improved, not deteriorated, during the Reagan era. In fact, the report simply noted, as have many others, that family incomes across the income spectrum rose in recent decades. That has nothing to do with mobility and everything to do with the widespread entry of spouses into the US workforce. Moreover, even family incomes have dwindled since, peaking in 1999, according to BLS statistics. An example of this misleading narrative is Michael Gerson's "America's Class Problem," *Washington Post*, July 13, 2012.

[19] Julia B. Isaacs, "Economic Mobility of Families Across Generations," November 2007.

[20] Emily Beller, "Bringing Intergenerational Social Mobility Research into the Twenty-first Century: Why Mothers Matter," *American Sociological Review* 74(4), 507–528. Emily Beller, "Moms and Mobility," *Pathways*, Stanford University, Fall 2009. Emily Beller and Michael Hout, "Intergenerational Social Mobility: The United States in Comparative Perspective," *The Future of Children* 16: 19–36 (2006).

[21] Kathleen Bradbury and Jane Katz, "Women's Labor Market Involvement and Family Income Mobility When Marriages End," *New England Economic Review* Q4: 41–74 (2002).

[22] Daniel Aaronson and Bhashkar Mazumder, "Intergenerational Economic Mobility in the United States, 1940 to 2000," *Journal of Human Resources* vol. 43, issue 1 (2008).

[23] Michael Kinsley, "Mobility vs. Nobility," *Washington Post*, June 5, 2005.

[24] Michael Gerson, "Head and Heart: Remembering Jack Kemp," *Washington Post*, May 4, 2009.

[25] As quoted by Erik Eckholm, "Study Says Education Gap Could Further Limit Poor," *New York Times*, Feb. 20, 2008.

[26] Jo Bladen, Paul Greeg, and Stephen Machin, "Intergenerational Mobility in Europe and North America," Centre for Economic Performance, London School of Economics, April 2005.

[27] "OECD Surveys: United States in 2012," Paris, OECD, 67.

[28] Jason DeParle, "Harder for Americans to Rise from Lower Rungs," *New York Times*, June 4, 2012.

[29] Anna-Cristina d'Addio, "Intergenerational Transmission of Disadvantage: Mobility or Immobility Across Generations? A Review of Evidence for OECD Countries," OECD Social, Employment, and Migration working paper no. 52, 2007:7 (2006).

[30] The d'Addio analysis is based on M. Jäntti, (University of Oslo), B. Bratsberg, K. Roed, O. Raaum, R. Naylor, E. Österbacka, A. Björklund, and T. Eriksson (2006), "American Exceptionalism in a New Light: A Comparison of Intergenerational Earnings Mobility in the Nordic Countries, the United Kingdom, and the United States," Institute for the Study of Labor (IZA), discussion paper no. 1938, Bonn. Additional research on France, Germany, and Australia from Miles Corak, "Do Poor Children Become Poor Adults? Lessons from a Cross-Country Comparison of Generational Earnings Mobility," IZA discussion paper no. 1993 (2006), Bonn. Surveys consistently conclude that US mobility is lower than in northern Europe; for example, see the chapter on social mobility in "Economic Policy Reforms: Going for Growth 2010," Paris, OECD, March 2010.

[31] "Inequality in America: The Rich, the Poor, and the Growing Gap Between Them," *Economist*, June 15, 2006.

[32] Isabel V. Sawhill, "Economic Mobility of Families Across Generations," *Getting Ahead or Losing Ground: Economic Mobility in America*, the Pew Charitable Trusts.

[33] Mrakus Jäntti, Bernt Bratsberg, Knut Roed, Oddbjorn Raaum, Robin Naylor, Eva Osterbacka, Anders Bjorklund, and Tor Eriksson: "American Exceptionalism in a New Light: A Comparison of Intergenerational Earnings Mobility in the Nordic Countries, the United Kingdom, and the United States," Nordic Program on Welfare Research, memorandum no. 34/2005, Department of Economics, University of Oslo. Also reproduced as discussion paper no. 1938, Bonn: Institute for the Study of Labor.

[34] There is evidence that the American income distribution violates evolved Darwinian standards about the societal optimum distribution learned through the eons by our ancestors. Eric Aiden Smith at the University of Washington examined five hunter-gatherer populations and determined that their average income inequality was comparable to northern Europe today, while the US is twice as extreme. See Natalie Angier, "Thirst for Fairness May Have Helped Us Survive," *New York Times*, July 5, 2011.

[35] Agence France-Presse, "Nine Out of Ten Threes in Kindergarten," *Handelsblatt*, June 12, 2012.

[36] "Enrollment Rates in Early Childhood and Primary Education, By Age (2005, 2010), Education At A Glance 2012, OECD Indicators," Indicator C2.1, Paris, OECD, September 2012, http://www.oecd.org/edu/eag2012.htm.

[37] DAP News, Agence France-Presse, "Schroeder Argues with Countries About Daycare Expansion," *Handelsblatt*, Oct. 17, 2012, http://www.handelsblatt.com/politik/deutschland/kinderbetreuung-schroeder-streitet-mit-laendern-ueber-kita-ausbau/7264504.html. See also Benita Dill, Katrin Elger, Katharine

Fuhrin, Christoph Hickmann, and Christoph Schwennicke, "Why Won't Germans Have More Babies," *Der Spiegel*, Sept. 12, 2011.

[38] Tarjei Havnes and Magne Mogstad, "No Child Left Behind: Subsidized Child Care and Children's Long-Run Outcomes," *American Economic Journal: Economic Policy* 3(2): 97–129 (2011).

[39] Lyndsey Layton and Susan Svrluga, "Brain Development Studies Fuel Push for Early Education," *Washington Post*, Feb. 14, 2013.

[40] "Comparability of State and Local Expenditures Among Schools Within Districts," Washington, DC, US Department of Education, November 2011. See also Sam Dillon, "Report: Districts Pay Less in Poor Schools," *New York Times*, Dec.1, 2011.

[41] Helen F. Ladd and Edward B. Fiske, "Class Matters: Why Won't We Admit It," *New York Times*, Dec. 12, 2011.

[42] Sabrina Tavernise, "Middle-Class Areas Shrink as Income Gap Grows, New Report Finds," *New York Times*, Nov. 16, 2011. Helen F. Ladd and Edward B. Fiske, "Class Matters: Why Won't We Admit It."

[43] Isabel V. Sawhill,"Economic Mobility of Families Across Generations," http://www.brookings.edu/~/media/research/files/reports/2008/2/economic%20mobility%20sawhill/02_economic_mobility_sawhill_overview.pdf.

[44] Ron Haskins, Harry Holzer, and Robert Lerman, "Promoting Economic Mobility by Increasing Postsecondary Education," the Economic Mobility Project, the Pew Charitable Trusts, May 2009, Washington, DC, fig. 2.

[45] Tamar Lewin, "Once in first place, Americans now lag in attaining college degrees," *New York Times*, Aug. 23, 2010.

[46] Haskins, Holzer, and Lerman, "Promoting Economic Mobility," fig. 5.

[47] Anthony P. Carnevale and Jeff Strohl, "How Increasing College Access Is Increasing Inequality, and What to Do About It," *The Century Foundation*, July 16, 2010.

[48] "The Way Up," *Economist*, April 17, 2010, 30.

[49] "Education At A Glance 2012: OECD Indicators," Paris, OECD, September 2012, http://www.oecd.org/edu/eag2012.htm. Daniel de Vise, "US Falls in Global Ranking of Young Adults Who Finish College," *Washington Post*, Sept. 13, 2011. Tamar Lewin, "Once in First Place, Americans Now Lag in Attaining College Degrees," *New York Times*, July 23, 2010.

[50] David Broder, "Rescuing a College Education," *Washington Post*, Dec. 7, 2008.

[51] David Brooks, "Middle Class Capitalists," *New York Times*, Jan. 11, 2008.

[52] E. J. Dionne, Jr.,"Our Silent Education Emergency," *Washington Post*, July 16, 2009.

[53] "Global Wage Report 2010/11," Geneva, ILO, Dec. 15, 2010, fig. 21 and 36.

[54] Cynthia Cohen, Arline Geronimus, and Maureen Phipps, "Getting a piece of the pie: The economic boom of the 1990s and declining teen birth rates in the United States," *Social Science and Medicine* vol. 63, issue 6, 2006, http://econpapers.repec.org/article/eeesocmed/v_3a63_3ay_3a2006_3ai_3a6_3ap_3a1531-1545.htm.

[55] Timothy M. Smeeding, "Poorer by Comparison," *Pathways*, Stanford University Center for the Study of Poverty and Inequality, Winter 2008.

[56] As quoted by Erik Eckholm, "To Avoid Student Turnover, Parents Can Get Help with Rent," *New York Times*, June 24, 2008.

[57] Ibid.

[58] Ezra Klein, "The Republicans' Free-Lunch Problem," *Washington Post*, April 10, 2012.

[59] As quoted by Joerg Blech, "How Hereditary Can Intelligence Be? Studies Show Nurture at Least as Important as Nature," *Der Spiegel*, Sept. 6, 2010, and E. Turkheimer, A. Haley, B. D'Onofrio, M. Waldron and I.I. Gottesman, "Socioeconomic status modifies heritability of IQ in young children," *Psychological Science* vol. 14, no. 6, 2003, pp. 623–628.

[60] Ibid.

CHAPTER 17

[1] Sabine Blaschke, Bernard Kittel, and Franz Traxler, *National Labour Relations in International Markets* (Oxford: Oxford University Press, 2001), 178.

[2] Ross Gittins, "We Could Get Richer by Beating Ourselves Up," *Sydney Morning Herald*, July 11, 2011.

[3] David Brooks, "The Spirit of Enterprise," *New York Times*, Dec. 2, 2011.

[4] Ruth Reichstein, "The End of a Success Story," *Handelsblatt*, Dec. 19, 2010.

[5] Blaschke, Kittel, and Traxler, *National Labour Relations in International Markets*, 178.

[6] Lane Kenworthy, "Wage Setting Coordination Scores," June 17, 2001, http://www.u.arizona.edu/~lkenwor/WageCoorScores.pdf.

[7] Marriner Eccles, as quoted by Jean-Pierre Robin, "The American Middle Class Mortgage Crisis Ends," *Le Figaro*, Feb. 7, 2011. For a review of Eccles' role in the New Deal, see Robert Reich, *Aftershock* (New York: Alfred A. Knopf, 2010).

[8] Sylvia Nasar, *Grand Pursuit*, 423.

[9] Jeffrey Pfeffer and Alison Konrad, "Do You Get What You Deserve? Factors Affecting the Relationship Between Productivity and Pay," *Administrative Science Quarterly* vol. 35: 258–285 (June 1990). Jeffrey Pfeffer and Alison Davis-Blake, "Determinants of Salary Dispersion in Organizations," *Industrial Relations*, 29: 38–58 (Winter 1990).

[10] Robert H. Frank, *The Darwin Economy* (Princeton, NJ: Princeton University Press, 2011), 135. Robert H. Frank, "Are Workers Paid Their Marginal Product?," *American Economic Review* vol. 74, no. 4 (September 1984).

[11] Stefan Sauer, "Curly, Cheated and Ripped Off," *Berliner Zeitung*, Oct. 23, 2012, http://www.berliner-zeitung.de/arbeit---soziales/arbeiter-betrogen-gelockt--geprellt-und-abgezockt,10808232,20686416.html.

[12] Ulrich Krökel, "Even a Small Rush," *Berliner Zeitung*, Sept. 9, 2011.

[13] Australian Bureau of Statistics, "Income Distribution: Trends in Earnings Distribution," *Australian Social Trends*, December 2012, http://www.abs.gov.au/AUSSTATS/abs@.nsf/2f762f95845417aeca25706c00834efa/962f9aed98c33606ca2570ec000e4b0a!OpenDocument.

[14] Ruth Reichstein, "The End of a Success Story," *Handelsblatt*, Oct. 19, 2010.

[15] Åge Johnsen and Jarmo Vakkuri, "Exploring Performance Management in the Public Sector: Political and Cultural Explanations Revisited," 32d Annual Conference of the European Group of Public Administration, Sept. 8, 2010, Toulouse.

[16] Julian Isherwood, "Unions Question 'Danish Model,'" *Der Spiegel*, Aug. 11, 2010.

[17] Eva Roth, "Growth in the Crisis Year," *Berliner Zeitung*, March 29, 2010. Stefan

Sauer, "Collective Bargaining Coverage in Germany: Wages No Lower Limit," *Berliner Zeitung*, Oct. 15, 2012, http://www.berliner-zeitung.de/wirtschaft/tarifbindung-in-deutschland-loehne-ohne-untergrenze,10808230,20706404.html.

[18] Jack Ewing, "VW Workers Agree to Pact Bolstering Share of Profit," *New York Times*, Feb. 8, 2011.

[19] "Germany's Collective Agreement System Is Changing," *Statistisches Bundesamt Deutschland*, 2009 Berlin.

[20] For a summary of the wage determination systems in the major European nations, see Carlos Yakubovich, "Collective Wage Bargaining and the Adoption of the Single Currency: A Comparison of Germany, Spain, France and Italy," *Données Sociales: La Société Française,* 2002–2003 edition, INSEE, Paris.

[21] Firms or branches in distress can claim exceptions in negotiations. Like print journalists everywhere, for example, German newspaper employees face job insecurity. In August 2011, editors there accepted guarantees of job preservation in exchange in some instances for reductions in holiday and Christmas bonuses and a real wage cut. See Eva Roth, "Wage Dispute Ended in Newspapers," *Berliner Zeitung*, Aug. 19, 2011.

[22] Reuters, "Wage Increases Linked to Productivity," *Le Figaro*, March 4, 2011.

[23] Sabine Bessière and Stéphanie Depil, "Les Salaires Dans Les Entreprises en 2006: Une Hausse Modérée," Département de l'Emploi et Des Revenus D'Activité, INSEE, January 2008, http://www.insee.fr/fr/themes/document.asp?ref_id=ip1174®_id=0; Productivity data from OECD.

[24] Matt Steinglass, "Dutch Unions Reorganize Amid Pensions Row," *Financial Times*, Dec. 5, 2011. Thomas Amosse and Maria-Teresa Pignoni, "The Changing Trade-Union Scene Since 1945," May 2006 (*Donnees Socials La Societe Francaise*).

[25] Another example is the "Irish Programme for National Recovery in 1988." See Barry Eichengreen, *The European Economy Since 1945*, 388, 390.

[26] Keith Whitfield, "The Australian Wage System and Its Labor Market Effects," *Industrial Relations* vol. 27, no. 2 (March 1988).

CHAPTER 18

[1] "Rich-Poor Divide Widens in Advanced Economies," Editorial, *Financial Times*, Dec. 5, 2011, drawing on Michael Förster, "Divided We Stand: Why Inequality Keeps Rising," OECD, December 2011.

[2] Sven Böll and Michael Sauga, "Kenneth Rogoff: Germany Has Been the Winner in the Globalization Process," *Der Spiegel*, Feb. 20, 2012.

[3] Anne Rodier, "For Employees, the Company Is Accountable to Society," *Le Monde*, June 28, 2011 (source: FIFG survey for the recruiting firm Michael Page, May 16–24, 2011; Correspondents are from larger French firms), http://ya20.com/2011/06/27/for-employees-the-company-is-accountable -to-society-2/.

[4] Chris Giles, "Globalization Backlash in Rich Nations," *Financial Times*, July 22, 2007.

[5] Stephan Kaufmann, "German Corporations Are the Winners of Globalization," *Berliner Zeitung*, April 30, 2011.

[6] Job losses abroad continue. The Dutch ship engine and propeller builder Wärtsilä, for example, lost 570 of its 1,500 employees in January 2010 to China. "Dutch Shipbuilders Lose Jobs to China," *Radio Netherlands Worldwide*, Amsterdam, Jan. 19, 2010.

[7] Florence Jaumotte and Irina Tytell, "The Globalization of Labor, 2007 World Economic Outlook," *International Monetary Fund*, chap. 5.

[8] Wolfgang F. Stolper and Paul A Samuelson, "Protection and Real Wages," *Review of Economic Studies* 9:58–73 (1941).

[9] Jaumotte and Tytell, "The Globalization of Labor."

[10] *Economic Surveys: United States 2012*, fig. 18, OECD, Paris, 2012. *Education at a Glance*, OECD, Paris, 2011.

[11] "48th Is Not a Good Place," Editorial, *New York Times* Oct. 12, 2010.

[12] Ibid.

[13] From Michael Förster, "Divided We Stand: Why Inequality Keeps Rising," OECD, December 2011.

[14] "Rich-Poor Divide Widens in Advanced Economies," Editorial, *Financial Times*, Dec. 5, 2011, www.ft.com/cms/s/0/8d936858-1e8b-11e1-bae4-00144feabdc0.html.

CHAPTER 19

[1] Chris Evans, "Fair Work: The Big Picture," Ninth Annual Workforce Conference, Melbourne, Nov. 22, 2010.

[2] David Neumark and William L. Wascher, *Minimum Wages* (Cambridge, MA: MIT Press, 2008), 193.

[3] "Insecure Work a Scourge on Nation's Productivity: Howe," *Workplace Insights*, Thomson Reuters, May 23, 2012.

[4] See for example, Greg Thompson, Tim Murray, and Patrick Jomini (Australian Productivity Commission), chap. 5, "Trade, Employment and Structural Change: The Australian Experience, Policy Priorities for International Trade and Jobs," OECD, September 2012, 126, http://www.oecd.org/site/tadicite/policyprioritiesforinternationaltradeandjobs.htm.

[5] David R. Cameron, "The Expansion of the Public Economy: A Comparative Analysis," *American Political Science Review* vol. 72, no. 4, 1243–1261 (December 1978), http://www.jstor.org/discover/10.2307/1954537?uid=3739936&uid=2&uid=4&uid=3739256&sid=21100916185691.

[6] Anna Maria Mayda, Kevin H. O'Rourke, and Richard Sinnott, "Risk, Government and Globalization: International Survey Evidence," NBER working paper 13037, April 2007, http://www.princeton.edu/~pcglobal/conferences/globdem/papers/w13037.pdf.

[7] Dani Rodrik, *The Globalization Paradox* (New York: Norton, 2011), 16–17.

[8] Dani Rodrik, Ibid.

[9] Sylvia Nasar, *Grand Pursuit*, 9–10.

[10] Sam Dillon, "Many Nations Passing US in Education, Expert Says," *New York Times*, May 10, 2010.

[11] Clive Cook, "America's Classroom Equality Battle," *Financial Times,* May 19, 2009.

[12] Annie Lowrey, "Big Study Links Good Teachers to Lasting Gains," *New York Times*, Jan. 6, 2012.

[13] "Ratios of Students to Teaching Staff in Educational Institutions, 2005," "Education at a Glance," OECD, table D2.2.

[14] Lucile Quillet, "France Is Reducing Its Spending Per Student," *Le Figaro*, Nov. 2, 2012, http://etudiant.lefigaro.fr/les-news/actu/detail/article/la-france-reduit-ses-depenses-par-etudiant-344/.

[15]"In 25 Years, France Has Created More Than 3 Million Jobs: In What Areas, at What Levels?," *Le Monde,* Sept. 14, 2011.

[16]"Safety Net or Windfall? Examining Changes to Income-Based Repayment for Federal Student Loans," Federal Education Budget Project, New American Foundation, October 2012.

[17]Julian Isherwood, "Re-training Causes Jobless to Rise," *Politiken*, Copenhagen, August 26, 2010.

[18]Barbara Gill and Kalus Stratmann, "Companies give poor students a chance," *Handelsblatt,* Oct. 21, 2010 and DPA, "Apprenticeships are still 100,000 Unfilled," *Handelsblatt,* August 8, 2012.

[19]Navy Rabreau, "Have a Billion Euros More for Employment," *Le Figaro*, Feb. 2, 2011.

[20]"Trends in the Percentage of Young Males in Education and Not in Education (1995–2005)," table C4.4b, Paris, OECD.

[21]Gerrit Wiesmann, "Germany Sets Gold Standard for Training," *Financial Times,* July 9, 2012.

[22]"Employment Outlook 2007," Paris, OECD, box 2.1.

[23]Andrea Bassanini and Wooseok Ok, "How Do Firms' and Individuals' Incentives to Invest in Human Capital Vary Across Groups," Paris, OECD, 2004.

[24]Barry Eichengreen, *The European Economy Since 1945*, 260.

[25]Karl Fluch, "The Street Bankers," *Der Standard*, Vienna, Aug. 1, 2011.

[26]Florence Jaumotte and Irina Tytell, "The Globalization of Labor, 2007 World Economic Outlook," table 5.11, IMF.

[27]Howard F. Rosen, "Reforming Unemployment Insurance for the 21st Century Workforce," Peterson Institute for International Economics (Testimony before the Income Security and Family Support Subcommittee, House Ways and Means Committee, March 15, 2007), http://www.piie.com/publications/testimony/testimony.cfm?ResearchID=727.

[28]Casey B. Mulligan, "Unemployment Compensation Over Time," Economix, *New York Times*, Dec. 21, 2011. National Employment Law Project, "Recovery Act's Unemployment Insurance Modernization Incentives Produce Bipartisan State Reforms in Eight States in 2010," Sept. 3, 2010.

[29]Casey Mulligan, "In Europe, a Longer Perspective on Unemployment Benefits," Economix, *New York Times,* Jan. 11, 2012.

[30]"Employment Outlook 2007," Statistical Annex, table J, Paris, OECD.

[31]Ibid., 76

[32]Michael Luo, "Job Retraining May Fall Short of High Hopes," *New York Times*, July 6, 2009.

[33]Ibid.

[34]Stefan Sauer, "Many Students, Some Apprentices," *Berliner Zeitung*, Aug. 30, 2012.

[35]Adam Cohen, "After 75 Years, the Working Poor Still Struggle for a Fair Wage," *New York Times,* June 17, 2008.

[36]"Working Poor, from the Editor's Desk," Washington, DC, Bureau of Labor Statistics, US Department of Labor, April 4, 2012.

[37]Peter Martin, "Surge in Wage Increase," *Sydney Morning Herald*, Nov. 18, 2010. Ben Schneiders, "$19 a Week Minimum Wage Rise," *Sydney Morning Herald*, June 3, 2011.

[38] Marie Bartnik, "The Minimum Wage Increased by 0.3% to 1430 Euros Gross Per Month," *Le Figaro*, Dec. 17, 2012, http://www.lefigaro.fr/social/2012/12/16/09010-20121216ARTFIG00071-la-hausse-du-smic-au-1er-janvier-limitee-a-l-inflation.php.

[39] Judy Dempsey "Germany's Economic Miracle Eludes the Country's Lowest-Paid Workers," *New York Times*, Aug. 19, 2011. RTR and AFP, "Low Pay Is Normal," *Berliner Zeitung*, Sept. 10, 2012.

[40] "The High Cost of Germany's Economic Success," *Der Spiegel*, May 4, 2012, http://www.spiegel.de/international/business/0,1518, druck-830972,00.html.

[41] "Profits at the Expense of the Taxpayers,'" *Berliner Zeitung*, Jan. 30, 2010.

[42] Ezekiel Emanuel and Victor R. Fuchs, "Solved," *Washington Monthly*, June 2005.

[43] Andrea Bassanini and Wooseok Ok, "How do Firms' and Individuals' Incentives To Invest In Human Capital Vary Across Groups," Paris, OECD, December 2004. See also "Wage and Benefits," OECD, Directorate for Employment, Labour and Social Affairs, ELSA/WD?SEM (2007)9, table 5.2.

[44] Andrea Bassanini and Danielle Venn, "Assessing the Impact of Labour Market Policies on Productivity: A Difference-in-Difference Approach," "OECD Employment Outlook 2007," Paris, OECD, fig. 2.5.

[45] "The Hourly Minimum Wage Increase to 9 Euros Gross in 2011," *Le Monde*, Nov. 17, 2010. AAP, "Low Wage Workers Win Wage Rise," *Business Spectator*, June 3, 2010.

[46] "Characteristics of Minimum Wage Workers: 2007," Washington, DC, Bureau of Labor Statistics, US Department of Labor, 2007, table 10.

[47] Steven Greenhouse, "Raising the Floor on Pay," *New York Times*, April 10, 2012.

[48] Ibid.

[49] David Card and Alan B. Krueger, "A Living Wage: The Effects of the Minimum Wage on the Distribution of Wages, the Distribution of Family Incomes and Poverty," working paper no. 333, Industrial Relations Section, Princeton University (October 1994), http://davidcard.berkeley.edu/papers/minwage%20fam.pdf.

[50] David S. Lee, "Wage Inequality in the United States During the 1980s: Rising Dispersion or Falling Minimum Wage?," *Quarterly Journal of Economics* vol. 114: 977–1023, 1999.

[51] Larry M. Bartels, *Unequal Democracy*, 247. For a discussion of the Earned Income Tax Credit (EITC), see V. Joseph Hotz and John Karl Scholz, "Not Perfect, But Still Pretty Good: The EITC and Other Policies to Support the US Low-Wage Labour Market," Economic Studies, OECD, 2000, and the survey by Gordon Berlin, "Transforming the EITC to Reduce Poverty and Inequality," *Pathways*, Stanford University (Winter 2009).

[52] Chris Hanger, "Inside the Journals," The Churchill Centre, Washington, DC.

[53] Adam Smith, *The Wealth of Nations*, 94.

[54] Paul Gregg, "The Use of Wage Floors as Policy Tools," *OECD Economic Studies* no. 31 (2000), Paris, OECD.

[55] "U.K. Low Pay Commission," 2008, vi-vii, and "Global Wage Report 2010/11," Geneva, ILO, Dec. 15, 2010, 68.

[56] Peter Dolton, Rosazza-Bondibene Chiara, and Jonathan Wadsworth "Employment, Inequality, and the UK National Minimum Wage Over the Medium Term,"*Oxford Bulletin of Economics and Statistics*, August 2011.

[57] Eva Roth, "Everyone Benefits From the Minimum Wage," *Berliner Zeitung*, Oct. 27, 2011.

[58] Arindrajit Dube, T. William Lester, and Michael Reich, "Minimum Wage Effects Across State Borders: Estimates Using Contiguous Counties," *The Review of Economics and Statistics* 92(4): 945–964 (November 2010). Nancy Folbre, "Along the Minimum Wage Battlefront," Economix, *New York Times*, Nov. 1, 2010.

[59] John Schmitt & David Rosnick, "The Wage and Employment Impact of Minimum-Wage Laws in Three Cities, CEPR Reports and Issue Briefs 2011-07," Center for Economic and Policy Research (CEPR). See also, "A Minimum Wage Increase," Editorial, *New York Times,* March 27, 2011.

[60] The latest update is from David Card and Alan B. Krueger, "Minimum Wages and Employment: A Case Study of the Fast-Food Industry in New Jersey and Pennsylvania: Reply," *The American Economic Review*, December 2000, http://www.krueger.princeton.edu/90051397.pdf. A host of other analyses are available, including: David H. Autor, Alan Manning, and Christopher L. Smith, "The Minimum Wage's Role in the Evolution of US Wage Inequality over Three Decades: A Modest Reassessment," MIT working paper October 2009 (revised from October 2008); David H. Autor, Lawrence F. Katz, and Melissa S. Kearney, "Trends in US Wage Inequality: Revising the Revisionists," *Review of Economics and Statistics* (May 2008); and David Card and Alan B. Krueger, *Myth and Measurement: The New Economics of the Minimum Wage* (Princeton, NJ: Princeton University Press, 1995).

[61] Larry Bartels, *Unequal Democracy*, 249.

[62] George J. Stigler, "The Economics of Minimum Wage Legislation," *American Economic Review* 36 (1946), 358–65.

[63] Paul Gregg, "The Use of Wage Floors as Policy Tools," *OECD Economic Studies* no. 31(2000), Paris, OECD, 136.

[64] Charles Lane, "Better Than the Minimum Wage," *Washington Post,* Feb. 20, 2013.

[65] David Neumark and William L. Wascher, *Minimum Wages,* 251.

[66] "John Martin and Herwig Immervoll, "The Minimum Wage: Making It Pay," *OECD Observer*, May 2007, 3. See also OECD, "Special Feature: The Tax Treatment of Minimum Wages, Taxing Wages 2005/2006," 26 and Table S.3, http://www.oecd.org/about/39005490.pdf.

[67] Bruno Crepon and Rozenn Desplatz, "A New Evaluation of the Effects of Reduced Social Security Charges on Low Wages," *Economie et statistique* no. 348, Insee, May 2002.

[68] David Neumark and William L. Wascher, *Minimum Wages,* 97.

[69] Ibid., 248, 252.

CHAPTER 20

[1] "Manufacturing: A Better Future for America," ed. Richard McCormack, Alliance for American Manufacturing, 2009.

[2] Robert Reich, *Aftershock*, 56.

[3] Steven Pearlstein, "The Bleak Truth About Unemployment," *Washington Post*, Sept. 8, 2010.

[4] Tyler Cowen, "The Sad Statistic That Trumps the Others," *New York Times*, Aug. 21, 2011.

[5] Jeffrey Immelt, "Renewing American Leadership," General Electric, Dec. 9, 2009.

[6] Max Hastings "The West's Crisis of Honest Leaders," *Financial Times,* Aug. 15, 2011.

[7] "Public Says American Work Life Is Worsening, But Most Workers Remain Satisfied with Their Jobs," Social Trends Project, Pew Research Center, September 2006.

[8] "The Story so Far," *Economist*, Jan. 19, 2013, 5.

[9] Justin R. Pierce and Peter K. Schott, "The surprisingly swift decline of US manufacturing employment," NBER working paper w18655, http://papers.ssrn.com/sol3/papers.cfm?abstract_id=2194778##. See also Binyamin Appelbaum, "The benefits of uncertainty," Economix, *New York Times*, Jan. 7, 2012.

[10] Robert E. Scott, "The High Price of 'Free' Trade," Economic Policy Institute, briefing paper, Nov. 17, 2003.

[11] Alan Blinder, "Offshoring: The Next Industrial Revolution," *Foreign Affairs* vol. 85, no. 2, (March–April 2006), 113–128.

[12] Michael A. Fletcher and Jia Lynn Yang, "A Push to Bring Foreign Profits Home," *Washington Post*, Sept. 25, 2010.

[13] Bernie Woodall, Ben Klalyman, and Jan Schwartz," UAW Takes Aim at Foreign Automakers," Reuters, as reported on AutosonMSNBC.com, Dec. 29, 2011.

[14] Gabor Steingart, "America's Middle Class Has Become Globalization's Loser," *Der Spiegel*, Oct. 24, 2006.

[15] Kate Bronfenbrenner and Stephanie Luce, "The Changing Nature of Corporate Global Restructuring: The Impact of Production Shifts on Jobs in the U.S., China and Around the World," U.S.–China Economic and Security Review Commission, Oct. 14, 2004.

[16] A recent study found little net employment impact of American outsourcing. I. Gianmarco, P. Ottaviano, Giovanni Peri, and Greg C. Wright, "Immigration, Offshoring, and American Jobs," London School of Economics and Political Science, Center for Economic Performance, CEP discussion paper 1147, May 2012, http://cep.lse.ac.uk/pubs/download/dp1147.pdf.

[17] David Wessel, "Big US Firms Shift Hiring Abroad," *Wall Street Journal*, April 29, 2011.

[18] As reported by Catherine Rampell, "Is a Multinational CEO the Best Jobs Czar?," *New York Times*, Jan. 27, 2011. Another study by Sullivan referencing statistics presented by Ray Mataloni in the November 2007 BLS *Survey of Current Business* drew on somewhat different data, concluding that US multinationals reduced their domestic jobs by 1.238 million between 1999 and 2005, while concurrently adding 1.113 million new jobs abroad. Martin Sullivan, "Offshore Jobs and Taxes: Will Democrats Attack?," *Tax Analysts*, 2008. A Business Roundtable study concluded that US multinationals cut 2.2 million American jobs between 2000 and 2006, while adding 1.3 million at their foreign affiliates: Matthew J. Slaughter, "How US Multinational Companies Strengthen the US Economy," Business Roundtable and the United States Council Foundation, Spring 2009.

[19] Kate Bronfenbrenner and Stephanie Luce, "Offshoring: The Evolving Profile of Corporate Global Restructuring," Third World Traveler, *Multinational Monitor*, December 2004, http://www.thirdworldtraveler.com/Corporate_Welfare/Offshoring.html.

[20] "Study Says Share of Service Firms with Offshoring Plans Grows to 53 percent," *Daily Labor Report* 153 A-12 (August 2009). See also Daniel Marschall and Laura Clawson, "Outsourced: Sending Jobs Overseas: The Cost to America's Economy and Working Families," Working America and AFL-CIO, Washington, DC, http://staging.workingamerica.org/upload/OutsourcingReport.pdf.

[21] Kathrin Hille, "Foxconn to Shift Some of Apple Assembly," *Financial Times,* June 28, 2010.

[22] David Segal, "Apple's Retail Army, Long on Loyalty but Short on Pay," *New York Times,* June 24, 2012.

[23] Barney Jopson and Tim Bradshaw, "Apple Stores Most Productive US Shops," *Financial Times*, Nov. 12, 2012.

[24] "Social Tension Mounts in French Apple Stores," *Le Figaro*, Sept. 18, 2012, http://www.lefigaro.fr/societes/2012/09/18/20005-20120918ARTFIG00416-la-tension-sociale-monte-dans-les-apple-store-francais.php.

[25] Julian Mertens, "Apple Store Selects Workers," *Berliner Zeitung*, Nov. 11, 2012, http://www.berliner-zeitung.de/politik/apple-store-frankfurt-apple-store-waehlt-betriebsrat,10808018,20844026.html.

[26] Charles Duhigg and Keith Bradsher, "How US Lost Out on iPhone Work," *New York Times,* Jan. 22, 2012. (Apple sells about 40 percent of its products in the United States. At $65 per unit, American-sourcing 40 percent of its 159 million iPhones, iPads, MacBooks, and other items produced in 2011 would have added about $2 billion in costs to Apple [assuming Apple and purchasers split the cost]. The company's income before taxes that year was $34.2 billion.)

[27] Elsa Bembaron, "The iPhone Has Reported $50 Billion to Apple" *Le Figaro*, Aug. 10, 2012, http://bourse.lefigaro.fr/indices-actions/actu-conseils/l-iphone-a-rapporte-50-milliards-de-dollars-a-apple-260813.

[28] Apple's unit sales are proprietary, but US sales were revealed in its patent and design dispute with Samsung in August 2012 to total less than 70 million iPhones, iPads, and iPod touch units in 2012. Producing them in the United States would have added perhaps $2.5 billion to costs, assuming consumers pay about one-half the higher costs. See the following: "Apple's Tax Under the Microscope,"*Sydney Morning Herald*, Nov. 5, 2012, http://www.smh.com.au/business/world-business/apples-tax-under-the-microscope-20121105-28sse.html; Eric Slivka, "Apple and Samsung Reveal US Mobile Device Sales in Court Case," MacRumors, Aug. 10, 2012, http://www.macrumors.com/2012/08/10/apple-and-samsung-reveal-u-s-mobile-device-sales-in-court-case/; Chris Velazco, "Apple's Fiscal Q4 2012 Results: $36 Billion In Revenue, Net Profit Of $8.2 Billion, Earnings Of $8.67 Per Share," *Tech Crunch*, Oct. 25, 2012, http://techcrunch.com/2012/10/25/apple-q4-2012-earnings/; and Charles Duhigg and Keith Bradsher, "How US Lost Out on iPhone Work," *New York Times,* Jan. 22, 2012.

[29] Charles Duhigg and Keith Bradsher, "How US Lost Out on iPhone Work."

[30] David Brooks, "The Missing Fifth," *New York Times*, May 10, 2011.

[31] See Michael Mandel, "Innovation Failure," *Innovation*, Oct. 5, 2010. Mark Thoma, "Michael Mandel: Phantom GDP?," Economist's View, *Businessweek*, June 8, 2007.

[32] Keith Bradsher, "Hybrid in a Trade Squeeze," *New York Times*, Sept. 6, 2011.

[33] Nancy Folbre, "Super Sad True Jobs Story," Economix, *New York Times*, May 2, 2011.

[34] Ibid.

[35] Roger Lowenstein, "The New Joblessness," *New York Times Magazine*, July 26, 2009.

[36] Robert Shapiro, "The New Normal in Job Creation," *Washington Post*, Feb. 15, 2013.

CHAPTER 21

[1] Chris Evans, "Fair Work: The Big Picture," Ninth Annual Workforce Conference, Melbourne, Nov. 22, 2010.

[2] Robert J. Gitter and Markus Scheuer, "U.S. and German youths: unemployment and the transition from school to work," *Monthly Labor Review*, BLS, March 1997.

[3] Harold Meyerson, "Building a Better Capitalism," *Washington Post*, March 12, 2009.

[4] David Brooks, "The Party of Work," *New York Times*, Nov. 9, 2012.

[5] Sheryl Gay Stolberg, "A Growing Trend: Young, Liberal and Open to Big Government," *New York Times*, Feb. 11, 2013.

[6] Frédéric Lemaître, "Why Angela Merkel Has Blocked the Project EADS-BAE," *Le Monde*, Oct. 10, 2012, http://www.lemonde.fr/economie/article /2012/10/10 /pourquoi-angela-merkel-a-bloque-le-projet-eads-bae_1773074_3234.html.

[7] Marc Landré, "Xavier Bertrand Warns PSA on Employment," *Le Figaro*, Feb. 23, 2012.

[8] Peter Marsh, "Mittal Ugcs 'Buy European' Programme," *Financial Times*, May 10, 2012.

[9] Cyrille Pluyette, "The Ten Best-Selling Cars in France in 2012," *Le Figaro*, Jan. 5, 2013, http://lefigaro.fr/conjoncture/2013/01/05/20002-20130105DIMFIG 00288-les-dix-voitures-les-plus-vendues-en-france-en-2012.php.

[10] Isabelle de Foucaud, "How to Find the French Equivalent of a Foreign Product," *Le Figaro*, April 2, 2012.

[11] "Christmas Pay More for Made in France," *Le Figaro*, Oct. 25, 2012, http://www.lefigaro.fr/flash-eco/2012/10/25/97002-20121025FILWWW00415 -noel-payer-plus-pour-du-made-in-france.php.

[12] AFP, "90 % des Français Pour un Label France," *Le Figaro*, April 10, 2012.

[13] Charlotte Haunhorst, "Food From Nowhere: Producers Reject Calls For Stricter Labels," *Der Spiegel*, Oct. 17, 2012, http://www.spiegel.de/international/business/consumer-watchdogs-call-for-more-detail-on-processed-food-labels-a-861411.html#ref=rss.

[14] See Paul Krugman, "Winners and Losers from Trade," Economist's View, *New York Times*, May 14, 2007. (Krugman was awarded a Nobel Prize for his analysis of international trade issues.)

[15] Dani Rodrik, *The Globalization Paradox*, 56–57.

[16] Ibid., xix.

[17] Stephen Castle, "Europe Plan Spells Out Retaliation Over Bids," *New York Times*, March 22, 2012.

[18] Lionel Barber, Bertrand Benoit, and Hugh Williamson, "March to the Middle: Merkel Celebrates Germany's Social Market Model," *Financial Times,* June 10, 2008.

[19] Alan Blinder, "Offshoring: The Next Industrial Revolution," *Foreign Affairs* vol. 85, no. 2 (March-April 2006), 113–128. See also Robert Kuttner, "The Trade Debate We Need," *American Prospect*, May 27, 2008. Dani Rodrik, *The Globalization Paradox*, 86–87.

[20] Paul Krugman, "Divided Over Trade," *New York Times*, May 14, 2007 and "Winners and Losers From Trade," Economists View, *New York Times,* May 14, 2007.

[21] Lawrence Summers, "America Needs to Make a New Case for Trade" *Financial Times*, April 27, 2008, and "A Strategy to Promote Healthy Globalisation," *Financial Times*, May 4, 2008.

[22] As quoted by Peter Whoriskey, "A Bargain for BMW Means Jobs for 1,000 in South Carolina," *Washington Post*, Oct. 27, 2010.

[23] "Staying Put," *Economist*, Jan. 19, 2013, special report, 8.

[24] See Thomas I. Palley, "Trade, Employment, and Outsourcing: Some Observations on US-China Economic Relations," eds. Paul Auer, Genevieve Besse, and Dominique Meda, "Offshoring and the Internationalization of Employment," ILO Symposium, Annecy, 2005, 215.

[25] Mary Bartnik, "Offshoring Destroys 36,000 jobs Per Year," *Le Figaro*, May 28, 2010.

[26] "Business: A Lack of Enterprise," *Economist,* Nov. 17, 2101.

[27] As reported by Cecile Crouzel, "Internationalized Firms Create Jobs in France," *Le Figaro,* March 5, 2010.

[28] Stephan Kaufmann, "German Corporations Are the Winners of Globalization," *Berliner Zeitung*," April 30, 2011.

[29] Martin Falk and Bertrand M. Koebel "Outsourcing, Imports, and Labour Demand," *Scandinavian Journal of Economics* 104:4 (2002).

[30] Dalia Marin, "A Nation of Poets and Thinkers—Less So with Eastern Enlargement? Austria and Germany," Center for Economic Policy Research discussion paper 4358, 2004, London.

[31] As quoted by Cecile Corbiere, "Germany Less Inclined by Offshoring," *Le Figaro*, Feb. 29, 2008.

CHAPTER 22

[1] Scott Adams, "Dilbert" (Dogbert the CEO), *Washington Post*, July 28, 2009.

[2] Gary Pisano and Willy Shine, "Restoring American Competitiveness," *Harvard Business Review*, July 2009.

[3] Jeff Immelt, "Innovation Can Give America Back Its Greatness," *Financial Times,* July 8, 2009.

[4] Lawrence Mitchell, "Protect Industry from Predatory Speculators," *Financial Times,* July 8, 2009.

[5] As quoted by Ralph Atkins and Matt Steinglass, "Employment: A Fix That Functions," *Financial Times,* Aug. 3, 2011.

[6] Ibid.

[7] Phillippe Jacque, "Toyota Will Produce in France for the US Market," *Le Monde*, June 25, 2012.

[8] Peter G. Peterson, "The Morning After," *Atlantic Monthly*, October 1987.

[9] Barry Eichengreen, *The European Economy since 1945*, 423.

[10] Ibid.

[11] Paul Kennedy, *The Rise and Fall of the Great Powers,* 475.

[12] Peter G. Peterson, "The Morning After."

[13] Michael Mandel and Susan Houseman, "Not All Productivity Gains Are the Same—Here's Why," *What Matters*, McKinsey & Company, June 1, 2011. See also Michael Mandel, "Innovation Failure," *Innovation*, Oct. 5, 2010 and Mark Thoma, "Michael Mandel: Phantom GDP?"

[14] Ross Douthat, "The Pessimism Bubble," *New York Times*, July 5, 2010.

[15] "More Jobs But Less Productive? The Impact of Labour Market Policies on Productivity," Working paper on employment, Paris, OECD, March 2007, 29–30 [delsa/elsa/wp5(2007)2].

[16] Francis Wheen, "Mrs T and Sympathy," *Financial Times*, Nov. 5, 2010.

[17] Max Hastings, "The End of Britain's Long Weekend," *Financial Times,* Dec. 21, 2011.

[18] "Executive Pay," Editorial, *Financial Times,* Feb. 7, 2010.

[19] Michael Mandel, "Bob Gordon Has Bad News about Productivity," *Businessweek*, March 9, 2010.

[20] These layoffs spiked productivity even as productivity growth slowed in northern Europe for the opposite reason as employers stockpiled employees in expectation that economic growth would continue.

[21] John P. Hussman, "Misallocating Resources," *Weekly Market Comment*, July 12, 2010, http://www.hussmanfunds.com/wmc/wmc100712.htm.

[22] Paul Kennedy, *The Rise and Fall of the Great Powers,* 434–435.

[23] "Growth and Renewal in the United States: Retooling America's Economic Engine," Mckinsey Global Institute, McKinsey & Company, February 2011.

[24] As quoted by Mark Hawthorne, "Buzz around building productivity levels," *Sydney Morning Herald*, Aug. 7, 2012. Thomas Bevington and Danny Samson, *Implementing Strategic Change: Managing Processes and Interfaces to Develop a Highly Productive Organisation* (London, Philadelphia, and New Delhi: Kogan Page Unlimited, 2012). Kindle edition. The sluggish growth rate in Australia has sparked calls for a re-examination of regulations to improve labor market flexibility. See Saul Eslake and Marcus Walsh, "Australia's Productivity Challenge," Grattan Institute Report no. 2011-1, February 2011.

[25] Edith Ginglinger, William Megginson, and Timothée Waxin, "Employee Ownership, Board Representation, and Corporate Financial Policies," *Journal of Corporate Finance* 17 (2011), p. 8, http://halshs.archives-ouvertes.fr/docs/00/62/63/10/PDF/Employee-Ownership-Paper-JCF2011.pdf.

[26] Ibid., 1, 18.

[27] Peter G. Peterson, "The Morning After."

[28] Benjamin Friedman, "Sorting Out the Debt," *New Perspectives Quarterly* vol. 4, no. 3 (Fall 1987). For a trenchant criticism of the Reagan

Administration's debt policies, see Friedman's *Day of Reckoning* (New York: Random House, 1989).

[29] Peter G. Peterson, "The Morning After."

[30] John P. Hussman, "Misallocating Resources."

[31] Joseph Stiglitz, *The Price of Inequality* (New York: Norton, 2012).

CHAPTER 23

[1] As quoted by Stephen S. Cohen and John Zysman, "Business Forum: Can Services Survive Without Manufacturing?; The Myth of a Post-Industrial Economy," *New York Times,* May 17, 1987.

[2] "US International Competitiveness: Perception and Reality," New York Stock Exchange, August 1984, 30–32. See also Alan Tonelson, "Up From Globalism," Notebook, *Harper's Magazine,* January 2010.

[3] Jeffrey Immelt, "Renewing American Leadership," West Point, NY.

[4] As quoted by Jon Gertner, "I Make," *New York Times Magazine,* Aug. 28, 2011.

[5] As quoted by Jia Lynn Yang, "Employing Industrial Policy," *Washington Post,* June 8, 2011.

[6] Gillian Tett, "Manufacturing Is All Over the Place," *Financial Times,* March 18, 2011.

[7] Timothy H. Parsons, *The Rule of Empires,* 131.

[8] Ibid.

[9] As quoted by Steven Mufson, "Peering Over the Cliff, Saying, 'I Told You So,'" *Washington Post,* Sept. 19, 2008.

[10] Peter Boone and Simon Johnson, "The Recession Is Over–for Now," *New York Times,* Sept. 20, 2009.

[11] Simon Johnson, "The Quiet Coup," *The Atlantic,* May 2009.

[12] Frank Rich, "Awake and Sing," *New York Times,* April 12, 2009.

[13] "48th Is Not a Good Place," Editorial, *New York Times,* Nov. 12, 2010.

[14] Steven Pearlstein, "Toward a New International Capitalism," *Washington Post,* Nov. 14, 2008.

[15] Benjamin Friedman, "Overmighty Finance Levies a Title on Growth," *Financial Times,* Aug. 26, 2009.

[16] John Joseph Wallis, "Did the New Deal Save Democracy and Capitalism? Implications for the 21st Century," *Lessons from the 1930s,* NBER, April 2010.

[17] Jean-Louis Arcand, Enrico Berkes, and Ugo Panizza, "Too Much Finance?," working paper 12/161, International Monetary Fund, June, 2012.

[18] Subal C. Kumbhakar and George Mavrotas, "Financial Sector Development and Productivity Growth," United Nations University–World Institute for Development Economic Research, research paper no. 2005/68, Helsinki, December 2005.

[19] Benjamin Friedman, "Overmighty Finance Levies a Title on Growth."

[20] Tom Braithwaite, "Greenspan Warns on Dodd-Frank Reforms," *Financial Times,* March 29, 2011.

[21] Wolfgang Münchau, "Barnier Is No Threat But Shame About His Job," *Financial Times,* Dec. 6, 2009.

[22] Alan Greenspan, "Dodd-Frank Fails to Meet Test of Our Times," *Financial Times,* March 29, 2011.

[23] As quoted by Daniel Gross, "A Tale of Two Productivity Figures," *International Herald Tribune*, Aug. 20, 2005.

[24] Alan Tonelson, "Up From Globalism," *Harper's Magazine Notebook*, January 2012.

[25] Ed Crooks, "Jobs Boost Fuels Hope for US Industry," *Financial Times*, Jan. 17, 2012.

[26] Ibid.

[27] Harold Meyerson, "Building a Better Capitalism."

[28] Gary P. Pisano and Willy C. Shih, "Restoring American Competitiveness," *Harvard Business Review*, July 2009. Steven Greenhouse, "GE to Add Two New US Plants as Unions Agree on Cost Controls."

[29] Peter G. Peterson, "The Morning After," *Atlantic Monthly*, October 1987.

[30] Paul Kennedy, *The Rise and Fall of the Great Powers*, 529.

[31] Alan Tonelson, "Up From Globalism."

[32] "Staying Put," *Economist*, Jan. 19, 2013, special report p. 8.

[33] John Markoff, "Google Taking a Retro Route: Made in US," *New York Times*, June 28, 2012.

[34] "OECD Economic Surveys: United States 2012," Paris, OECD. See also: L. Branstetter, "Are Knowledge Spillovers International or Intranational in Scope? Macroeconomic evidence from the US and Japan," *Journal of International Economics* 53, 55–79 (2001); M. Greenstone, R. Hornbeck, and E. Moretti, "Identifying Agglomeration Spillovers: Evidence from Million-Dollar Plants," NBER working paper no. 13833 (2008); and W. Keller, "International Trade, Foreign Direct Investment and Technology Spillovers," *Handbook of the Economics of Innovation*, eds. B. Hall and N. Rosenberg (North Holland:, April 14, 2010). PDF e-book.

[35] Eduardo Porter, "The Promise of Today's Factory Jobs," *New York Times*, April 4, 2012.

[36] As quoted by Alexander Jung, "Yuan Revaluation Won't Allow the Americans to Export More Goods," *Der Spiegel*, Oct. 18, 2010.

[37] Gabor Steingart, "America's Middle Class Has Become Globalization's Loser," *Der Spiegel*, Oct. 26, 2006.

[38] Kevin Phillips, *Bad Money*, 208.

[39] Harold Meyerson, "Building a Better Capitalism."

[40] Dean Praetorius, "Gamers Decode AIDS Protein That Stumped Researchers for 15 Years in Just 3 Weeks," *Huffington Post*, Sept. 19, 2011.

[41] Thomas Mason and Persis Drell, "Topic A: What's Lost in the House Budget Cuts," *Washington Post*, Feb. 27, 2011.

[42] "Global Innovation/National Competitiveness," Center for Strategic and International Studies, Washington, DC, 1996.

[43] Interview with Eric D. Isaacs, "Powering the National Labs as Engines of Discovery," *Science News*, Jan. 16, 2010.

[44] Yuqing Xing and Neal Detert, "How the iPhone Widens the United States Trade Deficit with the People's Republic of China," ADBI working paper no. 257, Asian Development Bank Institute (Dec. 14, 2010).

[45] Judy Estrin, *Closing the Innovation Gap* (New York: McGraw-Hill, 2009). See also Claire Cain Miller, "Another Voice Warns of Innovation Slowdown," *New York Times*, Sept. 2, 2008.

[46] "China Increases Its Number of Patents," *Berliner Zeitung*, Jan. 20, 2012.

[47] "Special Report: Innovation in Emerging Markets," *Economist,* April 17, 2010.

[48] Gary P. Pisano and Willy C. Shih, "Restoring American Competitiveness," *Harvard Business Review*, July 2009.

[49] Laura D'Andrea Tyson, "Why Manufacturing Still Matters," *New York Times,* Feb. 10, 2012.

[50] Judy Estrin, *Closing the Innovation Gap*, 2009. See also Claire Cain Miller, "Another Voice Warns of Innovation Slowdown," *New York Times*, Sept. 1, 2008.

[51] "Science Stats, Science and Engineering Indicators," *Science News (*2008).

[52] David Brooks, "Carpe Diem Nation," *New York Times*, Feb. 12, 2013.

[53] Michael Arndt, "US Patents Take a Fall," *Businessweek*, Dec. 17, 2009.

[54] Cezary Podkul, "Behind the Curve," *Washington Post,* Oct. 23, 2011.

[55] Luce provides a lucid and compelling review of the eroding US innovation foundation and outlook in *Time to Start Thinking: America in the Age of Descent* (New York: Atlantic Monthly Press, 2012).

[56] Robert D. Atkinson and Scott M. Andes, "The Atlantic Century: Benchmarking EU and US Innovation and Competitiveness," Information Technology and Innovation Foundation, Feb. 25, 2009, www.itif.org/publications/atlantic-century-benchmarking-eu-and-us-innovation-and-competitiveness, and updated July 19, 2011, www.itif.org/publications/atlantic-century-2011-benchmarking-us-and-eu-innovation-and-competitiveness.

[57] Chris Nuttall, "Intel Takes Helm of Scheme to Enhance US Competitiveness," *Financial Times*, Feb. 23, 2010.

[58] Steven Pearlstein, "Obama vs. Big Business: A Losing Battle for All," *Washington Post*, July 7, 2010.

[59] Matthew J. Slaughter, "How US Multinational Companies Strengthen the US Economy," Business Roundtable and the United States Council Foundation, Spring 2009.

[60] Robert J. Gordon, "Revisiting US Productivity Growth Over the Past Century with a View of the Future," NBER working paper 15834 (March 2010).

[61] Robert J. Gordon, "Is US Economic Growth Over? Faltering Innovation Confronts the Six Headwinds," NBER working paper 18315 (August 2012).

[62] Sam Ro, "Jeremy Grantham's US Economic Growth Forecast Through 2050 is the Most Depressing Forecast You'll Ever See," *Business Insider*, Nov. 20, 2012, http://www.businessinsider.com/jeremy-grantham-us-growth-forecast-2012-11.

[63] "An Update to the Budget and Economic Outlook: Fiscal Years 2012-2022," Washington, DC, Congressional Budget Office, August 2012 , table 2.3, http://www.cbo.gov/sites/default/files/cbofiles/attachments/08-22-2012-Update_to_Outlook.pdf.

CHAPTER 24

[1] "American Children, the Poorest in the Developed World," *Le Figaro*, Nov. 3, 2009, and Jason DeParle and Robert M. Gebeloff, "Living on Nothing But Food Stamps," *New York Times,* Jan. 3, 2010.

[2] Timothy M. Smeeding, "Poorer by Comparison," *Pathways*, Stanford University Center for the Study of Poverty and Inequality (Winter 2008).

[3] Ron Haskins and Isabel Sawhill, *Creating an Opportunity Society* (Washington, DC: Brookings Institution Press, 2009), 7.

[4] Carol Morello, "Census Releases Alternative Formulas for Gauging Poverty," *Washington Post,* Jan. 5, 2011.

[5] Geranda Notten and Chris de Neubourg, "Poverty in Europe and the USA: Exchanging Official Measurement Methods," Graduate School of Commerce, Maastricht University, August 2007.

[6] Peter Adamson, "The Children Left Behind," Innocenti Research Centre, Report Card 9, UNICEF, Fig 2e, http://www.unicef-irc.org/publications/pdf/rc9_eng.pdf.

[7] "Single Parent Households: 1980–2009," *Statistical Abstract of the United States,* U.S. Census Bureau, 2012, table 1337.

[8] Isabel Sawhill, "Families at Risk, Setting National Priorities: The 2000 Election and Beyond," Washington, DC: Brookings Institution Press, 1999, eds. Henry Aaron and Robert D. Reischauer. Robert I. Lerman, "The Impact of Changing US Family Structure on Child Poverty and Income Inequality," *Economica* vol. 63 (1996).

[9] "American Children, the Poorest in the Developed World," *Le Figaro*, Nov. 3, 2009.

[10] "Working Poor, from the Editor's Desk," Washington, DC, Bureau of Labor Statistics, US Department of Labor, April 5, 2012.

[11] "Global Wage Report 2010/1/1" Geneva, ILO, fig. 21, 36.

CHAPTER 25

[1] Floyd Norris, "The Number of Those Working Past 65 Is at a Record High," *New York Times*, May 19, 2012.

[2] Brigid Schulte, "No Longer Ready to Retire," *Washington Post*, September 21, 2008.

[3] Teresa Ghilarducci, "Our Ridiculous Approach to Retirement," *New York Times*, Sept. 22, 2012.

[4] As quoted by Michael A. Fletcher, "Future Retirees at Greater Fiscal Risk," *Washington Post*, Feb. 17, 2013.

[5] Nancy Trejos, "Bleaker Hopes for a Good Retirement," *Washington Post,* April 8, 2008.

[6] Ghilarducci, "Our Ridiculous Approach to Retirement."

[7] "National Compensation Survey: Employee Benefits in Private Industry in the United States," Washington, DC, Bureau of Labor Statistics, US Department of Labor, March 2007.

[8] Michael A. Fletcher, "Future Retirees at Greater Fiscal Risk," *Washington Post*, Feb 17, 2013.

[9] Phyllis Korkki, "Turning 65? Maybe It's not Time to Quit," *New York Times,* Sept. 28, 2008.

[10] Vickie Elmer, "Staying on the Job," *Washington Post*, July 29, 2008.

[11] Floyd Norris, "The Number of Those Working Past 65 Is at a Record High," *New York Times*, May 19, 2012.

[12] Catherine Rampell, "Seniors Outnumber Teenagers in Job Force,"Economix, *New York Times,* July 15, 2010.

[13] As quoted by Schulte, "No Longer Ready to Retire."

[14] "Length of Working Life and Retirement," *Le Économie Française*, June 2001.

[15] Thomas Schulz, "The Erosion of America's Middle Class," *Der Spiegel*, Aug. 19, 2010.

[16] Daniel Baumann, "Live Longer, Work Longer," *Berliner Zeitung*, Sept. 22, 2010. Firms are pleased with the trend, which belies the theory of Hoover Institution economist Edward Lazear years ago that older workers are less productive and thus overpaid relatively to younger ones. German researchers, including Axel Borsch-Supan of the Mannheim Institute of Economic and Demographic Change, have found the groups equally productive, with older employees showing better judgment. See John Pennekamp, "The Power of the Ancients," *Handelsblatt*, Sept. 10, 2010.

[17] Marc Landré, "Two Million More Active by 2030," *Le Figaro*, Oct. 3, 2011.

CHAPTER 26

[1] Christopher Caldwell, "The 'Right' to Work until 70," *Financial Times,* Nov. 21, 2008.

[2] "Schumpeter: The French Way of Work," *Economist*, Nov. 19, 2011.

[3] Petula Dvorak, "The High Cost of Work Weights on Some Parents," *Washington Post*, Jan. 26, 2010.

[4] Agence France-Presse and DAP, "Municipalities Want to Use Unskilled Workers in Day Care Centers," *Handelsblatt*, May 26, 2012.

[5] Tarjei Havnes and Magne Mogstad, "No Child Left Behind: Subsidized Child Care and Children's Long-Run Outcomes," *American Economic Journal: Economic Policy* 3(2): 97-129 (2011).

[6] As quoted by Louis Uchitelle, "Job Security, Too, May Have a Happy Medium," *New York Times*, Feb. 25, 2007.

[7] "Economic Survey of The Netherlands," OECD Paris, 2008, 8, 9.

[8] For background, see Joshua Cohen and Charles Sabgel, "Flexicurity," *Pathways*, Stanford University, Spring 2009, 11-14. Lou Uchitelle, "Job Security, Too, May Have a Happy Medium," *New York Times*, Feb. 25, 2007. EU reforms have also included deregulating services to eliminate collusive fees by professions and unbundling energy production from distribution. See Guglielmo Barone and Federico Cingano, "Service Regulation and Growth: Evidence from OECD Countries," Bank of Italy, August 2010.

[9] As quoted by Michael Schuman, "How Germany Became the China of Europe," *Time Magazine*, Feb. 24, 2011.

[10] Liz Alderman, "Denmark Starts to Trim Its Admired Safety Net," *New York Times*, Aug. 17, 2010.

[11] Robert Kuttner, *The Squandering of America*, 213.

[12] Ric Battellino, "Twenty Years of Economic Growth," address to Moreton Bay Regional Council, Redcliffe, Queensland, Aug. 20, 2010.

[13] Robert Kuttner, "The Copenhagen Consensus, Reading Adam Smith in Denmark," *Foreign Affairs*, March/April 2008.

[14] As quoted by Patricia Veldhuis "Unemployment at 3.7 Percent—a Dutch Miracle?," NRC Netherlands, *Handelsblatt*, Dec. 9, 2010.

[15] Steven Greenhouse, "Former NLRB Member to Take Post in a Big Union," *New York Times*, May 23, 2012.

[16] Jody Heymann, Alison Earle, and Jeffrey Hayes, "How Does the United States Measure Up? The Work, Family, and Equity Index," Ford

Foundation, the Harvard-McGill University Project on Global Working Families and the Institute for Health and Social Policy, 2007.

[17] "Insecure Work a Scourge on Nation's Productivity: Howe," *Workplace Insight, Australia*, Thomson Reuters, May 24, 2012.

[18] Deepankar Basu and Duncan K. Foley, "Dynamics of Output and Employment in the U.S. Economy," Political Economy Research Institute, February 8, 2011.

[19] As quoted by Nelson D. Schwartz, "Europe's Focus on Saving Jobs Pays Off in a Recession," *New York Times*, Feb. 4, 2010.

[20] These top-ups are paid with funds accumulated during normal periods from taxes on both employees and employers, like unemployment compensation taxes in America. A wrinkle common in Germany and at French firms such as PSA Peugeot Citroën is for employees to stockpile overtime wage premiums in short-work programs. Including such top-ups, workers during the 2008–2009 downturn on reduced time at Peugeot received 95 percent of net earnings. For a broad discussion of short-work programs, see Alexander Hijzen and Danielle Venn, "The Role of Short-Time Work Schemes during the 2008–2009 recession," OECD Social, Employment, and Migration working paper no. 115, OECD, January 2011. For a discussion of the German short-time program, see Bernhard Honnigfort, "Better Short Than Not at All," *Berliner Zeitung*, June 7, 2010; for France, see Agence France-Presse, "Week of Unemployment for 20,000 Employees of PSA," *Le Monde*, Jan. 31, 2012.

[21] Dietrich Creutzburg, "Short-Time Working on the Retreat," *Handelsblatt*, July 30, 2010.

[22] Agence France Presse, "The Partial Unemployment Has Cost the State 300 Million Euros in 2009," *Le Monde*, Dec. 3, 2009.

[23] "Job Engine Almost Stable Middle Class in Crisis," *Berliner Zeitung*, May 20, 2010.

[24] Matthias Loke, "Jobsicherung in Crisis," *Berliner Zeitung*, Jan. 20, 2010.

[25] "Germany: 1.2 Million Jobs Saved," *Le Figaro*, Feb. 2, 2010.

[26] Alexander Hijzen and Danielle Venn, "The Role of Short Time Work Schemes during the 2008–09 Recession," OECD Social, Employment, and Migration, working paper no. 115, OECD, January 2011.

[27] Marc Landré, "12% Unemployment in France (blog)" *Le Figaro*, March 5, 2010.

[28] "Global Wage Report 2010/11," Geneva, ILO, 58.

[29] As quoted by Richard Milne, Brian Groom, and Jonathan Birchall, "Time Will Tell," *Financial Times*, June 30, 2009.

[30] DAP News, "Ford Plans to Short-Time Working in Cologne," *Berliner Zeitung*, April 25, 2012.

[31] As quoted by Markus Dettmer and Janko Tietz, "Germany's Massive Job-Saving Program Could Still Fail," *Der Spiegel*, Dec. 30, 2009.

[32] As quoted by Nelson D. Schwartz, "Europe's Focus on Saving Jobs Pays Off in a Recession," *New York Times*, Feb. 4, 2010.

[33] As quoted by Patricia Veldhuis, "Unemployment at 3.7 Percent—A Dutch Miracle?," NRC (Netherlands) *Handelsblatt*, Dec. 9, 2009.

[34] As quoted by Daniel Schaefer, "Credits in Jobs Bank," *Financial Times*, Feb. 25, 2009.

SECTION 4

CHAPTER 27

[1] Chrystia Freeland, "What Toronto Can Teach New York and London," *Financial Times*, Jan. 29, 2010.

[2] Richard Lambert, "Sir Ralph's Lessons on Short-Termism," *Financial Times*, May 22, 2011.

[3] Alexandra Petri, "State of the Millennial Union: Underemployed and Overlooked," *Washington Post*, Feb. 16, 2013.

[4] Sam Ro, "Jeremy Grantham's US Economic Growth Forecast Through 2050 Is the Most Depressing Forecast You'll Ever See," *Business Insider*, Nov. 20, 2012, http://www.businessinsider.com/jeremy-grantham-us-growth-forecast-2012 -11.

[5] Robert J. Gordon, "Is US Economic Growth Over? Faltering Innovation Confronts the Six Headwinds," NBER working paper 18315, August 2012.

[6] Ibid.

[7] Jim Clifton, *The Coming Jobs War* (New York: Gallup Press, 2012), 2.

[8] Ben Austen, "End of the Road," *Harper's Magazine*, August 2009.

[9] Joseph Stiglitz, *The Price of Inequality*, Norton, 2012.

[10] Daron Acemoglu and James Robinson, *Why Nations Fail*, (New York: Crown Business, Random House, 2012), p. 156, 159.

[11] Ibid., pp. 157, 427.

[12] Rich Morin, "Rising Share of Americans See Conflict Between Rich and Poor," Pew Research Center, Pew Social and Demographic Trends, Jan. 11, 2012, http://www.pewsocialtrends.org/2012/01/11/rising-share-of-americans-see-conflict-between-rich-and-poor/Top of Form.

[13] Francesco Guerrera, "A Need to Reconnect," *Financial Times*, March 12, 2009.

[14] John P. Hussman, "Misallocating Resources," *Weekly Market Comment*, July 12, 2010, http://www.hussmanfunds.com/wmc/wmc100712.htm.

[15] Simon Johnson, "The Quiet Coup," *The Atlantic,* May 2009.

[16] Richard Wilkinson and Kate Pickett, *The Spirit Level: Why Greater Equality Makes Societies Stronger* (New York: Bloomsbury Press, 2009). Leon Gettler, "The Wealth Time Bomb," *Sydney Morning Herald*, Oct. 28, 2010, http://www.smh.com.au/business/the-wealth-time-bomb-20101027 -173xm.html#ixzz1ndiT7ObQ.

[17] Nancy Folbre, "Defining Economic Interest," Economix, *New York Times*, Aug. 8, 2011.

[18] Michael I. Norton and Dan Ariely, "Building a Better America—One Wealth Quintile at a Time," *Perspectives on Psychological Science*, January 2011, http://pps.sagepub.com/content/6/1.toc.

[19] Paul Krugman, "Moochers Against Welfare," *New York Times*, Feb. 17, *2012.*

[20] Larry M. Bartels, *Unequal Democracy* (Princeton, NJ: Princeton University Press, 2008), 124.

[21] David Brooks, "Workers of the World, Unite!" *New York Times*, Jan. 3, 2012.

[22] Nancy Folbre, "Defining Economic Interest."

[23] Mancur Olson, *The Rise and Decline of Nations* (New Haven, CT: Yale University Press, 1982) and *The Logic of Collective Action* (Cambridge, MA: Harvard University Press, 1965).

[24] Joan C. Williams, "Learn to Bridge the Class Divide," *Washington Post*, Sept. 26, 2010.

[25] Dani Rodrik, *The Globalization Paradox* (New York: WW Norton, 2011), 146.

[26] Ross Garnaut, "Climate Change, China Booms and Australia's Governance Struggle in a Changing World," 2010 Hamer Oration, University of Melbourne, Aug. 5, 2010.

[27] David Brooks, "The Day After Tomorrow," *New York Times*, Sept. 14, 2010.

[28] Ross Garnaut, "Climate Change, China Booms and Australia's Governance Struggle in a Changing World."

[29] Tim Colebatch, "Adapt Or Die–RBAs Bitter Medicine," *Sydney Morning Herald*, June 13, 2012.

CHAPTER 28

[1] John Kay, "Powerful Interests Are Trying to Control the Market," *Financial Times*, Nov. 10, 2009.

[2] Edmund S. Phelps, "The Economy Needs a Bit of Ingenuity," *New York Times*, Aug. 7, 2010.

[3] Martin Wolf, "America's Inequalilty Need Not Determine the Future of Britain," *Financial Times*, Dec. 22, 2011.

[4] The forerunners are Jeff P. Faux (*The Global Class War: How America's Bipartisan Elite Lost Our Future; What It Will Take to Win*) and Clyde V. Prestowitz, Jr. (*Trading Places: How We Are Giving Our Future to Japan and How to Reclaim It*). A far from exhaustive list includes the following: Robert H. Frank and Philip Cook (*The Winner-Take-All Society*); Jacob S. Hacker and Paul Pierson (*Winner-Take-All Politics: How Washington Made the Rich Richer—and Turned its Back on the Middle Class*); David Cay Johnston (*Free Lunch*); Paul Krugman (*End This Depression Now!*); Robert Kuttner (*The Squandering of America*); Lawrence Lessig (*Republic, Lost: How Money Corrupts Congress–and a Plan to Stop It*); Timothy Noah (*The Great Divergence: America's Growing Inequality Crisis and What We Can Do About It*); Kevin Phillips (*Bad Money*); Joseph Stiglitz (*The Price of Inequality*); and Edward N. Wolff (*Top Heavy*).

[5] The revolving door evidence on civil servants is more mixed, with at least one study suggesting that firms hiring former SEC enforcement attorneys did not subsequently receive lenient treatment. See Edward Wyatt, "Study Questions Risk of S.E.C. Revolving Door," *New York Times*, Aug. 6, 2012.

[6] Dietmar Newer, "The Uncanny Power of Lobbyists," *Handelsblatt*, Sept. 20, 2012, http://www.handelsblatt.com/politik/deutschland/gefahr-fuer-die-demokratie-die-unheimliche-macht-der-lobbyisten-seite-all/7154788-all.html.

[7] See the investigative reporting of Kimberfly Kinday, Scott Higham, David S. Fallis, and Dan Keating, "High-Level Talks, Then Changes to Holdings," *Washington Post*, June 25, 2012.

[8] David S. Fallis and Dan Keating, "Lobbyists Can Try to Influence Bills That Go Before Relatives," *Washington Post*, Dec. 30, 2012.

[9] Edmund Phelps, "Uncertainty Bedevils the Best System," *Financial Times*, April 14, 2009.

[10] Michael Schuman, "How Germany Became the China of Europe," *Time Magazine*, Feb. 24, 2011. Thomas Schulz, "How The German Economy Became a Model," *Der Spiegel*, March 21, 2012.

[11] "Shareholder Value Reevaluated," Editorial, *Financial Times*, March 15, 2009.

[12] Francesco Guerrera, "Welch Denounces Corporate Obsessions," *Financial Times*, March 13, 2009.

[13] John Gillespie and David Zweig, *Money for Nothing* (New York: Free Press, 2011), 34.

[14] Paul Myners, "We Need More Responsible Corporate Ownership," *Financial Times*, Nov. 21, 2009.

[15] See Justin Fox and Jay W. Lorsch, "What Good Are Shareholders?," *Harvard Business Review*, July–August 2011.

[16] Larry Fauver and Michael E. Fuerst, "Does Good Corporate Governance Include Employee Representation? Evidence from German Corporate Boards," *Journal of Financial Economics* vol. 82 (December 2006), 7.

[17] Louis Uchitelle, "2 US Social Scientists Share Nobel in Economics," *New York Times*, Oct. 13, 2009.

[18] Forest L. Reinhardt, Robert N. Stavins, and Richard H.K. Vietor, "Corporate Social Responsibility Through an Economic Lens," *Review of Environmental Economics and Policy* vol. 2, issue 2 (Summer 2008).

[19] As reported by Stefan Stern, "Dean Poised to Shake Up Business," *Financial Times*, May 10, 2010.

[20] John Gapper, "Business Should Help the Heartland," *Financial Times*, March 7, 2012.

[21] Michael Skapinker, "Should MBA Students Do the Perp Walk?," *Financial Times*, Sept. 20, 2010.

[22] Francesco Guerrera, "GE Chief Attacks Executive 'Greed,'" *Financial Times*, Dec. 9, 2009.

[23] Robert Kuttner, *The Squandering of America* (New York: Vintage, 2008), 303. Larry Bartels, *Unequal Democracy*, 249.

[24] Jim Malewitz, "Minimum Wages About to Go Up in 10 States," *Washington Post*, Dec. 24, 2012.

[25] Wil Blechman, "Infants, Toddlers Need Our Attention," *Miami Herald*, Sept. 30, 2011.

[26] "Paying for University Education, Year Book Australia, 2005," Australian Bureau of Statistics, 1301.0. "A Political Trauma, but a Policy Success," *Financial Times*, Dec. 29, 2011.

[27] See Robert Lerman, "Training Tomorrow's Workforce," Center for American Progress, Dec. 9, 2009. James J. Heckman, Rebecca L. Roselius, and Jeffrey A. Smith, "US Education and Training Policy: A Reevaluation of the Underlying Assumptions Behind the 'New Consensus,'" working paper 94-1, Center for Social Program Evaluation, University of Chicago (1993).

[28] German Press Agency, "OECD Study of the US Education System, Labor Market Weakens," *Handelsblatt*, June 26, 2012.

[29] "This Year's Model," Editorial, *Washington Post*, Jan. 27, 2012.

[30] Andrew Liveris, *Make It In America* (Hoboken, NJ: John Wiley & Sons, Inc. 2011). See also Ed Crooks, "America: Riveting Prospects," *Financial Times*, Jan. 6, 2011.

[31] Edward Luce, *Time to Start Thinking: America in the Age of Descent* (New York: Atlantic Monthly Press, 2012).

[32] See Anthony Howe, *Free Trade and Liberal England, 1846–1946* (New

York: Clarendon Press Oxford, 1998). Stephen N. Broadberry, "How Did the United States and Germany Overtake Britain?: A Sectional Analysis of Comparative Productivity Levels, 1870–1990," *Journal of Economic History* vol. 58, no. 2 (1998).

[33] Charles Feinstein, "Slowing Down and Falling Behind," *ReFRESH 10* (Spring 1990), U.K. Economic History Society, http://www.ehs.org.uk/ehs/refresh/assets/Feinstein10b.pdf.

[34] Andrew Liveris, *Make It In America* (Hoboken, NJ: John Wiley & Sons, 2011).

[35] Ullrich Fichtner, Hans Hoyng, Marc Hujer, and Gregor Peter Schmitz, "Divided States of America: Notes on the Decline of a Great Nation," *Der Spiegel*, Nov. 5, 2012, http://www.spiegel.de/international/world/divided-states-of-america-notes-on-the-decline-of-a-great-nation-a-865295-2.html.

[36] Erik Schelzig, "Volkswagen Victim of Industrial Espionage in China?," Agence France-Presse/*Le Monde*, July 27, 2012.

[37] Alan Beattie, "Global Economy: Tricks of the Trade Law," *Financial Times*, Oct. 28, 2012.

[38] A good summary is Howard Schneider, "Racks Up Wins Over China, But Spoils Are Uncertain," *Washington Post*, Aug. 9, 2012.

[39] Martin Jacques, "Welcome to China's Millennium," *The Guardian*, June 23, 2009.

[40] Dani Rodrik, *The Globalization Paradox*, 278.

[41] As quoted by Bill Vlasic, Hiroko Taabuchi, and Charles Duhigg, "An American Model for Tech Jobs?," *New York Times*, Aug. 5, 2012.

[42] Hugh Carnegy, "Titan Hits Out at French Productivity," *Financial Times*, Feb 20, 2013.

[43] Agence France-Presse, "EU Tax on Chinese Mandarin," *Le Figaro*, Feb. 22, 2013. http://www.lefigaro.fr/flash-eco/2013/02/22/97002-20130222 FILWWW00619-ue-une-taxe-sur-les-mandarines-chinoises.php.

[44] Erin Hatton, "The Rise of the Permanent Temp Economy," *New York Times*, Jan. 26, 2013.

[45] Steven Greenhouse, "A Part-Time Life, as Hours Shrink and Shift," *New York Times*, Oct. 28, 2012.

[46] Ibid.

[47] Guy Standing, *The Precariat: The New Dangerous Class* (London: Bloomsbury Academic, 2012).

[48] Thomas Magenheim-Hörmann, "Shut Up and Keep Working," *Berliner Zeitung*, March 29, 2012.

[49] Chris Zappone, "Bad Jobs Trap Looms for Workers," *Sydney Morning Herald*, Nov. 1, 2012, http://www.smh.com.au/business/the-economy/bad-jobs-trap-looms-for-workers-20121101-28lf2.html.

[50] Tim Colebatch, "BHP Wants to Be Free of Unions," *Sydney Morning Herald*, May 18, 2012.

[51] Steve Greenhouse, "Working Life (High and Low)," *New York Times*, April 20, 2008. Clay Lucas, "A Precarious Life," *Sydney Morning Herald*, March 28, 2012.

[52] Eva Roth, "Temporary Workers Brought to Fair Wages," *Berliner Zeitung*, Nov. 26, 2012, http://www.berliner-zeitung.de/arbeit-soziales/zeitarbeit-arbeits

markt-leiharbeiter-um-gerechten-lohn-gebracht,10808232,20968776.html.

[53] ADP, "Temporary Workers Earn Only Half," *Berliner Zeitung*, March 26, 2012.

[54] Floyd Norris, "Tax Reform Might Start with a Look at '86," *New York Times, Nov. 23, 2012.*

[55] Thomas L. Hungerford, "Taxes and the Economy: An Economic Analysis of the Top Rates Since 1945," Congressional Research Service, Sept. 14, 2012, http://graphics8.nytimes.com/news/business/0915taxesandeconomy.pdf.

[56] Anthony Faiola and Mary Jordan, "Tax-Haven Blacklist Stirs Nations," *Washington Post*, April 4, 2009.

[57] Vanessa Houlder, "OECD Presents Plan to Close Tax Loopholes," *Financial Times*, Feb. 12, 2013.

[58] Gretchen Morgenson, "Death of a Loophole and Swiss Banks Will Mourn," *New York Times*, March 27, 2010.

[59] Stéphane Kovacsle, "Swiss Households Tax Exiles," *Le Figaro*, June 24, 2012, http://www.lefigaro.fr/impots/2012/09/23/05003-20120923ART FIG00169-la-suisse-menage-les-exiles-fiscaux.php.

[60] David Jolly, "US and Switzerland Reach Deal on Sharing of Financial Account Data," *New York Times*, June 22, 2012.

[61] German Press Agency, "European Banks Stop Serving American Customers," *Der Spiegel*, Dec. 14, 2011.

[62] Dina El Boghdady, "UBS Whistleblower Awarded $104 Million," *Washington Post*, Sept. 11, 2012, http://www.washingtonpost.com/business/economy/ubs-whistleblower-awarded-104m-by-irs-for-helping-in-swiss-bank-probe/2012/09/11/1a7232a2-fc28-11e1-b153-218509a954e1_story.html.

[63] Vanessa Houlder, "London Moves to Buy Stolen Bank Data," *Financial Times*, Feb. 5, 2010.

[64] "Secrets and Tax," Editorial, *Financial Times*, Feb. 7, 2010.

[65] Rob Turner, "Swiss Tax Dodge Probe Could Net Twice the Amount of Cash Expected," *Handelsblatt*, April 2, 2010.

[66] Michael Evans, "Untold Riches, Untold Taxes: a Royal Battle," *Sydney Morning Herald*, Sept. 1, 2012.

[67] "Stashed in the Alps: A Tax Evasion Bonanza Hidden in a Swiss Bank," *Der Spiegel*, Dec. 4, 2012, http://www.spiegel.de/international/germany/german-city-finds-3-billion-euros-hidden-by-tax-evaders-in-swiss-bank-a-870831.html#ref=rss.

[68] Holger Alich, "Switzerland Poses Germany's Organized Crime," *Handelsblatt*, Aug. 22, 2012. "Switzerland Anger Against Obama," *Le Figaro*, Aug. 22, 2012. "Purchase of Tax-Protected CDs Supreme Court," *Handelsblatt*, Aug. 23, 2012.

[69] Sven Böll, Dietmar Hipp, Alexander Neubacher, and Barbara Schmid, "Tax Deal Rewards Germans with Swiss Bank Accounts," *Der Spiegel*, April 16, 2012, http://www.spiegel.de/international/germany/0,1518,druck-827748,00.html. See also "Switzerland Seeks Tax Traitor," *Berliner Zeitung*, Nov. 5, 2012, http://www.berliner-zeitung.dewirtschaft/ermittlungen-wegen-steuer-cd-schweiz-sucht-den-steuer-verraeter,10808230,20791546.html.

[70] Agence France-Presse, "Tax Exiles in Switzerland Will Pay a Little More Tax," *Le Monde*, Sept. 13, 2012, http://www.lemonde.fr/economie/

article/2012/09/13/les-exiles-fiscaux-en-suisse-vont-payer-un-peu-plus-d-impots_1759812_3234.html. See also Vanessa Houlder, "Cash-Strapped Nations Raise Heat on Rich," *Financial Times*, May 4, 2009.

71 Harry F. Grubert, "Foreign Taxes and the Growing Share of U.S. Multination Company Income Abroad: Profits, Not Sales, are Being Globalized," Office of Tax Analysis, working paper no. 103, February 2012, p. 15, http://www.treasury.gov/resource-center/tax-policy/tax-analysis/Documents/OTA-W2012-103-Multinational-Income-Globalized-Feb-2012.pdf.

72 (Editorial), "Walking the Walk on Global Taxation," *Financial Times*, Nov. 6, 2012.

73 Eric Pfanner, "European Countries Seek More Taxes from U.S. Multinational Companies, *New York Times*, Nov. 19, 2012.

74 "Options for Taxing Multinational Corporations," Congressional Budget Office report, Jan. 8, 2013. http://www.cbo.gov/publication/43764?utm_source=feedblitz&utm_medium=FeedBlitzEmail&utm_content=812526&utm_campaign=0.

75 "Addressing Base Erosion and Profit Shifting," OECD Publishing, Paris 2013, http://dx.doi.org/10.1787/9789264192744-en.

76 Ian Verrender, "Australia Loses Its Reputation for Being Cheap and Easy," *Sydney Morning Herald*, Dec. 4, 2010.

77 Clancy Yeates, "Tax Flow for Private Equity Funds," *Sydney Morning Herald*, Dec. 2, 2010.

78 As quoted by Christopher Caldwell, "Not Malevolent, but Mediocre," *Financial Times*, Feb. 15, 2009.

79 Joseph Stiglitz, "Europe's Morality Play," *Sydney Morning Herald*, Dec. 7, 2011.

80 Martin Wolf, "Banking Reforms after the Libor Scandal," *Financial Times*, July 2, 2012.

81 Andrew Trotman, "Fed Boss Calls for Breakup of Wall Street Giants," *Sydney Morning Herald*, Feb. 25, 2011. Shahien Nasiripour, "Top Fed Official Suggests US Bank Size Cap," *Financial Times*, Oct. 11, 2012.

82 Gretchen Morgenson, "Do You Have Any Reforms in Size XL?," *New York Times*, April 25, 2010.

83 Gretchen Morgenson, "The Fattest or the Fittest," *New York Times*, Dec. 11, 2011.

84 (Editorial), "Stand by Liikanen," *Financial Times*, Feb. 3, 2013.

85 (Editorial), "Split the Difference," *Financial Times*, Oct. 18, 2012, and Peter Eavis, "Federal Governor Offers Way to Limit Bank Size," Dealbook, *New York Times*, Oct. 16, 2012. UK bankers Philip Augar and John McFall, chairman of the British Commons Treasury committee, have also proposed breaking up Red Queens. See Philip Augar and John McFall, "To Fix the System We Must Break Up the Banks," *Financial Times*, Sept. 10, 2009.

86 Andrew G. Haldane, "On Being the Right Size," Institute of Economic Affairs' 22nd Annual Series, 2012, Beesley Lectures, London, Oct. 25, 2012, 13. http://www.bankofengland.co.uk/publications/Documents/speeches /2012 / speech615.pdf.

87 Nassim Nicholas Taleb, "End Bonuses for Bankers," *New York Times*, Nov. 8, 2011.

88 "Final Report of the High Pay Commission," High Pay Commission, Joseph Rowntree Charitable Trust, Nov. 22, 2011, http://highpaycommission.

co.uk/wp-content/uploads/2011/11/HPC_final_report_WEB.pdf. "Managing High Pay in Companies," Editorial, *Financial Times*, Nov. 21, 2011.

[89] Michael Skapinker, "CEOs Need to Join the 20 Times Club Now," *Financial Times*, Nov. 30, 2011.

[90] Adele Ferguson, "More Transparency Needed for Executive Pay Reports," *Sydney Morning Herald*, Sept. 18, 2012.

[91] Michael Skapinker, "CEOs Need to Join the 20 Times Club Now."

[92] Julia Werdigier, "Shareholder Votes on Pay to Be Binding in Britain," *New York Times*, June 21, 2012.

[93] "Irresistible Rise of the Angry Investor," Editorial, *Financial Times*, May 4, 2012 .

[94] Richard Milne, "Europe: A Meeting of the Minds," *Financial Times*, Feb. 28, 2010.

[95] Michael West, "Two Strikes' Holds Boards to Account," *Sydney Morning Herald*, Nov. 17, 2012.

[96] Colin Kruger, "Crown Gets Approval for Executive Pay," *Sydney Morning Herald*, Oct. 30, 2012. Brian Robins, "Sirtex Just Avoids 'Second Strike,'" *Sydney Morning Herald*, Jan. 23, 2012.

[97] Brian Robins, "Penrice Soda First Company to Strike Out," *Sydney Morning Herald*, Oct. 30, 2012, http://www.smh.com.au/business/penrice-soda-first-company-to-strike-out-20121030-28hbc.html. See chart on strike votes outcome: *Sydney Morning Herald*, Nov. 5, 2012, http://images.smh.com.au/file/2012/11/01/3761569/Table%2520-%2520pay%2520development%2520after%2520first%2520strike.pdf .

[98] Georgia Wilkins, "Two-Strike Rule Hits Directors," Sydney Morning Herald, Oct. 8, 2012. Madeleine Heffernan, "Cochlear Cops First 'Strike' of the Season," *Sydney Morning Herald*, Oct. 16, 2012.

[99] See Ulrike Malmendier, Enrico Moretti, and Florian S. Peters, "Winning by Losing: Evidence on the Long-Run Effects of Mergers," working paper 18024, National Bureau of Economic Research, April 2012, http://emlab.berkeley.edu/~moretti/mergers.pdf.

[100] Lucian A. Bebchuk, Alma Cohen, and Holger Spamann, "The Wages of Failure: Executive Compensation at Bear Stearns and Lehman 2000-2008," Program on Corporate Governance at Harvard Law School, November 22, 2009. http://www.law.harvard.edu/faculty/bebchuk/pdfs/BCS-Wages-of-Failure-Nov09.pdf.

[101] Louise Story, "Executives Kept Wealth as Firms Failed, Study Says," *New York Times*, Nov. 23, 2009.

[102] Floyd Norris, "We Do It Right, but Those Others Don't," *New York Times*, Nov. 1, 2010.

[103] Hayat Gazzane, "GDF Suez Abandons Stock Options," *Le Figaro*, Jan. 6, 2011.

[104] Marie Bartnik, "L'Oreal Reopens the Debate on Stock Options," *Le Figaro*, Feb. 20, 2012.

[105] Tom Burgis, "The Liikanen Report Decoded," *Financial Times*, Oct. 2, 2012.

[106] "The Netherlands: ING Bonuses," World Business Briefing, *New York Times*, March 24, 2009.

[107] Sharlene Goff, "Lloyds to Claw Back Bonuses in Wake of PPPI Scandal," *Financial Times, Feb. 19, 2012.*

[108] Robert J. Shiller, "Help Prevent a Sequel, Delay Some Pay," *New York Times*, June 20, 2010. See also, Sewell Chan, "Fifteen Economists Issue Crisis-Prevention Manual," *New York Times*, June 16, 2010. Other experts including John Gillespie, David Zweig, Lucian A. Bebchuk, Jesse M. Fried, and Xavier Gabaix have also produced a variety of specific suggestions short of board recomposition, including simple and complete access to board ballots by shareholders and abolition of staggered board terms. See, for example, Bebchuk and Fried, "Tackling the Managerial Power Problem: the Key to Improving Executive Compensation," *Pathways*, Stanford Center for Poverty and Inequality, (Summer 2010).

[109] Gerhard Cromme, "Remarks by the Chairman of the Supervisory Board of Siemens AG," Jan. 26, 2010. "Briefing: Germany Introduces New Rules on Management Board Compensation," Freshfields Bruckhaus Deringer LLP, August 2009.

[110] Alex Barker, "EU Agrees to Cap Bankers' Bonuses," *Financial Times*, Feb. 28, 2013.

[111] David Brooks, "The Day After Tomorrow," *New York Times*, Sept. 14, 2010.

[112] Floyd Norris, "How the Public Sees Business Rules," *New York Times*, Jan. 28, 2012.

[113] Benjamin M. Friedman, "The No-Growth Trap," *National Interest*, Oct. 25, 2011.

INDEX

C

D

H

P

R

T

U

V

W

X

Z

ABOUT THE AUTHOR

George R. Tyler is an economist who has a varied background as an American and international government official and successful entrepreneur in the U.S. and Europe. He examines the troubled American economy from a uniquely international perspective.

George began his career working in the United States Congress as an economic adviser to Senators Hubert H. Humphrey of Minnesota and Lloyd M. Bentsen of Texas and as Senior Economist on the Congressional Joint Economic Committee. Appointed by President Clinton as a Deputy Treasury Assistant Secretary in 1993, George worked closely with the international financial institutions and in 1995 became a senior official at the World Bank.

Turning to the private sector in 1997, George founded a multimillion real estate firm with interests in California and Florida, which has developed a number of resort-residential subdivisions in Virginia.

George is active in the Washington-based NGO Bikes for the World (BfW), serving as board Treasurer (bikesfortheworld.org). Partnering with a number of organizations abroad, BfW collects more than ten thousand used bicycles and parts each year for recycling to nations in the Caribbean, Central America, Asia, and Africa. Its domestic partners include Chicago-based Working Bike Cooperative (workingbikes.org), Dicks Sporting Goods, (dickssportinggoods.com), REI, and numerous local bicycle shops.

George attended the University of Colorado and the Ph.D program in economics at the University of Virginia.